The Library
Hadlow College
Hadlow
Tonbridge
Kent TN11 0AL
Tel: **01732 853245**

Hadlow
college

Date of Return	Date of Return	Date of Return
25/07/2011 - NO RECORDED USAGE		
19/10/2011, checked by teaching Staff. Please keep G.D		

Please note that fines will be charged if this book is returned late

D1333380

Scarce Plants in Britain

THIS BOOK IS DEDICATED TO THE MEMORY OF

R.W. DAVID
(1912-1993)

WHOSE STUDIES OF SCARCE SEDGE SPECIES INSPIRED OUR APPROACH

AND WHO DEVOTED MUCH TIME TO THE PROJECT

UNTIL HIS DEATH IN APRIL 1993

Scarce Plants in Britain

Compiled and edited by

A. STEWART
Joint Nature Conservation Committee

D.A. PEARMAN
Botanical Society of the British Isles

and

C.D. PRESTON
Institute of Terrestrial Ecology

© JNCC 1994

First published in 1994 by JNCC, Monkstone House, City Road, Peterborough, PE1 1JY, U.K.

Typeset by PCL Type & Graphics, Birmingham   Printed and bound by W. Lake, Birmingham

ISBN 1 873701 66 7

Contents

List of tables

List of figures

Foreword

Forty years elapsed between the Botanical Society of the British Isles (BSBI) setting out to map the distribution of the British flora and the publication of *Scarce plants in Britain*. During this time enormous changes have taken place in our aims and objectives, as well as in the human and technical resources available to carry out the work involved in compiling maps.

Those who promoted the need for the *Atlas of the British flora* wanted to know more about the distribution of our vascular plants and their relationship to climate, topography and soils. This was not available from the county summaries published by G.C. Druce in 1932 in *The comital flora of the British Isles* and its predecessors, or from the incomplete coverage of local floras, many from the 19th century, which then existed.

The BSBI was astonished at the response from members and non-members. The gathering of 1½ million records in 5 years far exceeded expectations. However, in the 32 years that the *Atlas* has been in print, the maps have been used increasingly for other purposes, such as the selection of species as candidates for Red Data Books and as a basis for monitoring changes in distribution. For some species the information was satisfactory, but for others it was much less so: these differences relate to the way in which data were gathered in preparing the *Atlas* maps.

For the approximately 400 rarest species, those recorded from not more than 20 vice-counties in the *Comital flora*, detailed research in herbaria and in the literature, combined with local knowledge from field botanists, ensured that maps of these species in the *Atlas* included all the data which were available at that time. Subsequent selection of Red Data Book plants, and the intensive recent field work on these species, means that knowledge of the distribution of the majority of the rarest species is relatively complete.

However, for the 700 species in the *Atlas* recorded from 21 to 100 vice-counties in the *Comital flora,* the *Atlas* treatment was far less intensive. The outline of the known distribution was fairly represented, but those species which were rare or local over most of their range were often severely under-recorded during the one or two days fieldwork which was all that hundreds of 10 km squares received, with the time and man-power available in the 1950s.

It is the rarest 300 of those 700 species (plants which were recorded in 16-100 of the 10 km squares) which are the subject of this volume and have been mapped comprehensively for the first time. This was possible only because of the intensive fieldwork which has been carried out by BSBI members over the last 35 years and because of support given by the Biological Records Centre, the Nature Conservancy Council and (since 1991) the Joint Nature Conservation Committee. Since 1960, much of Great Britain has been covered by local mapping projects using either 'tetrads' (2 km × 2 km squares) or 5 km × 5 km squares as the mapping unit. These methods resulted in a thorough search being made and much more comprehensive information being gathered than that on which the *Atlas* was based.

Furthermore, the tetrad surveys have made it possible to map some species in more detail. For these, maps show the number of tetrads in which the species was found per 10 km square and provide more quantitative information than has hitherto been possible. Such maps will be a powerful tool for monitoring in the future, and may even become a routine product.

The potential for mapping plants at intervals is also demonstrated here, with series of maps showing distribution at different periods of time. Even allowing for difficulties of interpretation, because of the different level of survey now compared with that in the past, these suggest significant changes in our flora and that losses of some species have been extensive and alarming.

Many of the scarce species have suffered significant losses. The most serious declines are shown by lowland species of inland situations, some of which now occur in less that 70% of the 10 km squares from which they were formerly recorded, e.g. *Silene gallica* and *Sium latifolium* - arable and wetland species respectively.

It is this lowland flora, which has been subjected to severe habitat destruction over the last 40 years, that it is desirable to map again in detail now. So, whilst we can all be justly proud of *Scarce plants in Britain* and look forward to the next edition of the *Red Data Book,* currently being prepared by the Joint Nature Conservation Committee, the major challenge for the BSBI is to complete a resurvey of all the commoner species, many of which are lowland, and prepare a comprehensive new *Atlas of the British flora* before the end of the millennium. Only then will the work begun in 1954 have been truly completed.

Franklyn Perring
President, BSBI
Green Acre, Wood Lane, Oundle, July 1994

Introduction

The publication of the *Atlas of the British Flora* in 1962 had many far-reaching consequences both for botany and for other branches of natural history in Britain and Europe. One of these was the fact that the objective mapping of records in 10 kilometre squares, pioneered by the *Atlas,* provided a crude but effective index to the rarity of plants in Britain and Ireland. In 1967 a detailed survey of the rarest British species, defined as those which were present in 15 or fewer 10 km squares, was initiated. The results were published in the *British Red Data Book:1 Vascular Plants* (Perring & Farrell 1977), and updated in a second edition which appeared six years later (Perring & Farrell 1983). Since 1983 the Red Data Book species have continued to be monitored intensively, and work on a new edition of the *Red Data Book* was started by the Joint Nature Conservation Committee, in co-operation with the Botanical Society of the British Isles, in 1993. Rare species in Ireland are covered by a separate *Red Data Book* (Curtis & McGough 1988).

Many of the species which are not sufficiently rare to qualify for the *Red Data Book* are nevertheless of considerable interest to conservationists. The next tier of rarity which is recognised in Britain comprises the nationally scarce species, which are defined as those which are recorded nationally in 16-100 10 km squares. These species are used in evaluating the conservation importance of sites: their presence is one of the criteria used to select Sites of Special Scientific Interest (Nature Conservancy Council 1989). Scarce species also have considerable potential as indicators of environmental change, and a study of trends in their distribution is likely to highlight the impact of changes in the countryside on the British flora. Despite the importance of the scarce species, they were inevitably rather neglected during the period in which attention was concentrated on the very rarest species. This book presents an updated picture of the distribution of scarce species in Britain, based on the results of a project jointly undertaken by the Botanical Society of the British Isles, the Biological Records Centre of the Institute of Terrestrial Ecology and the Joint Nature Conservation Committee (which took over the project from the Nature Conservancy Council).

The species covered by the current study are those which at the start of the project were thought to be present in 16-100 10 km squares. These included those species which were mapped in this range of squares in the *Atlas of the British Flora*, plus some additional species which were mapped in more squares in the *Atlas* but which were thought to have declined significantly since then. The main aim of the project was to assemble into a database details of all the sites at which the species have been reliably recorded since 1970. A welcome result of the project has been the revelation that some species are more frequent than had been supposed, and now occur in more than 100 10 km squares. Sadly, it is also true that a few species appear to be rarer than they were and now qualify for inclusion in the *Red Data Book*. In presenting the results of the project we have reassessed the list of scarce species, and distinguished between those species which are still regarded as scarce, those which are now rare and those which are too frequent to qualify for the scarce category.

The main part of this book is an account of the individual species covered by the project. The distribution of each species is summarised as a 10 km square distribution map which distinguishes records in or after 1970 from earlier records. This is accompanied by a text which outlines the habitat of the species, summarises its reproductive biology, comments on any historic changes in its distribution, assesses current threats and outlines the distribution of the species outside Britain.

From the beginning of the project we have been conscious that the standard dot-distribution map, although invaluable, is a very simplified summary of the detailed data which are available for many species. Ever since the publication of the original *Atlas*, critics have pointed out that a presence of a dot in a 10 km square only shows that the species is present, but does not distinguish between squares in which it is abundant and those in which there is only a single individual. In presenting the results of this project we have therefore tried to provide maps for some scarce species which not only show presence in a square but also give an indication of frequency within that square as well. We believe that this presents a more valuable means of assessing the conservation status of species, and we hope that it will be possible to extend this approach to other species in the future.

Aims and methods of the project

Aims

The main aim of the scarce species project was to create a computer database of records of nationally scarce vascular plants. The definition of a nationally scarce plant adopted for the project was a species which had been recorded as a native plant in 16-100 10 km squares of the Ordnance Survey national grid from 1970 onwards. The choice of this cut-off date was a compromise between the desire to obtain the most up-to-date information and the need for the geographical and taxonomic coverage to be as complete as possible. A later cut-off date, such as 1980, would have meant that accepted records were more recent but that the geographical coverage would have been inadequate, particularly for some remote areas and critical taxa. The definition of a scarce species was, however, extended to cover some species, all of them arable weeds, which are known to have declined rapidly and which had been recorded in 16-100 10 km squares from 1980 onwards. We attempted to collect localised records of all the sites where scarce species had been recorded since 1970. A subsidiary aim of the project was to gather sufficient pre-1970 records to provide an indication of the distribution of the species before 1970 at the 10 km square scale. At the end of the project the aim was to revise the list of nationally scarce plant species and to publish the records of all the species covered in summary form.

Organisation

The project was a co-operative venture which originally involved three organisations: the Nature Conservancy Council (NCC), the Institute of Terrestrial Ecology (ITE), through the Biological Records Centre (BRC), and the Botanical Society of the British Isles (BSBI). A project to survey the plants in 16-30 10 km squares was suggested by BRC in 1987 and subsequently expanded to include all the scarce species. It was started in 1990 with funding from NCC as part of the Great Britain Nature Conservation Review Strategy. The Joint Nature Conservation Committee (JNCC) took over NCC's responsibility for the project when NCC was disbanded in April 1991.

Alison Stewart was employed by NCC in October 1990 on a two-year contract to work on the project, and was based at ITE's Monks Wood station. Miss C. Ward (October 1990-May 1991) and Miss S.E. Yates (June 1991-October 1992) were also employed by NCC/JNCC as her assistants. The other members of the project team were D.A. Pearman (BSBI) and C.D. Preston (BRC). The main sources of new plant records were the vice-county recorders of the BSBI, volunteers who are appointed by the BSBI to maintain records from the Watsonian vice-counties. A map of the vice-counties is given as Figure 1.

Geographical coverage

The project covered the whole of Great Britain, the Isle of Man and the Channel Islands. However, we have followed the traditional definition of scarce plants which includes those which occur in 16-100 10 km squares in Britain and the Isle of Man; records from the Channel Islands are excluded. All 10 km squares are included in the total, including coastal squares which do not contain a full 100 square kilometres of land.

Taxonomic coverage

The aim of the project was to include all nationally scarce species of vascular plants. Fortunately the *New Flora of the British Isles* (Stace 1991) was published during the period that the project was running and we have followed its taxonomy and nomenclature. Like Stace (1991), we have excluded species in the large apomictic or facultatively apomictic genera *Hieracium*, *Rubus* and *Taraxacum*. This is not because we regard the conservation of these species as less important than that of other vascular plants, but because the task of assembling data on their distribution would need a different approach from that which was adopted for the more easily identified species. The only departure from Stace's (1991) taxonomy lies in our treatment of the *Limonium binervosum* group. We have aggregated records into a single broadly defined species. Stace (1991) recognises 22 species and subspecies within this aggregate but admits that the species are difficult to distinguish and the subspecies are even less easy to define. We did not have sufficient data to assess their distribution and ecology adequately.

The plants covered by the project are those described in 325 individual accounts later in this book. The species included were basically those listed as nationally scarce by the Nature Conservancy Council (1989), a list which is based on the maps in the *Atlas of the British Flora* (Perring & Walters 1962) and the *Atlas of Ferns* (Jermy *et al.* 1978) with modifications in the light of later evidence. We excluded from this list a number of introductions or probable introductions (*Anisantha diandra*, *Chenopodium*

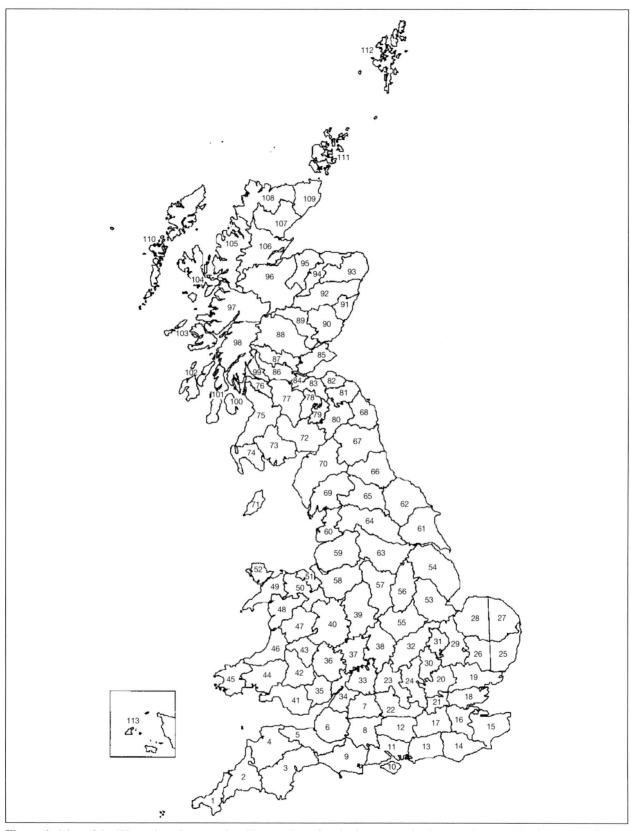

Figure 1 Map of the Watsonian vice-counties. The number of each vice-county is given on the map. For the names of the vice-counties, see Table 3.

glaucum, Fagopyrum esculentum, Festuca longifolia auct.), hybrids (*Dryopteris* × *deweveri, D.* × *tavelii, Equisetum* × *litorale, Polystichum* × *bicknellii*), infraspecific taxa (*Asplenium trichomanes* subsp. *trichomanes, Epilobium tetragonum* subsp. *lamyi, Euphrasia arctica* subsp. *arctica*) and species which were already known to occur in more than 100 10 km squares (*Carex diandra, Draba incana, Geranium rotundifolium, Raphanus maritimus, Valerianella carinata*). We added to the list three species which had apparently been omitted by accident (*Ajuga pyramidalis, Calamagrostis stricta, Lepidium latifolium*) and eleven species which were included in the *Red Data Book* (Perring & Farrell 1983), or were added to the list of species qualifying for the *Red Data Book* by the Nature Conservancy Council (1989), but were now believed to occur in more than 15 10 km squares (*Ajuga chamaepitys, Arabis glabra, Atriplex longipes, Centaurea cyanus, Elatine hydropiper, Fallopia dumetorum, Juncus filiformis, Najas flexilis, Orobanche maritima, Silene conica* and *Spiranthes romanzoffiana*). We also included a further 16 species which appeared from evidence from the BSBI Monitoring Scheme (Rich & Woodruff 1990) or from other sources to have declined appreciably (*Carex elata, Chamaemelum nobile, Epilobium lanceolatum, Galeopsis angustifolia, Gnaphalium sylvaticum, Hydrocharis morsus-ranae, Hyoscyamus niger, Hypochaeris glabra, Orchis morio, Polygala calcarea, Potentilla argentea, Ranunculus parviflorus, Silene noctiflora, Teesdalia nudicaulis, Ulex minor* and *Ulmus plotii*).

We had begun to collect data for the project before the appearance of Stace's *New Flora* (1991). A few of the species included in the scope of the project are treated by Stace (1991) as introductions (*Briza minor, Poa palustris*), are relegated to infraspecific status (*Orobanche maritima*) or are placed in taxonomic limbo (*Cochlearia scotica*). We have presented the results of the project for these species but have not considered them for inclusion in the revised list of scarce species. We attempted to obtain data on *Centaurium capitatum*, treated by Stace as *C. erythraea* var. *capitatum*, but the available records proved to be inadequate because of the taxonomic uncertainty which surrounds this plant and we have not included the results in this volume.

If a species which qualifies as scarce in Britain is represented by more than one native subspecies we have attempted to collect records of the subspecies separately. However, if a species is represented by both a native and an alien subspecies we have restricted our attention to the native taxon.

It is unfortunate that in making our initial assessment of species which are likely to be present in 16-100 10 km squares we have had to rely on the maps in the *Atlas of the British Flora*, which are largely based on a field survey carried out between 1954 and 1959. This reliance is unavoidable as this was the last geographically comprehensive survey of the British flora. There must be a strong possibility that some species which are shown in well over 100 squares in the *Atlas* have declined since 1962 and would now qualify as scarce species. We have included in the survey species which were shown to have suffered a marked decline in the BSBI Monitoring Scheme, but this was only based on a sample of squares and it was not designed to detect trends in the distribution of relatively uncommon species. The work on the scarce species project, like that on the Monitoring Scheme (Rich & Woodruff 1990), has emphasised the need for an updated atlas of vascular plants.

Acquisition of data

Data on the species covered by the project were acquired and processed in the following stages.

1. Existing data on the selected species held by the Biological Records Centre were computerised, if not already held on computer file. The data held by BRC are the records collected for publication in the *Atlas of the British Flora* and additional data sent in since then. The latter included records submitted for revised maps of ferns (Jermy *et al.* 1978), sedges (Jermy, Chater & David 1982) and crucifers (Rich 1991) and records of other species sent because they represented additional 10 km square records to those published in the *Atlas*. Relevant data from other surveys are also held by BRC, notably the results of the BSBI Monitoring Scheme (Rich & Woodruff 1990) and surveys of arable weeds (Smith 1989) and limestone pavements (Ward & Evans 1976).

2. Print-outs of records for individual vice-counties and draft distribution maps were circulated to BSBI vice-county recorders or their nominated representatives. Recorders were asked to check the accuracy of existing records for each species, to provide later records from known sites and to report additional sites. Records were sent by recorders to BRC as manuscript lists, on standard record cards or in computerised form.

    The BSBI vice-county recorders are the main source of information on the detailed distribution of the British flora. They are usually active fieldworkers themselves and often have their own network of botanists reporting to them. Some recorders based their responses to the print-outs on the records they already held; others organised fieldwork in 1991 and 1992 to check on the current status of scarce species in their vice-counties.

3. The list of species covered by the project was published in *BSBI News*, and details were also placed in the newsletters of the Wild Flower Society and the British Pteridological Society. In addition to a general request

for records of the species covered, individuals with a particular interest in one or more species were invited to 'adopt' the species and compile records from literature or herbarium sources or survey the plant in the field. Experts on critical species were invited to work with the project to ensure that the records of these taxa were taxonomically reliable.

4. The records of all species were reviewed by D.A. Pearman, who took particular responsibility for adding records from published county floras and other literature sources which were not reaching the project by other routes.

5. All records which were submitted to the project as a result of stages 2, 3 and 4 were added to the database. Revised print-outs of records from individual vice-counties and a set of draft distribution maps were sent to vice-county recorders for final checking.

As they were incorporated into the database the records were subjected to standard BRC checking programs to ensure the consistency of the geographical and other information, eg the vice-county was checked against the grid reference.

Additional sources of data were available for 28 aquatic plants, as these were the subject of a concurrent project jointly funded by the Institute of Terrestrial Ecology, the Joint Nature Conservation Committee and the National Rivers Authority. The sources of data for this project are described by Preston & Croft (1992).

Distinguishing native records of a species

The definition of a scarce species that we have adopted refers to 10 km squares where the species is present as a native. This presents no problem for those species which can be assumed to be native at all their sites in the sense that they have arrived at the locality without being deliberately or accidentally transported there by man. However, there are many species which are believed or known to be native in some of their localities but are introduced elsewhere. In many cases recorders have been able to specify whether the species was native or introduced, but it is often impossible to decide whether a species is native on the basis of fieldwork alone as historical evidence must also be assessed (Webb 1985). The most experienced recorders have sometimes been the most reluctant to express an opinion. We as editors have therefore had to use our own judgement in assessing the status of species in particular 10 km squares. In making these decisions we have normally been guided by the treatment of the species in the *Atlas of the British Flora*. We think that this presents a realistic assessment of the status of most species, and also recognise that there is an

arbitrary element to the decisions which have to be made and there is no point in presenting alternative opinions if the evidence to support them is equally weak. Some of the species which would qualify as scarce are only doubtfully native to Britain as a whole. In deciding whether or not to include these we have followed Stace (1991).

The decisions about the native status of species at particular sites have been the most difficult and unsatisfactory ones we have had to make as editors. This distinction is undoubtedly worth making in some cases, particularly if the introduced populations are not persistent, but we have sometimes wondered whether it would not be better for conservationists to accept the distribution of species such as *Helleborus foetidus*, *Hippophae rhamnoides*, *Meconopsis cambrica* and *Nymphoides peltata* as it is, rather than to continue to attempt to maintain a theoretical distinction which has little relevance to the behaviour of the plant in the field.

Preparation of accounts of individual species

Botanists who had offered to 'adopt' a particular species were invited to draft an account of that species for publication with the distribution maps. Other authors were recruited to draft accounts of plants which they knew well or which grew in habitats which they had studied. We attempted to find authors who were not vice-county recorders, as the request for species texts came at a time when recorders were fully occupied in providing distributional data to the project. After the draft texts had been assembled they were circulated to a few vice-county recorders, covering geographically disparate areas, who had offered to read the accounts of all the species from their region. Draft texts were also sent to other botanists with relevant experience of the species concerned. The final accounts are basically those submitted by the original author but most have been modified in some degree in the light of the comments we received, or because of the need to edit all the texts into a consistent format.

Structure of the database

All records in the project database are held by BRC on the ORACLE database management system. The following details can be held on computer for an individual record. Data in some fields (eg species, vice-county, grid reference) are available for all or almost all of the records on file; data in other fields (eg altitude, population size) have been computerised if they were provided by the recorder but they are not available for all records. Fields which are merely present for internal database management reasons are omitted from the following list.

Species: code number of species

Identification: code which tags doubtful records (these do not appear on the distribution map or in the statistics for the species)

Vice-county: number of the Watsonian vice-county

Grid reference: Ordnance Survey grid reference. If the grid reference is only approximate this fact is tagged in a separate field.

Tetrad: code letter for the tetrad

Locality: name of locality (in words)

Altitude: altitude (in metres)

Date: date of record (day, month and year as separate fields). In some cases this might be the date of publication if that is the only date available.

Dateclass: code letters which tag approximate dates, dates of publication, etc.

Recorder(s): code number for recorder(s)

Determiner(s): code number for determiner(s), if they differ from the recorders

Status: distinguishes records of plants which are thought to be native at the site in question from established introductions and casual occurrences

Source: code for source (field, herbarium or literature record). The standard herbarium abbreviation or a code for the literature source is given in a separate field.

Population size: the number of individuals in the population, given as a number or (if only an approximate estimate is available) allocated to the range 1-10, 11-100, 101-1000 or over 1000 plants.

Extinct: used to tag populations which are believed to be extinct. A separate code is used for populations which have been searched for without success but which cannot yet be adjudged extinct with any confidence.

Confidential: used to tag confidential records.

Evenness of the survey

Most BSBI vice-county recorders responded enthusiastically to the scarce species initiative, and data have been received from almost the entire area covered by the project (Figure 2). The only vice-counties from which it was not possible to obtain data were Renfrewshire, Kincardineshire and Stirlingshire. However, there were also a number of counties (marked on the map) from which we received the best data available but where there had been insufficient fieldwork since 1970 to give a true picture of the current localities for scarce species.

A total of 138,099 records were submitted and processed during the course of the survey. These were added to the 29,432 records held by BRC on computer file before the beginning of the project to give a total database of 167,531 records. Some 75% of these records are for dates from 1950 onwards, 50% are for the period from 1970 and 17% date from 1988 or later, and were therefore made after the last major national botanical survey, the BSBI Monitoring Scheme. Over 1,100 botanists took part in fieldwork for the project in 1991 and 1992.

The number of records of all the species covered by the project are shown for individual 10 km squares in Figure 3; the records dating from 1970 onwards are shown in Figure 4 and Figure 5 illustrates the number of records made in 1991-92. It should be emphasised that the absence of a large number of 1991-92 records may reflect no discredit on the botanists in the counties concerned, as a county which had just completed a detailed floristic survey, for example, would have little need for new fieldwork. The records made from 1970 onwards are summarised in Figure 6 as the mean number of records per species recorded.

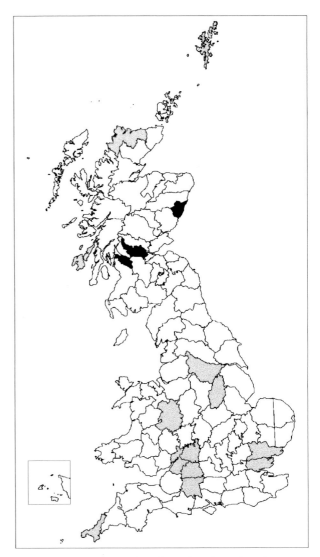

Figure 2 Records received from the Watsonian vice-counties. Adequate records were received from all the unshaded vice-counties. The records received from the vice-counties shaded grey are believed to be inadequate to identify all the recent localities for scarce species. No records were received from the vice-counties shaded black.

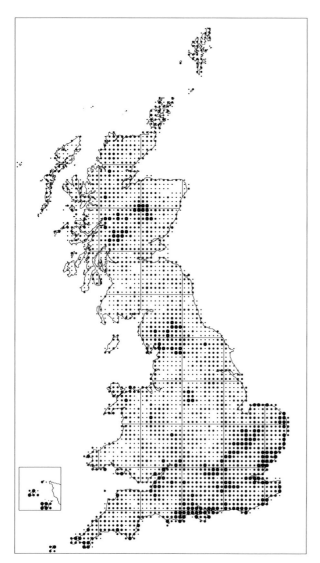

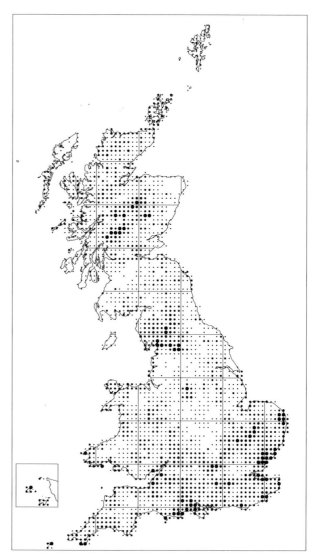

Figure 3 Total number of records of all species covered by the project, mapped in 10 km squares. Dots of increasing size indicate that 1-9 records, 10-49 records, 50-99 records and 100 or more records are available for the square.

Figure 4 Number of records of all species covered by the project dating from 1970 onwards, mapped in 10 km squares. Dots of increasing size indicate that 1-9 records, 10-49 records, 50-99 records and 100 or more records are available for the square.

16

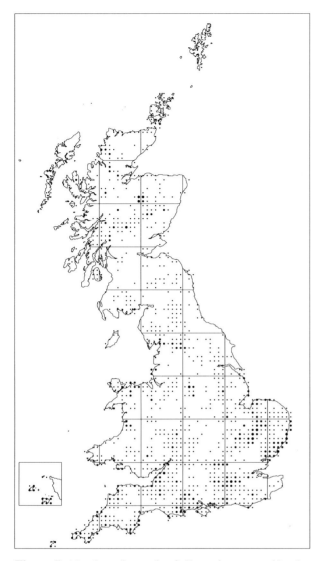 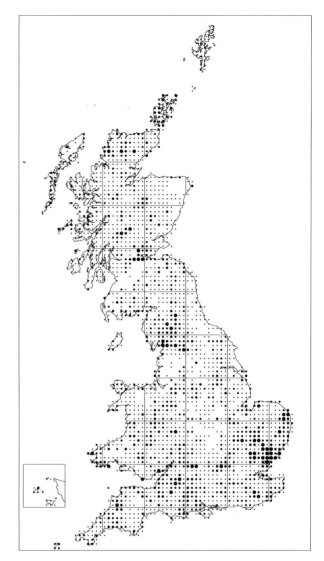

Figure 5 Number of records of all species covered by the project dating from 1991-92, mapped in 10 km squares. Dots of increasing size indicate that 1-9 records, 10-49 records, 50-99 records and 100 or more records are available for the square.

Figure 6 Mean number of records per species covered by the project dating from 1970 onwards, mapped in 10 km squares. To obtain this figure the number of records for all species covered by the project which date from 1970 onwards has been divided by the number of species recorded since 1970. Dots of increasing size indicate that 1-2 records, 3-5 records, 6-9 records and 10 or more records per species are available.

Revised list of scarce species

The species which have been recorded from 16-100 10 km squares from 1970 onwards are listed in Table 1. A number of arable weeds which have been recorded in more than 100 km squares since 1970 but are known to have declined rapidly and have been recorded in only 16-100 squares since 1980 are also included in the list. This constitutes the revised list of 254 scarce species which should now replace that published by the Nature Conservancy Council (1989).

Nine species covered by the project have been recorded in fewer than 16 10 km squares since 1970. These are listed in Table 2. Four of these species are thought to be genuinely restricted to fewer than 16 squares but the remaining five are probably under-recorded, and almost certainly await rediscovery in some of the squares for which there are only pre-1970 records. *Mentha pulegium* is included in this list as this well-recorded and declining species has been found in fewer than 16 squares from 1980 onwards.

The number of scarce species ever recorded from each vice-county is listed in Table 3, where it is compared to the number recorded since 1970. These figures are based on the revised list of scarce species in Table 1 and the species in Table 2.

The total number of scarce species ever recorded in each 10 km square is mapped in Figure 7. The number recorded in each square from 1970 onwards is mapped in Figure 8. The difference between the total number of species recorded in each square and the number seen since 1970 is mapped in Figure 9. These maps are also based on the revised list of species in Table 1 and the species in Table 2.

Species which are included in the latest edition of the *Red Data Book* are listed in the index. The *Red Data Book* is currently being revised by JNCC in a project led by M.J. Wigginton. Some species which are now known in 15 or fewer squares might be found in over 15 squares as a result of this work. A further revision of the list of scarce species may therefore become necessary when the new edition of the *Red Data Book* is available.

Table 1 Revised list of nationally scarce species. Species which are included in the *Red Data Book* (Perring & Farrell 1983) but are now known to occur in over 15 10 km squares are marked with an asterisk.

Aceras anthropophorum	*Atriplex longipes	Carex rupestris	Dactylorhiza traunsteineri
Aconitum napellus	Atriplex praecox	Carex saxatilis	Daphne mezereum
Actaea spicata	Betula nana	Carex vaginata	Deschampsia setacea
Adiantum capillus-veneris	Brassica oleracea	Centaurea cyanus	Dianthus armeria
Ajuga chamaepitys	Bromopsis benekenii	Centaurium littorale	Dianthus deltoides
Ajuga pyramidalis	Bupleurum tenuissimum	Cephalanthera longifolia	Draba muralis
Alchemilla glomerulans	Callitriche truncata	Cerastium alpinum	Draba norvegica
Alchemilla wichurae	Campanula patula	Cerastium arcticum	Dryas octopetala
Allium schoenoprasum	Cardamine bulbifera	Cerastium cerastoides	Dryopteris submontana
Alopecurus borealis	Cardamine impatiens	Cerastium pumilum	Elatine hexandra
Alopecurus bulbosus	Carex appropinquata	Chamaemelum nobile	*Elatine hydropiper
Althaea officinalis	Carex atrata	Cicendia filiformis	Epipactis atrorubens
Apera interrupta	Carex capillaris	Cicuta virosa	Epipactis leptochila
Apera spica-venti	Carex digitata	Circaea alpina	Epipactis phyllanthes
Arabis glabra	Carex divisa	Clinopodium calamintha	Equisetum pratense
Arabis petraea	Carex elongata	Coincya monensis subsp.	Equisetum variegatum
Arctostaphylos alpinus	Carex ericetorum	monensis	Erodium moschatum
Arum italicum subsp.	Carex humilis	Corallorhiza trifida	Euphorbia platyphyllos
neglectum	Carex magellanica	Crassula tillaea	Euphorbia portlandica
Asplenium obovatum	Carex maritima	Crepis mollis	Euphrasia foulaensis
Asplenium septentrionale	Carex montana	Cuscuta europaea	Euphrasia frigida
Athyrium distentifolium	Carex punctata	Cyperus longus	Euphrasia ostenfeldii

continued

Euphrasia pseudokerneri
Euphrasia rostkoviana
  subsp. montana
Euphrasia rostkoviana
  subsp. rostkoviana
Fallopia dumetorum
Festuca arenaria
Frankenia laevis
Fritillaria meleagris
Fumaria densiflora
Fumaria parviflora
Fumaria purpurea
Fumaria vaillantii
Galeopsis angustifolia
Galium parisiense
Galium pumilum
Gentiana pneumonanthe
Gentianella anglica
Gentianella germanica
Goodyera repens
Gymnocarpium
  robertianum
Hammarbya paludosa
Helianthemum canum
Helleborus foetidus
Herminium monorchis
Hippophae rhamnoides
Hordelymus europaeus
Hordeum marinum
Hornungia petraea
Hypericum undulatum
Hypochaeris glabra
Iberis amara
Illecebrum verticillatum
Impatiens noli-tangere
Inula crithmoides
Isoetes echinospora
Juncus acutus
Juncus alpinoarticulatus
Juncus balticus
Juncus biglumis
Juncus castaneus
*Juncus filiformis
Lathyrus aphaca
Lathyrus japonicus

Lathyrus palustris
Lepidium latifolium
Limonium humile
Limosella aquatica
Linnaea borealis
Linum perenne
Lotus subbiflorus
Luronium natans
Lycopodiella inundata
Lycopodium annotinum
Lysimachia thyrsiflora
Marrubium vulgare
Meconopsis cambrica
Medicago minima
Medicago polymorpha
Medicago sativa subsp.
  falcata
Melampyrum cristatum
Melampyrum sylvaticum
Melittis melissophyllum
Mertensia maritima
Meum athamanticum
Minuartia hybrida
Minuartia sedoides
Minuartia verna
Myosotis stolonifera
Myriophyllum
  verticillatum
Nuphar pumila
Nymphoides peltata
Oenanthe silaifolia
Ophioglossum azoricum
Orchis purpurea
Orchis ustulata
Ornithogalum pyrenaicum
Orobanche alba
Orobanche hederae
Orobanche rapum-genistae
Parapholis incurva
Persicaria laxiflora
Peucedanum palustre
Phleum alpinum
Phyteuma orbiculare
Pilularia globulifera
Pinus sylvestris

Poa alpina
Poa bulbosa
Poa glauca
Polygonatum odoratum
Polygonum boreale
Polypogon monspeliensis
Potamogeton coloratus
Potamogeton compressus
Potamogeton filiformis
Potamogeton trichoides
Potentilla crantzii
Potentilla neumanniana
Primula elatior
Primula farinosa
Primula scotica
Puccinellia fasciculata
Puccinellia rupestris
Pulmonaria longifolia
Pulsatilla vulgaris
Pyrola media
Pyrola rotundifolia subsp.
  maritima
Pyrola rotundifolia subsp.
  rotundifolia
Ranunculus tripartitus
Rhynchospora fusca
Ribes alpinum
Ribes spicatum
Ruppia cirrhosa
Sagina saginoides
Salicornia pusilla
Salix arbuscula
Salix lapponum
Salix myrsinites
Salix reticulata
Sarcocornia perennis
Saxifraga nivalis
Scandix pecten-veneris
Scilla autumnalis
Sedum forsterianum
Sedum villosum
Sesleria caerulea
Sibbaldia procumbens
Sibthorpia europaea
Silene conica

Silene gallica
Silene nutans
Sium latifolium
Sonchus palustris
Sorbus devoniensis
Sorbus porrigentiformis
Sorbus rupicola
Spartina maritima
*Spiranthes romanzoffiana
Stratiotes aloides
Suaeda vera
Tephroseris integrifolia
  subsp. integrifolia
Thelypteris palustris
Thesium humifusum
Thlaspi caerulescens
Tilia platyphyllos
Torilis arvensis
Trifolium glomeratum
Trifolium occidentale
Trifolium ochroleucon
Trifolium squamosum
Trifolium suffocatum
Ulmus plotii
Vaccinium microcarpum
Verbascum lychnitis
Verbascum
  pulverulentum
Verbascum virgatum
Veronica alpina
Veronica spicata subsp.
  hybrida
Vicia bithynica
Vicia lutea
Vicia parviflora
Viola lactea
Vulpia ciliata subsp.
  ambigua
Vulpia fasciculata
Vulpia unilateralis
Wolffia arrhiza
Zostera angustifolia
Zostera marina
Zostera noltii

Table 2 Species covered by the project which are recorded in 15 or fewer 10 km squares. Those marked with an asterisk are believed to be under-recorded.

*Calamagrostis stricta
Carex vulpina
Chenopodium
  chenopodioides

Corynephorus canescens
*Cystopteris montana
*Euphrasia marshallii
*Luzula arcuata

Mentha pulegium
*Najas flexilis

19

Table 3 The number of native scarce species in each vice-county. Only species listed in Table 1 and Table 2 are included in these totals.

Vice-county	Scarce species recorded	Scarce species recorded since 1970	Percentage of scarce species recorded since 1970
1, W. Cornwall	61	51	84
2, E. Cornwall	61	45	74
3, S. Devon	89	67	75
4, N. Devon	62	38	61
5, S. Somerset	62	47	76
6, N. Somerset	94	71	76
7, N. Wilts.	48	29	60
8, S. Wilts.	54	30	56
9, Dorset	110	92	84
10, Wight	74	44	59
11, S. Hants.	112	89	79
12, N. Hants.	68	53	78
13, W. Sussex	106	75	71
14, E. Sussex	96	68	71
15, E. Kent	101	77	76
16, W. Kent	94	62	66
17, Surrey	83	58	70
18, S. Essex	73	42	58
19, N. Essex	88	54	61
20, Herts.	58	35	60
21, Middlesex	48	13	27
22, Berks.	73	46	63
23, Oxon.	59	49	83
24, Bucks.	60	33	55
25, E. Suffolk	96	71	74
26, W. Suffolk	67	47	70
27, E. Norfolk	90	59	66
28, W. Norfolk	96	64	67
29, Cambs.	74	52	70
30, Beds.	52	33	63
31, Hunts.	37	21	57
32, Northants.	44	14	32
33, E. Gloucs.	52	37	71
34, W. Gloucs.	78	54	69
35, Mons.	49	34	69
36, Herefs.	54	29	54
37, Worcs.	61	39	64
38, Warks.	37	15	41
39, Staffs.	45	22	49

Vice-county	Scarce species recorded	Scarce species recorded since 1970	Percentage of scarce species recorded since 1970
40, Salop.	54	38	70
41, Glam.	80	49	61
42, Brecs.	33	28	85
43, Rads.	27	17	63
44, Carms.	53	35	66
45, Pembs.	57	47	82
46, Cards.	36	27	75
47, Monts.	29	21	72
48, Merioneth	51	40	78
49, Caerns.	86	60	70
50, Denbs.	43	29	67
51, Flints.	35	20	57
52, Anglesey	49	32	65
53, S. Lincs.	60	40	67
54, N. Lincs.	70	44	63
55, Leics.	44	15	34
56, Notts.	44	18	41
57, Derbys.	48	37	77
58, Cheshire	44	12	27
59, S. Lancs.	49	14	29
60, W. Lancs.	52	35	67
61, S.E. Yorks.	54	34	63
62, N.E. Yorks.	63	19	30
63, S.W. Yorks.	50	16	32
64, Mid-W. Yorks.	75	54	72
65, N.W. Yorks.	67	45	67
66, Co. Durham	68	35	51
67, S. Northumb.	46	34	74
68, Cheviot	49	36	73
69, Westmorland	96	78	81
70, Cumberland	75	51	68
71, Man	23	13	57
72, Dumfriess.	42	26	62
73, Kirkcudbrights.	39	31	79
74, Wigtowns.	23	15	65
75, Ayrs.	33	19	58
76, Renfrews.	19	9	47
77, Lanarks.	21	13	62
78, Peebless.	14	6	43

continued

Vice-county	Scarce species recorded	Scarce species recorded since 1970	Percentage of scarce species recorded since 1970
79, Selkirks.	16	14	88
80, Roxburghs.	28	20	71
81, Berwicks.	24	10	42
82, E. Lothian	28	14	50
83, Midlothian	36	12	33
84, W. Lothian	15	4	27
85, Fife	36	21	58
86, Stirlings.	39	13	33
87, W. Perth	53	41	77
88, Mid Perth	72	59	82
89, E. Perth	62	50	81
90, Angus	82	56	68
91, Kincardines.	28	9	32
92, S. Aberdeen	69	52	75
93, N. Aberdeen	23	16	70
94, Banffs.	52	43	83
95, Moray	42	31	74
96, Easterness	76	71	93
97, Westerness	65	59	91
98, Main Argyll	65	55	85
99, Dunbarton	36	26	72
100, Clyde Is.	22	11	50
101, Kintyre	26	21	81
102, S. Ebudes	28	17	61
103, Mid Ebudes	36	27	75
104, N. Ebudes	49	44	90
105, W. Ross	65	48	74
106, E. Ross	69	52	75
107, E. Sutherland	58	41	71
108, W. Sutherland	64	47	73
109, Caithness	31	25	81
110, Outer Hebrides	28	23	82
111, Orkney	24	20	83
112, Shetland	17	16	94
113, Channel Islands	76	50	66

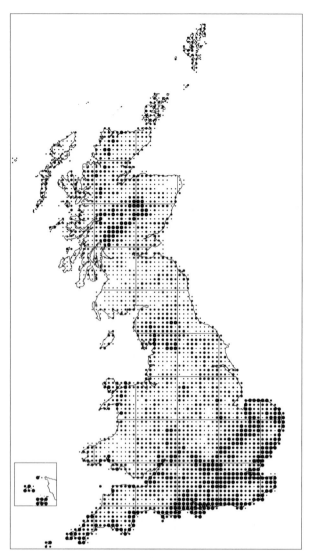

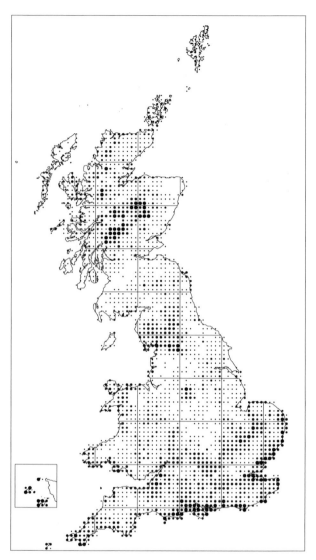

Figure 7 Number of scarce species recorded in each 10 km square. The species mapped are listed in Tables 1 and 2. Dots of increasing size indicate 1-4 species, 5-9 species, 10-19 species and 20 or more species per square.

Figure 8 Number of scarce species recorded from 1970 onwards in each 10 km square. The species mapped are listed in Tables 1 and 2. Dots of increasing size indicate 1-4 species, 5-9 species, 10-19 species and 20 or more species per square.

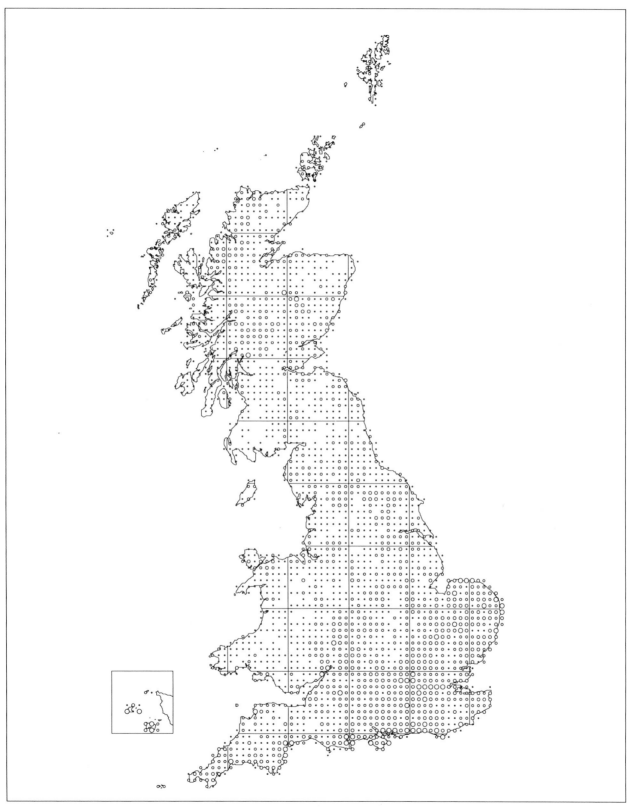

Figure 9 Number of scarce species in each 10 km square which were recorded before 1970 but have not subsequently been refound. The species mapped are listed in Tables 1 and 2. Circles of increasing size indicate 1-4 species, 5-9 species, 10-19 species and 20 or more species per square.

Accounts of individual species

Explanation of the maps and accompanying text

The scientific and English names at the head of each account are taken from Stace (1991). The revised status of each species is also given. The following terms are used:

Rare: recorded in 15 or fewer 10 km squares from 1970 onwards.

Scarce: recorded in 16-100 10 km squares from 1970 onwards or (for a few species) from 1980 onwards. If a 1980 cut-off date has been used this is explained in the text for that species.

Not scarce: recorded in more than 100 10 km squares from 1970 onwards.

A few cases which do not fit into these categories are explained individually. Species which are specially protected under the provisions of Schedule 8 of the Wildlife and Countryside Act 1981 (as amended) are noted as 'WCA Schedule 8 species'.

The distribution of each species is illustrated by a distribution map which plots the records for that species in the 10 × 10 km squares of the Ordnance Survey national grid. The Channel Islands are shown in an inset and records from there are plotted in the 10 × 10 km squares of the Universal Transverse Mercator Grid. The maps have been plotted using the DMAP program for distribution and coincidence map plotting, written by Dr A. J. Morton.

The following symbols are used on the standard maps for each species:

●   Record of native plant(s) made in or after 1970

○   Record of native plant(s) made before 1970

×   Record of introduced plant(s)

The symbols are listed above in the order of priority in which they appear. If there is a native record made in or after 1970 for a square, a solid dot will appear. If there are pre-1970 native records and post-1970 introductions, the symbol plotted will be an open circle.

Briza minor and *Poa palustris*, the two species covered by the survey which are now thought to be introductions throughout their British range, are mapped with the symbols used for native populations of other species. It

has not been possible to distinguish native from introduced records of *Hyoscyamus niger* and so all records are mapped as if they were native.

The total number of squares from which a species is recorded is shown in a table beneath the map. The number of squares in which the plant is mapped as a native from 1970 onwards, the number of squares in which there are only earlier native records and the number of additional squares in which the plant has occurred as an introduction are listed under the heading 'Current map'. These figures are compared with the equivalent values on the maps in the *Atlas of the British Flora* (Perring & Walters 1962), abbreviated to 'Atlas', or its *Critical Supplement* (Perring & Sell 1968), abbreviated to 'Atlas (S)'. In cases where these publications distinguished records made from 1930 onwards, separate counts are given in the table. In some cases all records of a species were mapped as a single symbol, irrespective of date, and these counts are given as 'All records'.

Other aspects of the distribution of some scarce species are shown on separate maps. We have illustrated the frequency of some species in 10 km squares by plotting the number of tetrads in which they have been recorded since 1970. Tetrads are individual 2 × 2 km squares of the national grid; there are 25 tetrads in each 10 km square. The mapping of records in tetrads has become a very popular method of presenting distributional data in local floras since the publication of J.G. Dony's *Flora of Hertfordshire* in 1967. Many local recording schemes have since collected distributional data systematically on a tetrad basis, particularly in southern England where botanists are most numerous. In mapping the frequency of scarce species in tetrads for areas which have not been recorded systematically tetrad by tetrad we run the risk of underestimating their occurrence, as recorders may have simply noted the grid reference for the main colony of a species and ignored the fact that it just extended into another tetrad. However, we have selected species for this sort of map only if they were well recorded at a tetrad scale in most of their British range, and we have noted any areas in which individual species are likely to be under-recorded in the caption to the map.

It would have been possible to map the frequency of some well-recorded species in 1 km squares, but we have preferred to present these data as tetrad maps so that they are directly comparable to the rest. Similarly we could have mapped the number of sites at which some species occurred but the definition of sites can be problematic, and trial maps were essentially similar to the maps of the same species on a tetrad basis.

We have illustrated the changing distribution of some species over time by means of a series of maps. If a species is essentially sedentary, and rarely colonises new localities, all records are aggregated into an initial map and subsequent maps illustrate the records made after successive cut-off dates. The risk of this approach is that the maps will exaggerate the decline of a species if the species is mobile and tends to disappear from some localities, and colonise others. For mobile species the implicit assumption that the initial map of all records represents the distribution of the species at the start of botanical recording will be invalid. We have therefore mapped the distribution of species which are known to be mobile in specific time periods. This is a more satisfactory method, but it requires detailed research to obtain adequate historical records.

The final type of map we have used is one which shows the distribution of the species after a later cut-off date than 1970. These maps have been used for species which have declined markedly since 1970. When examining these maps it is important to remember that the scarce species project was designed to collect records from 1970 onwards, and there might therefore be a danger that we do not have a complete coverage for the period from 1980 onwards.

The first paragraph of the text for each species outlines its habitat and altitudinal range. The word 'lowland' is used to indicate that a species is confined to altitudes below 300 metres. The second paragraph deals with the reproductive biology of the plant. The following terms used to describe the breeding system of a plant may require explanation:

Autogamous: automatically self-pollinating.

Self-compatible: able to set seed by self-pollination.

Self-incompatible: unable to set seed by self-pollination.

Apomictic: producing seed which is formed, without fertilisation, solely from maternal tissue.

The following types of apomixis may be distinguished:

Facultative: able to reproduce sexually or by apomixis.

Pseudogamous: requiring pollination but not fertilisation for the production of seed.

Obligate: always reproducing by apomixis.

The reproduction of some scarce species has been studied in detail, but there are many species for which even basic facts, such as the extent to which the plant reproduces by seed, are apparently unknown. Worthwhile studies of population biology can be carried out with very little technical equipment and this field of research offers a great deal of scope to amateur naturalists.

The third paragraph assesses any historical trends in the distribution of the species and comments on current and potential threats to the extant populations. The wider distribution of the plant is outlined in the next paragraph. This information has often been drawn from the invaluable distribution maps published by Hultén & Fries (1986). Additional comments may be given in a fifth paragraph.

Aceras anthropophorum (L.) Aiton f.

Status: scarce

Man orchid

This is a lowland plant of old chalk and limestone quarries, calcareous pastures and roadsides. It is able to tolerate considerable shade and grows best at the edge of scrub, often among coarse grasses such as *Brachypodium pinnatum*. It does not do well in heavily grazed pastures and can be eliminated by continuous, heavy grazing. It usually grows in association with other orchids, such as *Anacamptis pyramidalis*, *Dactylorhiza fuchsii*, *Gymnadenia conopsea* and *Listera ovata*.

A. anthropophorum persists vegetatively by annual 'side-by-side' tuber replacement, whereby the ovoid tuber used in producing an inflorescence is replaced by a new tuber which began growth about eight months previously. Leaves push through in November and are winter green, usually dying as flowers on the inflorescence open in late May or early June. Capsules are formed and copious seed dispersed by late June, early July. Studies of individually marked plants at Totternhoe, over a period of 20 years, have established that individual plants live for up to ten years and that flowering may occur for up to five years in succession (the species is only rarely monocarpic). The fate of the huge quantities of seed produced is not known, but most must perish as new localities for this species are rare. Germination of the seed will occur only in the presence of a compatible fungal associate, but details of such a relationship are at present inadequately researched.

A. anthropophorum has decreased in Britain. Most East Anglian populations were extinct by 1930 (Perring & Walters 1962) as a result of the ploughing of chalky pastures in the late 19th century. Further Suffolk sites were ploughed up or used as airfields in wartime or were on roadside verges which have deteriorated because of inappropriate cutting regimes or spray-drift (Sanford 1991). The species is, however, still plentiful at sites in Kent and at certain favourable localities elsewhere, and populations in excess of 10,000 plants have been reported from old quarry sites, such as Barnack Hills and Holes, in some years. Some chalk-pit sites are threatened by use as rubbish tips, euphemistically termed 'land-fill'.

A. anthropophorum has a distinctly southern and western distribution in Europe, reaching its northernmost limit in England and extending in the Mediterranean region as far east as Rhodes and Cyprus; it also occurs in Morocco and Algeria.

T. C. E. Wells

Current map	No	Atlas	No
1970 →	50	1930 →	58
Pre-1970	59	Pre-1930	41
Introductions	2	Introductions	0

continued →

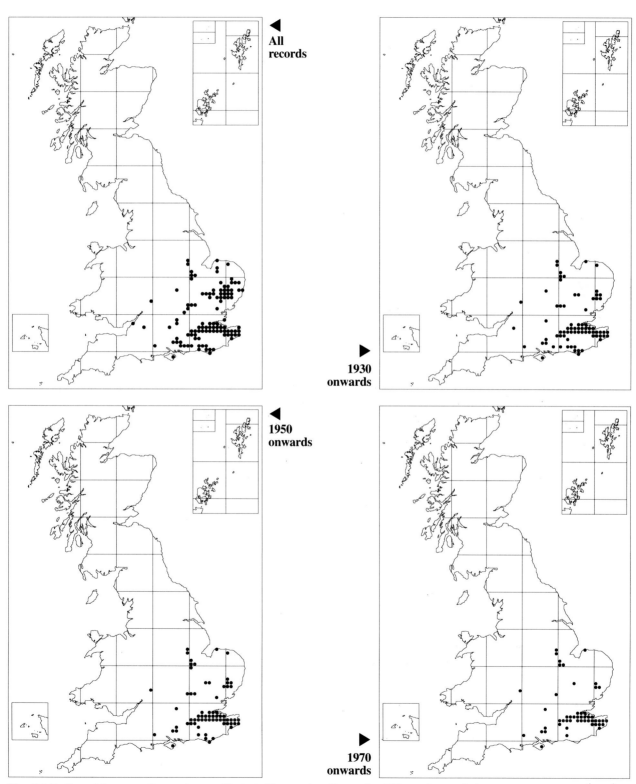

The distribution of *Aceras anthropophorum*, illustrated by a series of maps for different time periods.

continued →

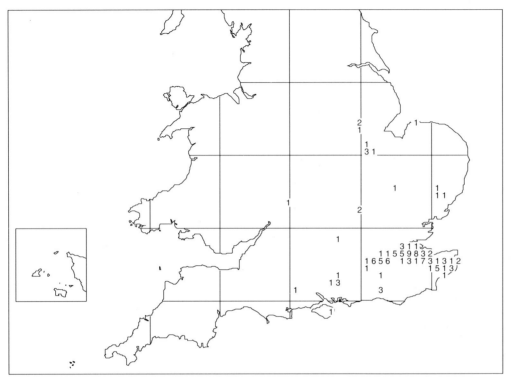

The number of tetrads in each 10 km square in which *Aceras anthropophorum* has been recorded as a native species from 1970 onwards. Squares in which the species is recorded in 9 or more tetrads are plotted as 9: *A. anthropophorum* is actually recorded from 10 tetrads in TQ66. The species has been found in a total of 120 tetrads from 1970 onwards.

Aconitum napellus L.

Status: scarce

Monk's-hood

This plant is found in shady wet hazel, alder and oak woodland, mostly near or along the banks of streams, but it occasionally grows where there are only scattered trees. As a native plant it is exclusively lowland, but garden escapes have been recorded up to 460 metres at Quarnford.

The plant is perennial, forming clumps by the growth of the tuberous rhizomes. It flowers in May and June, and is self-incompatible.

A. napellus has decreased in recent years, but it is still locally common in parts of the Welsh borders, Somerset and Devon. It is poisonous to stock, and Cooper & Johnson (1984) suggest that it may have been removed from places where animals can eat it. Nevertheless, it is grown for ornament in gardens, and is often naturalised. The native distribution of the species has been obscured by the presence of these alien populations. However, many naturalised plants reported as *A napellus* are probably the hybrid *A. napellus* × *A. variegatum* (*A.* × *cammarum*) which commonly escapes from gardens (Rich & Rich 1988).

A. napellus is a variable species that is endemic to western and central Europe, extending southwards to central Spain and eastwards to the Carpathians, mainly in the mountains. It is absent as a native species from Scandinavia. The British plants of *A. napellus*, distinguished by less deeply cut and more finely pointed leaf-segments and a slightly earlier flowering period, belong to subsp. *napellus* (subsp. *anglicum*). This is restricted to western Britain and south west France (Jalas & Suominen 1989).

J. R. Akeroyd

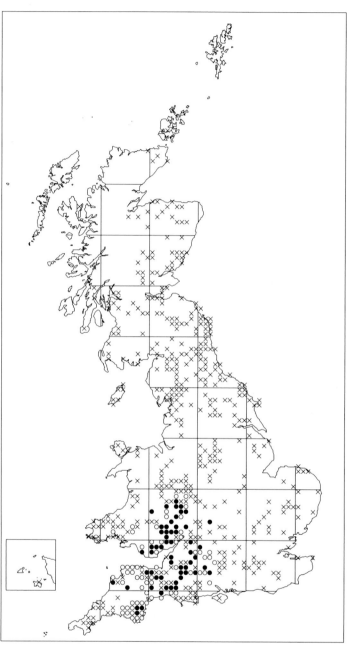

Current map	No	Atlas *	No
1970 →	56		
Pre-1970	62	Native records	76
Introductions	436	Introductions	38

* The *Atlas* mapped introduced populations of *A. napellus* subsp. *napellus* only; the current map includes introduced plants referable to *A. napellus sensu lato*.

Actaea spicata L.   **Baneberry**
Status: scarce

A. spicata is a plant of shaded sites on calcareous
soils, growing in deciduous woods at low altitudes
and, in the uplands, in grikes in limestone pavement
or on scar ledges. In the latter situation, it can
sometimes be found in the shade of a single tree. The
altitudinal range varies from 25 metres in Airedale to
450 metres at Hawkswick Clowder near Malham.

It is a perennial species pollinated by small insects.
The fruit is a berry, which is unusual in the
Ranunculaceae.

A. spicata will apparently tolerate dense shade, but
not competition from more vigorous plants. It may
have been lost from one of its lowland sites by
competition from *Rubus fruticosus*. Generally,
however, populations are stable but usually small,
varying little, if at all, from year to year.

It is widely but sparsely distributed in Europe, though
in the south only in mountains (Jalas & Suominen
1989). It extends as far as China in north temperate
Asia.

The plant has an offensive smell and is reputed to be
highly toxic but, if one believes the herbals, it must at
one time have been almost a panacea, or perhaps used
in desperation as a kill or cure treatment (Clapham,
Tutin & Warburg 1962; Grieve 1931; Potterton
1983)!

For a detailed account of the distribution of this
species in Yorkshire, see Garnett & Sledge (1967).

P. P. Abbott

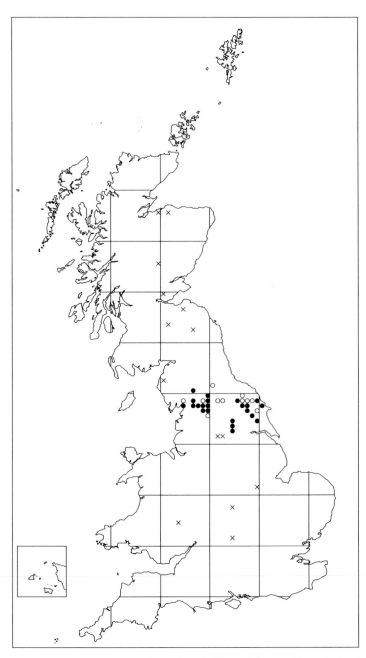

Current map	No	Atlas	No
1970 →	22	1930 →	12
Pre-1970	11	Pre-1930	15
Introductions	14	Introductions	6

Adiantum capillus-veneris L.

Status: scarce

Maidenhair fern

A limestone-loving plant, this fern is found naturally in lowland Britain on calcium-bearing rocks in shady coastal sites. Where water seeps through the rock it can form large colonies. The species was highly sought after in Victorian times as a house-plant; spores are easily spread and establish in crevices of mortared walls, where the microclimate is suitable. Other populations have spread from native habitats onto artificial substrates. Such populations may exist for a considerable period.

A. capillus-veneris is a long-lived perennial, which usually produces viable spores. Sporelings are not uncommon. Plants are highly frost-sensitive and this limits the potential distribution of the species.

In the late nineteenth century native populations were in jeopardy because of collecting for horticulture, but this species is so common in cultivation that this is unlikely to occur now. Coastal defence works may be a threat at some sites.

A. capillus-veneris has a Mediterranean-Atlantic distribution, reaching its northern limit in Britain and Ireland (Jalas & Suominen 1972). It also occurs in other warm areas of the Old World and it is found in South America, but probably only as an adventive.

A. C. Jermy

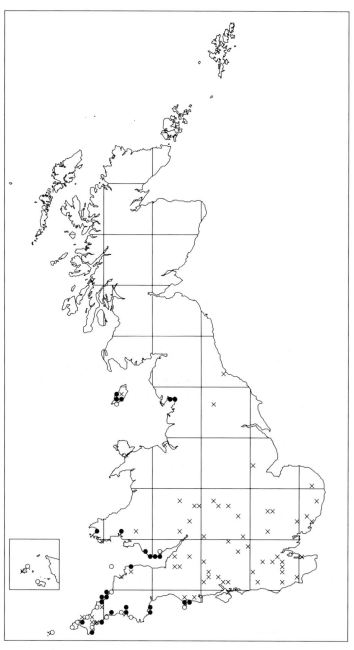

Current map	No	Atlas	No
1970 →	26	1930 →	14
Pre-1970	14	Pre-1930	15
Introductions	62	Introductions	15

Ajuga chamaepitys (L.) Schreber
Status: scarce

Ground-pine
WCA Schedule 8 species

Typically this is a species of open chalk downland habitats in southern England, most often on arable field margins but occasionally in open grassland sites. Where it does occur as an arable weed, it is usually indicative of a site that has escaped the normal intensive farming regime, and it is often associated with other rare species such as *Filago pyramidata* or *Teucrium botrys*. This lowland species appears to favour the top end of a south-facing slope, where the soils are more freely draining and warmer, and where there is usually less competition from the crop itself. The plant benefits from the activity of rabbits in reducing the crop canopy and opening up areas by scraping. In chalk grassland it also colonises areas disturbed by rabbits or human activity.

A. chamaepitys is an annual or biennial. Its main germination period is in the autumn (August/ September), with a further flush from January to February. It is vulnerable to cold, wet, prolonged winters which kill off autumn-germinated seedlings. This may help to explain its sporadic appearance in its regular sites. In cold years the seeds fail to ripen (Grubb 1976). The seed can remain dormant for some years.

This plant is at the northern limit of its range in Britain, and is restricted to south-east England by its requirements for warm calcareous soils. It has declined considerably under the impact of modern intensive farming regimes: it cannot compete effectively in enriched soils and is susceptible to herbicide treatments. In some areas it is now more frequent in disturbed areas, such as places where trees have been uprooted or pipelines laid, than on arable margins. This species has become so scarce in many of its sites that it is now listed on Schedule 8 of the Wildlife and Countryside Act (1981). At some sites it is encouraged by a programme of regular ploughing or scraping of turf. The introduction of low intensity arable regimes (such as 'conservation headlands') on remaining sites would enhance its prospects of survival.

Found throughout Europe except for the far north, it has declined considerably in northern and western Europe. Its distribution extends eastwards into the Lebanon and Palestine, and southwards into North Africa.

A. chamaepitys has been known to persist at some sites for more than a century, and to recur in these sites after a period of time in which plants were not found, usually after a deep plough.

A. Smith

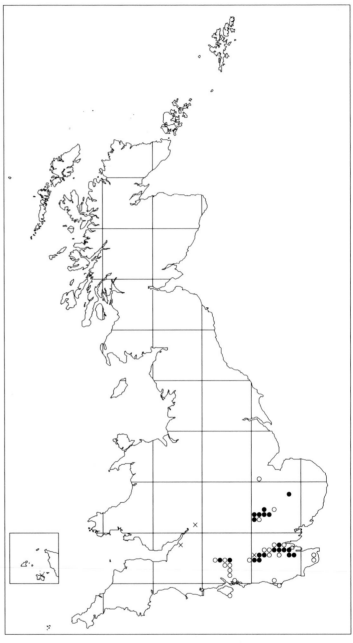

Current map	No	Atlas	No
1970 →	20	1930 →	23
Pre-1970	22	Pre-1930	15
Introductions	3	Introductions	2

continued →

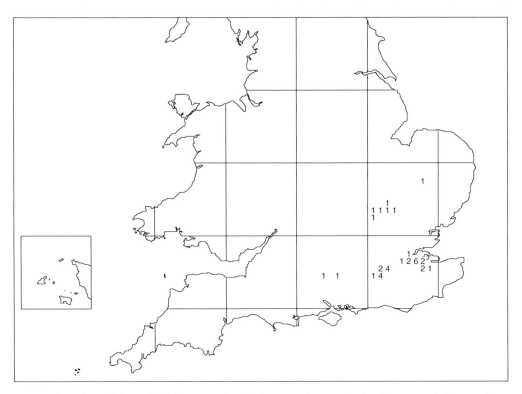

The number of tetrads in each 10 km square in which *Ajuga chamaepitys* has been recorded as a native species from 1970 onwards. The species has been found in a total of 35 tetrads from 1970 onwards.

Ajuga pyramidalis L.

Status: scarce

A. pyramidalis grows on low-lying, free-draining, steep, sunny slopes with incomplete vegetation cover. It occurs in dry heathland, which is frequently species-rich, or in grassland. Associated species include *Arctostaphylos alpinus*, *Calluna vulgaris*, *Erica cinerea*, *Festuca ovina*, *Thymus polytrichus* and *Teucrium scorodonia*. The soils are usually of medium base status such as have been derived from old red sandstone or conglomerate rocks. In south-west Sutherland it is widespread and even locally abundant on Lewisian gneiss. In altitude it ranges from sea level, as at Lochinver, to 650 metres above Troutbeck.

A perennial, but unlike its close relative *Ajuga reptans*, *A. pyramidalis* does not produce stolons and relies entirely on seed for reproduction. The flower spikes are frequently eaten by deer and sheep, which limits seed production. Initial observations indicate that the seeds of *A. pyramidalis* can remain viable in the soil for long periods and that germination may only occur once the ground is disturbed. The plant therefore may rely upon a seedbank to take advantage of disturbances such as fire or frost action.

This plant still occurs in some of the earliest recorded sites. However, it is easily overlooked and has certainly been under-recorded in the past. Its distribution is better understood now, particularly in the Scottish Highlands, although there are probably still new sites awaiting discovery. The main threat to this species is not so much habitat destruction but habitat change due to the colonisation of bare ground by shrubs or grasses where grazing pressure has been reduced.

In Europe, *A. pyramidalis* has a boreal-montane distribution, occurring from northern Norway south to the mountains of Iberia, northern Italy and Bulgaria.

P. Wortham

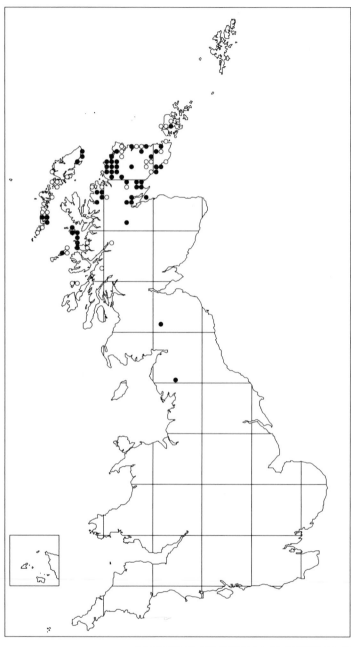

Current map	No	Atlas	No
1970 →	53	1930 →	35
Pre-1970	37	Pre-1930	17
Introductions	0	Introductions	0

Alchemilla glomerulans Buser
Status: scarce

This is a distinctive plant, and sometimes the only species of *Alchemilla*, in a variety of ungrazed or lightly grazed habitats on base-poor rocks in the higher Scottish mountains. It may grow on well-drained rock-ledges where *Alchemilla glabra*, *Coeloglossum viride* and *Gnaphalium norvegicum* might be associates; in lush herb-rich sites in the flushed screes below cliffs, with *Geranium sylvaticum* and *Trollius europaeus*; and on dripping ledges in very inhospitable gloomy corries on the granite, with *Deschampsia cespitosa* or in drier sites with *Carex lachenalii* and *Veronica alpina*. It often grows in a depauperate form with *A. filicaulis* subsp. *filicaulis* and *A. glabra* in heavily sheep-grazed turf around the base of cliffs. In Teesdale it is found in species-rich hay meadows and roadsides. In altitude it ranges from 185 metres in Upper Teesdale to at least 970 metres on Sgurr na Lapaich.

This species reproduces apomictically and vegetatively. It soon reappeared in a resown hayfield in Teesdale, apparently from seed.

A. glomerulans probably had a wider distribution in Scotland, but if so it has been eliminated from many sites by intense sheep-grazing. There is a shortage of post-1970 records of this critical species, but it is unlikely to have disappeared from many of the sites for which only pre-1970 records are available. Given the trickle of new records in the relatively well-recorded south of its range, it seems likely that the species is still somewhat overlooked elsewhere.

A. glomerulans is rare in the central European mountains, but more frequent in northern Europe east to the northern Urals, and extends west to Greenland and Labrador.

There is some variation in this species in Scotland. There are some closely related taxa in northern Scandinavia, and relatively glabrous plants in Scotland may be referable to one of these.

F. J. Roberts

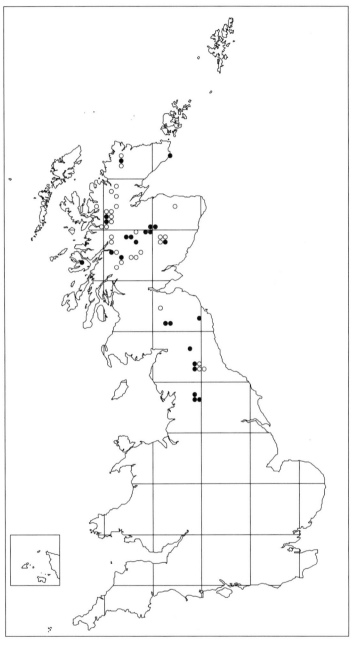

Current map	No	Atlas (S)	No
1970 →	24	1930 →	26
Pre-1970	30	Pre-1930	8
Introductions	0	Introductions	0

Alchemilla wichurae (Buser) Stéfansson
Status: scarce

This is a montane plant of basic soils. It grows as a
component of herb-rich ledges on outcrops and cliffs,
recurring in upland grasslands where grazing or
mowing keep the vegetation suitably short. In both
types of habitat it seems to prefer damper soils, and
indeed is common by waterfalls or seepages on cliffs.
However, it tolerates immersion or splashing less well
than its almost constant companion *A. glabra*. It may
also colonise bare cracks in hard limestones and
basalt, and scree where this is well-vegetated and
moist. In the Yorkshire Dales, tracksides are a
favoured habitat, where it often grows with
A. glaucescens. It grows from sea level to at least
990 metres on Ben Lawers.

A. wichurae is an obligate apomict. It appears to
regenerate vigorously both from seed and from
portions of rhizomes detached in the frequent falls of
accumulated soil from ledges. Many colonies in long-
established grassland appear to reproduce
vegetatively.

Like *A. glomerulans*, there is a shortage of post-1970
records of this critical species. In its cliff sites
A. wichurae is scarcely threatened: with its low
stature the species is much less frequent in
haymeadows than other grosser lady's-mantles, and
its preference for shallower soils renders many of its
sites safe from ploughing. However, it is readily
overgrown by coarse grasses on road-sides when
these become enriched. The tracksides on which it
grows are being damaged by walkers and off-road
vehicles in Yorkshire.

A. wichurae is restricted to northern Europe,
including the Faeroes and Iceland. It reaches its
southern limit in the Sudeten mountains.

This is usually a distinctive plant, but there are
populations in Breadalbane and elsewhere which are
less easily distinguished from *A. glabra* and whose
taxonomic status is unclear.

F. J. Roberts

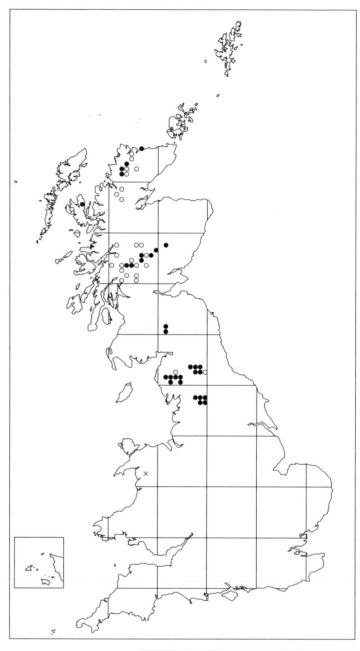

Current map	No	Atlas (S)	No
1970 →	30	1930 →	37
Pre-1970	26	Pre-1930	7
Introductions	1	Introductions	0

Allium oleraceum L.

Status: not scarce

Field garlic

This perennial generally occurs in predominantly south-facing dry grassy sites which are subject to summer drought. It often forms locally dense swards. It is found on steep slopes over chalk, oolitic and Carboniferous limestone, on field borders and on freely-draining banks on roadside verges. It is, however, most frequent as a riparian species, either as a component of the banks of floodplain meadows or in open sandy banks in the middle reaches of river systems. In these sites it will tolerate winter flooding, and it frequently occurs with other species with bulbs, bulbils or fleshy structures which are dispersed by water, such as *Aegopodium podagraria* (expanded leaf bases), *Allium scorodoprasum*, *Allium ursinum*, *Gagea lutea*, *Ranunculus ficaria* and *Saxifraga granulata*. It is virtually confined to the lowlands, but it is recorded up to 365 metres in Dovedale, and 335 metres in Kingsdale.

In riparian situations it appears to colonise new sand-banks from bulb fragments, offsets and bulbils re-deposited from plants eroded out of established colonies. On roadside verges and in grazed situations it probably spreads vegetatively, as reproductive heads of bulbils, with or without flowers, are often removed by mowing or grazing. Fruit seems to be produced very rarely in Britain.

The main centres of distribution are based on major river complexes: the Vale of York, Trent, Ure, Severn and Avon. The apparent decline in records within these complexes is probably due to under-recording, especially outside riparian habitats.

It is widespread in Europe from Scandinavia and northern Russia to northern Spain, Corsica, central Italy, Yugoslavia, Bulgaria and the Caucasus.

Once one is familiar with its 'jizz', it is most easily located early in the season, before flowering, owing to its prominent and distinctive growth prior to the main flush of grasses. Subsequently it becomes more difficult to locate as grasses grow up and swards are mown and grazed. It is treated as a native species by Stace (1991) and Kent (1992) but W. T. Stearn (in Oswald 1993) considers that all the British *Allium* species except *A. schoenoprasum* and *A. ursinum* are long-established aliens.

H. E. Stace & T. E. Dixon

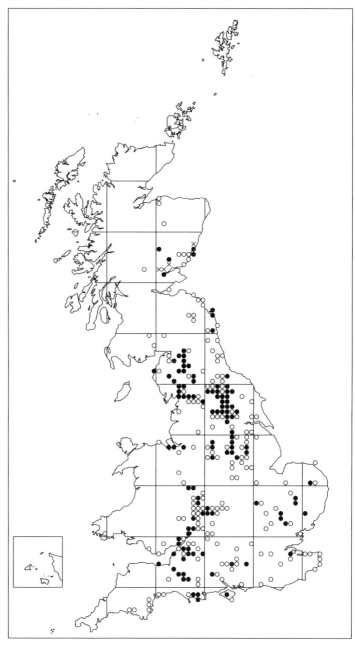

Current map	No	Atlas	No
1970 →	112	1930 →	94
Pre-1970	170	Pre-1930	89
Introductions	4	Introductions	4

Allium schoenoprasum L.

Chives

Status: scarce

Native populations are typically found on thin soil in sparsely vegetated, rocky habitats that fluctuate between very wet and bone-dry. Sea-cliff habitats include rock crevices and stabilised boulders or scree, with typical maritime associates such as *Armeria maritima*, *Cochlearia officinalis*, *Crithmum maritimum*, *Plantago coronopus*, *P. maritima* and *Scilla verna*. It is also occasionally found in deeper soil among lush grasses, including *Dactylis glomerata* and *Festuca rubra*. This species occurs in similar habitats inland on limestone cliffs and in shallow, stony depressions over outcrops of rock amongst dense heath or grassland. At the Lizard peninsula it grows on serpentine with drought-tolerant perennials, whereas on the Whin Sill in Northumberland most associates are winter annuals. Deep crevices in riverside outcrops of bedrock provide another habitat. As a native plant *A. schoenoprasum* is restricted to lowland areas. It is widely recorded as an escape from cultivation, but such populations are often short-lived.

This species is self-compatible, hermaphrodite, bulbous and perennial. It lies dormant over winter, producing new leaf growth in early spring. Cliff and riverside plants flower profusely in early summer, and a high level of outcrossing occurs (Stevens & Bougourd 1988b). Seed may germinate immediately (e.g. by the River Wye) or during the autumn and following spring. Bulb reproduction also occurs producing clumps. In rocky depressions where plants are stunted, flowering is much less common, and in some populations reproduction is predominantly asexual. Grazing, mainly by rabbits, reduces the seed output in some localities.

The inhospitable habitats of *A. schoenoprasum* are not currently threatened and its British distribution is apparently stable.

A. schoenoprasum has a circumboreal distribution, occurring in Europe, Asia and North America. It is widely distributed in arctic and alpine regions of Europe, penetrating lowland regions along river courses. Habitats in continental Europe are wetter than those in Britain and support a more varied, denser flora (Stevens 1985).

This plant is very variable, with many morphologically distinct populations (Bougourd 1977; Stevens & Bougourd 1988a). It is diploid (2n = 16), with some structural chromosome variation (Stevens & Bougourd 1991) and b-chromosomes have been found in one locality (Bougourd & Parker 1975; Bougourd & Parker 1979).

S. M. Bougourd

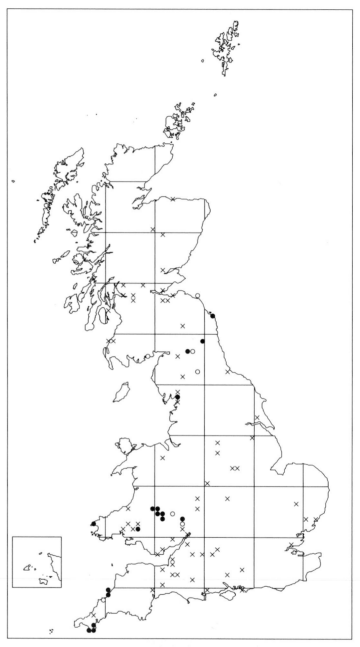

Current map	No	Atlas	No
1970 →	17	1930 →	9
Pre-1970	7	Pre-1930	11
Introductions	67	Introductions	4

Allium scorodoprasum L.

Status: not scarce

Sand leek

This is a bulbous plant of grassland, scrub and open woodland on dry, sandy soils. It is occasionally found on riversides, mainly on gravel and sandy banks. It is often found in limited numbers, sparsely scattered. It is virtually confined to the lowlands, but reaches 370 metres in Silverdale.

It is a perennial and reproduces by bulb offsets and by bulbils.

There are many more records in northern England now than were available to the editors of the *Atlas of the British Flora* (Perring & Walters 1962). This probably reflects the recent recording efforts in this area, but the plant may also have become more obvious by increased flowering with the warm, dry summers experienced over the last few years.

The British plant is *A. scorodoprasum* subsp. *scorodoprasum*. This has a scattered distribution in northern and central Europe, reaching its northern limit in Scotland and southern Finland, and extending south to Bulgaria and the Crimea. Three other subspecies are recognised in Europe, and have more southerly distributions.

Like *A. oleraceum* this plant may be a long-established alien in Britain, and its wide and scattered distribution in Europe may be partly due to its former cultivation as a culinary plant (Tutin *et al.* 1980).

L. Farrell

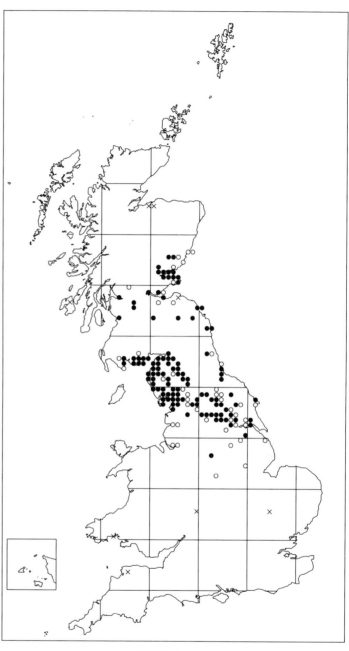

Current map	No	Atlas	No
1970 →	113	1930 →	75
Pre-1970	45	Pre-1930	8
Introductions	8	Introductions	2

Alopecurus aequalis Sobol.

Status: not scarce

Orange foxtail

This species is found on the margins of shallow ponds, of gravel pits and of reservoirs, always in the proximity of fresh water. It is not often seen in shallow water but occurs on mud as the water level recedes. In some of the Breckland meres, where the water level fluctuates markedly from year to year, it can occur in great abundance. Its associates in these meres include *Agrostis stolonifera, Chenopodium rubrum, Juncus articulatus, Mentha aquatica, Myosoton aquaticum, Oenanthe aquatica, Persicaria amphibia, Phalaris arundinacea, Potentilla anserina, Rorippa amphibia, R. palustris, Rumex maritimus* and *Sagina nodosa*.

It is an annual plant, which reproduces by seed. Culms ascend from a decumbent base and root at the nodes, a habit which adds to the density of the colony. Populations vary greatly in number from year to year, being largest when water levels are low and much mud is exposed. In years of high water level the plant may only be present as dormant seed.

In the long term this species may be considered under threat. Old ponds have been reclaimed and many wet habitats have been drained. Suitable remaining habitats are in danger of pollution. It has, however, recently been seen as a weed in a number of aquatic garden centres and it might therefore be expected to spread into garden ponds.

This is a widespread species which occurs in the boreal and temperate zones throughout the northern hemisphere. In Europe it is rare in the oceanic western fringe and virtually absent from the Mediterranean region.

P. J. O. Trist

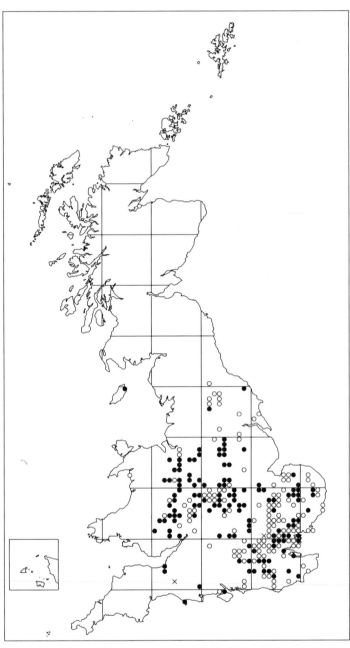

Current map	No	Atlas	No
1970 →	128	1930 →	84
Pre-1970	126	Pre-1930	26
Introductions	2	Introductions	0

Alopecurus borealis Trin.
Status: scarce

Alpine foxtail

This rare grass is found in oligotrophic mountain springs and flushes, often associated with late snow-beds. Plants usually grow in the centres of flushes with percolating water, where associates include *Caltha palustris*, *Chrysosplenium oppositifolium*, *Epilobium anagallidifolium*, *Montia fontana*, *Saxifraga stellaris*, *Stellaria uliginosa* and *Veronica serpyllifolia* and bryophytes such as *Dicranella squarrosa*, *Philonotis fontana* and *Scapania uliginosa*. Inflorescences may occur more commonly along the drier edges of flushes where taller growing species such as *Carex nigra* and *Eriophorum angustifolium* give some protection from the heavy grazing pressures of sheep and deer. *A. borealis* is found over a wide range of acidic or slightly basic substrates. Although *Phleum alpinum* is an associate at some sites in the Scottish Highlands, *A. borealis* has a more eastern tendency, being absent from suitable habitats in the Western Highlands where *P. alpinum* occurs. It ranges in altitude from 450 metres on Widdybank Fell to 1220 metres on Braeriach.

A. borealis is a loosely tufted perennial with slender rhizomes. Flower production varies considerably between years. Little is known of its reproduction.

It was unknown outside the Highlands until 1956, when it was discovered in the Southern Uplands (Ratcliffe 1959). Since then further populations have been found in southern Scotland and northern England (Ratcliffe & Eddy 1960). Over-grazing and trampling are threats to the habitat, as is the occasional scrambler motorbike which churns through flushes.

The British sites and those on Svalbard are the only ones in Europe for this predominantly High Arctic circumpolar grass which reaches 83° N in Greenland. A closely related species, *A. magellanica* Lam., occurs in the southern Andes, Falkland Islands and South Georgia.

R. W. M. Corner

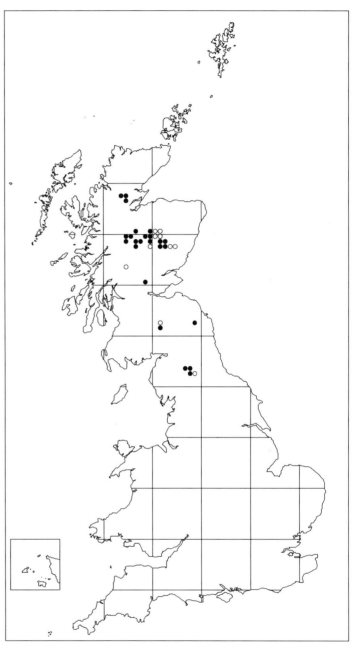

Current map	No	Atlas	No
1970 →	24	1930 →	15
Pre-1970	10	Pre-1930	6
Introductions	0	Introductions	0

continued →

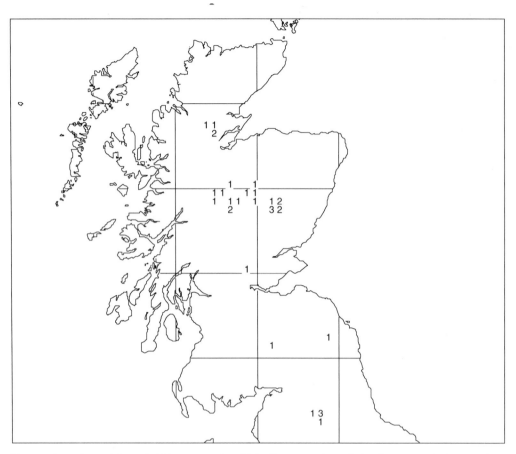

The number of tetrads in each 10 km square in which *Alopecurus borealis* has been recorded as a native species from 1970 onwards. The species has been found in a total of 32 tetrads from 1970 onwards.

Alopecurus bulbosus Gouan
Status: scarce

Bulbous foxtail

This coastal species is a perennial grass of damp brackish turf, found in winter-wet hollows in unimproved grazing marshes, at ditch edges and on trampled cattle droves at the base of sea and river walls. In these habitats it is usually the dominant species, but it can also occur in mixed swards where saline water reduces competition. It tolerates quite high levels of salinity, but is a species of brackish grasslands, not a salt-marsh plant. The most faithful associates are *Carex divisa*, *Festuca rubra*, *Juncus gerardii*, *Poa humilis*, *P. pratensis* and *Trifolium fragiferum*, with *Ranunculus sardous* at the drier edges of populations. The common *A. geniculatus* is often present with *A. bulbosus*, growing in the wettest parts of the sites and the two species can grow in close enough proximity to produce the hybrid *A. ×plettkei*. *Puccinellia distans* can occur at particularly brackish, wet sites.

A. bulbosus has two quite short growth periods, in the autumn to start new leaves, and for about 100 days between mid-April and July to flower and seed (Trist 1981). The rest of the time it is dormant and inconspicuous.

It appears to have been under-recorded in the 1960s and 70s, probably because of its flowering so early, for only about three weeks from mid-May into June - with the spikes quickly breaking up afterwards. However, searches made in the 1980s showed that this species persists in many of the areas with historical records (FitzGerald 1989; Pearman 1990; Trist 1981). In dormant periods in particular, its 'bulbs', the swollen stem bases, can survive flooding with full strength seawater and major disturbance such as ploughing and earth moving. However, in spite of its excellent adaptations for withstanding such traumas and its decline since 1900 being less drastic than had been supposed, *A. bulbosus* is threatened by exploitation of its habitat. It can be obliterated by intensive drainage and agricultural changes, and by industrial and leisure developments. The pressure on the deceptively empty-looking expanses of grazing marshes, and 'useless' areas of marginal coastal grassland, is increasingly fierce.

This species is endemic to Europe, where it is found on northern and western coasts, and as far east as northwest Yugoslavia.

R. FitzGerald

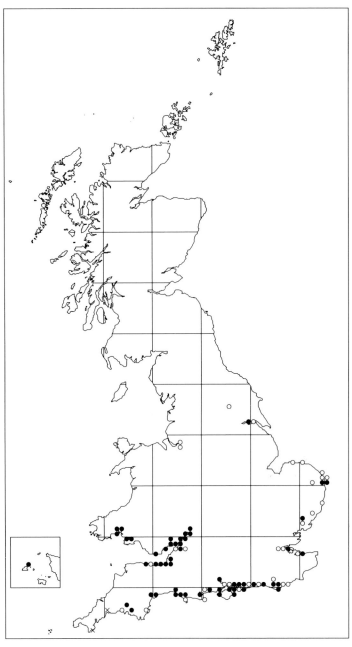

Current map	No	Atlas	No
1970 →	54	1930 →	26
Pre-1970	32	Pre-1930	36
Introductions	2	Introductions	2

continued →

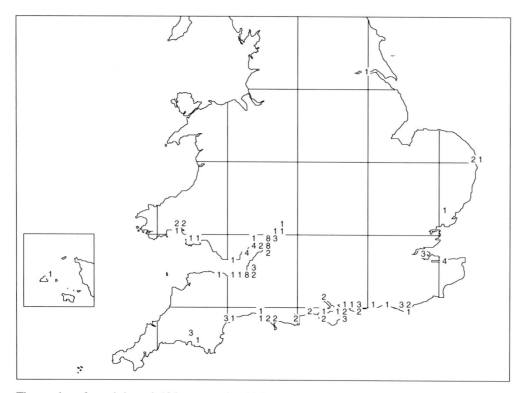

The number of tetrads in each 10 km square in which *Alopecurus bulbosus* has been recorded as a native species from 1970 onwards. The species has been found in a total of 116 tetrads from 1970 onwards.

A. officinalis is locally frequent in the coastal zone, growing on the banks of ditches with brackish water or where the upper parts of saltmarsh give way to freshwater habitats. It is particularly common by ditches in grazing marshes which have been converted to arable land, as it is notably intolerant of grazing and cutting. It can form a dominant sward in brackish pastures from which stock have been removed. It is a shade-tolerant species, found under *Quercus robur* by the Solent estuary where ancient woodland borders saltmarsh. The distribution of *A. officinalis* is strictly lowland, and at coastal sites it grows mainly on alluvial soils. It is also recorded as an escape from cultivation away from the coast.

A. officinalis is a perennial, flowering in the late summer and reproducing by seeds.

This species has declined through most of its British range, partly due to drainage and partly due to the development of the coastal zone for industry and housing. The decline was first noted in the last century (Hanbury & Marshall 1899) and still continues except where sites survive on waterlogged soils, near the sea, but protected from stock.

A. officinalis reaches its northern limit in Europe in Britain, Denmark and central Russia, also occurring in north Africa and west Asia, and as a rare introduction in North America.

The past use of *A. officinalis* for the production of sweetmeat and its ornamental appearance are responsible for its introduction well outside its native range.

J. O. Mountford

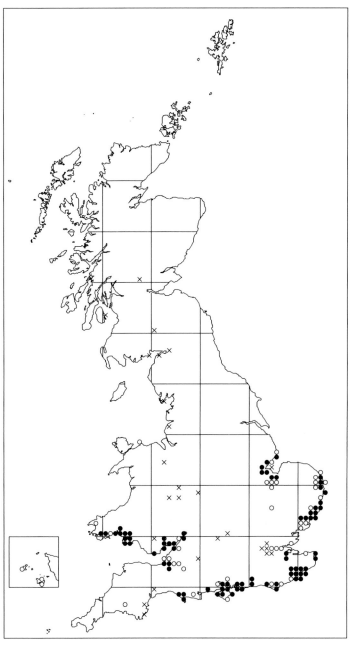

Current map	No	Atlas	No
1970 →	77	1930 →	73
Pre-1970	40	Pre-1930	12
Introductions	27	Introductions	17

Andromeda polifolia L.
Status: not scarce

Bog-rosemary

This is exclusively a species of raised mires, growing almost invariably amongst living sphagnum in a substrate largely composed of sphagnum peat, in the pH range 2.8-4.8. It is most commonly found on relatively undisturbed (i.e. not drained or regularly burnt) raised ombrogenous mires on the tops or sides of hummocks of *Sphagnum magellanicum*, *S. papillosum*, or less commonly, *S. capillifolium* and *S. fuscum*. The most frequent higher plant associates are *Deschampsia flexuosa*, *Drosera rotundifolia*, *Erica tetralix*, *Eriophorum vaginatum* and *Vaccinium oxycoccos*. Its altitudinal range is from near sea-level up to 530 metres at Ward's Stone and Bottom Head Fell, and 735 metres on Mount Keen.

A. polifolia is an evergreen perennial plant most usually occurring as simple or weakly branched single stems, but low horizontal branches frequently layer to form small clonal colonies. The homogamous flowers are chiefly visited by small beetles and flies, but also by bees and butterflies. It may flower more freely after fires (Sinker *et al*. 1985). Capsules seldom develop and the species is probably self-incompatible. The small seeds are wind dispersed. Successful seedling establishment probably requires a mycorrhizal association.

The undisturbed raised mire habitat has suffered severely from drainage, afforestation, heather burning and peat digging in recent years, and *A. polifolia* has correspondingly become more local. Amongst higher plants, this is the raised mire specialist *par excellence*.

This species occurs in the boreal zone of Europe, Asia and North America. It extends south in Europe to northern Spain. It occurs throughout Scandinavia, so that it is difficult to account for the absence of this species from much of Scotland on the basis of its European distribution. It is less of a sphagnum mire specialist in some other countries, where it is usually associated with wet acidic peat but is occasionally present in base-rich fen.

For details of the habitat of *A. polifolia* at the recently discovered site in north-east Scotland, see Birse (1980).

A. J. Richards

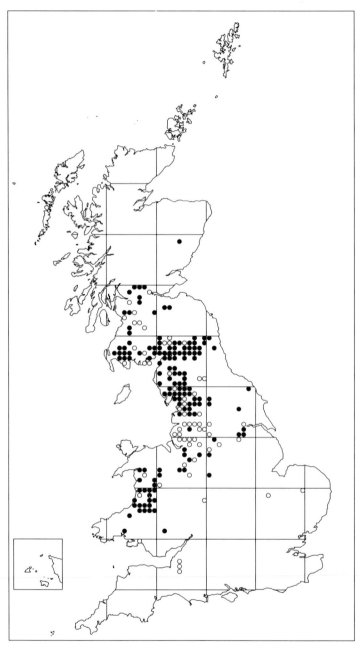

Current map	No	Atlas	No
1970 →	140	1930 →	69
Pre-1970	60	Pre-1930	32
Introductions	0	Introductions	0

Apera interrupta (L.) P. Beauv.

Status: scarce

Dense silky-bent

This grass is a shallow rooted, lowland annual of arable land, which also colonises road and rail verges and chalk and gravel excavations. It is mostly confined to field headlands but has become a troublesome weed at a few sites. More significantly, there are a number of long established populations on grassland or heathland where mammals have maintained a close-cropped habitat. On trackways and heathland it is usually a very low plant growing alongside *Arenaria serpyllifolia*, *Catapodium rigidum* and *Sagina procumbens*, attracting attention only by its silky green coloration which is especially noticeable when other species have blanched in the sun. In contrast, in the enriched arable soils it is usually a tall, leaning grass half a metre high.

This annual grass produces a large number of light-weight grains, each with a long, rough-awned lemma which should facilitate a wide dispersal. However, the inability of the seeds to germinate where any sort of competition from established plants exists restricts its spread. Longevity of seed enables it to survive at its strongholds, where it often appears after an apparent absence of several years, and explains its frequent appearance after soil disturbance where long buried seeds are brought to the surface.

Probably native only on the light soils of eastern England. Other records are mainly of a casual nature or are the result of introductions with agricultural seed, wool-shoddy or aggregates from gravel pits where the plant grows as a native. At these sites it is usually a short-lived invader which fails to survive competition from other species.

A. interrupta is patchily distributed across Europe and North Africa to Asiatic Russia and has been introduced into North America (Hubbard 1954).

In ancient times it may have grown on sheepwalks on the sands and chalklands of eastern England. Easy (1992) presented evidence that this is a native species; it is described as introduced by Stace (1991) but not by Kent (1992).

G. M. S. Easy

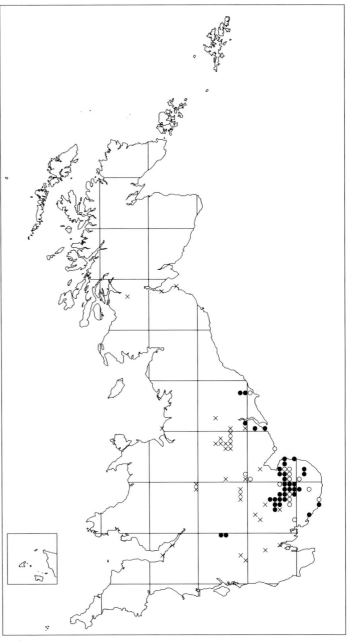

Current map	No	Atlas	No
1970 →	35	1930 →	17
Pre-1970	16	Pre-1930	10
Introductions	34	Introductions	9

Apera spica-venti (L.) P. Beauv.
Status: scarce

Loose silky-bent

This is an elegant annual grass, best known as a plant of arable land; indeed, in some localities it has been regarded as a troublesome weed. On the light soils of Breckland it often grows alongside *A. interrupta*, but unlike that species there is little evidence of populations which persist for long periods despite its widespread occurrence there. Some populations do persist on disturbed waste ground and sandy tracks, having spread from nearby farmland or having been dumped with waste soil. It is a lowland species, although it was recently recorded as a casual on a made-up path at 690 metres on Ingleborough.

The height of *A. spica-venti* plants, up to a metre, and the prolific production of long-awned, light-weight grain often allows a swift build-up of seedlings some distance around the parent plants. This enables dense swards to smother crops a few years after its introduction and makes the species difficult to eradicate in traditional corn-growing areas. In contrast, its appearance following introduction with grass seed, as along roadside verges, is usually short-lived due to regular mowing or eventual domination by perennial species.

The wide distribution across lowland England and the Channel Isles belies the fact that this is mostly a garden escape, casual, or arable weed, and it is rarely established at any one site over a significant period of time.

A. spica-venti is well distributed across Europe into northern Asia and has been introduced into North America and New Zealand.

A. spica-venti is treated as a native by both Stace (1991) and Kent (1992). However, the transient nature of the British distribution, even in Breckland, indicates that it is not truly native. Surprisingly, its history goes back to 1670 (Perring, Sell & Walters 1964), whereas *A. interrupta* was not noted until the mid nineteenth century. Even in ancient times, aliens were being introduced with imported European corn.

G. M. S. Easy

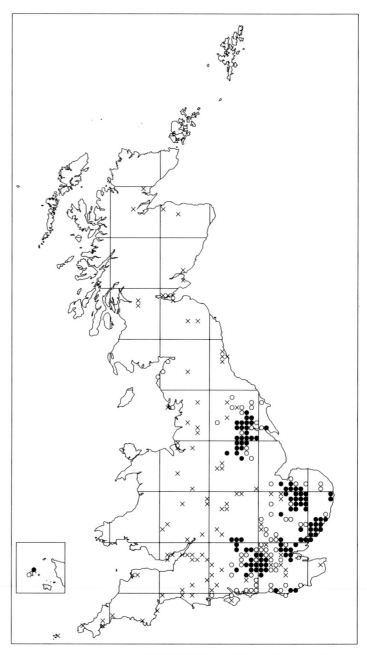

Current map	No	Atlas *	No
1970 →	99	1930 →	80
Pre-1970	74	Pre-1930	76
Introductions	94	Introductions	-

* Introductions were not distinguished on the *Atlas* map.

Arabis glabra (L.) Bernh.

Status: scarce

Tower mustard

A. glabra occurs on light, sandy soils over chalk and limestone, found on disturbed ground as long as it is free draining. In the Breckland of East Anglia, it thrives where it can re-colonise ground in clear-felled coniferous plantations and on waste ground such as the sites of old straw stacks, but always where the underlying soils are calcareous. When these sites become overgrown with a dense cover of grasses or are shaded by newly planted trees, individual plants appear able to hold their own but, with no open space for seedlings, this species does not survive for long. It is often found in association with *Lactuca serriola* and *Verbascum thapsus*, both being species that can take advantage of temporary clearances and open soil, and it often behaves like an invasive weed. It is a lowland species.

A. glabra is a biennial or sometimes a short-lived perennial species, and produces large quantities of seed. At some sites it has reappeared after long intervals, presumably from buried seed (Lousley 1976).

This species has undoubtedly declined in most of its British range. It has, however, increased in numbers in parts of the Norfolk Breckland in recent years. In the *Ecological Flora of Breckland*, Trist (1979) describes it as usually occurring singly, but some colonies now consist of thousands of plants, although they occupy only very restricted areas.

It has a very wide distribution throughout the world, being found in Europe up to 70° N, and in Africa, Asia, North America and Australia. It is believed to be native in Europe and western Asia and introduced elsewhere (Hultén & Fries 1986).

Because of its invasive tendency in Breckland, this may not be a plant to encourage in sensitive areas.

G. Beckett

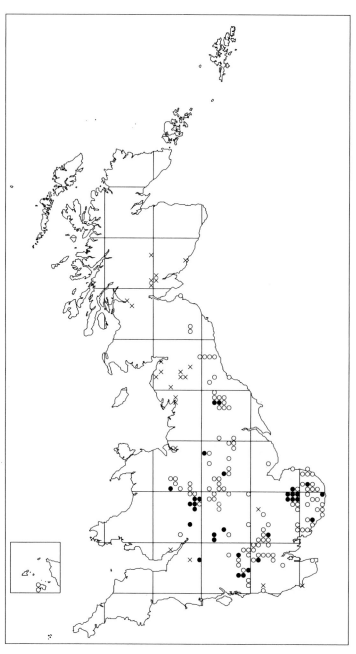

Current map	No	Atlas	No
1970 →	31	1930 →	32
Pre-1970	111	Pre-1930	75
Introductions	25	Introductions	14

continued →

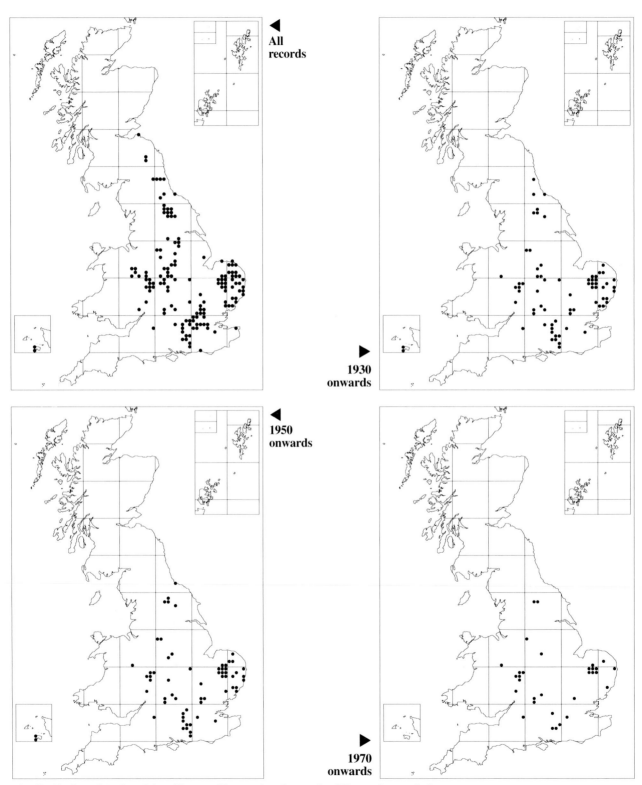

The distribution of *Arabis glabra*, illustrated by a series of maps for different time periods.

Arabis petraea (L.) Lam.
Status: scarce

Northern rock-cress

This is an extremely local and erratically distributed montane species. It is usually in dry to slightly moist, markedly open habitats, on cliff faces, screes, exposed soil and gravel, river alluvium and shingle. *A. petraea* is especially abundant on basic and ultra-basic igneous rocks in the western Highlands and Inner Hebrides, but also has another stronghold on the granite of the Cairngorms. There are occurrences on serpentine, limestone, hornblende schist, Lewisian gneiss and Torridonian sandstone, so that range of substrate base-status is extremely wide. Yet it is absent from a great many apparently suitable places. Commonly associated species include *Alchemilla alpina, Antennaria dioica, Cerastium arcticum, Festuca vivipara, Luzula spicata, Saxifraga oppositifolia, Silene acaulis, Thymus polytrichus* and *Racomitrium lanuginosum*. The altitudinal range is wide, from near sea level in Shetland to at least 1220 metres on Braeriach.

This perennial herb evidently propagates by seed quite freely, at least in some localities. Any limitation by high summer temperature is unlikely, as indicated by the altitudinal range. Its occurrence on low-lying river gravels and shingle suggests establishment from down-washed seed, but could also represent ancient populations.

Many pre-1970 records of *A. petraea* are probably still extant. This plant is often in places grazed by sheep and deer, but appears to be less threatened than many montane species. Smaller populations would be vulnerable to collecting, but many are large and not at risk.

A. petraea is an arctic-alpine species of wide distribution in the Old World and extending to Alaska in North America.

D. A. Ratcliffe

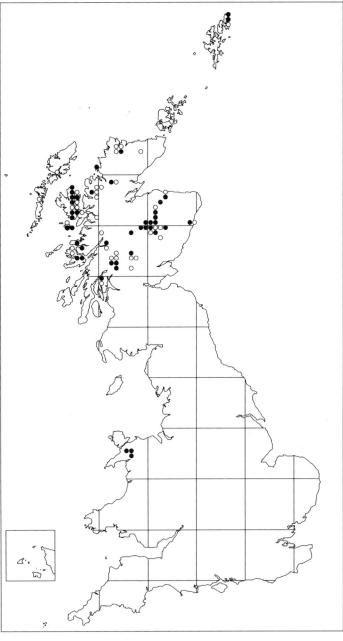

Current map	No	Atlas	No
1970 →	43	1930 →	49
Pre-1970	36	Pre-1930	13
Introductions	0	Introductions	0

Arctostaphylos alpinus (L.) Sprengel
Status: scarce

Mountain bearberry

The best known habitat for this plant is on dry, windswept ridges and moraines at about 600 metres altitude (Raven & Walters 1956). In this montane heath habitat its associates include prostrate *Calluna vulgaris*, *Carex bigelowii*, *Empetrum nigrum* subsp. *hermaphroditicum*, *Loiseleuria procumbens*, *Salix herbacea*, *Racomitrium lanuginosum* and lichens. Where the vegetation becomes taller, *A. alpinus* tends to disappear. In the northern Highlands it also grows in undisturbed blanket bog with *Betula nana*, *Calluna vulgaris* and *Eriophorum vaginatum* (McVean & Ratcliffe 1962). In all its Scottish habitats, *A. alpinus* is a strict calcifuge, growing on acidic mineral or peat substrates. It is mainly a middle elevation plant, but reaches at least 945 metres on Tom a'Choinich above Glen Affric, and descends to 130 metres in Sutherland.

A. alpina is a woody perennial, possibly with a long life-span, flowering in May or June before the leaves expand. The white bell-flowers are small and have small openings so that self-pollination may be the rule (Raven & Walters 1956). Fruits ripen in late July or August, but crops are commonly sparse. The plant is partially deciduous, many leaves displaying brilliant scarlet autumn colours and some surviving the winter. As the winter winds remove snow from its habitat, it may be left vulnerable to grazing. Bird-carried berries are possibly the source of new populations.

There is little evidence for a widespread decline of this species, which is probably still present in most of the 10 km squares for which only pre-1970 records are available. However, it appears to retreat when its habitats are burned, recovering only slowly after moorland fires.

A. alpina has a typical arctic-alpine distribution, occurring widely in Fennoscandia, through the Eurasian Arctic and in North America and Greenland. Southwards it reaches the Alps, Pyrenees and New Hampshire mountains.

The south-eastern edge of the plant's distribution closely follows the mean July isotherm for 14.5°C. Horticulturists find difficulty with the plant to the east of this isotherm (R. Macbeath pers. comm.). A few outlying colonies occur but at a higher altitude. The less distinct western edge runs near the mean January isotherm for 4°C, which passes through Skye near Kylerhea, where J. Lightfoot found the plant in 1772. Further attempts to find the species here failed until it was rediscovered by Mrs C. W. Murray in 1990 (Murray 1991).

A. Slack

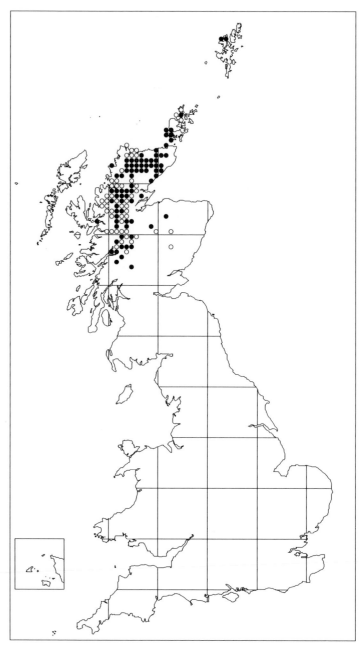

Current map	No	Atlas	No
1970 →	78	1930 →	62
Pre-1970	50	Pre-1930	17
Introductions	0	Introductions	0

Arum italicum Miller

Status: scarce

Italian lords-and-ladies

This plant grows in relatively humid environments in a range of lowland wooded and sheltered coastal habitats. Towards the east of its native range it is almost wholly confined to inland 'hanger' woods of upper greensand and chalk scarps. A number of colonies are known from former woodpasture commons, now overgrown by trees. This suggests that *A. italicum* is tolerant of grazing by domestic livestock. This plant is known from both ancient and secondary woods. Towards the west of the range, it is found in a wider variety of habitats including hedgebanks, secondary woods developed over formerly cultivated land, and open scrub. In the extreme west of its range, it is the only *Arum* species present. With the exception of the inland hanger woodland populations, it is strongly associated with coastal land. It is remarkably tolerant of dense shade and thus may be found under beech or sycamore canopies where only a limited range of species such as *Hedera helix* and *Phyllitis scolopendrium* persist. These shaded areas are often of relatively recent origin and are associated with aggressive ornamental tree species.

This plant is a perennial which reproduces from seed, and by natural division of the rhizomatous rootstock. Whilst the plant flowers freely, the flowers are often destroyed by animals consuming the spadix, and thus little seed is set. This is particularly so towards the east of its British range.

The native distribution of this species is probably stable. There is scope for the expansion of native populations into scrub and secondary woodlands that are colonising ungrazed coastal slopes and undercliffs.

This species is found as a native in western and southern Europe from England southwards, and in North Africa and Macaronesia.

All records of *A. italicum* are shown on the map. The native plant is *A. italicum* subsp. *neglectum*. *A. italicum* subsp. *italicum* is widely cultivated particularly as cultivar 'Marmoratum' (often called 'Pictum'), and is often naturalised. Despite the fact that this ornamental form is readily separable from subsp. *neglectum*, there are inconsistencies in recording. *A. italicum* subsp. *neglectum* is known to produce a sterile hybrid with *A. maculatum*. There is evidence to suggest introgression between the two. For detailed accounts of the British *Arum* species, see Prime (1954, 1960).

C. Chatters

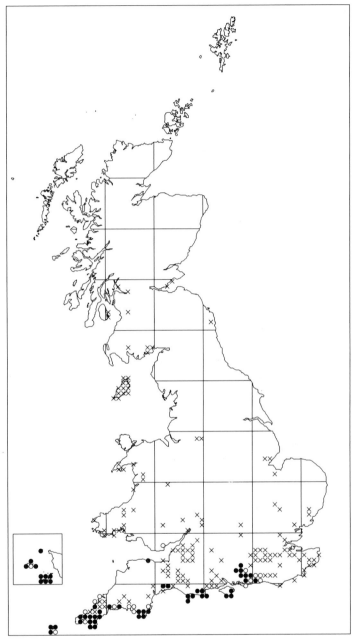

Current map	No	Atlas	No
1970 →	43	1930 →	38
Pre-1970	17	Pre-1930	0
Introductions	144	Introductions	29

Asplenium obovatum Viv.
Status: scarce

Lanceolate spleenwort

This Atlantic fern requires the frost-free environment found in sheltered, shady crevices and ledges on maritime cliffs or on rocky outcrops. It is a calcifuge, found on granite and other siliceous rocks and also on serpentine. It rarely grows far from the sea. In these situations it is associated with *Armeria maritima*, *Crithmum maritimum*, *Silene uniflora* and *Umbilicus rupestris*, but it is not tolerant of dense vegetation. It is recorded from inland sites on drystone walls but is never vigorous in these colder areas. Its presence in West Sutherland is interesting and it may be elsewhere on this northwest coast warmed by the Gulf Stream.

This is a perennial species which retains its green fronds throughout the winter. Little is known about its reproductive capacity, but, like other lithophytes, it must find suitable moist crevices for spores to germinate.

The distribution of this species appears to be stable, although the plant may have been lost from some inland sites by shading from colonising scrub.

A. obovatum subsp. *lanceolatum* is confined to southwest Europe and Macaronesia, being most common in northwest France, western Pyrenees and Portugal and reaching as far as western Italy and Pantellaria (Jalas & Suominen 1972).

The British plant is *A. obovatum* subsp. *lanceolatum* (Fiori) Pinto da Silva. This is derived from the diploid subsp. *obovatum*, which has a predominantly Mediterranean distribution but is found as far north as northwest France. Subsp. *obovatum* may yet be found in the Channel Islands or in mainland Britain and our populations should be examined for it.

A. C. Jermy

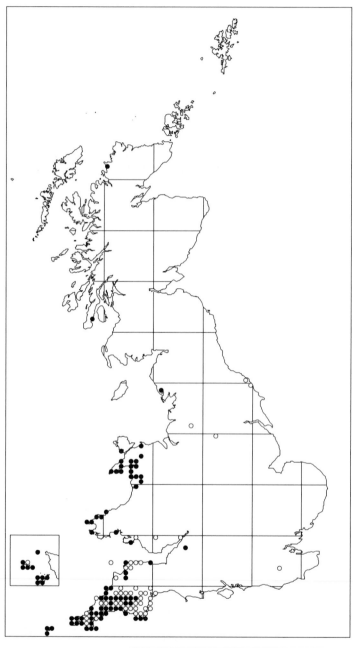

Current map	No	Atlas	No
1970 →	77	1930 →	34
Pre-1970	47	Pre-1930	48
Introductions	0	Introductions	0

Asplenium septentrionale (L.) Hoffm.

Forked spleenwort

Status: scarce

This fern is characteristic of rock crevices and earthy, unmortared walls on dry, south-facing, unshaded slopes. It usually grows on hard, base-poor, dark-coloured rocks, in crevices on vertical surfaces and on the sides more often than on the tops of walls, and is also occasionally found on spoil heaps of metalliferous mines and on old, mortared walls. Commonly associated species include *Agrostis capillaris, Asplenium ruta-muraria, A. trichomanes* subsp. *trichomanes, Athyrium filix-femina, Festuca ovina, Teucrium scorodonia, Thymus polytrichus, Ulex europaeus, U. gallii* and, on mine waste, *Racomitrium lanuginosum*. The reasons for its association with metalliferous mines are uncertain. It has been found at low to moderate elevations, mostly in mountainous districts, from sea level in northwest Scotland to 460 metres at Blake Rigg and Cwmorthin, but is perhaps gone from the latter.

A. septentrionale is a winter-green, clump-forming, usually gregarious perennial. The clumps are slow-growing and long-lived. Establishment and spread can be rapid on old earthy walls, some populations in mid Wales having increased tenfold in the last three or four decades, but on natural rock, establishment of new plants must be a rare event, as also is spread to new sites. A particular stage in the decay of earthy walls seems to favour colonisation. Dark-coloured rock may provide valuable thermal qualities, while shade and waterlogging seem to be deleterious.

It is decreasing in natural sites but increasing in some synanthropic ones. This species has probably disappeared from at least half its former sites in Scotland, England and North Wales. Most populations consist of very few plants. However, populations in Cardigan, where there are now some 1200 plants chiefly associated with lead-mine remains, are expanding rapidly and several new sites seem to have been colonised, but there is no spread to natural rock sites. Past extinctions were at least partly caused by collecting, while more recent losses have probably been caused mostly by shading resulting from scrub encroachment and afforestation.

Widespread throughout the northern hemisphere, especially in the mountains, and generally continental or northern-montane. It is thus probably under unusual stress in the cool, wet, oceanic zone where the suitable sites for it in Britain are found. In Europe it is rare around the Mediterranean (Jalas & Suominen 1972).

For stimulating accounts of its ecology, from which much of the above was drawn, see Page (1982, 1988).

A. O. Chater

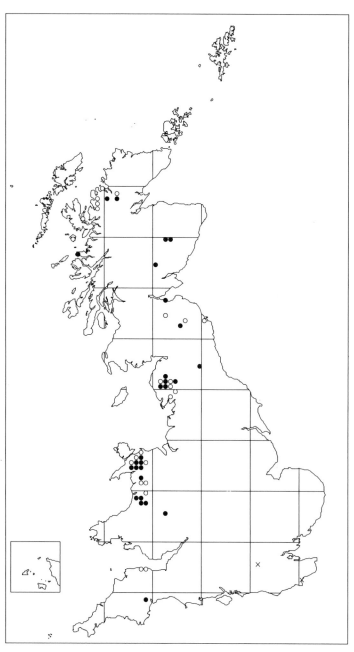

Current map	No	Atlas	No
1970 →	27	1930 →	19
Pre-1970	24	Pre-1930	18
Introductions	2	Introductions	1

continued →

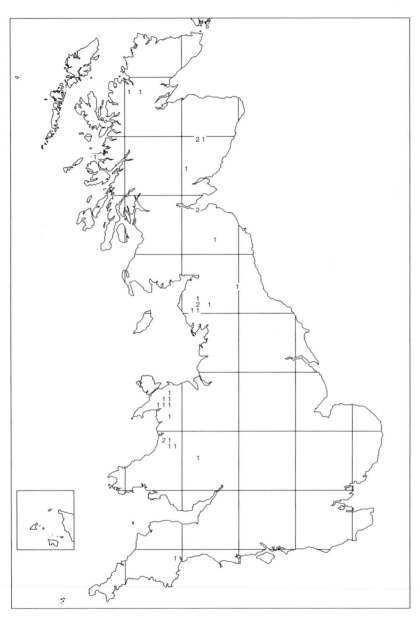

The number of tetrads in each 10 km square in which *Asplenium septentrionale* has been recorded as a native species since 1970. The species has been found in a total of 31 tetrads from 1970 onwards.

Athyrium distentifolium Tausch ex Opiz

Status: scarce

Alpine lady-fern

This is primarily a plant of block screes and gullies with a north or north-easterly aspect, growing on lee slopes where snow accumulates and where low insolation often enables the snow cover to persist into the early summer. It favours the more stable, acid block screes with a degree of infill, where meltwater remains near the surface. In this habitat vascular plant associates are few, possibly the most consistent being *Cryptogramma crispa*, *Deschampsia cespitosa*, *Galium saxatile*, *Saxifraga stellaris* and *Vaccinium myrtillus*. Bryophyte associates are rather more numerous and include *Barbilophozia floerkei*, *Hylocomium umbratum*, *Plagiothecium undulatum* and rarer chionophilous species such as *Brachythecium glaciale*, *B. reflexum* and *Kiaeria starkei*. *A. distentifolium* is an alpine plant, seldom occurring below 600 metres and reaching at least 1220 metres on Ben Macdui.

A. distentifolium is a perennial species. Spores are produced readily but large clumps are presumably built up by the branching rhizome system.

There is no reason to believe that this plant has decreased and some individual colonies are very large. It is probably still under-recorded.

It has a circumboreal distribution in Europe and Asia, extending south to the Pyrenees, southern Alps, Carpathians, Bulgaria and the Caucasus. For a map of its European distribution, see Jalas & Suominen (1972). Closely related variants occur in N. America.

The closely related *A. flexile*, treated as *A. distentifolium* var. *flexile* (Newman) Jermy by Tutin *et al.* (1993), is a rarer plant which if regarded as a species qualifies for inclusion in the Red Data Book.

G. P. Rothero

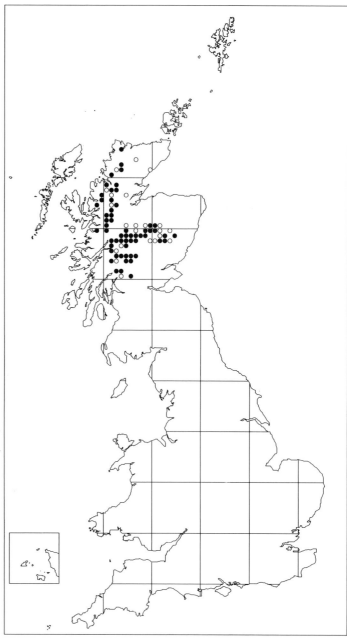

Current map	No	Atlas	No
1970 →	57	1930 →	51
Pre-1970	22	Pre-1930	9
Introductions	0	Introductions	0

Atriplex longipes Drejer
Status: scarce

Long-stalked orache

This species is usually found in tall, estuarine saltmarsh vegetation, especially in silty, brackish sites. Associated species include a perennial variant of *Aster tripolium*, *Cochlearia anglica*, *Juncus maritimus* and *Phragmites australis*.

A. longipes is an annual that is capable of self-pollination but also exhibits protogyny, which promotes outcrossing (Taschereau 1985). The flowers, to a large extent wind-pollinated, are produced during July and August.

A. longipes was not widely recognised as a British plant until its presence here was confirmed by Taschereau (1977). It is almost certainly under-recorded. It hybridises extensively with *A. glabriuscula* and *A. prostrata*, making identification difficult.

A. longipes sensu stricto is endemic to Europe, occuring on the coasts of southern Scandinavia and the Baltic (Jalas & Suominen 1980). Scandinavian botanists usually treat the closely related *A. praecox* (q.v.) as a subspecies of *A. longipes*.

J. R. Akeroyd

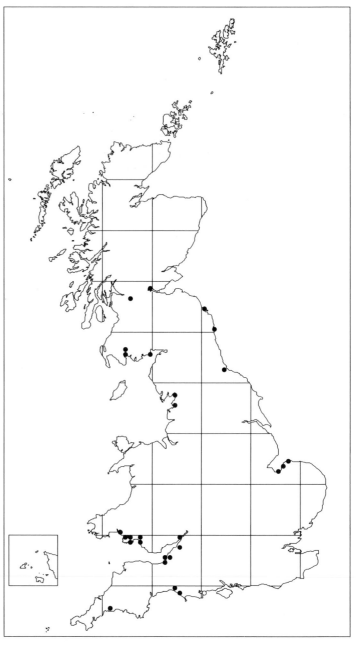

Current map	No
1970 →	27
Pre-1970	1
Introductions	0

Atriplex praecox Hülph.

Early orache

Status: scarce

This is a tiny annual plant, rarely more than 10 cm tall, that occurs in the lowest part of open strand communities. Its most characteristic habitat is sand and shingle beaches on the sheltered shores of Scottish sea-lochs.

The plant is capable of self-pollination but also exhibits protogyny, which promotes outcrossing (Taschereau 1985). The flowers, to a great extent wind-pollinated, are produced in June and July, earlier than those of other coastal species of *Atriplex*.

A. praecox was first reported in Britain only in 1975 (Taschereau 1977) and is almost certainly under-recorded.

This species occurs on the coasts of most of north-eastern Europe from Iceland to arctic Russia, extending southwards to Britain and southern Sweden (Jalas & Suominen 1980); it also occurs in North America.

Scandinavian botanists usually treat it as subsp. *praecox* (Hülph.) Turesson of *A. longipes*.

J. R. Akeroyd

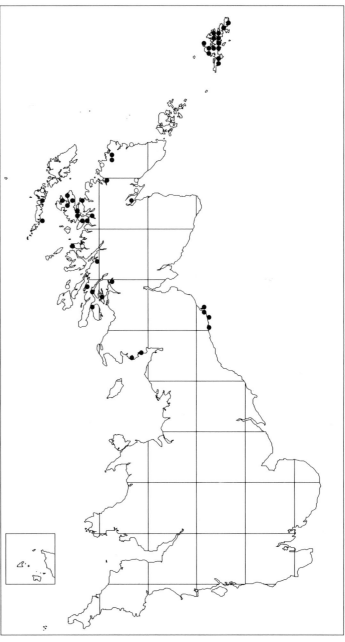

Current map	No
1970 →	43
Pre-1970	7
Introductions	0

Betula nana L.
Status: scarce

Dwarf birch

B. nana is a plant of wet upland heaths and blanket bogs on ground varying from moderately dry and sloping to completely flat and waterlogged. Although its usual substrate is acidic peat or mor humus, it occasionally roots in rock crevices. In favourable habitats populations are spread over many hectares (e.g. on Ben Wyvis), but others are small and patchy. Frequent associates include *Calluna vulgaris, Empetrum nigrum, Erica tetralix, Eriophorum angustifolium, E. vaginatum, Molinia caerulea, Narthecium ossifragum, Rubus chamaemorus, Trichophorum cespitosum* and *Sphagnum* spp. Altitudinal range is from 120 metres in Sutherland to 860 metres above Glen Cannich.

B. nana is a perennial shrub. Although it is successfully grown from native seed in nurseries, seedlings are seldom found in the wild in Britain. Although germination may occur (and be overlooked), further development of seedlings is probably prevented by grazing.

Fossil remains of *B. nana* are abundant in glacial and early post-glacial deposits throughout Britain and Ireland (Godwin 1975). While *B. nana* had probably suffered a major post-glacial restriction of range by the onset of the Atlantic period, it has evidently continued to lose ground through overgrazing and burning, and is often of somewhat depauperate growth. Despite a large extent of apparently suitable habitat, only two small populations are known south of the Highlands. Overgrazing, burning and the recent trend to peatland afforestation present continuing threats, though new colonies continue to be found in the Highlands.

Betula nana is a widespread circumpolar arctic-alpine species, and in Europe extends south at high altitudes to the Alps and Carpathians (Jalas & Suominen 1976). It is an important dominant of communities in the Boreal and Arctic regions.

Outside Britain, *B. nana* grows in a wider range of habitats and more frequently on well-drained mineral soils; and in a wider variety of variants, from completely prostrate plants to tall, bushy and upright shrubs which result from introgressive hybridisation with *B. pubescens* (Elkington 1968). Widespread though infrequent hybridisation with *B. pubescens* is reported, both in Britain and worldwide.

R. H. Scott

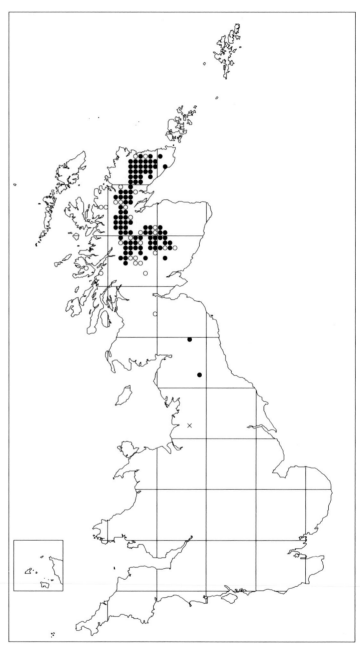

Current map	No	Atlas	No
1970 →	93	1930 →	48
Pre-1970	27	Pre-1930	11
Introductions	1	Introductions	0

Brassica oleracea L. var. *oleracea*
Status: scarce

Wild cabbage

B. oleracea is found on maritime cliffs, most often on calcareous substrates, but also on base-rich sandstones, shales, and less commonly on clay. It often behaves as a chasmophyte, but competes well in grassland and mixed herb communities at the top or base of the cliff, although it is usually less long-lived here. It is typically found near centres of human population, and often does not persist on unpopulated coastlines. Associated species include *Armeria maritima*, *Cochlearia officinalis*, *Daucus carota*, *Plantago coronopus*, *Raphanus raphanistrum* subsp. *maritimus*, *Silene uniflora* and *Tripleurospermum maritimum*.

B. oleracea var. *oleracea* is a relatively short-lived (rarely to 20 years) evergreen perennial without means of vegetative multiplication. It forms woody trunks with annual groups of leaf-scars by which it can be aged. There is a range of pollinators, especially bees and hoverflies, and it is fully self-incompatible; the Tynemouth population contains in excess of 20 sporophytic S-alleles. Up to 100,000 seeds are produced per plant (more commonly about 10,000). Seeds germinate best at 20°C in a long day, after dark chilling. Viability scarcely drops after 4 years storage.

Many southern populations seem to be fairly stable and are not threatened. The species is not very hardy, and suffers after very severe winters. In some areas, fluctuating populations may be reinforced by introductions from cultivated plants in gardens and allotments.

Outside Britain, *B. oleracea* var. *oleracea* is found on Heligoland and locally on the Channel and Atlantic coasts of France. Subsp. *robertiana* (Gay) Rouy & Fouc. occurs in France, Italy, Corsica, Sardinia and Yugoslavia. *B. oleracea sensu lato* is also recorded as an introduction in North America and Australasia.

B. oleracea has long been known in Britain, where it was first found on Dover cliffs by W. Turner in 1548. Mitchell (1976) and Mitchell & Richards (1979) argue that *B. oleracea* is not native in northern Europe, but was introduced, probably by the Romans, and has been able to persist in a feral state on sea-cliffs. However, in many areas it may be maintained by reintroductions which morphologically soon revert to 'wild' phenotypes. As the distinction between 'native' and 'introduced' is therefore meaningless for maritime populations, all established coastal colonies are mapped as if they were native.

A. J. Richards

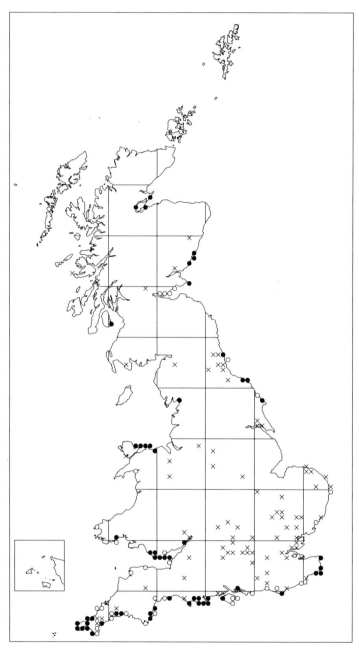

Current map	No	Atlas	No
1970 →	55	1930 →	33
Pre-1970	33	Pre-1930	21
Casuals	82	Introductions	9

Briza minor L.

Status: introduced

B. minor is a small annual grass largely confined in Britain to arable habitats. As an established species it is restricted to parts of the country with relatively mild winters, where it is found mainly on light, base-poor soils. It is most abundant in the Isles of Scilly, where it is found not only in bulb and potato fields, but also as a ruderal species by roadsides and similar situations. It is frequently associated with other uncommon arable annuals including *Chrysanthemum segetum* and *Misopates orontium*, although showing a greater preference for autumn-cultivated land than these species. In one Hampshire site it occurs with the nationally rare *Gastridium ventricosum. B. minor* is a lowland species, the majority of its sites being within 10 km of the sea.

Relatively little is known about the biology of this species. It is an annual, germinating mainly in the autumn. Nothing is known about its dormancy mechanism or length of persistence in the soil. In common with other arable annuals, it is a poor competitor and requires regular disturbance for seedling establishment. On the mainland it flowers from mid- to late summer, while in the more favourable climate of the Isles of Scilly it flowers from March onwards. Its climatic restriction suggests a degree of frost sensitivity in the seedlings.

As with many other arable annuals, *B. minor* appears to be declining as a result of agricultural intensification. Threats include the use of herbicides (often directed specifically against grasses) and the increased competitiveness of modern crop varieties under high levels of nitrogen application. This species appears to survive best where agriculture is less intensive, or of an unusual nature (e.g. on the Isles of Scilly).

B. minor has a predominantly Mediterranean and western European distribution; and Britain is towards the northern edge of its range. It is naturalised in South Africa, Japan, North and South America and Australia. Although traditionally regarded as a native member of the British flora, both Stace (1991) and Kent (1992) treat this species as an introduction.

P. J. Wilson

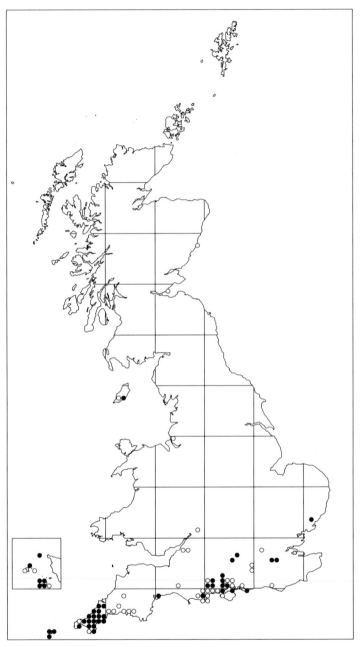

Current map	No	Atlas	No
1970 →	38	1930 →	13
Pre-1970	35	Pre-1930	28
		Introductions	8

Bromopsis benekenii (Lange) Holub

Status: scarce

Lesser hairy-brome

This grass is apparently largely confined to woods on shallow chalk, limestone or other calcareous soils in steep valleys. It is frequently recorded in beech woods but also occurs in other deciduous woods, and woodland margins and scrub. It grows in small to medium-sized patches among the species-rich ground layer on moderate humus in light shade and grows best on a slight slope.

B. benekenii is a perennial species which grows in small tufts. Little is known of its reproductive biology.

This is a little known and probably under-recorded species. It is treated by some authorities as *B. ramosa* subsp. *benekenii* (Lange) Tzvelev, and several competent recorders have found it difficult to distinguish from *B. ramosa*, with which it sometimes grows. *B. benekenii* may therefore still be present in the areas for which only pre-1970 records are available.

It is found in central and eastern Europe and at scattered localities eastwards to the Yangtze River in China.

A. L. Newton

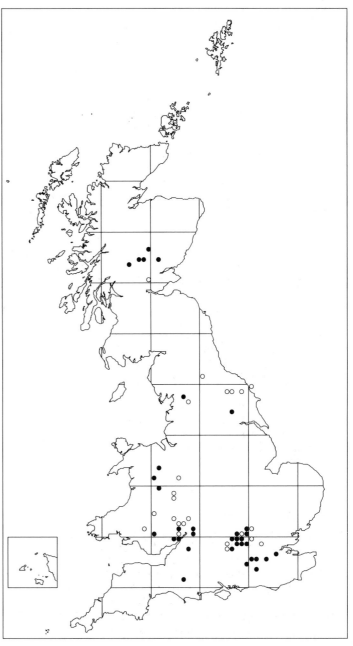

Current map	No	Atlas	No
1970 →	34	1930 →	22
Pre-1970	23	Pre-1930	0
Introductions	0	Introductions	0

Bupleurum tenuissimum L.
Status: scarce

This is a plant of dry, usually brackish, grassland on sea-walls, drained grazing marshes and, less frequently, on the upper (often disturbed) parts of saltmarshes. It typically occurs in short turf with plenty of bare ground, and can be locally abundant in disturbed areas, for example alongside trackways, ditches and spoil dumps, and in areas subject to poaching by livestock. Associated species are varied, and include several other nationally scarce plants with similar habitat requirements and geographical distribution, e.g. *Hordeum marinum*, *Parapholis incurva* and *Trifolium squamosum*. The only recent inland records are from Worcestershire, where it still occurs on several commons. It is confined to the lowlands.

B. tenuissimum is an annual, flowering from July to September. Seed germinates in autumn and spring, and the fact that plants normally grow in open situations suggests that bare ground is important for germination and successful seedling establishment. As with many annual species, population size can vary considerably from year to year. However, it is uncertain whether it develops a persistent 'bank' of buried seed.

B. tenuissimum has disappeared from almost all its inland stations. On the coast, too, there have been some losses, particularly towards the northern edge of its range. Many *B. tenuissimum* populations are closely associated with sea-walls, and these are likely to be at risk from engineering schemes to upgrade coastal defences.

It is found on the coasts of western Europe northwards to southern Scandinavia (Denmark and Sweden), also locally inland. In southern Europe it occurs by the Mediterranean and from there eastwards to the Middle East.

S. J. Leach

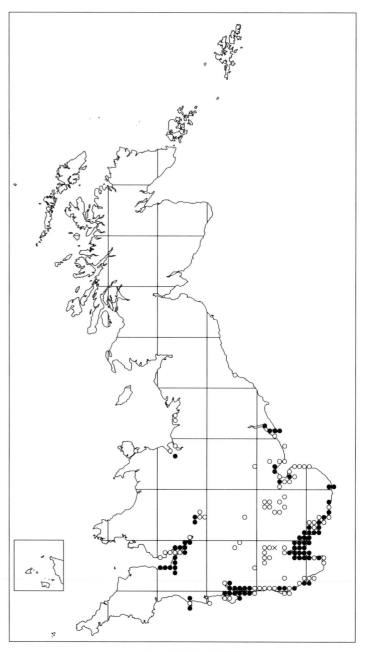

Current map	No	Atlas	No
1970 →	76	1930 →	59
Pre-1970	81	Pre-1930	36
Introductions	1	Introductions	0

Calamagrostis stricta (Timm) Koeler

Status: rare?

Narrow small-reed

A plant of near-neutral bogs and marshes. At a site near Dalmellington it grows with *Deschampsia cespitosa*, *Filipendula ulmaria*, *Juncus effusus* and *Phalaris arundinacea*. In Yorkshire it is found as an emergent at the edge of the Leven Canal. It is primarily a lowland species, but ascends to 340 metres at Kingside Loch.

C. stricta is a tufted perennial, with slender creeping rhizomes. It flowers in June and July. Little is known of its reproductive biology.

It is difficult to assess trends in the distribution of *C. stricta* as it has previously been confused with *C. scotica*, *C. purpurea* and hybrids with *C. canescens* and perhaps with other species. It has certainly been lost from some sites through drainage.

C. stricta has a circumpolar distribution. It is widespread in the boreal zone of Europe, Asia and North America, and occurs very locally in mountains further south.

British populations of *C. stricta* are variable, perhaps because of past hybridisation and introgression with other species (Stace 1975). Where *C. stricta* grows with *C. scotica* in Caithness there is little sign of hybridisation between them, but some plants in populations of *C. stricta* in Selkirkshire show some similarity to *C. scotica* although they are well outside the southern limit of that species.

As this species has been recorded in only 15 10 km squares since 1970, it qualifies for inclusion in the *Red Data Book* (Perring & Farrell 1983) under the current criteria. However it will probably be recorded in more than 15 10 km squares, when, as seems likely, it is refound in some of its old localities.

O. M. Stewart

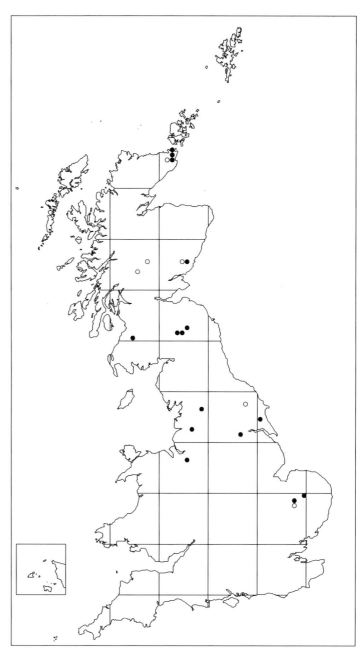

Records of *C. stricta* were not distinguished from those of *C. scotica* in the *Atlas*.

Current map	No
1970 →	15
Pre-1970	6
Introductions	0

continued →

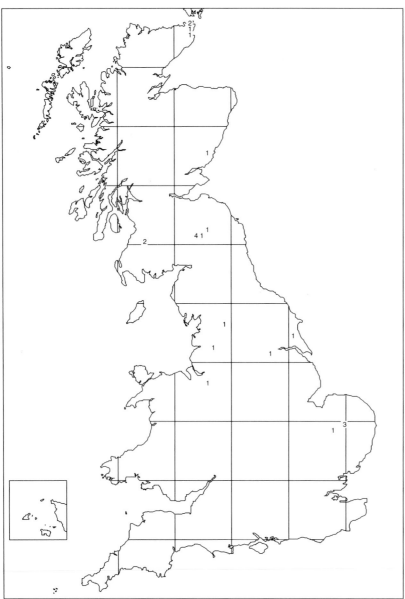

The number of tetrads in each 10 km square in which *Calamagrostis stricta* has been recorded as a native species from 1970 onwards. The species has been found in a total of 22 tetrads from 1970 onwards.

Callitriche hermaphroditica L.
Status: not scarce

Autumnal water-starwort

This aquatic species usually grows on silty substrates in mesotrophic or eutrophic lakes. It can be found in shallow water at the edges of sheltered lakes, but in more exposed sites it is confined to deeper water. Species such as *Myriophyllum alterniflorum*, *Potamogeton gramineus*, *P. × nitens* and *Nitella flexilis* are often found in its more mesotrophic localities, where less frequent associates include *Najas flexilis* and *Potamogeton praelongus*. Unlike these scarce species, *C. hermaphroditica* is also found in abundance in some eutrophic waters, such as the Anglesey lakes, where it can be found with *Potamogeton crispus*, *P. pusillus* and *Zannichellia palustris*. *C. hermaphroditica* has also been recorded as a colonist of canals and flooded gravel pits. It is a predominantly lowland species, recorded up to 350 metres (Kingside Loch) and 380 metres (Malham Tarn, where its occurrence may have been transient). A record from 425 metres in Perthshire (White 1898) requires confirmation and one from 915 metres in Inverness-shire (McCallum Webster 1978) is erroneous.

C. hermaphroditica is a shallow-rooted annual. The flowers are submerged and pollinated under water. Plants fruit freely. Fruiting plants are often uprooted by autumn winds. Little is known about its germination requirements.

Like many aquatics, *C. hermaphroditica* was under-recorded in the *Atlas of the British Flora* (Perring & Walters 1962) and it is difficult to assess any changes in its distribution. There is no evidence to suggest that it has declined, and its tolerance of eutrophication suggests that it is unlikely to be threatened by changes in water quality. In 1985 it was discovered in gravel pits in Lincolnshire, a significant extension of its British distribution.

It is a widespread circumboreal species, occurring in Europe, Asia and North America. In Europe it has a predominantly northern distribution, extending south as far the British Isles, northern Germany and Rumania; it is absent from the Alps.

Although a relatively distinct species, *C. hermaphroditica* has sometimes been confused with *C. hamulata*. Many of the records cited by McCallum Webster (1978) are erroneous.

C. D. Preston

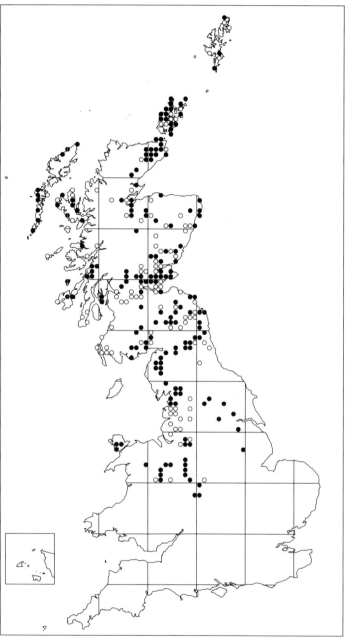

Current map	No	Atlas	No
1970 →	179	1930 →	83
Pre-1970	105	Pre-1930	34
Introductions	0	Introductions	0

Callitriche truncata Guss.
Status: scarce

Short-leaved water-starwort

C. truncata is an aquatic plant which grows totally submerged in shallow lowland waters, extending down to a depth of 1.5 metres. It is a pioneer which often appears before other species in newly created habitats such as gravel pits, or after herbicide treatment, dredging or other major management operations in ditches, drains, ponds, lakes, reservoirs, rivers and canals. It is tolerant of a range of water chemistry, but it is usually found in base-rich, mesotrophic or somewhat eutrophic waters. It is also found over a wide range of substrates, from pebbles and stones to soft organic mud. Plants are most vigorous in clear, still or very slowly flowing water but are occasionally found in sites where the water flows steadily but rather more rapidly, and can sometimes grow in turbid conditions. *C. truncata* often grows by itself, or with *Lemna minor* and *Sparganium erectum* in still water and *Myriophyllum spicatum* and *Ranunculus penicillatus* subsp. *pseudofluitans* in flowing water; *Elodea canadensis* is a frequent associate in both habitats.

Plants break up in autumn and float on the surface; they can overwinter as vegetative fragments. Recent observations indicate that *C. truncata* fruits freely at most of its British sites, producing large numbers of seeds (Barry & Wade 1986). These contrast with previous reports of populations which fruit only sparingly. Dispersal of seed is by water or possibly by wildfowl; seed fed to ducks has germinated when recovered from the faeces. Seeds have no innate dormancy, but in the wild seeds shed in autumn do not germinate until spring. Like many pioneers the species can be erratic in its appearance and sometimes reappears in a site after a long absence.

C. truncata is still present in most of the areas in which it has previously been recorded, although it is apparently extinct in Sussex, Kent, Gloucestershire and Guernsey. The reasons for these disappearances are not clear. They have been compensated for by the recent discovery of new localities, including two reservoirs and a fishing lake in Essex, a county from which it has not previously been reported.

C. truncata has a Mediterranean-Atlantic distribution. The British plant is subsp. *occidentalis*, which also occurs in Spain, Portugal, Belgium, France and Ireland. Subsp. *truncata* is found in the central and eastern Mediterranean region, and subsp. *fimbriata* Schotsman occurs in Russia.

For more details of the ecology of this species see Barry & Wade (1986), on which the above account is based.

C. D. Preston

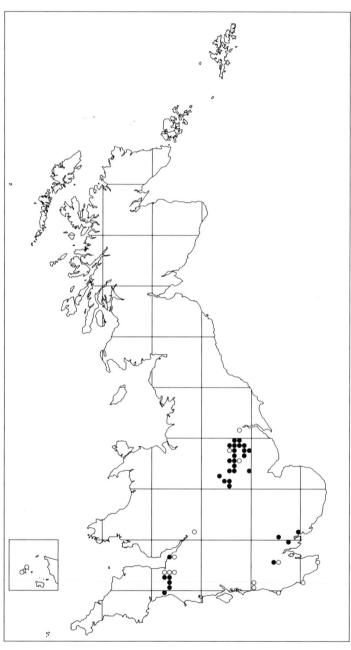

Current map	No	Atlas	No
1970 →	31	1930 →	11
Pre-1970	14	Pre-1930	3
Introductions	0	Introductions	0

Campanula patula L.
Status: scarce

Spreading bellflower

C. patula is a plant of open woodland, wood borders and rock outcrops. It is most frequently found on banks by hedges, roads, railways and rivers, particularly in disturbed sites, and it has been found on spoil heaps and land slips. It is thermophilous, normally favouring dry, well-drained, sunny sites on fairly infertile, sandy or gravelly soils with a low nutrient status and a mildly acidic to neutral reaction. It can tolerate partial shade but does not persist long in competition with taller more vigorous plants. It is tolerant of heavy grazing but may persist under lightly grazed regimes including open horse-grazed swards and orchards. It is strongly associated with the forest areas of England and is seldom found far from areas of ancient woodland. It is confined to the lowlands.

C. patula is a biennial reproducing entirely by seed. The seeds may need disturbed and sunny sites for germination and establishment. Second year plants can compete and flower in taller vegetation. Seeds in the soil appear to have a long viability. Plants occur in unrecorded sites following soil disturbance and may reappear in old stations after long absences. In the absence of competition it may be extremely persistent and it has been recorded for more than 130 years on one rock outcrop. Plants can colonise new sites and spread along corridors such as railway banks where there is suitable habitat.

It is in long-term decline and has suffered a considerable range contraction. Even in its core area on the Welsh Borders it is very reduced. Most populations are small. Early accounts indicate local abundance or profusion (Lees 1851; Lees 1867; Rea 1897; Turner & Dillwyn 1805). Direct habitat loss has contributed to the decline, but the plant has disappeared from many sites following the increased use of agricultural fertilisers, herbicide use along roadsides, and the cessation of traditional woodland management practices, particularly coppicing.

C. patula is found throughout Europe east to Central Russia. It has a distinctly continental distribution and is rare in the Iberian peninsula and western France.

J. J. Day

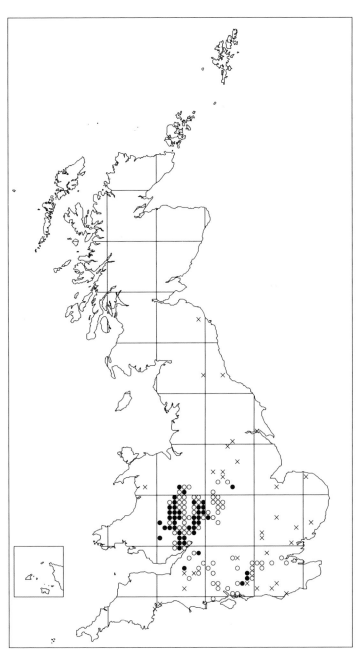

Current map	No	Atlas	No
1970 →	44	1930 →	26
Pre-1970	74	Pre-1930	60
Introductions	31	Introductions	19

Cardamine bulbifera (L.) Crantz

Coralroot

Status: scarce

This is a plant with two contrasting habitats. In the Chilterns it is found in beech woodland on relatively dry slopes with underlying chalk, generally close to tracks and paths. It grows as patches 1-2 metres in diameter, in areas which are free of most other vegetation; or more thinly scattered and then associated with *Rubus fruticosus*, *Mercurialis perennis* and the typical ground flora of such woodland. In the Kent and Sussex Weald it grows in damp woodlands on Wealden clay, often closely associated with streams and damp places, frequently on the steep banks of a stream, in smaller patches and deeper into the woodland than in the Chilterns; often with *Carpinus betulus* as the tree cover and *Cardamine flexuosa*, *Carex pendula* and *Hyacinthoides non-scripta* in the ground flora. It flourishes in both types of habitat for a few years when the tree canopy is opened up but forms much more stable colonies where there is little interference and the light intensity is relatively low. It is confined to the lowlands.

C. bulbifera is perennial with a cream-coloured, coral-like rhizome. Many mature plants flower (though only for a short period) and bear axillary bulbils. The remainder produce bulbils but no flowers. Reproduction is normally by means of these bulbils but a few plants in some colonies sometimes produce viable seed, remaining green and leafy long after the others have withered away and the bulbils fallen. There are generally many times more juvenile plants in a colony than mature plants. It flowers from seed or bulbil after 3-4 years.

Although *C. bulbifera* has been well-recorded in the past, it is still possible to discover new sites but there is no evidence to suggest that these are not hitherto overlooked populations. It has disappeared from only a few localities, these being where a wood has been clear-felled or replanted with conifers. On the whole the distribution appears stable.

In Europe this species occurs from southern Scandinavia and France to the Black Sea, often in the mountains. It does not extend to the Mediterranean area. It is also found in south-west Asia, reaching its eastern limit in the Caucasus.

C. bulbifera has been introduced in a number of places in Britain and in many it still persists. In the West Country, forma *ptarmicifolia*, a bigger plant with larger leaves and browner bulbils than the native one, is a common introduction.

For a detailed account of this species, see Showler & Rich (1993).

A. J. Showler

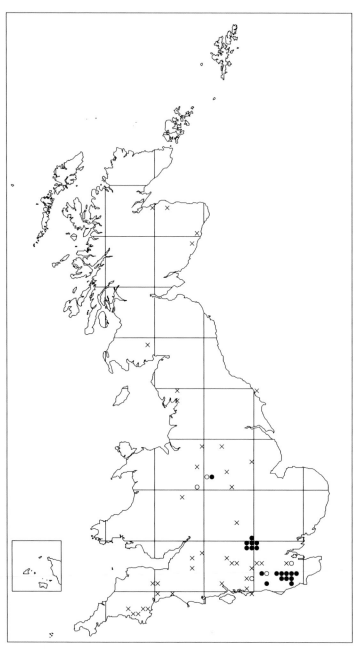

Current map	No	Atlas	No
1970 →	19	1930 →	19
Pre-1970	5	Pre-1930	4
Introductions	39	Introductions	10

continued →

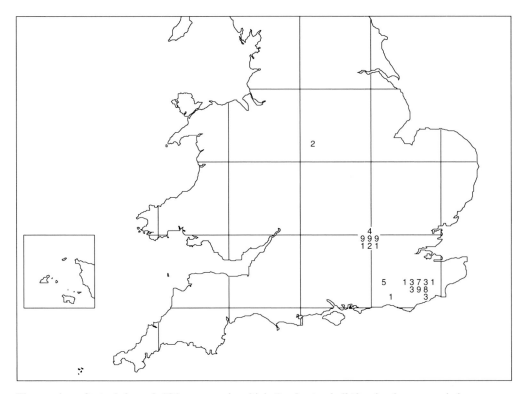

The number of tetrads in each 10 km square in which *Cardamine bulbifera* has been recorded as a native species from 1970 onwards. Squares in which the species is recorded in 9 or more tetrads are plotted as 9: *C. bulbifera* is actually recorded from 9 tetrads in SU99, 11 in TQ62 and 12 in SU89 and TQ09. The species has been found in a total of 81 tetrads from 1970 onwards.

Cardamine impatiens L.
Status: scarce

Narrow-leaved bitter-cress

This is a plant of varied habitats, including shady woodland, rocks and screes, shady banks of rivers and streams, and damp roadsides. In the south this species frequently grows in clearings in ash woods, and in northern England it can be found in the damp shady grikes of limestone pavement. It is often on calcareous rocks, but it also grows frequently in neutral soils. It ascends from sea-level to 610 metres on Ingleborough.

C. impatiens is a biennial. The ripe seeds are dispersed explosively. In southern ashwoods seedlings appear in cleared sites within the year following felling. The flowering stems from over-wintering rosettes fruit freely, but few of the seedlings in the following year survive the competing vegetation. By the third year after felling very few *C. impatiens* plants survive. New colonies are found after felling in each suitable new area of woodland, as dormant seeds buried in the soil remain viable for many years (Briggs 1990).

There is little evidence for a marked decline of this species, which is still locally abundant in the south and west of England and in Wales. It has been planted in gardens, from where it can be self-sown, and occasionally it is also recorded as a casual with aliens at docks and on waste ground.

It is widely distributed throughout temperate Europe, where it grows in mountain woods and pastures, and colonises stony man-made habitats such as reservoir edges. It extends through the Caucasus and central Asia to the Far East, and is recorded as an introduction in N. America.

For further information, see Rich (1991).

M. Briggs

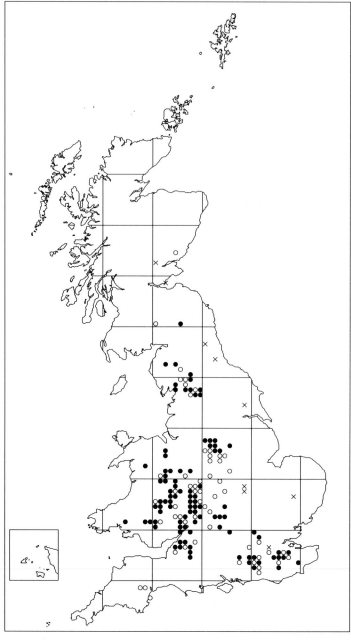

Current map	No	Atlas	No
1970 →	95	1930 →	48
Pre-1970	56	Pre-1930	51
Introductions	9	Introductions	2

Carex appropinquata Schum.
Status: scarce

Fibrous tussock-sedge

C. appropinquata is a plant of lowland herbaceous fen. When *C. appropinquata* grows in the same site as *C. paniculata* it is often found in slightly drier places, but it is the first of the two to disappear when the water level falls. It can be found in fen carr, where it may be a relic of a time when conditions were more open. It is predominantly a lowland plant, but is found up to 380 metres at Malham Tarn.

C. appropinquata is a tufted perennial. Its method of reproduction is by seed, which is abundantly produced.

It is now extinct in its southernmost station in Britain on the Middlesex-Hertfordshire-Buckinghamshire borders. In East Anglia it has recently suffered much from invasion by scrub and *Phragmites australis* following drought, excessive water extraction and lack of management. Some colonies (e.g. that at Wicken Fen) consist of large tussocks and there has been no regeneration in recent years. However, it is locally abundant in Broadland and very locally abundant in Yorkshire. In the last twenty years it has been found in several new sites in the Scottish Borders. Reports from Wales were errors (S.B. Evans 1989). The species must be regarded as very vulnerable outside its Broadland strongholds because of the small number of sites to which it is now restricted.

It is widespread in central and eastern Europe, extending north to northern Scandinavia and eastward to Siberia.

European studies, particularly in Czechoslovakia, have seemed to show that it requires more acid conditions than its congener *C. paniculata*, but the fact that its largest congregations in Britain and Ireland are in calcareous fens in East Anglia and County Westmeath suggest that the opposite is true in western Europe.

R. W. David

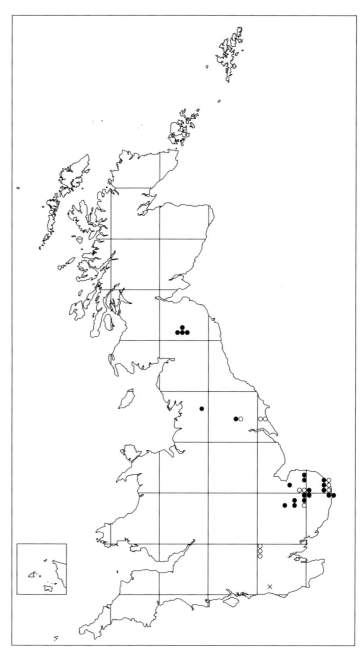

Current map	No	Atlas	No
1970 →	21	1930 →	17
Pre-1970	12	Pre-1930	9
Introductions	1	Introductions	1

continued →

73

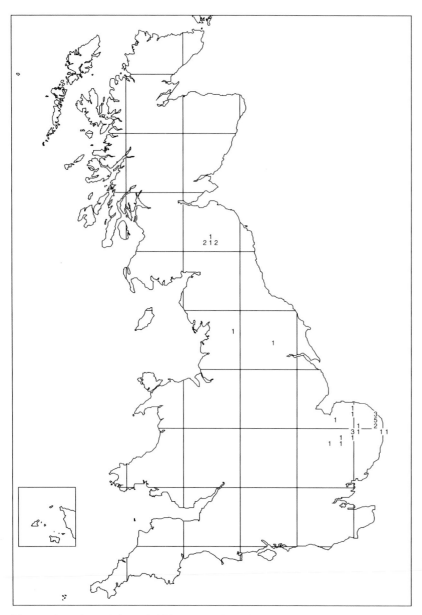

The number of tetrads in each 10 km square in which *Carex appropinquata* has been recorded as a native species from 1970 onwards. The species has been found in a total of 32 tetrads from 1970 onwards.

Carex aquatilis Wahlenb.

Status: not scarce

Water sedge

This is a species of mires and swamps. In lowland lake basins it frequently forms large stands with *Carex rostrata*, *C. vesicaria* and *Equisetum fluviatile* at the upper end of the basin. It can be dominant in swamps alongside slow-flowing rivers, with *Carex acutiformis*, *C. vesicaria*, *Phalaris arundinacea* and *Phragmites australis*. In upland areas it is found on gently sloping mires on deep peat, with *Carex curta*, *C. nigra*, *C. rariflora*, *C. rostrata* and several *Sphagnum* species and bryoid mosses. It also occurs by drainage channels in upland mires and occasionally alongside fairly fast flowing upland rivers. In these habitats plants are notably shorter than those in the lowlands. It has a wide altitudinal range from sea-level to 750 metres on Glas Maol.

It is a rhizomatous perennial. The rhizome is far-creeping and the plant therefore has a considerable potential for vegetative spread. Plants are often sterile over large areas, especially where populations are shaded or where there have been changes in water level. *C. aquatilis* is wind pollinated and hybridises readily with other members of the *C. nigra* group. Many populations appear to be hybrid swarms.

Some lowland populations are disappearing due to land-use changes, but those in the Scottish Highlands are not threatened except very locally in areas selected for ski developments where ski-tows and downhill running could be detrimental.

This is a circumpolar species. In Europe it extends south to Wales, northern Germany and central Russia but in western North America it occurs as far south as Arizona and California.

A. C. Jermy

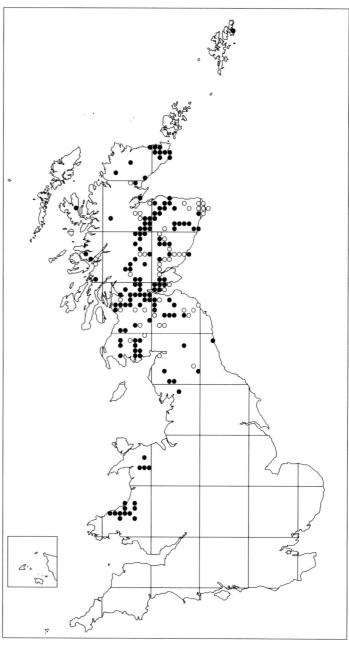

Current map	No	Atlas	No
1970 →	137	1930 →	44
Pre-1970	49	Pre-1930	52
Introductions	0	Introductions	0

75

Carex atrata L.　　　　　　　　　　　　　　　　　　　　**Black alpine-sedge**
Status: scarce

A strictly montane plant, *C. atrata* grows on ungrazed faces and ledges of calcareous cliffs of the higher mountains, as scattered tufts or small clumps in both dry and moist places. Typical associates are other montane calcicoles, such as *Carex capillaris, Cerastium alpinum, Dryas octopetala, Persicaria vivipara, Poa alpina, Saxifraga aizoides, S. nivalis, S. oppositifolia, Silene acaulis* and *Thalictrum alpinum*; and more widespread plants such as *Carex flacca, Festuca ovina* agg. and *Thymus polytrichus*. On more stable ledges with taller herbaceous communities, it grows with *Angelica sylvestris, Geum rivale, Oxyria digyna, Saussurea alpina, Sedum rosea* and *Trollius europaeus*. *C. atrata* also occurs amongst open growths of *Salix lapponum* and other montane willows. The altitudinal range is from 550 metres at Coire Ghamhnain in Glen Orchy to 1060 metres on Beinn Heasgarnich.

A perennial, *C. atrata* flowers and produces ripe fruits in most localities, but there is no information on germination. Probably most populations are maintained by vegetative growth, and this species appears to have little capacity for spread under present conditions, although this may be mainly a grazing limitation.

South of the Scottish Highlands, the best population is on Snowdon, and it is very rare elsewhere. It is almost plentiful on the Breadalbane mountains, but is nowhere abundant. It may once have had a wider distribution at high levels, and if so it has evidently become restricted to steep rock habitats through grazing. It is probably still present in most of the 10 km squares for which only pre-1970 records are available.

This is a circumpolar arctic-alpine species, occurring in the high mountain systems of central Europe, Asia and the Rockies, as well as widely at higher latitudes. In southern Norway it grows in open birchwood and willow scrub as well as in montane herbaceous and rock communities, while in Norwegian Lapland it grows down to sea level in closed herb-rich grassland.

D. A. Ratcliffe

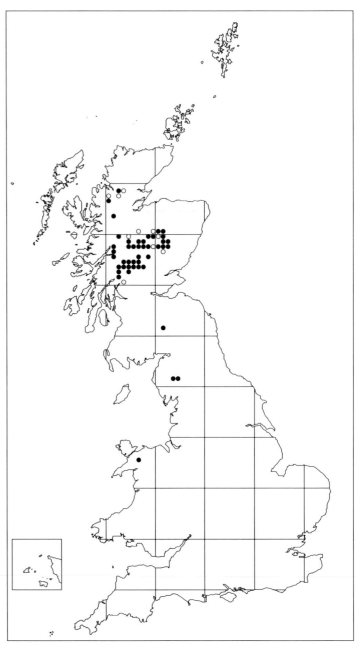

Current map	No	Atlas	No
1970 →	44	1930 →	28
Pre-1970	10	Pre-1930	13
Introductions	0	Introductions	0

Carex capillaris L.

Status: scarce

Hair sedge

This is a montane sedge growing in short herb-rich grassland, closed marshes with low vegetation, open hummocky marshes and flushes, and on steep rock faces and ledges. It is a strict calcicole, growing especially on limestone and calcareous mica-schists, but also on lime-rich dolerite, gneiss, greywackes, sandstones and blown shell sand. Substrates vary from dry to permanently wet, though usually with some lateral water movement. *C. capillaris* has a wide variety of associates, from species such as *C. rupestris, Dryas octopetala, Festuca vivipara, Persicaria vivipara, Potentilla crantzii, Salix reticulata, Silene acaulis* and *Thymus polytrichus* in dry habitats; to *C. dioica, Carex pulicaris, C. viridula* subsp. *brachyrrhyncha, C. viridula* subsp. *oedocarpa, Juncus triglumis, Kobresia simpliciuscula, Saxifraga aizoides, Selaginella selaginoides, Thalictrum alpinum* and *Tofieldia pusilla* in moist situations. Its altitudinal range is from almost sea level on the north Scottish coast to at least 1025 metres on Ben Lawers.

C. capillaris is a perennial species which spreads locally by short rhizomes. Little is known of its reproduction by seed.

While it can grow in very open boreal woodland, *C. capillaris* may have been favoured by the destruction of forest and scrub. Although intolerant of competition from taller plants, it grows well in short swards and withstands moderate grazing; but its restriction to steep rocks in some localities suggests that this sedge may succumb to heavy grazing. In common with many calcicoles, it is adversely affected by application of fertilisers in pasture improvement. Upper Teesdale has the only large populations south of the Highlands. It is probably still present in most Scottish 10 km squares for which only pre-1970 records are available.

This is a circumpolar arctic-alpine species, occurring at sea-level on tundras in the far north but confined to high mountains further south.

D. A. Ratcliffe

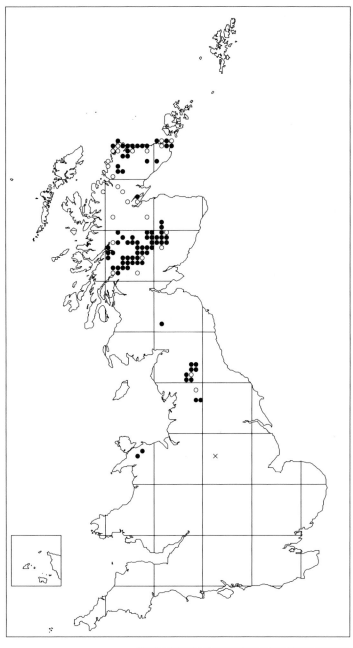

Current map	No	Atlas	No
1970 →	79	1930 →	69
Pre-1970	26	Pre-1930	10
Introductions	1	Introductions	0

Carex digitata L.
Status: scarce

Fingered sedge

This sedge is locally abundant in open woods and on scree and the shaded ledges of quarries in limestone areas. It requires soil with a high calcium content (pH 7.3 - 8.0), and good drainage yet with some protection against drying out. Colonies tend to be concentrated on the broken banks at the edges of woodland rides, particularly on south-facing slopes, where they receive more light than in the wood proper. They are confined to lowland habitats.

Individual tufts of this perennial species may not be long-lived, but they set abundant seed if not too shaded. The plant requires some shade but may disappear from a site if it becomes too densely shaded, reappearing from a dormant seed bank only after disturbance.

Some populations have been reduced in numbers or eliminated by afforestation, the destruction of limestone pavements and excessive public pressure. The Dorset record is based on a single, imprecisely localised herbarium specimen. The species as a whole is not at risk in Britain; recent survey work has revealed more sites than were previously known and the species may still be somewhat under-recorded.

It is widespread in suitable situations throughout Europe from southern Lapland to northern Spain and central Italy but absent from Greece. It extends eastward to the Caucasus and the Urals.

For a detailed account of its British distribution, see David (1978a, 1982a).

R .W. David

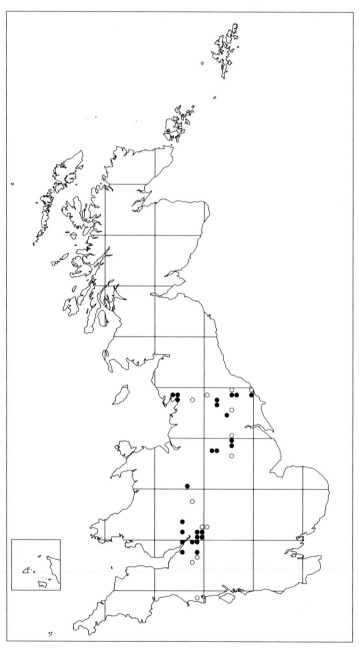

Current map	No	Atlas	No
1970 →	25	1930 →	14
Pre-1970	13	Pre-1930	17
Introductions	0	Introductions	0

continued →

78

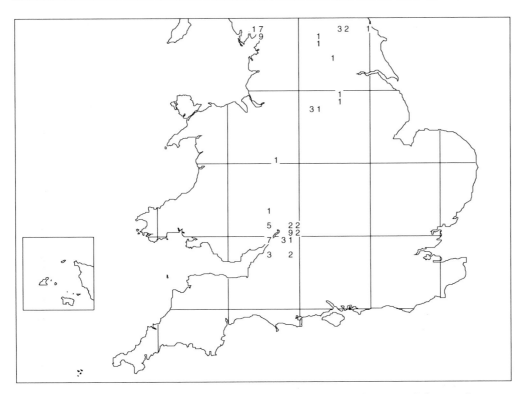

The number of tetrads in each 10 km square in which *Carex digitata* has been recorded as a native species from 1970 onwards. Squares in which the species is recorded in 9 or more tetrads are plotted as 9: *C. digitata* is actually recorded from 10 tetrads in SD47 and SO80. The species has been found in a total of 72 tetrads from 1970 onwards.

Carex divisa Hudson

Divided sedge

Status: scarce

A perennial sedge of grassland near the sea, *C. divisa* is moderately tolerant of salt, but absent from saltmarshes themselves. It is particularly characteristic of lightly grazed depressions in coastal pastures and the margin of grazing-marsh ditches on alluvial or sandy soils. It often accompanies *Carex distans*, *Oenanthe lachenalii* and *Trifolium fragiferum* in the damp brackish sward. *C. divisa* rarely occurs above 10 metres altitude, although it does occur on the inland margins of grazing marshes.

C. divisa has a far-creeping rhizome and much of its local spread is by vegetative means. Longer-distance dispersal by seed is frequent.

C. divisa is declining within most of its British range, and has disappeared from its inland sites. Many populations have been lost as a result of ploughing, drainage and industrial development of coastal grasslands (in particular the conversion of grazing marsh to arable land); increasing control of tidal water may also have contributed to its demise on some sites, by reducing the occurrence of brackish conditions inland.

C. divisa occurs inland in southern and south-central Europe, but is mainly coastal further north; it reaches its northern limit in Britain. It is also widespread in Mediterranean north Africa and west Asia.

J. O. Mountford

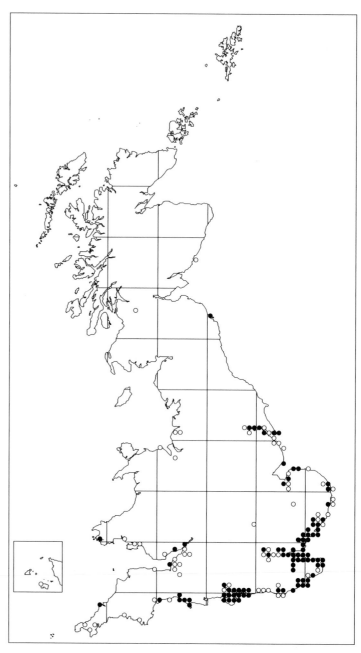

Current map	No	Atlas	No
1970 →	89	1930 →	76
Pre-1970	63	Pre-1930	20
Introductions	0	Introductions	0

Status: not scarce

This is a plant of ditches, lake- and river-sides and reed-swamps, in eutrophic conditions. It often forms extensive stands, and usually in places subject to seasonal flooding. In East Anglian reedswamps its common associates are *C. acutiformis*, *C. riparia*, *Cladium mariscus* and *Phragmites australis*.

Being a tussock-forming plant without leading rhizomes, reproduction is presumably entirely by seed. Like other members of this group of sedges it often fails to flower or set seed if water levels or other habitat factors are not right.

This perennial species has suffered from wetland drainage, and some sites are probably still vulnerable to drainage and to widening and deepening of ditches. However, many sites for *C. elata* are of great conservation interest and are nature reserves or designated as SSSIs and current populations seem stable.

C. elata is widespread in Europe although absent from the arctic and much of the boreal zone and very rare in the Mediterranean region. It is scattered across Asia to Manchuria. Eastern populations have been distinguished as subsp. *omskiana* (Meinsh.) Jalas.

Because of confusion with tussock forms of *C. nigra* and with partially fertile hybrids with this and other members of the section *Phacocystis,* the exact distribution of the species requires further investigation.

R. W. David

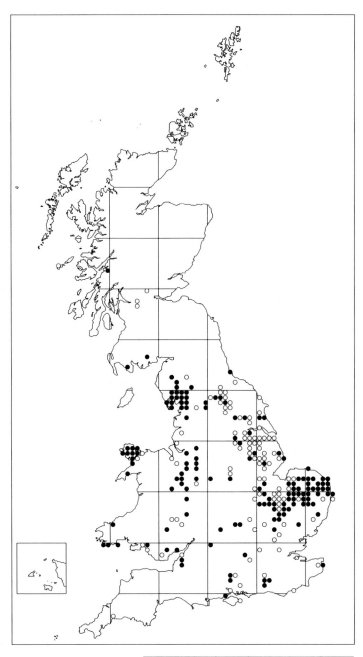

Current map	No	Atlas	No
1970 →	146	1930 →	108
Pre-1970	103	Pre-1930	15
Introductions	0	Introductions	0

Carex elongata L.

Status: scarce

Elongated sedge

C. elongata is a plant of lowland ponds, canal sides and wet woods and is more rarely found beside lakes in occasionally flooded meadows. It cannot tolerate continuous swamp conditions and benefits from winter flooding and drying out in summer. A characteristic habitat is decaying alder or willow carr, where the plant is often epiphytic on fallen boughs that keep it above summer water level with its roots still wet. It also favours stagnant ditches in water-meadows, and canals where the ancient wooden camp-sheathing provides the kind of pedestal that it enjoys.

C. elongata is a perennial species. In suitable conditions and not too much shade it seeds freely, but one of the largest and most floriferous colonies in England at Askham Bog seldom sets viable seed (Fitter & Smith 1979). Individual tussocks may become substantial but soon decay if conditions are not right. The plant seems unable to colonise newly exposed mud either vegetatively (the rhizomes are very short) or by seed.

Reclamation of marshes, the rehabilitation of canals for recreation, especially that involving strengthening of the banks with metal sheathing, and the infilling of pits and ponds have greatly reduced or extinguished many populations. The early British records were mostly from canals in the Manchester area, where the sedge was abundant, but the whole area has been reclaimed and the sedge has now gone. In recent years fine colonies have been discovered in Wales and several around Loch Lomond.

In Europe this sedge reaches as far north as the subarctic zone in Norway and Russia but is not found south of central France and northern Spain and Italy. It extends eastward to the Caucasus.

For a detailed account of the British distribution, see David (1978b, 1982a).

R. W. David

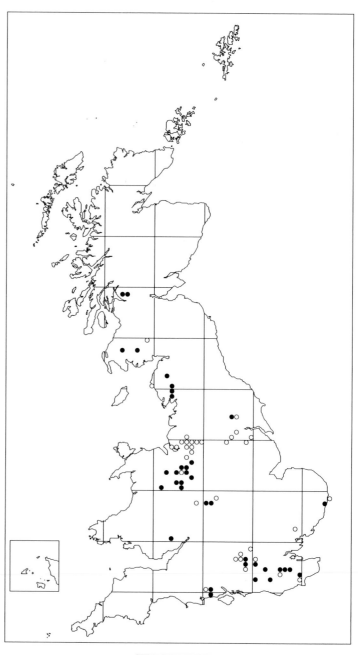

Current map	No	Atlas	No
1970 →	36	1930 →	25
Pre-1970	34	Pre-1930	22
Introductions	0	Introductions	0

continued →

Carex elongata
continued

Elongated sedge

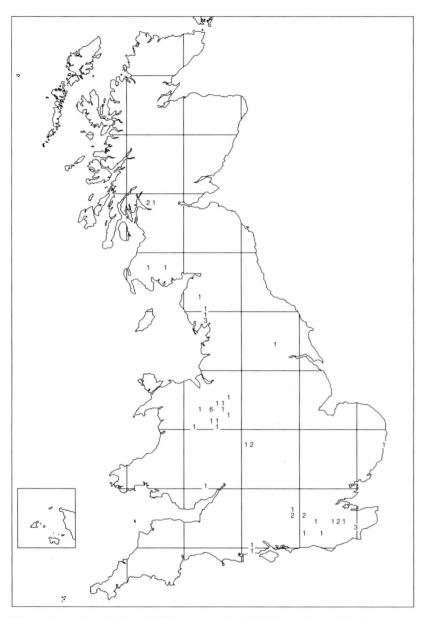

The number of tetrads in each 10 km square in which *Carex elongata* has been recorded as a native species from 1970 onwards. The species has been found in a total of 50 tetrads from 1970 onwards.

Carex ericetorum Pollich

Status: scarce

Rare spring-sedge

This is a plant of short grassland, on chalk and limestone. Unlike *C. caryophyllea*, which often grows with it, it is confined to highly calcareous soils. In Breckland the most frequent associates in the short, closed, rabbit-grazed swards in which it grows are *Astragalus danicus*, *Festuca ovina*, *Galium verum*, *Linum catharticum*, *Lotus corniculatus*, *Pilosella officinarum* and *Thymus pulegioides*. It is a lowland plant in East Anglia, but ascends to 400 metres at Long Scar Pike and at Crosby Ravensworth Fell.

C. ericetorum is a mat-forming perennial. The individual tufts extend slowly by means of pioneering rhizomes. The species also reproduces by seed, although in some seasons the plant flowers only sparingly.

First recognised as a British plant in 1861, though the sedge had been collected in East Anglia by Babington as early as 1838. A number of East Anglian sites have been lost because of ploughing or other disturbance of its native grasslands, or by competition from coarse grasses following the reduction of grazing.

This sedge is scattered in suitable sites throughout northern and central Europe from Scandinavia and Russia (to 68° N), as far south as northern Spain, central France, northern Italy, Yugoslavia, Bulgaria and the Caucasus, ascending to 2460 metres in the mountains. It is also found in Siberia (Urals).

For a detailed account of the British distribution, see David (1981a).

R. W. David

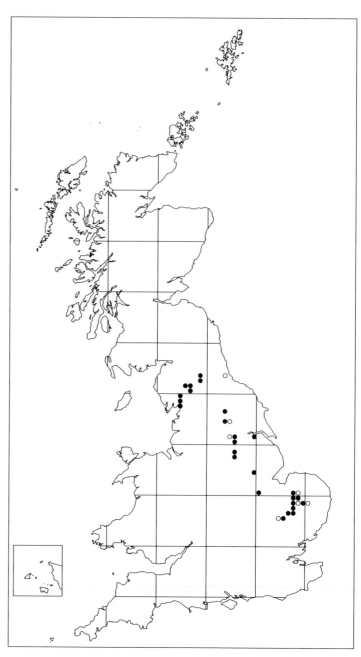

Current map	No	Atlas	No
1970 →	26	1930 →	22
Pre-1970	7	Pre-1930	2
Introductions	0	Introductions	0

continued →

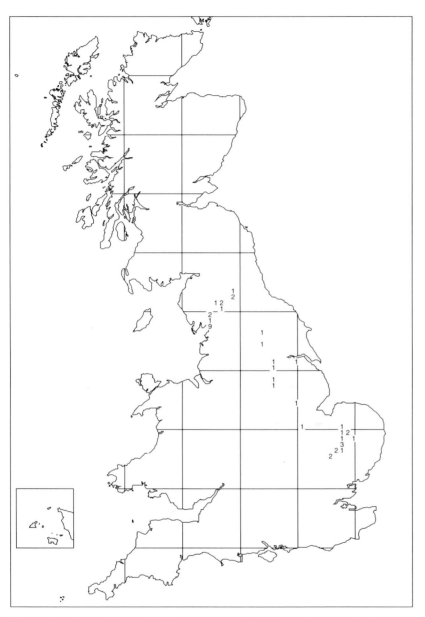

The number of tetrads in each 10 km square in which *Carex ericetorum* has been recorded as a native species from 1970 onwards. The species has been found in a total of 42 tetrads from 1970 onwards.

Carex humilis Leysser

Status: scarce

Dwarf sedge

This species is locally abundant in closed turf on close-grazed chalk downland, with a few outliers in more open conditions on Carboniferous limestone rocks to the west. It is now almost restricted to steeper slopes and earthworks, out of reach of ploughing. It favours southerly and south-westerly aspects as it is able to withstand drought, and in such situations competition from other species is presumably much reduced. Associated species on chalk downland occasionally include the nationally scarce species *Tephroseris integrifolia* and *Thesium humifusum*. On the Carboniferous limestone it occurs in a community with a large number of nationally rare and scarce species, including *Helianthemum apenninum*, *Koeleria vallesiana*, *Trinia glauca* and the moss *Scorpiurium circinnatum*. Experimental studies in the Avon Gorge indicate that *C. humilis* benefits from the addition of mineral nutrient mixtures which are deficient in phosphorus (Willis 1989). It is confined to the lowlands.

C. humilis is a long-lived perennial, gradually spreading vegetatively to form mats 15 cm or more across. Recent observations have shown that ripe seed is spread by ants and seedlings are occasionally found on bare ground in the Avon Gorge (Lovatt 1982) and at Brean Down. It is also able to spread by the re-rooting of detached pieces (David 1979a; Lovatt 1982), especially on steeper slopes, and possibly where it is ploughed, and its presence on ancient earthworks may result from this, unless they were thatched with turves. Although the species rarely behaves as a colonist, at Blandford Camp it has succeeded in establishing itself on a variety of man-made habitats, including recreation fields and the central reservations of roads.

Although the map shows little contraction of range, very many individual sites have been lost. In Dorset 17 out of a total of 49 sites were lost between 1860 and 1990, and many others in Dorset and Wiltshire much reduced in size. This reduction is continuing where sites are not being grazed or where cattle, with their extra weight, rather than sheep, are used. Aerial fertilising has also reduced some populations, especially in Wiltshire. In the Wye Valley trampling has completely destroyed some sites. It has been much reduced but not completely eliminated by public pressure at Stonehenge.

It is widespread in Europe, except Scandinavia, and extends east to Manchuria.

For a detailed account of the British distribution, see David (1979a, 1982a).

D. A. Pearman

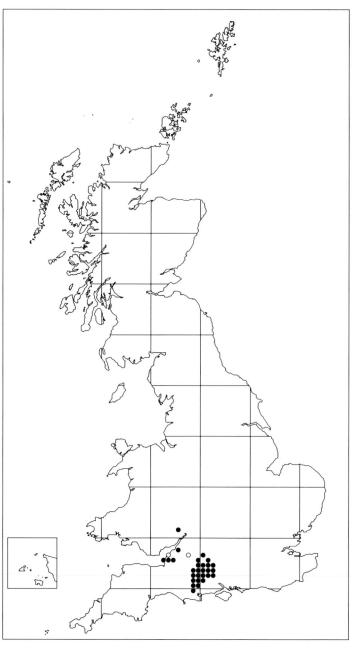

Current map	No	Atlas	No
1970 →	28	1930 →	22
Pre-1970	2	Pre-1930	1
Introductions	0	Introductions	0

continued →

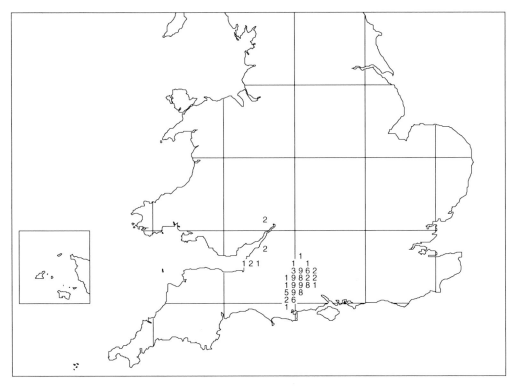

The number of tetrads in each 10 km square in which *Carex humilis* has been recorded as a native species from 1970 onwards. Squares in which the species is recorded in 9 or more tetrads are plotted as 9: *C. humilis* is actually recorded from 9 tetrads in ST91 and ST93, 11 in ST92, 13 in SU04 and 15 in SU02. The species has been found in a total of 124 tetrads from 1970 onwards.

Carex magellanica Lam.

Status: scarce

Tall bog-sedge

This is a perennial plant of wet level moorlands and occasionally clearings in swampy woods, where it grows in *Sphagnum* lawns and infilled hollows but, unlike its ally *C. limosa*, seldom in standing water. The two species sometimes grow close together in the same bog, but appear to have slightly different habitat requirements. *C. magellanica* is a sub-montane plant, mainly of upland blanket bogs and valley mires, from 170 metres to 658 metres near Cononish. Typical associates include *Carex curta*, *C. echinata*, *C. pauciflora*, *Drosera rotundifolia*, *Narthecium ossifragum*, *Vaccinium oxycoccos*, *Viola palustris*, *Aulacomnium palustre*, *Sphagnum cuspidatum*, *S. papillosum* and *S. rubellum*.

Unlike *C. limosa*, *C. magellanica* produces only short rhizomes and its often extensive colonies must be generated largely by seeds, although in some seasons the plants are very shy-flowering. Growth is often rather sparse but distinct tussocks occur on Armboth Fells.

It is surprisingly rare in the Scottish Highlands, and more frequent in Cumbria, while in the last thirty years, a number of colonies have been discovered on the borders of Montgomery and Merioneth and in Cardiganshire. Several sites have been destroyed by forestry operations and the plant is at risk from moor draining. It is probably still present in most of the 10 km squares for which only pre-1970 records are available.

This sedge is widespread in northern Europe from Iceland (where it is found at sea level) to Finland and northern Russia, but further south occurs only on the higher mountains. In Asia it is found in Siberia and Japan. In North America it is again frequent from Greenland to British Columbia, and locally as far south as Utah and Pennsylvania. The plant of the northern hemisphere is subspecies *irrigua* (Wahlenb.) Hiit. Subsp. *magellanica* occurs in Chile and Patagonia near the Straits of Magellan.

R. W. David

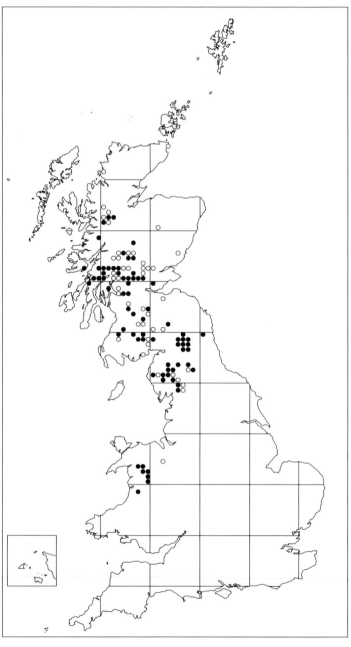

Current map	No	Atlas	No
1970 →	73	1930 →	46
Pre-1970	44	Pre-1930	23
Introductions	0	Introductions	0

Carex maritima Gunnerus
Status: scarce

Curved sedge

This sedge is found in wet sandy places by the sea. In Britain it occurs on open damp sand, often at the mouth of a stream debouching onto the beach for it requires plentiful fresh water, in wet dune slacks, and in turf beside rock pools. In dune slacks it is often found in quite dense turf provided that it is kept short by grazing livestock or rabbits. Surprisingly, the largest British colonies are on the fairways of golf-courses at St Andrews, where it is found in intermittently flooded turf (Leach 1986). Common associates are *Carex distans, C. extensa, Juncus gerardii, Plantago maritima*, and in slacks, *Agrostis stolonifera, Carex nigra* and *Hydrocotyle vulgaris*.

The perennial *C. maritima* usually forms extensive patches, spreading vegetatively by means of its long rhizomes. It may also reproduce by the abundant seed, which is planted in the soil by the bending of the mature fruit-stalk. It colonises open ground rapidly.

In Britain it is now confined to the northern and eastern coasts of Scotland. It was formerly known as far south as Blyth in the east and once seen (in 1971) at Humphrey Head in Lancashire but now is apparently extinct in both places. Many Scottish sites have been destroyed by the construction of leisure facilities such as car-parks, seaside bungalows, camping sites and golf courses, although once re-established on a golf course, the sedge may find the conditions very congenial.

C. maritima is an arctic-alpine, which is locally abundant along the whole northern coast of Europe and Asia from Iceland to Kamchatka, including the islands of Spitzbergen and Novaya Zemlya; and similarly from Greenland westward along the coasts of Canada and Alaska to British Columbia. In the Antarctic it is found on coasts near the Straits of Magellan. It also appears on the mountains of Europe (Pyrenees, Alps) in wet sandy or gravelly areas, in the Himalayas (to 4500 metres), in the Rockies as far south as Colorado, and in the southern Andes.

For a detailed account of its British distribution, see David (1982b).

R. W. David

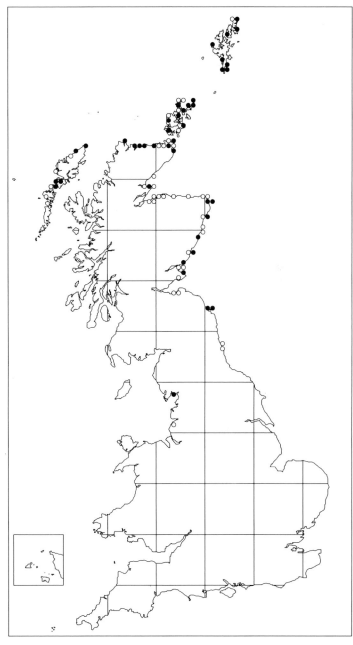

Current map	No	Atlas	No
1970 →	41	1930 →	26
Pre-1970	38	Pre-1930	27
Introductions	1	Introductions	0

Carex montana L.

Status: scarce

Soft-leaved sedge

A plant of neutral to acidic grasslands, and in light shade in woodlands. The underlying rock is often Carboniferous limestone, or basic rocks such as serpentine (at the Lizard Peninsula), but usually the solid rock is covered with a layer of non-calcareous 'drift' (probably of aeolian origin; this is the case in its Mendip and Wye Valley sites). In the New Forest it is relatively common in heathland and wood-pasture. It has recently been found in quantity in *Erica vagans* heath on the Lizard Peninsula. Although mainly a lowland species, it is found at 560 metres on Carreg yr Ogof.

C. montana is a perennial species. It appears incapable of re-rooting after disturbance, and regeneration is only by seed which, except in heavily shaded sites, is set abundantly.

It is very local, but often extremely abundant where it occurs. Its sites are less susceptible to trampling than those of *C. humilis* which sometimes grows nearby on calcareous soils, but at Symonds Yat one site of *C. montana* has been severely damaged by abseiling from the edge of a cliff. The original British station in Sussex was destroyed by building in 1969-71.

In Europe *C. montana* is not found further north than England, southern Sweden and central Russia, or further south than northern Spain, Corsica, northern Italy, Yugoslavia and Bulgaria. It also occurs in the Caucasus, Urals and east Siberia.

Detailed accounts of its British distribution were provided by David (1977, 1982a) but since then the species has been discovered in Cornwall and many new sites have been found in Hampshire.

R. W. David

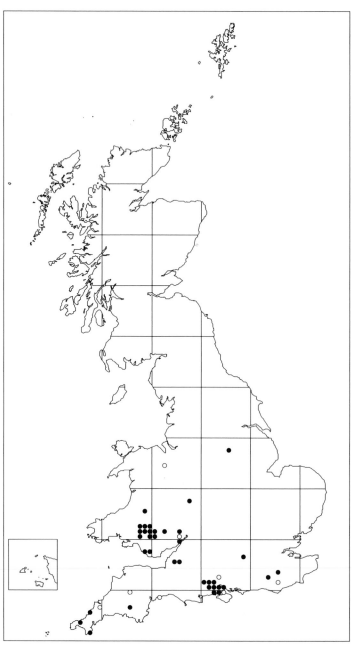

Current map	No	Atlas	No
1970 →	36	1930 →	14
Pre-1970	8	Pre-1930	12
Introductions	0	Introductions	0

continued →

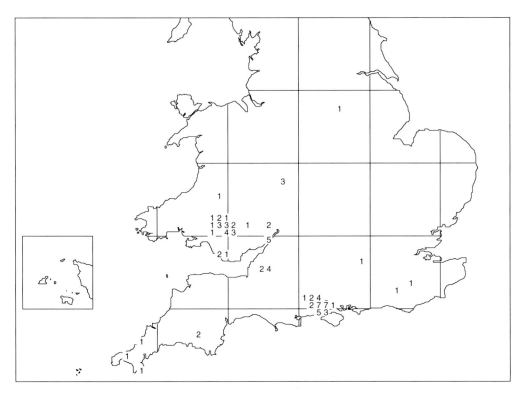

The number of tetrads in each 10 km square in which *Carex montana* has been recorded as a native species from 1970 onwards. The species has been found in a total of 83 tetrads from 1970 onwards.

Carex punctata Gaudin

Status: scarce

Dotted sedge

This coastal sedge needs shelter and abundant fresh water. It is therefore usually found in nooks of sea cliffs where a trickle of water descends, on wet sandy patches in saltmarshes or where a stream enters a beach, rather than on rocks exposed to wind and salt spray. It also occurs in dune-slacks, and in estuarine alder-carr.

C. punctata is a perennial; individual plants are short-lived but they set abundant seed. The species is rather mobile: populations tend to appear and disappear or to shift their ground.

The distribution of this sedge in Britain has been masked by confusion with its close ally *C. distans*. Here it is a purely coastal plant, being favoured by the milder climates of the south and west. Colonies are scattered and usually small. It is liable to be destroyed by tourist developments such as car-parks and seaside bungalows.

C. punctata occurs at intervals all along the Mediterranean coast from Greece to southern Spain and up the Atlantic coast and the English Channel to southern Scandinavia. It is abundant in south-west Ireland. It is also found sporadically as a mountain plant in the Alps and elsewhere. Isolated populations are known in Asia Minor and Algeria, and a variety is found in the Azores.

For a detailed account of its British distribution, see David (1981b).

R. W. David

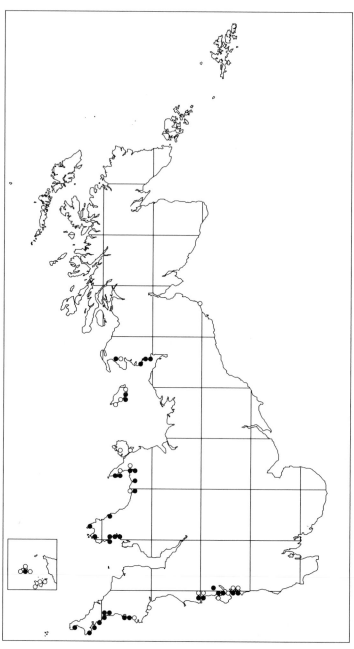

Current map	No	Atlas	No
1970 →	35	1930 →	23
Pre-1970	18	Pre-1930	13
Introductions	0	Introductions	0

continued →

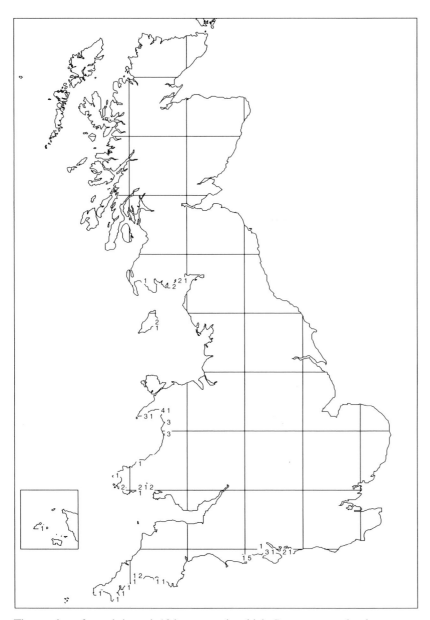

The number of tetrads in each 10 km square in which *Carex punctata* has been recorded as a native species from 1970 onwards. The species has been found in a total of 59 tetrads from 1970 onwards.

Carex rupestris All.
Status: scarce

Rock sedge

This sedge is aptly named for it is most often found, frequently with *Dryas octopetala*, on steep cliffs to which its conglomerate tufts are anchored by the deep penetration of their rhizomes into cracks in the rock; but it may also colonise damp moraines and grazed turf of ground below cliffs. It is a strict calcicole which forms extensive but very local colonies on the calcareous mica-schists of the Grampians and Cairngorms and on the dolomitic limestones of Skye, Kishorn and Sutherland. Its typical associates include *C. capillaris*, *C. flacca*, *Festuca ovina*, *Galium boreale*, *Linum catharticum*, *Persicaria vivipara*, *Saxifraga aizoides*, *Thymus polytrichus*, *Viola riviniana*, *Ctenidium molluscum* and *Tortella tortuosa*. In the central Highlands it is a montane species growing above 600 metres and reaching 900 metres at Fin Glen in Glen Lyon, but in the far north it descends to near sea level at Durness.

In some localities it flowers only very sparingly, but in others sets abundant seed. In any case the tufts are evidently long-lived.

C. rupestris has been overlooked in many places until recently, and there is little evidence of significant decline. Threats are probably few, but might arise from proposals to quarry Durness limestone outcrops.

An arctic-alpine, *C. rupestris* is found all along the arctic coasts of Europe (including Spitzbergen and Novaya Zemlya), Asia and America from Kamchatka to Alaska. It descends the chain of the Rockies as far south as Colorado; and occurs on suitable soils in all the higher mountains (Pyrenees, Alps, Caucasus, Urals, Himalayas).

For a detailed account of its British distribution, see David (1979b).

R. W. David

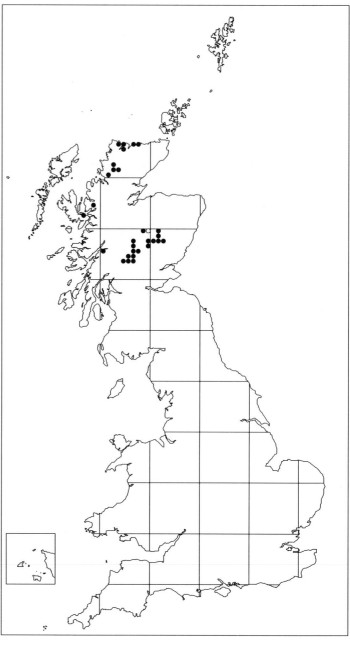

Current map	No	Atlas	No
1970 →	29	1930 →	14
Pre-1970	1	Pre-1930	0
Introductions	0	Introductions	0

continued →

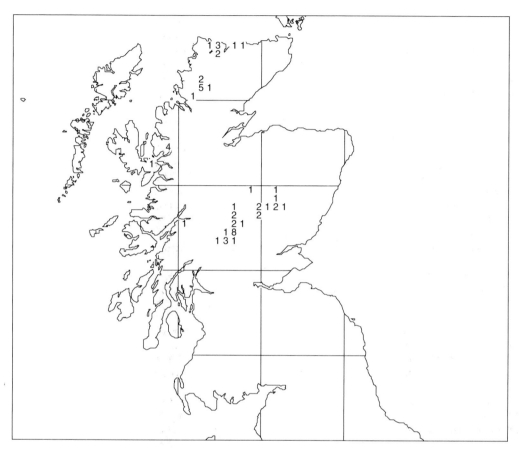

The number of tetrads in each 10 km square in which *Carex rupestris* has been recorded as a native species from 1970 onwards. The species has been found in a total of 54 tetrads from 1970 onwards.

Carex saxatilis L.

Status: scarce

Russet sedge

This is a strictly montane sedge, confined to the higher mountains of the Scottish Highlands and somewhat local even there. Its main stronghold is on the Dalradian calcareous mica-schist Breadalbane range in Perthshire. Here it occurs as a local dominant, though with other low sedges, in small marshes (flush bogs) with lateral water seepage on high slopes and in corries where snow lies until well into the early summer. Characteristic montane associates are *Juncus biglumis*, *J. castaneus*, *J. triglumis* and *Thalictrum alpinum*. More widespread species of these habitats are *C. viridula* subsp. *oedocarpa*, *Eriophorum angustifolium*, *Persicaria vivipara* and *Selaginella selaginoides*. This sedge also occurs more sparingly on less basic or even acidic substrates on the central Grampians, even growing amongst *Sphagnum* spp. in places. It is much rarer in the Cairngorms and Clova Hills, and its scattered outposts north of the Great Glen are mainly on basic mountains. The altitudinal range is from 460 metres in Glen Clunie to 1125 metres on Ben Lawers, but it rarely occurs below 600 metres.

A perennial, *C. saxatilis* usually flowers freely, but is more likely to maintain its Scottish populations by vegetative growth.

It is probably not much affected by grazing, and may be a species limited to the montane zone by adversely high summer temperatures at lower levels. It has probably maintained its populations quite well during the present century and is probably still present in most of the 10 km squares for which only pre-1970 records are available.

Matthews (1955) classifies this as an arctic-subarctic species, and it has a wide distribution in mountainous circumpolar regions. Its most southerly localities are in Scotland.

D. A. Ratcliffe

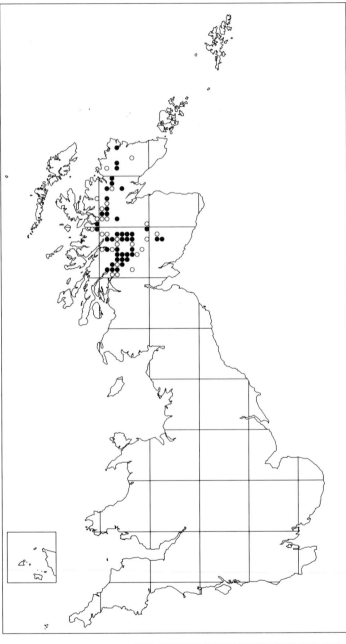

Current map	No	Atlas	No
1970 →	41	1930 →	46
Pre-1970	26	Pre-1930	7
Introductions	0	Introductions	0

Carex vaginata Tausch

Sheathed sedge

Status: scarce

In Britain this sedge is confined to Scottish mountains, where its characteristic habitat is flushed grassland on neutral or slightly acid soils, in particular the 'sills' where a descending burn increases its gradient. It also grows in flush bogs and on rock ledges. Typical associates are *C. bigelowii*, *C. echinata*, *C. saxatilis*, *Festuca ovina*, *Juncus squarrosus*, *Leontodon autumnalis*, *Persicaria vivipara*, *Selaginella selaginoides* and *Thalictrum alpinum*. Although found mostly in only moderately base-rich habitats, it is most abundant on the calcareous mountains of the central Highlands. It is usually found over 700 metres, reaching 1150 metres on Cairn Toul, but descends to 380 metres at Meikle Kilrannoch.

C. vaginata is a perennial. Only a small proportion of plants flower in any one year and the species is therefore easily overlooked, although the prostrate, parallel-sided leaves, often with yellowing tips, are distinctive. It spreads vegetatively by means of long rhizomes and may form extensive patches.

This species appears to be fairly tolerant of grazing, and most of its habitats are not threatened by change.

C. vaginata is a circumboreal arctic-alpine, extending south in Europe to scattered sites in the Massif Central, Pyrenees, Alps and Harz Mountains.

R. W. David

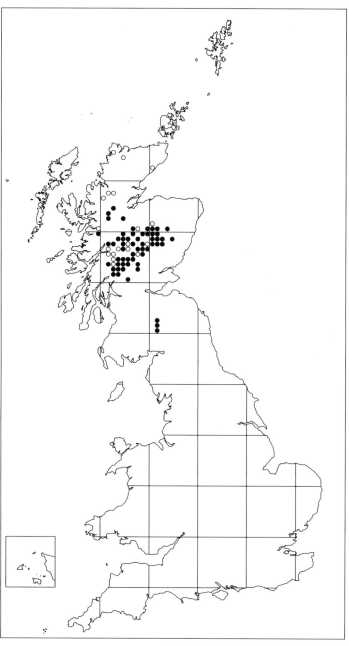

Current map	No	Atlas	No
1970 →	57	1930 →	39
Pre-1970	19	Pre-1930	9
Introductions	0	Introductions	0

Carex vulpina L.   True fox-sedge

Status: rare

C. vulpina is a lowland plant of wet ditches and pond-sides, for the most part on chalk or limestone. It requires wetter conditions than does the closely related *C. otrubae*; where the two grow together (as they often do), *C. otrubae* is likely to be on the bank of the ditch and *C. vulpina* in the standing water.

In open sites this perennial sedge may form a large clump, but it spreads by abundant seed rather than vegetatively. In shade it soon ceases to flower and dwindles to extinction.

In Britain, this species was not recognised as distinct from the closely related *C. otrubae* until 1939, and its full distribution may still be masked by confusion between the two. It is commonest in the south-east (Kent). In the last twenty years many British colonies have disappeared owing to drought and/or water-extraction, the clearing of ditches and filling of ponds, and shading by invasive scrub.

C. vulpina occurs in suitable situations throughout Europe south of 60° N, though becoming much scarcer in the west and south. As in Britain, it has been confused with *C. otrubae* and its distribution in Asia is not fully known.

R. W. David

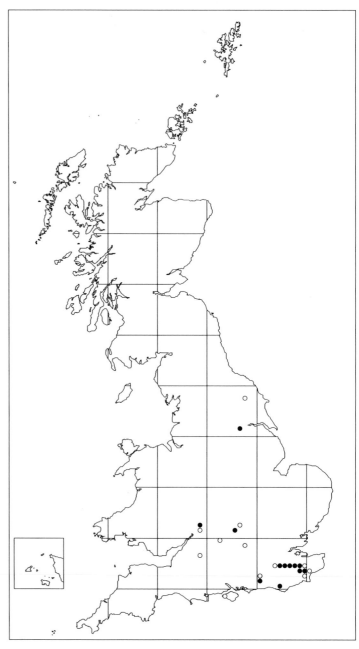

Current map	No	Atlas	No
1970 →	12	1930 →	19
Pre-1970	12	Pre-1930	1
Introductions	0	Introductions	0

continued →

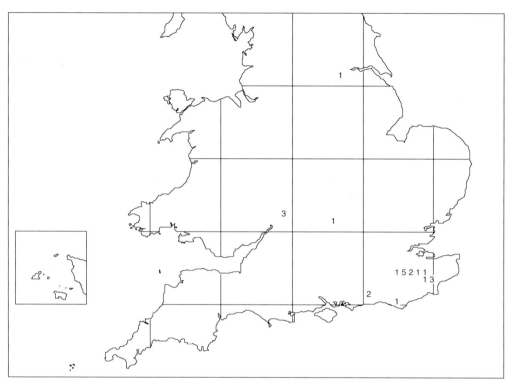

The number of tetrads in each 10 km square in which *Carex vulpina* has been recorded as a native species from 1970 onwards. This species has been found in a total of 22 tetrads from 1970 onwards.

Centaurea cyanus L.

Status: scarce

Cornflower

This plant was formerly a weed of arable land, particularly on sandy, rather acidic soils where it was associated with *Chrysanthemum segetum*. *C. cyanus* used to grow mainly in crops of rye, but it could occur in other spring and winter crops and as a ruderal, provided competition from other plants was slight. In the eighteenth and nineteenth centuries, it constituted a serious agricultural weed and possibly maintained its population with continuous reintroductions in rye seed from eastern Europe and Russia. Now it is more often seen as a cultivar in gardens or where 'wild flower seed' has been sown.

C. cyanus is an annual. There are peaks of germination in September/October and May/June. The flowers open in long days and are self-incompatible. They are cross-pollinated by bumble bees. Fruits are relatively large and heavy and can be harvested with the grain. Although germination is greatest in the first year after sowing, viability can be retained for at least 4 years (Svensson & Wigren 1985). This enables it to survive crop rotations as long as perennial leys are not included and the competition pressure is not too high. It occasionally overwinters.

This species has the potential to occur on suitable sites throughout Britain, and the poet John Clare referred to its "destroying beauty". The species declined rapidly with the introduction of seed screening and, later, with the advent of chemical herbicides such as 2,4-D and MCPA. This species is now known from only one persistent site in Britain, in mid-Suffolk. Isolated plants still occur over a large area of the south and east of England although these rarely persist for longer than a year. Large numbers sometimes occur when there are deep excavations for roads and pipelines. Although there are records from 127 10 km squares from 1970 onwards, this declining species is classified as scarce as it has been recorded in only 78 10 km squares from 1980 onwards.

This species is thought to have originated in south-east Europe but it has spread with agriculture and is now widespread in both the northern and southern hemispheres.

Godwin (1975) suggest that this species once grew in natural communities on scree slopes and alluvial deposits of the late-glacial tundra.

A. Smith

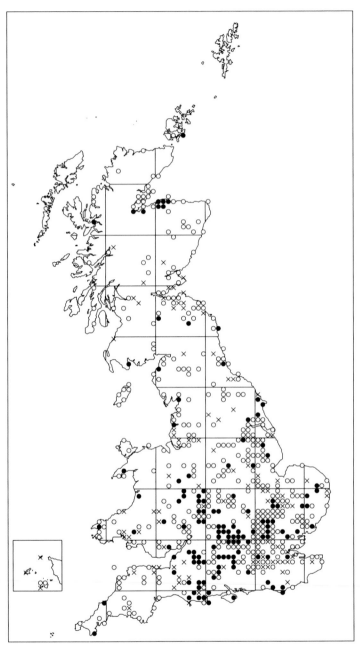

Current map	No	Atlas	No
1970 →	127	1930 →	267
Pre-1970	374	Pre-1930	88
Introductions	90	Introductions	0

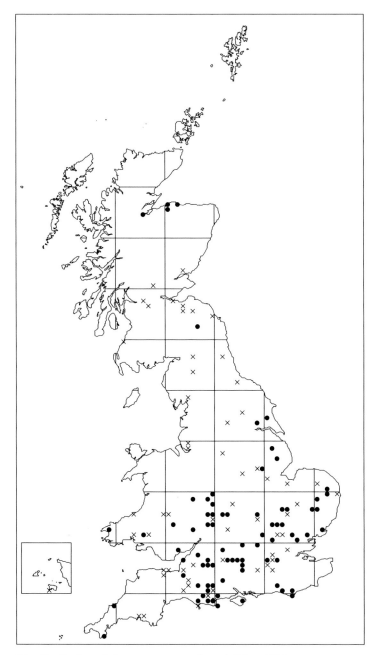

The distribution of *Centaurea cyanus* from 1980 to 1992.

Centaurium littorale (Turner ex Sm.) Gilmour

Status: scarce

Seaside centaury

This plant is confined to sandy areas near the sea, most usually associated with large areas of relatively undisturbed sand dune. It is typical of rather open but stable species-rich turf on calcareous sand with a high admixture of humus (pH range 6.2-7.2) which remains moist throughout the year, but does not withstand regular flooding, so that it often occurs around the edges of wet dune slacks. Associated species include *Carex arenaria*, *Euphrasia* spp., *Festuca rubra*, *Gentianella amarella*, *Glaux maritima*, *Lotus corniculatus*, *Salix repens* and *Samolus valerandi*. It is restricted to the lowlands.

It is a monocarpic winter annual or short-lived perennial, germinating in the autumn and usually flowering during the next or the following summer. Plants flowering in their second year are often larger. It is visited by a range of small insects, especially hoverflies, but it is also self-pollinating and self-fertile. Seeds have no specialised means of dispersal, and colonies are often highly gregarious.

C. littorale is threatened by damage to its habitat, especially by eutrophication caused when cattle are over-wintered on sand dunes. It is a very poor competitor, and in the absence of grazing by rabbits or sheep will quickly disappear, or else will become confined to areas kept open by human trampling. Records from Dorset and Hampshire have not been confirmed and are omitted from the maps.

It is found in coastal districts of western Europe from the central Baltic and southern Norway to Brittany (subsp. *littorale*). Subsp. *uliginosum* occurs in inland salt marshes in central and eastern Europe.

A. J. Richards

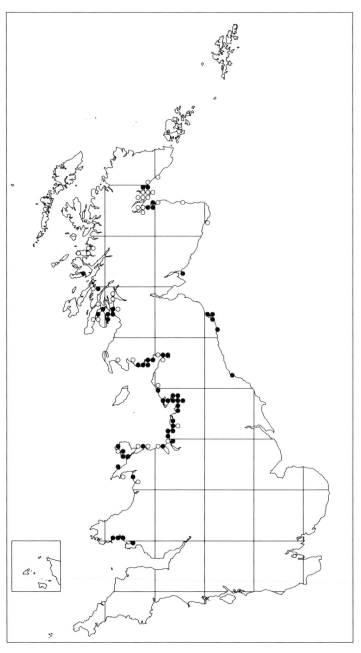

Current map	No	Atlas	No
1970 →	54	1930 →	44
Pre-1970	38	Pre-1930	12
Introductions	1	Introductions	0

Cephalanthera longifolia (L.) Fritsch

Status: scarce

Narrow-leaved helleborine

This species is a light-demanding orchid of lowland woods on hard limestone, chalk and, more rarely, on other lime-rich substrates. It is found in a variety of woodland types, particularly beech and oak-ash. *C. longifolia* perhaps most typically occurs on steep slopes where the tree canopy is naturally thin and patchy, including limestone gorges, woodlands on limestone ridges or outcrops and chalk hangers. Well illuminated woodland rides and forest margins are also a favoured habitat, and it even occurs under conifers on dune sand where the canopy is sufficiently broken and on dumped chalk on heathlands. It has a poor ability to adapt rapidly to changing light intensities, and is not typically a coppice woodland plant, but instead is best regarded as a glade species where a broken tree cover permits relatively permanent high levels of light. The range of associates of *C. longifolia* is broad and typically includes *Ajuga reptans*, *Dactylorhiza fuchsii*, *Epipactis helleborine*, *Fragaria vesca*, *Hedera helix*, *Ligustrum vulgare*, *Mercurialis perennis*, *Rosa arvensis*, *Sanicula europaea* and *Viola riviniana*.

C. longifolia is a long-lived perennial with apparently poor reproductive abilities. It is cross-pollinated by small bees.

The plant has undergone a massive decline during this century, and has become rare in many former strong-holds such as the Wye Valley. Today it is extinct in at least 23 vice-counties, whilst its hold in others is often tenuous indeed. Only a few colonies of over a few hundred plants exist, and most are declining or at best static. Collection has often been quoted as a principal cause of extinction at many sites; it certainly contributed to the plant's decline to extinction in the Durham magnesian limestone denes where it has not been reliably recorded this century (Graham 1988), whilst collecting severely reduced or eliminated one colony in Worcestershire as recently as the mid 1980s. However, natural, subtle changes in woodland composition and changes in forestry practice (principally resulting in reduced levels of insolation) probably account for most declines and eventual extinctions. *C. longifolia* is a difficult plant to conserve successfully in the long term: increased shading as the tree canopy closes soon results in a diminution of the population, whilst too much light results in desiccation of plants, together with a vigorous growth of competing coarse vegetation.

C. longifolia is widespread in southern and central Europe, extending north to 60° N in Scandinavia, with isolated occurrences in North Africa and east to the Himalayas.

A. J. Byfield

Current map	No	Atlas	No
1970 →	41	1930 →	29
Pre-1970	79	Pre-1930	63
Introductions	2	Introductions	0

continued →

Cephalanthera longifolia
continued

Narrow-leaved helleborine

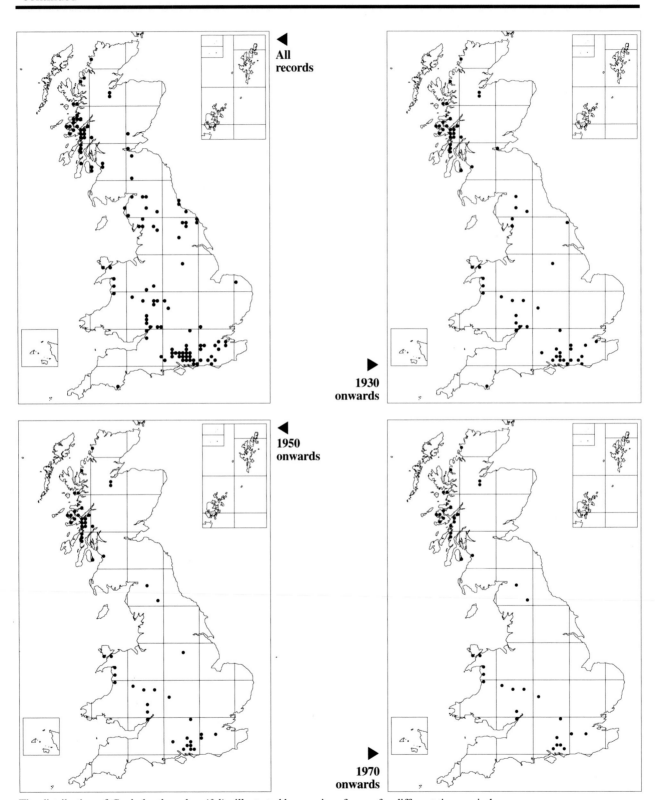

The distribution of *Cephalanthera longifolia*, illustrated by a series of maps for different time periods.

Cerastium alpinum L.

Status: scarce

Alpine mouse-ear

C. alpinum is a montane plant which is usually found on the softer mica schists and limestones but can occur on more acid rocks if there is some basic flushing. It is basicolous rather than calcicolous, as it occurs on serpentine where magnesium tends to be the major basic ion and calcium can be at quite low levels. The plant grows on ledges, scree and in base-rich montane grassland and in the species-rich mountains of Breadalbane and Caenlochan can accompany many of the conspicuous montane rarities. It is similar to *C. arcticum* in many respects but grows in more base-rich places. *C. alpinum* has a wide altitudinal range within the montane zone, ranging from 300 metres on Seana Braigh to 1210 metres on Ben Lawers.

C. alpinum is a mat-forming perennial and reproduction is both sexual and vegetative.

Its distribution is fairly stable and any major alteration to its British status is most likely to be brought about by climate change. This plant is likely to be over- rather than under-recorded as most mistakes are made when *C. arcticum* is misidentified as *C. alpinum*. There are also other awkward taxa including large-flowered upland forms of *C. fontanum* and putative hybrids between *C. fontanum* and *C. alpinum* which cause problems in recording.

C. alpinum is a circumboreal arctic-alpine with a wide distribution outside Britain in northern Europe, Asia and North America. In Europe it is widespread in the north, extending south on mountain ranges to the Pyrenees and the Balkans (Jalas & Suominen 1983). This distribution covers the species as a whole and includes several subspecies. British material is generally referred to subsp. *lanatum*. For a detailed discussion, see Hultén (1956).

P. S. Lusby

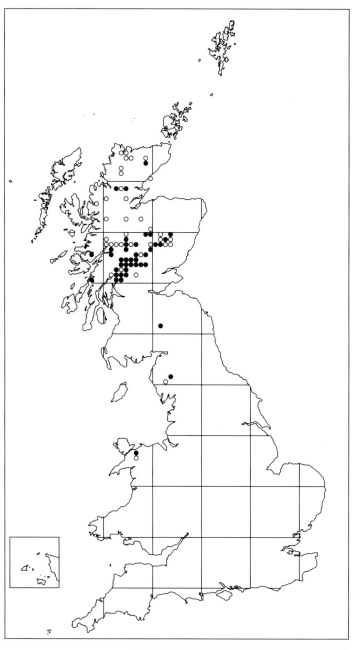

Current map	No	Atlas	No
1970 →	40	1930 →	49
Pre-1970	35	Pre-1930	6
Introductions	0	Introductions	0

Cerastium arcticum Lange

Status: scarce

Arctic mouse-ear

Rather scarcer than the closely related *C. alpinum*, *C. arcticum* is a montane plant of north-facing corrie walls and mountain cliffs. It is generally found on acid mountains but also occurs on the harder basic igneous rocks such as the gabbro and basalt on Skye and on calcareous Moine schists in Ross. In its corrie habitat it grows on narrow ledges and in crevices but can also become established on block scree and wet montane grassland below mountain cliffs. Characteristic associates are *Alchemilla alpina*, *Arabis petraea*, *Cochlearia officinalis*, *Luzula spicata*, *Poa alpina*, *Saxifraga hypnoides*, the rare *S. rivularis*, *S. stellaris* and *Sedum rosea*. The Trotternish ridge is one of the very few (or possibly the only place) in Britain where the plant occurs on very gently sloping ground. Here it accompanies *Koenigia islandica*, forming a plant assemblage that is characteristic of the Faeroese fellfields where *C. arcticum* and *Koenigia islandica* are widespread. *C. arcticum* rarely occurs below 600 metres, and is only likely to do so when washed down from higher rocks. It is usually found above 800 metres, reaching its highest altitude at 1190 metres on Beinn Dearg.

A perennial herb which spreads by long, slender stolons. It also reproduces by seed.

The distribution of *C. arcticum* appears to be stable, and its habitats are mostly secure from human interference.

Outside Britain, *C. arcticum* occurs in Iceland, the Faeroe Islands, Fennoscandia, Greenland, Spitzbergen, Russia and arctic America. For a map of its distribution in Europe, see Jalas & Suominen (1983).

Two varieties of this species have been recorded in Britain. *C. arcticum* var. *alpinopilosum* is the commoner and is thought to possess genes of *C. alpinum*. Var. *arcticum* has also been recorded from three British localities. A further variant recorded from the eastern Cairngorms approaches var. *arcticum* but differs markedly in hair structure and is probably a new taxon. The Shetland endemic *C. nigrescens* is very closely related to *C. arcticum* and is thought to be conspecific by some botanists (Brummitt *et al.* 1987). This plant occurs at a much lower altitude. It is treated as *C. arcticum* subsp. *edmondstonii* in the *Red Data Book* (Perring & Farrell 1983). Other varieties of *C. arcticum* recognised by Hultén extend to Jan Mayen, Novaya Zemlya and Franz Josef Land but have not been recorded in Britain. Hultén explains these varieties in terms of introgressive hybridisation between *C. arcticum* and *C. alpinum* (Hultén 1956).

P. S. Lusby

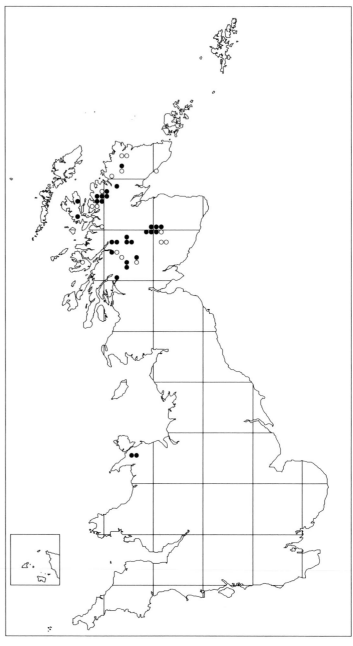

Current map	No	Atlas	No
1970 →	28	1930 →	24
Pre-1970	16	Pre-1930	4
Introductions	0	Introductions	0

Cerastium cerastoides (L.) Britton
Status: scarce

Starwort mouse-ear

This is a plant of moist to wet places on high acidic mountains, often where snow lies late. *C. cerastoides* occurs in small sparse colonies up to several square metres in extent. It is found most frequently in oligotrophic bryophyte-rich springs, especially ones dominated by *Philonotis fontana* and *Pohlia albicans* var. *glacialis*, in rocky ground on the sides or floors of corries. Here it occurs with such plants as *Caltha palustris*, *Chrysosplenium oppositifolium*, *Epilobium anagallidifolium*, *Ranunculus acris*, *Saxifraga stellaris*, *Stellaria uliginosa*, *Veronica serpyllifolia* and *Viola palustris*. The plant is also found on wet, bryophyte-covered rocks and stony ground in and beside rivulets. A somewhat different habitat where it occurs occasionally is fine scree stabilised by bryophytes in gullies and crevices, at the foot of cliffs and in depressions on slopes and ridges. Associates here include *Alchemilla alpina*, *Deschampsia cespitosa* and *Gnaphalium supinum*, as well as some of those listed above. On a few mountains the plant is locally frequent, but on many others, apparently just as suitable, it seems to be very thinly distributed or absent. It is usually found above 750 metres although it has been recorded at 335 metres near Mar Lodge where seeds may have been washed down from higher ground; it ascends to 1220 metres on Ben Macdui.

C. cerastoides is a perennial which flowers freely but appears to set seed infrequently, unless capsule-bearing plants are overlooked. Being a straggling plant generally growing in fairly unstable habitats near running water, dispersal presumably also occurs when rooted parts of plants are washed downhill.

C. cerastoides is under no obvious threats and is still likely to be present in any areas where it was once found. However, because of former uncertainties in *Cerastium* taxonomy, early records which have not been confirmed may well have been based on mistaken identifications. Nevertheless, it is an inconspicuous plant and is almost certainly much under-recorded.

It is found in Arctic Europe, western Asia and eastern North America, extending south on the mountains of central Europe and Asia. For a map of its European distribution, see Jalas & Suominen (1983).

A. G. Payne

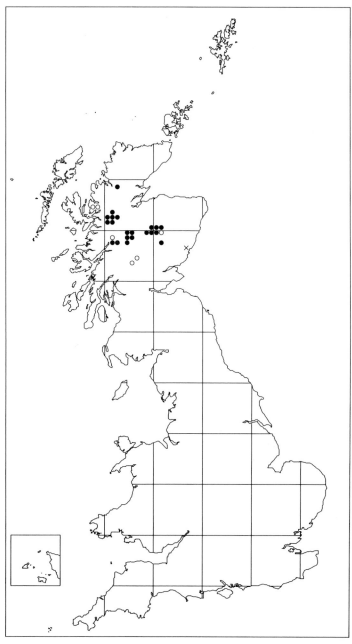

Current map	No	Atlas	No
1970 →	21	1930 →	16
Pre-1970	6	Pre-1930	3
Introductions	2	Introductions	0

Cerastium pumilum Curtis

Status: scarce

Dwarf mouse-ear

C. pumilum is a calcicolous winter annual, typically found on dry grassy banks with thin overlying soils and open vegetation. Quarries also provide suitable habitat. There are localities on chalk and both Carboniferous and oolitic limestones. Associates in the Avon Gorge include *Arabis scabra, Erophila verna, Festuca ovina, Helianthemum nummularium, Linum catharticum, Origanum vulgare, Potentilla neumanniana, Sanguisorba minor* and *Saxifraga tridactylites*. On the Purbeck coast it grows on limestone spoil heaps with *Arenaria serpyllifolia, Festuca ovina, Hippocrepis comosa, Medicago lupulina, Polygala calcarea* and *Ranunculus parviflorus*. Some colonies have been observed on railway lines but these are seldom persistent. It is confined to the lowlands.

C. pumilum is an early-flowering annual which sets seed by May. Populations tend to fluctuate, being greatest in years following droughts. A hot dry early spring can cause significant seedling mortality.

C. pumilum is apparently decreasing in the eastern part of its range; populations on the western limestone appear to be more stable.

It is found from southern Britain south and east across Europe to the Black Sea; there are also populations in southern Scandinavia, Russia, the Iberian peninsula, North Africa and on the west coast of Turkey. For a map of its European distribution, see Jalas & Suominen (1983).

Due to confusion with the similar species *C. diffusum* and *C. semidecandrum*, with which it can occur, some historical records have been found to be erroneous.

M. A. R. Kitchen

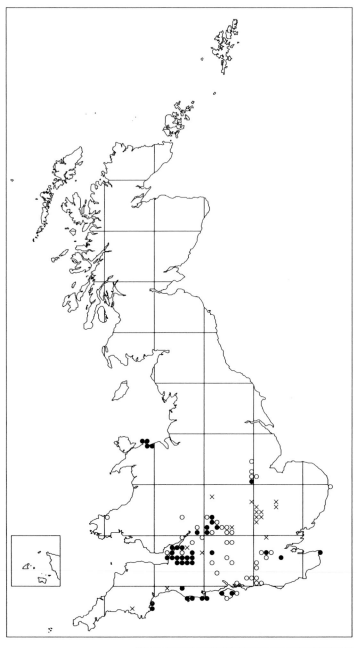

Current map	No	Atlas	No
1970 →	39	1930 →	31
Pre-1970	39	Pre-1930	34
Introductions	16	Introductions	0

Ceratophyllum submersum L.

Soft hornwort

Status: not scarce

This is a perennial aquatic plant of shallow, sheltered, eutrophic waters. It is one of the few British vascular plants which lack roots, growing as a floating mass or lightly anchored to the substrate by buried stems. In coastal sites its most characteristic habitats are shallow ponds and ditches (including grazing marsh ditches), where it grows with other plants which tolerate slightly brackish conditions such as *Myriophyllum spicatum*, *Potamogeton pectinatus*, *Ranunculus baudotii* and *Zannichellia palustris*, as well as species of wider habitat range. At inland localities it grows in similar habitats to the commoner *C. demersum*, including small field ponds, lakes and flooded gravel pits. It is shade-tolerant, and can be found in ditches or small ponds surrounded by tall emergents. In both coastal and inland sites it can be so abundant that it virtually excludes all competitors. It is confined to the lowlands.

Plants flower freely but mature fruit is less frequent (*C. demersum* is known to require high temperatures for the maturation of its fruit). Vegetative reproduction is probably frequent as plants are brittle and are able to regenerate from fragments. Plants survive the winter as sunken stems, but are unable to tolerate prolonged freezing.

The simple vegetative distinction between *C. submersum* and *C. demersum* was not understood until 1927 (Sandwith 1927). Older records of *C. submersum* are unreliable, and have been accepted only if supported by herbarium specimens. It is therefore difficult to assess changes in the distribution of the species. *C. submersum* is being recorded with increasing frequency in inland sites, but it is not clear if this reflects a real increase or whether it was previously overlooked. As a species of eutrophic water, it is unlikely to be threatened by changes in water quality.

C. submersum sensu lato is widespread in Europe, north to southern Scandinavia (Jalas & Suominen 1989). It is also found in Asia, Africa and North and South America, but it is absent from Australasia. For a map of its world distribution, see Wilmot-Dear (1985).

C. D. Preston

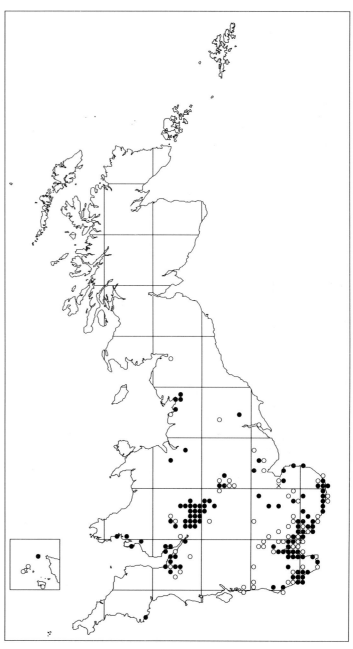

Current map	No	Atlas	No
1970 →	111	1930 →	37
Pre-1970	63	Pre-1930	50
Introductions	1	Introductions	0

Chamaemelum nobile (L.) All.

Chamomile

Status: scarce

C. nobile is most frequently found in herb-rich, closely grazed, moderately acidic, lowland grassland which has not been fertilised or sprayed. It flourishes in relatively high nutrient situations providing that sufficient grazing, mowing or trampling occurs to prevent grasses and taller plants from dominating the sward. Although a plant of dry, sandy or gleyed soils, a common requirement is to be seasonally wet, usually in winter. The sun also often bakes sandy soil hard in the summer, rendering it slowly permeable thus leading to temporary waterlogging in winter. Its common associates are *Agrostis capillaris*, *Lotus corniculatus*, *Plantago coronopus*, *P. lanceolata* and *Potentilla erecta* but rarer species such as *Cicendia filiformis*, *Corrigiola litoralis*, *Galium constrictum*, *Illecebrum verticillatum*, *Mentha pulegium*, *Persicaria minor*, *Pilularia globulifera* and *Pulicaria vulgaris* have been recorded at particular sites. *C. nobile* also occurs in maritime grassland, where salt spray and exposure keep the sward short. Here the flora is less rich, but typically includes *Carex panicea*, *Festuca rubra*, *Pulicaria dysenterica* and *Sagina procumbens*. A further habitat is on cricket and football pitches where regular cutting and rolling mimic grazing pressure, but here again the flora is less diverse.

A perennial, producing shoots in the first year of growth which normally form a rosette of leaves, which do not flower until the second year. It is long-lived, reproducing both by clonal spread, and in some populations, by seed. Under heavy grazing pressures it adopts a semi-prostrate, often non-flowering form where the stems creep out parallel to the ground and thus avoid being nibbled (Westerhoff & Clark 1992).

C. nobile has declined dramatically in recent years, principally because of cessation of grazing. It cannot compete with taller herbs or scrub, and quickly disappears together with its rich associated flora. It is often eliminated by drainage, and it has vanished from its roadside sites as they are fenced, and as the vegetation becomes coarse and tall. It survives in the New Forest and Dartmoor because of grazing by ponies and cattle and on the cliffs of the south-west because of climatic conditions. The map is believed to be an accurate summary of the current position with the exception of Dartmoor, where the plant has not been surveyed since 1970.

It is widespread in western Europe from Belgium, where it may be adventive, southwards to Algeria and the Azores.

H. Winship & C. Chatters

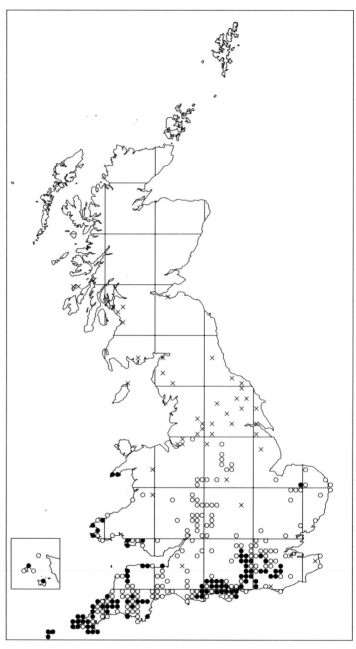

Current map	No	Atlas	No
1970 →	96	1930 →	148
Pre-1970	165	Pre-1930	51
Introductions	47	Introductions	23

Chenopodium chenopodioides (L.) Aellen

Status: rare

Saltmarsh goosefoot

This little-known annual is characteristic of a restricted estuarine habitat, growing on dry brackish mud seasonally exposed on ditch sides and in the shallow winter inundations (or 'fleets') of saltings and grazing marshes. Associated species are mostly annual, often including *Chenopodium rubrum*, *Parapholis strigosa*, *Salicornia* spp. and *Suaeda maritima*, with the nationally scarce *Hordeum marinum*, *Polypogon monspeliensis* (and sometimes ×*Agropogon littoralis*, its rare hybrid with *Agrostis stolonifera*), *Puccinellia fasciculata*, and occasionally *P. rupestris*. Of the rarities, *C. chenopodioides* probably has the narrowest range of tolerance. Perennial associates are usually *Glaux maritima*, *Juncus gerardii* and *Spergularia* spp.

Like most annuals of exposed mud, *C. chenopodioides* can appear in great quantity in suitable years, when the mud dries and warms early, but is scarce or even absent when water levels remain high. It appears to germinate from dormant seed only when the mud is exposed to the air, and flowering is normally only just beginning in July, but can build up to spectacular displays by mid September when fruiting plants turn bright red. Plant sizes vary, but like its close relative *C. rubrum* when on mud, *C. chenopodioides* is often present as minute plants producing good seed in late years, or in very ephemeral habitats such as hoofprints.

The restricted habitat and exacting requirements make *C. chenopodioides* a vulnerable and threatened species. Traditional management with fluctuating water levels and stock trampling the drying ditch edges was ideal, but grazing marshes have been much reclaimed for arable, or drained with stabilised levels in the ditches. The few colonies recorded outside the core populations of the Thames estuary (including a wildfowl scrape in a coastal reserve and damp hollows on a sandy golf course, both in Sussex) are probably extinct.

This species is endemic to central and southern Europe, extending to Denmark and south-east Russia, but excluding the central and southern Mediterranean. For a map of its European distribution, see Jalas & Suominen (1980).

Some past records may have been mis-determinations of the dwarf ephemeral form of *C. rubrum*, but the taxonomy is now clearly understood. Recorders no longer have to rely on the rather subjective character given by Fitt (1844), that "when fresh-gathered, the smell is like that of the pods of green peas".

R. FitzGerald

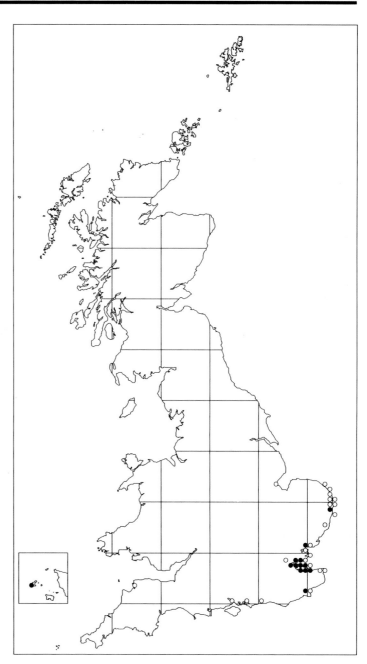

Current map	No	Atlas	No
1970 →	12	1930 →	16
Pre-1970	23	Pre-1930	11
Introductions	0	Introductions	0

Cicendia filiformis (L.) Delarbre

Yellow centaury

Status: scarce

C. filiformis is a diminutive annual of heathlands on soils which have a relatively high base status and are damp in winter and spring. It is most frequently associated with winter-flooded pools, cart tracks and ditches, but also very locally abundant in heavily grazed damp pasture. Such sites are usually on mildly acid, base-rich clays (e.g. New Forest and Dorset) or loess overlying serpentine and gabbro (Lizard Peninsula). At one site on the Lizard Peninsula it is associated with serpentine erosion pans and rock outcrops. Reduced competition is essential: this is effected by winter flooding, high levels of rough grazing, and disturbance. It is often found with many other rare and local species, suggesting the great age, and continuity of management, of such habitats. At the Lizard Peninsula, associates on rutted tracks include *Juncus pygmaeus*, *Pilularia globulifera*, *Ranunculus tripartitus* and *Chara fragifera*. On the sand and clay heaths of south-central England, *Anagallis minima*, *Chamaemelum nobile*, *Galium constrictum*, *Illecebrum verticillatum*, *Ludwigia palustris*, *Mentha pulegium* and *Radiola linoides* also occur.

C. filiformis is a short-lived summer annual, germinating in spring on bare ground exposed after winter flooding. Like many such annuals, it may be extremely abundant over small areas during favourable seasons, but absent in other years.

Many sites have been lost by the extensive destruction of heathland or by infilling or drainage of its favoured microhabitats. Now that most extant sites are SSSIs or nature reserves, the greatest threat arises from lack of suitable management. Stock grazing is especially critical: in its absence *C. filiformis* soon disappears as succession to grassland and scrub occurs. Thus with the cessation of grazing and other traditional management practices over many of the heathland districts of lowland Britain, the range of *C. filiformis* has contracted severely. Another threat lies in the upgrading of heathland tracks to improve access for vehicles. Today the plant is only widespread on the Lizard Peninsula and in the New Forest. In former strongholds, such as Dorset, it is likely to appear only at rare intervals following chance disturbance unless traditional management practices are reinstated.

C. filiformis is most widespread in western Europe south to the Mediterranean, and is also found in the Azores, North Africa and western Turkey.

A. J. Byfield

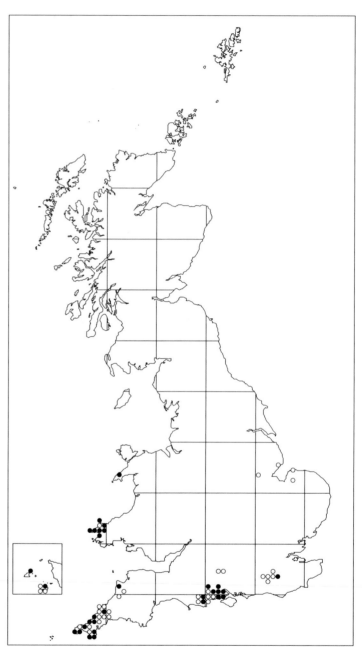

Current map	No	Atlas	No
1970 →	29	1930 →	29
Pre-1970	31	Pre-1930	22
Introductions	0	Introductions	0

continued →

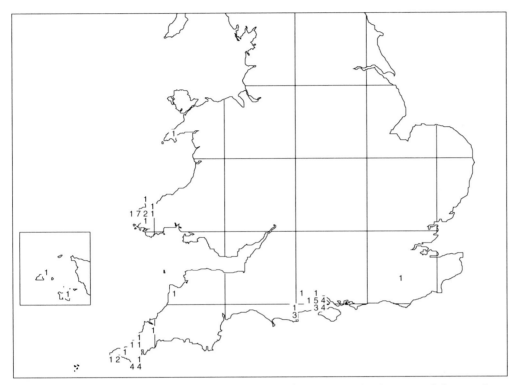

The number of tetrads in each 10 km square in which *Cicendia filiformis* has been recorded as a native species from 1970 onwards. The species has been found in a total of 59 tetrads from 1970 onwards.

Cicuta virosa L.   **Cowbane**
Status: scarce

This is an aquatic species of lake shores, pond margins, mires and ditches. It grows in shallow water or on a floating mat of vegetation and has a wide pH tolerance. Associates include such species as *Angelica sylvestris*, *Carex paniculata*, *C. riparia*, *C. rostrata*, *Phalaris arundinacea*, *Phragmites australis*, *Potentilla palustris*, *Ranunculus hederaceus*, *R. lingua*, *R. sceleratus* and *Typha latifolia*. It is restricted to the lowlands.

C. virosa is perennial. It reproduces by seed and sometimes forms rather dense colonies in mires.

C. virosa has probably always been local. It has disappeared from many sites in eastern England because of drainage. It contains a convulsant poison, cicutoxin, which is frequently fatal to cattle, and has perhaps been selectively eliminated from some areas by man. Many of the remaining populations are stable. It persists in sites where the water has become eutrophic and many submerged species have disappeared.

Widespread from Britain and Ireland east to eastern Siberia and Japan, becoming more scattered in the western part of its range and virtually absent from the Mediterranean region. Closely related species occur in North America.

M. E. Braithwaite

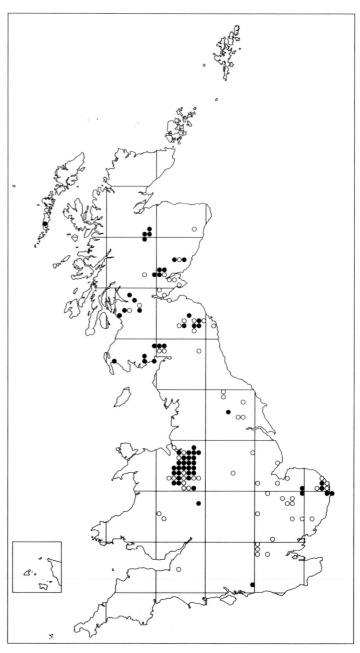

Current map	No	Atlas	No
1970 →	63	1930 →	29
Pre-1970	65	Pre-1930	46
Introductions	0	Introductions	0

continued →

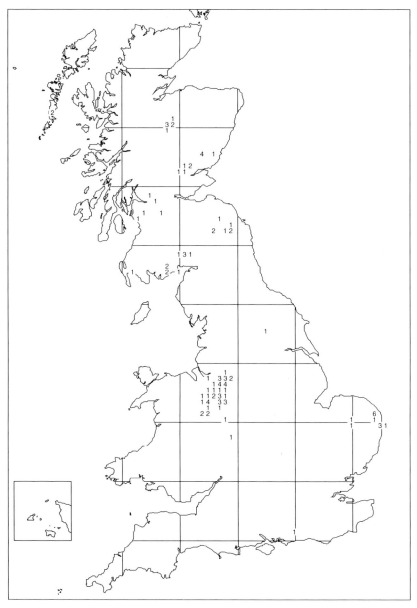

The number of tetrads in each 10 km square in which *Cicuta virosa* has been recorded as a native species from 1970 onwards. The species has been found in a total of 107 tetrads from 1970 onwards.

Circaea alpina L.
Status: scarce

Alpine enchanter's-nightshade

A small, delicate, inconspicuous plant of open and usually shaded or north-facing seepage areas and streamsides. In the Lake District it is characteristic of rocky, bryophyte-rich submontane *Quercus petraea* woodland, where it is often associated with *C. × intermedia* and *Chrysosplenium oppositifolium*. Here, as on Arran, it also occurs on open hillsides in block scree, among boulders by the sides of streams and by waterfalls, also under bracken and even amongst sphagnum. It descends virtually to sea-level on Arran. All sites are below 400 metres except one at 750 metres in a limestone sinkhole near Cross Fell.

The main method of reproduction is probably by rhizome. It does, however, fruit freely, the flowers being self-pollinated.

Its status and distribution in the British Isles were considerably clarified by Raven (1963). There has been much confusion in the past between *C. alpina* and the much commoner sterile hybrid *C. × intermedia* and this confusion unfortunately still persists. The extremely restricted and relict distribution of *C. alpina* is in marked contrast to the present wide distribution of *C. × intermedia*. This is probably the result both of the decrease of *C. alpina*, perhaps due to competition from *C. × intermedia*, and the increase of the latter with its more vigorous vegetative propagation.

C. alpina is represented in Europe only by subsp. *alpina*. This has a wide distribution throughout the northern boreal zone, being most frequent in the mountains of central and northern Europe, eastern North America and Japan. Other subspecies occur in Asia and western North America.

G. Halliday

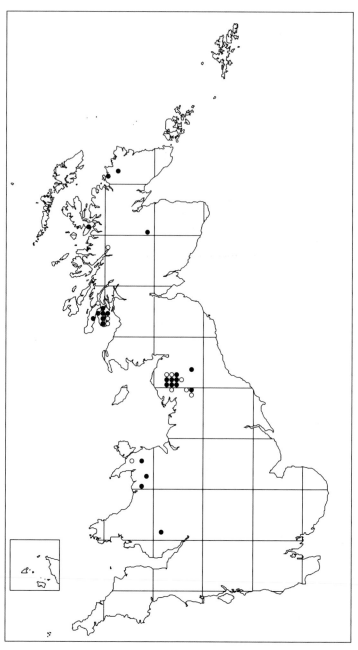

Current map	No	Atlas (S)	No
1970 →	24		
Pre-1970	11		
Introductions	0	All records	17

Clinopodium calamintha (L.) Stace

Lesser calamint

Status: scarce

A warmth-loving species with a preference for dry, south-facing banks which produce sun traps. It is almost certainly native in a restricted area of lowland England, typically on calcareous sandy and gravelly glacial deposits. It was formerly characteristic of hillocky or south-facing lightly-grazed pastures, but is now a truly wayside plant largely confined to churchyards, verges of tracks and roadsides, railway banks and waste ground.

C. calamintha is a short-lived perennial. Flowering plants are conspicuous in late summer and autumn and flowering extends well into November. The hairs in the mouth of the calyx delay seed drop. Overwintering plants have a shallow spreading, easily uprooted rootstock with short woody stems from the previous year's growth. Plants are destroyed in cold winters and regenerate from a generally copious seedbank. Seedling establishment depends on lack of competition, but plants are readily established on dry ground, rockeries, and in cracks between paving stones. Seed dispersal is inefficient, but may have been better in the days of wooden carts and muddy unmetalled roads.

The outlying localities may be relics of a former, more general spread in eastern and southern England; alternatively, the species may have been planted as a herb outside its main range. The contraction apparent from the map cannot be solely due to confusion with the closely related *C. ascendens*. Existing colonies are threatened by the flailing of verges, which unless it is delayed until winter or spring prevents new seed replenishing the seed bank. In churchyards and cemeteries the increasing use of rotary mowers is destroying many colonies.

It is widespread across central and southern Europe, into North Africa, the Middle East and Asia. Scattered introductions of this herb south to New Zealand were made by European colonists.

G. M. S. Easy & K. J. Adams

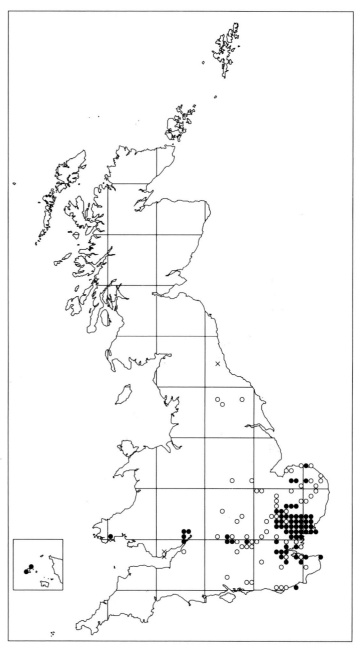

Current map	No	Atlas	No
1970 →	63	1930 →	46
Pre-1970	60	Pre-1930	54
Introductions	3	Introductions	0

continued →

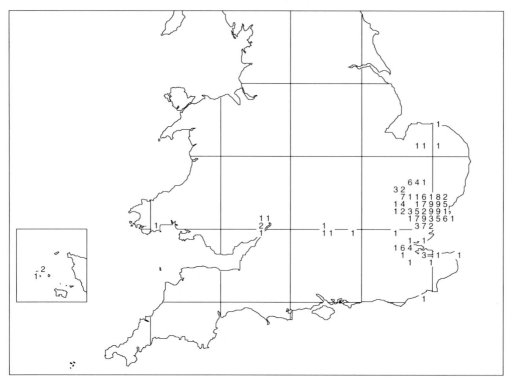

The number of tetrads in each 10 km square in which *Clinopodium calamintha* has been recorded as a native species from 1970 onwards. Squares in which the species is recorded in 9 or more tetrads are plotted as 9: *C. calamintha* is actually recorded from 13 tetrads in TL81 and TM02,16 in TL93 and TM03 and 18 in TL92. The species has been found in a total of 225 tetrads from 1970 onwards.

Cochlearia scotica Druce
Status: taxonomically uncertain

This species is reported from a variety of northern coastal habitats. These include cliff-top grasslands (especially when heavily rabbit-grazed), mature dune grasslands and the tops of shingle spits close to the sea. In Shetland it is found on peat now subject to tidal inundation. It is also found on rather open stony shores with little competition, and it often grows in soil-filled crevices in rocks near the upper tidal level. Additionally it has been recorded from the serpentine debris field on the Keen of Hamar on Unst.

Little is known of reproduction in this species, although material collected from Shetland sets seed in a Surrey garden (probably after self-pollination), and seedlings are abundant. The plant is biennial or perhaps a short-lived perennial.

The distribution map shows that most records were made before 1970, but this is almost certainly a result of botanists' loss of confidence in the existence of the species rather than any real change in status. It can be very common locally in suitable sites.

This species does not appear to be recorded from outside the British Isles. Superficially similar plants from the Norwegian coast are grouped under three subspecies of *C. officinalis* (Nordal & Stabbetorpe 1990).

Opinions differ greatly as to the taxonomic status of *C. scotica*, as summarised by Dalby (Rich 1991). It is possible that plants from cliffs and higher levels on the shore are salt-stressed forms of *C. alpina*, whilst those from the lower level of the *Puccinellia maritima* zone or below, especially on stony sea shores in the Inner and Outer Hebrides, are *C. atlantica* or (in the case of the Norwegian plants) other geographically restricted segregates. The consensus appears to be against recognising *C. scotica* as a species in its own right.

D. H. Dalby

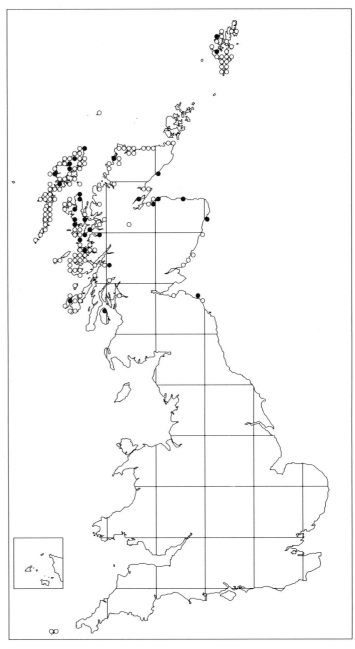

Current map	No	Atlas	No
1970 →	30	1930 →	76
Pre-1970	136	Pre-1930	7
Introductions	0	Introductions	0

Coincya monensis (L.) Greuter & Burdet subsp. *monensis*
Status: scarce

Isle of Man Cabbage

This lowland plant grows on sand dunes, sandy ground and sometimes cliffs by or near the sea. Its usual habitat is unfixed 'yellow dune' with *Ammophila arenaria*. It sometimes occurs as a casual inland and in recent years has been found in ruderal communities in central Scotland.

It is an annual to short-lived perennial, capable of self-pollination. It flowers from June to September.

It is a local species, but reasonably common on the Isle of Man, on parts of the western coast of northern England and the estuary of the River Clyde. There has been some decline in its distribution, with the loss of outlying populations on Mull and elsewhere.

Subsp. *monensis* is endemic to Britain. Subsp. *recurvata*, a more erect and hispid plant with smaller seeds, is native to south-west Europe, and is naturalised on waste and sandy ground in south-west England and south Wales.

J. R. Akeroyd

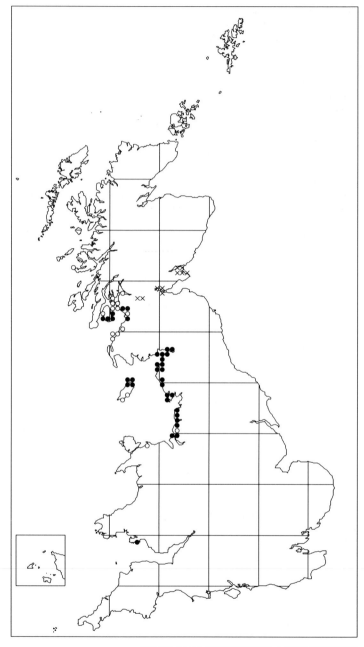

Current map	No	Atlas	No
1970 →	33	1930 →	18
Pre-1970	17	Pre-1930	19
Introductions	10	Introductions	11

Corallorrhiza trifida Châtel.
Status: scarce

Coralroot orchid

This saprophytic orchid is most often found amongst moss cushions and thick leaf mould in damp pine and birch woods (including pine plantations where it grows with *Goodyera repens* and *Moneses uniflora*), and in willow and alder carr. Deep shade is not essential though, and *C. trifida* also grows in the open in damp dune slacks, invariably with *Salix repens* and sometimes with *Juncus balticus* and *Schoenus nigricans*. Less typically it has been found in tall herb fen, with young *Salix cinerea*, amongst *Carex* spp. and on sphagnum hummocks; on dunes with *Ammophila arenaria*, where the water table is near the surface; amongst rank *Molinia caerulea*; in heather moorland; and under willows on the damp stony ledges of a quarry. It seems to have exacting water table requirements, sometimes growing only by tree bases, or following the margins of a dune slack. It is normally found in the lowlands, but reaches 365 metres at Braemar.

Plants survive as underground rhizomes except while flowering for a few weeks between April and August (usually in June and July). Most flowers set seed. Self-pollination is normal, though insects are attracted by the slight scent and may cause some cross-pollination. The number of flower spikes can fluctuate wildly from year to year but it is not clear what causes this fluctuation. Vegetative reproduction occurs by fragmentation of the rhizome.

C. trifida is inconspicuous and easily overlooked, and large new populations are still being found. Fluctuating numbers of flowering spikes may lead to populations appearing to vanish in some years.

C. trifida is a circumboreal species. In Europe it is found from northern Scandinavia south to the Pyrenees, northern Italy, northern Greece and the Crimea.

C. trifida is extremely unusual in obtaining its nutrients by photosynthesis, parasitism and saprophytism.

E. J. MacKintosh

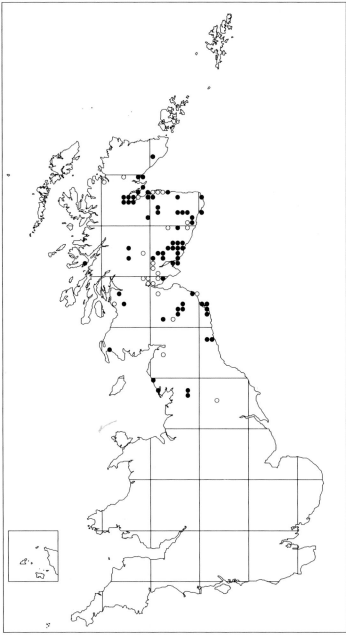

Current map	No	Atlas	No
1970 →	65	1930 →	19
Pre-1970	24	Pre-1930	21
Introductions	0	Introductions	0

Corynephorus canescens (L.) P. Beauv.

Status: rare

Grey hair-grass

This is a mainly coastal species found in short sandy turf on beaches and on dunes to the landward side of shingle ridges. It also occurs on inland areas of mobile sand. This species survives only where an annual accretion of sand around the base of the plants allows bud growth (and hence the development of roots and new shoots) low down on the culm. Dispersal of plants over a wide area is unusual and most are found in confined areas with an open community. In areas with low rainfall, plants are well spaced and elsewhere any formation approaching a sward is rare. Its common associates are *Agrostis vinealis*, *Ammophila arenaria*, *Carex arenaria* and *Hypochaeris radicata*. In very dry sand it is also found with *Cladonia gracilis*, *C. impexa*, *C. pyxidata* agg. and *Corniculata aculeata*. It is confined to the lowlands.

C. canescens is a perennial reproducing by seed. There is no vegetative spread beyond individual plants arising from the parent position. Germination is erratic. This species does not colonise new sites readily.

The distribution is probably stable, although there are annual variations in colony populations. Prolonged gales will unseat plants in loose sand and beach colonies are occasionally in danger from tidal encroachment and from the public. Management for this species must ensure that colonies remain exposed to wind and hence subject to sand movement. An adjacent conifer plantation will shelter plants from wind as will the encroachment of bracken and gorse. The presence of some rabbits will help to control *Carex arenaria* by grazing, and their liking for *C. canescens* stems is offset by vegetative reproduction. For details of the introduced populations in Scotland, see Trist (1993).

C. canescens is found in Europe from the southern Baltic to southern Portugal, northern Italy and central Ukraine. It is local in the eastern part of its range. It is also recorded from North Africa, and occurs as an introduction in North America.

For further information on the ecology of this species, see Marshall (1967).

P. J. O. Trist

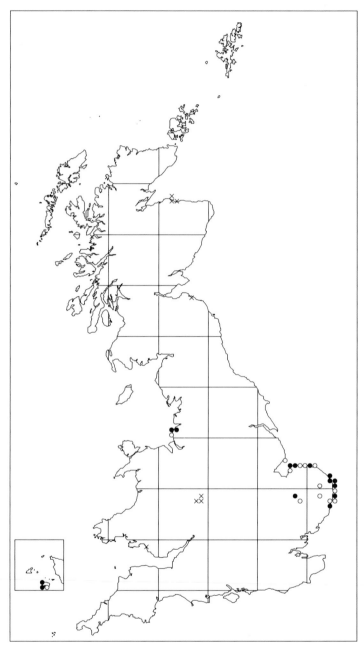

Current map	No	Atlas	No
1970 →	12	1930 →	14
Pre-1970	12	Pre-1930	8
Introductions	9	Introductions	1

Crambe maritima L.

Sea-kale

Status: not scarce

This maritime plant is found on shingle beaches, or on dunes but only where these rest on a shingle beach (Salisbury 1952). It is also occasionally found on cliffs as at Sidmouth and Burton Bradstock. It often grows in pure stands and its only associates are those of a shore-line vegetation, such as *Beta vulgaris* subsp. *maritima*, *Glaucium flavum*, *Rumex crispus* and *Silene uniflora* with very occasional occurrences of the scarce species *Lathyrus japonicus* and *Mertensia maritima*.

C. maritima is a perennial, long-lived herb, growing into very large clumps. It sets seed readily, other than in the north of its range (Scott & Randall 1976) and these few heavy but buoyant seeds are dispersed by the sea. Some humus, in the form of buried seaweed, and a fine substrate seem to be necessary for the germination of the seed. Vegetative reproduction may occur from broken portions of roots, particularly after heavy storms. This was very apparent after the 1990 storms on Chesil Beach where many plants were uncovered and destroyed. By 1992 there were more colonies than before.

In some areas of southern England this species seems to be increasing. It may be that it was formerly collected for sea-kale: it is much more common now on Chesil Beach than in Good's day, when he remarked that it was much gathered for culinary use (Good 1948). In other areas it has undoubtedly declined, notably in South Wales. Its decline may be because of human trampling and possibly coastal development and sea defence works.

It occurs in northern France and around the Baltic, with outlying populations in northern Spain and Ireland. There is also a population around the Black Sea.

D. A. Pearman & A. McG. Stirling

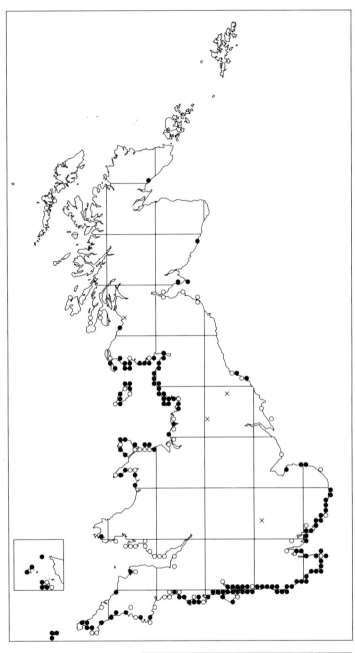

Current map	No	Atlas	No
1970 →	137	1930 →	88
Pre-1970	71	Pre-1930	21
Introductions	4	Introductions	0

Crassula tillaea Lester-Garl.

Status: scarce

Mossy stonecrop

This plant is restricted to open, bare sandy soils, of pH 5.0 to 6.1, often growing where there is a certain amount of compaction and hence occasional flooding in winter. It grows in heathland tracks, sandy tracks by the sea and in sandy areas used as car parks. Because of its small size, less than 5 cm in height and generally prostrate, it prefers places devoid of other vegetation. However, species found in the same vegetation include *Agrostis capillaris*, *Aira praecox*, *Aphanes inexspectata*, *Carex arenaria*, *Erodium cicutarium*, *Festuca ovina*, *Hypochaeris radicata*, *Koeleria macrantha*, *Ornithopus perpusillus*, *Plantago coronopus*, *P. lanceolata*, *Rumex acetosella* subsp. *acetosella*, *Sagina apetala*, *Scleranthus annuus*, *Trifolium arvense*, *T. suffocatum* and *Hypnum cupressiforme* (Trist 1979). It is a lowland plant, probably always occurring below 100 metres.

It is an annual, often bright yellow-green in the earlier part of the year, and turning a characteristic vivid red in summer. Reproduction is by seed.

Some sites have been lost in eastern England, especially at inland localities, because of heathland destruction. The species appears to have expanded its range in south-west England in recent years, with the discovery of many new sites in Dorset, some of them very substantial, and colonies in Somerset and Cornwall. This expansion may have been favoured by recent summer droughts and by the reduction in competition at coastal sites because of increased public pressure.

C. tillaea is found in the Mediterranean area, western Europe, north-west Germany and Macaronesia.

L. Farrell

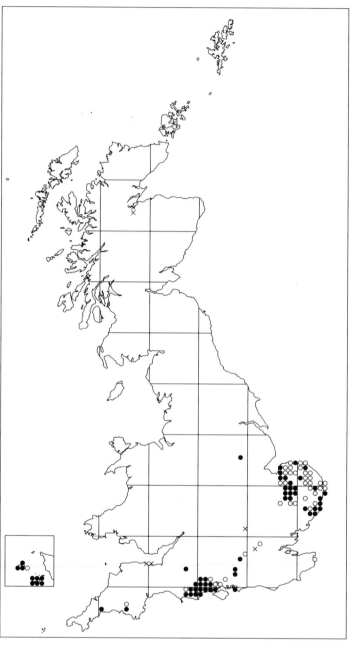

Current map	No	Atlas	No
1970 →	49	1930 →	40
Pre-1970	38	Pre-1930	32
Introductions	6	Introductions	0

Crepis mollis (Jacq.) Asch.
Status: scarce

Northern hawk's-beard

Found in herb-rich grassland or wood pasture on shallow, slightly flushed, base-rich soils, often on north-facing slopes. At those of its localities by upland burns, which are typically associated with intrusive rocks, it is found on banks away from the burn. In this it differs from *C. paludosa*, which is often present nearby in a much wetter habitat. It may be associated with other yellow composites including *Hieracium* spp., *Hypochaeris radicata*, *Leontodon autumnalis* and *L. hispidus*, together with basic grassland species such as *Briza media* and *Coeloglossum viride*, or, in more shaded situations, with *Fragaria vesca*, *Fraxinus excelsior*, *Geum rivale*, *G. urbanum*, *Lathyrus linifolius*, *Prunus padus*, *Saxifraga granulata* and *Viola riviniana*. It is usually found between 150 and 400 metres, descends to 90 metres in Northumberland and reaches 670 metres at Caenlochan.

It is a winter-green perennial forming a dense root mass from a short rhizome. Fresh rosettes frequently replace the parent rosette after flowering. Seed germinates more readily in spring than autumn. The flowers are relished by rabbits.

C. mollis is local and apparently declining, but still somewhat under-recorded. It cannot be refound at a number of the stations where it was recorded in the late nineteenth century. Many new sites in Northumberland and Durham have, however, been discovered in recent years and new sites have also been found in the Scottish Borders. It is plentiful at a few sites.

It is a continental species, occurring in central Europe from the Pyrenees, northern Italy and southern Russia northwards to Germany, Poland and central Russia.

M. E. Braithwaite

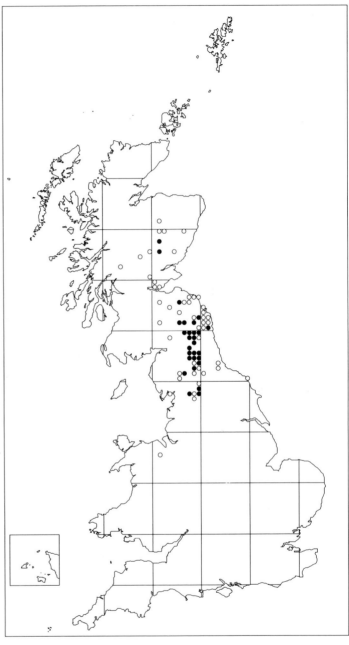

Current map	No	Atlas	No
1970 →	28	1930 →	9
Pre-1970	46	Pre-1930	31
Introductions	0	Introductions	0

Cuscuta europaea L.

Status: scarce

Greater dodder

This plant is a rootless parasite which, upon germination, attaches to a primary host. The host is almost invariably *Urtica dioica*, but rarely *Humulus lupulus*. *C. europaea* then parasitises a broad spectrum of secondary hosts - over 40 species in many families have been recorded. It is generally found on the banks of streams and rivers but in some areas it is more frequent on roadside hedges and ditch banks. It always grows in damp nitrophilous conditions where its primary host occurs in abundance. It was once recorded as a casual on potatoes. It is restricted to the lowlands.

C. europaea is usually annual but it could possibly perennate on certain hosts. It flowers in August and September. Seeds may be dispersed down stream following winter flooding.

This species has been confused with other members of the genus, and some old records shown in the *Atlas of the British Flora* are now regarded as unreliable. It has always been uncommon and may be in decline in some areas, though the reasons for this are not clear. Herbicide spraying to combat its primary host may in part be responsible. The recent discovery of the plant in North Essex (Tarpey & Heath 1990) suggests that it may be overlooked in its painful and otherwise botanically unpromising habitat.

This plant has a scattered distribution throughout much of Europe but is absent from the far north and from many of the islands. It is montane at the southern end of its range. It is also found in North Africa and temperate Asia, and known as an introduction in North America.

It is known in Gloucestershire, and perhaps elsewhere, as devil's guts. For a more detailed account of its ecology, see Verdcourt (1948).

F. J. Rumsey

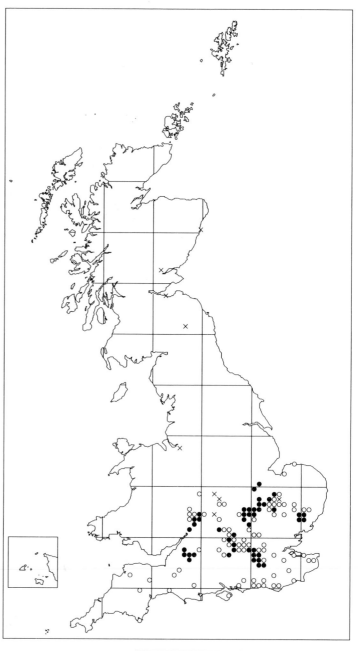

Current map	No	Atlas	No
1970 →	45	1930 →	36
Pre-1970	75	Pre-1930	118
Introductions	9	Introductions	0

Cyperus longus L.

Galingale

Status: scarce

C. longus is found in marshes and wet pastures near the coast, particularly in valleys and also in base-rich flushes on the cliffs.

It is a rhizomatous perennial, forming vigorously spreading patches that may extend over a considerable area, eliminating most competition. The seed may well not ripen in Britain (Syme 1870).

The species seems to have declined in localities where it is almost indisputably native. However, it was used agriculturally in the Channel Islands and so it may have been planted at some of these sites. It has gone from many of the coastal sites shown in the *Atlas* (Perring & Walters 1962), through drainage and agricultural improvement of habitat, and through cessation of grazing which has led to outcompetition by *Oenanthe crocata*, or invasion by alder scrub. However, there are also many recent records from ponds and ditches all over southern England. It is widely available horticulturally, especially at aquatic garden centres, and at many sites is clearly deliberately introduced.

It is common over all western, central and southern Europe, east to central Asia, and in North and East Africa.

D. A. Pearman

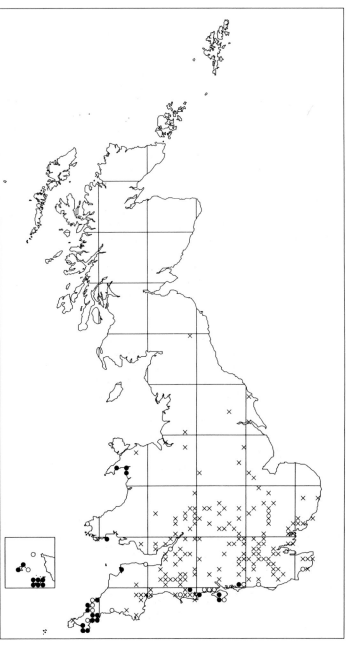

Current map	No	Atlas	No
1970 →	20	1930 →	17
Pre-1970	16	Pre-1930	14
Introductions	156	Introductions	26

Cystopteris montana (Lam.) Desv.

Status: rare?

Mountain bladder-fern

This is a perennial fern of sheltered, humid habitats, usually on steep north-facing crags in sites where there is at least periodic irrigation. It is strongly calcicolous, favouring ledges and slopes of unstable micaceous gravel with a high calcium content and usually with a cover of bryophytes and mat-forming vascular plants. In this species-rich habitat there are numerous associates, including *Arabis petraea*, *Cochlearia* spp., *Cystopteris fragilis*, *Philonotis fontana*, *Saxifraga aizoides*, *S. oppositifolia*, *S. stellaris*, *Sedum rosea* and *Ctenidium molluscum*. It grows at altitudes from 490 metres on Ben Lui to 1070 metres on Bidean nan Bian and Aonach Beag.

The plant produces spores but it seems likely that the small, local populations are built up by the creeping rhizome system.

C. montana is extinct in the Lake District where it was only seen once, but its status is probably little changed in Scotland. It probably survives in most of the Scottish 10 km squares from which only pre-1970 records are available. The main cause for concern would seem to be the plant's propensity towards small isolated populations.

It is a circumboreal species. In Europe it extends south to the Pyrenees, Apennines, the Carpathians and the Caucasus (Jalas & Suominen 1972).

As this species has been recorded in only 15 10 km squares since 1970, it qualifies for inclusion in the *Red Data Book* (Perring & Farrell 1983) under the current criteria. However it will probably be recorded in more than 15 10 km squares, when, as seems likely, it is refound in some of its old localities.

G. P. Rothero

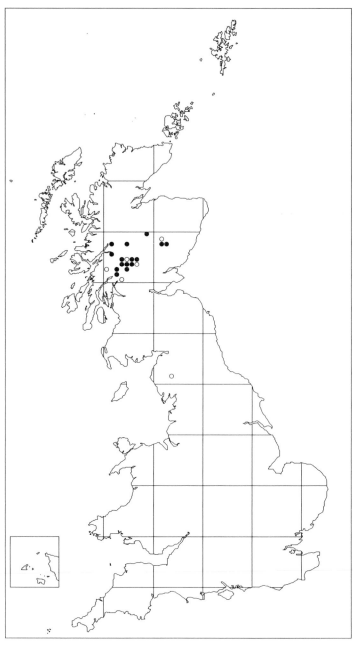

Current map	No	Atlas	No
1970 →	15	1930 →	10
Pre-1970	6	Pre-1930	4
Introductions	0	Introductions	0

Dactylorhiza traunsteineri (Sauter ex Reichb.) Soó
Status: scarce

Narrow-leaved marsh-orchid

D. traunsteineri is confined to wet, base-rich habitats, in particular to fens and flushes. Although very local, it is sometimes present in considerable numbers, loosely rooted in the moist substrate in areas where there is only modest competition. It is usually accompanied by *Schoenus nigricans*, whilst other frequent associates include *Menyanthes trifoliata*, *Pinguicula vulgaris*, *Primula farinosa*, *Valeriana dioica* and *Carex* species typical of base-rich flushes.

This is a perennial species. Reproduction is by seed, and as with other *Dactylorhiza* species, it is amongst the quickest of terrestrial orchids to achieve maturity and to flower. Mature plants will often produce lateral shoots which later develop into new tubers. These tubers can then become detached and form separate plants.

At present, populations appear to be stable in numbers, but by requiring a damp habitat, threats to their survival will come from direct drainage and from any activities which cause a general lowering of the water-table. Planting of conifers within close proximity also imposes a similar drying-out effect, whilst a reduction in grazing places *D. traunsteineri* at a competitive disadvantage.

D. traunsteineri is the principal member of a complex range of closely-related taxa. True *D. traunsteineri* is known to occur in the Alps and surrounding regions as well as from central and north-west Europe. The conspecificity of our plant with that from the Alps and Scandinavia has sometimes been doubted (Bateman & Denholm 1983) but has recently been demonstrated by Roberts (1988) and Foley (1990). In the Baltic states and parts of western Russia, it intergrades with *D. russowii*, and in northern Scandinavia with *D. lapponica*. The latter has also recently been recorded from Scotland and is probably only subspecifically distinct from *D. traunsteineri*.

Like most species of marsh-orchid, it is variable in form both within and between populations. It has in the past been a rather misunderstood plant and is still probably overlooked at higher altitudes, especially in Scotland. It hybridises readily with *D. fuchsii* and *D. maculata* and to a lesser extent with other *Dactylorhiza* species. Hybrids persist at some sites from which *D. traunsteineri* has apparently been lost.

M. J. Y. Foley

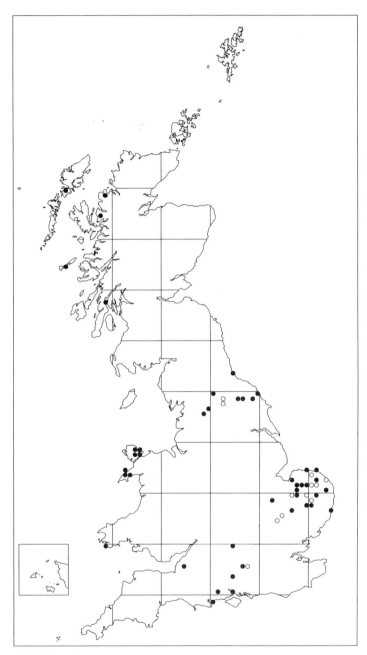

Current map	No	Atlas	No
1970 →	44	1930 →	12
Pre-1970	12	Pre-1930	1
Introductions	0	Introductions	0

continued →

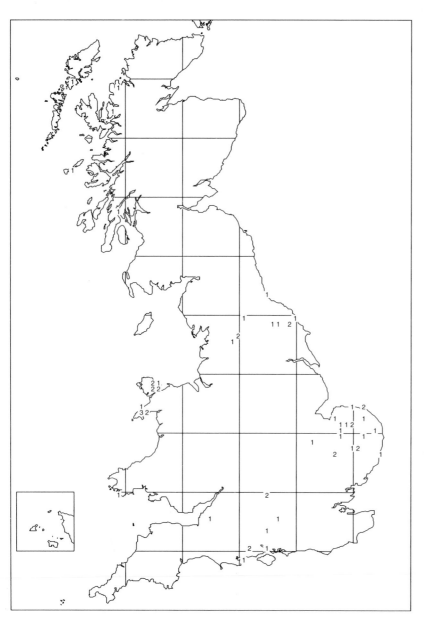

The number of tetrads in each 10 km square in which *Dactylorhiza traunsteineri* has been recorded as a native species from 1970 onwards. The species has been found in a total of 58 tetrads from 1970 onwards.

Daphne mezereum L.
Status: scarce

Mezereon

This shrub grows in both ancient and recent secondary woodland on calcareous soils. In dry sites its associates include *Acer pseudoplatanus, Betula* spp., *Brachypodium sylvaticum, Carex sylvatica, Corylus avellana, Crataegus monogyna, Fraxinus excelsior, Hedera helix, Hyacinthoides non-scripta, Ligustrum vulgare, Lonicera periclymenum, Mercurialis perennis, Rubus* spp. and some common woodland mosses. It has been recorded from several chalk pits where there is relatively little competition from other ground flora. As a dense canopy develops and it is shaded, it may fail to flower. In Dorset and Hampshire there are substantial colonies in very wet, species rich fens with invading alder scrub. It is a mainly lowland species, but is found up to 335 metres at Ling Gill in Ribblesdale.

It is a perennial, deciduous shrub which produces fragrant, pink-purple flowers very early in the year before the leaves unfold in late spring. It is pollinated by moths and bees and reproduces by seeds, which turn bright red when ripe in late summer and are eaten by birds. Germination can occur quickly with green seed, but riper seed requires removal of the red flesh and some abrasion of the seed coat, so germination is assisted by partial digestion by birds. *D. mezereum* probably requires open ground for germination.

It is difficult to assess trends in this species as it has long been cultivated. Plants have been taken into cultivation from the wild but also colonise semi-natural habitats from cultivated stock. Native populations have declined over a long period, perhaps because of habitat destruction and collection. Plants are also susceptible to virus and most species of *Daphne* are known to be relatively short-lived in cultivation.

D. mezereum is a continental species, widespread in Europe and Asia from Spain east to the Altai Mountains. It is also established as an escape from cultivation in North America.

There is some debate about its native range in Britain. It is poisonous to humans, pigs and wolves. Gerarde (1597) informs us that "The leaves of Mezereon do purge downward, flegme, choler and waterish humors with great violence. Also if a drunkard do eate one graine or berrie of this plant, he cannot be allured to drinke any drinke at that time; such will be the heate of his mouth and choking in the throte".

L. Farrell

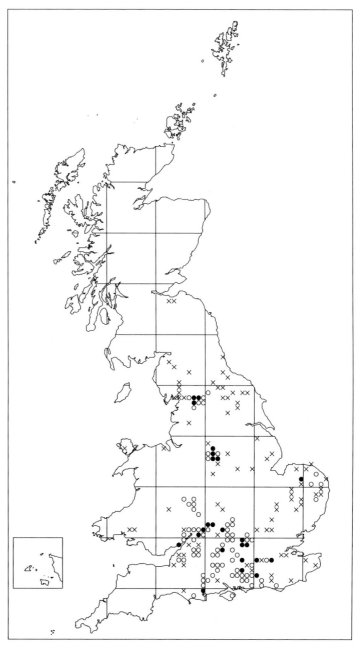

Current map	No	Atlas	No
1970 →	24	1930 →	12
Pre-1970	76	Pre-1930	62
Introductions	83	Introductions	55

Deschampsia cespitosa (L.) P. Beauv. subsp. *alpina* (L.) Hook. f.

Status: insufficiently known

Alpine tufted hair-grass

This grass grows on high mountains where it occurs in open communities on rock ledges and peaty and gravelly flushes in corries and on high plateaux, often where the snow lies late. It seems relatively indifferent to soil type, its main requirement being the absence of competition. In most of its habitats much of the soil is either bare of vegetation or dominated by bryophytes, and in many cases these are the only associated species. Associated vascular plants include *Cerastium cerastoides*, *Huperzia selago*, *Oxyria digyna* and *Saxifraga stellaris*. It is usually found above 800 metres, although it descends lower on Rum. It reaches 1200 metres on Aonach Beag.

It is a tufted perennial reproducing by means of proliferous (viviparous) spikelets. It is more capable of reproducing by propagules in a shorter, colder growing season than almost any other species, proliferous forms of *Poa alpina*, *P. flexuosa* and *Saxifraga cespitosa* perhaps being its equal. The plantlets are capable of independent existence almost as soon as the panicle emerges from the sheath. They require a continuously moist substrate on which to become established, being intolerant of desiccation. Reproduction appears to be solely vegetative in present European populations though the plant shows variation and several clones are present in the British Isles. Seed-bearing populations are known in eastern North America.

The distribution of *D. cespitosa* subsp. *alpina* is probably stable with no obvious threats. In Britain this diploid taxon has always been confused with the proliferous forms of the tetraploid *D. cespitosa* (which are known only from the British Isles). *D. cespitosa* subsp. *alpina* is difficult to distinguish from triploids which are presumed to be hybrids with diploid *D. cespitosa*. All records attributed to *D. cespitosa* subsp. *alpina sensu lato* are included on the main map. Confirmed records of *D. cespitosa* subsp. *alpina*, proliferous forms of subsp. *cespitosa* and putative hybrids between the two subspecies are shown on separate maps.

D. cespitosa subsp. *alpina* occurs in arctic and subarctic regions from Russia through Scandinavia, Iceland and Greenland to the eastern North American seaboard (Hultén 1958). Outlying occurrences in Siberia and the Far East may be referable to this subspecies.

H. A. McAllister

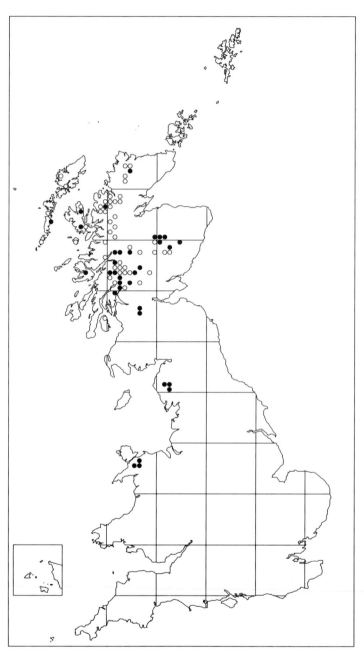

Current map	No	Atlas	No
1970 →	33	1930 →	52
Pre-1970	46	Pre-1930	5
Introductions	0	Introductions	0

continued →

Deschampsia cespitosa subsp. *alpina*

continued

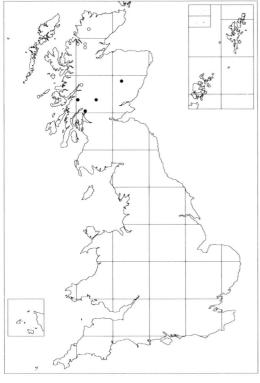

◀ The distribution of *Deschampsia cespitosa* subsp. *alpina* (confirmed records).

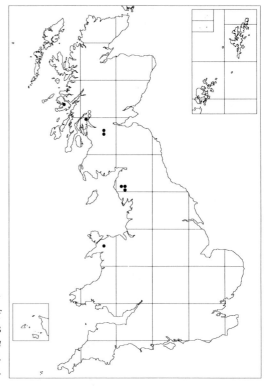

▶ The distribution of proliferous forms of *Deschampsia cespitosa* subsp. *cespitosa*.

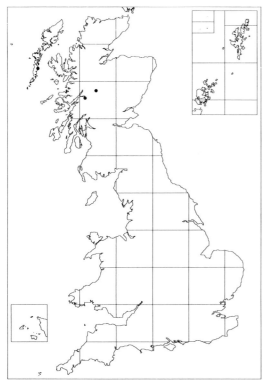

◀ The distribution of *Deschampsia cespitosa* subsp. *alpina* × subsp. *cespitosa*.

133

Deschampsia setacea (Hudson) Hackel
Status: scarce

Bog hair-grass

A grass of the bare, sometimes stony, margins of shallow pools; of seasonally inundated depressions on heaths, with *Molinia caerulea*, *Eleocharis multicaulis* and species of algae; and of acid bogs principally on lowland heaths. In the south of England it grows in wetter areas than *Agrostis curtisii,* which can look very similar. Winter inundation seems to be a requirement (Baker 1866), as does drying out in summer (Hughes 1983), and it may also be necessary that this water is moving, no matter how slightly. It will not grow on dry ground. *D. setacea* prefers an open situation, and can gradually be crowded out by more aggressive plants. It fares better where bare soil is present in quadrats than where many species are recorded (Hughes 1984). *Molinia caerulea* is a constant associate. The majority of sites in Britain are lowland and coastal, but it is found up to 320 metres, by Loch Morlich.

It is a densely tufted perennial with many vegetative shoots. It presumably spreads by seed, but little is known of its reproductive method, nor why the plant is in such small quantity at most of its stations. It is occasionally viviparous.

There are now more records from north and north-west Scotland than were known to Perring & Walters (1962), purely because of increased recording, and the species may still be at many of its sites in the Outer Hebrides for which only pre-1970 records are available. Further south, there are few recent records, and the rank state of many heaths may be responsible for this. However, it is difficult to see in flower, and very elusive indeed in its vegetative state (Lousley 1976).

D. setacea is an oceanic species which is endemic to western Europe, from Norway and Poland southwards to Spain. It is threatened by habitat destruction in much of its European range.

D. A. Pearman

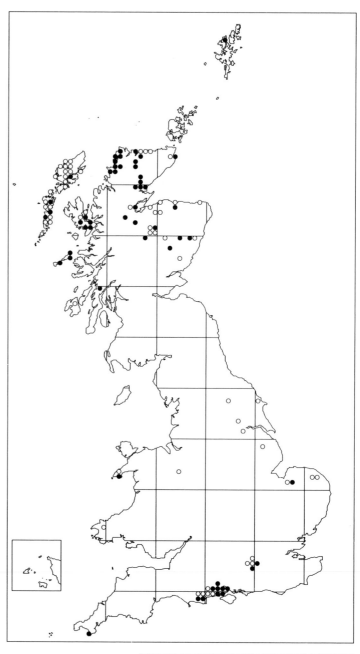

Current map	No	Atlas	No
1970 →	55	1930 →	37
Pre-1970	58	Pre-1930	26
Introductions	0	Introductions	0

Dianthus armeria L.

Status: scarce

Deptford pink

This is a plant of dry pastures, field borders and hedgerows. It prefers short grassland, where there is some open ground maintained either by grazing or some other form of disturbance, and dies out when shaded by coarse grasses or scrub invasion. It is found on light, sandy, slightly basic soil where associates include *Achillea millefolium, Daucus carota, Lotus corniculatus, Ranunculus repens* and *Trifolium repens.* It formerly grew on peaty soil of pH 4.8 at Woodwalton Fen (Wells 1967) where its commoner associates were *Agrostis capillaris, Festuca rubra, Luzula campestris, Plantago lanceolata* and *Potentilla erecta.* It is confined to the lowlands.

D. armeria can behave as an annual or biennial. The flowers lack scent and are seldom visited by insects and the plant is generally self-pollinated. It produces abundant seed, about 400 per plant, with 70% germination after 6 months' storage at room temperature. However, there may be an inhibiting factor which delays germination for up to 5 months after seeds are shed (Farrell, pers. obs.; Wells 1967).

The species has declined throughout southern England, mainly due to the conversion of pasture to arable or building land (Smith 1986).

D. armeria occurs widely across western and central Europe, extending eastwards to the Crimea and southwards to central Spain and Sicily (Jalas & Suominen 1986). It is also found in Anatolia and the Caucasus. It has been introduced into North America.

The beneficial effects of grazing by Galloway cattle, rabbits and hares are discussed by Wells (1967).

L. Farrell

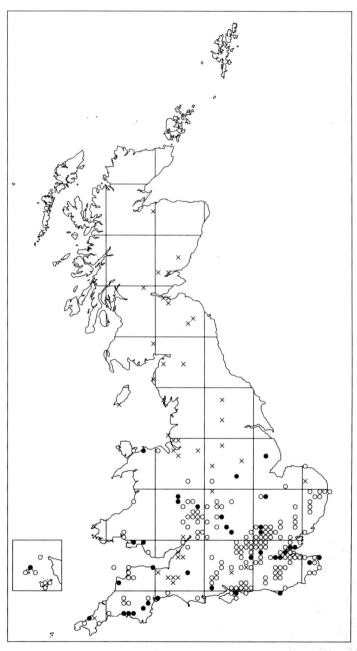

Current map	No	Atlas	No
1970 →	36	1930 →	40
Pre-1970	149	Pre-1930	91
Introductions	42	Introductions	22

continued →

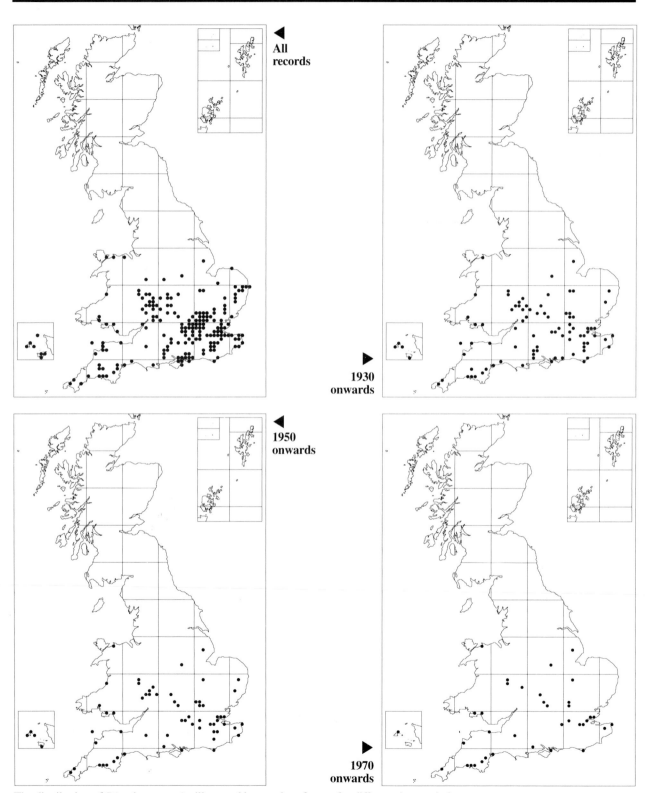

The distribution of *Dianthus armeria*, illustrated by a series of maps for different time periods.

Dianthus deltoides L.

Status: scarce

Maiden pink

Found in sandy grassland or heath and amongst detritus on rocky outcrops, *D. deltoides* favours sunny slopes on soils with some base content, such as those derived from Silurian sandstones, basalt, mica-schist, Carboniferous limestone or chalk. It usually grows in areas where the sward is broken by bare rock or bare soil. Although it occurs in species-rich grassland, it does not grow in close proximity to the more characteristic species such as *Helianthemum nummularium*, *Saxifraga granulata* and *Viola lutea* but rather with commoner species such as *Agrostis capillaris*, *Aira praecox*, *Dactylis glomerata*, *Festuca ovina*, *F. rubra*, *Galium verum*, *Plantago lanceolata*, *Thymus polytrichus* and *Ulex europaeus*. Colonies on Silurian rocks may be restricted to a particular stratum on which the flora is not otherwise notably different from the surroundings. In Derbyshire it occurs in fairly tall species-rich vegetation on metalliferous spoil. It is mostly confined to the lowlands, but occurs at 355 metres at Parsley Hay.

D. deltoides is a loosely tufted perennial reproducing by seed. Colonies typically consist of a mixture of long-established plants and young plants on the more open areas.

D. deltoides is now largely confined to small refugia whose fate is linked to the management of a wider area. It has suffered from over-grazing following partial re-seeding, from the total removal of grazing and from the conversion of its sites to conifer plantations. There are few large colonies.

Its range covers all Europe north to Norway, Finland and Russia, and temperate Asia. In Europe it is a somewhat continental species, being much less frequent in western Europe than it is further east (Jalas & Suominen 1986).

M. E. Braithwaite

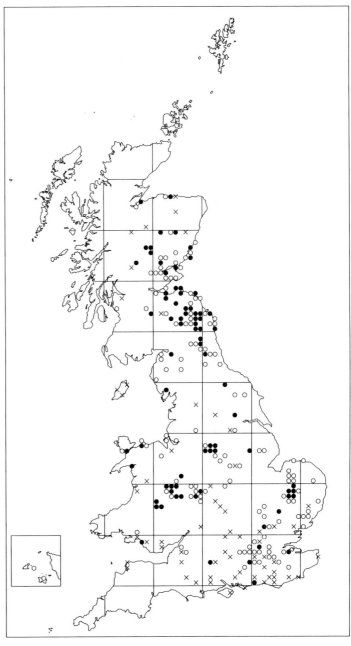

Current map	No	Atlas	No
1970 →	77	1930 →	58
Pre-1970	125	Pre-1930	72
Introductions	63	Introductions	36

Draba muralis L.

Status: scarce

Wall whitlowgrass

This overwintering annual has very similar Carboniferous limestone habitats to *Hornungia petraea*, with which it is occasionally associated. Other annual associates include *Arabidopsis thaliana*, *Arenaria serpyllifolia*, *Cardamine hirsuta*, *Erophila verna* and *Saxifraga tridactylites*. It is also found on stony ground, such as the edges of screes or quarry debris where there is enough soil to support it, sometimes in very open ash woodland; and, rarely, on north-facing slopes. However, it avoids the shallowest and driest soils. In its natural range the species shows no tendency to spread but it has frequently been recorded on forest roads and as a garden weed, principally on old walls where the summer-dry winter-moist conditions of its usual habitat are duplicated. Past spread can be traced to nurseries, and to botanic gardens. One possibly native site has recently been discovered on basalt in southern Scotland. It occurs mostly in the lowlands but up to 390 metres at Great Close Scar, Malham, and reported by Lees (1888) up to 490 metres elsewhere in the Craven Pennines.

Germination behaviour and subsequent growth and survival are closely similar to *Hornungia petraea*, and it shares the winter-hardiness of that species. Flowering starts in April or May and may continue until June or early July unless drought intervenes. Good seed set is ensured by self-pollination.

Populations seem to be stable, though none are large, and habitat destruction by excessive disturbance by trampling or grazing is the main, though unlikely, hazard. One site on the Staffordshire bank of the River Dove, where it was associated with *Hornungia petraea* on the edge of a small scree, has probably been lost by removal of the major part of the scree for footpath material.

It is widely distributed in suitable habitats in southern Scandinavia, and the eastern Baltic area and western central and southern Europe, extending to north west Africa, Asia Minor and southern Russia and the Caucasus.

For a more detailed account of the ecology of this species, see Ratcliffe (1960).

D. Ratcliffe

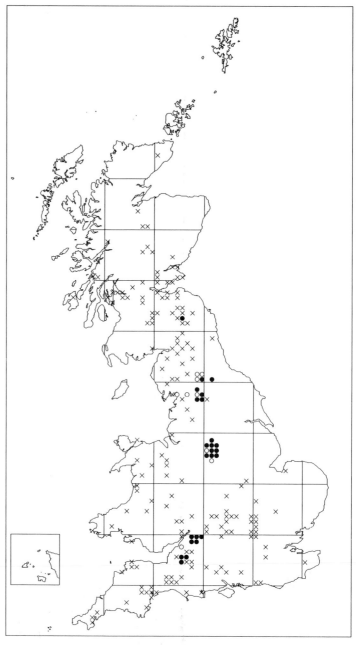

Current map	No	Atlas	No
1970 →	24		
Pre-1970	9	Native records	20
Introductions	166	Introductions	87

Draba norvegica Gunnerus

Rock whitlowgrass

Status: scarce

This is a rare, densely tufted plant of lime-rich rocks, where its preferred habitat is rock ledges and crevices of steep faces, consolidated scree and similar bare places. *D. norvegica* grows on calcareous mica-schists of the Dalradian and Moine series, hornblende schist, Lewisian gneiss and Old Red Sandstone. Frequent associates are *Alchemilla alpina, Carex atrata, C. capillaris, Cerastium alpinum, Festuca ovina, Minuartia sedoides, Poa alpina, Salix reticulata, Saxifraga nivalis, S. oppositifolia* and *Silene acaulis*, though it occurs in heterogeneous rock face communities rather than readily recognisable types. It is known from as low as 500 metres in Sutherland but is more frequently recorded at higher altitudes, reaches 1210 metres near the summit of Ben Lawers.

D. norvegica is a perennial, flowering in July. It is usually self-pollinated and sets abundant seed.

At present it appears to be under little threat, but collecting would certainly affect the mostly small populations. A number of new colonies have been discovered in Scotland in recent years, suggesting that it is probably under-recorded.

This is an arctic-subarctic species with a widespread distribution, occurring westwards to the Hudson Bay area of Canada and eastwards to northern Russia. In Scotland it is at its southern limit in Europe.

Scottish plants show little character variation, but elsewhere variability is appreciable. Plants similar to those from Scotland are known from various parts of Scandinavia, and have been described as a separate species, *D. rupestris*. It is more likely, however, that all are members of a widespread Arctic complex. Hybridisation with *D. incana* is thought to occur, and apparent intermediates grow in Strath Carron.

M. J. Y. Foley

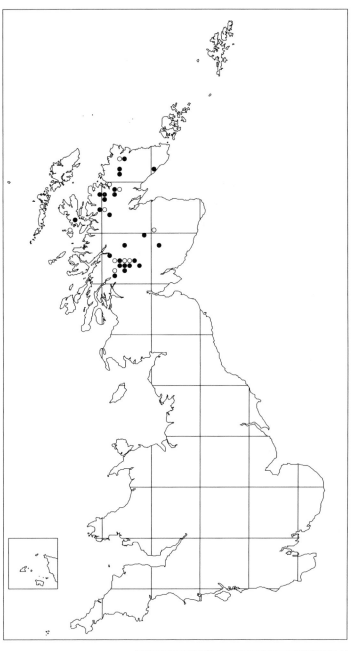

Current map	No	Atlas	No
1970 →	24	1930 →	12
Pre-1970	10	Pre-1930	6
Introductions	0	Introductions	0

Dryas octopetala L.

Mountain avens

Status: scarce

Dryas octopetala normally grows on basic rocks, usually where the soil is not too deep and drainage is very good. Sites tend to be relatively exposed. Commonly associated plants include *Carex flacca* and *Saxifraga oppositifolia*. In north-west Scotland it grows at unusually high densities, the densest sites being found at sea level on wind-blown shell sand where it forms a thick sward. At Invernaver it is a component of a *Juniperus communis* heath and is found growing amongst *Betula pubescens* woodland at Loch Cill Chriosd and at Loch Urigill. *D. octopetala* is found from sea level in the extreme north west of Scotland, as at Durness, to about 1035 metres on Ben Avon.

D. octopetala is a perennial plant flowering in June and July. Pollination is by insects. The seeds are wind dispersed and germinate best on eroded or bare sites. Few new sites have been recorded, indicating that seedling establishment does not occur readily although the plant is widely acknowledged as a colonising species. The plant is creeping in nature and can easily reproduce vegetatively.

The range of this species does not appear to be expanding or contracting significantly, though a number of potential pressures can be identified. One of the major threats to some sites is erosion caused by the large numbers of walkers or grazing stock. In many cases the biggest threat appears to be overgrazing by rabbits which are prolific at several sites.

D. octopetala sensu lato is a circumpolar arctic-alpine species. In Europe it is found in montane communities as far south as central Italy.

The characteristic leaves of *D. octopetala* are found in glacial and late glacial deposits in sites south of its current range in Britain, and elsewhere in north-west Europe (Godwin 1975). For a more detailed account of its present-day ecology, see Elkington (1971). As this plant does not seem to grow on wind-blown shell sand elsewhere in Europe, Scottish populations are internationally significant.

M. Currie

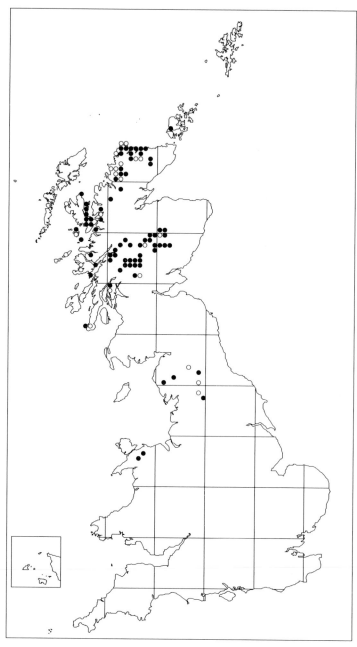

Current map	No	Atlas	No
1970 →	74	1930 →	57
Pre-1970	24	Pre-1930	8
Introductions	0	Introductions	0

Dryopteris submontana (Fraser-Jenkins & Jermy) Fraser-Jenkins

Status: scarce

Rigid buckler-fern

This fern grows on Carboniferous limestone pavement, rough screes and similar crevices from sea-level to 465 metres at Highfolds Scar, Malham. It is often associated with *Asplenium trichomanes-ramosum*, *Geranium robertianum*, *Gymnocarpium robertianum*, *Phyllitis scolopendrium* and *Sesleria caerulea*. It is a plant that needs shelter from winds if its full reproductive capacity is to be attained (Gilbert 1970). The records from Snowdonia, authenticated by herbarium specimens, are from Ordovician rocks with a high base content (Gilbert 1966).

D. submontana is a perennial species. Spores germinate readily on soil in crevices (Gilbert 1970), but in damper situations moss competition can prevent establishment of the sporophyte.

It is a common plant of the Great Scar limestone of northern England, provided it is well protected by grikes and deep crevices from over-grazing. A major threat is from limestone quarrying and the removal of limestone pavement. In its southern sites, both in the Pennines and Wales, it is more vulnerable to both sheep grazing and quarrying. It is probably due to grazing that it was lost from Snowdonia and Arran.

In Europe this species has a scattered distribution on limestone mountains from northern Spain to Rumania, and into Turkey and the Caucasus (Jalas & Suominen 1972). It is also found in Algeria. *D. submontana* is part of the southern European *D. pallida-D. villarii* complex and earlier European literature records are confusing due to name changes. All records in Britain refer to the tetraploid form now put under this name.

A. C. Jermy

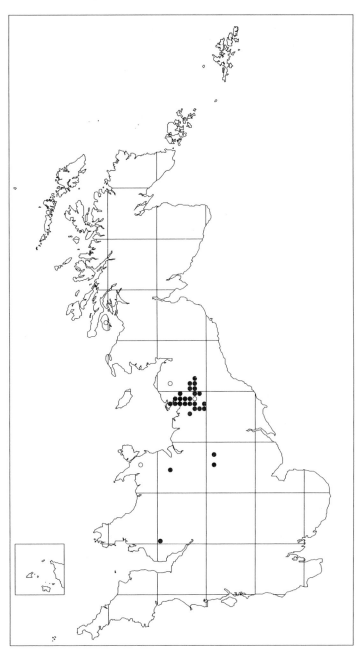

Current map	No	Atlas	No
1970 →	27	1930 →	14
Pre-1970	4	Pre-1930	3
Introductions	0	Introductions	0

continued →

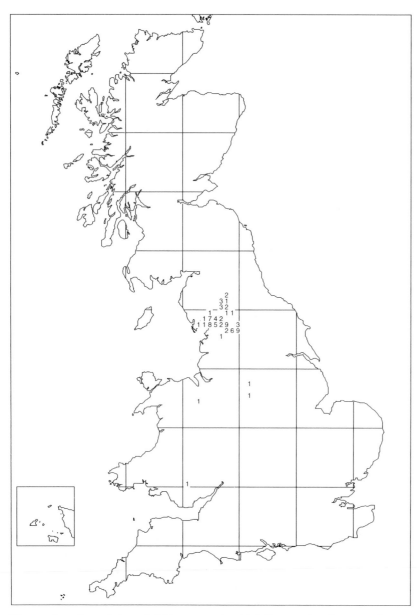

The number of tetrads in each 10 km square in which *Dryopteris submontana* has been recorded as a native species from 1970 onwards. Squares in which the species is recorded in 9 or more tetrads are plotted as 9: *D. submontana* is actually recorded from 9 tetrads in SD96 and 15 in SD77. The species has been found in a total of 85 tetrads from 1970 onwards.

Elatine hexandra (Lapierre) DC.

Status: scarce

Six-stamened waterwort

This is an aquatic plant, often behaving as an ephemeral on exposed, wet mud. Plants may persist in the vegetative state at depths of 1 metre or more, where, even if noticed, they may be misrecorded as young *Callitriche* spp. When exposed during summer droughts, *E. hexandra* can dominate substantial areas. It tolerates a wide range of nutrient conditions and substrata, preferring soft, sandy or peaty mud, but can occur on almost pure sand or even some types of fine gravel. Occasionally it can occur on peat at the edges of moorland lakes. It often occurs in moderately nutrient rich water and can even persist in shallow water at the edges of highly turbid eutrophic water bodies which receive substantial amounts of fertiliser run-off. A common associate of submerged plants is *Eleocharis acicularis*, and other associates in shallow water or on mud may include its rarer relative *E. hydropiper*, *Littorella uniflora* and *Subularia aquatica*. Peatier sites will normally have *Baldellia ranunculoides* and *Juncus bulbosus*. It grows predominantly in the lowlands, ascending to 425 metres at Llyn Gynon; a record from nearly 500 metres in the Scottish Highlands (Hooker 1884) has not been localised.

It is an annual to short-lived perennial, capable of flowering in shallow water but showing rapid germination, maturation, and abundant seed-set, on seasonally exposed mud. Limited vegetative spread is possible, but reproduction is apparently mainly by seed, with replenishment of the seed bank in drought years. Populations may fluctuate considerably from one year to the next.

Although suffering local loss of habitat and apparent decline in the south of its range, *E. hexandra* does not appear to be generally under threat. It is better known to botanists than in the past and is consequently being discovered at new sites. It is still apparently under-recorded.

It is widespread in Europe, extending north to southern Scandinavia, and also occurs in North and West Africa.

A. J. Silverside

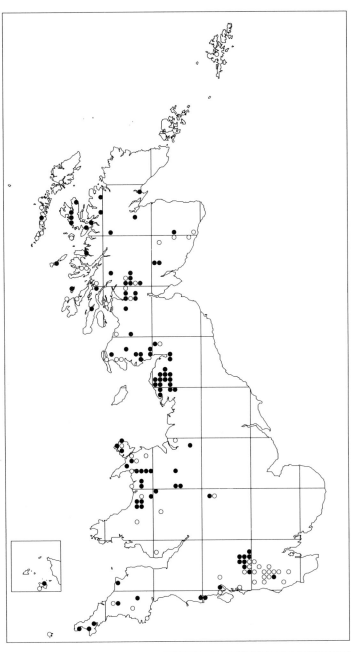

Current map	No	Atlas	No
1970 →	97	1930 →	38
Pre-1970	62	Pre-1930	44
Introductions	0	Introductions	0

Elatine hydropiper L.
Status: scarce

Eight-stamened waterwort

This aquatic plant colonises bare mud and silty sand above and below the water surface. In clear water, *E. hydropiper* can germinate in depths of up to 0.75 metres. When exposed or lightly covered by water, the compact plants root at every node, but in deeper water the elongated stems take on a straggly growth form as they reach upwards towards the light. It is restricted to a narrower range of trophic conditions than the closely related *E. hexandra*, having never been known to occur in the oligotrophic waters of Lakeland or the Scottish Highlands for example. The most frequently noted associates are *Callitriche hermaphroditica*, *C. stagnalis*, *E. hexandra*, *Eleocharis acicularis*, *Littorella uniflora* and *Lythrum portula*. It is confined to the lowlands.

E. hydropiper is a self-fertilising annual, although there seems no reason why cross-pollination by insects visiting open flowers should not take place. Prolific seed production occurs in exposed plants. Long range dispersal is almost certainly assisted by seeds becoming embedded in mud adhering to water fowl. Buried seeds may remain dormant in the mud for many years, until stimulated by increased light intensity brought about by abnormally low water levels during the summer months.

Population trends in Britain are difficult to assess, as the species has more than once been reported to have been lost from a locality, only to reappear in abundance when conditions for germination became more favourable. Nevertheless, its recent retraction of range in England and expansion in Central Scotland is undoubtedly real. The principal threat is from excessive eutrophication of the habitat, particularly from agricultural fertilisers, transforming the water bodies' firm substrate into a soft ooze. Premature die-back and eventual loss of one well-established and large colony on drying-out mud was suggestive of some form of metal ion toxicity.

It is found in northern and central Europe, only locally extending east and south, and in North America.

E. hydropiper grows in brackish water in some north European countries, but it has not been found in this habitat in Britain.

J. Mitchell

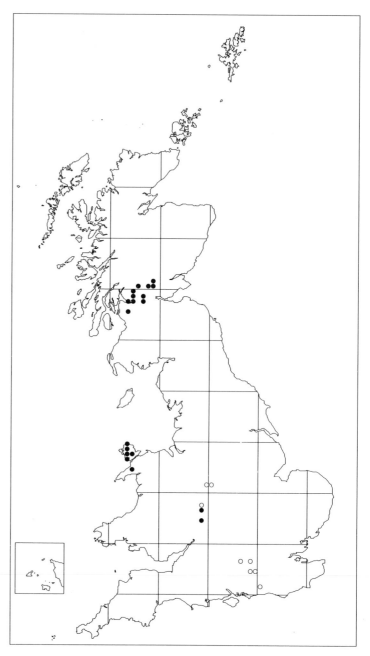

Current map	No	Atlas	No
1970 →	19	1930 →	4
Pre-1970	8	Pre-1930	5
Introductions	0	Introductions	0

continued →

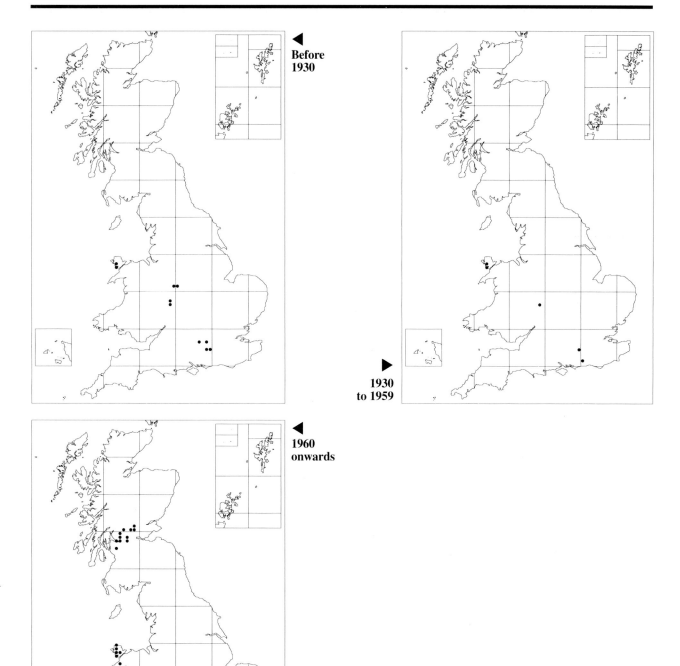

The distribution of *Elatine hydropiper*, illustrated by a series of maps for different time periods.

continued →

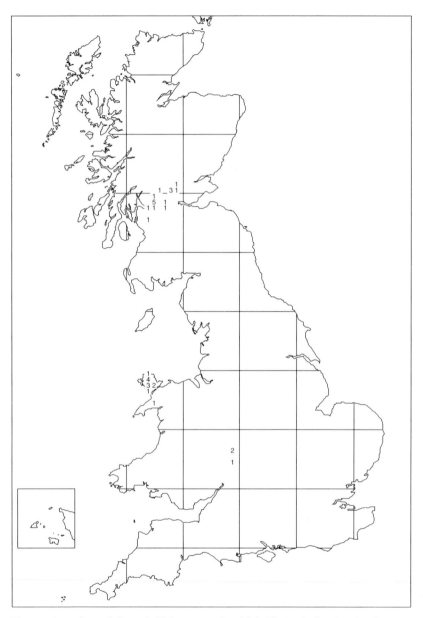

The number of tetrads in each 10 km square in which *Elatine hydropiper* has been recorded as a native since 1970. The species has been found in a total of 32 tetrads from 1970 onwards.

Eleocharis acicularis (L.) Roemer & Schultes

Needle spike-rush

Status: not scarce

E. acicularis can grow both as a terrestrial species and as a submerged aquatic. As an aquatic it is found in shallow, eutrophic water (usually less than 50 cm deep) in sheltered lakes and reservoirs, the still backwaters of rivers, slow-flowing streams, canals, fenland lodes and ditches and flooded sand or gravel pits. It is more frequently found growing on damp silt, sandy soil or sandy shingle at the edge of such water bodies, in areas which are flooded in winter but not in summer, and it occasionally occurs in abundance on mud dredged from them or on the beds of newly drained reservoirs. Although terrestrial plants are often present in pure stands, they can be accompanied by such species as *Chenopodium rubrum*, *Gnaphalium uliginosum*, *Juncus bufonius*, *Persicaria* spp. and *Rorippa palustris*. *E. acicularis* is a predominantly lowland species, ascending to 365 metres at Loch Kinardochy.

This plant is a perennial with a slender rhizome. Submerged plants do not normally flower, but terrestrial plants flower and fruit freely. Little is known of its germination requirements. As with many species of seasonally flooded habitats, populations vary in size from year to year and flowering plants are often particularly abundant in seasons when water levels are low. The seeds may be dispersed by birds. This species can be purchased in garden centres but there is no evidence to suggest that such plants have been introduced into the wild.

Aquatic plants of *E. acicularis* are often overlooked and even terrestrial individuals are inconspicuous unless present in quantity. This species therefore tends to be under-recorded. The apparent decline shown by the map resembles that of *Limosella aquatica*, and is unlikely to be completely attributable to under-recording. *E. acicularis* has become extinct in some canals and has probably suffered from the fact that many small ponds have become overgrown, have completely dried out or have been engulfed by urban sprawl.

It is widespread in Europe, although absent from the far north and rare in the Mediterranean area. It also occurs in North Africa, northern Asia, and North and South America. It has been reported from Australia by numerous authorities but not by Aston (1973).

C. D. Preston

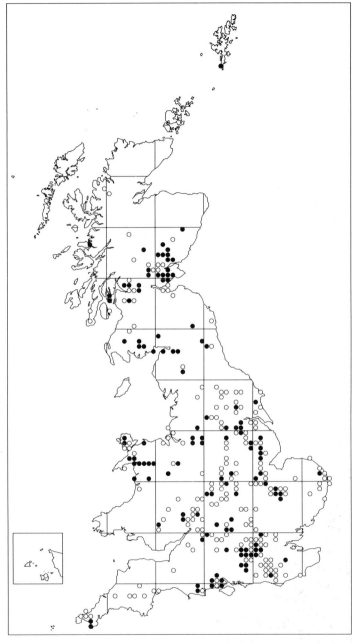

Current map	No	Atlas	No
1970 →	123	1930 →	86
Pre-1970	190	Pre-1930	114
Introductions	0	Introductions	0

Epilobium alsinifolium Villars
Status: not scarce

Chickweed willowherb

This is a plant of hillside springs, usually occurring in closed communities with a high bryophyte cover. In the Lake District and northern Pennines these springs may be rather base-poor, associated species being *Cardamine pratensis, Cerastium fontanum, Cochlearia pyrenaica, Montia fontana, Ranunculus omiophyllus, Saxifraga stellaris, Stellaria uliginosa, Dicranella palustris, Philonotis fontana, Pohlia* spp. and *Scapania undulata*. Interesting associates locally are *Cardamine amara* (Corner 1990) and *Myosotis stolonifera*. Over more calcareous rock, as locally in the northern Pennines and particularly in central and north-west Scotland, the spring communities are more species-rich and characterised by *Carex nigra, C. panicea, Festuca rubra, Saxifraga aizoides, Cratoneuron commutatum* and *C. filicinum*. It may also occur, though rarely, in semi-open calcareous, stony flushes which are often found below the spring vegetation. Other habitats are on irrigated rock ledges and by mountain streamsides, especially in steep, shaded gullies, where the mass of willowherb stolons are usually rooted in bryophyte cushions. It occurs up to 1140 metres in Glen Coe and descends to 120 metres on Eigg and 150 metres in the Lune Gorge.

This is a perennial herb which is probably self-pollinated. It spreads by stolons.

Plants in the more open accessible sites suffer from grazing and this may have resulted in the disappearance of the species from some of its more peripheral montane localities.

Its world distribution extends through the mountains of northern and central Europe, with outlying stations in southern Spain and Greece and single localities in west Greenland and north-west Ireland.

R. W. M. Corner & G. Halliday

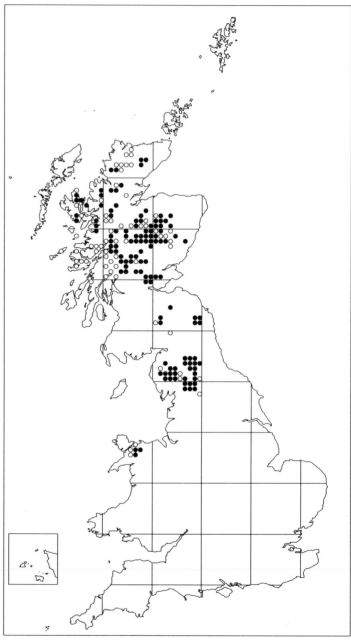

Current map	No	Atlas	No
1970 →	123	1930 →	83
Pre-1970	65	Pre-1930	11
Introductions	0	Introductions	0

Epilobium lanceolatum Sebast. and Mauri

Spear-leaved willowherb

Status: not scarce

E. lanceolatum grows in a wide range of disturbed sites where the vegetation cover is open and competition is low. It is found on sand dunes, open banks, walls and quarries and as a garden weed, typically in drier habitats than most *Epilobium* species. In Europe, it is typical of screes of siliceous rocks in a habitat mimicked in Britain by the loose granitic ballast and cinder along railway lines. A typical associate in central Europe and in the artificial British habitat is *Senecio viscosus*. Although primarily a lowland plant, *E. lanceolatum* reaches over 400 metres on Dartmoor.

E. lanceolatum is a perennial, reproducing both by wind-borne seeds and vegetatively in late autumn by above-ground stolons that terminate in leaf-rosettes.

The trends in its distribution are difficult to establish, due to apparent confusion with other willowherbs. There is some suggestion of a decline in England but new records on the rail network and as a garden weed in Wales and the Midlands partly offset this trend. The numerous pre-1970 records from Devon were extracted from Ivimey-Cook (1984); there has been no recent survey of this species in the county.

E. lanceolatum is found in west and southern Europe (from Britain, France and Belgium to the Balkans) and around the Mediterranean including North Africa and the Near East, as far east as the Caucasus mountains.

J. O. Mountford

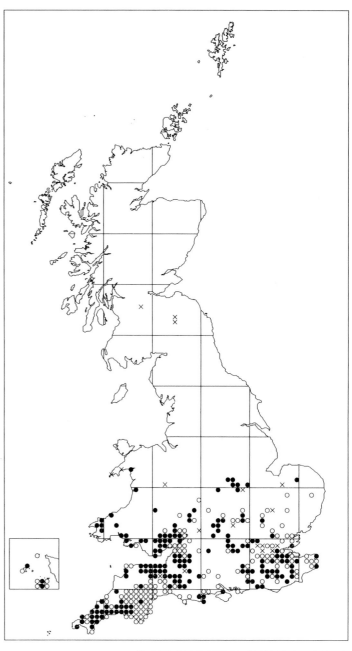

Current map	No	Atlas	No
1970 →	166	1930 →	102
Pre-1970	132	Pre-1930	14
Introductions	18	Introductions	0

Epipactis atrorubens (Hoffm.) Besser

Status: scarce

Dark-red helleborine

E. atrorubens is confined to limestone, growing on Carboniferous and magnesian limestone in Wales and northern England and the Durness and Dalradian limestones of Scotland. Its habitat ranges from exposed, bare scree to well-wooded pavement with moderate shade, but it favours wide, shallow grikes, filled with small, broken scree in thinly wooded situations. On the Great Orme it is mostly restricted to narrow ledges on cliff faces. Typical associated species include *Carex flacca*, *Corylus avellana*, *Fraxinus excelsior*, *Teucrium scorodonia* and *Sesleria caerulea*. Most English and all Welsh sites are below 270 metres, but it occurs at 400 metres in eastern Cumbria and at over 500 metres on Cronkley Fell. It ranges from near sea-level on the north coast of Scotland to 610 metres in Glen Beg.

It is a perennial reproducing by seed. Many populations are characterised by small numbers of plants and by non-flowering individuals. The largest populations are on the Magnesian limestone of Durham, where one site may well contain more plants (c. 2000) than all the remaining British localities. It can flower prolifically.

Damage by deer and rabbits reduces its reproductive capacity and quarrying sometimes poses a threat to populations.

It is found in Europe, northwards to Arctic Scandinavia and is frequent in some areas (e.g. Switzerland). It extends east to Central Asia.

R. Wilson

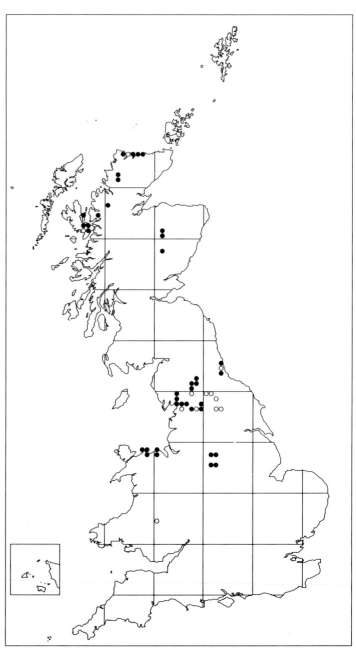

Current map	No	Atlas	No
1970 →	38	1930 →	28
Pre-1970	12	Pre-1930	7
Introductions	0	Introductions	0

continued →

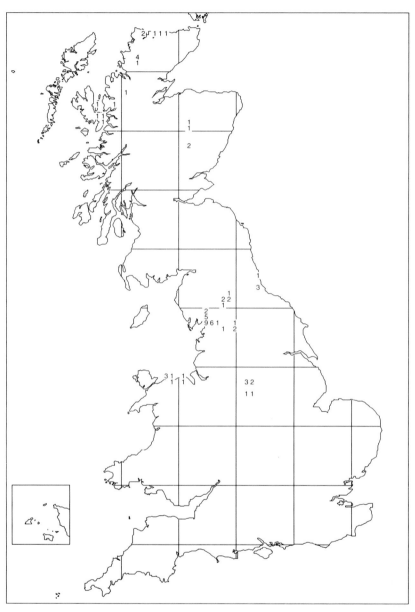

The number of tetrads in each 10 km square in which *Epipactis atrorubens* has been recorded as a native species from 1970 onwards. Squares in which the species is recorded in 9 or more tetrads are plotted as 9: *E. atrorubens* is actually recorded from 10 tetrads in SD47. The species has been found in a total of 72 tetrads from 1970 onwards.

Epipactis leptochila (Godfery) Godfery

Narrow-lipped helleborine

Status: scarce

In Britain it is found in three very distinct lowland habitats: in the south, on decomposed litter in woods, especially beechwoods, on calcareous substrates in deep shade with a very sparse ground cover; inland in the north under birch on well-drained stony substrates kept open through such diverse influences as the presence of lead and zinc tailings (Richards & Swan 1976), old aerodrome runways, and coal spoil; and on the edges of dune-slacks and the stabilised sides of sandhills, usually growing amongst *Salix repens*.

This plant is a long-lived perennial which takes at least four years to flower from seed and then appears above ground irregularly. It is self-fertile, and automatically self-pollinating. However, the flowers are sometimes visited by wasps and cross-pollination of the disintegrating pollinia can occur (Richards 1986). Each capsule forms 1000-2000 tiny wind-blown seeds which develop by mycorrhizal association.

The apparent size of colonies varies dramatically from year to year, but dormant (subterranean) population sizes may be more stable and much greater, as can sometimes be demonstrated by the rapid reappearance of *E. leptochila* following scrub clearance. Light levels appear to be critical. It is intolerant of direct sunlight in the south, but in the north it fails to flower and then disappears from temporarily disturbed sites as shade increases with seral development. Dune populations are very sensitive to levels of grazing: large rabbit populations bite off all the flowering stems, but if rabbit populations are too low, the plants cannot compete with the surrounding vegetation.

On the continent, the *E. leptochila* complex is distributed from Belgium and central France through the Alps to Hungary and northern Greece. It is doubtful whether *E. muelleri, E. albensis, E. bugacensis, E. olympica* or *E. danubialis* are specifically distinct.

British dune populations, previously known as *E. dunensis*, have a short recurved epichile, but are identical to some plants occurring inland in northern England in populations where other individuals closely resemble southern *E. leptochila* with longer straight epichiles. Some southern beechwood populations, previously known as *E. cleistogama* and *E. leptochila* var. *cordata*, are very similar to *E. dunensis*, as are French populations of *E. muelleri*. All these taxa, with a short recurved epichile, are best treated as *E. leptochila* var. *dunensis*.

A. J. Richards

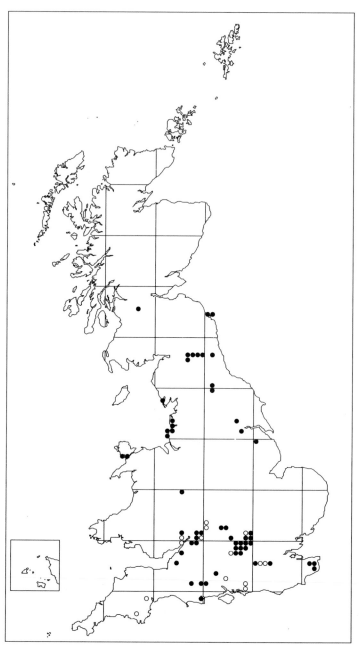

Current map	No	Atlas	No
1970 →	56	1930 →	24
Pre-1970	14	Pre-1930	6
Introductions	0	Introductions	0

Epipactis phyllanthes G. E. Sm.

Status: scarce

Green-flowered helleborine

This plant is found in a variety of rather bare, dry, shaded sites under trees on well-drained, usually somewhat acidic, soils with a relatively low humus content. It is frequently associated with *Pyrola minor*. Typical sites include beechwoods on flint capping, or on sandstone, Scots pine/birch scrub on Bagshot Sands, hazel coppice on sandy alluvium, pine plantations on sand-dunes and on sand-dunes themselves. It can also be found in riverside *Salix* scrub, where it tolerates occasional flooding. It is confined to the lowlands.

E. phyllanthes is a completely autogamous perennial; indeed in some populations the flowers are partially (var. *vectensis*) or more or less completely (var. *degenera*, var. *phyllanthes*) cleistogamous. Well-developed individuals are rarely encountered, apparently because of drought stress.

Above-ground populations fluctuate markedly in size, and *E. phyllanthes* disappears from well-known sites and appears in totally new areas in a most unpredictable manner. Site occupancy seems rarely to exceed 30 years. In recent years it has become noticeably less widespread in central southern England, but has been recorded in several new sites in the north. One of these, in which a few individuals were first recorded in 1974 (Richards & Swan 1976), now probably holds the largest regular population in the country, with more than 100 spikes annually. The apparent irrationality in its choice of site, and its absence from most apparently suitable areas in districts where it does occur, makes it difficult to prepare a coherent conservation strategy for this species.

It is recorded from southern Sweden, Denmark and northern Germany (usually as *E. confusa*, which cannot be clearly separated), and from France as far south as the Pyrenees and the western Alps. *E. nordeniorum* from Austria is also very closely related (although with puberulent stems), while plants apparently identical to *E. phyllanthes* occur in the Prin, south Bulgaria. The distribution of this species east of the Alps is not yet well understood, and may include at least some populations known as *E. persica*.

E. phyllanthes represents a series of local autogamous populations which individually tend to be uniform, but which vary greatly between populations.

A. J. Richards

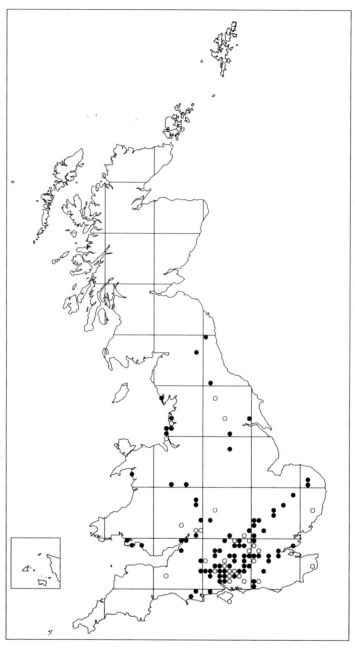

Current map	No	Atlas	No
1970 →	85	1930 →	54
Pre-1970	30	Pre-1930	13
Introductions	0	Introductions	0

Equisetum pratense Ehrh.

Status: scarce

Shade horsetail

A plant of often sloping, and thus well-drained, sites, on alluvial silt or similar sandy soils. It requires a fairly high base content in the soil and develops best in shady situations where calcium- or magnesium-rich water flushes the site, where it often grows with *Crepis paludosa*, *Galium odoratum*, *Melica nutans* and *Trollius europaeus*. In areas of higher rainfall it can become a moorland plant on micaceous schistose soils, but it is then often small in stature. It ranges from sea-level in the Hebrides to 850 metres on Sgorr Dhearg in Glen Coe.

E. pratense is a rhizomatous perennial. According to Page (1982), cone production is extremely poor and spasmodic in most British populations, a fact that he relates to the general trend for milder winters. The species is, however, persistent in the vegetative state.

Most of the sites known a century or more ago are still extant. It appears that many of the pre-1970 records are moorland sites where *E. sylvaticum* may have been erroneously recorded as *E. pratense* in the past or where *E. pratense* may have been overlooked in recent years.

E. pratense is an arctic-alpine species. It is common in Iceland and Scandinavia, and extends south to the Alps and Romania; central and northern Asia and the Caucasus. Its European distribution is mapped by Jalas & Suominen (1972). In North America it is found from Alaska to Nova Scotia, and south to New York, Michigan and South Dakota.

A. C. Jermy

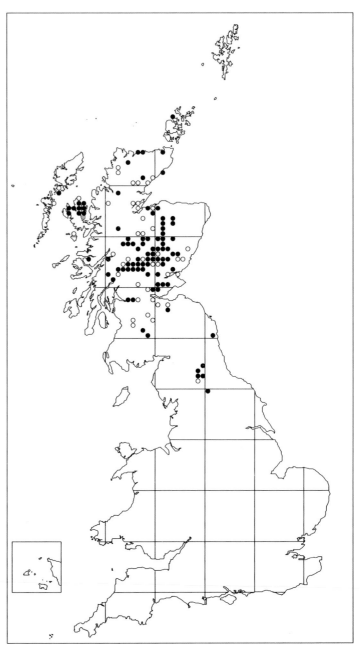

Current map	No	Atlas	No
1970 →	89	1930 →	32
Pre-1970	43	Pre-1930	21
Introductions	0	Introductions	0

Equisetum variegatum Schleicher

Status: scarce

Variegated horsetail

This is a plant of a wide variety of open habitats, ranging from sand dune slacks at sea-level to mountain ledges. The species frequently dominates the lowest and most frequently flooded areas of dune slacks. At middle altitudes it can be found on river gravels and in many upland sites it is associated with flushes and calcareous springs. All sites are base-rich to some extent, and characteristic associates include *Carex capillaris*, *C. flacca*, *C. viridula* subsp. *brachyrryncha*, *Saxifraga aizoides*, *Selaginella selaginoides*, *Cratoneuron commutatum*, *Ctenidium molluscum*, *Philonotis calcarea* and *Scorpidium scorpioides*. It ascends to at least 1040 metres on Ben Lawers.

Established plants spread by rhizomes. Populations in all sites produce cones readily and gametophytes could presumably colonise nearby open habitats.

There is little evidence of a decline and it is probably still present in many of the upland 10 km squares for which only pre-1970 records are available.

This is a northern montane species, scarce or scattered in the Baltic basin but frequent in the Pyrenees and the central European mountains (Jalas & Suominen 1972). It is found in mountainous areas across Asia to northern Japan, and through northern North America south to Pennsylvania and in the Rockies to Colorado.

E. variegatum is variable morphologically as well as physio-ecologically and both coastal populations and those of mountain streamsides and ledges should be conserved.

A. C. Jermy

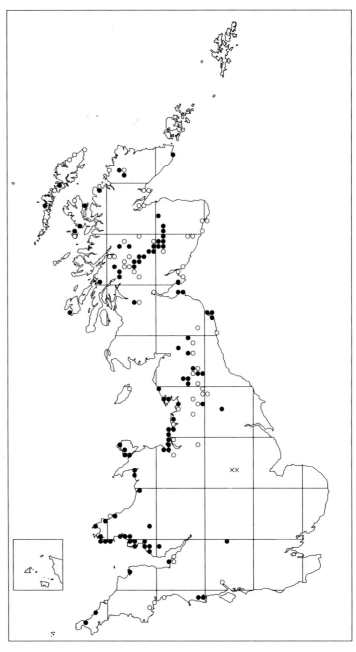

Current map	No	Atlas	No
1970 →	95	1930 →	71
Pre-1970	61	Pre-1930	23
Introductions	2	Introductions	0

Erodium maritimum (L.) L'Hér.

Status: not scarce

Sea stork's-bill

E. maritimum grows in a wide variety of open coastal sites where competition is reduced by drought, fire, trampling or other disturbances. Characteristic habitats include dry, rocky cliff ledges and coastal banks, short rabbit- or sheep-grazed turf, disturbed sand dunes, trampled paths and view points, burnt heath and gull-infested cliff tops. Like many ruderals, *E. maritimum* can take advantage of high nutrient levels and plants in such sites are much larger than those in less eutrophic localities. In trampled or closely-grazed localities *E. maritimum* is prostrate (and often grows with small rosette-forming species such as *Leontodon saxatilis* and *Plantago coronopus*) but in short coastal scrub its stems can be scrambling and almost erect. Inland habitats for this species include sandy tracks and disturbed grassland associated with gravel workings in Dorset and short, trampled turf over Carboniferous limestone in the Mendips; it formerly also grew inland in sand pits and other open sandy habitats on heaths.

E. maritimum is an annual, usually germinating in late summer or autumn. Plants may flower as early as March, and usually continue flowering until they succumb to summer drought. In wet summers populations can be found with all age classes from seedlings to fruiting plants. The flowers often lack petals and are probably self-pollinating; they usually set a full complement of viable fruit. Populations vary in size depending on the amount of open habitat available and are often large in the season following a hot summer.

There is no indication that *E. maritimum* has declined in coastal localities in the period for which we have botanical records. In the longer timescale it has probably been favoured by human disturbance, and has doubtless spread from native habitats such as cliff ledges and gull colonies into habitats opened up by human activity.

In Europe *E. maritimum* is found in the western Mediterranean countries, and along the Atlantic coast from Spain and France to Britain and Ireland. It is at its northern world limit in Scotland. Outside Europe it is known only from Tenerife and Tunisia.

C. D. Preston

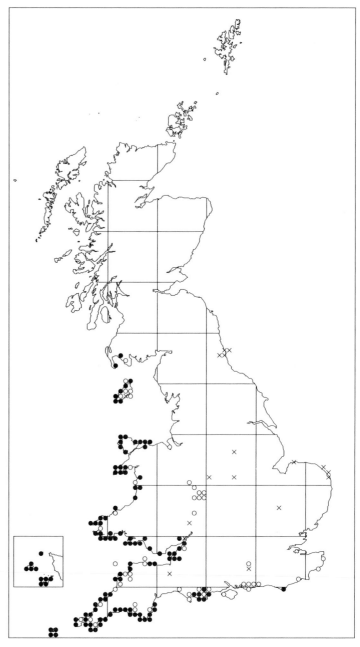

Current map	No	Atlas	No
1970 →	108	1930 →	72
Pre-1970	51	Pre-1930	27
Introductions	17	Introductions	6

Erodium moschatum (L.) L'Hér.

Status: scarce

Musk stork's-bill

This species only occasionally occurs in semi-natural habitats in Britain. In the Mendips it grows with other annuals on shallow soils over Carboniferous limestone, and elsewhere in south-west England it can be found in open, drought-prone coastal grassland on thin, often sandy soils and rarely, on coastal rock outcrops. Most of the persistent populations, however, grow in ruderal habitats near the sea, and are typically found on roadside banks and verges, pathsides, the sides and tops of Cornish 'hedges', trampled turf and waste ground. *Medicago arabica*, another coastal ruderal, is a frequent associate, as is *E. cicutarium* where the soil is sandy. In the Isles of Scilly, *E. moschatum* is a weed of bulb and potato fields, growing with species such as *Ranunculus muricatus* and *R. parviflorus*. It is often found as a casual inland, presumably originating from foreign seed, and it was regularly introduced with wool shoddy. It is confined to the lowlands.

Seeds of *E. moschatum* germinate in autumn, and in a mild season plants begin to flower in February. If conditions are favourable they continue flowering until October, the plants becoming larger and coarser as the year advances. Although basically an annual, autumn-flowering plants sometimes persist through the winter to flower again the following spring. Viable fruit is produced by almost all flowers. Populations tend to be small but many of them are surprisingly persistent.

The ruderal habitat of *E. moschatum* makes it difficult to assess changes in its distribution or abundance, but there is no evidence of marked changes in either. Populations in some semi-natural grasslands may be at risk from scrub encroachment following the cessation of grazing.

E. moschatum is widespread in southern and western Europe, and occurs throughout the Mediterranean region. It is also known as an alien in South Africa, North and South America, Australia and New Zealand.

Although this plant is described as native (Clapham, Tutin and Warburg 1962; Kent 1992; Stace 1991), it may be a long-established alien. It was formerly cultivated as a pot herb for 'the sweete smell that the whole plant is possessed with' (Gerarde 1597), although the scent now seems barely detectable. Populations in semi-natural habitats may have originated from cultivated plants.

C.D. Preston

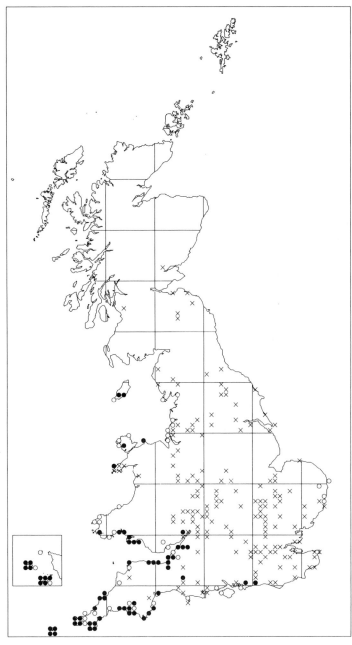

Current map	No	Atlas	No
1970 →	54	1930 →	31
Pre-1970	39	Pre-1930	20
Introductions	162	Introductions	96

Euphorbia paralias L.

Status: not scarce

Sea spurge

This species is most characteristic of free-draining mobile or semi-stable sand dunes and may also be found along the drift line on sandy foreshores. It is often associated on foreshores with such species as *Cakile maritima* and *Salsola kali*. At Chesil Beach the sole remaining Dorset colony is on coarse shingle, where it is accompanied by *Crithmum maritimum*. It is a perennial with many adaptations to drought conditions. This species is a good stress tolerator but not a good competitor.

E. paralias is a deep rooted perennial which reproduces by seed.

This species shows little evidence of decline nationally, although locally it has retreated from excessively disturbed dune systems.

E. paralias is found along the coast of western and southern Europe from the Netherlands to Romania. It is also found in Morocco and the Canaries.

E. paralias has a similar distribution to *E. portlandica* and they are often found together. A partially sterile hybrid between *E. paralias* and *E. portlandica* which is morphologically intermediate between the parents has been recorded at several Welsh localities on fixed dunes and sandy or gravelly banks (Stace 1975).

H. Ainsworth

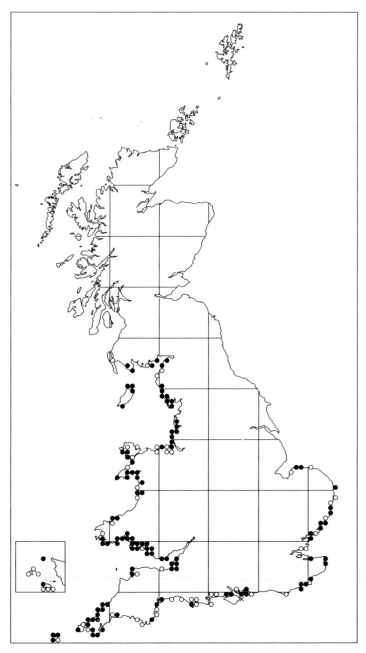

Current map	No	Atlas	No
1970 →	112	1930 →	89
Pre-1970	47	Pre-1930	12
Introductions	1	Introductions	0

Euphorbia platyphyllos L.

Broad-leaved spurge

Status: scarce

This is a plant of cultivated and waste land, usually found on calcareous clay but also on lighter chalky soils. It is generally encountered on the field margins, often growing in small numbers in places where crop density is reduced and which have been missed by herbicide sprays. It rarely occurs on ruderal sites such as roadsides. It is often found with other uncommon weeds such as *Euphorbia exigua, Kickxia elatine, K. spuria, Ranunculus arvensis, Scandix pecten-veneris, Valerianella dentata* and *V. rimosa*.

An annual, this spurge germinates in spring and autumn. Its seed is thought to possess considerable longevity in the soil seed bank.

Once locally common in southern England, from Somerset to Kent and Norfolk, it has now virtually disappeared from most of East Anglia and is of reduced incidence in most of its former range. This decline is primarily due to the effects of modern herbicides. It is now most frequent on the clays of Somerset and Surrey. Although there are records from 108 10 km squares from 1970 onwards, this declining species is classified as scarce as it has been recorded in only 74 10 km squares from 1980 onwards.

It appears to be declining in north-west Europe, being better adapted to the warmer, and less-intensively farmed, countries of southern Europe.

A. Smith

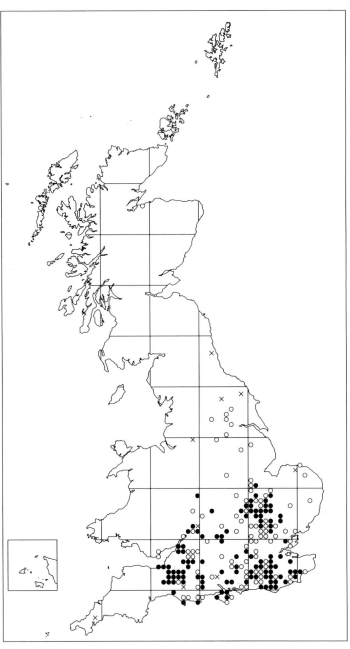

Current map	No	Atlas	No
1970 →	108	1930 →	42
Pre-1970	93	Pre-1930	36
Introductions	10	Introductions	2

continued →

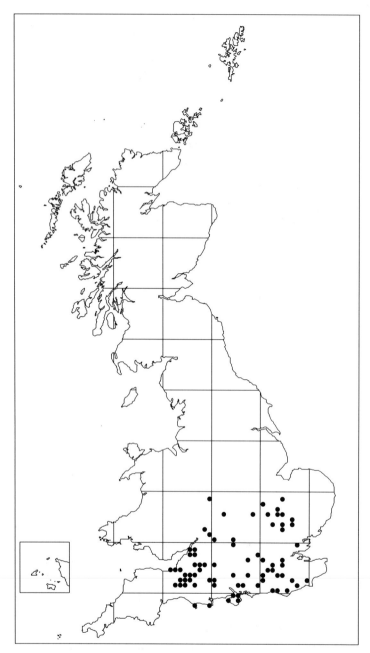

The distribution of *Euphorbia platyphyllos* from 1980 to 1992.

Euphorbia portlandica L.
Status: scarce

Portland spurge

This species is found in a variety of coastal habitats. It frequently occurs on cliffs, rocky slopes and steep maritime grasslands over a wide range of rocks from chalk and limestone to granite. In coastal grasslands frequent associates include *Dactylis glomerata*, *Daucus carota*, *Festuca rubra*, *Holcus lanatus*, *Jasione montana*, *Plantago maritima* and *Scilla verna*; on some calcareous cliffs it can also be found with several nationally rare or scarce species including *Helianthemum apenninum*, *Scilla autumnalis* and *Trinia glauca*. It also occurs on shingle, and on sheltered or semi-fixed sand-dunes in vegetation dominated by *Ammophila arenaria*, *Festuca rubra* or a mixture of the two. Unlike *E. paralias*, it is not usually found on the most exposed and mobile dune systems.

E. portlandica is a biennial or short-lived perennial, flowering from April or May to September. It presumably germinates in the spring. Reproduction is entirely by seed.

The distribution of *E. portlandica* in Britain has probably changed very little during the present century. However, there may have been a slight contraction of range with its disappearance from several localities in north-western England and southern Scotland. Paradoxically, on the north coast of the Isle of Man *E. portlandica* is thought to be a recent arrival, having been unrecorded there until 1939 (Allen 1984).

The species is found along the coasts of western Europe from Portugal to France, Britain and Ireland. It is at its northern limit in the British Isles.

S. J. Leach

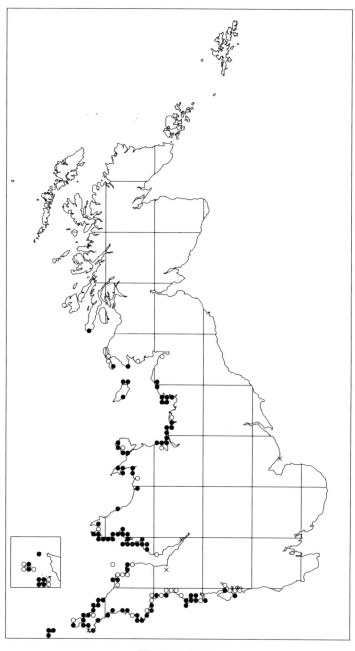

Current map	No	Atlas	No
1970 →	94	1930 →	70
Pre-1970	33	Pre-1930	10
Introductions	4	Introductions	0

Euphrasia foulaensis F. Towns. ex Wettst.

Status: scarce

This is the characteristic *Euphrasia* of damp turf on northern Scottish cliff-tops. It is also frequent at the tops of saltmarshes. Grazing, normally by sheep or rabbits, appears to be essential in these sites. *E. foulaensis* seems unable to survive in ranker turf, though it can also occur in thin, ungrazed turf on coastal rocks. Cliff-top sites are invariably within the range of blown sea-spray. It is typically absent from the *Plantago maritima-P. coronopus* community that occupies the tips of exposed headlands, but in the slightly more sheltered conditions at the landward edges of such sites *E. foulaensis* often occurs in considerable abundance. *Primula scotica* is a notable associate at a few sites, when there is some slight basic flushing, and, in very few localities, authentic *E. rotundifolia* also occurs. It is confined to the lowlands.

E. foulaensis is a hemiparasitic annual, presumably germinating in spring and attaching to a suitable host when root contact is first made. No information is available on host plants, but it is unlikely to be host specific. Individual plants begin to flower from mid-summer onwards and populations set seed over a long period.

While many sites may be lost locally through agricultural improvement or cessation of grazing, the plant is so abundant within its range that it is not subject to any currently foreseeable threat. Lack of post 1970 records from some 10 km squares almost certainly reflects the lack of recent critical recording.

Outside Britain, *E. foulaensis* occurs only in the Faeroes, where, however, it is local and often taxonomically rather ill-defined. Populations rarely show any substantial degree of hybridisation, though, when they occur, hybrids can form locally uniform and distinctive populations, leading to incipient speciation.

A. J. Silverside

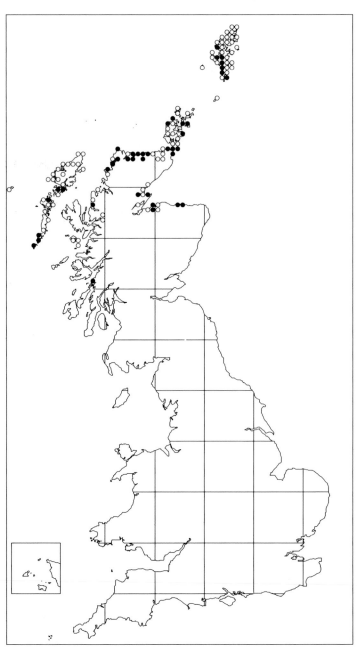

Current map	No	Atlas (S)	No
1970 →	41		
Pre-1970	81		
Introductions	0	All records	72

Euphrasia frigida Pugsley
Status: scarce

This is a strictly montane species, occurring on damp to wet, usually rather basic, ledges. It occurs with a variety of other arctic and arctic-alpine species, *Oxyria digyna* and *Rhinanthus minor* subsp. *borealis* perhaps being particularly frequent associates. In such habitats it is usually the only *Euphrasia* species present, but on wet ground below alpine cliffs or along streamsides, it commonly forms extensive hybrid populations involving *E. scottica*. It occurs at 200 metres on Foula, but is usually found above 400 metres and ascends to 1100 metres on Am Binnein.

E. frigida is a hemiparasitic annual, presumably germinating in late spring and attaching to a suitable host when root contact is first made. No information is available on host plants, but it is unlikely to be host specific. Small individuals commonly occur in bare soil or thin, wet moss mats, in the apparent absence of other vascular plants and apparently not host-established. Such plants nevertheless normally mature one or more capsules. Plants may produce their first flowers as low as the second node, presumably increasing the chance of successful seed-set in difficult climatic conditions and allowing efficient allocation of resources in individuals lacking hosts.

This is one of the better-known species of the genus and there appears to be no evidence of population change, nor of any serious foreseeable threat. Lack of post-1970 records from some 10 km squares almost certainly reflects the lack of recent critical recording.

E. frigida is a circumpolar, boreal and arctic species, its distribution including Greenland, northern Europe (south to Belgium and Czechoslovakia), Russia and North America.

A. J. Silverside

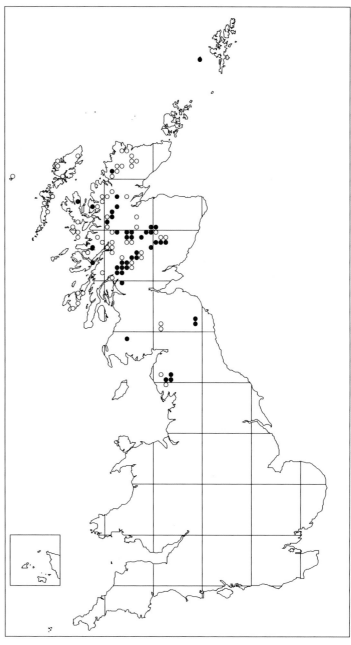

Current map	No	Atlas (S)	No
1970 →	42		
Pre-1970	59		
Introductions	0	All records	66

163

Euphrasia marshallii Pugsley
Status: rare?

This is a strictly coastal plant of rocks and eroding sea-cliff edges, often on moderately basic sites, with such species as *Carex capillaris*, *Coeloglossum viride*, *Gentianella amarella* subsp. *septentrionalis*, *Gentianella campestris*, *Oxytropis halleri* and *Scilla verna*. However, the most characteristic plants are found in rather leached or less basic sites below maritime *Calluna-Empetrum* heath, with *Festuca rubra*, *Plantago* spp. and *Thymus polytrichus*. It occupies equivalent habitats to *E. ostenfeldii* further north and *E. tetraquetra* to the south, growing and hybridising with the latter species on Skye. It is confined to the lowlands.

E. marshallii is a hemiparasitic annual, presumably germinating in spring and attaching to a suitable host when root contact is first made. No information is available on host plants, but it is unlikely to be host specific. It commonly occurs in very close association with *Plantago maritima* and it has also been observed growing with *P. lanceolata* in the apparent absence of other vascular plants, *P. lanceolata* being a generally suitable host for *Euphrasia* spp. in cultivation.

Taxonomic confusion with other hairy taxa and lack of detailed monitoring make it difficult to assess any changes in distribution. The majority of past records from Orkney and Shetland are suspect, especially those made as "*E. marshallii* var. *pygmaea*", which are mostly referable to *E. foulaensis* × *ostenfeldii* or to *E. ostenfeldii* itself. *E. marshallii* hybridises readily with *E. arctica*, and since the latter becomes an invasive grassland species in the north, cultivation of cliff tops for hay has led to genetic alterations in adjacent *E. marshallii* populations. On dunes and limestone cliffs, or where cliffs have been enriched by blown shell sand, *E. marshallii* is often replaced by its hybrid with *E. nemorosa*. Impressions suggest that these are serious threats to the species, but most collecting and fieldwork has been done at the most accessible parts of the coastline, where these threats are at their greatest. There are many miles of unsurveyed and apparently suitable cliff habitat away from these influences.

E. marshallii is endemic to Britain.

As this species has been recorded in only 15 10 km squares since 1970, it qualifies for inclusion in the *Red Data Book* (Perring & Farrell 1983) under the current criteria. However, it will probably be recorded in more than 15 10 km squares when, as seems likely, it is refound in some of its old localities.

A. J. Silverside

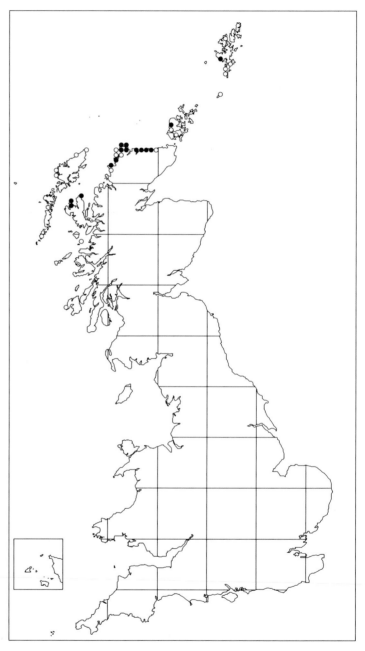

Current map	No	Atlas (S)	No
1970 →	15		
Pre-1970	20		
Introductions	0	All records	24

Euphrasia ostenfeldii (Pugsley) Yeo
Status: scarce

This is a plant of exposed and very well drained habitats, usually with very limited vascular plant cover. It occurs in such habitats as rather dry limestone rock-ledges, eroding edges of sea-cliffs, fine gravel screes and, rarely, sandy coastal turf. In Shetland, it is of occasional occurrence in thin turf on sea cliffs, but it is particularly characteristic of almost bare serpentine debris on Fetlar and Unst. It grows from sea level in North Scotland to over 600 metres on Fraochaidh, and over 760 metres on Cul Mor. It is probably always found above 300 metres in England and Wales.

It is a hemiparasitic annual, presumably germinating in spring and attaching to a suitable host when root contact is first made. No information is available on host plants, but it is unlikely to be host specific. In open rock debris, small plants often occur in thin moss carpets in the apparent absence of other vascular plants and appear not to be host-established. Flowering commences in mid-summer and even very small plants normally produce some seed.

E. ostenfeldii was grouped with an assortment of other hairy taxa and hybrids under '*E. curta*' until given separate recognition by Yeo (1971). It continues to be confused with *E. marshallii* and *E. rotundifolia*, the position being well stated by Scott & Palmer (1987). In North Scotland, a number of coastal populations are hybridised to varying extents with *E. foulaensis*. As an often inconspicuous member of a highly critical genus, it is also substantially under-recorded. Against this background of taxonomic confusion, it is difficult to recognise any changes in distribution, but it is likely to have suffered only localised habitat loss. There is a lack of recent critical fieldwork in some areas.

It is confined to Britain, the Faeroes and Iceland. In the Faeroes it is locally frequent and better differentiated taxonomically than in Britain.

Populations in Snowdonia were formerly given separate recognition as *E. curta* var. *rupestris*. They are matched by an old collection from Teesdale and by certain Lake District material and may merit subspecific status.

A. J. Silverside

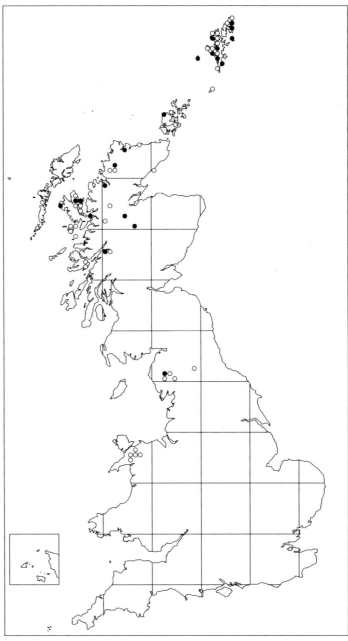

Current map	No
1970 →	21
Pre-1970	37
Introductions	0

E. ostenfeldii as currently defined was not mapped in the *Atlas of the British Flora* or its *Critical Supplement*.

165

Euphrasia pseudokerneri Pugsley
Status: scarce

This is a lowland plant of grazed, well drained, herb-rich turf on chalk and other soft limestones. It is characteristic of floristically rich sites of high conservation value, occurring in the same turf as such species as *Gentianella germanica* and *Pulsatilla vulgaris*. On chalk downs, *E. pseudokerneri* frequently occurs on the higher slopes, with *E. nemorosa* replacing it on the lower slopes or in rougher grass and scrub. Substantial hybrid zones and swarms are to be expected wherever the two species meet. In Norfolk, tall, slender plants (forma *elongata* Pugsley) occur in damp fen turf. On a localised area of the Cardiganshire coast, plants matching *E. pseudokerneri* have recently been recorded from three flush and cliff-top sites, but require further investigation.

It is a hemiparasitic annual, germinating in spring after an obligatory cold period (Yeo 1961) and attaching to a suitable host when root contact is first made. No information is available on host plants in the wild, but in cultivation experiments Wilkins (1963) showed that it can attach to *Festuca ovina*, *Plantago coronopus* and *Trifolium repens*, or mature without host establishment. It is reasonable to suppose that wild plants are attached to a diversity of species. Although capable of germinating from January onwards, *E. pseudokerneri* plants do not normally flower until August or September, later flowering plants perhaps having some reproductive isolation from *E. nemorosa*.

Hybridisation with *E. nemorosa* creates difficulties for recorders, with *E. pseudokerneri* apparently being over-recorded through confusion with hybrids and yet also locally under-recorded, being a critical and late-flowering species. There has been substantial loss of habitat through ploughing and agricultural improvement, while disturbance or reduction in grazing favours *E. nemorosa* and consequent hybridisation. It appears that pure *E. pseudokerneri* is no longer to be found in some areas.

Outside Britain, it occurs only in western Ireland and perhaps in France.

A. J. Silverside

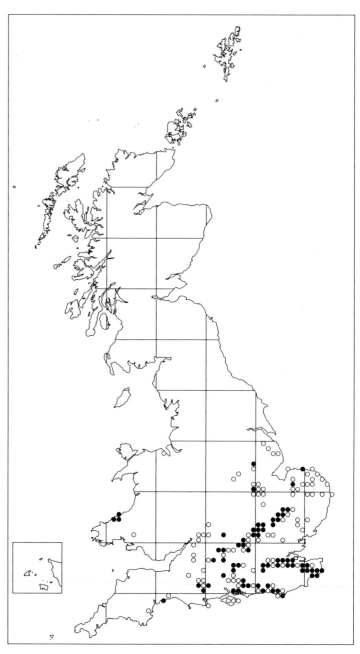

Current map	No	Atlas (S)	No
1970 →	68		
Pre-1970	92		
Introductions	0	All records	104

Euphrasia rostkoviana Hayne subsp. *montana* (Jordan) Wettst.

Status: scarce

This is a plant of upland hay-meadows, recorded mainly from relatively dry sites but also in wet meadows and upland fens. It seems to be rare throughout its range, but it is frequently difficult to separate from subsp. *rostkoviana*, which makes precise assessment of its distribution and status difficult. There is evidence of the two subspecies meeting and hybridising in the Lake District. The altitudinal range is equally difficult to assess, but it is authentically recorded as low as 100 metres and typically occurs at altitudes between 200 and 500 metres.

It is a hemiparasitic annual, presumably germinating in spring and attaching to a suitable host when root contact is first made. No information is available on host plants, but it is unlikely to be host specific. It begins to flower in early to mid-summer, the first flowers typically occurring at the third or fourth node. It thus appears adapted to mature a substantial proportion of its potential seed before the hay is cut. Parallel variation is seen in upland hay-meadow variants of *E. arctica*.

The loss of floristically rich meadows owing to agricultural improvement has undoubtedly caused this plant to become less common, though the difficulty of correctly identifying it has meant that there is a lack of detailed evidence. Nevertheless, its recent rediscovery in South Wales may indicate that it is overlooked in some localities. It rarely, if ever, colonises 'improved' grasslands.

It has a scattered distribution throughout much of Europe, eastwards to central Russia, but is considered extinct in Scandinavia and believed to be declining in much of its range.

The nomenclature used here is not accepted by Silverside (1991), who treats the taxon as *E. officinalis* subsp. *monticola* Silverside.

A. J. Silverside

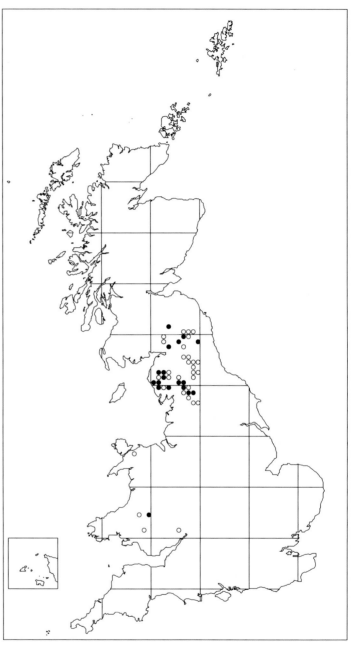

Current map	No	Atlas (S)	No
1970 →	18		
Pre-1970	30		
Introductions	0	All records	22

Euphrasia rostkoviana Hayne subsp. *rostkoviana*
Status: scarce

Primarily a plant of rather damp, herb-rich hay meadows, this plant also occurs in riverside grassland, lightly grazed pastures and on grassy roadsides on fertile soils. Its habitat requirements are not clearly distinct from those of *E. arctica*, with which it may grow and probably compete. To some extent, particularly in Scotland, its distribution may be restricted by competitive exclusion from apparently suitable habitats. In the Scottish Central Highlands its populations tend to be small, isolated, surrounded by *E. arctica* subsp. *borealis* and showing strong signs of introgression. In shorter turf and particularly in more acid sites, it is locally replaced by the very closely related *E. anglica*, entirely so in south-west England. (The few reports of *E. rostkoviana* in south-west England mostly refer to *E. anglica* or *E. anglica* × *arctica*.) Usually it is found in the lowlands, but reaches 370 metres in the Honister Pass.

It is a hemiparasitic annual, germinating in spring after an obligatory cold period, and attaching to a suitable host when root contact is first made. No information is available on host plants in the wild, but, in cultivation experiments reviewed by Yeo (1961), it is said to have formed haustorial attachments to a number of plants, including grasses. Flowering commences in mid-summer. In hay meadows, much seed production is likely to be from growth of side branches after the first cutting of the hay.

This taxon is probably declining through agricultural improvement and loss of habitat. Surviving colonies on roadsides are liable to suffer competition and introgression from the more invasive *E. arctica*, despite their different ploidy levels and consequent sterility barrier.

E. rostkoviana subsp. *rostkoviana* occurs throughout most of Europe, extending to Turkey and into the Caucasus mountains. In north-east Scandinavia and northern Russia it is replaced as a native by *E. officinalis sensu stricto*, from which it is scarcely even subspecifically separable.

This taxon shows complete intergradation with *E. anglica*, particularly in Wales, and Silverside (1991) considers both taxa to be subspecies of *E. officinalis*.

A. J. Silverside

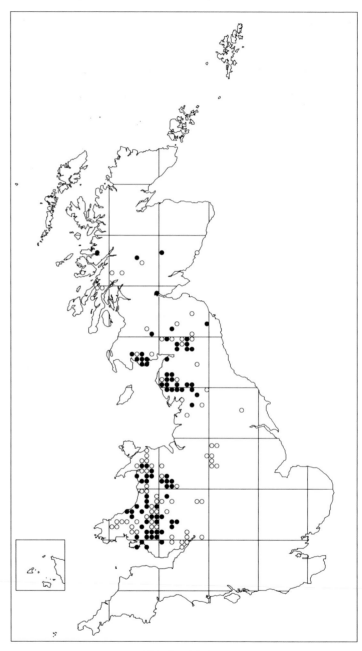

Current map	No	Atlas (S)	No
1970 →	83		
Pre-1970	79		
Introductions	1	All records	94

168

Fallopia dumetorum (L.) Holub

Status: scarce

Copse-bindweed

This is a plant of woodland margins, open woodland, coppices and hedges on well-drained soils.

It is an annual and probably largely self-pollinated. Plants produce an immense number of fruits which appear to remain viable for many years. Germination is stimulated by disturbance of the soil, and the species can appear in quantity when woods are felled or coppiced.

This species has always been local, but it has probably decreased in Britain over the last 30 years. The reasons for this are obscure, but the decline in woodland management may be partly responsible.

F. dumetorum occurs over much of Europe northwards to northern Sweden, but is scarce over much of the Iberian Peninsula and the Mediterranean region (Jalas & Suominen 1979). It extends eastwards across most of Asia. *F. scandens* (L.) Holub from North America may be conspecific.

J. R. Akeroyd

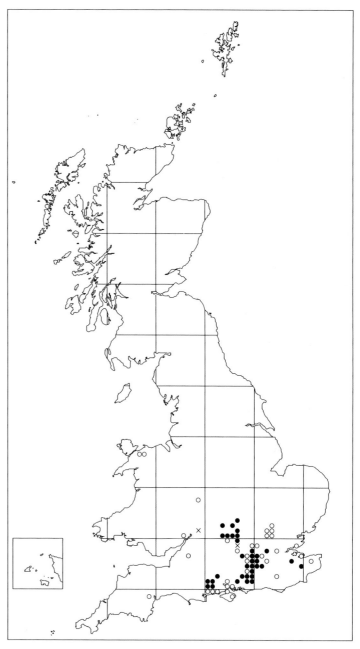

Current map	No	Atlas	No
1970 →	34	1930 →	19
Pre-1970	33	Pre-1930	34
Introductions	2	Introductions	2

Festuca altissima All.

Wood fescue

Status: not scarce

This species grows in shaded, fairly dry but humid situations in wooded ravines. It is found in crevices and on small ledges where it forms large, leafy tufts which trap soil around them. It prefers slightly basic conditions and other mildly calcicolous species such as *Galium odoratum*, *Melica* spp., *Polystichum* spp. and *Sanicula europaea* frequently occur nearby. Its outlying sites in south-east England are on sandstone outcrops. Although it is largely restricted to upland districts, it is restricted to low altitudes, being recorded from sea-level at Roudsea Wood to 300 metres in Ribblesdale.

This is a perennial species and the tufts are evidently long-lived.

There is no indication that this plant is decreasing, and recent more thorough investigations of its rather inaccessible habitat have shown it to be much more frequent than previously thought.

This species is scattered across Europe, extending from northern Spain, Italy and northern Greece to central Norway. It occurs very locally to 90 °E in central Asia.

N. F. Stewart

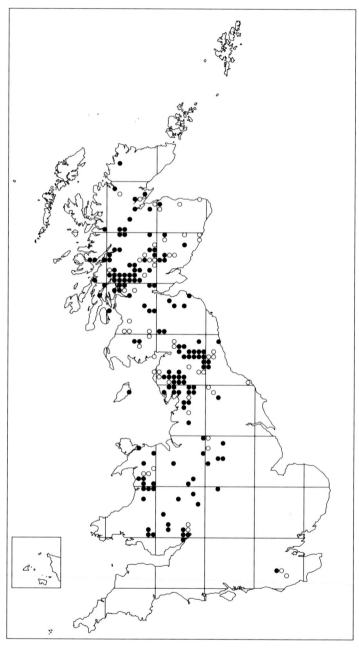

Current map	No	Atlas	No
1970 →	148	1930 →	56
Pre-1970	56	Pre-1930	17
Introductions	0	Introductions	0

Festuca arenaria Osbeck
Status: scarce

Rush-leaved fescue

This grass is confined to sand dunes, or to very sandy places close to the sea that mimic sand dunes, such as rough ground and cliff tops or ledges. These latter places are probably secondary habitats colonised from sand dunes, although in some cases the sand dune populations have died out locally. Its most characteristic habitat is open, semi-mobile fore dunes, almost invariably with *Ammophila arenaria* as its most abundant, and often its only, associate. *Leymus arenarius* is also a characteristic associate. It usually does not occur on the most seaward parts of dunes, but sometimes overlaps with the most characteristic grass of such areas, *Elytrigia juncea*. On the landward side it is replaced by *Festuca rubra* as the dune vegetation becomes more closed, but often the two do not overlap.

F. arenaria is a vigorously rhizomatous plant that also sets abundant seed, so it has two effective and independent methods of spread. It colonises virgin sand and serves to bind it. Observations on establishment in the wild are needed, but seedling germination and growth should be highly successful in the open habitats involved. The species requires winter vernalisation in order to flower, and is less than 3% self-fertile.

Although the map shows that *F. arenaria* occurs on both eastern and western coasts of Britain up to northern Scotland, it is very much more abundant on the east coast, and is in fact very rare on the west coast north of South Wales. Most of the western sites north of there have only pre-1970 records (e.g. there are no known extant sites in Lancashire), and might have been short-lived occurrences. Where the plant is sparse it is in danger from habitat destruction.

F. arenaria occurs on the Atlantic and Baltic coasts of Europe from northern Spain to southern Norway, Sweden and Finland.

The concept of *F. arenaria* used here covers both *F. juncifolia* Chaub. and *F. rubra* subsp. *arenaria* (Osbeck) F. Aresch., which cannot be separated. Even so, it remains difficult in some cases to separate *F. arenaria* from *F. rubra*. The best characters are the densely pubescent spikelets (though glabrous variants occur) and adaxial leaf ribs, the rounded abaxial leaf keel, and the distribution of leaf sclerenchyma. Hybrids with *Vulpia fasciculata* have been found in west Sussex and east Kent, but none with *F. rubra* have been reported.

For further information see Al-Bermani (1991) and Stace (1991).

C. A. Stace

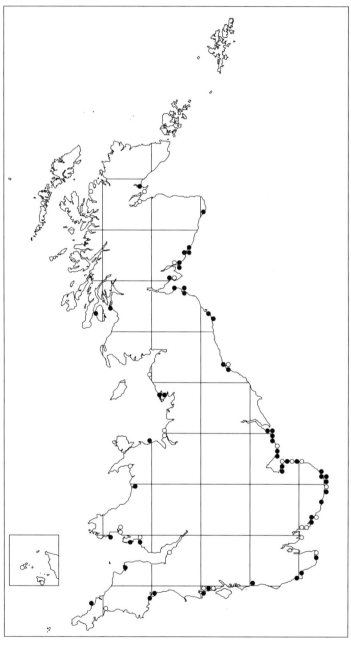

Current map	No	Atlas	No
1970 →	52	1930 →	13
Pre-1970	27	Pre-1930	2
Introductions	0	Introductions	0

Frankenia laevis L.
Status: scarce

Sea-heath

F. laevis is a prostrate, wiry perennial which occupies a particular zone in English salt marshes, where the wet silt of the marsh proper gives way to the dry sand of adjacent dunes and beaches. In Norfolk, transitional vegetation of this kind is also the primary habitat of *Limonium bellidifolium*. More rarely, *F. laevis* is found on shingle and, in Kent, at the foot of chalk cliffs, forming a turf on eroded ledges within the splash zone. Being strictly coastal, *F. laevis* reaches a maximum altitude of 5 metres on the cliffs near Dover.

F. laevis can spread vegetatively, the procumbent shoots rooting to produce new individuals. In localities where populations are small and plants somewhat isolated only 10% of the flowers produce capsules containing seed; in larger and denser populations over half the flowers produce seeds. The average number of seeds set per flower is also higher in larger populations. Germination probably occurs in the spring.

F. laevis has declined in eastern England, due to disturbance of salt marshes and their destruction through improved sea-defences, urbanisation and industrial development. *F. laevis* is, rather surprisingly, grown as a rock-garden plant and sometimes escapes from cultivation to become established in coastal habitats. In Dorset it has become well naturalised in recent years on bare clay cliffs. The species was first recorded in Wales in 1965 on an Anglesey salt-marsh, where the population increased gradually over the next ten years (Roberts 1975). It has subsequently been found in Glamorgan (Waldren 1982). It is not known whether these populations are garden escapes, but they are treated as introductions on the map.

It is a species of the coasts of Western Europe and the Mediterranean, from Norfolk to south-east Italy. *F. laevis* also occurs on the adjacent coast of North Africa and in Macaronesia.

For a detailed account of the ecology of this species, including a map of its European distribution, see Brightmore (1979).

J. O. Mountford

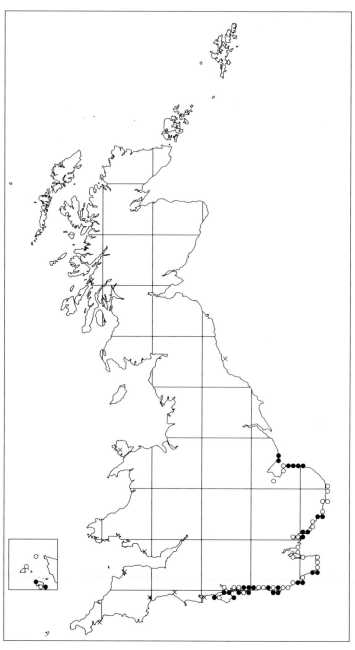

Current map	No	Atlas	No
1970 →	28	1930 →	21
Pre-1970	31	Pre-1930	25
Introductions	8	Introductions	0

Fritillaria meleagris L.

Fritillary

Status: scarce

This is a grassland plant which thrives best where the usual form of management is a hay cut followed by aftermath grazing. This enables plants which have all their leaves on the flowering stem, as does *F. meleagris*, to complete their life cycles. The fact that this species often occurs in grassland subjected to flooding may have more to do with the resultant past agricultural tendency to treat such land as a hay meadow than with any ecological dependence on flooding *per se*. Classic sites for *F. meleagris* are, or were, meadows adjacent to lowland rivers where the flora consists of twelve or more grasses, a few sedges and a wide range of herbs associated with damp loam soils. Associated species of note are *Cardamine pratensis*, *Ophioglossum vulgatum*, *Sanguisorba officinalis*, *Silaum silaus* and *Thalictrum flavum*.

F. meleagris is a perennial which flowers freely in the open but is inhibited by shade from dense scrub. Seed production is of the order of 100 seeds per capsule and germination is in the spring. Survival of the species is likely to be mainly by vegetative reproduction of the bulb. Colonisation of new sites is uncommon, if it occurs at all, possibly because of inhospitable grassland sites created by modern agricultural methods.

This species declined rapidly after 1940 following agricultural intensification by chemicals and mechanisation. Current threats are from gravel extraction but most major sites now have some form of protection.

F. meleagris is endemic to Europe, where it extends from the Alps and Yugoslavia northwards to Britain and Russia; it is also naturalised in Scandinavia.

A detailed account of the ecology and population dynamics of this species in Sweden is given by Zhang (1983). For an account of its occurrence in England, see King & Wells (1993).

D. A. Wells

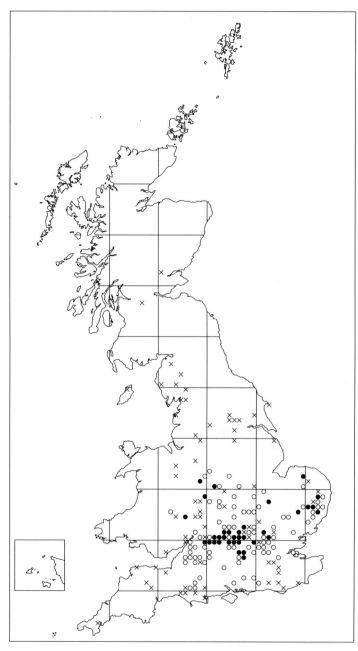

Current map	No	Atlas	No
1970 →	34	1930 →	32
Pre-1970	82	Pre-1930	76
Introductions	71	Introductions	15

continued →

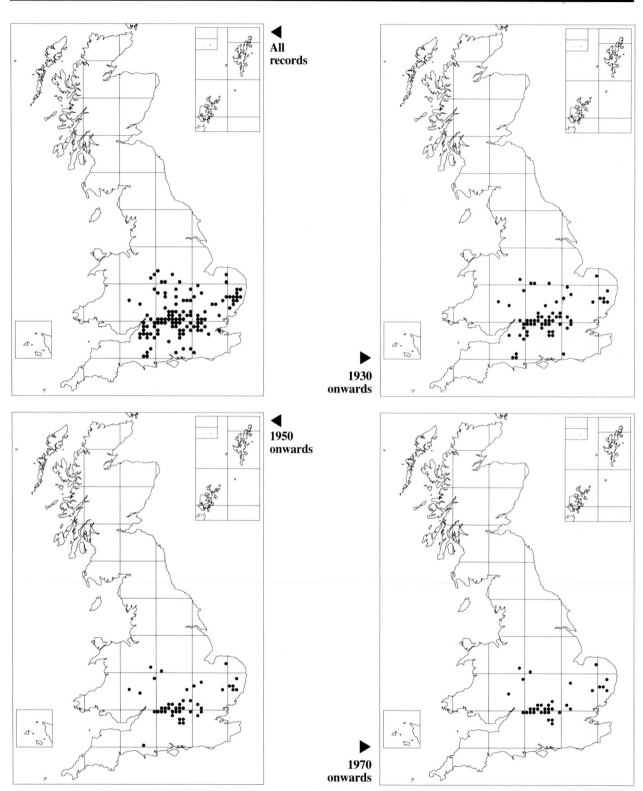

The distribution of *Fritillaria meleagris*, illustrated by a series of maps for different time periods.

continued →

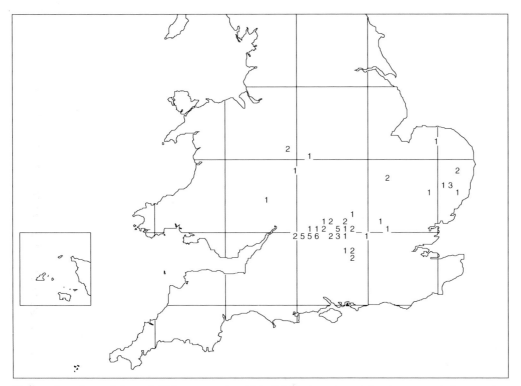

The number of tetrads in each 10 km square in which *Fritillaria meleagris* has been recorded as a native species from 1970 onwards. The species has been found in a total of 66 tetrads from 1970 onwards.

Fumaria bastardii Boreau

Status: not scarce

This is a weed of disturbed ground in gardens, cultivated fields, market gardens, newly made-up roadside verges and dumped soil. Unlike the other western species *F. capreolata* and *F. purpurea* it is only occasionally found scrambling over walls and hedges, or on cliff slopes. It is confined to the lowlands.

F. bastardii is a self-compatible, cleistogamous species which set seeds freely.

There is little evidence to suggest that the distribution is changing. The map shows that it is still frequent in areas which have been systematically surveyed since 1970; the absence of records from other areas such as Devon perhaps reflects a lack of recent, critical recording.

F. bastardii is widespread in the Mediterranean region and extends north in western Europe to Britain and Ireland (Jalas & Suominen 1991). It is naturalised in India, North and South America and Australia (Lidén 1986).

This is a variable species, both in Britain and in its wider range. The principal variants in Britain are var. *bastardii*, var. *gussonei* (Boiss.) Pugsley and var. *hibernica* Pugsley (Sell 1989b). Var. *bastardii* is frequent. Var. *gussonei* occurs only in the Isles of Scilly and the Channel Islands but is common in the Mediterranean region. Var. *hibernica* is frequent and endemic to the British Isles.

D. A. Pearman & C. D. Preston

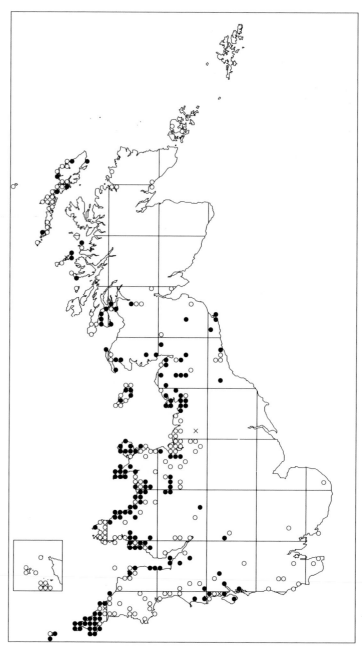

Current map	No	Atlas	No
1970 →	155		
Pre-1970	165		
Introductions	4	All records	151

Fumaria capreolata L.
Status: not scarce

White ramping-fumitory

F. capreolata is usually found scrambling up hedge-banks, old walls or on warm, partially scrub-covered slopes and coastal cliffs, where it often grows to a large size. It often appears in abundance after a disturbance, such as the clearance of coastal gorse scrub (Margetts 1988). It is also found as a weed of cultivated fields and gardens, although it is less frequent in this habitat than some other fumitories. It is confined to the lowlands.

F. capreolata is a winter annual. It is a self-compatible, cleistogamous species which sets seed freely. In shade the flowers are smaller and paler than they are in the open.

There is no evidence that this species is declining. In most areas which have been surveyed recently it appears to be as frequent as it ever was; the absence of recent records from Devon is probably due to under-recording.

F. capreolata is frequent in the Mediterranean region and extends north in western Europe to Britain and Ireland. Its European distribution is mapped by Jalas & Suominen (1991).

The British and Irish populations of *F. capreolata* are the endemic subsp. *babingtonii* (Pugsley) Sell, but some plants on the south coast verge towards subsp. *capreolata*. Those in the Channel Islands are referable to the continental subsp. *capreolata*.

D. A. Pearman & C. D. Preston

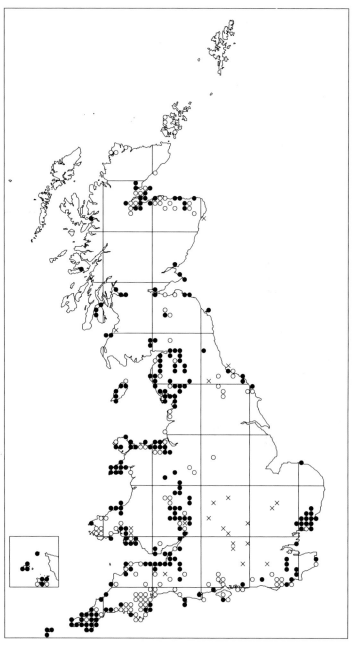

Current map	No	Atlas	No
1970 →	220		
Pre-1970	130	Native records	129
Introductions	21	Introductions	9

177

Fumaria densiflora DC.
Status: scarce

Dense-flowered fumitory

This is a species of lowland arable land which is usually found as a weed of cereal, root and vegetable crops. It is predominantly a plant of well-drained calcareous soils, which is most frequently found on chalk but also known from sandy loams in the Hampshire basin and calcareous clay soils in East Anglia. It also occurs in eastern Scotland in coastal fields where the soil is enriched by calcareous sand. In south-east England it often grows with other uncommon arable weeds of calcareous soils such as *Papaver argemone, P. hybridum, Silene noctiflora* and *Valerianella dentata*. It may also be found in small quantity on bare soil on roadsides, hedgebanks and waste ground, usually in sites adjacent to arable fields.

F. densiflora is a self-compatible, cleistogamous annual which fruits freely. It has peaks of germination in spring (April-May) and autumn (September-October). Experimental work has shown that few seedlings emerge in the year they are sown, and the species has a persistent seed bank (Roberts & Boddrell 1983; Roberts & Feast 1973).

This species has declined in abundance in recent years because of the routine use of herbicides and the application of massive amounts of nitrogen to highly competitive modern crop varieties. It is now usually confined to the outermost parts of fields, where the application of herbicides and fertilisers is less efficient. It can still occasionally be found in quantity where dormant seed has germinated in fields which have escaped spraying or on other areas of disturbed ground. It may now be more frequent in potato and sugar-beet fields, and in vegetable crops such as carrots and onions, than it is in cereals. It is possible that it persists, unknown to botanists, as a weed in gardens. Although there are records from 161 10 km squares from 1970 onwards, this declining species is classified as scarce as it has been recorded in only 89 10 km squares from 1980 onwards.

F. densiflora is widespread in the Mediterranean region and extends northwards in western Europe to Britain and Ireland (Jalas & Suominen 1991). It is, however, a rare plant in many areas (Lidén 1986).

P. J. Wilson

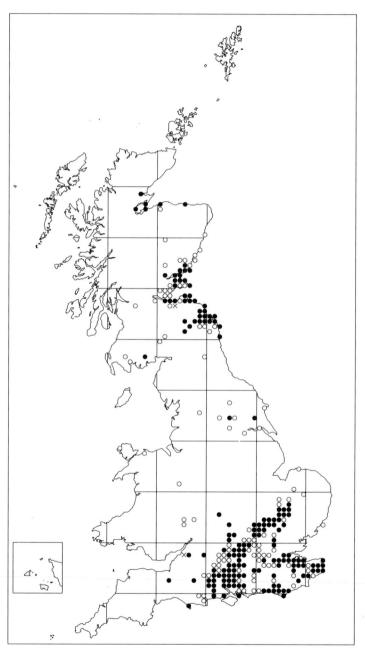

Current map	No	Atlas	No
1970 →	161		
Pre-1970	102		
Introductions	2	All records	139

continued →

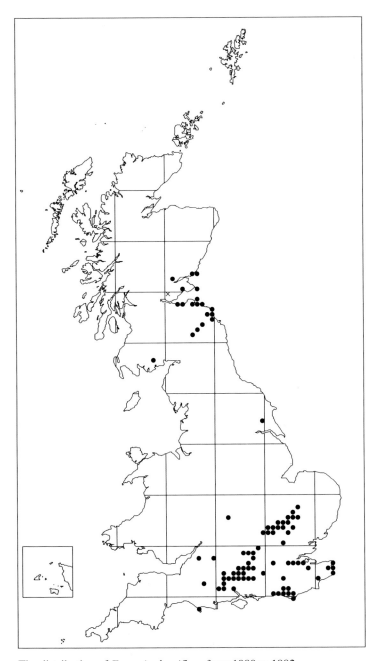

The distribution of *Fumaria densiflora* from 1980 to 1992.

Fumaria parviflora Lam.
Status: scarce

Fine-leaved fumitory

This weed is virtually confined to arable fields on the chalk, although it can occasionally be found on other areas of disturbed ground in the vicinity of the arable populations. In Breckland it was regarded as "a plant of the early phase of colonisation following the breaking-up of chalk grassland... as soon as the vegetation becomes dense the plant disappears" (Petch & Swann 1968). It is usually associated with other uncommon arable weeds, including *Fumaria vaillantii*, *Legousia hybrida*, *Papaver argemone*, *P. hybridum* and *Valerianella dentata*.

F. parviflora is a self-compatible, cleistogamous annual which fruits freely. Little is known about its germination requirements, but the seeds probably possess similar dormancy characteristics to *F. densiflora*.

This plant never grew in the same abundance as some arable weeds such as *Centaurea cyanus* and *Ranunculus arvensis,* but it was always more common than *F. vaillantii*. It has almost certainly become much more local since 1950, and even in sites where it has been known since the early 19th century, such as the Gog Magog Hills, it is now difficult to find. It has declined for the same reasons as *F. densiflora*: the widespread use of herbicides and its inability to compete with highly fertilised modern crop varieties.

This species is very common throughout the Mediterranean region, and extends north in western Europe to Britain (Jalas & Suominen 1991; Lidén 1986). It is also recorded from Macaronesia and is naturalised in both North and South America.

Three varieties of *F. parviflora*, differing in the shape of their fruits, are recognised in Britain (Rich & Rich 1988). Var. *parviflora* and var. *acuminata* Clavaud are the most frequent variants. The endemic var. *symei* Pugsley has only been recorded once in recent years.

P. J. Wilson

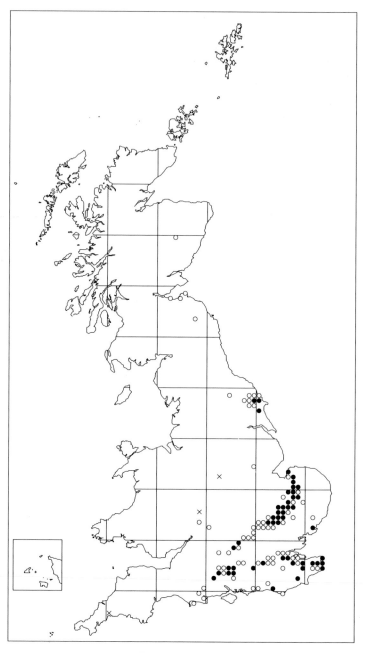

Current map	No	Atlas	No
1970 →	48		
Pre-1970	68		
Introductions	3	All records	86

Fumaria purpurea Pugsley

Status: scarce

Purple ramping-fumitory

F. purpurea is a climbing or scrambling herb which grows amongst bushes, on hedge banks, in cultivated fields and waste ground and occasionally on earthy sea-cliffs. In Cornwall it also grows on earth-core walls and in the Isles of Scilly it is found as a weed of bulb-fields. It is usually most abundant in sites which have recently been disturbed by animals or farm machinery or in habitats opened up by summer drought.

Like other fumitories, this species is a self-compatible, cleistogamous annual.

It is difficult to assess trends in the distribution of this plant. It was not described as a species until 1902, and it is easily overlooked by botanists who are not familiar with it. Its distribution appears to be stable in the areas where it is most frequent, Cornwall and West Lancashire. The map suggests that it has declined elsewhere, but at some of its older sites it may be overlooked or it may have been only a casual.

F. purpurea is endemic to Britain, Ireland and the Channel Islands. Lidén (1986) suggests that it may have originated as an allopolyploid hybrid of *F. muralis* subsp. *boraei* and *F. officinalis*.

D. A. Pearman & C. D. Preston

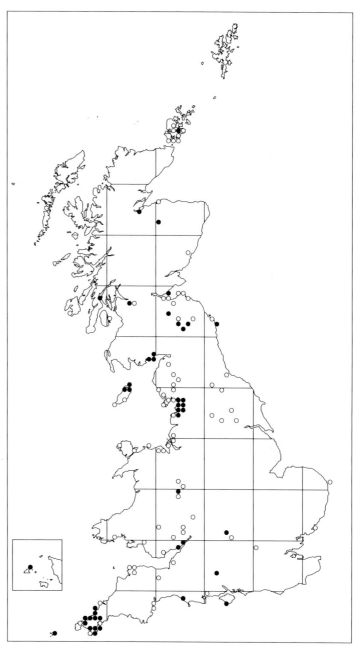

Current map	No	Atlas	No
1970 →	43		
Pre-1970	76		
Introductions	1	All records	70

Fumaria vaillantii Lois.
Status: scarce

Few-flowered fumitory

F. vaillantii is predominantly a weed of arable land, being very rarely found in other disturbed ground. It is a weed of cereal or root crops or of other vegetables. It is virtually restricted to chalky soils. Other uncommon arable weeds, such as *Legousia hybrida*, *Papaver argemone*, *P. hybridum* and *Valerianella dentata*, can often be found in the same field.

F. vaillantii is a self-compatible, cleistogamous annual which fruits freely. Little is known of its germination requirements, but it probably possesses similar dormancy characteristics to *F. densiflora*.

This species, has often been confused with *F. officinalis* subsp. *wirtgenii*. Like the other rare fumitories of disturbed ground, was never common but it now appears to be much less frequent than it once was. Only occasionally is it possible to find a field in which fumitories occur in abundance, perhaps because climatic conditions have been particularly suitable and the plants have escaped applications of herbicide. *F. densiflora*, *F. officinalis* var. *minor*, *F. officinalis* var. *wirtgenii* and *F. vaillantii* were, for instance, all found in a single onion field in 1985 by Sell (1985).

F. vaillantii is widespread in Europe and western Asia, extending north to southern Scandinavia (Jalas & Suominen 1991). It is much rarer than *F. parviflora* in the Mediterranean region. It is also recorded in the mountains of Morocco and Algeria (Lidén 1986).

Most populations of *F. vaillantii* are referable to var. *vaillantii*. A variant with reddish flowers, var. *chavinii* (Reuter) Rouy & Fouc., has only been seen once in recent years.

P. J. Wilson

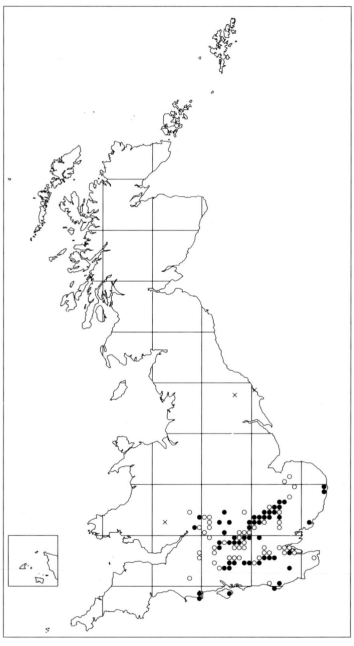

Current map	No	Atlas	No
1970 →	51		
Pre-1970	50		
Introductions	3	All records	52

182

Gagea lutea (L.) Ker Gawler

Status: not scarce

Yellow star-of-Bethlehem

This is a small bulbous perennial, flowering during March and April. It occurs very locally in small, moist, base-rich woodlands, woodland borders, wooded limestone pavements, pastures and shady river banks. In this last situation it is often found in areas of silt deposition in association with *Chrysosplenium alternifolium*. It is virtually confined to the lowlands, but is recorded from 320 metres near Llanarmon-yr-Ial and 340 metres near Ribblehead.

Although it can occur as scattered individuals, colonies are often quite dense but may be of limited extent, just a few square metres in area. Some of these appear to persist for many years in a vegetative state, others are very free-flowering, and the density of the tree canopy is probably a controlling factor.

Some populations have been lost, mainly through felling of their woodland habitat, but adverse agricultural practices and river bank reinforcements also take their toll. Losses due to erosion are probably less important as displaced plants may re-establish themselves downstream.

The plant is widely distributed throughout western and central Europe, extending eastwards into Russia with outlying populations in northern Scandinavia. It also occurs in eastern Asia and the western Himalayas, Japan and the Kamchatka peninsula, Russia.

Systematic searching for this easily overlooked species has resulted in the discovery of many new colonies in recent years. Non-flowering plants can be easily confused with *Hyacinthoides non-scripta*, especially when they are immature.

M. J. Y. Foley

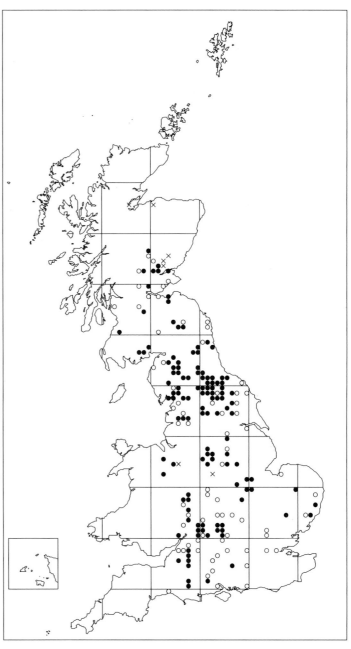

Current map	No	Atlas	No
1970 →	123	1930 →	64
Pre-1970	71	Pre-1930	45
Introductions	7	Introductions	3

Galeopsis angustifolia Ehrh. ex Hoffm.

Red hemp-nettle

Status: scarce

This lowland species is normally found in arable fields on calcareous soils. It is also known to occur on coastal sands and shingle in southern counties of England and Wales. It prefers well-drained, warm soils, faring best where competition is not too great. It is quite often associated with *Euphorbia exigua*, *Fumaria densiflora*, *Kickxia elatine*, *K. spuria*, *Legousia hybrida*, *Lithospermum arvense*, *Papaver argemone* and *P. hybrida*. On occasion it has such uncommon associates as *Adonis annua*, *Torilis arvensis* and *Valerianella dentata*.

This summer annual tends to germinate quite late in spring and consequently plants may fail to set seed before they are eradicated after the harvest. It is most frequently encountered in spring-sown crops and grows rapidly after harvest, setting much seed in stubbles if they are left in the late summer.

The decline of this species is apparent from the map. It competes poorly with dense, fully fertilised crops, and the increase in levels of nitrogen application and herbicide use, the switch from spring to winter sowing and the early ploughing of stubbles have probably contributed to its decline. Although there are records from 116 10 km squares from 1970 onwards, this declining species is classified as scarce as it has been recorded in only 61 10 km squares from 1980 onwards.

This species is found in western, central and southern Europe, eastwards to Poland and Bulgaria. It occurs as far north as southern Sweden, where it has been introduced.

A. Smith & P. J. Wilson

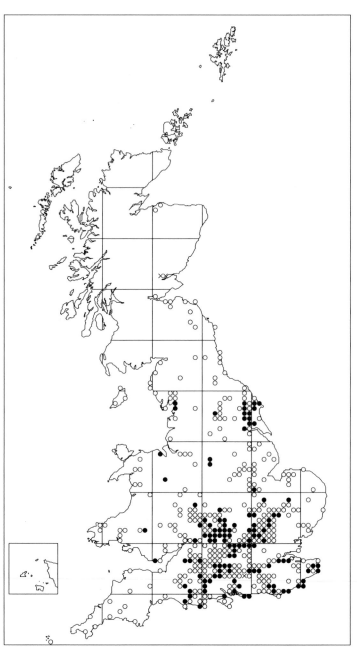

Current map	No	Atlas	No
1970 →	116	1930 →	233
Pre-1970	312	Pre-1930	72
Introductions	3	Introductions	0

continued →

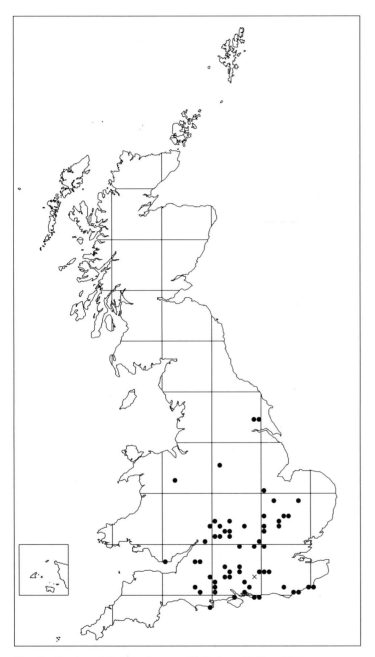

The distribution of *Galeopsis angustifolia* from 1980 to 1992.

Galium parisiense L.

Status: scarce

Wall bedstraw

G. parisiense is a small annual of bare ground and walls, where it occurs alone or in the company of *Arenaria serpyllifolia*, especially subsp. *leptoclados*, *Catapodium rigidum*, *Erophila* spp., *Sagina apetala*, *Saxifraga tridactylites* and various mosses and lichens. The flowering plants listed are all shallowly rooting species which cannot survive if the habitat becomes sufficiently enriched to allow the establishment of more vigorous competitors. Trist (1979) lists as associates of *G. parisiense* a number of larger or perennial species recorded within the same square metre; it must be assumed that these constituted a fairly closed vegetation in which the smaller annuals were confined to the discontinuities.

G. parisiense can reproduce only by seed. Germination is triggered by a spell of warm weather following a wet period. In the Mediterranean climatic regime germination is always in spring, whereas in Britain it can also occur following unusual weather conditions in summer and autumn. Seed is set within two or three months of germination. Where the plant occurs on walls, subsidiary colonies may often be found at the base if there is suitable gravel, but it has no way of spreading further. Autumn-germinated plants on the ground are likely to be killed by frosts.

The colonies of *G. parisiense* on old walls are probably well recorded, whereas plants on the ground are much more easily overlooked. The outlying locality in Devon, discovered in 1954, is of this type, but as the plant lasted only until 1966 (Ivimey-Cook 1984) it might represent an accidental introduction. The nature of such accidents is extremely obscure. Some are indicated by the crosses on the map and others are hidden among the circles, most notably a colony at Tottenham, on the concrete remains of sewage filter beds, discovered in 1984 and still thriving in 1992. There may be other colonies of this inconspicuous plant waiting to be found in unexpected places.

Outside Britain, *G. parisiense* is common in the west and central Mediterranean region, but rare north of the Alps. The most northerly localities in Germany are even more isolated than the British ones (Haeupler & Schönfelder 1989). It is tempting to speculate that this species was able to spread rapidly northwards in western and central Europe during the period of warmer climate between 1150 and about 1300 (Lamb 1977), and outside its main range has been steadily decreasing ever since. This suggestion is supported by the observation by G. Beckett (pers. comm.) that five of the six old walls in west Norfolk where it still grows are of no later than 13th century origin.

R. M. Burton

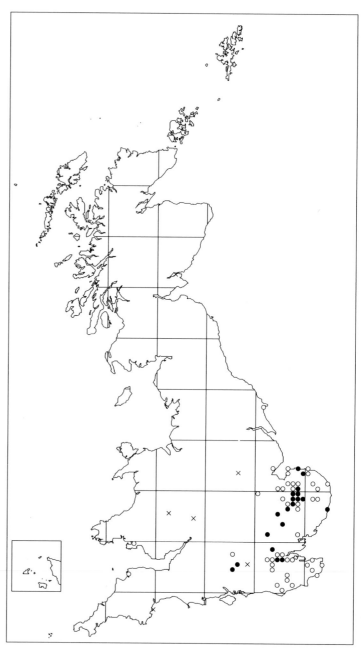

Current map	No	Atlas	No
1970 →	19	1930 →	24
Pre-1970	44	Pre-1930	27
Introductions	6	Introductions	0

continued →

continued

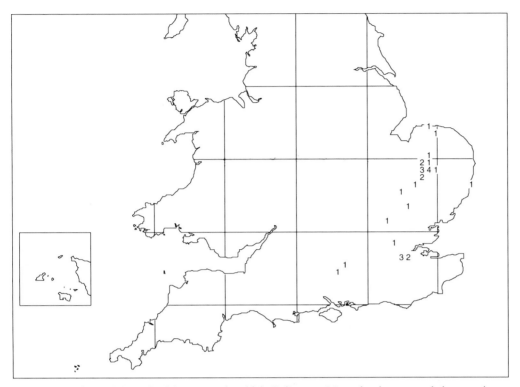

The number of tetrads in each 10 km square in which *Galium parisiense* has been recorded as a native species from 1970 onwards. The species has been found in a total of 29 tetrads from 1970 onwards.

Galium pumilum Murray
Status: scarce

Slender bedstraw

This is a perennial bedstraw of herb-rich chalk grassland. *G. pumilum* thrives at sites where the turf is grazed, mown or kept short and thin by exposure, and the open texture gives adequate light and lowers competition. *Bromopsis erecta*, *Festuca ovina* and *Helictotrichon pubescens* are usually the characteristic grass species present, with plants such as *Anacamptis pyramidalis*, *Asperula cynanchica*, *Cirsium acaule*, *Gymnadenia conopsea*, *Helianthemum nummularium*, *Hippocrepis comosa*, *Polygala calcarea* and the scarce species *Aceras anthropophorum*. There is an interesting connection with *Euphorbia cyparissias*, formerly present with *G. pumilum* at five Kent sites (Rose & Géhu 1960), in Berkshire and in Sussex. They are still found together at a Dover site near where this continental spurge was first recognised as a native in 1876.

Populations seem to remain as small isolated patches persisting in exact locations. This implies that vegetative spread is not vigorous and seedling establishment is rare. However, hundreds of young plants were found in very short turf at Colley Hill in 1992 and these had presumably originated from seed.

Historical records are confusing, as the specific status of this group of bedstraws has been much argued. *G. pumilum* was formerly lumped with the northern limestone species *G. sterneri* and the doubtfully distinct Cheddar Gorge species *G. fleurotii* as 'G. *sylvestre* Pollich', though plants of the southern chalk were distinguished as *G. sylvestre* var. *nitidulum* by the 1880s. There was also considerable discussion about whether it was an alien or not, "introduced with grass seed" being argued against "may be a native" (Druce 1900, 1926), and at this time the presence of *Euphorbia cyparissias* suggested that it was a garden escape. However it is almost certain that all records from ancient chalk grassland in south-east England are for *G. pumilum*, while limestone plants from the north and west are variously distinct. Because of these past uncertainties and its rather inconspicuous habit the plant may be under-recorded, but destruction of chalk grassland, and cessation of grazing on much of what remains, has undoubtedly caused considerable losses.

It is found throughout western and central Europe, north to Denmark and east to the Baltic. The exact distribution is not quite clear because of the existence of many hybrids and chromosomal differences between the many forms of this variable species.

R. FitzGerald

Current map	No	Atlas	No
1970 →	19		
Pre-1970	44		
Introductions	1	All records	51

188

Galium sterneri Ehrend.
Status: not scarce

Limestone bedstraw

G. sterneri grows in base-rich short grassland often on steep slopes and ledges where the turf is fragmentary. The plant also occurs in bare rock crevices. In the Scottish Highlands its associates at high altitude include *G. boreale, Geum rivale, Linum catharticum, Persicaria vivipara, Saxifraga aizoides* and *Thalictrum alpinum*. In northern England the main habitat for *G. sterneri* is *Sesleria caerulea* grassland where it is a constant species. Here the main associates are *Briza media, Campanula rotundifolia, Carex flacca, Festuca ovina, Helianthemum nummularium, Koeleria macrantha, Thymus polytrichus* and *Ctenidium molluscum. Helianthemum canum* may replace *H. nummularium* as an associate at some localities in northern England. Other rare associates include *Gentiana verna, Minuartia verna* and *Myosotis alpestris*. It may occur in sites subject to some basic flushing, and tends to avoid heavily droughted vegetation. It is found from sea-level to 975 metres on Creag Mhor.

G. sterneri is a perennial herb which in spring sends out creeping shoots forming a spreading mat. Later, in June, July or even August, it produces upright flowering shoots with longish peduncles forming a rather open, somewhat flat-topped, inflorescence. The creamy flowers are visited by small flies, and fruits are commonly produced.

Recognition of *G. sterneri* as a distinct species has been slow. In the nineteenth century, Floras noted *G. saxatile*, the common heath bedstraw and a rarer heath bedstraw with various names, including *G. pumilum, G. sylvestre* and *G. pusillum* (Hennedy 1891; Hooker 1870). In the present century the southern plants of this rarer group were separated as *G. pumilum* and the more numerous northern group became *G. sterneri*. Acceptance of this move was slow, but was assisted perhaps by a BSBI exhibit in 1955 (Goodway 1955). The relatively brief period since this species was recognised makes it difficult to judge whether its abundance or range is changing.

This species is confined to north-west Europe, where it occurs in Denmark, Germany, Norway and the Faeroes as well as in Britain and Ireland. The closely related *G. normanii* occurs in Iceland and Norway.

Both diploid and tetraploid populations of this species are found in Britain, but they are morphologically indistinguishable.

P .J. Lusby & A. Slack

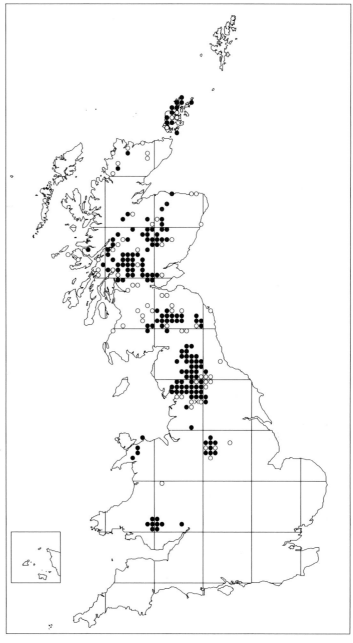

Current map	No	Atlas	No
1970 →	166		
Pre-1970	70		
Introductions	1	All records	141

Gentiana pneumonanthe L.

Status: scarce

Marsh gentian

This plant grows in damp acid grassland and heathland in the lowlands, typically associated with *Erica tetralix* and *Molinia caerulea*. In the New Forest it is frequently associated with *M. caerulea* tussocks, growing where there is a seasonal steady movement of surface water, usually on relatively enriched soils. Plants grow out of the tussocks themselves rather than from the intervening swards (Tubbs 1986).

It is a long-lived perennial, having a mean life expectancy of about 20 years. Reproduction is by seed, with open conditions being required for seedling establishment. Flowering is variable between individuals and from year to year. Plants in more open conditions tend to flower more than those in denser vegetation. Enhanced flowering may occur in summers following a warm year, or after burning. Seeds do not remain viable for more than about 5 years. Survival depends upon plants persisting in a non-flowering state until climate or disturbance initiate flowering and the enhancement of the population.

While the limits of the distribution of this species have not changed, there has been a considerable loss of sites, and a reduction in the sizes of populations at extant sites. Losses have resulted from habitat destruction (e.g. by ploughing, drainage or afforestation) and by the reduction of grazing or of other physical disturbance on remaining heathland. Uncontrolled and excessive burning can also threaten the species. However, the plant may be more abundant on some sites than is thought as non-flowering individuals are difficult to locate.

G. pneumonanthe is distributed over much of Europe, from southern Scandinavia to the mountains of Spain, Italy and the Balkans, but is everywhere subject to similar losses and reductions as in Britain. It extends eastwards to central Asia.

For detailed accounts of this species see Chapman, Rose & Clarke (1989) and Simmonds (1946).

S. B. Chapman

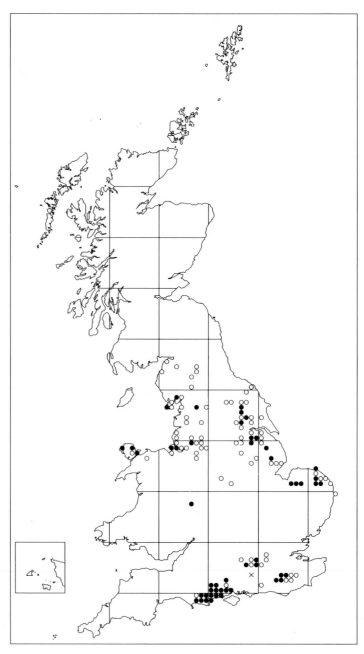

Current map	No	Atlas	No
1970 →	50	1930 →	36
Pre-1970	76	Pre-1930	36
Introductions	1	Introductions	0

continued →

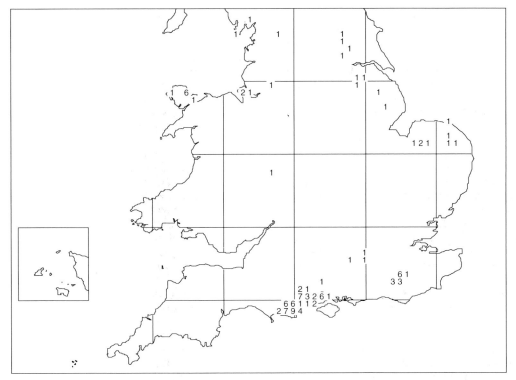

The number of tetrads in each 10 km square in which *Gentiana pneumonanthe* has been recorded as a native species from 1970 onwards. Squares in which the species is recorded in 9 or more tetrads are plotted as 9: *G. pneumonanthe* is actually recorded from 13 tetrads in SY98. The species has been found in a total of 114 tetrads from 1970 onwards.

Gentianella anglica (Pugsley) E. Warb.
Status: scarce

Early gentian
WCA Schedule 8 species

This is a plant of sparsely vegetated base-rich parched grasslands. It is found in localities such as cliff tops, dunes, coastal slopes, south-facing chalk downs or mineral workings where bare ground is maintained by trampling, grazing, soil creep, exposure to wind and insolation. It usually grows in old established grasslands but it is also found on ancient and modern earthworks, including tumuli and 1940s rifle butts, chalk rubble dumped on lowland grazed heathland, and arable land which has reverted to grassland within the last 150 years. It is confined to the lowlands.

This plant is an annual which usually germinates in spring. It is an opportunistic species whose numbers fluctuate from year to year. Fluctuations probably reflect the relative abundance of bare ground for germination and soil moisture conditions. The re-appearance of plants after apparent absence suggests that the seed is viable for a number of years. Many extant colonies consist of only a few irregularly appearing plants.

Genuinely large colonies are almost wholly confined to the Isles of Wight and Purbeck and the coast of North Devon and Cornwall. Away from this area the species has suffered a marked decline, presumably caused by the widespread destruction of calcareous grassland and the changing character of the remaining sites. Most fragments of surviving grasslands are unsuitable as the cessation of traditional grazing regimes has allowed rank grassland and scrub to replace the closely grazed swards required by this species. Populations within SSSIs and nature reserves are still threatened because of the practical difficulties of grazing grassland fragments, cliff edges and coastal slopes. There is also a difficulty within fragmented sites in balancing the requirements of this species with other species worthy of conservation.

G. anglica is endemic to England and has recently received special protection under Appendix I of the Bern Convention and Annexes II and IV of the European Community Habitats and Species Directive. It is also protected under Schedule 8 of the Wildlife and Countryside Act 1981 (as amended).

This gentian is found as two subspecies. Subsp. *anglica* is confined to chalk and limestone, whereas subsp. *cornubiensis* is found on cliff top grasslands and calcareous dunes in Devon and Cornwall. Subsp. *cornubiensis* produces fertile hybrids with *G. amarella* in some sand dune sites (Margetts 1987). There are no suggestions that subsp. *anglica* has been known to hybridise with *G. amarella*, the flowering periods being distinct.

C. Chatters

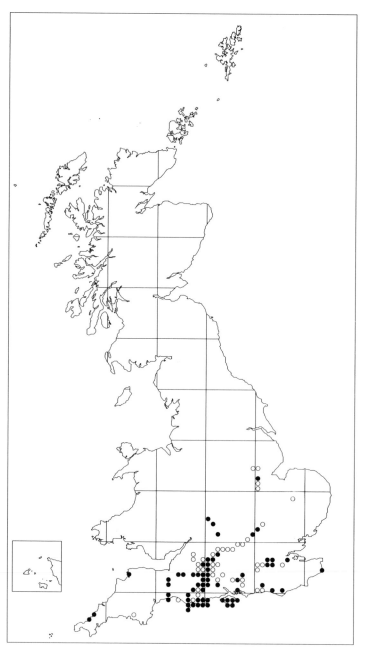

Current map	No	Atlas	No
1970 →	62	1930 →	34
Pre-1970	40	Pre-1930	32
Introductions	0	Introductions	0

continued →

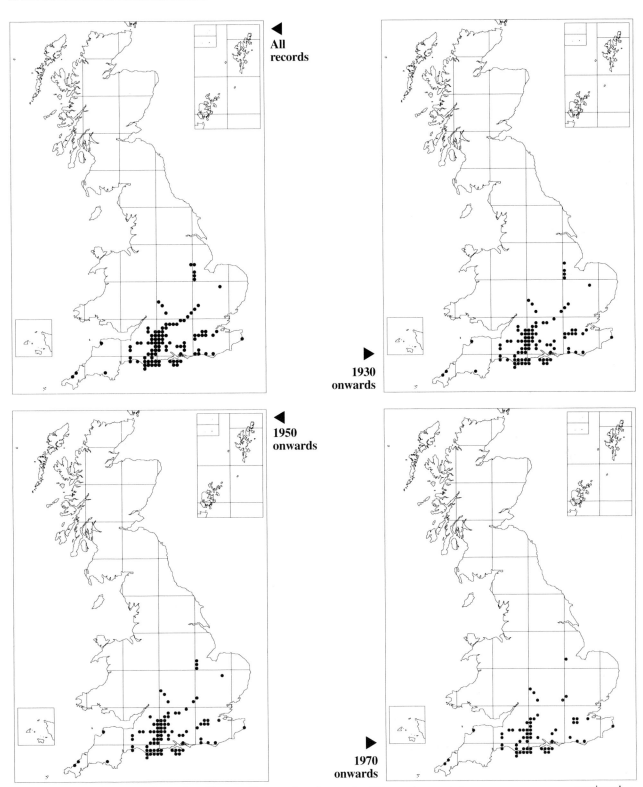

The distribution of *Gentianella anglica*, illustrated by a series of maps for different time periods.

continued →

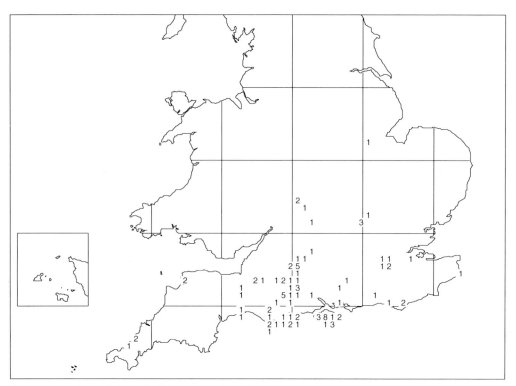

The number of tetrads in each 10 km square in which *Gentianella anglica* has been recorded as a native species from 1970 onwards. The species has been found in a total of 98 tetrads from 1970 onwards.

Gentianella germanica (Willd.) Boerner
Status: scarce

Chiltern gentian

This is a plant of chalk downland and chalk pits, found particularly in places where the soil has been disturbed. It is also found at woodland margins and on slightly scrubby ground on suitable soils. In general it occurs in similar localities to *G. amarella* subsp. *amarella* but requires a more sheltered site and is unable to withstand as much competition from other vegetation. It is a successful coloniser of bare chalk ground in some chalk pits, where populations of several thousand have occurred. Among associated species here are *Anthyllis vulneraria*, *Euphrasia nemorosa*, *G. amarella*, *Lotus corniculatus* and *Rhinanthus minor*. The maintenance of such habitats is often occasioned by motorcycle and 4-wheel drive activity! In more natural situations it favours areas where rabbit activity has broken the ground and reduced the height of the vegetation. It is confined to the lowlands.

G. germanica is predominantly a biennial and reproduction is by seed. Annual forms do occur which are, in general, significantly smaller in all their parts. It hybridises freely with *G. amarella*, but this occurrence is much reduced because of the later flowering of *G. germanica*. The hybrids are fertile.

The species is extinct at some of its former sites. This is certainly in part due to the loss of habitat by quarrying but, in some cases, this activity has caused significant increases in population. A secondary cause of decline may be hybridisation with the more vigorous *G. amarella* subsp. *amarella* which, eventually, appears to be the only species remaining (Pritchard 1961).

This species is endemic to west and central Europe, occurring from southern Britain eastwards to the southern Alps and eastern Carpathians.

C. R. Boon

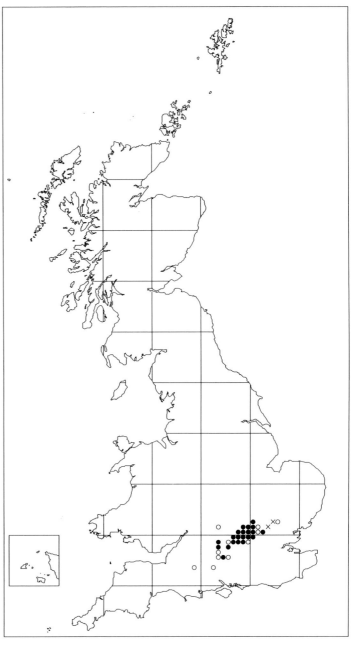

Current map	No	Atlas	No
1970 →	21	1930 →	14
Pre-1970	11	Pre-1930	11
Introductions	2	Introductions	0

continued →

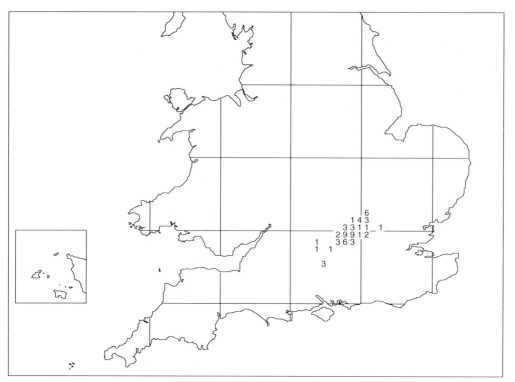

The number of tetrads in each 10 km square in which *Gentianella germanica* has been recorded as a native species from 1970 onwards. Squares in which the species is recorded in 9 or more tetrads are plotted as 9: *G. germanica* is actually recorded in 9 tetrads in SU89 and 10 in SU79. The species has been found in a total of 65 tetrads from 1970 onwards.

Gnaphalium sylvaticum L.
Status: not scarce

Heath cudweed

This calcifuge is found on moorland and forestry tracks in the north and in dry, open woods, heaths and sandy field edges elsewhere. It often grows in open patches on the edges of grazed rides in woodland. Typical associates include *Agrostis capillaris*, *Anthoxanthum odoratum*, *Betula pubescens*, *Cerastium fontanum* subsp. *holosteoides*, *Galium saxatile*, *Pteridium aquilinum*, *Rumex acetosella* and *Veronica officinalis*. This is essentially a lowland species, but it occurs up to 950 metres at Knockchoilum.

It is a short-lived perennial, with small flowers, which are little visited by insects and probably wind-pollinated. It reproduces by seed. Populations can vary greatly in numbers from year to year.

The results of the BSBI Monitoring Scheme suggested that this species had declined, and this is supported by the distribution map. A more detailed study is required to establish the reasons for this apparent decline. The species may be under-recorded in some areas, especially as it is often found in small populations.

This is an amphi-atlantic species, found in Europe north to northern Norway and in western and central Asia and also in eastern North America. It is recorded as an introduction in New Zealand.

L. Farrell

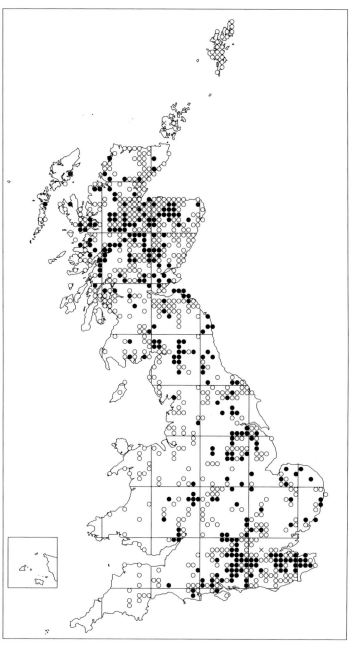

Current map	No	Atlas	No
1970 →	290	1930 →	525
Pre-1970	574	Pre-1930	60
Introductions	2	Introductions	0

Goodyera repens (L.) R.Br.
Status: scarce

Creeping lady's-tresses

G. repens is primarily a plant of coniferous woodlands, both semi-natural and planted, with, in almost every case, a considerable proportion of *Pinus sylvestris* and often some *Betula* spp. It appears to grow best in a moist layer of moss and pine-needles and is accompanied by other calcifuge plants which can thrive in slight or moderate shade. These include *Calluna vulgaris*, *Galium saxatile*, *Vaccinium myrtillus* and *Veronica officinalis*, while *Listera cordata* and *Pyrola minor* may also occur nearby. It is also found on old sand dunes. In favoured sites *G. repens* can spread and cover large areas and is abundant in some localities in north-east Scotland. It is generally a lowland plant but has been recorded at 336 metres near Morinsh.

G. repens is an evergreen perennial, with rosettes which can be found throughout the year, often most easily in winter. Established plants flower freely in July and August and seed is very often set but it appears that, within colonies, vegetative reproduction predominates, with stolons spreading just below the surface of the moss and giving rise to new plants. The fine, windblown seed serves to establish new colonies (Summerhayes 1951). Once established in an area *G. repens* can spread rapidly to other nearby sites, thus forming clusters of colonies. However, it often fails to spread far if an area of unsuitable land intervenes and there are many apparently ideal sites in northern England and the Borders which are, as yet, uncolonised.

The map indicates that *G. repens* may be declining. Being so dependent on *Pinus sylvestris*, it is extremely vulnerable to clear-felling and replanting with other conifers and a large number of sites has been lost in this way. It is also susceptible to shading by scrub and brambles.

G. repens is a circumboreal species. In Europe it extends south in the mountains to the Pyrenees, northern Italy and the Balkans.

It is generally considered that the East Anglian colonies developed from plants inadvertently introduced with seedling pines from sources in north-east Scotland, and populations in northern England and the Borders may well have developed in the same way. However, it is also possible that these sites were colonised by wind-blown seed.

M. S. Porter

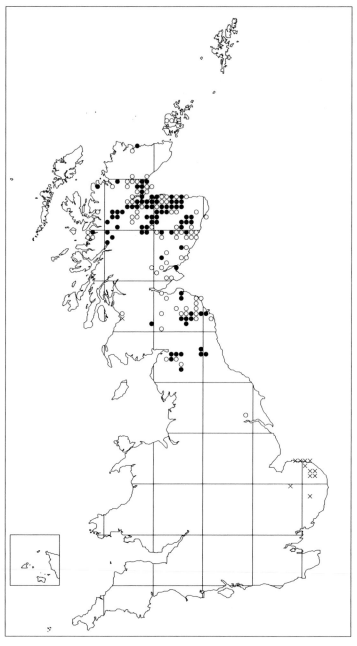

Current map	No	Atlas	No
1970 →	84	1930 →	79
Pre-1970	80	Pre-1930	32
Introductions	12	Introductions	3

Gymnocarpium robertianum (Hoffm.) Newman   **Limestone fern**

Status: scarce

This fern is confined to calcium-rich substrates and usually grows on natural limestone screes and pavement. It is usually found on Carboniferous and oolitic limestone, but there is at least one locality on hard chalk. It is favoured by open sunny situations, although it may get established in shady grikes. *G. robertianum* is associated with other limestone species such as *Asplenium trichomanes-ramosum*, *Cystopteris fragilis*, *Geranium robertianum*, *Mercurialis perennis*, *Oxalis acetosella* and *Phyllitis scolopendrium*. It rarely grows above 450 metres altitude, but reaches 585 metres on Carreg yr Ogof in the Black Mountains.

This perennial species is easily grown from spores and is a favourite with fern gardeners. It often escapes and establishes itself on man-made walls and in culverts even in the drier and colder parts of the country.

In its natural habitats *G. robertianum* can be ousted by competition with *Mercurialis perennis* and hawthorn scrub, and limestone quarrying has taken its toll of its localities.

This is a circumboreal species. In Europe it is most frequent in central Europe, extending south to the Pyrenees and north to northern Norway (Jalas & Suominen 1972).

A. C. Jermy

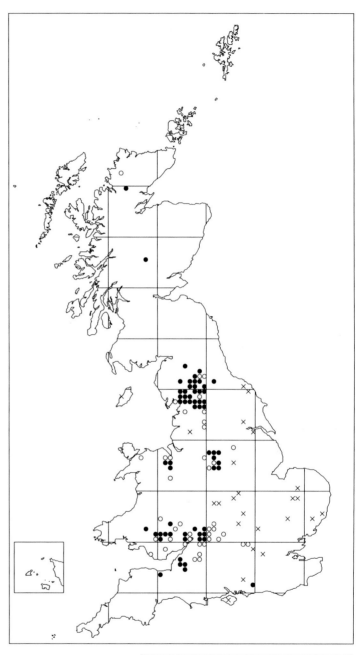

Current map	No	Atlas	No
1970 →	61	1930 →	37
Pre-1970	41	Pre-1930	22
Introductions	24	Introductions	10

Hammarbya paludosa (L.) Kuntze

Bog orchid

Status: scarce

H. paludosa is found in boggy areas where the drainage water is moderately acidic. It frequently grows in sphagnum and can also be found on peaty mud and among grasses on the edges of runnels. In most sites it is associated with some water movement. Associated species are numerous but often include *Carex echinata, Drosera rotundifolia, Erica tetralix, Molinia caerulea, Nardus stricta* and *Rhynchospora alba*. In some sites *Vaccinium oxycoccos* is quite frequent. In Merioneth, and perhaps elsewhere, it tends to occur where bogs are flushed with water from base-rich rocks, growing with base-demanding sphagna such as *S. contortum, S. teres* and *S. warnstorfii*. *H. paludosa* is generally a lowland species, though it has been recorded up to 500 metres on Millfore and at Llyn Anafon.

H. paludosa is a perennial with a long flowering season: there may be plants in flower in one colony from the end of June until the second half of September. Though seed is often set, this species also reproduces vegetatively by means of bulbils which develop on the leaf tips and which, having become detached, develop into new plants (Summerhayes 1951).

The drainage of bogs has brought about a dramatic decrease in the number of recorded sites, especially in lowland England. In lowland mires systems such as the New Forest the species depends on grazing to maintain open runnels, flushes and *Molinia*-free mires in which it grows. The tiny, shallow-rooted plants are vulnerable to nearby trampling which can cause them to pop out of the ground. However, there are many areas in Scotland where *H. paludosa* could well be thriving unseen. More sites are known in Cumbria, for example, than at any time in the past simply as a result of recent intensive recording.

H. paludosa is most frequent in northern and central Europe, but it is also recorded at scattered localities in the boreal zone of Asia and North America. It is considered to be under threat in Europe as a whole .

Because of its small stature (sometimes under 3 cm in height), sporadic appearance and pale coloration, *H. paludosa* is notoriously difficult to find and may often escape detection. It could well be holding its own in the more western and northern parts of Great Britain.

M. S. Porter

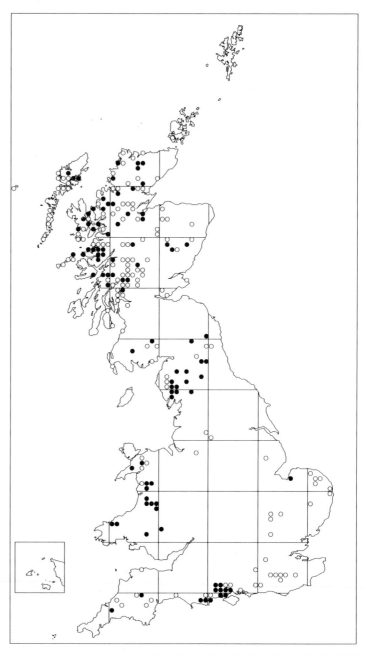

Current map	No	Atlas	No
1970 →	95	1930 →	66
Pre-1970	142	Pre-1930	72
Introductions	0	Introductions	0

Helianthemum canum (L.) Baumg.

Hoary rock-rose

Status: scarce

H. canum is restricted to Carboniferous limestone. It is found on rocky outcrops and on the face of scars and cliffs, often on the upper parts of outcrops and in sparse vegetation on shallow soil near the edges of cliffs. It can be very abundant on steep, rocky, exposed, often south-facing sites, which are prone to summer drought. Its associates include a number of typical limestone plants, particularly *Anthyllis vulneraria*, *Helianthemum nummularium*, *Hippocrepis comosa*, *Lotus corniculatus*, *Scabiosa columbaria* and *Thymus polytrichus*. In Teesdale it is found on sugar limestone, an extremely porous and free-draining metamorphosed Carboniferous limestone. It is almost exclusively lowland but occurs at 535 metres on Cronkley Fell.

H. canum is a shrubby, mat-forming perennial. Plants flower freely and set abundant seed unless they are subjected to particularly heavy grazing. There is no specialised means of dispersal. Seeds produced in one summer germinate gradually over a long period but the successful establishment of seedlings requires a period of damp weather long enough for young plants to develop a root system which will withstand subsequent drought (Griffiths & Proctor 1956).

Its major British stronghold is on the Great Orme. Some smaller populations may be threatened by competition from invading native trees and shrubs, and aliens such as *Cotoneaster* spp. and *Rhamnus alaternus*.

H. canum is also found on the west coast of Ireland, central and southern Europe, Öland (Sweden), Asia Minor, the Caucasus and North Africa.

Two subspecies are recognised in Britain. The widespread plant is subsp. *canum* which occurs almost throughout the range of the species. The plant on Cronkley Fell is an endemic subspecies, subsp. *laevigatum* M. Proctor.

R. Wilson

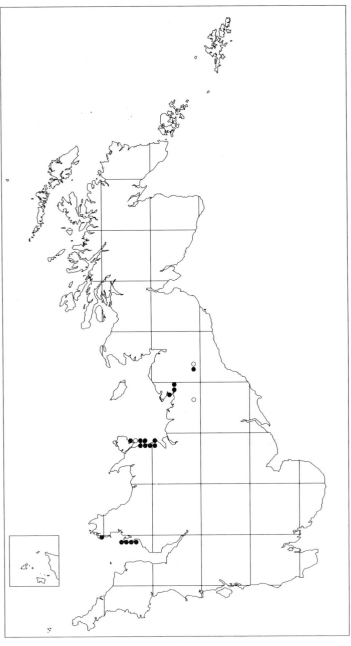

Current map	No	Atlas	No
1970 →	17	1930 →	15
Pre-1970	3	Pre-1930	2
Introductions	0	Introductions	0

continued →

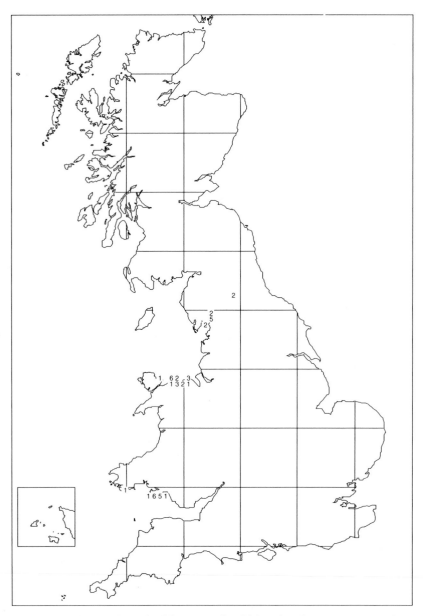

The number of tetrads in each 10 km square in which *Helianthemum canum* has been recorded as a native species from 1970 onwards. The species has been found in a total of 44 tetrads from 1970 onwards.

Helleborus foetidus L.

Status: scarce

Stinking hellebore

H. foetidus is confined largely to calcareous soils, growing on scree and shallow soil over chalk and also over calcareous clays. It is found both in exposed and partially shaded situations but rarely in deep shade. In beechwoods it tends to occur as isolated plants or colonies in more open areas. In hedgerows it is often absent from the northerly aspect and where competition is dense. In scrub it occurs in more open areas between shrubs.

Individual plants are short-lived perennials, with leafy overwintering stems, and they usually die after four or five years. Flowering starts early in the year, sometimes in January, and, in spite of the relative shortage of pollinators, reproduction is entirely by seed. Reduced seed set is compounded by mice eating buds, flowers and immature seed pods. A major factor in reduced longevity and poor seed set, particularly where surrounding vegetation creates a humid atmosphere in winter, is the fungus *Coniothyrium hellebori*. This attacks the overwintering flowering stems at the base causing death of the shoots before seed set. Seeds are distributed by ants, but most seem to germinate immediately around parent plants. Spread to new sites is limited.

This species is decreasing over much of its range, partly as the result of the disappearance of hedgerows and also the cruder management of those that remain. Herbicide drift and the destruction of flowering stems by tractors during winter flailing of hedges are also important factors. An accurate assessment of the status of this species is confused by the frequent occurrence of individuals and small populations as garden escapes which persist for only a relatively short period.

A western European species, which extends from Britain, Spain and Portugal to Italy and Germany (Jalas & Suominen 1989). It is also found in Morocco.

A wider range of forms introduced from southern and eastern Europe are being cultivated in gardens. Unusually vigorous forms, and plants with enlarged bracts and without the characteristic purple rim to the flower, may soon appear as garden escapes.

G. Rice

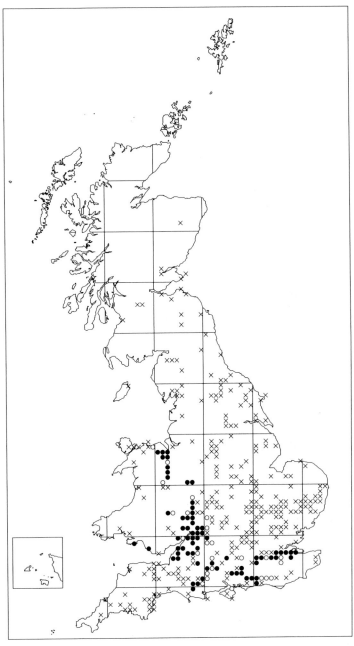

Current map	No	Atlas	No
1970 →	69	1930 →	55
Pre-1970	25	Pre-1930	15
Introductions	268	Introductions	138

Herminium monorchis (L.) R.Br.   **Musk orchid**

Status: scarce

One of the smallest of our native orchids, *H. monorchis* grows in short turf in calcareous grassland. It grows particularly well on narrow terracettes formed on steep slopes by soil creep. It also favours the floors of old quarries, where infertile soils and compaction restrict the growth of other taller-growing species. It is confined to the lowlands.

It multiplies vegetatively by producing tubers on the end of slender root-like rhizomes, forming small colonies around a 'mother' plant, but separated from it by as much as 10 cm. Large colonies can arise by this means over a number of favourable years.

Flowering fluctuates greatly from year to year. In dry years, populations may cease to flower completely but individuals survive as small rosettes of leaves which are easily over-looked. The flower-spike is produced in late June or July and consists of many yellowish-green or green, sweetly scented flowers, closely packed together. Capsules are set and seeds dispersed by August. Leaves die down in late September and do not appear again until late May the following year.

H. monorchis has been lost from many of its former downland localities, especially in East Anglia, but it does have the ability to colonise new sites such as quarry floors.

H. monorchis is a member of the Northern Eurasian group of British orchids and is widely distributed throughout the northern parts of these two continents. Elsewhere in Europe it is not restricted to calcareous soils and it often grows in much damper places than those in which it is found in Britain.

T. C. E. Wells

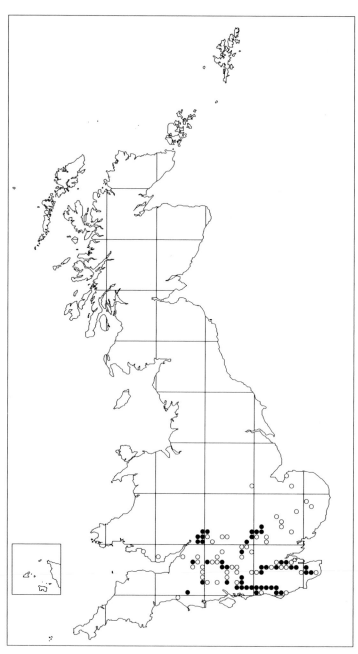

Current map	No	Atlas	No
1970 →	46	1930 →	40
Pre-1970	54	Pre-1930	39
Introductions	0	Introductions	0

continued →

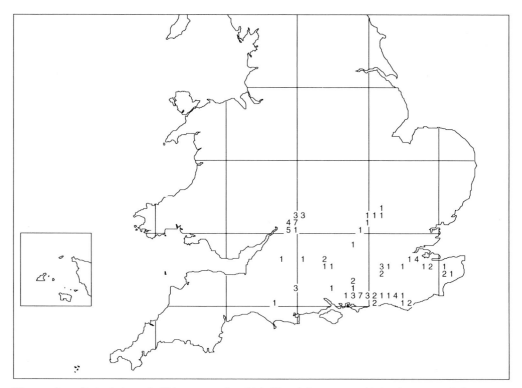

The number of tetrads in each 10 km square in which *Herminium monorchis* has been recorded as a native species from 1970 onwards. The species has been found in a total of 87 tetrads from 1970 onwards.

Hippophae rhamnoides L.
Status: scarce

Sea-buckthorn

This is a thorny deciduous shrub or small tree of less mobile dune sand and occasionally soft sea cliffs. In its coastal habitat, it grows most vigorously where it is sheltered from the wind, in places such as dune hollows and the leeward or landward side of ridges rather than on dune crests. It is intolerant of shade and does not penetrate into woods and forests, except locally in clearings and by trackways. Plants which were present before *Hippophae* invades (e.g. *Ammophila arenaria*, *Festuca rubra*) often persist for a period under the canopy. The shrub later becomes dominant, forming dense stands in which *Urtica dioica* often grows (Pearson & Rogers 1962). It is often planted in gardens or amenity plantations and introduced plants are sometimes found on river sand and gravel banks inland.

Initial invasion may be by seed because, though the species is dioecious, fruiting can be prolific and birds can transport the seed some distance. Germination requires a cold pre-treatment (2 to 5 °C) (Ranwell 1972) but such a need is generally met in early winter and viability can be high. Seeds can withstand at least 12 weeks at a temperature of -20 °C and still remain viable. Young plants can withstand some accretion, as long as they are not completely buried. The mature plant does not show any signs of frost damage. Established plants produce vigorous suckers.

H. rhamnoides is considered native only on the eastern coast of England. Introductions and the natural spread from introduced populations have now obscured the native range. It was seen initially as a possible solution to problems associated with dune erosion, but more recently *H. rhamnoides* has given cause for concern in some dune sites, presenting a real threat to botanical interest. In some areas steps have been taken to eradicate this species.

It occurs along the coast of north-west Europe, Norway and the Baltic. It is also found on the shores of the northern Mediterranean, the Black and Caspian Seas and Lake Baikal. Its inland distribution embraces most of the major mountain ranges from the Pyrenees and Alps to the Caucasus, Carpathians and the Himalayas, occurring as far east as south-west China (Pearson & Rogers 1962).

H. rhamnoides was widespread in Britain in the Late Glacial in both coastal and inland sites. With the spread of forest it became restricted to coastal sites. In Scandinavia it has a similar history, but there it survives in montane refugia as well as in coastal sites (Godwin 1975).

H. Ainsworth

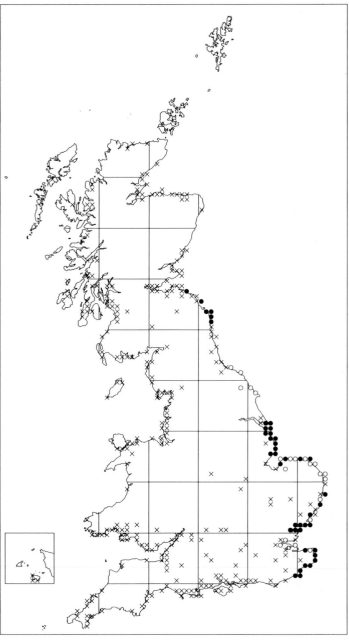

Current map	No	Atlas	No
1970 →	41		
Pre-1970	21	Native records	36
Introductions	270	Introductions	186

Hordelymus europaeus (L.) Jessen

Wood barley

Status: scarce

This grass usually grows on wood banks and hedgerows, often occurring on or near medieval woodland boundary banks. It is often found under the high canopy of *Ulmus* spp. and in the shade of shrubs such as *Corylus avellana* and *Sambucus nigra* in sites near the edge of the wood where some light penetrates from the margin. Most sites are over chalk and limestone; it is less frequent on calcareous boulder clay. Plant associates include several common woodland species such as *Anthriscus sylvestris, Galium aparine, Geum urbanum, Glechoma hederacea, Hedera helix, Heracleum sphondylium, Hyacinthoides non-scripta, Mercurialis perennis, Rubus* spp. and *Urtica dioica*.

It is a perennial reproducing by seed.

H. europaeus is usually found in a wood as discrete colonies, which are often small. It persists in woods which are managed by coppicing or periodic clear-felling, and the only real threat lies in the destruction of old woodland.

H. europaeus is found in Europe, North Africa and western Asia. It is widespread in this area but has a curiously discontinuous distribution (Hultén & Fries 1986).

P. J. O. Trist

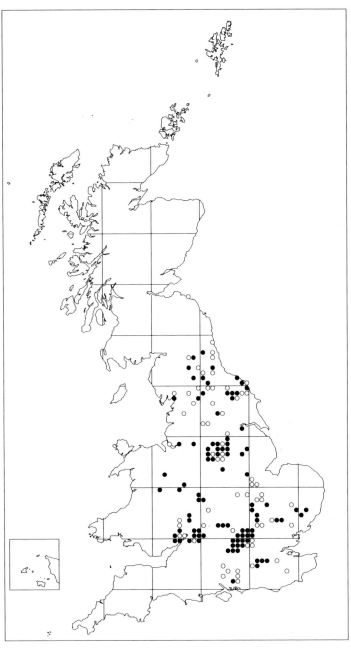

Current map	No	Atlas	No
1970 →	93	1930 →	51
Pre-1970	64	Pre-1930	34
Introductions	0	Introductions	0

continued →

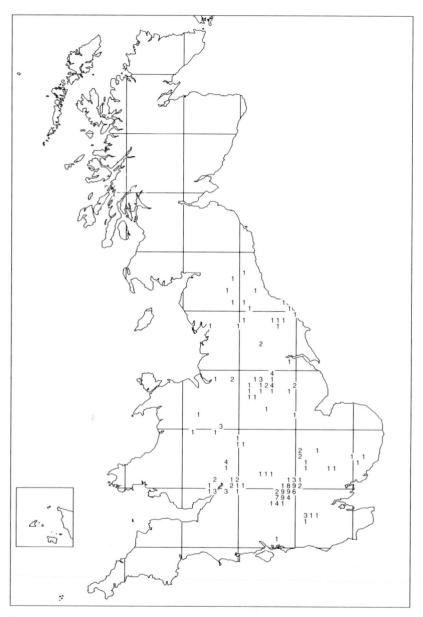

The number of tetrads in each 10 km square in which *Hordelymus europaeus* has been recorded as a native species from 1970 onwards. Squares in which the species is recorded in 9 or more tetrads are plotted as 9: *H. europaeus* is actually recorded in 9 tetrads in SP90,12 in SU78, 21 in SU89 and 22 in SU79. The species has been found in a total of 209 tetrads from 1970 onwards. The tetrad data are inadequate in Gloucestershire, where the species is still plentiful (Holland 1986).

Hordeum marinum Hudson
Status: scarce

Sea barley

This is an annual grass of bare soils along the coast. It favours brackish sites which are occasionally flooded in winter but baked hard and dry by midsummer, so it is frequently found by the edges of dried-up pools and ditches, or on ground on the landward side of sea walls which has been rutted by vehicles or trampled by cattle. Characteristic associates in these open communities include *Puccinellia distans*, *Spergularia marina* and the scarce species *Polypogon monspeliensis*, *Puccinellia fasciculata* and *P. rupestris*. In a few places it also occurs on the upper parts of salt-marshes, especially where these are grazed and trampled by cattle or sheep; associates in these sites can include *Festuca rubra*, *Glaux maritima*, *Juncus gerardii*, *Parapholis strigosa*, *Plantago coronopus* and *Puccinellia maritima*.

H. marinum is free-flowering and strictly annual, reproduction being entirely from seed. The mature spikes are very brittle and break up into little clusters of spikelets which tend to disperse together. Dispersal of spikelets is probably assisted by flooding, as winter flood-lines around pools are often marked the following summer by narrow banks of *H. marinum*. Seedlings occur in spring and autumn but the latter may not survive the winter.

H. marinum appears to be decreasing, particularly along the south coast. This is probably the result of the loss of coastal grazing marsh, filling-in of pools and small ditches, and the strengthening and upgrading of sea defences. It is susceptible to successional changes, tending to be overpowered by perennial grasses (notably *Elytrigia atherica*), and thus it requires the continuous creation of open ground.

It is widely distributed in the Mediterranean region, where it grows on both maritime sands and on disturbed ground away from the coast, and extends along the coast of western Europe to reach its northern limit in the British Isles.

A. J. Gray

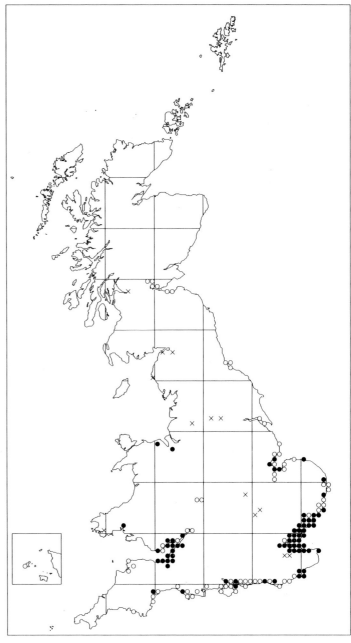

Current map	No	Atlas	No
1970 →	70	1930 →	59
Pre-1970	66	Pre-1930	46
Introductions	13	Introductions	7

Hornungia petraea (L.) Reichb.

Hutchinsia

Status: scarce

This small species has two habitats in Britain: south or south-west facing slopes on Carboniferous limestone, and calcareous sand dunes. In both it is restricted to open vegetation with bare soil which is dry in summer and moist in winter. On limestone it avoids the rockiest and driest situations and continuous grass cover. Its most typical habitat is a shallow humus-rich but skeletal soil on a broken rocky slope with an intermittent cover of *Festuca ovina*. It is usually associated with other overwintering annuals such as *Arabidopsis thaliana*, *Aphanes arvensis*, *Arenaria serpyllifolia*, *Cardamine hirsuta* and rarely *Draba muralis*. On sand dunes it is occasionally found at the early fixed stage, more usually at a later stage but where the turf is open owing to instability or disturbance. *H. petraea* ranges from near sea-level in South Wales to *c*. 490 metres near Hawes, but normally grows below 300 metres.

H. petraea is a winter annual. Soil moistening and lower temperatures in the autumn stimulate germination and seedlings surviving the early stages have a high probability of reproductive success, as the leaf rosettes are capable of withstanding low temperature, exposure and snow cover. Flowering can start as early as January in warm spells and continues until May or June but is usually curtailed earlier than this by spring drought. Plants are largest, and subsequent seed production is greatest, following mild winters when much-branched plants continue to grow and flower for long periods in the spring. A certain amount of disturbance by grazing can be beneficial by preventing development of a closed turf, and the species does well in the year following a dry summer when more bare soil is exposed by the death of perennial grasses. Self-pollination always ensures good seed production.

In most localities the population size, which varies from tens to many thousands, has been stable over many years and the only major threat is of habitat destruction, as in the ecologically similar *Draba muralis*.

It is widely distributed in suitable habitats in southern Scandinavia and the eastern Baltic, western, central and southern Europe, and extends to north-west Africa and Asia Minor.

For a more detailed account of this species, see Ratcliffe (1959).

D. Ratcliffe

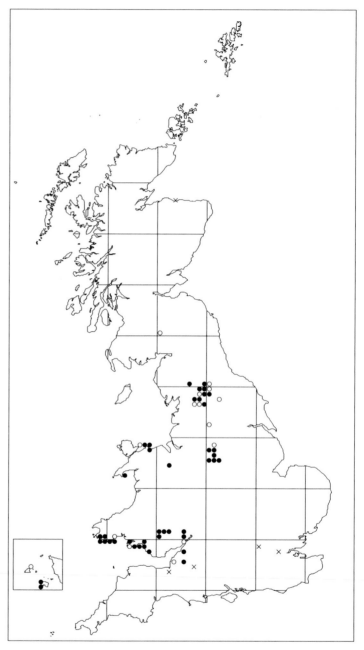

Current map	No	Atlas	No
1970 →	40	1930 →	26
Pre-1970	14	Pre-1930	12
Introductions	5	Introductions	2

continued →

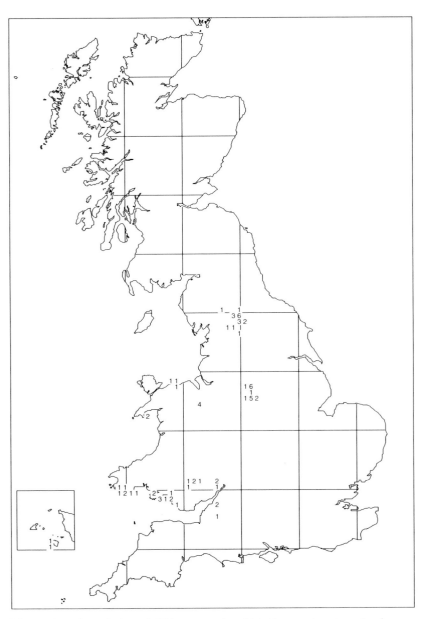

The number of tetrads in each 10 km square in which *Hornungia petraea* has been recorded as a native species from 1970 onwards. The species has been recorded in a total of 74 tetrads from 1970 onwards.

Hydrocharis morsus-ranae L.

Status: not scarce

Frogbit

H. morsus-ranae is a free-floating species which typically occurs as a dominant of grazing marsh ditches, although it is also widespread in farm ponds and canals. Its preferred habitat is still (or very slow-flowing) water which is neutral to base-rich with moderate levels of nitrogen and other nutrients. Characteristic associates include *Lemna gibba*, *L. trisulca, Spirodela polyrhiza* and, locally *Stratiotes aloides*. *H. morsus-ranae* is intolerant of shade from tall emergents such as *Phragmites australis* and competes poorly with water-lilies and other large floating-leaved species. It is much commoner in sheltered sites protected from the wind, and on grazing marshes is generally associated with narrow field ditches rather than with broader arterial drains. *H. morsus-ranae* is most common where marginal grazing or occasional mechanised clearing of ditches suppresses the growth of emergents. On grazing marshes, therefore, it rarely persists in ditches adjoining fields which have been converted to arable. It grows on both alluvial and peaty soils and is rarely found above 50 metres, although it occasionally occurs in ponds at higher altitudes and reaches 240 metres above Westbury-sub-Mendip.

H. morsus-ranae reproduces almost entirely vegetatively. It is a stoloniferous species, with daughter plants produced at the end of the stolons, and becoming detached. In autumn turions are produced which sink to the bottom of the water and in the spring float to the surface, producing a new plant. This species is a partly monoecious perennial, but fruits are rarely produced in Britain.

H. morsus-ranae has declined markedly in the last century except in those coastal flatlands (e.g. the Somerset Levels and Moors) which remain mostly under pasture. It has suffered from the conversion of grazing marsh to arable, the elimination of ditches and changes in their management. This rapid decrease has also been experienced by its relative and associate, *Stratiotes aloides*.

H. morsus-ranae is found throughout temperate Eurasia, but it is generally local and is probably declining throughout its range. It is rare in the Mediterranean region. It is naturalised in North America.

J. O. Mountford

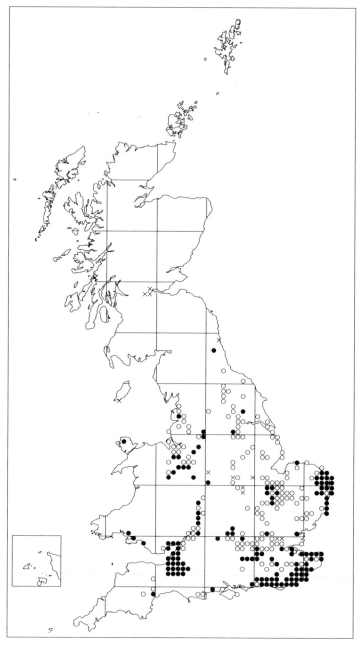

Current map	No	Atlas	No
1970 →	134	1930 →	173
Pre-1970	160	Pre-1930	49
Introductions	12	Introductions	5

Hyoscyamus niger L.

Status: not scarce

Henbane

This lowland, biennial herb tends to occur on disturbed ground and in sandy coastal areas. *H. niger* is usually to be found on calcareous soils where there is little competition from coarse vegetation. In some seaside sites it grows alone and thrives in very sandy soil where other plants which lack its deep tap-root are unable to maintain a foothold. It is frequently to be found inland on chalk downs, particularly around rabbit-warrens where other more palatable competing species have been grazed away and the soil is continually disturbed.

Reproduction is by means of its plentiful seeds. These germinate erratically and there is strong evidence that buried seeds remain viable for many years, awaiting disturbances that will bring them to the surface. Distribution of seeds to new sites is probably by wind, although many occurrences in new sites are clearly a result of human activities, since *H. niger* turns up regularly on refuse-tips where builders' rubble has been dumped.

H. niger is declining due to loss of suitable habitat to coastal development, to more intensive use of farmland and general 'tidying-up' of waste places. Several factors affect its prospects for future survival. Livestock farmers uproot and destroy *H. niger* on sight, since it is extremely poisonous to animals (and humans). However, it has been cultivated for many centuries for medical purposes, as a source of several important alkaloids, which may have assisted its spread. Recent records suggest that it may be introduced as a seed impurity in leguminous forage crops.

The native range of *H. niger* has been obscured by its spread as a medicinal plant. It probably originates in the Mediterranean region and western Asia, but is now widespread in the northern hemisphere and also recorded in Australasia.

In Britain, as in Europe, it is virtually impossible to separate localities where the species is native (or at least long-established) from those where it is a recent introduction. All records are therefore mapped together irrespective of status.

V. A. Johnstone

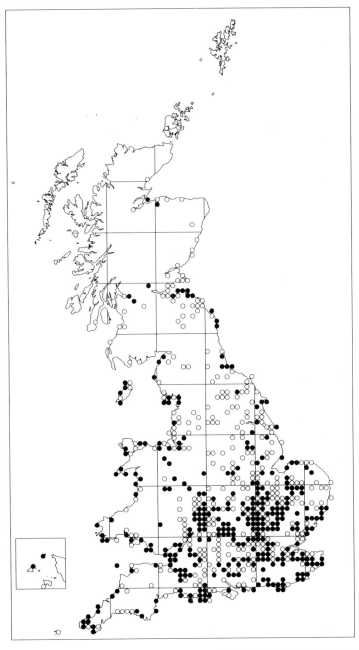

Current map	No	Atlas	No
1970 →	320	1930 →	249
Pre-1970	315	Pre-1930	60

Hypericum montanum L.
Status: not scarce

Pale St John's-wort

This is a lowland, southern species restricted to calcareous rocks: Carboniferous limestone in the north-west of England, Wales, and the Mendips, Permian limestone to the east of the Pennines and the chalk of the Lincolnshire Wolds and southern England. It also occurs on calcareous sandstone in Surrey. It prefers warm, well-drained soils and occurs on roadside banks, by thickets and among scrub, under light shade in ashwoods and in the grikes of limestone pavement. It occasionally grows in coarse, relatively species-poor grassland dominated by *Festuca ovina*, *Helictotrichon pratense*, *Holcus lanatus* and *Trisetum flavescens* in areas where grazing pressure is low. It ascends to 330 metres near Buxton.

The populations are generally small. Seed production is normal but, with its short, perennial rootstock, vegetative propagation is very slow. Each individual produces from one to three shoots per year, most of which flower.

The map shows a number of occurrences outside the areas referred to above. Some are undoubtedly correct, as for example the occurrence at Heysham Docks, and by railways in Cheshire and west Cornwall, but it seems likely that a number of apparently anomalous records are the result of confusion with *H. hirsutum*. The main threat to *H. montanum* is the continuing disappearance of lowland calcareous grassland.

H. montanum occurs throughout central Europe, extending south to central Spain, Italy and the northern Balkans, north to southern Scandinavia and east to the Ukraine, with disjunct occurrences in the Crimea and on the east side of the Black Sea. In the Alps it occurs locally in the subalpine zone but it typically grows lower down in somewhat open, mixed woodland on dry, calcareous soils.

G. Halliday

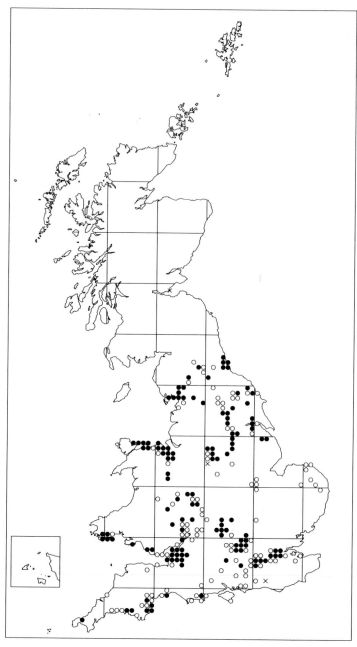

Current map	No	Atlas	No
1970 →	125	1930 →	94
Pre-1970	109	Pre-1930	58
Introductions	3	Introductions	0

Hypericum undulatum Schousboe ex Willd.

Status: scarce

Wavy St John's-wort

This is a plant of rushy pastures and damp heaths on non-calcareous soils. The vegetation in which *H. undulatum* occurs is usually dominated by mixtures of *Molinia caerulea* and *Juncus* species, particularly *J. acutiflorus* and *J. effusus*. A variety of herbs may be present, including *Angelica sylvestris*, *Cirsium palustre*, *Filipendula ulmaria*, *Galium palustre*, *Lotus pedunculatus*, *Mentha aquatica* and *Senecio aquaticus*. The western-oceanic species *Carum verticillatum* and *Scutellaria minor* also occur on many sites. Within this vegetation *H. undulatum* shows a preference for seasonally or permanently waterlogged areas subject to marked lateral water movement (giving slight base enrichment). It is confined to the lowlands.

H. undulatum is a stoloniferous perennial, flowering in August and September, and with seed germinating in the spring. In common with other members of this genus, *H. undulatum* may develop a persistent 'bank' of buried seed (F. Evans 1989). Seedlings probably require bare ground for successful establishment: in tussocky grassland the plant tends to occur in open areas, either on the sides of the *Molinia caerulea* tussocks or on cattle-poached ground between them. Population size can vary greatly from year to year, and may increase rapidly following reinstatement of grazing and burning on under-managed (overgrown) sites (F. Evans 1989).

The loss of *H. undulatum* from many of its former localities has been largely due to habitat destruction, particularly as a result of agricultural intensification (including the use of fertilisers, drainage, ploughing and reseeding). Evidence from north Devon is that in recent years the rate of loss of these western rush-pastures has been high (Devon Wildlife Trust 1992). Clearly the continued survival of *H. undulatum* in Britain will depend on the protection and appropriate management of its remaining sites. Management of grasslands with *H. undulatum* usually involves cattle-grazing in summer and occasional burning in winter to remove any accumulation of litter.

This species is confined to the Atlantic fringe of western Europe, from western Spain and Portugal northwards to Britain. It also occurs on Madeira and the Azores.

S. J. Leach & R. J. Wolton

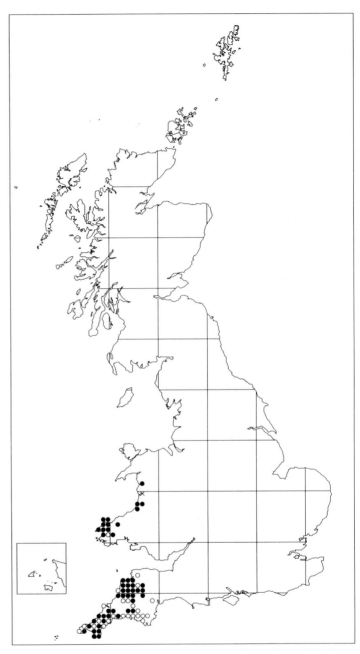

Current map	No	Atlas	No
1970 →	49	1930 →	24
Pre-1970	24	Pre-1930	27
Introductions	1	Introductions	0

continued →

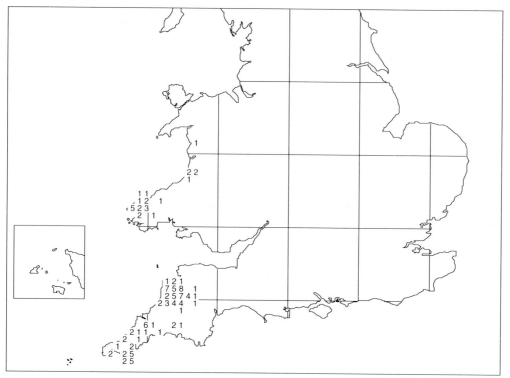

The number of tetrads in each 10 km square in which *Hypericum undulatum* has been recorded as a native species from 1970 onwards. The species has been found in a total of 121 tetrads from 1970 onwards.

Hypochaeris glabra L.

Status: scarce

Smooth cat's-ear

This plant grows on disturbed, usually nutrient-poor, light soils in acidic sandy, heathy and gravelly places. *H. glabra* prefers a sunny, warm and exposed situation, and is relatively intolerant of competition, growing, for instance, in open communities on sand dunes, with *Jasione montana* and occasionally *Corynephorus canescens*. It often occurs in resown sandy pastures, providing they are not fertilised or irrigated, with *Agrostis* spp., *Potentilla argentea*, *Radiola linoides*, *Trifolium* spp. and *Vicia lathyroides*. It was formerly found as a component of open arable communities with *Scleranthus annuus* and *Teesdalia nudicaulis*. It also colonises bare ground, along with other pioneer annuals such as *Aphanes arvensis*, *Filago minima*, *Rumex acetosella* and *Senecio sylvaticus* (Sinker *et al.* 1985).

H. glabra is a self-compatible annual herb, pollinated by bees. It produces fruit of two forms, which germinates after autumn rains have begun (Fone 1989).

There is no doubt that the range and frequency of *H. glabra* have been considerably reduced. It used to be more frequent as a weed of sandy arable land and also occurred as a shoddy weed (Silverside 1990). However, it is often overlooked because of its small size, and because it does not open its flowers until 9 a.m. and they shut again by 1 or 2 p.m. (Curtis 1777). Conversely, small forms of *H. radicata* are often optimistically recorded as *H. glabra*. The two occasionally hybridise (Stace 1975).

It is found in Europe, northwards to southern Scandinavia, and in North Africa and the Middle East. It is widely naturalised elsewhere.

D. A. Pearman

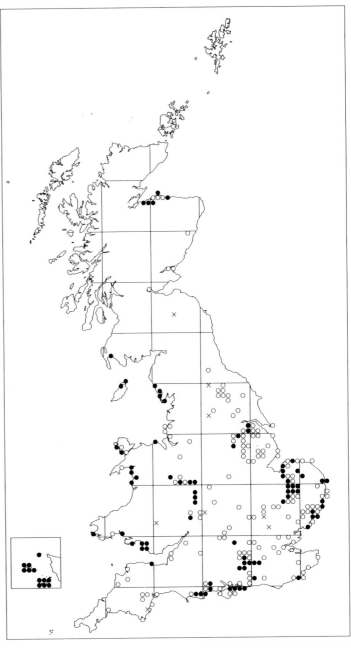

Current map	No	Atlas	No
1970 →	81	1930 →	134
Pre-1970	148	Pre-1930	42
Introductions	8	Introductions	2

Iberis amara L.

Status: scarce

Wild candytuft

This is a plant of chalk grassland, generally found on areas of bare ground, such as rabbit scratchings, and especially favouring steep south or south-west facing slopes. It may very occasionally be found in relatively tall grass and frequently in freshly disturbed sites, such as storm-damaged woodland where the canopy has been destroyed, in newly ploughed grassland or arable and in chalkpits. It can scarcely be said to have any true associates, simply the odd calcicole able to establish itself on the bare soil favoured by *I. amara*. At a later stage of succession many species invade such habitats and finally choke out *I. amara*. It is confined to the lowlands.

Plants flower and fruit freely; hillsides where it is frequent are sometimes described as quite white from a distance. Plants range in size from small and single-stemmed to large much-branched individuals. They are normally annuals and the dead plants persist and are easy to find even in winter. The seed is long-lived, surviving adverse conditions (e.g. the development of a dense ground flora and low light levels) and germinating when the soil surface is broken up and exposed to light and probably warmth.

The somewhat transient nature of this species makes it a little difficult to assess changes in the distribution over the years but it seems to be a little less common than in the past in most places but especially in Berkshire, probably due to the conversion of many areas of open downland to arable. However, it would undoubtedly reappear in many of its old sites here and elsewhere given the opportunity by ploughing or clearance. It has occurred in many places as an introduction, casual or garden escape, along with other similar *Iberis* spp.

It is found as a native in western and southern Europe and North Africa, but it is widely naturalised elsewhere.

A. J. Showler

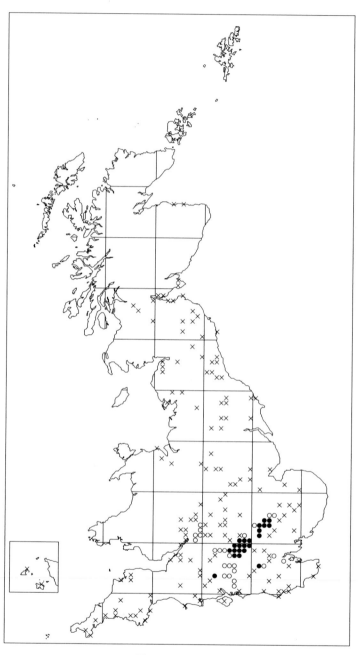

Current map	No	Atlas	No
1970 →	22	1930 →	21
Pre-1970	24	Pre-1930	15
Introductions	149	Introductions	0

continued →

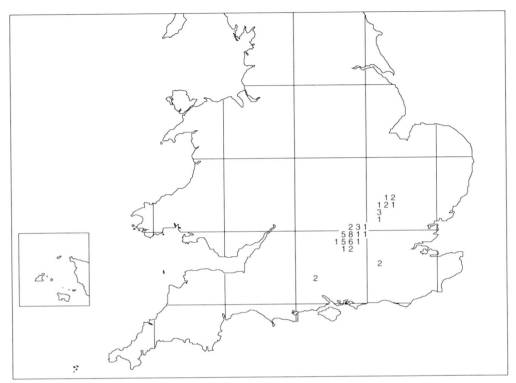

The number of tetrads in each 10 km square in which *Iberis amara* has been recorded as a native species from 1970 onwards. The species has been found in a total of 52 tetrads from 1970 onwards.

Illecebrum verticillatum L.

Status: scarce

I. verticillatum is an annual plant of neutral to acid soils, found in seasonally wet sandy or gravelly tracks. In the New Forest it occurs in very short heathy swards, heavily grazed 'lawns' near settlements, winter-wet hollows in tracks and at the edges of pools in the 'tide-mark' left when water levels drop. It is found in similar sites in Cornwall, but the largest Cornish populations are on the shallower edges of streams and the flooded ditches that branch off from them. Associates in tracks are *Gnaphalium uliginosum*, *Radiola linoides* and the scarce *Cicendia filiformis*. Around New Forest pools other species include *Galium constrictum*, *Hydrocotyle vulgaris*, *Littorella uniflora* with, at times, *Anagallis minima* and *Cicendia filiformis*. In Cornish streams, the main associates are *Eleogiton fluitans*, *Juncus articulatus*, *Lythrum portula* and *Potamogeton polygonifolius*.

The main flowering period is July to September, self-pollination being followed by the development of one-seeded fruits. Where the plant is growing in streams and pools it is noticeable that flowering takes place only on emergent stems. Seed germination can be held back by cold dry springs. In Cornwall the range of flowering time is more variable, and flowers have been found as early as June and as late as December.

This species is holding its own in the New Forest. It has, however, shown a marked decline in Cornwall where it has been recorded in only 10 of its 57 tetrads since 1987 and is now confined to strongholds in West Penwith, Goss Moor and Bodmin Moor. Outside its native range plants have become established on the moist gravels and clinker of disused railway lines. One population has been found in a disused china-clay pit.

This is a western European species, widespread from Spain to Germany and Poland and with a few scattered sites in the Mediterranean region (Jalas & Suominen 1983). It also occurs in the Azores and the Canaries.

R. J. Murphy

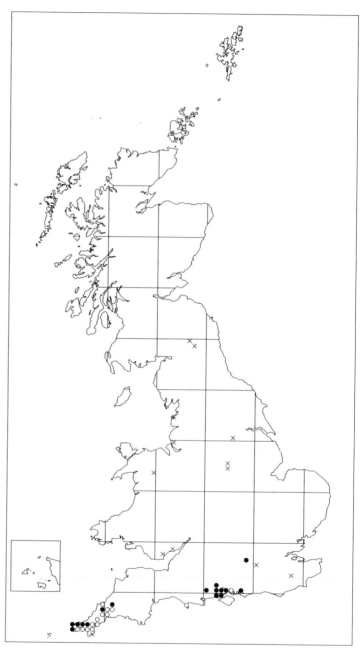

Current map	No	Atlas	No
1970 →	16	1930 →	10
Pre-1970	14	Pre-1930	14
Introductions	13	Introductions	4

continued →

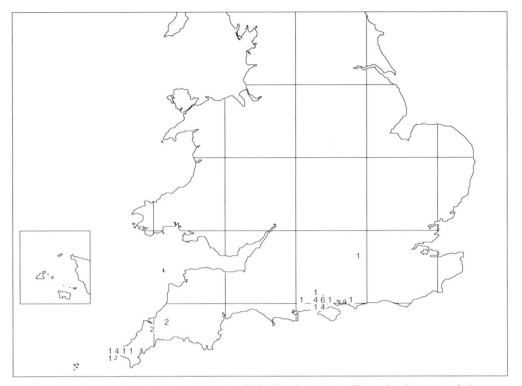

The number of tetrads in each 10 km square in which *Illecebrum verticillatum* has been recorded as a native species from 1970 onwards. The species has been found in a total of 32 tetrads from 1970 onwards.

Impatiens noli-tangere L.
Status: scarce

Touch-me-not balsam

This is essentially a woodland plant, occurring in damp, nutrient-rich soil in streamside silt and valleyside seepage areas. In the former it occurs chiefly under alder and oak and in the latter under oak and sometimes ash. Although an annual, it has few associated species and often forms pure stands. Most of the sites are below 100 metres but it reaches 200 metres at Dolgellau.

Flowering is from August onwards. Most flowers are produced in the more open, sunny and disturbed sites, as along woodland roads, around the bases of fallen trees and by car-parks. In shade, reproduction is most likely to be by cleistogamous flowers. The seeds probably have only a short viability and there is little evidence of a seed bank.

The populations are mostly small, 300-400 individuals, but some in the Lake District contain over 1000 plants. Although the Lake District populations fluctuate somewhat from year to year, they do not appear to be under any particular threat. However, populations on the Welsh borders have been reduced since 1950 by river management designed to increase flow rates.

This species is widespread throughout most of continental Europe, though absent from most of the Iberian peninsula, the extreme south-east and the extreme north. It ranges across Asia to Japan and in North America is largely confined to the north-west coast.

I. noli-tangere is probably native only in the Lake District, where it is locally frequent, around Dolgellau and in a small area on the Montgomery-Shropshire border, where it was found, new to Britain, by G. Bowles in 1632. The numerous records from outside these 'native' areas probably represent casual occurrences, originating perhaps as garden escapes or throw-outs, although it is rarely cultivated. Some may be the result of confusion with *I. parviflora*. Its claim to native status in the Lake District and Dolgellau is reinforced by the occurrence there of the only two British populations of the netted carpet moth *Eustoma reticulatum*, the larvae of which feed on *I. noli-tangere* (Hatcher & Alexander 1994), and by the presence of other oligophagous invertebrates (Coombe 1956).

P .E. Hatcher & G. Halliday

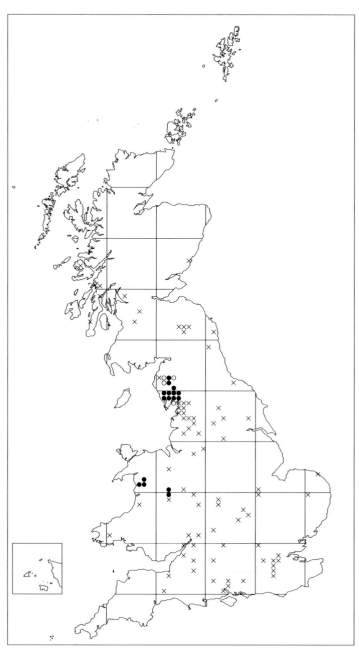

Current map	No	Atlas *	No
1970 →	16	1930 →	22
Pre-1970	4	Pre-1930	50
Introductions	78	Introductions	-

* Introductions were not distinguished on the *Atlas* map.

continued →

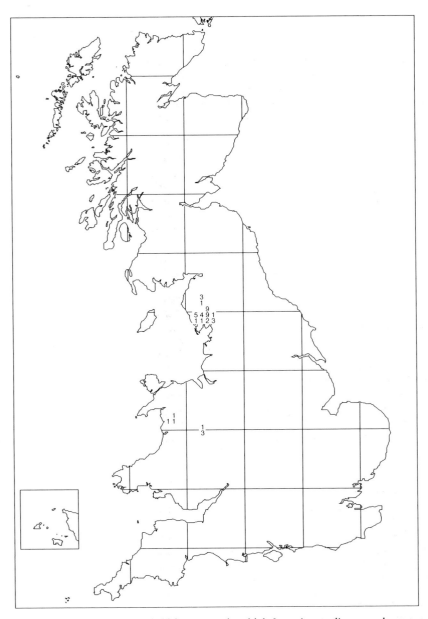

The number of tetrads in each 10 km square in which *Impatiens noli-tangere* has
been recorded as a native species from 1970 onwards. Squares in which the species is
recorded in 9 or more tetrads are plotted as 9: *I. noli-tangere* is actually recorded
from 9 tetrads in NY30 and 10 in SD39. The species has been found in a total of
47 tetrads from 1970 onwards.

Inula crithmoides L.

Status: scarce

Golden-samphire

I. crithmoides is found in several communities on seacliffs and saltmarshes. On seacliffs it is found in maritime rock crevices on calcareous rocks or crevices containing wind-blown shell sand, associated with *Aster tripolium*, *Crithmum maritimum*, *Limonium binervosum* (including several microspecies), *Parapholis incurva*, *Plantago coronopus* and *Spergularia rupicola*. Here the soil is of high (>7.0) pH, usually very shallow and usually well-drained and dry. A little further inland, it is found in *Festuca rubra-Armeria maritima* turf, usually on the seaward edge, associated with *Arenaria serpyllifolia*, *Bromus hordeaceus* subsp. *ferronii*, *Catapodium marinum*, *Euphorbia portlandica* and *Sedum acre*. In both these latter cases the soils are shallow and developed on chalk or limestone. On saltmarshes, *I. crithmoides* occurs in two distinct communities. The first is in low marsh areas developed on coarse sands, where it is associated with *Atriplex portulacoides*, *Limonium vulgare*, *Puccinellia maritima* and *Salicornia europaea*, and occasionally *Frankenia laevis* and *Sarcocornia perennis*. The second is on the upper marsh at about the drift line where the soil is highly organic and here *I. crithmoides* is associated with *Atriplex portulacoides* and *Elytrigia atherica*. It also occurs on the gravels of an accreting foreshore.

I. crithmoides is a long-lived perennial, producing groups of stems up to about 30 cm across. Germination is sporadic in the autumn, but chiefly occurs in spring. Flowering is from July to October, with fruit dispersal from September to November. In cold summers and in northern localities flowering and fruiting is delayed and may result in heavy seed abortion. Seedlings are resistant to saline conditions, but are sensitive to cold, with 70% being killed by exposure to -5 °C for six hours (none survived 1 hour at -10 °C). Seedlings are common in open bare areas near adult plants.

I. crithmoides is relatively stable in its distribution. The saltmarsh occurrences are mainly restricted to the Solent, West Sussex, the Thames estuary and Essex, whereas the cliff populations are found in Kent and Purbeck westwards. However, saltmarsh populations in Carmarthenshire may originate from seed washed round the coast from cliff populations in neighbouring counties. Almost all sites are unmanaged in any way, and are unlikely to be under any threat.

I. crithmoides has Mediterranean-Atlantic distribution, reaching about 55 °N in Britain.

A. J. C. Malloch

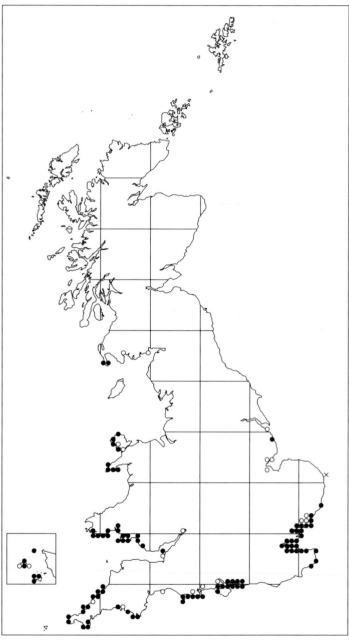

Current map	No	Atlas	No
1970 →	88	1930 →	56
Pre-1970	19	Pre-1930	4
Introductions	1	Introductions	0

Isoetes echinospora Durieu

Status: scarce

Spring quillwort

This is a submerged aquatic pteridophyte which forms open stands to a depth of 2 metres in mountain and moorland lakes on acid, gravelly, usually nutrient-poor substrates. It is associated with a few other macrophytes, e.g. *Littorella uniflora*, *Lobelia dortmanna*, *Potamogeton gramineus* and *Subularia aquatica*, but it usually grows in deeper water than the first two species. Occasionally it is found with filamentous green and blue-green algae. It is found from sea-level at Little Sea in shallow lagoons on sand in which *Potamogeton obtusifolius* and *Nitella* sp. are associates, to 500 metres at Loch Callater.

Plants of *I. echinospora* are perennial. Copious spores mature in the autumn at the leaf-bases and embed in the tight rosette. They are only distributed when plants are dislodged by wave action or by fish or birds, and then washed up on the strand line or moved by water currents or birds.

The increase in records since 1962 may reflect acidification of upland lake waters, but is more likely to be the result of more active botanical recording. There is the risk that pasture improvement by fertilisers or lime will, through eutrophication, increase competition by other plants to the detriment of *I. echinospora*.

It is a widespread plant in Scandinavia and in Iceland but rare and scattered in Europe south of 55 °N where it is threatened by eutrophication. Its European distribution is mapped by Jalas & Suominen (1972). It is a boreal species found across northern Asia (often under other names), and common in North America south to Pennsylvania and north California.

The ecology of this species has been discussed by Seddon (1965), but its absence or rarity in some areas where rock substrates appear suitable is an anomaly still to be studied and may be correlated with water temperatures and chemistry in early Pleistocene Britain.

A. C. Jermy

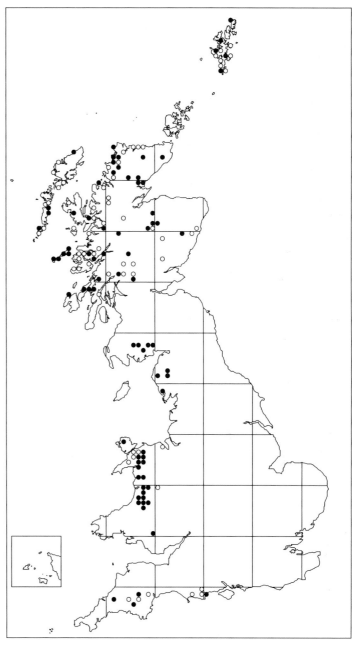

Current map	No	Atlas	No
1970 →	79		
Pre-1970	62		
Introductions	0	All records	51

Juncus acutus L.

Sharp rush

Status: scarce

This is a handsome perennial rush of brackish dune-slacks and the upper fringes of saltmarshes, where its tall, well-spaced, dense tussocks of stiff leaves are unmistakable. Its chief habitat is in low-lying, permanently moist dune-slacks which are more or less saline but rarely if ever flooded by the tide (Jones & Richards 1954). Typical associates here include *Agrostis stolonifera, Carex arenaria, Festuca arundinacea, F. rubra* and *Potentilla anserina*, all of which may find shelter from grazing animals beneath its formidably sharp-pointed leaves. In saltmarsh sites it grows with *Carex extensa, Centaurium pulchellum, Limonium binervosum* agg. (most frequently *L. procerum*), *Parapholis strigosa* and *Plantago coronopus*. Many sites are grazed by sheep, ponies or rabbits, which understandably avoid *J. acutus*. At one Cornish site it grows in a bare flush on the side of a cliff 30 metres above the sea, a most unusual habitat.

The tufts are extremely long-lived and persistent, increasing only slowly in diameter. Compatibility relations are not known but outbreeding is likely, with large amounts of pollen being released from the anemophilous flowers. Healthy tufts flower in June and July and seed profusely, producing long-lived seed capsules which can retain some viable seeds for a year or more although most of the small seeds are shed in the first autumn. Local seed dispersal is probably by wind (perhaps including tumbleweed dispersal of some detached inflorescences) and water (both rainsplash and floating on flooded slacks in winter). Wider dispersal may occur on the feet of grazing animals and by waterfowl. Establishment from seed appears to be rare.

Possible reasons for the disappearance of *J. acutus* from sites on the south and east coast include the discontinuation of grazing and the disturbance or destruction of small and vulnerable populations by road-building, seawall construction, saltmarsh pollution and industrial or recreational development. Most of the surviving dune-slack populations in western Britain are comparatively large, and many are protected within nature reserves. Its range in Britain may be limited by an intolerance of low winter temperature (Jones & Richards 1954; Willis 1985).

J. acutus grows in broadly similar saltmarsh and brackish-sand sites around the coasts of the Mediterranean and south-western Europe, and in areas of similar climate in North and South America and South Africa. It reaches its northern limit in the British Isles.

Q. O. N. Kay

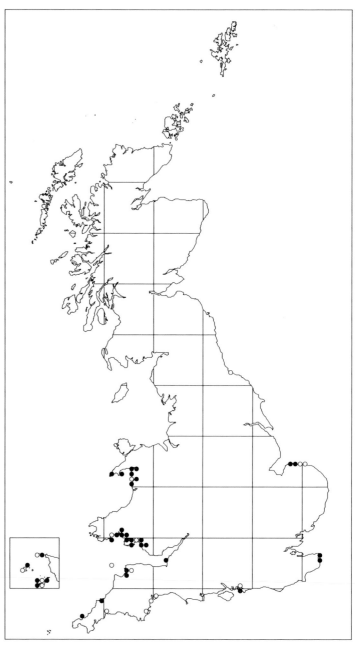

Current map	No	Atlas	No
1970 →	28	1930 →	21
Pre-1970	13	Pre-1930	11
Introductions	0	Introductions	0

Juncus alpinoarticulatus Chaix
Status: scarce

Alpine rush

A rare, northern and sub-montane to montane species of base-rich mires. In the Scottish Highlands it is a plant of open, base-rich flushes, lake margins and mossy marshes, growing with a wide variety of species including *Carex capillaris*, *Juncus triglumis*, *Saxifraga aizoides*, *Thalictrum alpinum*, *Tofieldia pusilla* and at two sites *Schoenus ferrugineus* and *Kobresia simpliciuscula*. In the Southern Uplands all these species are absent and *Parnassia palustris* is conspicuous. In Teesdale, it grows principally in open vegetation at the base of hummocks of the moss *Gymnostomum recurvirostrum* with most of its Highland associates. Here the soil is shallow, saturated and resting directly on solid rock (Clapham 1978). It occurs on limestones of the Carboniferous, Dalradian and Moine series, but is on calcareous Silurian greywackes and shales in the Southern Uplands. It ascends to 880 metres on the Ben Alder range but is found between 190 metres and 365 metres in the Southern Uplands (Corner 1970).

J. alpinoarticulatus is a rhizomatous perennial. Seed is set in abundance but little is known of its reproduction.

This species has been under-recorded in the past, and many new sites have been discovered in recent years. Populations in the Scottish Highlands appear to be stable, but those in the Southern Uplands are under continual threat from coniferisation and some populations have already been lost. The flooding of Cow Green in Upper Teesdale destroyed some of its sites there.

This species is widespread in the boreal zone of Europe, Asia and North America. In Europe it extends south in the mountains to Spain, Italy and the Balkans.

Three subspecies are known, of which subsp. *alpinoarticulatus* alone occurs in the British Isles. *J. nodulosus* is probably only a variety of this subspecies but more taxonomic work is needed. Hybrids occur very rarely with *J. articulatus*.

R. W. M. Corner

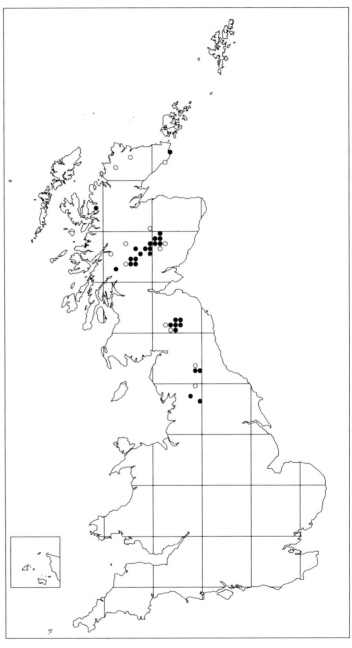

Current map	No	Atlas	No
1970 →	28	1930 →	10
Pre-1970	13	Pre-1930	10
Introductions	0	Introductions	0

Juncus balticus Willd.

Baltic rush

Status: scarce

J. balticus is mainly a plant of dune slacks and other damp areas in maritime sand, mud or peat, frequently beside river estuaries, occurring in a range of habitats from completely closed species-rich grass/sedge communities to bare ground. It is a coloniser of damp bare areas; it is resistant to grazing and trampling but succumbs to later stages of dune colonisation by tall herbs or shrubs. Although usually in damp ground, it rarely grows in long-term standing water and frequently the water-table is over 50 cm below the surface. Relatively high levels of sodium and chloride ions in the groundwater of almost all sites indicate contamination by seawater or spray, but *J. balticus* is essentially a plant of freshwater habitats. The number of closely associated species is large (over 60 in Lancashire alone), and their diversity renders a list of little value. Species common to Scottish and Lancastrian sites are *Agrostis stolonifera*, *Carex arenaria*, *Euphrasia* spp., *Festuca rubra*, *Holcus lanatus*, *Hypochaeris radicata*, *Lotus corniculatus*, *Plantago lanceolata*, *Poa pratensis*, *Rhinanthus minor* and *Trifolium repens*. *Salix repens* is also highly characteristic of the Lancashire sites. Less common species occurring in Lancashire include *Blysmus compressus*, *B. rufus*, *Centaurium littorale*, *Epipactis palustris*, *Equisetum variegatum* and *Pyrola rotundifolia* subsp. *maritima*. *J. balticus* also occupies a distinct inland habitat in the eastern Scottish Highlands on river terraces or flood-plains, usually on peat overlying sand and shingle, up to *c*. 400 metres on Slochd Mor. There it occurs in marshy places in closed vegetation dominated by grasses, sedges and other rushes.

J. balticus is rhizomatous and self-compatible, and sets abundant seed that readily germinates in fresh or brackish water (up to 15% seawater). The seeds are very sticky when wet and would adhere to birds' feet. The rhizomes can survive in seawater for up to three months, and in brackish water for longer.

This is an inconspicuous plant, which is easily overlooked in closed vegetation. There is no evidence that it is declining, and it is likely that many of its pre-1970 sites are still extant.

J. balticus is circumboreal, extending southwards in Europe as far as Lancashire and Holland, with closely related species in the Alps and Pyrenees.

For an account of the ecology and conservation of this species in Lancashire, including details of its hybrids with *J. effusus* and with *J. inflexus*, see Smith (1984).

C. A. Stace

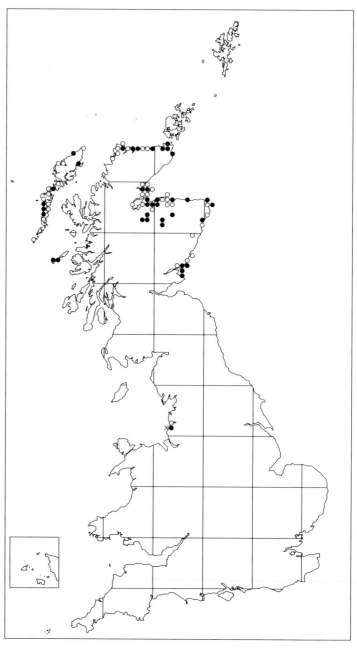

Current map	No	Atlas	No
1970 →	39	1930 →	47
Pre-1970	39	Pre-1930	17
Introductions	1	Introductions	0

Juncus biglumis L.
Status: scarce

Two-flowered rush

This is a rare and strictly montane species, growing in gravelly alpine flushes and small marshes with short and rather open vegetation, and on steep rock faces. Most habitats are permanently moist, with abundant bryophytes. Many populations are subject to irrigation by meltwater from late snow patches. *J. biglumis* is calcicolous and its main occurrences are on the calcareous Dalradian mica-schist mountains of Perth and Argyll. It grows on other base-rich rocks, such as Moine schist, Lewisian gneiss, Tertiary basalt (Skye) and peridotite (Rum). The more widespread *J. triglumis* usually grows near it, in the same habitats, and other typical associates are *Caltha palustris, Carex saxatilis, C. viridula* subsp. *oedocarpa, Cochlearia micacea, Epilobium anagallidifolium, J. castaneus, Persicaria vivipara, Saxifraga aizoides, S. oppositifolia, Selaginella selaginoides* and *Thalictrum alpinum. J. biglumis* needs freedom from competition, but may also be intolerant of high summer temperatures, since apparently suitable habitats (often with *J. triglumis*) are widespread at lower levels and further south. Its altitudinal range is from 460 metres on Rum to 1100 metres on Ben Lawers and Aonach Beag.

J. biglumis is a perennial which presumably regenerates from seed since it has neither rhizomes nor stolons.

J. biglumis has probably been over-collected in some localities, but is unlikely to be much influenced by grazing. It is probably still present in most of its pre-1970 sites.

This is a widespread arctic species, reaching over 83 °N in Greenland, with very few occurrences further south in the Alps, the mountains of central Asia and the Rocky Mountains of North America.

D. A. Ratcliffe

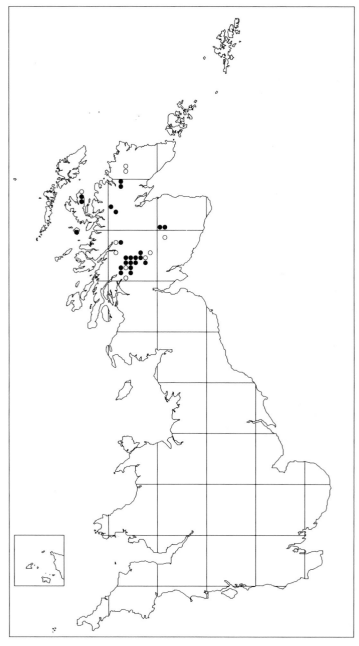

Current map	No	Atlas	No
1970 →	23	1930 →	19
Pre-1970	10	Pre-1930	1
Introductions	0	Introductions	0

Juncus castaneus Smith

Status: scarce

Chestnut rush

This rush grows in, or close to, base-rich flushes or mires in the mountains and on irrigated ledges of base-rich, montane crags. It is most frequent on calcareous, micaceous soils, preferring the grassy vegetation at the margin of flushes rather than the most open, stony part of the community. The largest populations are on Dalradian limestones and mica-schists, but it also grows on calcareous Moine schist and Lewissian gneiss. In these rich habitats there is a large number of associates but the most frequent are *Carex panicea*, *C. viridula* subsp. *oedocarpa*, *Juncus bulbosus*, *J. triglumis*, *Saxifraga aizoides* and *Thalictrum alpinum*. Other rare montane plants are often associated with these stands, particularly *Alopecurus borealis*, *Carex saxatilis* and *Juncus biglumis*. *J. castaneus* is a plant of the higher hills from 850 metres in the Grey Corries to 1030 metres on Beinn Heasgarnich.

This is a perennial species. Populations are presumably able to spread by growth of the stolons, and perhaps by seed, but little is known about its reproduction in the wild.

The populations of this rush are often very small and often in sites where heavy grazing is apparent. There may be some cause for concern here but further field work is necessary. It is probably still present in most of the 10 km squares for which only pre-1970 records are available.

This is an arctic-alpine species with a circumpolar distribution. It extends southwards to the Alps and Urals and to Quebec and New Mexico in North America.

This is not always an easy species to find, even in sites where it has been seen recently. The flushes where it grows are frequently heavily grazed and if the flowers have been nipped off then the search becomes very much more difficult.

G. P. Rothero

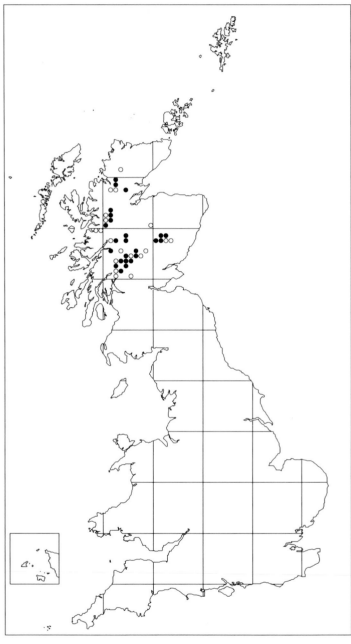

Current map	No	Atlas	No
1970 →	24	1930 →	23
Pre-1970	19	Pre-1930	4
Introductions	0	Introductions	0

Juncus filiformis L.

Status: scarce

Thread rush

In Britain, *J. filiformis* is confined to the edge of lakes and reservoirs. It most frequently occurs in a narrow fringing zone of periodically-flooded wet marshy pasture, with a range of associated species including *Agrostis* spp., *Deschampsia cespitosa*, *Eleocharis palustris*, *Galium palustre*, *Juncus acutiflorus*, *J. effusus*, *Mentha aquatica*, *Molinia caerulea*, *Persicaria hydropiper*, *Ranunculus flammula* and *Senecio aquaticus*. It also occasionally grows in more open communities on lake-shore sand and gravel, and at some sites it is found submerged with aquatics such as *Littorella uniflora*. Populations are often small and patchy, but in a few cases *J. filiformis* extends into larger expanses of alluvial flood-plain vegetation. All its sites are below 300 metres.

The reproductive biology of *J. filiformis* in Britain has not been studied in detail. Clonal spread by rhizomatous growth is often evident, and there appears to be at least moderate seed-set in many colonies. Water dispersal of rhizome fragments and seeds is likely, but transport to isolated reservoirs is probably via seed carried by migrating water birds. A large *J. filiformis* seed bank has been demonstrated at an undisturbed lake-shore locality in Nova Scotia (Wisheu & Keddy 1991).

J. filiformis was formerly thought to be rare enough to be included in the *Red Data Book*, but its British distribution has been extended through the colonisation of reservoirs (which date in construction from the late 19th century onwards). It is an inconspicuous species which may still be somewhat under-recorded.

J. filiformis is a circumboreal species with a somewhat continental distribution. In Europe it extends from Iceland and northernmost Scandinavia south to the Iberian peninsula, but it is rare towards the southern part of its range.

For accounts of the distribution and ecology of this species, see Blackstock (1981) and Richards (1943).

T. H. Blackstock

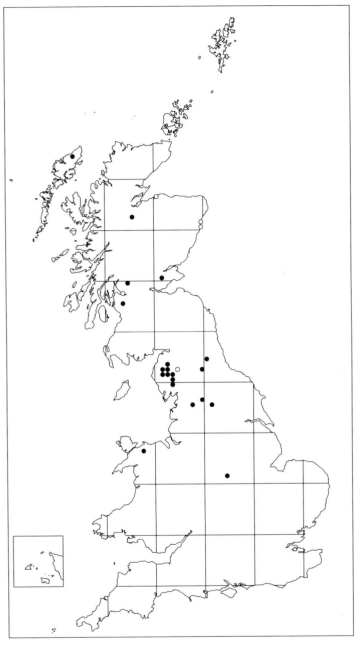

Current map	No	Atlas	No
1970 →	20	1930 →	10
Pre-1970	5	Pre-1930	3
Introductions	0	Introductions	0

Lathyrus aphaca L.
Status: scarce

Yellow vetchling

This species grows on lowland roadside verges, grassy waysides, low earthy cliffs by the sea and sea walls. It is generally found in ungrazed or lightly grazed calcareous grassland, particularly over clay but also on limestone in some coastal sites. These sites often have a rich legume flora, with species such as *Lathyrus nissolia*, *Vicia bithynica*, *V. lutea* and *V. parviflora* in similar vegetation and *Trifolium fragiferum* in shorter, more trampled, areas nearby. The species is also found as a casual in places such as mills, docks, railway banks, arable land and on waste ground.

This is an annual species which flowers from May to August. Germination takes place in the autumn.

L. aphaca may be a long-established introduction rather than a native species. In many areas such as Somerset (Roe 1981), Kent (Parkinson 1640), and Essex (Jermyn 1974), most of the early records are as an arable weed, and the species may have been introduced as a seed contaminant of leguminous crops. Many of the pre-1970 records date from the nineteenth century, and at some of these localities, the species may not have been well established. It is now more frequent in permanent habitats, particularly near the sea. The history of this species resembles that of *Gastridium ventricosum*, described by Trist (1986), and *L. aphaca* can often be found at sites for *G. ventricosum*.

L. aphaca is widespread in western, central and southern Europe, North Africa and south-west and central Asia. In Europe it is established northwards to Britain, Belgium, The Netherlands and Germany but it is believed to be an introduction in all these countries.

The established British plant is var. *aphaca*. The species is a variable one elsewhere, attaining its maximum variability in Anatolia.

F. J. Rumsey

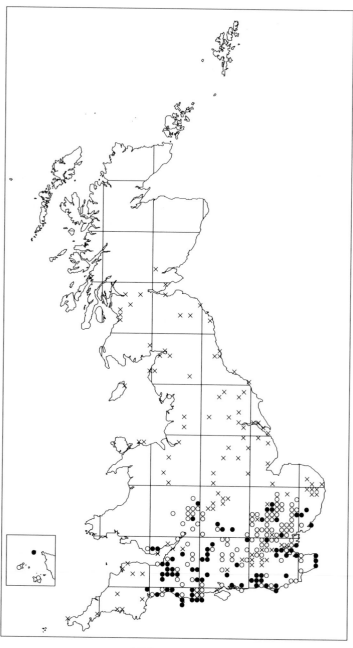

Current map	No	Atlas	No
1970 →	76	1930 →	56
Pre-1970	114	Pre-1930	39
Introductions	106	Introductions	60

Lathyrus japonicus Willd.   **Sea pea**

Status: scarce

This is a characteristic but local plant of coastal shingle beaches. It grows on bare or semi-vegetated shingle, a member of an open plant community with other colonists such as *Crambe maritima*, *Glaucium flavum* and *Rumex crispus* subsp. *littoreus*. In a few places it occurs on blown sand.

The plant is perennial and self-incompatible. It flowers from May to September. The flowers are protandrous and pollinated by bumble-bees (Brightmore & White 1963).

This species has long been abundant on the extensive coastal shingle formations of Suffolk, where the seeds were said to be plentiful enough in earlier centuries to sustain the inhabitants in times of famine. It is also locally common on the coast of Kent and East Sussex and on the Chesil Beach in Dorset, and in several places it is extending or consolidating its range (Randall 1977). However, to the west and north it has declined over the last 50 years, and Randall (1977) found that by the mid-1970s it had disappeared from over half of its known stations. Small populations are especially susceptible to trampling where there is public pressure on beaches.

L. japonicus is a plant of coasts throughout the boreal and arctic regions of the northern hemisphere (Brightmore & White 1963). In the far north of Europe and America the species occurs inland on the shores of lakes. In Europe it extends from southern England and Denmark (extinct in northern France) to the Arctic. The British plant is subsp. *maritimus* (L.) P.W. Ball. Populations on sand dunes in Angus and Shetland with narrow leaflets tapering at both ends have been referred to var. *acutifolius* Bab. (Duncan 1970; Scott & Palmer 1987). Plants from the Arctic, with fewer, somewhat larger flowers, belong to subsp. *japonicus*.

J. R. Akeroyd

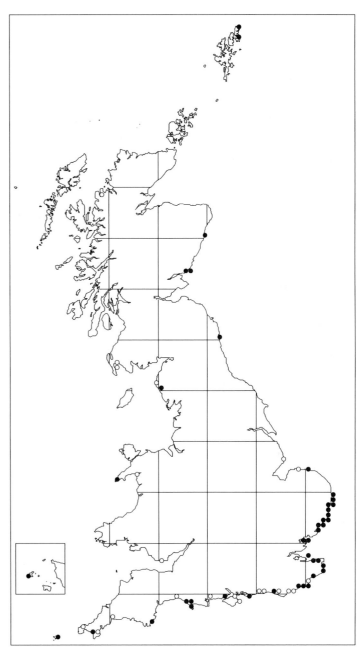

Current map	No	Atlas	No
1970 →	40	1930 →	23
Pre-1970	21	Pre-1930	16
Introductions	0	Introductions	0

Lathyrus palustris L.

Status: scarce

Marsh pea

L. palustris is a perennial that climbs and scrambles over coarse vegetation. Its preferred habitats are base-rich and wet with tall grass, reed or scrub cover. In particular it is characteristic of rich fens in Britain, although on the continent of Europe it is more typical of habitats such as wet coarse grasslands and hay meadows on peat. It prefers well-lit sites on base-rich soils which are deficient in nitrogen. Characteristic associates include *Calamagrostis canescens*, *Cladium mariscus*, *Eupatorium cannabinum*, *Juncus subnodulosus*, *Lysimachia vulgaris*, *Lythrum salicaria*, *Mentha aquatica* and *Phragmites australis*. *Peucedanum palustre* and *Thelypteris palustris* grow with *L. palustris* at several of its eastern localities. This species is confined to the lowlands of Britain.

L. palustris spreads by seeds, but is a long-lived perennial.

L. palustris is declining in the eastern half of its British range, even within its strongholds in Broadland. It has declined in Fenland due to drainage and site destruction, whilst in wet hay-meadows, grassland improvement and reseeding have eliminated or modified the habitat. In Wales, however, several sites have been discovered since 1970, and the species was also discovered in Kintyre in 1976.

L. palustris has a very wide world distribution, being found throughout Europe, temperate and arctic Russia east to the Pacific, and temperate North America. It is rare in the Mediterranean region.

The American var. *pilosus* (Cham.) Ledeb. persists at one site in a seasonally flooded dune slack at Tywyn Burrows (Vaughan 1978). It has been suggested that this population has its origins as a drift seed, having floated across from America on the North Atlantic Drift.

J. O. Mountford

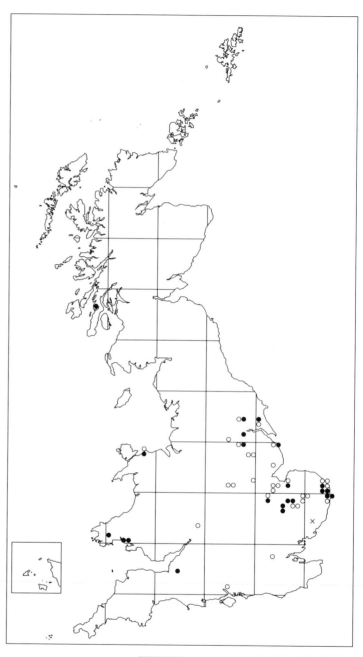

Current map	No	Atlas	No
1970 →	22	1930 →	15
Pre-1970	29	Pre-1930	25
Introductions	2	Introductions	0

continued →

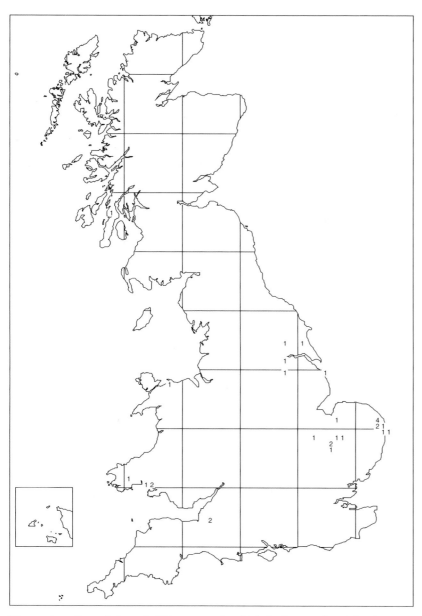

The number of tetrads in each 10 km square in which *Lathyrus palustris* has been recorded as a native species from 1970 onwards. The species has been found in a total of 29 tetrads from 1970 onwards.

Lavatera arborea L.

Tree-mallow

Status: not scarce

L. arborea is a strictly maritime species, very rarely found more than 100 metres from the coast. It usually grows on shallow soils (10-30 cm) which have developed over a range of rocks from granite to limestone. It occurs in two main habitats. The first is amongst the vegetation of sea bird roosts where the chief associates are *Armeria maritima*, *Atriplex* species, *Beta vulgaris* subsp. *maritima*, *Festuca rubra*, *Plantago coronopus* and *Silene uniflora*. The second consists of areas that have had nutrient enrichment, most usually from garden rubbish. Here the most commonly associated species are *Beta vulgaris* subsp. *maritima*, *Dactylis glomerata*, *Festuca rubra* and *Rumex crispus*. The soils where *L. arborea* grows are always nutrient enriched from guano or decomposing rubbish.

L. arborea is biennial or a very short-lived perennial and is generally monocarpic. Reproduction is exclusively by seed which is shed in late summer to early autumn. Germination is sporadic in autumn and commoner in the spring. Mature plants, and particularly the seedlings, are extremely frost sensitive, with a temperature of -5 °C for three hours killing all plants. No seedlings survived the winter in exposed situations in the Port Logan Botanical Garden (on the Galloway coast) though 40% survived in very sheltered situations. Mature plants are rather more tolerant and can survive very light frost of short duration. Establishment normally requires disturbed, open and moist conditions with a relatively low soil salinity level but more mature plants are very resistant to wind-borne salt spray. The quantity of fruit produced appears to be directly related to the size of the plant. Setting of fruit is usually good. Fruit dispersal is limited, with most of the rather heavy mericarps falling in the immediate vicinity of the parent.

L. arborea may be decreasing in some areas as a result of less intensive disturbance of sea-cliff vegetation and progressive restriction of sea-bird roosts to the more inaccessible offshore rocks. However, this is more than offset by the spread of the plant from coastal gardens onto disturbed and nutrient-enriched ground.

L. arborea is a species of Mediterranean-Atlantic distribution, reaching its northern limit of 55 °N in Britain.

Records from inland and east coast sites, reported as *L. arborea*, are more likely to be another *Lavatera* species. It has been confused with *L. olbia* in gardens.

A. J. C. Malloch

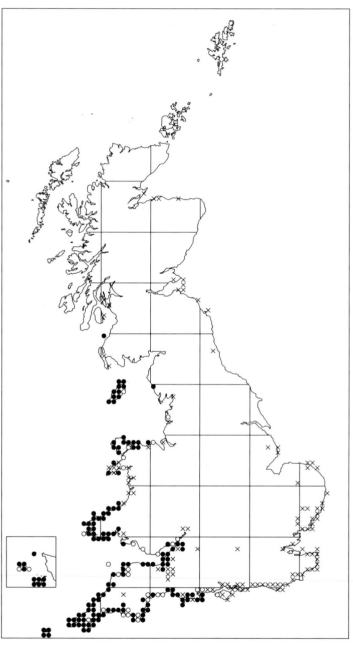

Current map	No	Atlas	No
1970 →	133	1930 →	70
Pre-1970	30	Pre-1930	2
Introductions	111	Introductions	53

Lepidium latifolium L.

Status: scarce

Dittander

The habitats of this plant are creeksides, ditches and brackish marshland in the upper reaches of estuaries; and less frequently on sea walls, in saltmarshes and on damp sand. Inland, it may become a persistent weed of bare waste places, in gravel pits, on railway banks and by canals, sometimes as a relic of past cultivation.

This is a patch-forming stoloniferous perennial, flowering from June to September. It has probably dispersed inland from native coastal sites as portions of rootstock in gravels and other ballast.

This plant was once used as a 'hot' flavouring but has been long since replaced by horse-radish and pepper. Because of this it is difficult to assess its true native range. It would appear to be maintaining its numbers in its East Anglian heartland, and is unquestionably increasing in its inland ruderal habitats.

L. latifolium is found throughout Europe to *c.* 60 °N, in north Africa and south-west Asia. It is known to have been introduced in North America and Australasia.

F. J. Rumsey

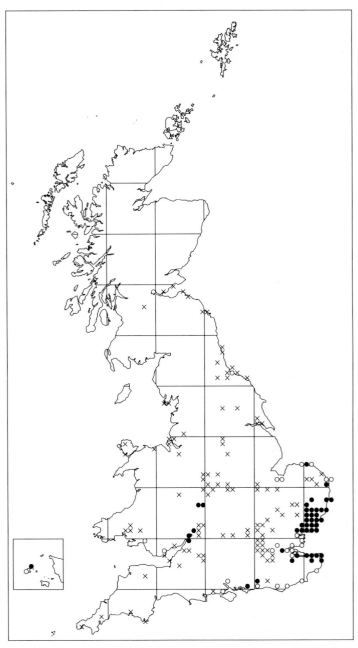

Current map	No	Atlas	No
1970 →	43	1930 →	27
Pre-1970	26	Pre-1930	27
Introductions	105	Introductions	31

Limonium binervosum (G.E. Smith) Salmon *sensu lato*   **Rock sea-lavender**
Status: not scarce

L. binervosum sensu lato occupies a range of maritime habitats, including sea-cliffs, coastal screes, saltmarshes, shingle banks and sand dunes. Associated species are equally varied, ranging from *Crithmum maritimum*, *Inula crithmoides* and *Spergularia rupicola* on western seacliffs, to *Atriplex portulacoides*, *Frankenia laevis* and *Limonium bellidifolium* on Norfolk saltmarshes and sand dunes. It is also found occasionally on dock walls.

L. binervosum is perennial and apomictic, flowering from June to September.

There is little evidence of *L. binervosum* having been lost from sites. Many populations, particularly in western Britain, are on remote sea-cliffs, and apparent losses here may not be real, but rather could simply reflect the practical difficulties of recording in such areas. Some populations on dock walls in Carmarthenshire have been lost by recent dock infilling.

L. binervosum sensu lato occurs in western Europe from Spain and Portugal northwards to France and Britain. It reaches its northern limit in south-west Scotland and Ireland (Co. Donegal).

The taxonomy of the *Limonium binervosum* complex in Britain and Ireland has recently been revised by Ingrouille & Stace (1986), who recognise nine species and numerous infraspecific taxa. Three species (*L. binervosum sensu stricto*, *L. britannicum* and *L. procerum*) are nationally scarce and the remainder (*L. dodartiforme*, *L. loganicum*, *L. paradoxum*, *L. parvum*, *L. recurvum* and *L. transwallianum*) are nationally rare. The following maps show the distribution of these segregate species, but our knowledge of the distribution of some of these species is still far from complete. Only one segregate, *L. binervosum sensu stricto*, is known to occur elsewhere in Europe; the other eight species are thought to be endemic to Britain and Ireland.

S. J. Leach

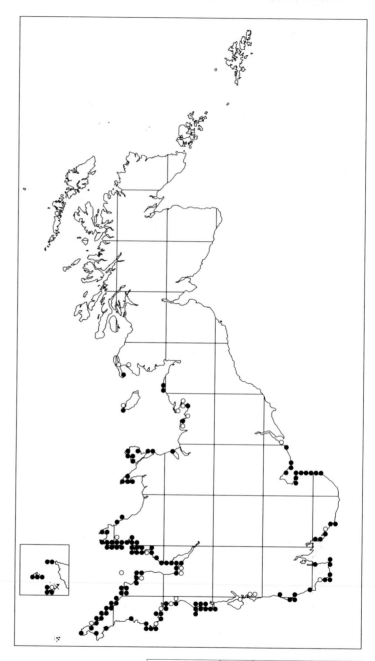

Current map	No	Atlas	No
1970 →	119	1930 →	70
Pre-1970	26	Pre-1930	15
Introductions	0	Introductions	0

continued →

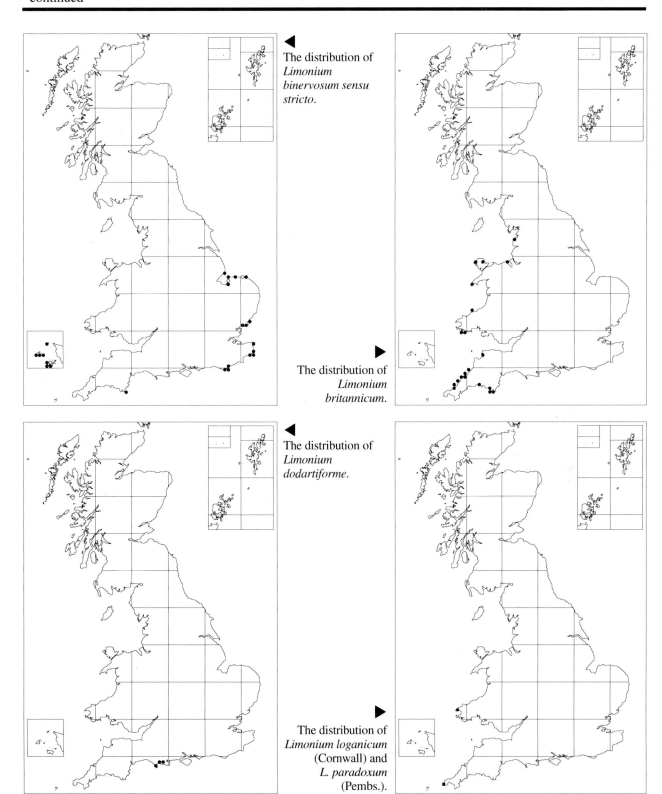

The distribution of *Limonium binervosum sensu stricto*.

The distribution of *Limonium britannicum*.

The distribution of *Limonium dodartiforme*.

The distribution of *Limonium loganicum* (Cornwall) and *L. paradoxum* (Pembs.).

continued →

Limonium binervosum
continued

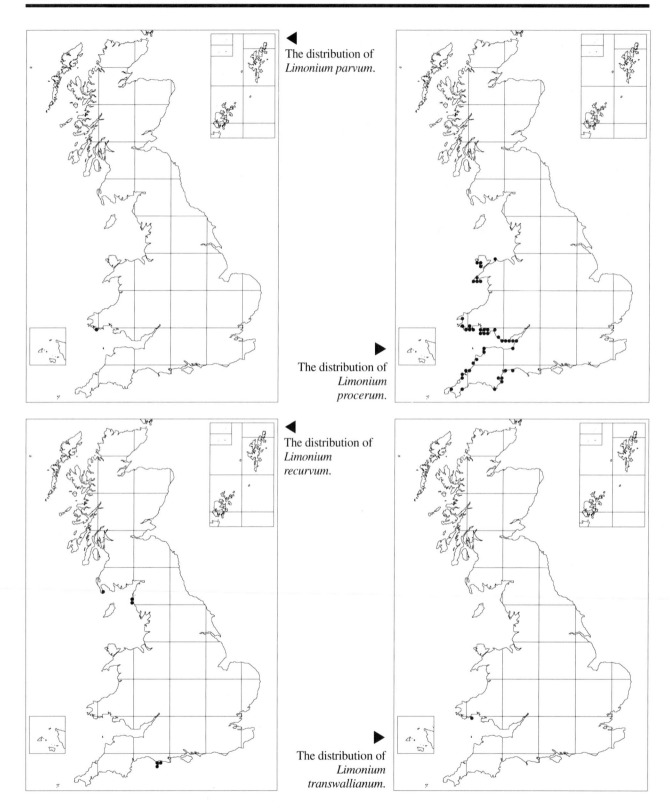

The distribution of *Limonium parvum*.

The distribution of *Limonium procerum*.

The distribution of *Limonium recurvum*.

The distribution of *Limonium transwallianum*.

Limonium humile Miller

Status: scarce

Lax-flowered sea-lavender

A species of muddy estuarine saltmarshes, where it generally grows close to mean high water. It has a preference for bare mud without other vegetation. It often grows in close proximity to *L. vulgare*, and on some marshes (e.g. in north-west England) it may largely replace its commoner relative. *L. humile* can occasionally be the dominant species along saltmarsh drift-lines.

L. humile is a perennial species. It is monomorphic and self-compatible. Plants colonise initially by seed, subsequent spread and infilling being largely vegetative. The flowers are insect-pollinated, visited by various species of bee, fly and beetle, and there is one seed per fruit. The seeds can survive and germinate in sea-water, and a pre-treatment in salt-water stimulates germination (Boorman 1967).

There is little evidence that *L. humile* has decreased, and there are still strong populations in many areas. John Ray (Ray 1704) records *L. humile* as 'Limonium Anglicum minus' "by the Tide-Mill at Walton in Essex...Mr. Dale. Found also by Mr. Sherard and Mr. Rand, at the Mouth of the River that runs from Chichester". It still survives in both these localities.

This is a species of north-western Europe, from Britain to Norway, Sweden and the western Baltic.

British populations of *L. humile* show some variation in chromosome number (Dawson 1990). Fertile intermediates between *L. humile* and *L. vulgare* occur, and are thought to be hybrids. However, Dawson (1990) suggests that at least some of the intermediates are simply forms of the variable *L. vulgare*. The variability of *L. vulgare* and the presence of intermediates may have resulted in some erroneous records of *L. humile*.

M. Briggs

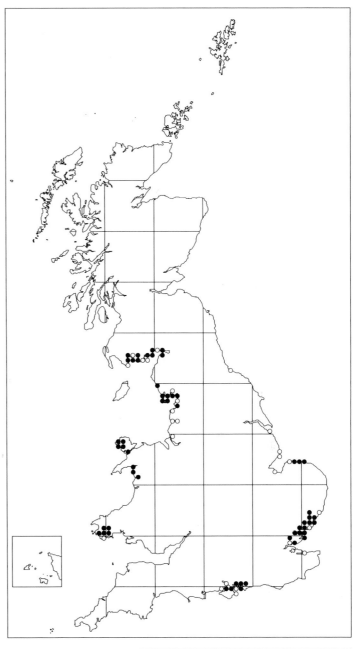

Current map	No	Atlas	No
1970 →	54	1930 →	48
Pre-1970	26	Pre-1930	6
Introductions	0	Introductions	0

Limosella aquatica L.
Status: scarce

Mudwort

L. aquatica grows on exposed mud at the edges of rivers, lakes, reservoirs, pools, ditches and winter-flooded ruts in tracks and unmetalled roads. It may be mildly calcifuge - many of its sites were on acidic soils on commons - and is perhaps favoured by nutrient enrichment from animal droppings. It is often found with other annual species, including *Eleocharis acicularis*, *Gnaphalium uliginosum*, *Juncus bufonius* and *Rorippa palustris*, and with stranded aquatics such as *Myriophyllum alterniflorum* or species of *Ranunculus*. It occurs in bare areas on saltmarshes in Hampshire. It is a predominantly lowland species, ascending to 450 metres on Malham Moor.

The species is an ephemeral which germinates very rapidly when mud becomes exposed in the summer and completes its life-cycle before the autumn. Populations vary greatly in size from year to year, and can be very large in those seasons when water levels are low. It has often been recorded at sites after an apparent absence of many years. Dry seeds yielded only 0.8% germination after 27 months (Salisbury 1970) but a greater proportion may remain viable in wet mud. For further details of the reproductive biology of this species, see Salisbury (1967).

L. aquatica is erratic in its appearance, and certainly could not have been found in any one year in all the 10 km squares for which there are pre-1970 records. Nevertheless, like several annuals of exposed mud in small pools, it has undoubtedly suffered a major decline in England and Wales (Salisbury 1970). The reasons for this probably include the surfacing of roads; the drainage of 'splashy places by the roadside' (Townsend 1883) and other ephemeral pools; and the fact that many ponds have dried out completely, become overgrown following the cessation of grazing or been engulfed by urban development. Lousley (1976) stresses the former role in Surrey of ducks and geese in creating muddy, nutrient-enriched areas around pools. The sites where the plant has survived tend to be larger waters rather than the small sites which were formerly its most characteristic habitat. It has, however, colonised some newly created habitats such as 'scrapes' dug for birds and the margins of gravel pits. In Scotland *L. aquatica* has been recorded with increasing frequency since 1950 (Leach, Stewart & Ballantyne 1984), probably because this inconspicuous species had been overlooked previously.

It is widespread in northern Europe, with scattered colonies in the mountains further south. It has a circumboreal distribution.

C. D. Preston

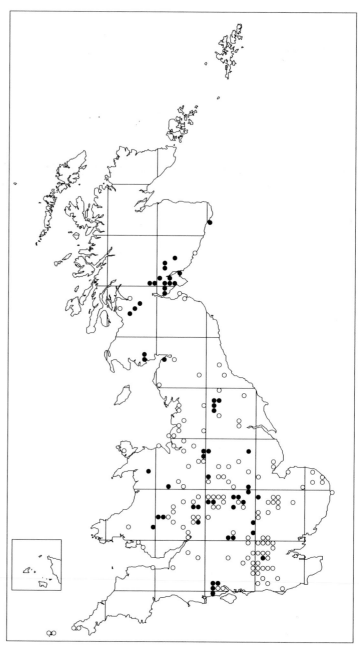

Current map	No	Atlas	No
1970 →	55	1930 →	22
Pre-1970	132	Pre-1930	103
Introductions	0	Introductions	0

Linnaea borealis L.   **Twinflower**
Status: scarce

L. borealis usually occurs in native pinewoods and old plantations. It grows as a spreading mat with horizontal creeping woody stems that produce adventitious roots. Typical associates in pinewoods are *Calluna vulgaris*, *Deschampsia flexuosa* and *Vaccinium myrtillus*. *Goodyera repens* is also a common associate and at some localities *Moneses uniflora* grows in proximity. The plant occasionally occurs outside woodland in more upland habitats, growing in the shade of mountain rocks. It has been recorded at *c*. 800 metres in the Grampians and *c*. 600 metres on Ben Chonzie (Wilson 1956).

L. borealis is a creeping woody perennial and regenerates by producing rejuvenating shoots from buds on the main axis and other parts of the plant (Hagerup 1921). The plant is therefore able to spread in any direction and in favourable conditions may rapidly cover several square metres. It requires slight shade to flower well and in conditions too dark for flowering it may persist in a vegetative state.
L. borealis is adapted for cross pollination although it is self-fertile. The funnel-shaped flowers are mainly suited to insects with short mouthparts. Flies, solitary bees, syrphids and some Lepidoptera are the main insect visitors (Barrett & Helenurm 1987; Knuth 1908). Fruits are adapted for animal dispersal by possessing two partially enclosed bracts with viscid hairs. The fruit breaks off below the bracts and sticks to fur and feathers (Ridley 1930). The fruits have been recorded on mountain hares, willow grouse and red grouse in Sweden (Ericson 1977; Ridley 1930). Seedling establishment seems to be rare and has been reported to any great extent only in disturbed ground (Ericson 1977).

L. borealis seems to be decreasing and there is little doubt that sites have been lost through clearance of native woodland. Many extant populations occur in old plantations where the timber is reaching or has reached economic maturity. Modern techniques of harvesting and ground preparation for replanting may exterminate these populations.

L. borealis has a circumpolar distribution. The three subspecies which are recognised differ slightly in leaf and flower shape. Subsp. *borealis* occurs from western Europe through northern Eurasia to Alaska, where it meets subsp. *americana* which occurs in most of North America and in Greenland. Subsp. *longiflora* is restricted to Pacific N. America (Hultén 1970; Hultén & Fries 1986).

P. S. Lusby

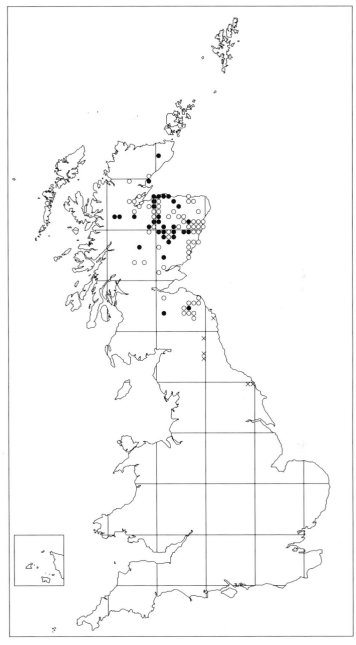

Current map	No	Atlas	No
1970 →	32	1930 →	16
Pre-1970	57	Pre-1930	51
Introductions	6	Introductions	0

243

Linum perenne L.
Status: scarce

Perennial flax

This plant grows in base-rich grassland over chalk, limestone or calcareous sand. It is found in open, sunny, well-drained situations on road verges, dry banks, lightly grazed grassland and similar habitats. Frequent associates include *Galium verum*, *Helianthemum nummularium*, *Linum catharticum*, *Lotus corniculatus*, *Sanguisorba minor* and *Scabiosa columbaria*. It is mainly a lowland plant, ranging from sea-level, where it grows in coastal sand in Kirkcudbrightshire, to 300 metres altitude on limestone grassland near Shap.

It is perennial, reproducing by seed, and is capable of colonising suitable open areas. However, it is slow growing and a poor competitor and is readily shaded out by encroaching scrub and tall plants. Overgrazing and repeated close mowing will also lead to its elimination. Individuals can be long-lived and capable of throwing up a large number of ascending, annual stems. The petals are fugacious and are shed soon after pollination, but new flowers open daily and the plant has a fairly protracted flowering season.

Within the last hundred years or so, the plant has become extinct in several localities and many of the present populations are small. Disturbance by man and reduced grazing have no doubt contributed towards this. However, there are at least three large populations containing many hundreds of plants, in Cambridgeshire, Co. Durham and Kirkcudbrightshire.

Our plant is subsp. *anglicum* (Miller) Ock. This subspecies is endemic to Britain and is the only member of the taxonomically-difficult *L. perenne* group to occur in this country. Variability can be appreciable, especially in habit and stem length and leaf size. In at least two populations (Cambridgeshire, Westmorland), a small proportion of plants have white flowers. *L. perenne sensu lato* is widespread but local in Europe, occurring from the Pyrenees to the Urals (Hultén & Fries 1986). Fossil seeds of *L. perenne* have been found in a number of deposits dating from the last glacial period, and particularly in eastern England. Godwin (1975) interprets its current distribution as a relic of a more widespread former range.

For further details of the ecology of this species, see Ockendon (1968).

M. J. Y. Foley

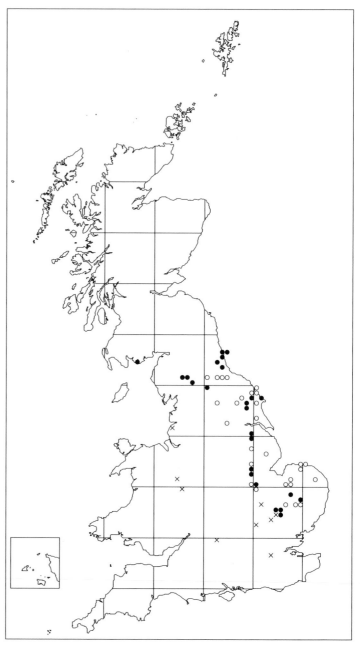

Current map	No	Atlas	No
1970 →	24	1930 →	18
Pre-1970	28	Pre-1930	25
Introductions	9	Introductions	0

continued →

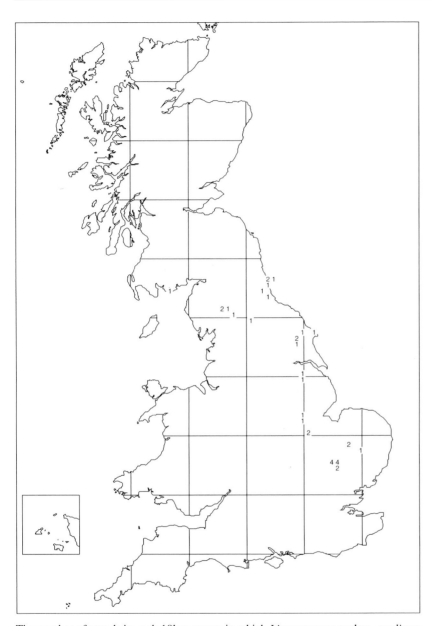

The number of tetrads in each 10km square in which *Linum perenne* subsp. *anglicum* has been recorded as a native species from 1970 onwards. The species has been found in a total of 36 tetrads from 1970 onwards.

Lotus subbiflorus Lag.
Status: scarce

Hairy bird's-foot-trefoil

Like its rarer congener *L. angustissimus*, this rather elusive species typically occurs on scrubby clifftops and dry grassy banks by the sea. It tends to avoid truly maritime swards where *Armeria maritima* and *Scilla verna* are abundant, preferring rather scruffier grasslands in more sheltered situations. Here it occurs in an open turf with such species as *Agrostis capillaris*, *Crepis capillaris*, *Dactylis glomerata*, *Hypochaeris radicata*, *Plantago coronopus*, *Rumex acetosella* and *Vulpia bromoides*, and with patches of gorse, bramble or bracken rarely far away. In Devon and Cornwall long stretches of coastline are now covered by impenetrable scrub, and in such areas it is often confined to narrow strips of open ground beside footpaths and trackways.

L. subbiflorus is an annual (perhaps rarely a short-lived perennial), germinating in autumn and possibly also in spring and flowering from July to September. An open turf is essential for successful germination and seedling establishment: scrub cutting, trampling, fire and summer droughts may all be of benefit for this reason. Population size can vary greatly from year to year. Buried seed probably remains viable for many years, enabling the species to appear intermittently whenever conditions are suitable.

L. subbiflorus may have been lost from some of its former localities, perhaps as a result of scrub encroachment following removal of traditional management practices such as grazing and burning, or due to agricultural improvement of clifftop grasslands. However, at some sites it could reappear from buried seed following, for example, the opening up or clearance of clifftop scrub or the reinstatement of grazing. In many 10 km squares in which it has not been seen since 1970 it probably does still occur, at least sporadically, in low numbers.

It is almost confined to Western Europe, extending through the Mediterranean eastwards as far as Sicily. It also occurs in North Africa. This species is at its northern limit in the British Isles.

S. J. Leach

Current map	No	Atlas	No
1970 →	52	1930 →	30
Pre-1970	26	Pre-1930	21
Introductions	3	Introductions	2

Luronium natans (L.) Raf.
Status: scarce

Floating water-plantain
WCA Schedule 8 species

L. natans is an aquatic plant which is currently found in two main habitats. Its most important natural habitat is in slightly acidic and oligotrophic lakes, where it grows in water up to 2 metres deep, with species such as *Callitriche hamulata*, *Isoetes lacustris*, *Littorella uniflora* and *Lobelia dortmanna*, or on bare mud exposed by falling water levels. It is also found in canals, where it grows in circumneutral or slightly basic, mesotrophic water, often with *Elodea nuttallii*, *Lemna minor*, *Sparganium emersum* and a range of *Potamogeton* species. In canals it apparently relies for its survival on periodic disturbance, which can be provided by light boat traffic in navigable waters or by periodic dredging or the control of marginal vegetation elsewhere. *L. natans* is also found in a slow-flowing, mesotrophic stretch of the Afon Teifi, and it was recorded in the past from a variety of other natural habitats, including streams, ditches, lowland lakes and pools. It is established as an introduction in the Norfolk Broads (Driscoll 1985) and also recorded as an alien in Scotland.

L. natans is a stoloniferous perennial. In fast-flowing water or deep water, or in sites which are shaded or turbid, it can persist as rosettes of submerged leaves. In shallow water or on wet mud it produces floating or terrestrial leaves and flowers and fruits freely. Reproduction is both vegetative and by seed. Populations in lakes appear to be largest when water levels are low and much mud is exposed, and in canals they are often greatest after major disturbance.

The populations in oligotrophic, upland lakes appear to be stable. During the nineteenth century the species spread into the canal system and these new sites more than offset losses of lowland, mesotrophic sites caused by eutrophication and habitat destruction. Since 1970 populations in canals have declined because of the increase in recreational boat traffic.

L. natans is endemic to Europe. It is a predominantly western European species, but extends eastwards to Yugoslavia, Bulgaria and Poland. It is rare and decreasing over much of its European range.

L. natans has recently received special protection under Appendix I of the Bern Convention and Annexes II and IV of the European Community Habitats & Species Directive. For a recent review of the ecology and conservation of this species in Britain, on which much of the above account is based, see Willby & Eaton (1993).

C. D. Preston

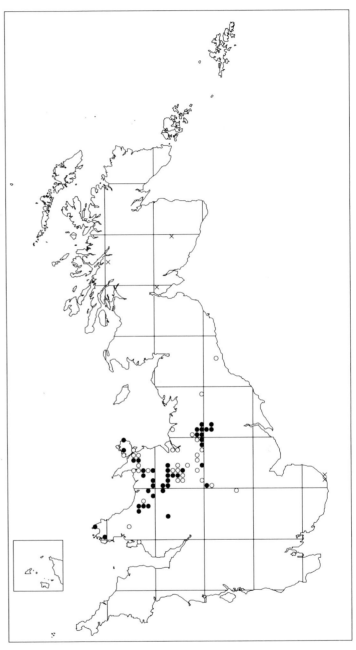

Current map	No	Atlas	No
1970 →	40	1930 →	28
Pre-1970	32	Pre-1930	30
Introductions	5	Introductions	4

continued →

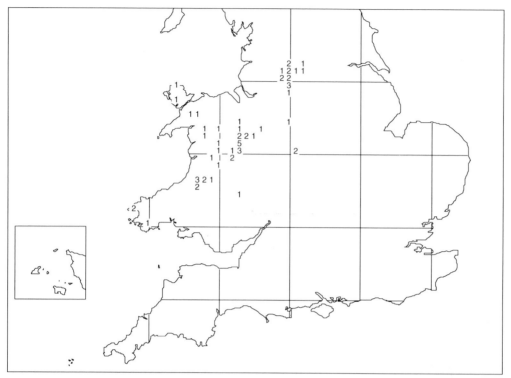

The number of tetrads in each 10 km square in which *Luronium natans* has been recorded as a native species from 1970 onwards. The species has been found in a total of 61 tetrads from 1970 onwards.

Luzula arcuata Sw.
Status: rare?

Curved wood-rush

This plant is found in one of the most uncompromising habitats on the highest of the Scottish hills. It grows in open, stony fell-field and rock debris on windswept summit ridges and plateaux where protective winter snow is stripped away by the wind leaving a scoured and harsh niche in which only a handful of vascular plants can survive. It appears to be calcifuge, growing on coarse, leached alpine soils derived from granite, quartzite, granulite and acidic schists. The most frequent associates are *Carex bigelowii* and *Juncus trifidus* with, less frequently, *Gnaphalium supinum* and *Luzula spicata*. The moss *Racomitrium lanuginosum* is also a common associate along with some lichen species. In higher and more open corries *L. arcuata* can extend down into more snow-loving vegetation with *Salix herbacea* and a variety of mosses and liverworts. The altitudinal range is from 760 metres on Slioch up to 1290 metres on Cairn Toul, making this one of the most exclusively montane of all British plants.

L. arcuata is a perennial species with short stolons and a creeping rhizome system.

There is nothing to suggest that this species is under any threat and it probably still occurs in most of the 10 km squares for which only pre-1970 records were available. In its Cairngorm stronghold it is still locally frequent.

This is an arctic species with a circumpolar distribution. It reaches its southern European limit in Scotland.

As this species has been recorded in only 12 10 km squares since 1970, it qualifies for inclusion in the *Red Data Book* (Perring & Farrell 1983) under the current criteria. However, it will probably be recorded in more than 15 squares when, as seems likely, it is refound in some of its old localities.

G. P. Rothero

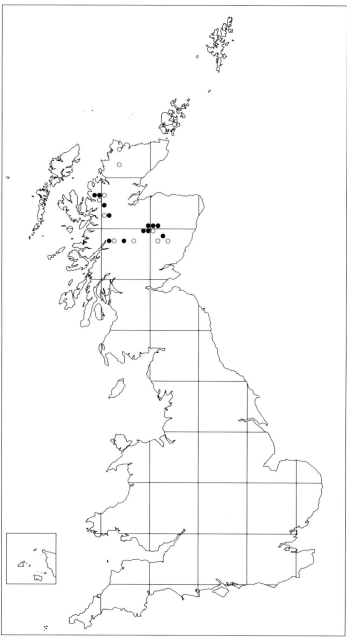

Current map	No	Atlas	No
1970 →	12	1930 →	13
Pre-1970	10	Pre-1930	4
Introductions	0	Introductions	0

Lycopodiella inundata (L.) Holub
Status: scarce

Marsh clubmoss

L. inundata is a short-lived perennial of bare peaty, occasionally silty or sandy, areas on mires, heaths, lake margins and sand and clay pits. These areas are normally submerged under water in winter and spring. It is most commonly associated with *Sphagnum auriculatum* and *Rhynchospora alba* on the edge of valley mires of the New Forest. *Rhynchospora fusca*, *Drosera intermedia* and *Hammarbya paludosa* are sometimes found growing with *L. inundata*. Human activities which provide areas of bare, seasonally flooded, well humified, acidic peat, such as tracks and old peat cuttings, favour this species. It is most common where high grazing pressure results in the poaching of wet heath and mire surfaces. Where bare ground is present it may become locally abundant. It is virtually restricted to lowland sites, but reaches 305 metres at Loch Ba.

Branches remain evergreen for two years, after which the clone fragments by disintegration of the older sections of the branches. It spreads relatively slowly at 2 to 10 cm each year. Strobili produced in summer mature in the autumn. Spores may be dispersed by air or by water within intact sporangia when the plant becomes submerged. The gametophyte stage is superficial and green and takes a few years to reach maturity. Other members of its genus reproduce more readily by sexual means than species of *Lycopodium*.

The drainage of bogs and successional changes in its habitat have resulted in this species disappearing from many sites in lowland England. In southern England it has increasingly become restricted to areas kept open by human disturbance. Until recently it has remained somewhat overlooked around the margins of Scottish lochs.

L. inundata is found throughout most of Europe, except the Mediterranean region, but it has declined markedly in recent times. Its European distribution is mapped by Jalas & Suominen (1972). It is also found on the eastern and western sides of North America.

A. D. Headley

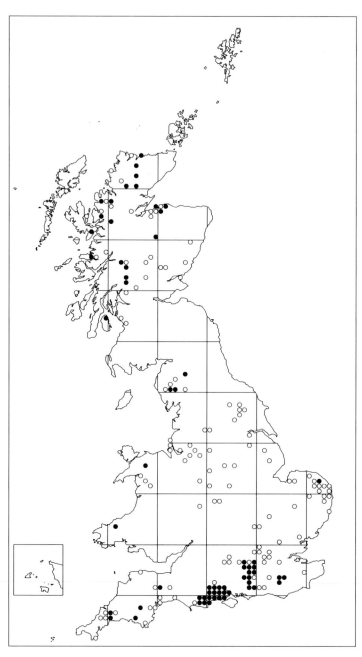

Current map	No	Atlas	No
1970 →	64	1930 →	49
Pre-1970	122	Pre-1930	87
Introductions	0	Introductions	0

continued →

Lycopodiella inundata

continued

Marsh clubmoss

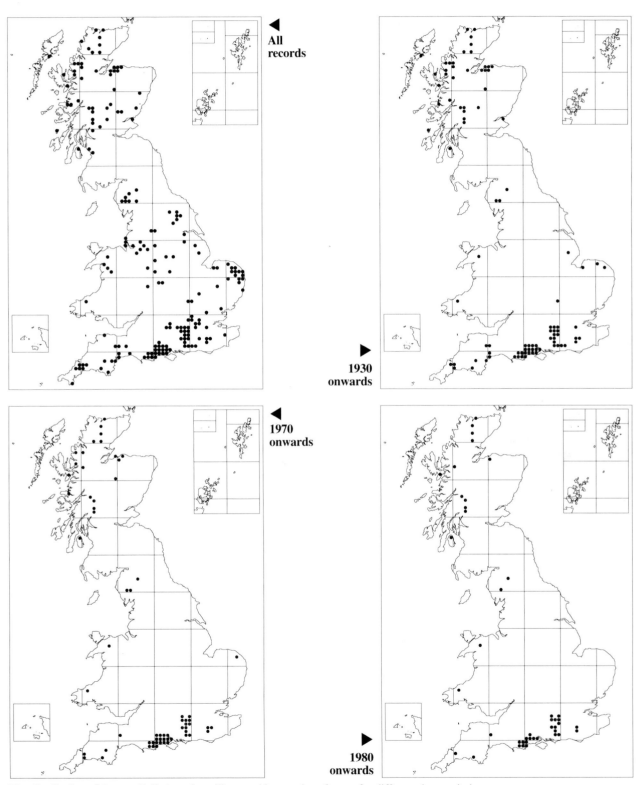

All records

1930 onwards

1970 onwards

1980 onwards

The distribution of *Lycopodiella inundata*, illustrated by a series of maps for different time periods.

Lycopodium annotinum L.

Status: scarce

Interrupted clubmoss

This is a plant of upland heaths, flushes, grassland and open woods, and is typically found in hollows and on steep slopes with late snow-lie in various sorts of *Calluna vulgaris* and *Vaccinium myrtillus* heath. It is a calcifuge growing on a range of base-poor substrates, usually well drained, but often with a surface layer of mor humus beneath a carpet of mosses. Associated species include numerous common heathland plants and relatively uncommon boreal species such as *Arctostaphylos uva-ursi*, *Cornus suecica*, *Juniperus communis* and *Vaccinium uliginosum*. In its southernmost extant locality in Langdale, it grows in acidic grassland with *Agrostis* spp., *Festuca ovina* and *Nardus stricta*. A predominantly upland plant, it reaches 950 metres in the Cairngorms, but descends to 45 metres on Mull. It is unaccountably rare to the north of Ross-shire.

L. annotinum is a long-lived perennial which spreads by means of stolons at a rate of 8 to 30 cm each year. Although sections of the plant may live for 15 to 20 years, the clone may persist at a site for at least 250 years. Strobili mature in late summer, but do not release their spores until October. The average number of spores produced per strobilus is close to a million and spore production may reach several hundred million. Spores have been estimated to take 6 to 7 years to germinate and the subterranean saprophytic gametophytes take at least 12 years to reach maturity. As a consequence the minimum time for completion of the life cycle is at least 25 years. Sexual reproduction is associated with disturbance, particularly fires, soil erosion and planting of conifers.

L. annotinum has a relatively stable distribution within the Scottish Highlands, but it is likely to be still under-recorded in this area. It has been lost from a few sites owing to frequent moor burning and the planting of conifers.

Within Europe *L. annotinum* is a widely distributed northern suboceanic plant, primarily found in boreal forests (Jalas & Suominen 1972). Almost circumboreal, it extends into the arctic and is found as far south as the Appalachian and Rocky mountains.

A. D. Headley

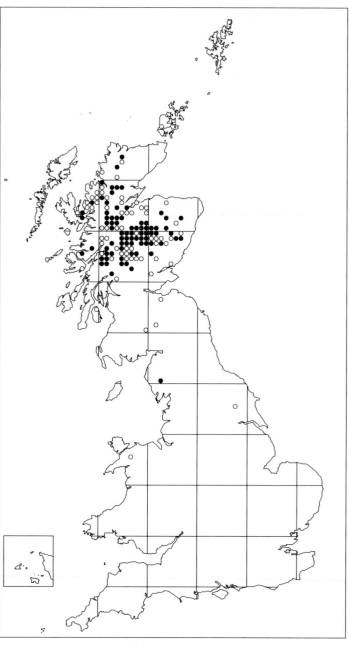

Current map	No	Atlas	No
1970 →	78	1930 →	56
Pre-1970	64	Pre-1930	25
Introductions	0	Introductions	0

Lysimachia thyrsiflora L.
Status: scarce

Tufted loosestrife

This is a species of fens and swamps where it usually grows among open, tall vegetation such as *Glyceria maxima* and large *Carex* species. It also occurs widely in rather less tall vegetation, growing with *Carex rostrata* and *Potentilla palustris*. Typical situations include fens on the flood plains of rivers and on lake margins, pools which have become overgrown by emergents and wet meadows. It is locally frequent along canals in central Scotland. Spectacular stands of this species developed on the marshy bed of the Union Canal in a stretch which lost its water following a breach of the bank near Kettlestoun (Anderson & Murphy 1987).

This is a perennial rhizomatous species.

This species has declined due to drainage and it is now very rare as a native plant in England. However, it is frequent in many of its remaining Scottish sites.

This species is widespread in the boreal zone of the northern hemisphere, occurring in Europe, Asia and North America. In Europe it extends from central France, the Alps, northern Yugoslavia and Bulgaria to northern Fennoscandia but it is most frequent in the eastern North Sea and Baltic Sea regions.

N. F. Stewart

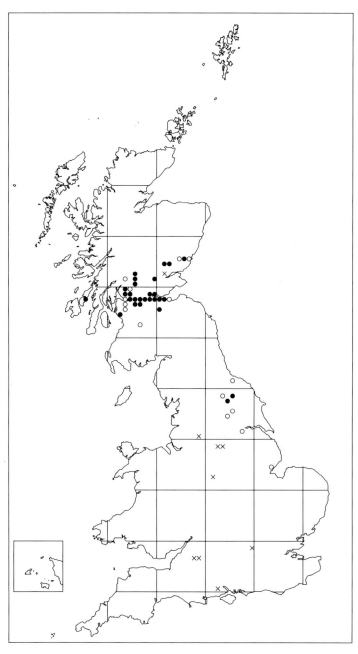

Current map	No	Atlas	No
1970 →	27	1930 →	16
Pre-1970	15	Pre-1930	16
Introductions	9	Introductions	6

continued →

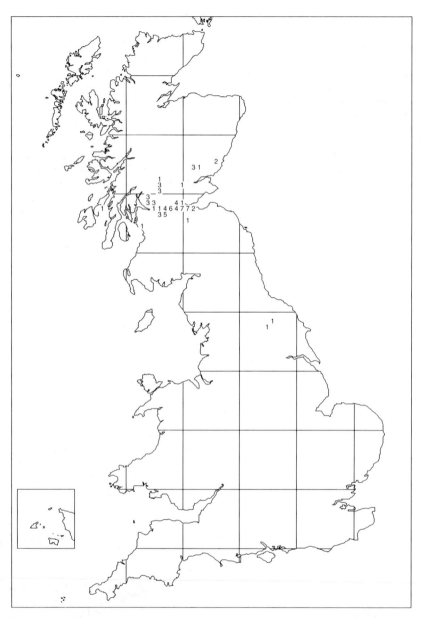

The number of tetrads in each 10 km square in which *Lysimachia thyrsiflora* has been recorded as a native species from 1970 onwards. The species has been found in a total of 73 tetrads from 1970 onwards.

Marrubium vulgare L.
Status: scarce

White horehound

This is an aromatic herbaceous perennial of lowland broken ground and parched calcareous grasslands. The 'native' coastal stations are open cliff-edge grasslands and coastal slopes subject to exposure to wind, soil creep, salt spray and insolation. These grasslands, in the presence of natural levels of herbivore grazing, are probably climax communities. *M. vulgare* tends to be found in relatively fertile, broken ground, or benefits from locally-intense rabbit or sheep dunging. The immediate associates may include *Cirsium arvense*, *Malva sylvestris* and *Picris echioides*. A wide range of notable species are found in association with *M. vulgare* in these habitats, including *Euphorbia portlandica*, *Helianthemum canum*, *Orobanche artemisiae-campestris* and *Torilis nodosa*.

Reproduction is by both seed and natural division of the herbaceous rootstock. Seed germinates freely in broken ground.

Long term trends in the distribution and abundance of this species are masked by the appearance and loss of naturalised colonies. The native coastal stations are under pressure from the elimination of natural grazing and the reluctance of the conservation managers to graze cliff tops and coastal slopes with domestic stock. The absence of any grazing is resulting in invasion by woody species or coarse herbs, which leave matted dead vegetation, resulting in the loss of open ground. Unlike annuals found in cliff top grasslands, *M. vulgare* is relatively tolerant of short term fluctuations in grazing pressure. It persists as a perennial even where bare ground is absent and plants cannot become established from seed. Where intensive grazing is present, the plant persists untouched by stock.

M. vulgare is found throughout Europe, except the far north. It also occurs in North Africa, the Middle East and further east through Asia.

The true natural distribution of the species in Britain is unclear. *M. vulgare* has long been regarded as a valuable herb and as an attractive ornamental plant. The widespread cultivation of this species has resulted in numerous inland naturalised colonies. The species is generally accepted to be native in coastal exposures of limestones and some of the harder chalk formations. There is a strong likelihood that some inland stations, especially those on limestone screes, crags and parched grasslands, are also native.

C. Chatters

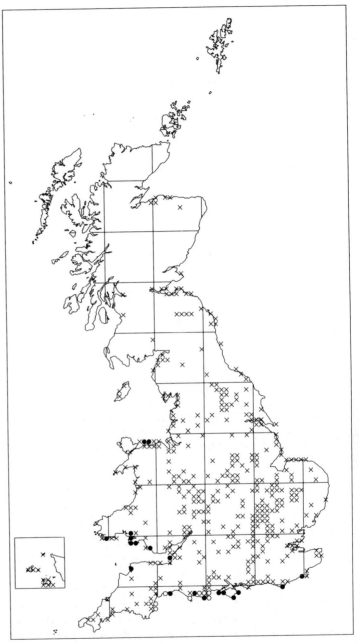

Current map	No	Atlas	No
1970 →	19	1930 →	13
Pre-1970	8	Pre-1930	0
Introductions	372	Introductions	131

Meconopsis cambrica (L.) Viguier

Welsh poppy

Status: scarce

This species shows a marked preference for moist shady, rocky places, often under trees and usually on base-rich soils. It also forms part of the arctic-alpine community in Wales, where associated species typically include *Arabis hirsuta*, *Crepis paludosa*, *Festuca vivipara*, *Hymenophyllum wilsonii*, *Luzula sylvatica*, *Oxyria digyna*, *Saxifraga hypnoides*, *S. oppositifolia*, *S. stellaris*, *Sedum rosea* and *Selaginella selaginoides* (Price Evans 1932; Price Evans 1944). Introduced populations occur along roadsides, hedges, walls and waste ground often some distance from habitation. It is confined, as a native, to land between 100 and 610 metres in Snowdonia, but introduced populations descend almost to sea-level in some areas.

M. cambrica is a long-lived perennial, flowering from June to September. Reproduction is entirely by seed.

This species is slowly decreasing as a native plant but is much grown in gardens and is now widespread and increasing as an established alien. Garden populations increase rapidly from self-sown seed but, paradoxically, native and some established populations seem reluctant to spread into apparently ideal habitats nearby.

M. cambrica is endemic to western Europe from western Ireland southwards to western France and northern Spain (Jalas & Suominen 1991). It is recorded as an introduction elsewhere in Europe. It is the only European representative of an otherwise Asiatic genus.

Native plants have predominantly yellow flowers, whilst those of established aliens may be yellow, orange or even scarlet, and are sometimes double (Huxley 1992).

R. G. Ellis

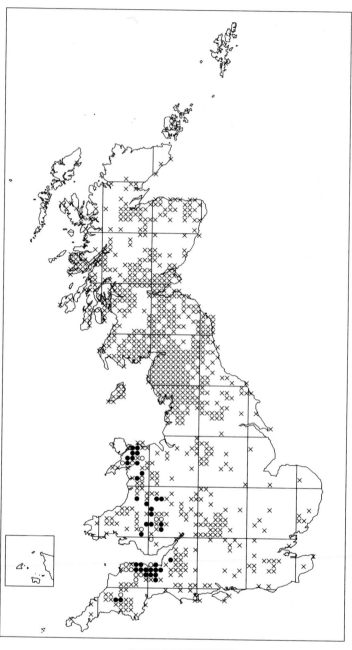

Current map	No	Atlas	No
1970 →	37	1930 →	37
Pre-1970	16	Pre-1930	8
Introductions	778	Introductions	293

Medicago minima (L.) L.

Status: scarce

Bur medick

This plant grows on dry sandy heaths in Breckland and in open sandy or gravelly places on the coast. It is a plant of open low vegetation which tolerates little competition. In Breckland it is found on low banks, on road verges, disturbed ground by rabbit warrens and it sometimes grows in small quantity. Its associates include *Achillea millefolium, Aphanes inexspectata, Arenaria serpyllifolia, Catapodium rigidum, Cerastium arvense, Erodium cicutarium, Galium verum* and *Rumex acetosella*. It is frequently recorded as a casual, often introduced with wool shoddy.

M. minima is an annual, reproducing entirely from seed, which germinates in autumn (Trist 1979).

It is still frequent in the Breckland, and in open places around the coast, but it is decreasing where lack of grazing has allowed its habitats to become more rank.

It is widespread in Europe, as far north as Britain and Denmark, and also found in Asia, Africa and parts of the New World.

D. A. Pearman

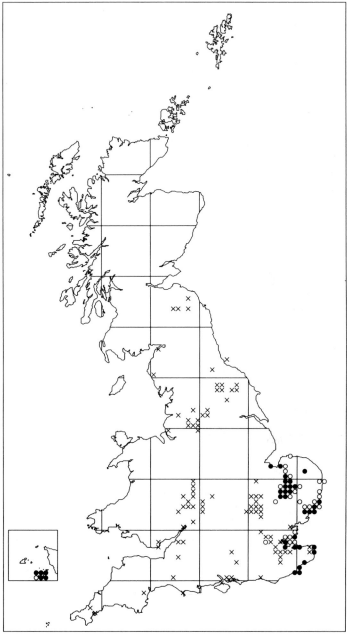

Current map	No	Atlas	No
1970 →	30	1930 →	23
Pre-1970	24	Pre-1930	15
Introductions	88	Introductions	58

Medicago polymorpha L.
Status: scarce

Toothed medick

This species is found in a variety of open, sandy or gravelly habitats near the sea. In south-west England, for example, it occurs in short summer-parched coastal grasslands with such species as *Arenaria serpyllifolia*, *Crepis capillaris*, *Medicago arabica*, *Torilis nodosa*, *Trifolium campestre* and *T. dubium*. It also grows in areas kept open by trampling. It occurs as an alien on road verges and rubbish tips, where it is usually casual but sometimes persists. It has often been introduced with wool shoddy.

It is an annual, reproducing entirely by seed, which germinates mainly in the autumn. It probably requires bare ground for germination and seedling establishment.

It appears to be much less frequent now than previously in its native habitats. Removal of grazing may have been responsible for its demise at some sites, and there are several populations in south-west England currently at risk from scrub encroachment following agricultural abandonment. Some sites may have been lost through habitat destruction, for example by sea-defence work and building developments. However, this species is probably under-recorded, as it can easily be overlooked, especially when accompanied by *M. arabica*.

M. polymorpha is widespread in Europe, extending northwards as a native to Britain but found as an occasional casual further north. It is also found in North Africa and throughout western Asia. Small & Jomphe (1989) describe it as "adventive where not limited by cold, drought, and waterlogging of soil".

The closely related *M. arabica*, which has a more northerly world distribution, has been a much more successful colonist of inland habitats.

S. J. Leach & D. A. Pearman

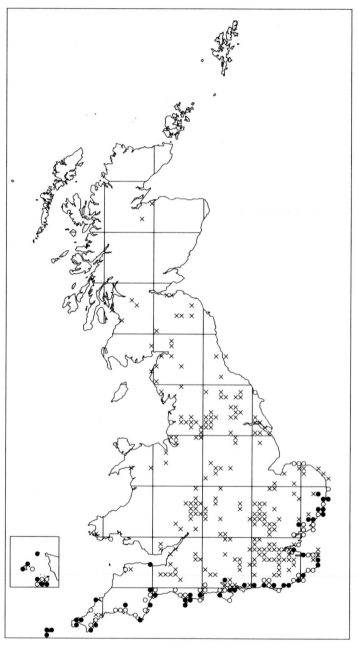

Current map	No	Atlas	No
1970 →	45	1930 →	39
Pre-1970	49	Pre-1930	22
Introductions	217	Introductions	130

Medicago sativa L. subsp. *falcata* (L.) Arcang.

Sickle medick

Status: scarce

This subspecies occurs as a native on slightly acid coarse sands and gravels, and on chalk grasslands, in sites where competition is reduced by summer drought. It thrives in open or closed swards of non-aggressive plants, on sand banks at the rear of wide road verges and beside tracks where there is no animal access. It will not withstand rabbit grazing and is therefore absent from open heaths. Its numerous associates include *Aira caryophyllea*, *Dactylis glomerata*, *Elytrigia repens*, *Galium verum* and *Ononis repens*. It is also found as a casual over a wide area, but rarely persists for long.

It is a deep-rooted drought-resisting perennial, which spreads by seed.

This is still frequent in the Breckland (Trist 1979), but has apparently declined on the coast and in adjoining heaths.

It is widespread in northern Europe and Asia, and widely introduced elsewhere. This subspecies has given rise to a few domesticated forms and is much used for breeding alfalfa resistant to cold, acid soils (Small & Jomphe 1989). It hybridises frequently with *M. sativa* subsp. *sativa* (lucerne, alfalfa). The hybrid, a fertile plant with a variety of flower colours, is locally frequent, especially on roadside verges.

D. A. Pearman

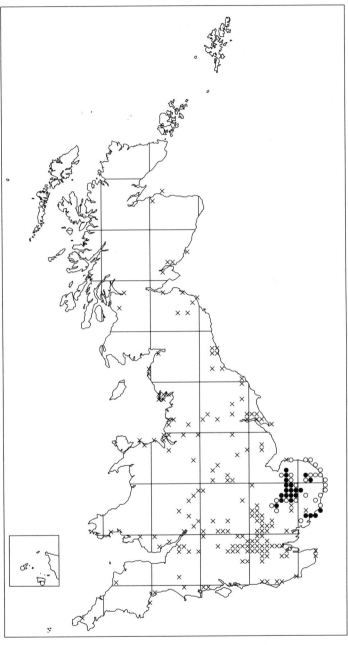

Current map	No	Atlas	No
1970 →	22	1930 →	23
Pre-1970	26	Pre-1930	17
Introductions	167	Introductions	99

Melampyrum cristatum L.
Status: scarce

Crested cow-wheat

This plant is an obligate hemiparasite of various woody and herbaceous species, predominantly found on the margins of ancient oak woodland and in its clearings and rides. It occasionally grows on roadside verges and hedgebanks where these have at some time bordered woodland. It occurs very exceptionally in open grassland. It is thermophilous on the continent and largely restricted to the most continental area of Great Britain where it grows on calcium-rich soils derived from boulder clay. It is restricted to the lowlands.

It is a summer annual which lives for about 7 months, flowering from the age of 4 months onward. Plants are pollinated by bumble-bees. If cross-pollination fails the stamens move to effect self-pollination. Seed dispersal is limited by the large seed size but the ant *Lasius flavus* acts as a dispersal agent in some British sites. The seed exhibits double dormancy and may persist for some years before germination is triggered by coppicing and soil disturbance.

This plant is apparently in decline, with its range contracting. Populations have been lost through cessation of traditional woodland management, removal of hedges and the increased use of weed killing sprays on verges and agricultural land.

Its distribution is centred on eastern Europe and western Russia, spreading westwards to northern Italy, northern Spain and Britain and eastwards to central Asia..

The autecology of this species is described by Horrill (1972).

F. J. Rumsey

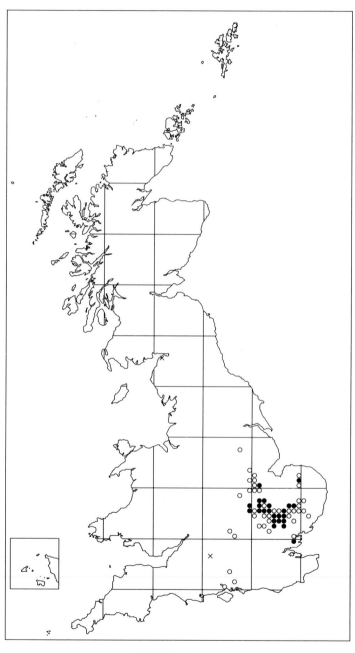

Current map	No	Atlas	No
1970 →	23	1930 →	21
Pre-1970	39	Pre-1930	33
Introductions	2	Introductions	0

continued →

Melampyrum cristatum
continued

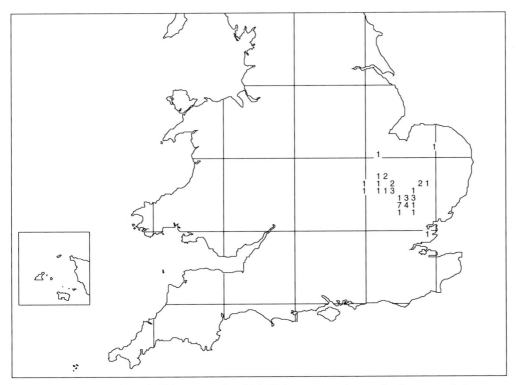

The number of tetrads in each 10 km square in which *Melampyrum cristatum* has been recorded as a native species from 1970 onwards. The species has been found in a total of 41 tetrads from 1970 onwards.

Melampyrum sylvaticum L.
Status: scarce

Small cow-wheat

This is an obligate hemiparasite of various woody and herbaceous species, usually found in wooded ravines and glens under birch, often with *M. pratense* which it may parasitise, and be parasitised by. Its sites are floristically similar to the *Geranium sylvaticum*-rich birch communities of the Norwegian mountains. It is more frequent in damper, more nutrient enriched, grassy species-rich areas than in *Vaccinium*- and *Empetrum*- dominated patches but it does appear there if not too dry. In some sites it is restricted to rock ledges. Its altitudinal range is from *c.* 60 metres to 760 metres on Aonach air Crith.

M. sylvaticum is a summer annual, flowering from June to August. It is probably pollinated by bumble bees but self-pollinates if cross-pollination fails.

M. sylvaticum was over-recorded in the past because of confusion with forms of *M. pratense*. Only reliable older records have been mapped. The species appears to be declining. It is extinct in Co. Durham, probably because of over-collecting, but still survives on the Yorkshire side of the R. Tees.

This species is confined to Europe. It extends from Iceland and Scandinavia southwards in montane areas to the Pyrenees, central Italy and southern Bulgaria.

F. J. Rumsey

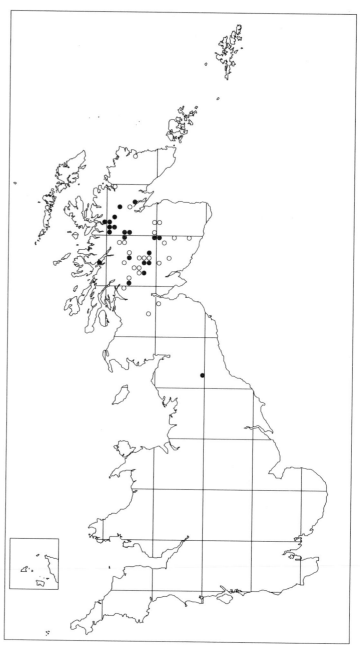

Current map	No	Atlas	No
1970 →	21	1930 →	12
Pre-1970	25	Pre-1930	12
Introductions	0	Introductions	0

Melittis melissophyllum L.
Status: scarce

Bastard balm

M. melissophyllum is a perennial plant of moisture-retentive, base-rich soils. It grows within and at the edges of woodland, on hedgebanks in sheltered river valleys, and in scrub. It responds well to coppicing and can be abundant in cleared areas of woodland. It appears to benefit from high humidity and light shade. In the New Forest it survives where the protection of brambles provides a refuge from pony-grazing. On the Lizard Peninsula, it flourishes in one place in coastal scrub under bracken. It is often associated with *Euphorbia amygdaloides* in its woodland sites, also with *Hedera helix*, *Lathyrus linifolius*, *Luzula pilosa*, *Mercurialis perennis* and *Viola riviniana*.

Flowering usually takes place in May and June, but it may be as early as April or as late as July. A great deal of nectar is produced, attracting insects such as bumble-bees and hawkmoths. Populations can be large, particularly in wooded areas, if the habitat is kept somewhat open.

M. melissophyllum has disappeared from many of its easternmost sites, but it is still frequent in Cornwall where it is not declining.

It is distributed through western, central and southern Europe, ranging from Britain eastwards to Lithuania and north-central Ukraine.

R. J. Murphy

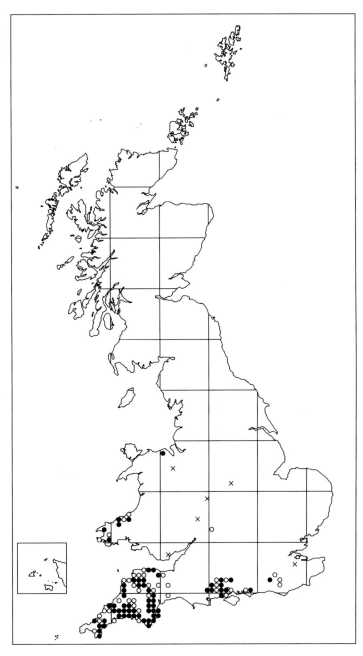

Current map	No	Atlas	No
1970 →	63	1930 →	53
Pre-1970	42	Pre-1930	21
Introductions	6	Introductions	3

continued →

263

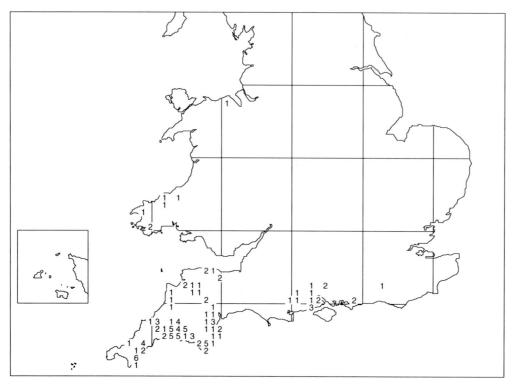

The number of tetrads in each 10 km square in which *Melittis melissophyllum* has been recorded as a native species from 1970 onwards. The species has been found in a total of 119 tetrads from 1970 onwards.

Mentha pulegium L.
Status: rare

This is a short-lived perennial herb of seasonally inundated grassland, usually appearing within and around ephemeral pools and runnels. The grasslands supporting *M. pulegium* are very short turf overlying clay and silt and are subjected to intense all year round grazing, trampling, dunging or disturbance by livestock or vehicles, causing poaching and ruts. This habitat is found within traditionally managed lowland village greens, settlement-edge lawns adjacent to open heath, and the verges of unmetalled trackways. Relic populations appear to persist in the presence of rutting and poaching in the absence of hard grazing. The ephemeral pools are typified by broken ground with grasses such as *Agrostis* spp. and the herbs *Chamaemelum nobile*, *Gnaphalium uliginosum*, *Lythrum portula* and *Ranunculus flammula*. The habitats supporting *M. pulegium* also contain a wide range of rare and scarce plants including *Cicendia filiformis*, *Galium constrictum*, *Pilularia globulifera* and *Pulicaria vulgaris*.

A mature plant of *M. pulegium* consists of a central group of rooted stems giving rise to a mass of weakly rooting arching non-flowering stems. When subject to trampling, rutting or 'mulching' by dung, the stems readily root. As each fragment of *M. pulegium* is short-lived, this process needs to be continuous if the plant is to persist. If conditions are suitable, the plant may become the dominant species in the turf. *M. pulegium* flowers freely and sets seed but seedlings have rarely, if ever, been seen in the wild.

As traditional management of village greens has become very scarce in the lowlands, this species has declined. It is only in the New Forest, where a pastoral economy persists, that the plant is found in the abundance historically reported from commons throughout the lowlands. *M. pulegium* is just one of a suite of species associated with village greens which have declined (Bratton 1990; Hare 1990). Even within land owned by conservation agencies, it is important to achieve a change in perception to permit the survival of these superficially untidy habitats (Byfield 1991). Threats come from ornamenting greens with flowering trees, excavating seasonally wet areas to 'save' village ponds, and filling ruts in tracks with hard core. Although there are records from 20 10 km squares from 1970 onwards, this declining species is classified as rare as it has been recorded in only 15 10 km squares since 1980.

Widespread in Europe, north to Ireland and Poland, and also present in Macaronesia, North Africa and the Near East. It has declined elsewhere in Europe.

C. Chatters

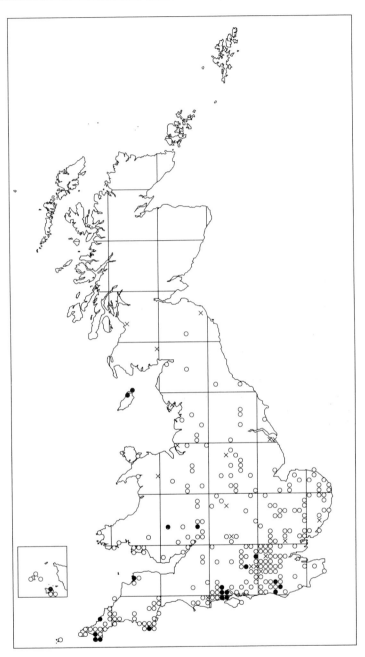

Current map	No	Atlas	No
1970 →	20	1930 →	43
Pre-1970	229	Pre-1930	126
Introductions	18	Introductions	7

continued →

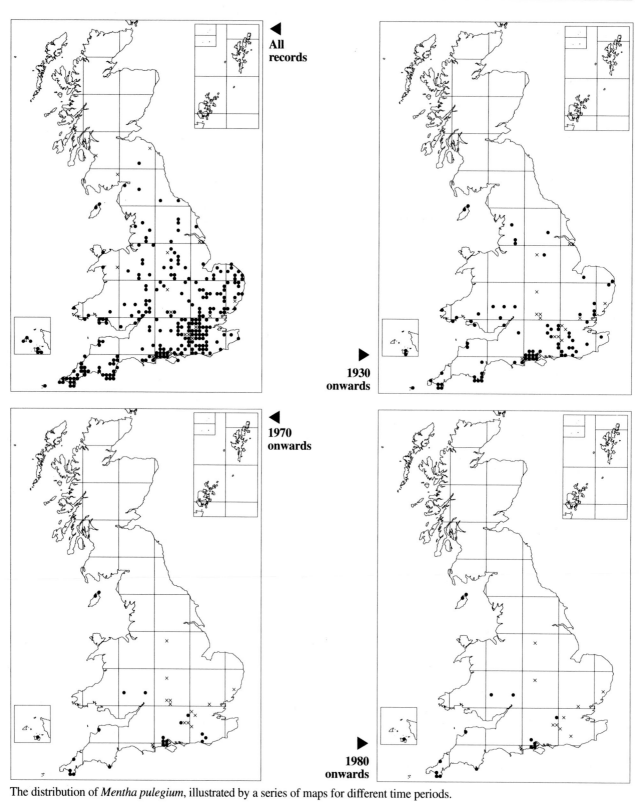

All
records

1930
onwards

1970
onwards

1980
onwards

The distribution of *Mentha pulegium*, illustrated by a series of maps for different time periods.

Mertensia maritima (L.) Gray

Status: scarce

Oysterplant

This plant grows on exposed beaches where it occurs among shingle or on shingle mixed with sand. More rarely it grows on pure sand, but such colonies are usually short-lived. It occurs around the zone reached by the highest storm tides, and it probably benefits from periodic deposition of decaying seaweed. Frequently it occurs near the mouths of streams, and in very exposed situations it often grows where there is some shelter from rocks to protect it from the full force of the waves. There are usually no associated plants, but occasionally it occurs with strandline species such as *Atriplex* spp., *Galium aparine*, *Honkenya peploides*, *Rumex crispus* and *Tripleurospermum maritimum*.

M. maritima is a perennial species with a large tap-root. The above-ground parts die back to ground level each winter. It is usually self-pollinated and the seeds are transported by wind and sea. Immersion in seawater does not affect seed germination and seeds have been known to travel at least 450 km. They also seem to be able to remain dormant *in situ* for several years. Some sand or organic matter is probably necessary for germination. Within individual colonies, numbers fluctuate as a result of erosion or accretion due to storms.

The map shows many old records and the plant is often stated to be declining. However it is a mobile plant which moves from site to site at the whim of storms. At some sites its occurrence for over 200 years is well documented, but at others there is good evidence that it occurred only as a casual for a few years. Within its main range there is no evidence to suggest that there has been an overall decrease, but at the southern edge of its range there is clear evidence of retreat. This is probably due to disturbance from human recreation and shingle removal. The largest and most important populations are in Orkney.

This is a boreal species which occurs around the north Atlantic, Pacific and the Arctic coast of America. On the east coast of Asia subsp. *maritima* is replaced by subsp. *asiatica* Takeda. In Europe its main stronghold is in Norway and Iceland, but it extends south to Ireland, Britain and, formerly, Denmark. Elsewhere its southern limit is approximately Maine (USA), Queen Charlotte Islands (Canada) and Riu Kiu Islands (Japan), but as in Europe the records peter into uncertainty. Its southern limit more or less corresponds with the mean January isotherm of 4.5 °C and the mean July isotherm of 19 °C (Scott 1963).

N. F. Stewart

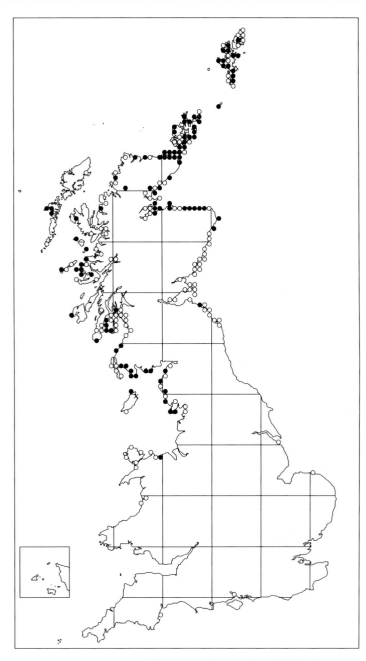

Current map	No	Atlas	No
1970 →	100	1930 →	53
Pre-1970	121	Pre-1930	73
Introductions	1	Introductions	0

continued →

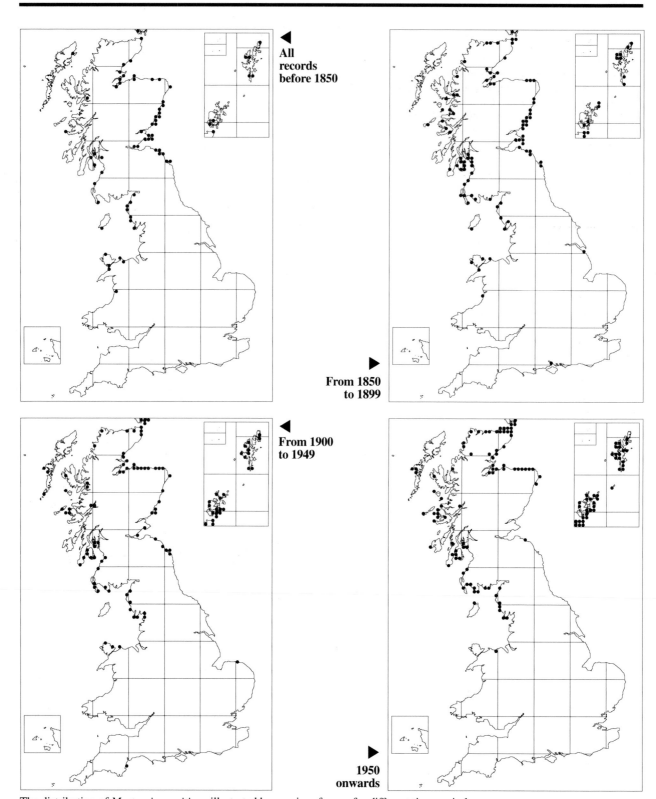

The distribution of *Mertensia maritima*, illustrated by a series of maps for different time periods.

Meum athamanticum Jacq.   **Spignel**

Status: scarce

This is a species of dry, neutral or acidic grassland in unimproved pastures, hay meadows and roadside banks. It is typically found over slightly acid soils but is absent from podsolic brown earths. It is sometimes associated with other 'northern hay meadow' species such as *Geranium sylvaticum*. It is largely restricted to upland districts but is not normally found above 300 metres, although it reaches 610 metres at White Coombe and Fealar.

This is a perennial species with a tough rootstock and it can probably survive being grazed over many years.

This species has probably suffered some decline due to agricultural improvement of grasslands, although in some areas it persists on banks in haymeadows which are too steep to cut and on roadsides. It is also unpopular with farmers because it is strongly aromatic and can taint cow's milk (although the rootstock had medicinal uses). The map probably over-emphasises the decline since some of its distribution is in areas where recent recording is inadequate.

It is a western European species which extends locally from northern Spain to southern Norway and east to Poland, Czechoslovakia and the Balkans.

N. F. Stewart

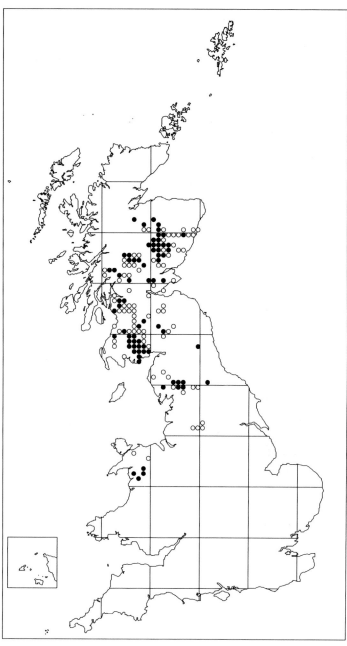

Current map	No	Atlas	No
1970 →	71	1930 →	63
Pre-1970	81	Pre-1930	36
Introductions	0	Introductions	0

Minuartia hybrida (Villars) Schischkin

Status: scarce

Fine-leaved sandwort

The natural habitat of *M. hybrida* is dry, weathered, calcareous rocky slopes. In Britain, this habitat is uncommon in the south and east. *M. hybrida* occurs in artificial sites instead, such as sandy arable fields over chalk, quarries, old walls, road verges and railway banks and sidings. It is particularly common in Breckland on abandoned arable land, often associated with other scarce or uncommon species such as *Medicago minima* and *Trifolium scabrum*. Although mainly lowland in distribution, *M. hybrida* reaches 400 metres at Langcliffe in the Craven Pennines.

A summer-flowering annual, *M. hybrida* reproduces by seed only.

M. hybrida has declined markedly in Britain over the last century, particularly in arable and grassland sites, with the increase of more intensive farming methods. New records on railways partly offset that decline and *M. hybrida* is cited in over fifteen county floras as a typical railway species.

M. hybrida reaches its northern limit in Europe in the British Isles (Jalas & Suominen 1983). Elsewhere it occurs from central Germany and the southern Ukraine, south to the North African coast, west to the Atlantic and east into western Asia. In the Netherlands it is undergoing a significant decline in its native habitats, but it has been discovered on railway verges (Witte 1992).

J. O. Mountford

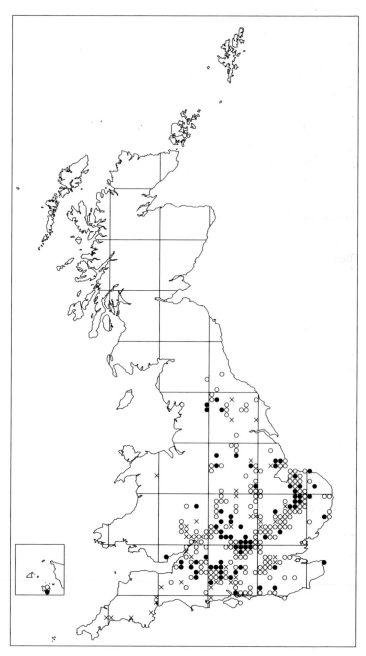

Current map	No	Atlas	No
1970 →	72	1930 →	100
Pre-1970	179	Pre-1930	106
Introductions	41	Introductions	0

Minuartia sedoides (L.) Hiern

Status: scarce

Cyphel

This is an alpine plant of open rocks, flushed grassland and exposed montane heath. In its more southerly localities it is limited to more base-rich rocks, particularly calcareous schists, but further north it occurs on rocks that are much less productive, a rather similar distribution pattern to *Silene acaulis*. Frequent associates in the southern Highlands are *Alchemilla alpina, Carex capillaris, Cerastium alpinum, S. acaulis* and a number of rare mountain plants. Further north, where it occurs in exposed situations on broad ridges and bealachs, the dominant associate is often the moss *Racomitrium lanuginosum* in a species-rich turf with *Armeria maritima, Gnaphalium supinum, Persicaria vivipara, Silene acaulis* and *Thymus polytrichus*. It is found from 335 metres in Skye to 1060 metres on Tom a'Choinich, and it is reported from 1200 metres on Ben Lawers.

M. sedoides is a perennial with flowers that are frequently protandrous and with abortive capsules.

There is no reason to believe that populations of this plant have decreased significantly, and it is probably still present in most of the 10 km squares for which only pre-1970 records are available.

It is unusual in being one of the few British alpines not also found in the Arctic. In Europe it is known from the Pyrenees and the Alps with isolated stations further east (Jalas & Suominen 1983).

G. P. Rothero

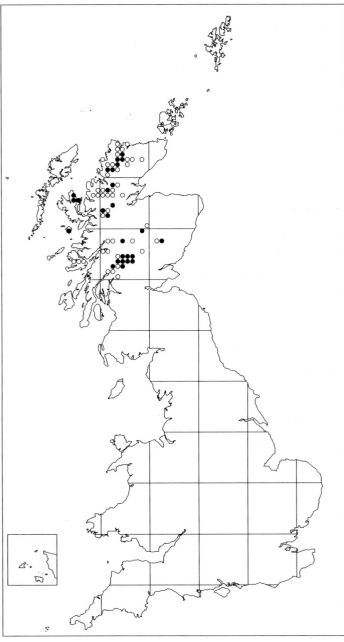

Current map	No	Atlas	No
1970 →	27	1930 →	47
Pre-1970	42	Pre-1930	10
Introductions	0	Introductions	0

Minuartia verna (L.) Hiern

Status: scarce

Spring sandwort

This is characteristically a plant of Carboniferous limestone, occurring on scars, in semi-open short grassland, in shallow soil-filled depressions on limestone pavement and in scree. It also occurs locally in base-rich gullies and rock ledges on other rock types such as basalt and serpentine. Common associates include *Linum catharticum, Saxifraga hypnoides, Thymus polytrichus, Ctenidium molluscum* and, on the limestone, *Galium sterneri*. In the Carboniferous limestone areas and in north-west Wales, it is frequent around old mine workings, chiefly of lead and zinc but also of copper in Wales. Many of these sites are simply open calcareous habitats with little or no heavy metal content. Others, although having considerable levels of 'available' metal, are non-toxic, the heavy metals being effectively 'neutralised' by the high pH. Some sites, however, are very definitely toxic, with a sparse, impoverished and characteristic flora of heavy-metal resistant ecotypes of *M. verna, Agrostis capillaris* and *Festuca ovina* and a pH around 5. *Thlaspi caerulescens* is a particularly characteristic associate on toxic sites in the north Pennines, Derbyshire and the Mendips. In North Wales it grows with some arctic-montane species. *M. verna* also occurs intermittently as an adventive on riverside gravels to the north and east of the Pennine mining sites. It rarely occurs above 600 metres, but it reaches 855 metres in the Lake District.

It is a short-lived perennial. The populations may be quite large, especially on the limestone, but those on thin exposed soil are very susceptible to periods of drought. Flowering is from May to September; the flowers are protandrous but there is some self-pollination. Seed production and germination are good.

This species is not obviously under threat.

In Ireland, *M. verna* occurs on the limestone of the Burren, and on basalt on the north-east coast. It occurs throughout the mountains of central and southern Europe (Jalas & Suominen 1983), extending into North Africa and eastwards to the mountains of central Asia. It also occurs in the north in a narrow band along the Arctic Circle in Russia as far as the Bering Sea.

The population on the Lizard serpentine is morphologically distinct. This is particularly evident in cultivation, the plants having broader and usually glandular pubescent leaves and shorter, broader petals (Halliday 1960).

G. Halliday

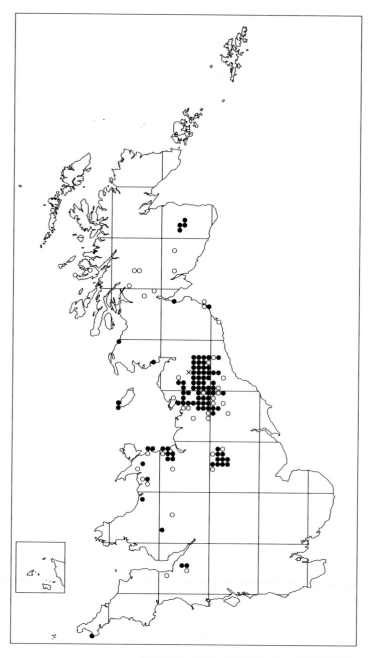

Current map	No	Atlas	No
1970 →	92	1930 →	77
Pre-1970	41	Pre-1930	25
Introductions	1	Introductions	0

continued →

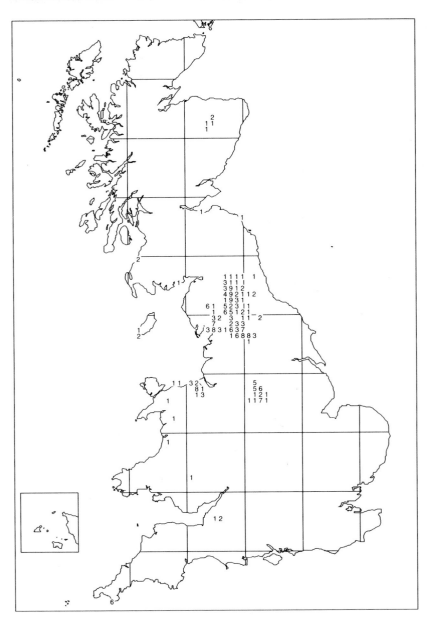

The number of tetrads in each 10 km square in which *Minuartia verna* has been recorded as a native species from 1970 onwards. Squares in which the species is recorded in 9 or more tetrads are plotted as 9: *M. verna* is actually recorded from 14 tetrads in NY73, 17 in NY74 and 19 in NY72. The species has been found in a total of 276 tetrads from 1970 onwards. The tetrad data are inadequate in Northumberland, as recording in this county has been in 5 × 5 km grid squares (Swan 1993).

Moenchia erecta (L.) Gaertner, Meyer and Scherb.

Upright chickweed

Status: not scarce

This plant grows on open broken soils that are at least seasonally parched. In coastal situations the plant is found on cliff tops, pathsides, dunes and other dry grasslands, often with *Cerastium diffusum*, *Sagina maritima* and *Sedum anglicum*. These grasslands are maintained by a combination of exposure to wind, insolation, soil creep and occasional grazing. The soils in these circumstances tend to be very shallow. The plant is locally abundant inland on the tightly-grazed grasslands and heaths of the New Forest, where it is sometimes found on soils which are waterlogged in winter. *M. erecta* is known from other scattered inland sites, both in natural habitats and often in adventitious circumstances such as on mineral workings and other disturbed ground. In dry grassland *M. erecta* may be found in association with *Ornithopus perpusillus*, and a range of *Trifolium* species including *T. glomeratum*, *T. ornithopodioides*, *T. scabrum* and *T. subterraneum*. On richer gley soils associates may include *Chamaemelum nobile*, *Cicendia filiformis*, *Illecebrum verticillatum* and *Radiola linoides*. It is a lowland plant, but reaches 400 metres near Widecombe on Dartmoor.

M. erecta is an annual, usually germinating in spring and setting seed and dying before mid-summer. The dried remains of flower stems may persist late into a dry summer. Seed is freely set and falls from the capsule. It readily germinates in bare and broken ground. Where conditions are suitable the plant may become locally abundant.

This plant was formerly widespread on lowland heaths and commons. With the cessation of heavy grazing many heathlands have lost open ground to dwarf shrubs (*Erica* spp. and *Calluna vulgaris*), rank grasses (*Holcus* spp. and *Molinia caerulea*) and tall scrub (*Betula* spp. and *Salix* spp.). As with so many other species, *M. erecta* is a casualty of socio-economic changes leading to a decline in pastoral management, combined with a reluctance of conservation managers to graze coastal slopes and heaths.

M. erecta subsp. *erecta* is confined to western Europe, with outliers in Italy, Greece and Turkey and it reaches its northern limit in Northumberland. Its distribution is mapped by Jalas & Suominen (1983). Subsp. *octandra* is found in the western Mediterranean region.

As a rather inconspicuous and early flowering species, this plant is possibly under-recorded.

C. Chatters

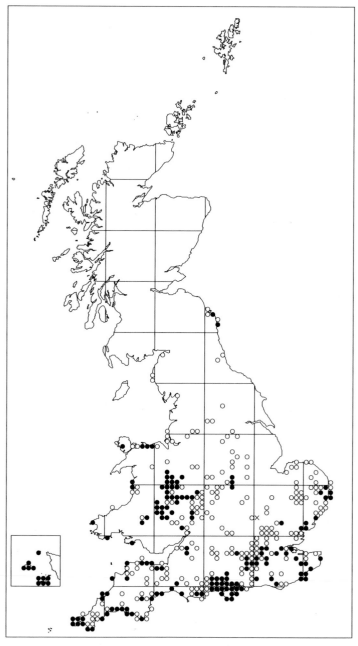

Current map	No	Atlas	No
1970 →	148	1930 →	84
Pre-1970	222	Pre-1930	129
Introductions	1	Introductions	0

Myosotis stolonifera (DC.) Gay ex Leresche & Levier

Pale forget-me-not

Status: scarce

This is a montane species, found over a wide variety of rocks although absent from limestone. It occurs in somewhat base-poor springs and seepage areas, soakways and flushes on the hillsides and in the valleys by pools, in ditches and in the backwaters of streams. The hillside springs and flushes are usually dominated by bryophytes, especially *Dicranella palustris* and *Philonotis fontana*; higher plant associates include *Cardamine pratensis*, *Chrysosplenium oppositifolium*, *Montia fontana*, *Saxifraga stellaris*, *Stellaria uliginosa* and, less frequently, *Epilobium alsinifolium*. *Myosotis secunda* and the more base-tolerant *Sphagnum* spp., such as *S. recurvum*, may be associated with it in valley pools. It descends to 130 metres in the Lune Gorge and ascends to 820 metres near Cross Fell.

The stems of this perennial species root freely at the nodes and during the latter part of the summer they branch freely, producing a dense, floating mass of vegetation which breaks up and is an effective means of vegetative propagation. Seed production is apparently normal.

This species was apparently first collected by A. Wilson near Sedbergh in 1892 but it was not recognised as a new British species until 1926 when it was described by C.E. Salmon as *M. brevifolia*. It was subsequently realised that it was conspecific with *M. stolonifera*. The near tripling in the number of records, compared with those in the Atlas (Perring & Walters 1962), probably reflects past confusion with *M. secunda* and also a greater awareness of the species. It is probably still under-recorded.

This species is endemic to Europe, and is confined to northern Portugal, Spain and Britain.

R. W. M. Corner & G. Halliday

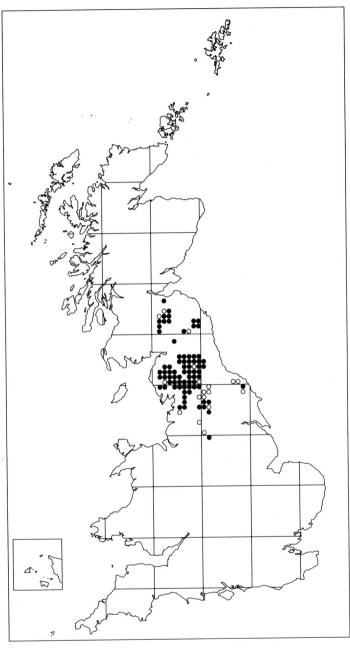

Current map	No	Atlas	No
1970 →	75	1930 →	32
Pre-1970	18	Pre-1930	1
Introductions	0	Introductions	0

continued →

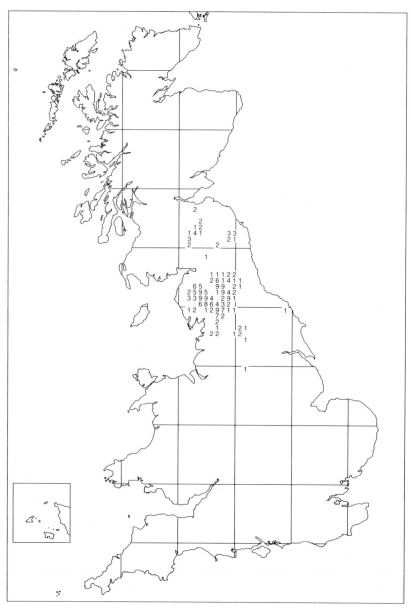

The number of tetrads in each 10 km square in which *Myosotis stolonifera* has been recorded as a native species from 1970 onwards. Squares in which the species is recorded in 9 or more tetrads are plotted as 9: *M. stolonifera* is actually recorded from 9 tetrads in NY32, NY63 and NY81, 10 in NY31, 11 in NY73, 12 in SD69, 13 in NY72 and 14 in NY41. The species has been found in a total of 254 tetrads from 1970 onwards.

Myosurus minimus L.

Status: not scarce

Mousetail

This is an annual plant of fertile broken ground which may be seasonally inundated and subject to trampling and compaction. *M. minimus* is found within a variety of lowland habitats, including cultivated land on the margins of arable fields and gardens as well as in grasslands and on the rutted or poached soil of tracks and gateways. As an arable weed, *M. minimus* is widely distributed but its appearance is unpredictable and sporadic. It grows on extensively grazed grasslands both within enclosed farmland and on commons and village greens. Here it is found in places where cattle or horses congregate and maintain bare muddy ground. Within more intensively managed grasslands, such as traditionally run small dairy farms, *M. minimus* is found in gateways and on tracksides along which livestock may pass daily. Where large populations are found, short lived satellite populations may occur on minor cattle paths and around drinking places.

Reproduction is by seed which is freely set. The seed invariably becomes trampled in the mud where it may germinate in bare ground in subsequent seasons. The seed-laden mud also adheres to hooves, tractor tyres and boot treads whereby it may be distributed to new sites. The seed floats and may be transported by flood waters.

M. minimus has declined throughout its range. This decline is partially concealed by the sporadic appearance of small populations; when mapped together these suggest a larger and more stable national population than actually exists. The decline is due to intensive arable and grassland management and the abandonment of extensive grazing of agriculturally marginal lowland grasslands, including commons. Without continued unintensive grazing, the fertile bare ground required by *M. minimus* is colonised by vigorous grasses and herbs.

M. minimus is widespread in Europe, North Africa, western Asia and North America. In Europe it is rare in the Mediterranean region and absent from the far north (Jalas & Suominen 1989). It is also recorded as an introduction in South Africa and Australia.

As a relatively inconspicuous species, growing in what are generally perceived as aesthetically and botanically unrewarding habitats, *M. minimus* is likely to be under-recorded.

C. Chatters

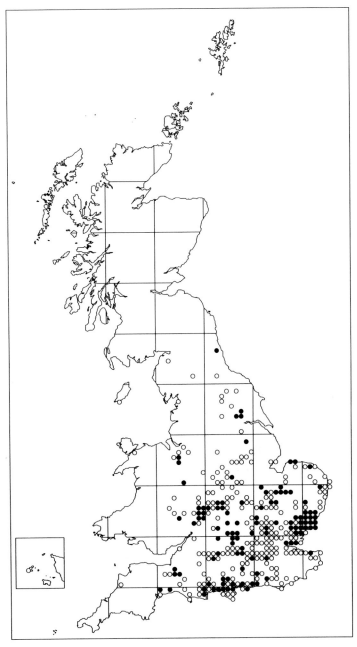

Current map	No	Atlas	No
1970 →	111	1930 →	58
Pre-1970	211	Pre-1930	181
Introductions	0	Introductions	0

Myriophyllum verticillatum L.
Status: scarce

Whorled water-milfoil

A submerged aquatic perennial with emergent flowering spikes, *M. verticillatum* occurs in ponds, ditches and lakes with base-rich water. It is a characteristic component of a still-water community rich in water-lilies and pondweeds. *M. verticillatum* is moderately tolerant of shade (i.e. turbid water) and occurs in water moderately rich in nutrients. It grows in grazing marshes with *M. spicatum*, but usually in more lime-rich water than its relative, and is strictly lowland in its distribution.

It is a creeping perennial rooted in the mud. Reproduction is mainly by vegetative means, with broken fragments rooting and by club-shaped turions produced in late summer and autumn.

M. verticillatum has been noted as declining throughout England and Wales, due to poorer water quality and habitat destruction. Open-water habitat has often been either over-deepened and canalised or colonised by tall emergents as the ditch has become redundant.

It is very widespread in Europe, absent only from a few peripheral islands. *M. verticillatum* is distributed throughout temperate Asia and North Africa, as well as both North and South America.

J. O. Mountford

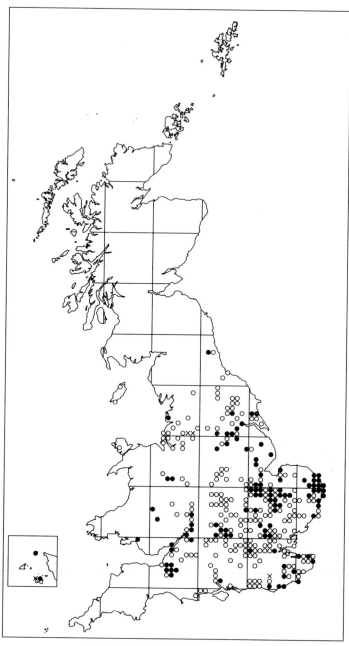

Current map	No	Atlas	No
1970 →	100	1930 →	92
Pre-1970	213	Pre-1930	81
Introductions	3	Introductions	0

Najas flexilis (Willd.) Rostkov & W. Schmidt

Slender naiad

Status: rare

WCA Schedule 8 species

N. flexilis is usually found over silty substrates in clear water in mesotrophic lowland lakes. It often occurs in sites which have slight base-enrichment from nearby basalt or limestone rock outcrops, or in machair lochs adjacent to calcareous dune sand. It is occasionally found in water less than 1 metre deep, as at Loch Ballyhaugh, where it grows with *Potamogeton rutilus* in a bed of *Chara aspera*. At most sites it grows in water over 1.5 metres deep, where associates can include *Callitriche hermaphroditica*, *Potamogeton praelongus* and the charophyte *Nitella flexilis*.

N. flexilis is an annual which reproduces by seed. Male and female flowers are found on the same plant. Pollination occurs under water and most mature plants appear to set seed.

N. flexilis was first discovered in Scotland in 1872 and at its only known English site, Esthwaite Water, in 1914. It is difficult to find as it grows out of sight of a shore-based observer, and it can usually be reached with a grapnel only where the water shelves rapidly. The number of sites from which it has been recorded has increased gradually in recent years, and further localities almost certainly await discovery. It has, however, become extinct at some sites in eastern Scotland as a result of eutrophication, which must be the most serious threat to this species. Although the more remote sites in western Scotland are less likely to receive enrichment from agricultural fertilisers, at least one is threatened by the presence of a fish farm.

N. flexilis has a northern distribution in Europe, extending south to Switzerland. It is rare throughout its European range. It is a circumboreal species, also found in northern Asia and North America. For a map of its world distribution, see Hultén & Fries (1986).

Fossil evidence indicates that *N. flexilis* was much more widespread in Britain and Europe in the Late Glacial and early Postglacial than it is today (Godwin 1975). As it has only been recorded from 15 10 km squares since 1970, it qualifies for inclusion in the *Red Data Book* under the current criteria. It is one of the species listed in Appendix I of the Bern Convention and Annexes II and IV of the European Community Habitats & Species Directive; the governments of the member states of the Council of Europe and the EC have an obligation to protect it.

C. D. Preston

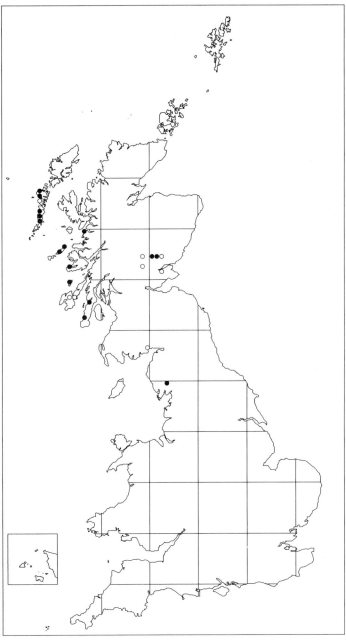

Current map	No	Atlas	No
1970 →	15	1930 →	9
Pre-1970	8	Pre-1930	3
Introductions	0	Introductions	0

Nuphar pumila (Timm) DC.

Status: scarce

Least water-lily

This water-lily grows in water 0.6-2.4 metres deep in sheltered lakes, in the oxbows and sheltered bays of rivers, in ditches and in pools in marshes and bogs. In Scotland it is found in oligotrophic, or, more frequently, mesotrophic sites, some of which receive base-rich drainage water. At the isolated sites in Shropshire it grows with *N. lutea* and *Persicaria amphibia* in sheltered bays in base-rich, eutrophic meres over glacial drift. These meres might, however, have been less eutrophic in former times. It is found over a range of substrates including mud, silt and peat. It ranges from near sea-level to 300 metres; a record from 520 metres near Lochan nan Damh (White 1898) is probably correct but requires confirmation.

N. pumila is a rhizomatous perennial. The flowers are not automatically self-pollinated but are visited by insects which may effect either self- or cross-pollination. The seeds lack morphological adaptations for animal dispersal, and are killed by desiccation and completely digested when eaten by birds or fish. The main chance of dispersal must be by water movement. Most populations are fertile, but at Avielochan a population shows reduced fertility, probably because the plants have undergone introgression with *N. lutea* (Heslop-Harrison 1953).

N. pumila was confused for many years by British botanists with the widespread hybrid *N. lutea* × *pumila* (*N.* × *spenneriana*). The taxonomy was clarified by Heslop-Harrison (1953) but the distribution cannot be revised adequately on the basis of herbarium material and a field survey is needed to establish the distribution of this species and the hybrid. There is no evidence that the species has declined in Scotland, but the plant has been lost from two of its three outlying sites in Shropshire, probably because of eutrophication.

N. pumila is a circumboreal species. It is frequent in northern Europe but is known from the Alps and other very scattered localities south to 43 °N in Spain. For maps of its European and world distributions, see Jalas & Suominen (1989) and Hultén & Fries (1986).

For an account of the ecology of this species, see Heslop-Harrison (1955).

C. D. Preston

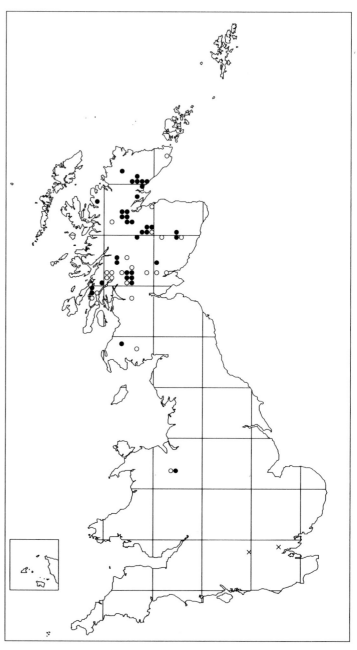

Current map	No	Atlas	No
1970 →	22	1930 →	16
Pre-1970	23	Pre-1930	14
Introductions	2	Introductions	0

Nymphoides peltata Kuntze
Status: scarce

Fringed water-lily

This is an aquatic plant, usually found in calcareous, relatively eutrophic water in larger water bodies. It is often found in a broad band along the edges of lakes, slowly flowing stretches of rivers and associated backwaters, fenland lodes and disused canals. Characteristic associates include *Ceratophyllum demersum*, *Elodea nuttallii*, *Myriophyllum spicatum*, *Potamogeton crispus*, *P. pectinatus* and *P. perfoliatus*. It is confined to the lowlands.

N. peltata is a rhizomatous perennial. It is heterostylous, with 'pin' and 'thrum' flowers on separate plants. Individual flowers last for only a day but colonies flower over a long period. Flowers are visited by a wide range of insects (Velde & Heiden 1981). Plants at some more northerly sites in Britain flower only sparingly. The seeds will stick to the webbed feet and to some parts of the plumage of waterfowl (Cook 1990). Little work has been done on the reproductive biology of this species in Britain.

N. peltata is thought to be native in the Thames valley, where both pin and thrum plants occur, and the East Anglian fenland, where only pin plants occur as natives but a thrum population has recently been found as an introduction. It is an attractive species which has been introduced and become established well outside its native range. It is still regularly planted in sites such as ornamental ponds, in gravel pits managed by anglers and in purpose-made fish ponds which may be far from houses. Studies in areas such as the Romney Marsh, where many aquatics have declined during the current century, show that this is one species which has increased in frequency (Mountford & Sheail 1989).

It is widespread in Europe north to England and the Baltic. It is also found in Asia in temperate latitudes from Turkey to Japan, and occurs as an introduction in North America. For a map of its world distribution, see Meusel *et al.* (1978).

C. D. Preston

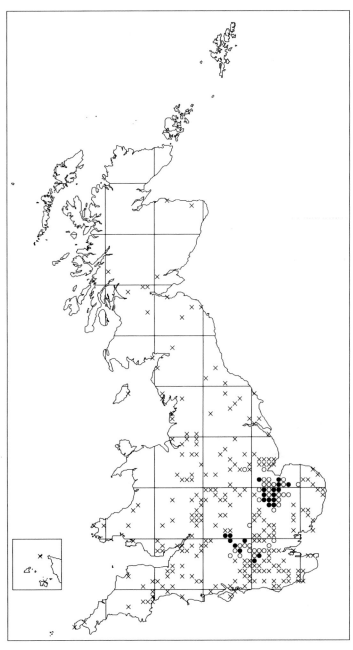

Current map	No	Atlas	No
1970 →	22	1930 →	27
Pre-1970	34	Pre-1930	23
Introductions	236	Introductions	47

Oenanthe fluviatilis (Bab.) Coleman

River water-dropwort

Status: not scarce

This plant is found only in flowing water in the lowlands. It most characteristically grows in large cylindrical masses in rapidly flowing, clear, calcareous streams and rivers. It is frequently associated with *Ranunculus penicillatus* subsp. *pseudofluitans*.

The perennial plant is usually seen vegetatively, and in some years at least the plant is green and visible in every month. Propagation is most commonly achieved by pieces of leaf and stem which break off and move downstream. Roots are very readily formed by almost any breakaway fragment. The plant does sometimes flower, always at a point where the flow is held up, and seed is set unless flood-water sinks the inflorescence.

This species is often overlooked by observers who are unfamiliar with the appearance of the leaves. It may have declined locally because of water-pollution. Searches in rivers in recent years have been more successful in urban and suburban areas than in agricultural districts.

O. fluviatilis is found only in north-western Europe, in Britain and Ireland and from France to Denmark. It has no doubt declined as industry and agriculture have increasingly affected water quality. The reported terrestrial variant from the River Elbe basin, *O. conioides* (Tutin *et al.* 1968), requires further study.

M. J. Southam

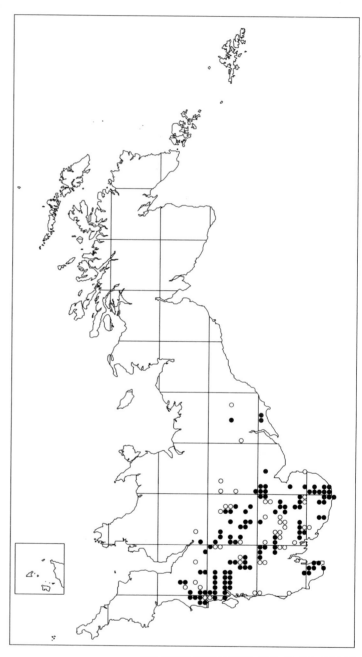

Current map	No	Atlas	No
1970 →	114	1930 →	79
Pre-1970	44	Pre-1930	26
Introductions	0	Introductions	0

Oenanthe pimpinelloides L.
Status: not scarce

Corky-fruited water-dropwort

This species generally occurs in lowland neutral pastures and hay-meadows, and on grassy banks and roadsides. It extends onto much drier ground than other British members of its genus, typically occurring with species such as *Agrostis capillaris*, *Anthoxanthum odoratum*, *Centaurea nigra*, *Cynosurus cristatus*, *Dactylis glomerata*, *Festuca rubra*, *Hypochaeris radicata*, *Ranunculus acris* and *Rumex acetosa*. It can continue to flourish under quite intensive management (although it usually keeps close to field edges in these circumstances), and there are cases of it persisting even in fields converted into village playgrounds and football pitches. In a few areas it has also been a successful colonist of roadside cuttings and embankments, for example on long stretches of the A38 in Devon and the M5 in Devon and Somerset.

O. pimpinelloides is a perennial, germinating in autumn and spring, and flowering from June to August. On regularly mown sites, its 'springy' flower stems tend to escape cutting, and even after repeated mowing and trampling it can send up secondary stems of reduced height which usually still manage to produce viable seed. Field observations suggest that gaps in the turf may be important for successful seedling establishment.

The decline of lowland herb-rich neutral grasslands, in particular by reseeding or conversion to arable, has undoubtedly caused this species to be lost from many sites. Even so, its ability to persist in more intensively managed grasslands, and its recent colonisation of roadside banks, suggests that the future conservation of this species is unlikely to be a problem. However, the reasons for its restricted distribution in Britain are far from clear, and would certainly merit further investigation.

It is widespread in southern and central Europe north to western Ireland, Britain and Belgium and eastwards to Asia Minor.

S. J. Leach & M. J. Southam

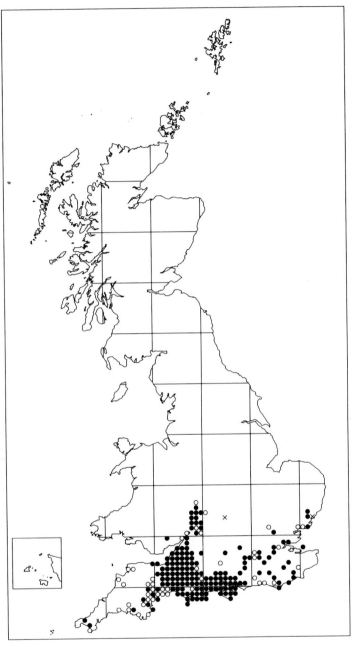

Current map	No	Atlas	No
1970 →	162	1930 →	94
Pre-1970	44	Pre-1930	19
Introductions	2	Introductions	0

Oenanthe silaifolia M. Bieb.
Status: scarce

Narrow-leaved water-dropwort

This species is found in unimproved damp meadows, primarily hay meadows on riverside alluvium, which receive calcareous flood-water in winter. Exceptionally, where such sites have undergone no improvement, the colonies may contain between 10,000 and 100,000 substantial plants. In more intensively farmed meadows, a few attenuated individuals are much more likely. It may grow on ground slightly raised above the water level, such as on floodbanks. In general it is not found near the sea, though the presence of a colony on the Isle of Sheppey suggests it could occur elsewhere on the coast. The plant is only readily detected during its brief flowering period.

Most plants are mown before shedding seed. This is apparently not harmful although there is no second flowering nor production of any further growth until the next winter rosette. Where seed is set, it is generally viable and may be distributed over the meadow from an uncut margin if flooding occurs. Colonisation downstream by seed does not seem to have been observed, and is perhaps unlikely under modern conditions. The cluster of tubers undergoes replenishment, enabling a plant to exist at the same spot for twenty or more years.

O. silaifolia is eliminated by quite modest agricultural intensification. 'Improvement' is its downfall.

It is quite widespread in western, central and southern Europe, east to Russia. It also occurs in north-west Africa, in Turkey and possibly further east, but confusion with other *Oenanthe* species may have artificially expanded this distribution.

M. J. Southam

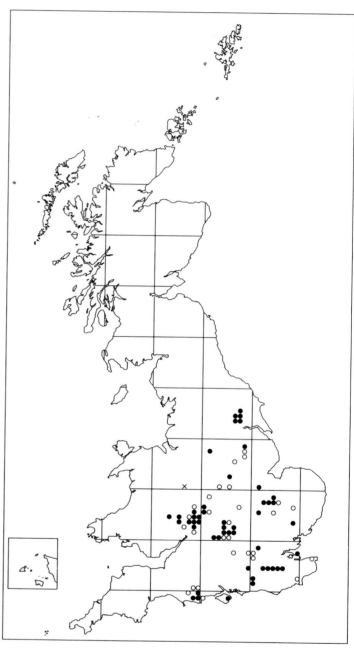

Current map	No	Atlas	No
1970 →	49	1930 →	13
Pre-1970	28	Pre-1930	27
Introductions	1	Introductions	0

continued →

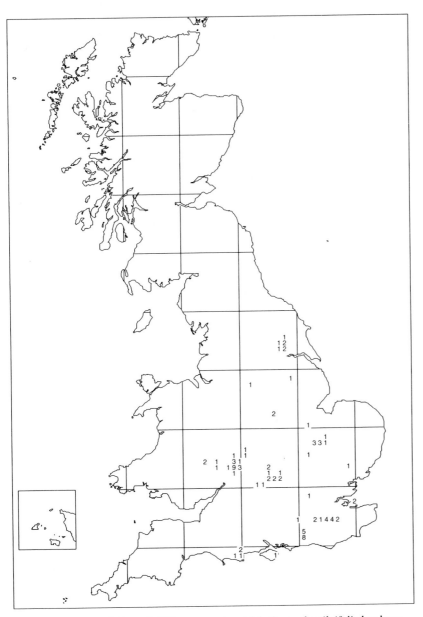

The number of tetrads in each 10 km square in which *Oenanthe silaifolia* has been recorded as a native species from 1970 onwards. The species has been found in a total of 94 tetrads from 1970 onwards.

Ophioglossum azoricum C. Presl
Status: scarce

Small adder's-tongue

This is a plant of well-drained maritime turf, being widespread on cliff tops and in damp sandy hollows in coastal dunes. In the New Forest, it grows in open damp hollows in *Calluna-Erica* heathland.

O. azoricum dies down in mid-summer and aestivates as dormant root-buds which become leafy the following spring. Its gametophytes are mycorrhizal and subterranean and little is known about their establishment. Ecological constraints on this stage of the life cycle could be a major factor in confining this species to a few sites.

The distinction between this species and the more widespread *O. vulgatum* is not always clear, and because of this *O. azoricum* may be under recorded. There seems to be little loss of sites, and it is almost certainly still present in those 10 km squares in the Outer Hebrides, Orkney and Shetland for which only pre-1970 records are available.

This species is confined to Europe and Macaronesia, there being scattered populations from Iceland (where it grows around hot springs) to Portugal (including the Azores and Madeira) in the west, eastwards in the Mediterranean to Corsica and Sardinia (Jalas & Suominen 1972). Central European records in Czechoslovakia and Poland require confirmation.

For a more detailed account of this species, see Paul (1987).

A. C. Jermy

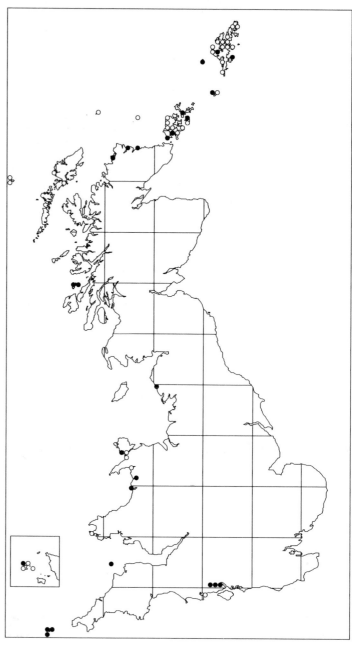

Current map	No	Atlas (S)	No
1970 →	24		
Pre-1970	32		
Introductions	0	All records	22

Orchis morio L.
Status: not scarce

Green-winged orchid

A plant of short damp and dry open lowland grassland. The orchid tolerates a wide range of soil conditions and grassland management. Soils in which it is found range from base-rich to base-poor and from open seasonally parched grasslands to wet alluvial soils and gleyed clays. Grassland management varies from traditionally cut hay meadows, seasonally grazed heavy clay pastures and extensively grazed unenclosed pastures which are open to livestock throughout the year. The species is usually regarded as a strong indicator of old agriculturally unimproved grasslands and is predominantly found in these situations. A number of colonies, however, have become established within relatively recently disturbed swards, particularly on freely draining nutrient-poor soils.

O. morio is a monocarpic perennial, which reproduces by seed. Plants can persist in a vegetative state for many years if the inflorescences are removed by mowing or grazing, eventually flowering and fruiting when this pressure is released.

This plant was formerly widespread and common throughout the lowlands of the south and east. It has declined since 1950 as many pastures have been ploughed and the remainder are much more intensively managed. The distribution of the species in many counties is now limited to nature reserves and other sites specifically managed for nature conservation. The distribution map belies the fact that within each 10 km square where the species is known to persist, the number of sites may have declined dramatically.

This species is found in Europe, western Asia and North Africa, extending north to Scotland and the southernmost areas of Scandinavia. The British plant is subsp. *morio*, which tends to be replaced by other subspecies towards the southern and eastern edge of its range.

Whilst there is an ineradicable public perception of the rarity of orchids, this 'rare' species is far more widespread and abundant than many other less obviously attractive and emotive plants.

C. Chatters

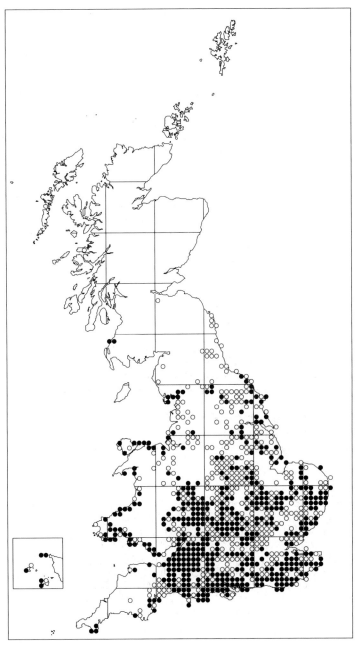

Current map	No	Atlas	No
1970 →	455		
Pre-1970	380		
Introductions	0	All records	420

Orchis purpurea Hudson
Status: scarce

Lady orchid

This is a species of open beech, ash or hazel woodland, of scrub, or sometimes of open grassland, on shallow, highly calcareous soils, nearly always on chalk, but also on Gault clay (where influenced by chalk drift) and on ragstone soils in Kent, and on Carboniferous limestone in Somerset. It sometimes grows with few associates at the more shady end of its habitat range, but generally it is associated with such species as *Daphne laureola, Mercurialis perennis, Sanicula europaea* and other orchids, particularly *Aceras anthropophorum, Listera ovata, Ophrys insectifera, Orchis mascula, Platanthera bifolia* and *P. chlorantha.*

O. purpurea is a tuberous perennial which may live at least ten years from the first production of flower spikes, flowering at least three times in this period. Reproduction is normally by seed but in vigorous populations, extra tubers may be formed, leading to clumps of plants formed by vegetative reproduction. In open situations, it may suffer frost damage in hard springs, but this is rarely obvious within a woodland canopy. Little is known of the conditions affecting seedling establishment. Seed-set is variable; in some years and sites this may be good, in other cases few capsules are set. Where deer are plentiful, they affect reproduction by biting off (and then dropping) the flower spikes. The species does not readily colonise new woods.

The species is remarkably stable at the present time. After some earlier declines in Surrey, Sussex and West Kent, it is now known that there are at least 100 separate sites for the species in Kent. Some populations may have over 1000 plants. It has been rediscovered in Oxfordshire in recent years, and has been found in a new site in Somerset. It is always threatened by picking or digging up, because of its attractiveness. Adequate light is clearly important for its flowering performance: it may almost disappear if a wood becomes too dense and dark, but felling or coppicing often leads to a spectacular reappearance.

It is widespread through much of western and south-western Europe from the Netherlands and Denmark to north-western Africa, and east through central Germany to Poland, Greece, and the Crimea. In parts of southern France and central Italy it is the commonest orchid on roadside banks, occurring also in very open places such as old vineyards.

For a more detailed account, see Rose (1948). Additional information about the outlying sites is provided by Kemp (1987) and Willis, Martin & Taylor (1991).

F. Rose

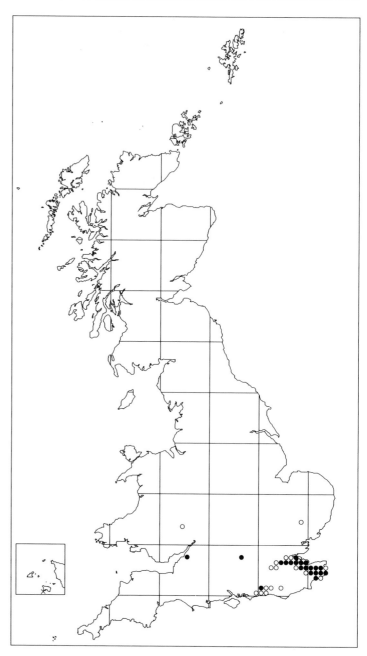

Current map	No	Atlas	No
1970 →	20	1930 →	22
Pre-1970	17	Pre-1930	9
Introductions	0	Introductions	0

continued →

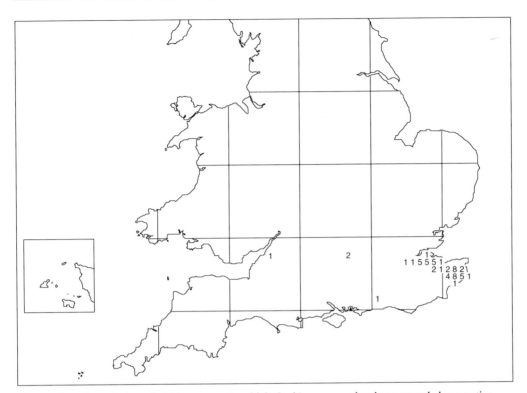

The number of tetrads in each 10 km square in which *Orchis purpurea* has been recorded as a native species from 1970 onwards. The species has been found in a total of 57 tetrads from 1970 onwards.

Orchis ustulata L.

Status: scarce

Burnt orchid

Confined to base-rich substrates, this is a plant of short, well-grazed limestone and chalk downland turf, particularly where there is a warm and sunny, more or less southerly, aspect. It often grows in association with *Orchis morio* as well as with other small herbs such as *Anthyllis vulneraria*, *Gentianella* spp., *Polygala* spp., *Sanguisorba minor*, *Primula veris* and *Rhinanthus minor*. It is not a strong competitor and may eventually be shaded out if the habitat is left ungrazed, although there are instances where plants have survived for considerable periods in quite tall meadowland.

Reproduction is by seed, but up to ten years may elapse before maturity and flowering. Further reproduction can occur through the mature plant's formation of secondary rhizomes, with small clusters of plants resulting.

The number of populations has decreased in the last fifty years mainly through adverse agricultural practices, such as ploughing, failure to maintain suitable grazing regimes, and the use of artificial fertilisers and herbicides. Encroachment by building and destruction of sites through quarrying have also contributed to the loss. It is now a very scarce plant although in Wiltshire it can occur in populations of considerable size; one of these is thought to be amongst the largest still surviving in western Europe. For a summary of the results of a detailed survey of its British distribution, see Foley (1992).

O. ustulata is found throughout most of central Europe and eastwards to beyond the Urals. It extends northwards to southern Scandinavia and southwards to the Mediterranean.

In southern England there occurs a form which flowers in July, much later than the normal late-May, but is otherwise doubtfully distinct from it. It is usually found in quite separate populations from the normal form and its origins are obscure, although there may be an ecological influence. It is also known from Europe where it has been described as subsp. *aestivalis* and has recently been studied in detail (Kümpel & Mrkvicka 1990). The totally white-flowered var. *albiflora* occurs very rarely in Britain.

M. J. Y. Foley

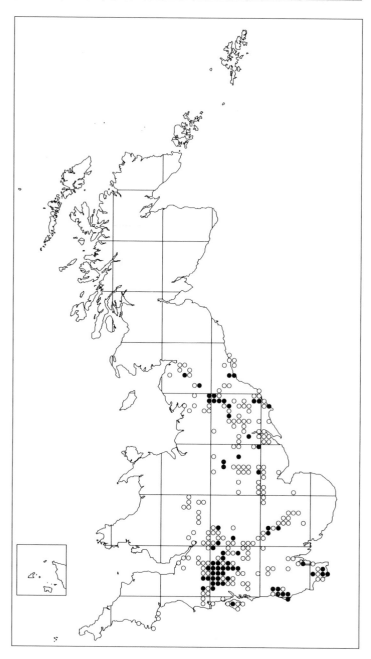

Current map	No	Atlas	No
1970 →	66	1930 →	67
Pre-1970	188	Pre-1930	147
Introductions	0	Introductions	0

continued →

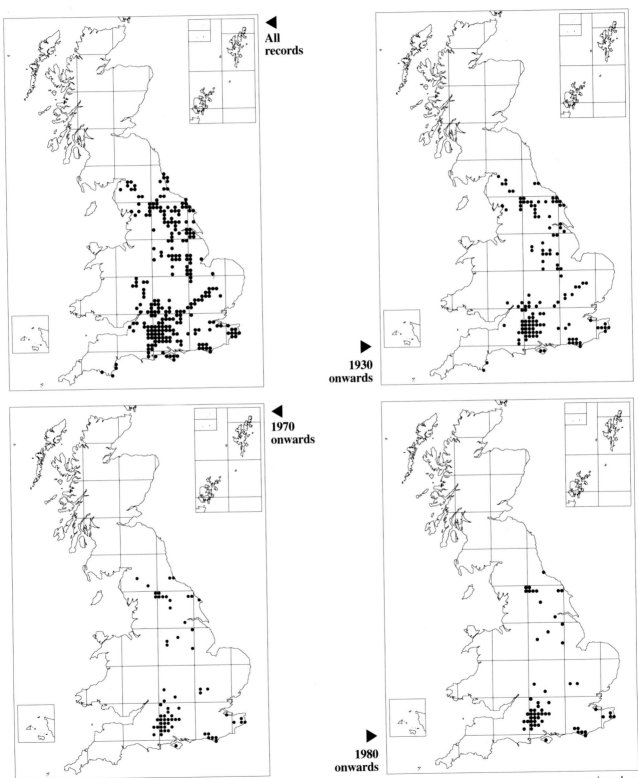

The distribution of *Orchis ustulata*, illustrated by a series of maps for different time periods.

continued →

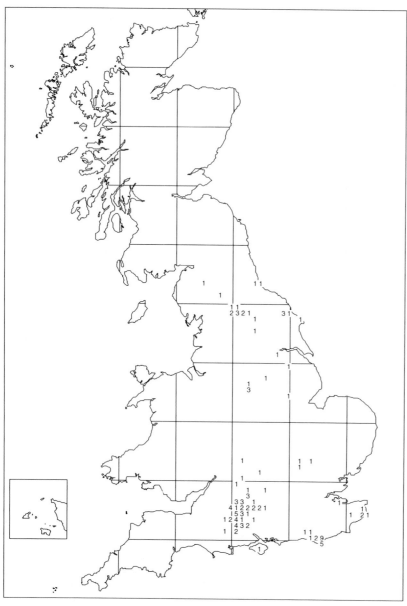

The number of tetrads in each 10 km square in which *Orchis ustulata* has been
recorded as a native species from 1970 onwards. The species has been found in a
total of 118 tetrads from 1970 onwards.

Ornithogalum pyrenaicum L.

Status: scarce

Spiked star-of-Bethlehem

This plant typically grows in hedges, copses and woods, especially on oolitic limestones and clays but occasionally on other calcareous substrates. It is often very abundant in ash-elm woodland, associated with *Allium ursinum* and *Hyacinthoides non-scripta*. It also occurs along old green lanes, in unimproved pasture and along river banks.

This is a bulbous perennial which flowers early in June. Seeds are large, and seedlings appear *en masse* in woodlands in early spring and require several seasons to develop to maturity. Vegetative reproduction occurs by means of lateral buds which develop from mature bulbs.

O. pyrenaicum is still abundant in its British stronghold near Bath. However, it has declined in elm-dominated woods where nettles have recently become very abundant following the death of standing trees by disease and the consequent admission of light and release of nutrients. Other sites in the Bath area have been lost to building land.

In Europe the plant occurs in Belgium, south-west Switzerland, Austria, the mountains of Spain, Portugal, Italy and Greece. Elsewhere, it is found in the Crimea, Asia Minor and Morocco.

The unopened flower spikes used to be collected and sold in bundles under the name Bath asparagus, a custom which has ceased in recent years. White (1912) considered that they were 'very little inferior to the cultivated esculent'.

D. E. Green

Current map	No	Atlas	No
1970 →	23	1930 →	22
Pre-1970	12	Pre-1930	5
Introductions	28	Introductions	0

continued →

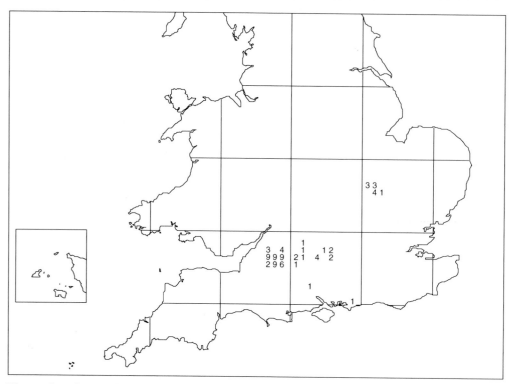

The number of tetrads in each 10 km square in which *Ornithogalum pyrenaicum* has been recorded as a native species from 1970 onwards. Squares in which the species is recorded in 9 or more tetrads are plotted as 9: *O. pyrenaicum* is actually recorded from 12 tetrads in ST66, 13 in ST76 and ST86 and 14 in ST75. The species has been found in a total of 95 tetrads from 1970 onwards.

Orobanche alba Stephan ex Willd.

Thyme broomrape

Status: scarce

This is principally a local plant of rocky slopes on the west coast of Britain, where it is a root parasite of *Thymus polytrichus*. It is confined to base-rich outcrops of rocks such as basalt, limestone or serpentine. It also occurs as a rare plant of the inland limestones of northern England where it occupies a specialised ecological niche on consolidated talus slopes immediately below low cliffs. It occurs from sea-level on the west coast up to 490 metres at Nappa Scar above Wensleydale.

It is thought to be normally annual but there is evidence that some plants are perennial. In common with all broomrapes, it produces large amounts of small seed and this may lie dormant for long periods. Emerging plants are palatable to grazing animals, especially rabbits, and in some seasons small populations are entirely grazed off. This can occur even before the flowers are fully open and the long term effect of this may be detrimental.

Populations of *O. alba* can fluctuate widely in numbers. It has apparently always been very scarce in Yorkshire and Fife; in Fife it may have suffered from collecting and one site is now occupied by a caravan site (Ballantyne 1992). Young plants can be eaten by rabbits before they set seed, but there appears to be little else to threaten the species. It may be under-recorded in Scotland and probably still persists in most of the 10 km squares for which only pre-1970 records are available..

The plant is widespread in Europe, north to Scotland, Belgium and central Russia, and it extends eastwards in Asia to the Himalayas.

Our plant has a fragrant odour and is of a noticeable reddish colouration, and in the latter respect differs markedly from the normal pale cream colour of the European plant. *O. alba* is known to vary appreciably throughout its range in both colour and form.

M. J. Y. Foley

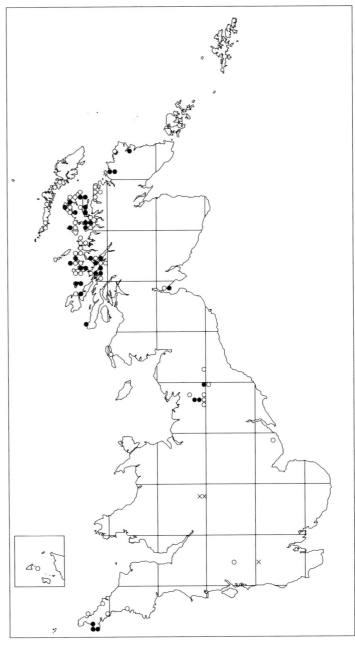

Current map	No	Atlas	No
1970 →	35	1930 →	33
Pre-1970	49	Pre-1930	16
Introductions	3	Introductions	0

Orobanche hederae Duby
Status: scarce

Ivy broomrape

O. hederae is a holoparasite of the Araliaceae, possibly restricted as a native to the Atlantic tetraploid cytotype of *Hedera helix,* subsp. *hibernica.* Its distribution closely reflects that of its host (McAllister & Rutherford 1990). *O. hederae* is essentially a maritime plant of coastal cliffs, undercliff woodlands and hedgebanks, but extending inland in sheltered sites such as gorges. It is grown as a curiosity and persists in gardens, parklands and cemeteries often at wall bases and under hedges.

It is an annual, or perhaps more frequently perennial, plant, probably reliant on self pollination. It has a longer flowering season than any other British broomrape, from late May to October, and is unique in the asynchronous appearance of plants within populations.

There is no threat to the native populations, and the species is apparently increasing through exploitation of cultivated Araliaceae to the east of its native range. All records on cultivated hosts have been mapped as introductions: some records may be of deliberate introductions and others may result from seed windborne from native sites. Its status in the Kent chalk pits is uncertain.

It is found in western, southern and southern central Europe, reaching its most northerly extent in Ireland. In Majorca, and perhaps elsewhere, it is now largely restricted to man-made habitats. Material thought to be of this species has been recorded as an introduction in North Carolina, USA (Musselman 1982). It is also known as an introduction in South Africa where it had been misidentified as *O. minor.*

O. hederae is often mistaken for the more frequent *O. minor* which may also grow on *Hedera* spp. All specimens reported to be of *O. hederae* from non-araliacean hosts have proved to be misidentifications. However, Jones (1987) claimed to have raised plants on *Trifolium pratense.* A yellow variant lacking anthocyanin has been reported on cultivated ivy in Hampshire (Brewis 1990).

F. J. Rumsey

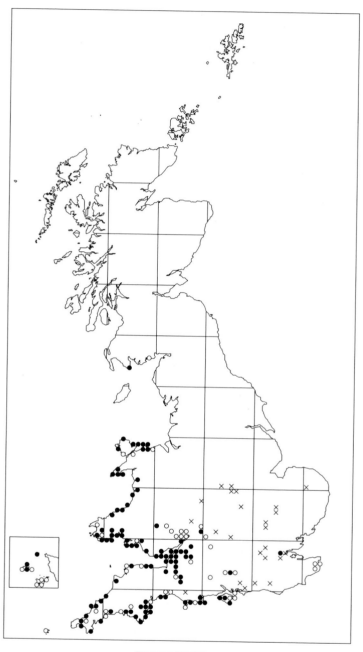

Current map	No	Atlas	No
1970 →	97	1930 →	58
Pre-1970	43	Pre-1930	9
Introductions	24	Introductions	7

Orobanche minor Smith var. *maritima* (Pugsley) Rumsey & Jury

Status: variety of *O. minor*

This is a parasite which is almost exclusively restricted to *Daucus carota* subsp. *gummifer*. It is reliably reported from *Plantago coronopus* and *Ononis repens*, but records from other hosts are suspect. Characteristically it is found in steeply sloping open grassland on the brink of south-facing sea cliffs. Common associates include *Brassica oleracea* subsp. *oleracea*, *Plantago lanceolata*, *Salvia verbenaca*, *Sonchus oleraceus* and a range of grasses, most notably *Bromus hordeaceus* subsp. *ferronii*. At the south-western extremes of its range, in the Channel Isles and Cornwall, it may also be found on fixed dune grassland. On more mobile dunes and elsewhere around our coasts it is replaced by other forms of the variable *O. minor*.

It is an annual or weakly perennial plant, probably largely reliant on self-pollination. Flowering occurs from late May to early August.

There is no real evidence of decline. Considerable fluctuations in population size routinely occur, with the plant apparently absent from well known sites for many years between occurrences. Abundance is linked to the size of the host population and climatic factors, being greatest following a very hot summer and mild winter. It is easily overlooked and confused with other taxa.

Its distribution outside Britain is not clear. Pugsley (1940) reported a possible specimen from Gibraltar. It is to be expected on the Atlantic coasts of France and northern Spain.

Of disputed taxonomic status, this plant is best regarded as a rather invariable segregate of the widespread and variable *O. minor*, from which it is only poorly morphologically defined. Cryptic speciation may be occurring as host-specific races become effectively isolated due to inbreeding. The association between parasite and host, both infraspecific taxa which intergrade with more widespread nominate types, suggests closely linked histories and subsequent dispersal.

F. J. Rumsey

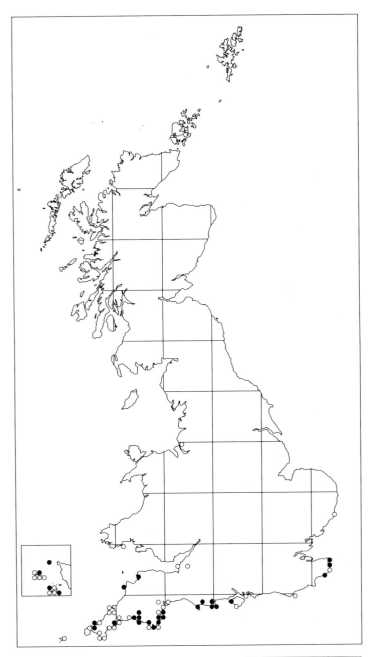

Current map	No	Atlas	No
1970 →	24	1930 →	15
Pre-1970	29	Pre-1930	20
Introductions	0	Introductions	0

Orobanche rapum-genistae Thuill.

Status: scarce

Greater broomrape

This broomrape is a root parasite of leguminous shrubs, especially *Cytisus scoparius* and *Ulex europaeus*. Its potential habitats are those of its hosts, namely hedgebanks, and scrubby areas on rough hillsides, but it has become increasingly confined to coastal areas. Its vigour is often increased after burning of the host plants.

It is apparently perennial, as evidenced by the previous year's dead spikes frequently persisting beside the following season's new growth. Reproduction is by seed and although this is very small and wind-dispersed, colonisation of new sites is rare, suggesting that other, as yet unknown, ecological factors play their part. Field observations have shown that through its parasitic life-style it can sometimes reduce the vigour of the host plant, occasionally fatally, and at sites where the latter is restricted, this may lead to the plant's ultimate extinction.

This plant was formerly widespread in the British Isles, when it was probably the most commonly encountered broomrape, but has declined appreciably during the present century and is now most often found to the south and west, often in coastal sites. This suggests a climatic cause for its decline. Although the host plants are still abundant, they are often destroyed by scrub clearance, and this may also have contributed to the reduction. The species probably continued to decline into the 1960s and the severe winter of 1962/3 eliminated several populations. Since then new sites have been discovered at a greater rate than they have been lost, even in Norfolk and Northumbria at the easterly extremities of its range. The great wind of 1987 opened up some afforested areas, allowing heathy scrub to regenerate and this species to reappear. It is almost certainly under-recorded on the western fringe of Britain due to the nature of its habitat. Even in localities where a host is abundant, this broomrape is very local and populations are usually small.

This species is found in the western Mediterranean region, extending northwards in western Europe to Britain.

Colour variants often occur in the larger populations, with the yellow-flowered forma *flavescens* Durand (forma *hypoxantha* G. Beck) being the most frequent.

M. J. Y. Foley

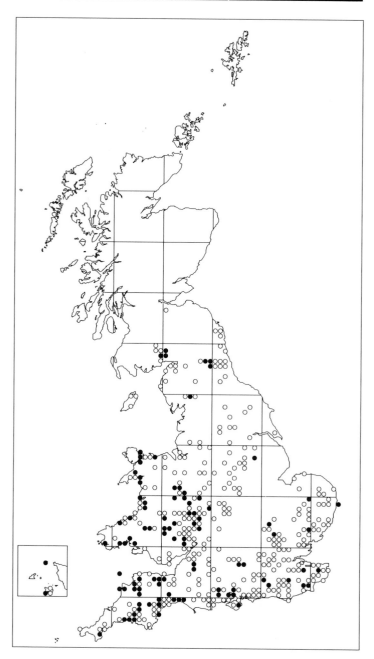

Current map	No	Atlas	No
1970 →	97	1930 →	36
Pre-1970	295	Pre-1930	248
Introductions	0	Introductions	0

continued →

continued

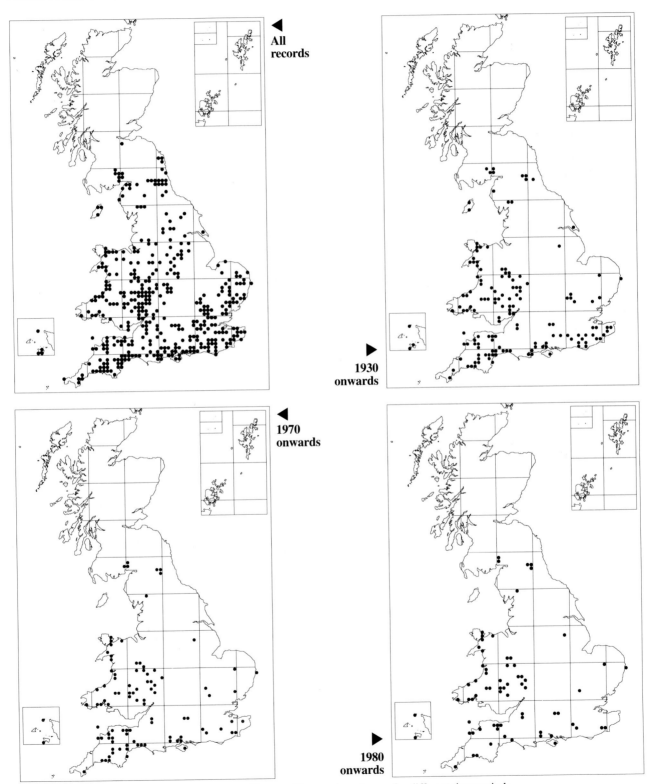

The distribution of *Orobanche rapum-genistae*, illustrated by a series of maps for different time periods.

Orthilia secunda (L.) House

Status: not scarce

Serrated wintergreen

This is a northern and sub-montane plant, rare and relict south of the Scottish Highlands. In its more southerly localities, *O. secunda* usually grows in narrow crevices of steep, broken and dry rocks, but often in rather humid ravines and gullies. In the Highlands it also frequently grows amongst moss under tall *Calluna vulgaris* and in *Vaccinium* heath on the mossy floor of both pine and birch woods. Substrates are usually acidic to only mildly basic, but in Glen Doll it grows on Dalradian limestone. Its altitudinal range is from 90 metres on the Culbin Sands to 690 metres at Craig an Dail Bheag; there is an unlocalised record from 730 metres in Ross-shire.

This is a perennial plant and its evergreen habit makes it most conspicuous in winter and early spring. It is seldom abundant even in northern localities, and some of the southern stations have only a few plants. Flowering is erratic or sparse in some southern outposts, and there is little evidence that *O. secunda* spreads by seed under present conditions. Regeneration under *Calluna vulgaris* after fire may be by seed or vegetatively.

Its absence from much heather moorland suggests that fire has greatly restricted its range. Grazing has probably also curtailed its present distribution. It is, however, probably still present in most of the 10 km squares from which only pre-1970 records are available.

Matthews (1955) classifies this species in his continental northern element. It is a characteristic plant of the boreal forests, occurring widely in northern Europe but also in the mountains of the south, and in North America.

D. A. Ratcliffe

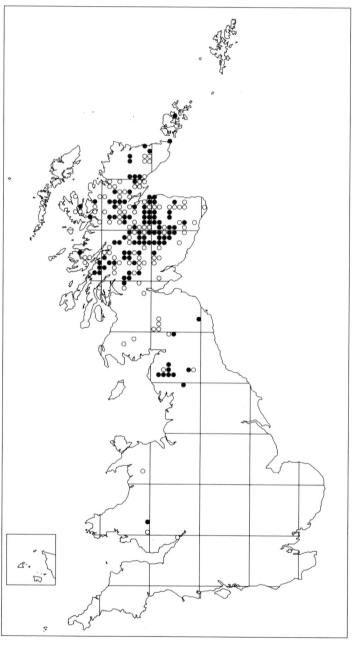

Current map	No	Atlas	No
1970 →	103	1930 →	56
Pre-1970	99	Pre-1930	40
Introductions	0	Introductions	0

Papaver argemone L.
Status: not scarce

The normal habitat for this species is arable field margins, mainly on poorer, light, sandy and calcareous soils in south and east England. It also occurs rarely on open waste land and railway banks in lowland areas. It is commonly associated with *P. rhoeas*, and occasionally with *P. dubium* or *P. hybridum*. Other common associates include *Anagallis arvensis*, *Anthemis cotula*, *Aphanes arvensis*, *Chaenorhinum minus*, *Euphorbia exigua*, *Fumaria densiflora*, *F. officinalis*, *Galium aparine*, *Lamium amplexicaule*, *Legousia hybrida*, *Matricaria recutita*, *Myosotis arvensis*, *Petroselinum segetum*, *Polygonum aviculare*, *Reseda lutea*, *Stellaria media*, *Valerianella dentata* and *Viola arvensis*.

An annual which germinates in autumn and spring, it is best represented in autumn-sown crops. The flowers are normally self-pollinated. In conditions where there is strong competition from other species, few seed heads develop. Seed dispersal is rather poor as many seeds remain in the capsule after ripening. Seed is capable of retaining its viability in the soil for some time, and germination is sporadic, being dependent on the erosion of the seed-coat.

This is a lowland species which in Britain has become rare in the south-west and occasional in most other areas of its former distribution. Although it is still locally frequent in the south and east, it is normally found in small numbers. It is susceptible to many herbicides, including some of the earliest invented. It is unable to tolerate competition with heavily fertilised modern crop varieties, and is usually found at the edges of fields or in unsprayed corners.

It is found throughout lowland Europe (Jalas & Suominen 1991) and eastwards to the Caucasus, Iran, Palestine and Cyprus, but it is generally introduced and of casual occurrence in the north, where it reaches Scandinavia. The centre of origin is possibly in the eastern Mediterranean.

For an account of the ecology of this species, see McNaughton & Harper (1964a).

A. Smith

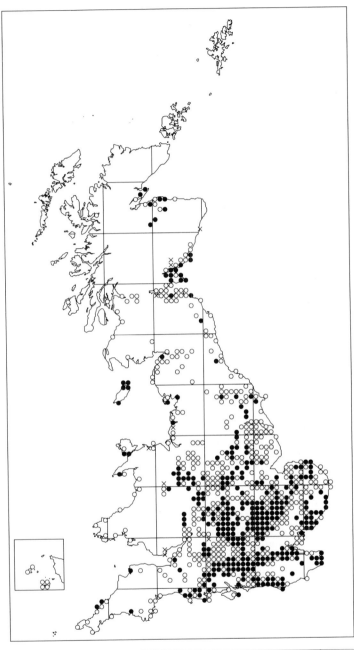

Current map	No	Atlas	No
1970 →	308		
Pre-1970	425		
Introductions	12	All records	394

Papaver hybridum L.
Status: not scarce

Rough poppy

This is a weed of calcareous, well-drained, and therefore light, soils. It normally occurs along the margins of autumn and spring-sown cereal crops, but can also be found on tracksides and waste land. *P. hybridum* is constantly associated with *P. rhoeas*, less so with *P. argemone* and *P. dubium*. It usually forms part of a species-rich community which may include some of the less common weed species such as *Euphorbia exigua*, *Fumaria densiflora*, *Legousia hybrida*, *Lithospermum arvense*, *Petroselinum segetum*, *Scandix pecten-veneris* and *Valerianella dentata*. It is confined to the lowlands.

An annual which is mostly self-pollinated. Although capable of producing 1500 seeds per plant, dispersal is inefficient with many seeds being retained in the capsule and hence germination is often close to the parent plant. It germinates in autumn and spring, but plants tend to be more vigorous in the less competitive spring-sown crops. *P. hybridum* normally exists as a few scattered individuals on the very edge of crop margins where regimes of herbicide and fertiliser applications are not so intense, but occasional larger populations can be found.

In Britain, *P. hybridum* has a more restricted range than that of *P. argemone*. It is another species which has diminished in response to the increased use of chemical herbicides and fertilisers since the 1950s.

It is distributed throughout the lowlands of central and southern Europe (Jalas & Suominen 1991), and eastwards to Iran and India. It is also found North Africa. In common with the other British *Papaver* species, it has almost certainly been introduced as an agricultural weed in ancient times. It is considered to be threatened with extinction or vulnerable in most of the countries of north-west Europe.

For a more detailed account of this species, see McNaughton & Harper (1964b).

A. Smith

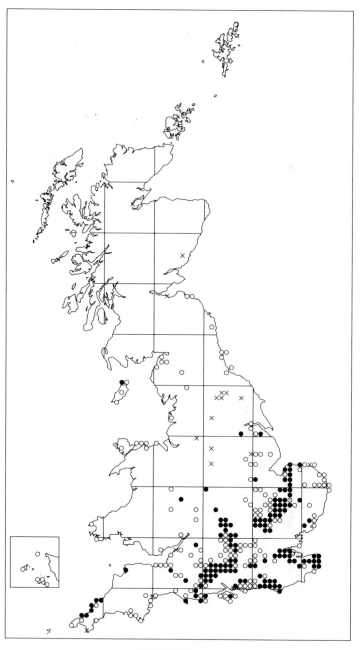

Current map	No	Atlas	No
1970 →	128	1930 →	80
Pre-1970	152	Pre-1930	74
Introductions	17	Introductions	5

Parapholis incurva (L.) C.E. Hubb.

Status: scarce

Curved hard-grass

Although confined to the coastal fringe, this delicate little grass occurs in a fairly wide range of habitats, including cliff-tops, sea-walls and on bare mud and shingle. It is, however, a plant most commonly associated with open gravelly mud and muddy shingle ridges above the high tide level, and tends to avoid the upper parts of saltmarshes where its congener *P. strigosa* is found. It has a strong preference for well-drained, saline soils. In many of its sites it is the only species present, but in others associates range from *Spergularia marina* in muddy habitats to *Rumex crispus* and *Silene maritima* on shingle.

P. incurva is an annual, reproducing entirely by seed. Small groups of plants, or even single plants, often appear in isolated situations, suggesting that the seeds are dispersed over long distances (or that they persist for several years in the seed bank). The species can sometimes occur in great abundance, but populations are known to vary greatly in size from year to year.

The distribution of *P. incurva* appears to be fairly stable, although it is likely to have been consistently under-recorded and is easily overlooked.

It is a western European and Mediterranean species, reaching its northern limit in Britain and Ireland.

A. J. Gray

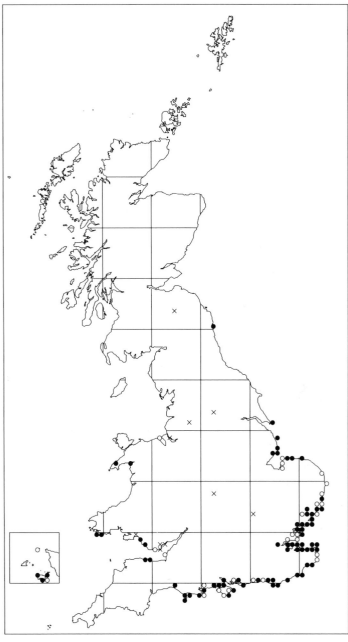

Current map	No	Atlas	No
1970 →	68	1930 →	35
Pre-1970	27	Pre-1930	4
Introductions	10	Introductions	6

Parentucellia viscosa (L.) Caruel

Status: not scarce

Yellow bartsia

A hemiparasitic annual of damp grassy places, this plant usually grows on sandy soils, often along track-sides or in ground which is patchily grazed. Fixed-dune grassland in dryish dune slacks is one characteristic habitat; poor pasture reclaimed from dampish heath is another. It sometimes occurs in abundance after disturbance, such as the felling of coniferous forests planted on sand dunes. Associated species include *Aira caryophyllea, Carex flacca, Centaurium erythraea, Leontodon saxatilis, Lotus corniculatus, Plantago coronopus, Rhinanthus minor, Vulpia bromoides* and *Salix repens*. It is confined to the lowlands.

It is an annual, reproducing entirely by seed. The British distribution, bounded roughly by the 5 °C mean January isotherm, suggests that this species requires a mild winter growing season.

P. viscosa appears to colonise new sites readily, and over much of its British range it is probably more widespread and frequent than formerly. The records suggest some decline in the south-west, particularly inland, perhaps due to re-seeding of old pastures.

It is widespread around the Mediterranean basin, and occurs in the Iberian Peninsula and western France; it reaches its northern limit in Scotland. It is also found in Macaronesia.

M. C. F. Proctor

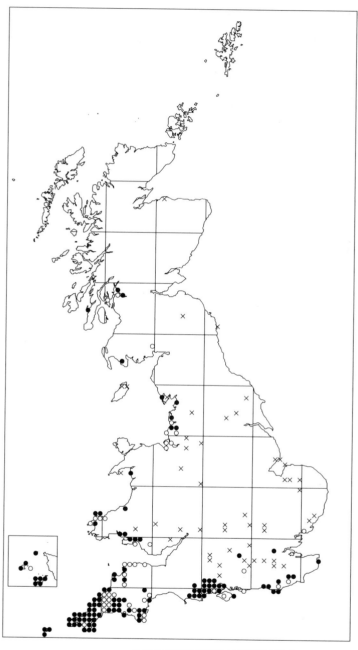

Current map	No	Atlas	No
1970 →	101	1930 →	64
Pre-1970	43	Pre-1930	11
Introductions	49	Introductions	18

Persicaria laxiflora (Weihe) Opiz

Status: scarce

Tasteless water-pepper

Together with its close relative *P. minor*, and the docks *Rumex maritimus* and *R. palustris*, *P. laxiflora* is typical of a distinctive community on wet muds or peat banks, left exposed in late summer as the water level drops. This open vegetation develops by ditches, in wet hollows, by cattle-trampled patches in pastures, by ponds and near former middens. In some areas, it is typical of abandoned peat-cuttings. It grows on wet or damp soils, rich in nutrients, but with no particular preference for soil reaction. The sites are well-illuminated and strictly lowland.

P. laxiflora is an annual, flowering in late summer, and reproducing entirely by seed.

P. laxiflora has frequently been confused with forms of *P. hydropiper*, as well as *P. minor*, such that trends in distribution can only be suggested with caution. However, it has apparently declined throughout England and Wales, probably as a result of closer regulation of water levels, elimination of ponds and fencing of ditches. All these factors contribute to the decrease of wet mud habitats.

P. laxiflora is widespread in Europe between 40 °N and 55 °N, but is rare in the north and in the Mediterranean region (Jalas & Suominen 1979). It has been reported from western Asia but the eastern limit of its range is uncertain because it has often been confused with other species.

J. O. Mountford

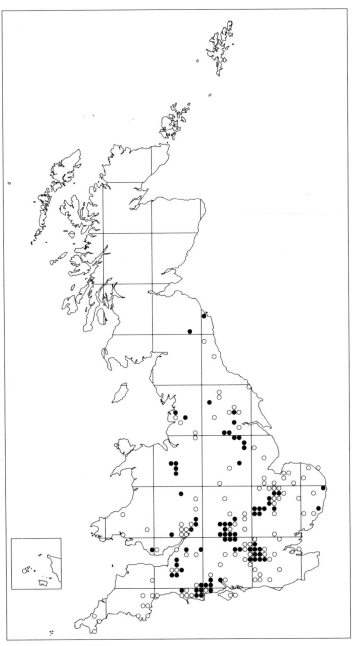

Current map	No	Atlas	No
1970 →	78	1930 →	44
Pre-1970	109	Pre-1930	45
Introductions	0	Introductions	0

Persicaria minor (Hudson) Opiz

Status: not scarce

Small water-pepper

P. minor has a similar distribution and ecology to its relative *P. laxiflora* and, indeed, the two species occasionally grow together, often accompanied by *P. hydropiper*. In southern England *P. minor* is typical of an open community of *Bidens cernua, B. tripartita, Catabrosa aquatica*, and with species of *Chenopodium* and *Rumex*. This community develops on nutrient-rich muds as the water level of ponds and ditches falls in the latter part of summer. These open conditions may also develop in cattle-poached sites or where peat-cutting removes the surface vegetation. In northern England and southern Scotland it is a plant of gravelly or sandy shores above the normal water level of lakes and in the draw-down zone of reservoirs. *P. minor* tends to occur in slightly more acidic conditions than *P. laxiflora* and somewhat more nitrogen-rich sites. Largely restricted to the lowlands in Britain, *P. minor* is found up to 315 metres at Skeggles Water.

P. minor is an annual, reproducing by seeds and, like *P. laxiflora*, requiring the open wet-mud habitat with low competition for successful germination.

As for *P. laxiflora*, past (and present) records have to be treated with caution owing to taxonomic confusion. However, there is considerable evidence for a decline in southern England. This decline follows both the decline of farm ponds and ditches and greater regulation of water levels, reducing the extent of wet mud. However, it was previously under-recorded and since 1962 it has been found in many new sites, especially in Cumbria and south-west Scotland.

P. minor is widespread in Europe between 45 °N and 65 °N, but absent from the arctic and from most of the Mediterranean region (Jalas & Suominen 1979). It extends eastwards to eastern Asia, and is a rare introduction in North America.

J. O. Mountford

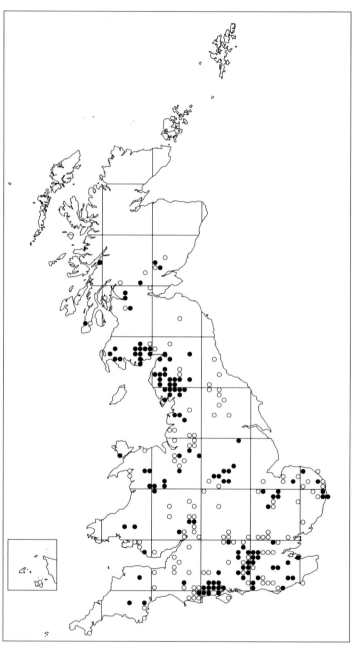

Current map	No	Atlas	No
1970 →	130	1930 →	45
Pre-1970	124	Pre-1930	88
Introductions	0	Introductions	0

Peucedanum palustre (L.) Moench

Milk-parsley

Status: scarce

P. palustre is one of the most characteristic plants of species-rich tall-herb fen, often occurring in the same sites as *Lathyrus palustris*, *Potentilla palustris* and *Thelypteris palustris*, or, more rarely, *Sonchus palustris*. Such vegetation developed where peat had a high water-table in summer, and often flooded in winter with calcareous water. As well as being a natural community of flood plains, tall-herb fen also developed in abandoned peat cuttings. Less frequently, *P. palustre* grows where the fen vegetation has been cut for hay, forming a fen meadow or 'litter' community. Where the herbaceous fen is colonised by shrubs, it can persist in alder or sallow carr, though usually with reduced frequency. *P. palustre* is most often found growing on peat of pH 5.0-6.5 (Meredith & Grubb 1993). It is strictly lowland in England, seldom growing above 50 metres.

P. palustre is normally a perennial, persisting by the development of axillary buds from the stem base, although each leaf rosette produces a flowering stem only once. Seeds are produced in large numbers (*c.* 4500 per stem at Wicken Fen) and dispersed over short distances by water and wind. Long distance dispersal to new sites occurs rarely or not at all. Seed germination is highest where the tall vegetation has been cut, a regular event in many managed fens. Seeds may be consumed by small mammals and seedlings by slugs. *P. palustre* survives best in vegetation that is rarely cut and most growth occurs at 50% of direct sunlight, where the soil is wet but not flooded (Harvey & Meredith 1981).

P. palustre has declined markedly in England over the past two centuries, as remnant rich fen has been drained for agriculture. Many of its surviving populations are in nature reserves, where occasional cutting (particularly in late autumn) and maintenance of high water tables favour its survival.

P. palustre is found throughout most of Europe, but is most common in the more continental east, being absent from the Iberian peninsula, the extreme south and most of the islands. Beyond Europe it extends into Central Asia.

The ecology of *P. palustre* has been studied in detail by Meredith & Grubb (1993). This species is also renowned as the larval foodplant of perhaps the most striking of the British butterflies, the swallowtail (*Papilio machaon* L.).

J. O. Mountford

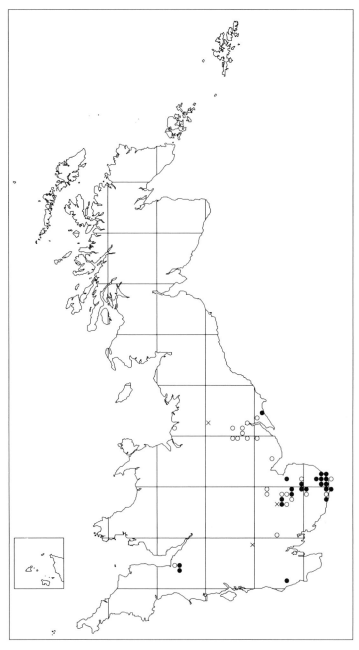

Current map	No	Atlas	No
1970 →	22	1930 →	23
Pre-1970	23	Pre-1930	16
Introductions	3	Introductions	2

continued →

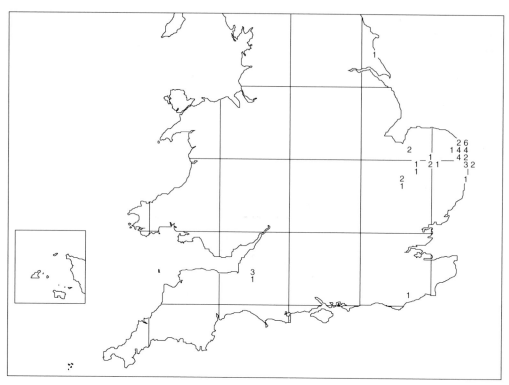

The number of tetrads in each 10 km square in which *Peucedanum palustre* has been recorded as a native species from 1970 onwards. The species has been found in a total of 46 tetrads from 1970 onwards.

Phleum alpinum L.
Status: scarce

Alpine cat's-tail

This is a strictly montane grass, growing sparingly in open, rocky habitats or in closed swards with other grasses, sedges and bryophytes. It is mainly found on base-rich substrates, and is therefore most frequent on the calcareous mountains of the central Scottish Highlands, but some habitats are on more acidic materials enriched by flushing or downwashed sediment. *P. alpinum* may grow on dry rock faces, but is more usually in slightly moist situations, sometimes receiving melt-water from late snow patches in high corries and hollows. The northernmost stations are in cliff gullies. It is often associated with *Agrostis* spp., *Carex bigelowii*, *C. saxatilis*, *Deschampsia cespitosa*, *Festuca rubra*, *Juncus castaneus*, *Luzula multiflora*, *Nardus stricta* and a variety of small herbs and mosses. *Alopecurus borealis* sometimes grows nearby but in spongier mossy springs. The altitudinal range is from 610 metres on Braeriach up to 1220 metres on Cairntoul.

Little is known about the reproduction of this perennial grass: probably vegetative growth maintains existing populations, but there is little evidence of a capacity for spread.

This plant survives precariously at two sites on Cross Fell, but it has not been seen in recent years on Helvellyn, the only other station recorded south of the Highlands. Most pre-1970 Scottish occurrences are probably still extant. Many habitats are lightly grazed, but heavy grazing appears to be a partial cause of its present restriction.

This is a circumpolar arctic-alpine species, widespread in northern regions and in the mountain ranges of Europe, Asia and North and South America.

D. A. Ratcliffe

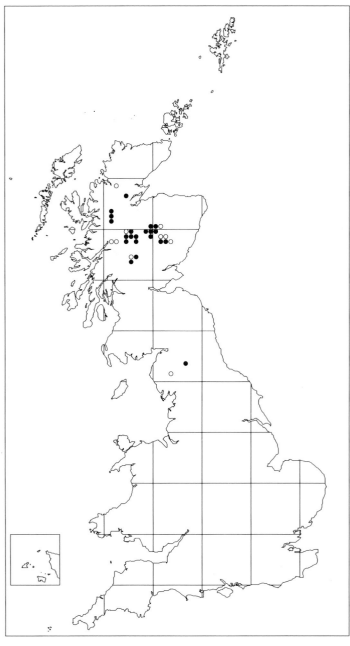

Current map	No	Atlas	No
1970 →	21	1930 →	19
Pre-1970	10	Pre-1930	5
Introductions	0	Introductions	0

Phyteuma orbiculare L.
Status: scarce

Round-headed rampion

A perennial species of ancient calcareous grassland, confined in Great Britain to lowland chalk. It occurs in *Bromopsis erecta*, *Festuca ovina* and *F. rubra* grasslands, and is associated with such species as *Anacamptis pyramidalis*, *Asperula cynanchica*, *Hippocrepis comosa*, *Lotus corniculatus* and sometimes rarer and more exacting calcicoles. As with most perennials adapted to chalk habitats, it can tolerate grazing, and under these conditions produces short-stemmed, leafy, open rosettes of basal leaves. Where it grows in the shade of *Brachypodium pinnatum* and *Bromopsis erecta* in ungrazed grassland, the basal leaves are reduced in number and have long petioles and narrower blades.

This is a perennial species. Some vegetative spread occurs by runners but reproduction appears to be mostly by seed, which is copiously produced.

The distribution seems to be fairly stable at present, but it no longer occurs in Kent, where it was recorded until *c.* 1940. It will tolerate fairly tall grass and some small degree of fertiliser enrichment, but cannot survive in dense scrub or with heavy fertiliser applications. The map does not make clear the extraordinary abundance of this species in the South Downs of Sussex and extreme E. Hants; elsewhere (in Wiltshire and the North Downs) it is much more local and scattered.

P. orbiculare is widespread in south-central Europe from Belgium southwards, but *P. tenerum sensu stricto* has an oceanic distribution (very like that of *Thesium humifusum* and *Gentianella amarella*) that is unusual among chalk grassland plants.

The British plant has been known as *P. tenerum* and the plants of north-west France (e.g. Fontainebleau) seem identical to ours; those further afield in central Europe and the Alps do look quite different with their large bract subtending the inflorescence.

F. Rose & D. E. Green

Current map	No	Atlas	No
1970 →	32	1930 →	33
Pre-1970	18	Pre-1930	14
Introductions	2	Introductions	0

Pilularia globulifera L.

Status: scarce

Pillwort

This fern is predominantly a lowland plant of silty or peaty lake and pond margins and shallow pans and pools resulting from brickearth or gravel extraction. It is an opportunist species, requiring open substrate which it will rapidly colonise, eventually to be ousted as the hydrosere progresses. It also colonises bare mud exposed by falling water levels. Characteristic associates include *Apium inundatum*, *Hydrocotyle vulgaris*, *Ranunculus flammula* and *Samolus valerandi*. Occasionally it maintains itself in denser plant communities as a submerged aquatic in base-poor pools around pH 6.0 and as a mire species with *Calliergon cuspidatum* and other hypnoid mosses, *Carex diandra* and *Menyanthes trifoliata*. In many sites competition may be kept to a minimum, and thus *P. globulifera* maintained, by cattle or horse trampling (poaching).

P. globulifera is a perennial species. Viable 'pills' (sporocarps containing sporangia) are formed in most populations except those in permanent deep water. They appear to have the potential of long-term storage in mud or silt but there is no evidence that this does happen. Spores released from the sporocarp in late summer can develop through the gametophyte phase to produce new sporophytes within seventeen days.

The number of lost sites reflects the changes in land-use that have taken place, especially between 1918 and 1950. Some of those that remain are probably stable; the species may disappear from others as a result of successional changes but these losses will perhaps be balanced by the colonisation of new sites. Populations can vary considerably in number from year to year, and plants can be particularly abundant in lakes and reservoirs in seasons when the water levels are exceptionally low.

This species is endemic to western Europe, with lowland areas in Britain, France, northern Germany and southern Sweden containing the bulk of the populations and outliers extending to Czechoslovakia, Italy and Portugal (Jalas & Suominen 1972). It is decreasing in much of mainland Europe and the British sites are therefore particularly important in a European context.

A. C. Jermy

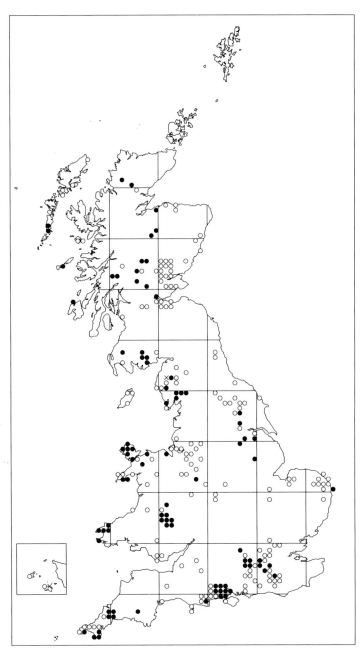

Current map	No	Atlas	No
1970 →	90	1930 →	47
Pre-1970	162	Pre-1930	84
Introductions	1	Introductions	0

continued →

311

continued

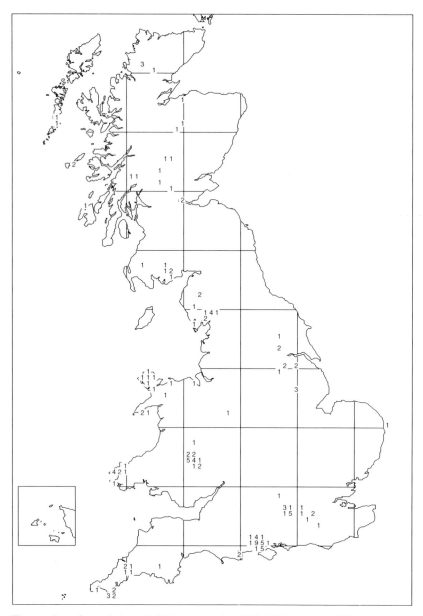

The number of tetrads in each 10 km square in which *Pilularia globulifera* has been recorded from 1970 onwards. Squares in which the species is recorded in 9 or more tetrads are plotted as 9: *P. globulifera* is actually recorded from 12 tetrads in SU20. The species has been found in a total of 155 tetrads from 1970 onwards.

Pinus sylvestris L.

Status: scarce

Scots pine

The Scots pine occurs either in pure stands or in association with other trees, mainly *Betula* spp. *P. sylvestris* tolerates a broad range of climatic and soil conditions, preferring freely-draining acid soils though it will also grow on deep waterlogged peats. In many woodlands there is a characteristic shrub layer of *Juniperus communis* and other species (notably *Salix* spp. and *Sorbus aucuparia*), and an ericaceous dwarf shrub layer (mainly *Calluna vulgaris* and *Vaccinium* spp.). It reaches altitudes over 600 metres in Speyside.

P. sylvestris is an evergreen tree, often surviving for 150-200 years and reproducing entirely by seed. High levels of selfing may occur, particularly in less dense stands, but these generally result in non-viable seed. All native pine woodlands have high levels of genetic variation (Giertych & Mátyás 1991; Kinloch, Westfall & Forrest 1986). Some western populations are genetically distinct from the rest, and north-western populations are especially resistant to extreme exposure.

P. sylvestris formerly covered much of the Scottish Highlands, but it is now reduced by exploitation and over-grazing to a small number of scattered remnant woodlands. In recent years high deer numbers have severely restricted natural regeneration. Interest in the conservation and amenity value of native pinewoods has stimulated several current schemes for their protection and extension, the encouragement of natural regeneration, and the creation of new woodlands using authentic native material (Forestry Commission 1989; Forest Enterprise 1992). Efforts are being made to maintain the regional genetic distinctions.

P. sylvestris is the most widely distributed conifer, extending from the Spanish coast to the far east of Russia, and from the Arctic circle to the Mediterranean. It is widely planted on both local and commercial scales throughout Britain from various native and continental origins.

The native British plant has been distinguished as subsp. *scotica* (P.K. Schott) E. Warb., but it is not possible to give a consistent formal taxonomic treatment to the variation in *P. sylvestris* (Tutin *et al.* 1993). Its native range is disputed; the interpretation here is close to that of Steven & Carlisle (1959) and Perring & Walters (1962), but it has been suggested that the plant is native as far south as Northumberland (Swan 1993). For a more detailed account of the ecology of the British plant see Carlisle & Brown (1968); descriptions of the native pinewoods are provided by Steven & Carlisle (1959).

G. I. Forrest

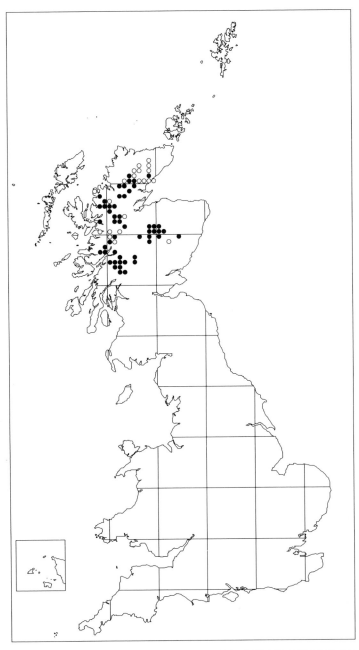

Current map	No	Atlas	No
1970 →	52	1930 →	38
Pre-1970	21	Pre-1930	0

In addition to the native records mapped above, the species is recorded as an introduction in an additional 1956 10 km squares.

Poa alpina L.
Status: scarce

Alpine meadow-grass

This montane grass usually grows in scattered small tufts on steep, open faces of calcareous rock, and its distribution is inevitably limited to the richer mountains, especially the calcareous schist formations of the central Scottish Highlands. Even here it could seldom be described as abundant. Some outlying populations are very small, and the plant is absent from a good many suitable habitats. Its open rock face associates include *Carex atrata*, *Cerastium alpinum*, *Draba incana*, *Poa glauca*, *Saxifraga oppositifolia*, *S. nivalis*, *Silene acaulis* and a range of mosses. This grass also grows sparingly in alpine/dwarf-herb swards and moss carpets on base-rich soils, where competition is slight. The altitudinal range is from 580 metres at Maize Beck up to 1140 metres on Bidean nan Bian in Glen Coe.

This is a perennial grass. Most British populations are viviparous, but seed-bearing forms are widespread and there is no particular pattern of occurrence for either. Spread by either mode is probably very limited under present conditions.

The potential habitat for *P. alpina* is probably greater than that which it currently occupies, and the species may be restricted by grazing. In Norway it is not confined to cliffs in areas in which grazing is light. It has also suffered from collecting in some outlying British localities, but most of the populations recorded before 1970 are probably still extant.

This is an arctic-alpine species with a wide circumpolar distribution.

D. A. Ratcliffe

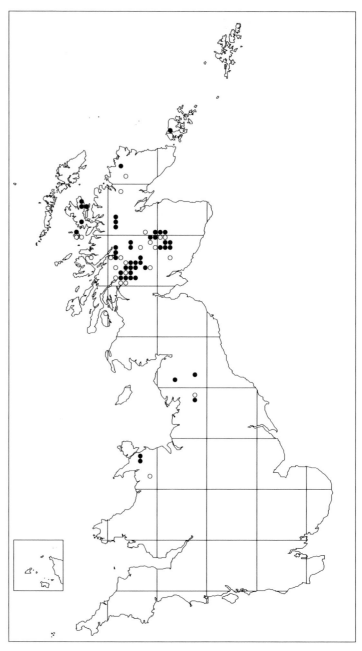

Current map	No	Atlas	No
1970 →	44	1930 →	44
Pre-1970	24	Pre-1930	12
Introductions	0	Introductions	0

Poa bulbosa L.
Status: scarce

Bulbous meadow-grass

This maritime grass is found in a range of habitats, typically on infertile sandy soils but also on shingle and chalk and in crevices in bare limestone. It usually grows in open sparse grassland and even occurs on bare sand in dune systems. Typical associates in these habitats include *Aira praecox*, *Plantago coronopus*, *Rumex acetosella*, *Trifolium striatum* and the mosses *Hypnum cupressiforme* and *Polytrichum piliferum*. It is confined to the lowlands.

It is a perennial plant forming small swollen bulb-like bases to the stem that remain after the rest of the plant dies. *P. bulbosa* flowers very early in the spring (March-May) and the above-ground parts wither soon after flowering. The 'bulbs' often lie on the surface and can be dispersed by wind over tens of metres. They regrow in autumn. A proportion of plants are viviparous (all plants in some populations such as those in South Wales), the flowers being replaced by tiny plantlets which are capable of rooting and becoming established as individual plants.

Its distribution is apparently stable, although this species is possibly overlooked in some places and new populations are discovered from time to time in regions where the plant has not been recorded in the past. It is difficult to know whether recently discovered plants, such as those in Surrey (Leslie 1987) and Berkshire, are hitherto-overlooked native populations, are the result of a natural extension of range, or are accidental introductions.

It is a widespread species in Europe, found in the Mediterranean area and the west coast north to southern Scandinavia and the Baltic. It also grows in temperate Asia and North Africa.

A. J. Gray

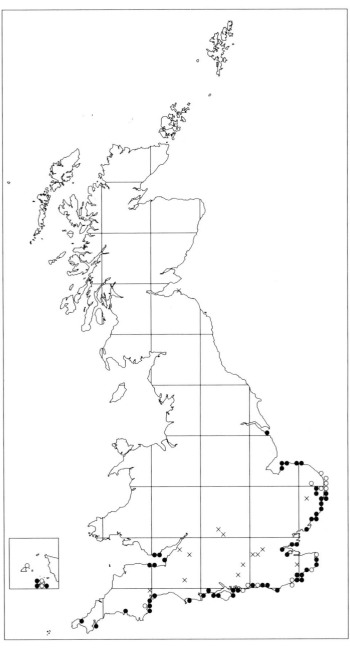

Current map	No	Atlas	No
1970 →	52	1930 →	23
Pre-1970	14	Pre-1930	16
Introductions	14	Introductions	4

Poa glauca Vahl
Status: scarce

Glaucous meadow-grass

This is a montane grass confined to steep, open faces of calcareous rock and scree, especially on the Dalradian schists of the central Scottish Highlands, where it grows as scattered small tufts. It is never present in quantity, even in the Highlands, and the more southerly populations are mostly small and highly relict. It does not occur in closed vegetation in Britain, and often grows close to *P. alpina*, sharing the same associates. The altitudinal range is from 550 metres on the Old Man of Coniston up to 1100 metres on Lochnagar but it is occasionally found washed down at lower latitudes.

This is a perennial grass. Flowering is quite usual in most localities, but there is no evidence of recent spread and it probably just maintains its scattered populations.

P. glauca appears to be grazing-sensitive, though it would be difficult to distinguish if growing sparsely in turf. Collecting may have reduced some smaller populations, but most of the pre-1970 occurrences probably still survive, and have simply not been re-sought. There is possible confusion with high altitude forms of *P. nemoralis* (some formerly distinguished as *P. balfourii*) which grow in the same habitats.

This is an arctic-alpine, Euro-Siberian and North American plant.

D. A. Ratcliffe

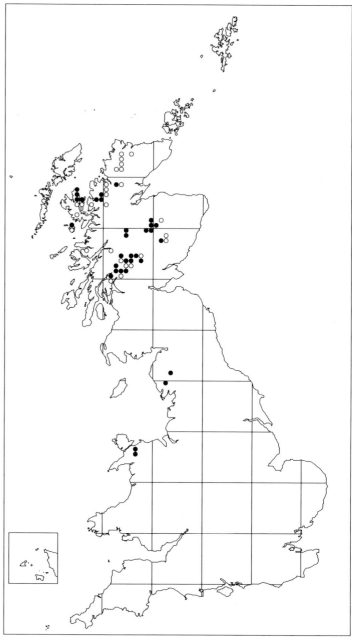

Current map	No	Atlas	No
1970 →	32	1930 →	32
Pre-1970	27	Pre-1930	6
Introductions	0	Introductions	0

Poa palustris L.
Status: introduced

Swamp meadow-grass

P. palustris is found principally in marshy areas such as ditches, willow carr and at the edges of ponds, streams and canals. In aquatic habitats, its associates include *Filipendula ulmaria, Galium uliginosum, Holcus lanatus, Juncus acutiflorus, J. effusus, Lythrum salicaria, Phalaris arundinacea, Phragmites australis, Persicaria amphibia, Ranunculus aquatilis* and *Senecio aquaticus*. Rarely, it occurs along railways and on waste ground in open urban habitats as a casual introduction.

P. palustris may be a facultative apomict. Seed dispersal is facilitated by a tuft of long sinuous hairs on the callus of the lemma.

P. palustris is thought to have been first introduced as a forage grass, but its lack of tolerance to competition in terrestrial habitats has prevented its wider establishment. It is generally frequent within its very restricted local areas of occurrence, but management of streamsides has reduced its frequency. In some localities where it has been recorded in natural habitats its occurrence was apparently only transient.

The distribution of *P. palustris* outside Britain extends from Scandinavia and western and central Europe through temperate parts of western, central and eastern Asia to Japan and China. It is also widespread in North America.

P. palustris is the only British species of the genus *Poa* with a preference for subaquatic habitats. Despite its distinctness as a species, it is often overlooked and its current status is therefore uncertain. It has been regarded as a native by some authors (e.g. Clapham, Tutin & Moore 1987) but this seems unlikely in view of the extremely sporadic distribution of early records. Stace (1991) regards it as an alien.

J. R. Edmondson

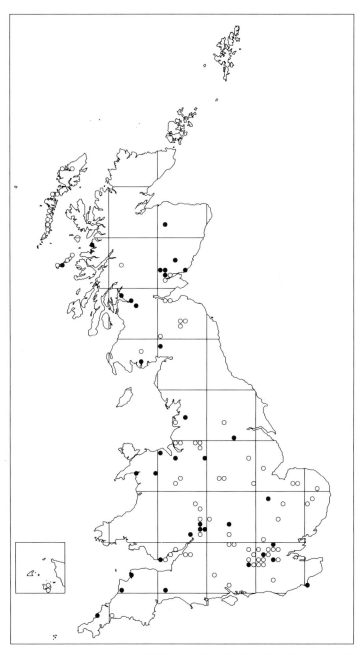

Current map	No	Atlas	No
1970 →	36	1930 →	39
Pre-1970	73	Pre-1930	18

Polygala calcarea F. Schultz
Status: not scarce

Chalk milkwort

This procumbent perennial is woody at the base with basal leaf-rosettes that persist throughout the winter. It grows in very short, ancient *Festuca ovina* grassland on chalk and Jurassic oolite, on very shallow soils, usually on warm, south-facing sites, often associated with *Hippocrepis comosa*, and sometimes with *Ophrys sphegodes, Tephroseris integrifolia* and *Thesium humifusum*. It is confined to the lowlands.

P. calcarea is a perennial and reproduces by both stolons and seed. It can colonise new sites adjacent to existing ones (e.g. chalk banks created by new or widened roads in downland areas) but not very rapidly.

This species is fairly stable in the core of its distribution but has retreated in places near the edge of its range in Somerset and in the outlying area in Leicestershire and Lincolnshire. It is very dependent on the maintenance of short, unfertilised turf such as that produced by sheep grazing, and it disappears if this is replaced by coarse grasses or scrub.

P. calcarea is a plant of calcareous grasslands in western Europe only, not extending north of Belgium or very far east of the Rhine.

P. calcarea has often been wrongly reported owing to confusion with *P. vulgaris*, particularly in certain areas of East Kent and West Sussex where there is no good evidence that it occurs, but the better description of it in modern Floras should avoid this in future. The blunt, obovate basal and stem leaves are diagnostic here, but flower colour varies enormously, as in *P. vulgaris*. The isolated populations in East Kent and on the Leicestershire-Lincolnshire oolite have smaller leaves and flowers than the main population from mid-Kent to Dorset, Somerset and the Cotswolds. More biometrical studies are required but the outliers appear to have been isolated for a long period.

F. Rose

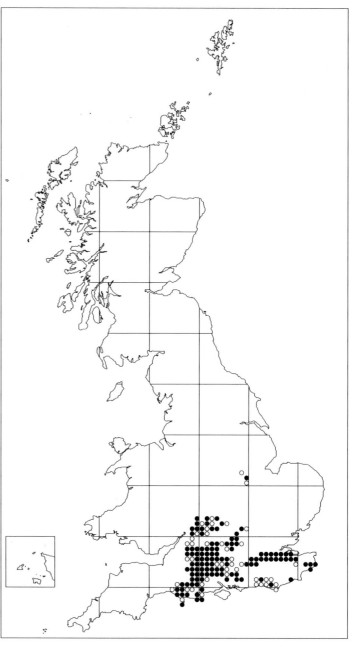

Current map	No	Atlas	No
1970 →	115	1930 →	104
Pre-1970	44	Pre-1930	15
Introductions	0	Introductions	0

Polygonatum odoratum (Miller) Druce

Angular Solomon's-seal

Status: scarce

P. odoratum is a rhizomatous creeping perennial herb of ancient limestone woodlands, preferring well-drained steep banks and lesser cliffs. In the Avon Gorge it often grows under *Fraxinus excelsior* and *Tilia cordata*, with associates which include *Anemone nemorosa*, *Convallaria majalis*, *Euphorbia amygdaloides*, *Mercurialis perennis*, *Rubia peregrina* and *Teucrium scorodonia*. Limestone pavements provide an additional niche for some of the more northerly populations. The plant appears equally at home on both Carboniferous and oolitic limestones and is usually a lowland species, although it ascends to nearly 400 metres at Malham. It has occasionally been recorded as an introduction.

Although populations flower and fruit freely, they do not appear readily able to colonise new localities. This is possibly because the fruits seem to suffer extensive predation by animals. Most colonies increase their size vegetatively and several colonies have spread in this manner from woodlands onto adjacent quarry faces.

Most populations appear stable, with the exception of those that have been reduced or destroyed through the quarrying of limestone or the removal of limestone pavement for horticultural use. This remains the main threat to this species in Britain.

P. odoratum occurs throughout Europe from central Scandinavia in the north, southwards to Morocco. The eastern range extends through Siberia and the western Himalayas as far as China.

Hybrids with *P. multiflorum* are widely grown as garden plants and are often naturalised (Stace 1991). Some of the records of *P. odoratum* as an introduction may be based on these hybrids.

M. A. R. Kitchen

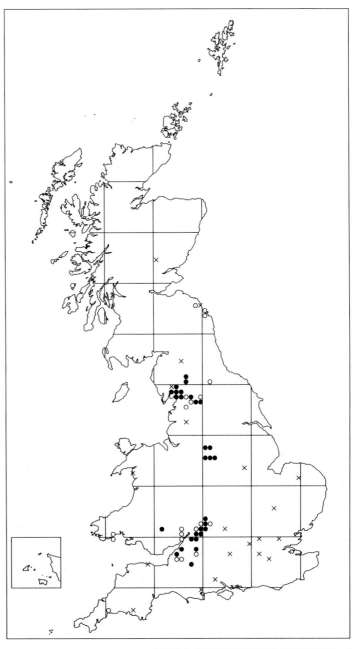

Current map	No	Atlas	No
1970 →	29	1930 →	23
Pre-1970	21	Pre-1930	13
Introductions	21	Introductions	11

continued →

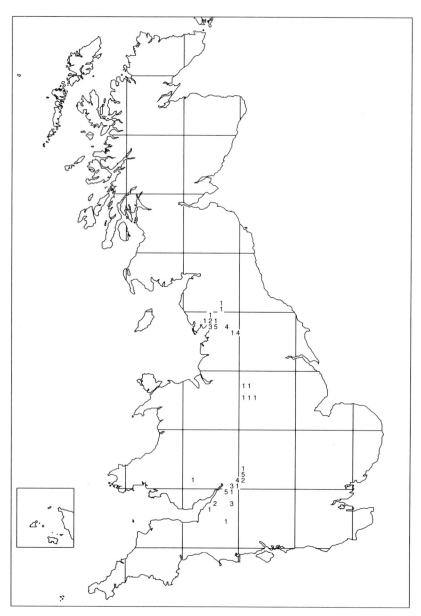

The number of tetrads in each 10 km square in which *Polygonatum odoratum* has been recorded as a native species from 1970 onwards. The species has been found in a total of 59 tetrads from 1970 onwards.

Polygonum boreale (Lange) Small

Status: scarce

Northern knotgrass

This is a plant of lowland, ruderal habitats, arable fields, gardens and coastal beaches. In the far north of Britain it occupies the same ecological niche as *P. aviculare*.

P. boreale is annual and probably to a great extent self-pollinated, although there is evidence that small *Polygonum* species may be pollinated by ants or other tiny insects.

Records are rather few, but the plant is abundant where it does occur. Although a number of observers from 1865 onwards noted that the Shetland 'P. aviculare' was distinct (Scott & Palmer 1987), it was not until 1962 that it was recognised as a distinct species (Styles 1962). *P. boreale* is widespread in Orkney and especially Shetland, where it apparently replaces *P. aviculare* entirely (Scott & Palmer 1987). It is probably still present in the 10 km squares shown as pre-1970 on the map. It is probably overlooked elsewhere in Scotland, especially in ruderal communities on the coasts.

P. boreale is circumpolar in distribution and in Europe it is restricted to northern Russia, northern and north-western Scandinavia, the Faeroes and Iceland. It is not a particularly variable species.

J. R. Akeroyd

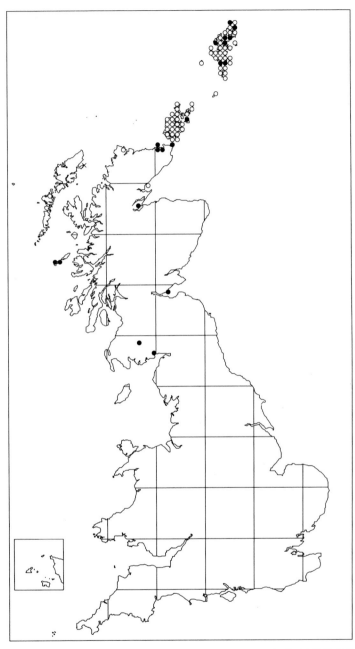

Current map	No	Atlas (S)	No
1970 →	19		
Pre-1970	54		
Introductions	1	All records	49

Polygonum oxyspermum C. Meyer & Bunge ex Ledeb.

Ray's knotgrass

Status: not scarce

This is a characteristic but local plant of strandlines on coastal sand, shingle and silty mud. Associated species include *Atriplex glabriuscula, A. laciniata, Cakile maritima* and *Salsola kali*. It also occurs above the strandline in embryonic foredunes.

It is an annual or short-lived perennial and is probably largely self-pollinated. It flowers from July to October.

This species has declined in some areas. It has always been rare in eastern England. Strandline plants are notoriously erratic in appearance (Webb & Akeroyd 1991), so disappearance from a particular locality does not always imply a decline. Nevertheless, this plant has suffered from the increased disturbance of many beaches, with consequent damage to strandline and foredune communities. It may be under-recorded on the west coast of Scotland.

The species occurs along most of the coasts of Europe, except southern and western Spain (Jalas & Suominen 1979). Subsp. *raii* extends from north-western Spain to arctic Russia, with almost indistinguishable plants from the coasts of the Black Sea having been called *P. mesembricum*. Subsp. *oxyspermum*, with longer, more greenish-brown fruits than subsp. *raii*, occurs in the Baltic and southern Norway. Longer-lived perennial plants from the western and central Mediterranean coasts belong to subsp. *robertii* (an epithet erroneously ascribed to British material in the past).

The British plant is subsp. *raii* (Bab.) D. Webb & Chater. Some plants from Scotland, especially from Arran, are close to subsp. *oxyspermum* and require further investigation.

J. R. Akeroyd

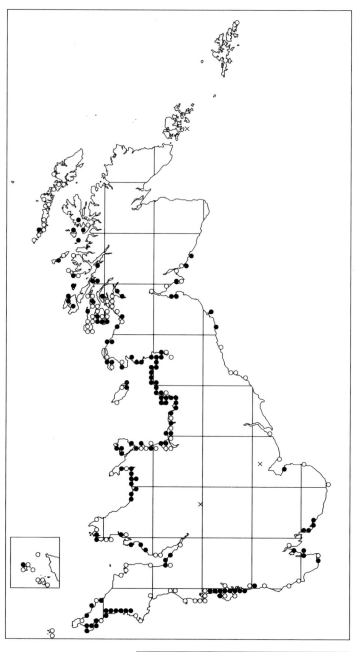

Current map	No	Atlas	No
1970 →	129	1930 →	66
Pre-1970	107	Pre-1930	59
Introductions	3	Introductions	0

Polygonum rurivagum Jordan ex Boreau

Status: not scarce

Cornfield knotgrass

This is a plant of arable fields on calcareous or light soils, especially on the chalk. It sometimes occurs as a ruderal and on disturbed road-verges.

The plant is annual and usually self-pollinated. It begins to flower in late July or August, later than related species of *Polygonum*, continuing to flower after fields have been harvested until November.

Although there has apparently been a decline in southern and south-eastern England, the species has been recorded over a wider range in recent years. This may indicate that it has been overlooked and recent records from western Wales suggest that it should be sought more widely. Few recorders report it, but those that do seem to find it repeatedly.

The European distribution is still not fully known, but there are records for most territories in south-western to western-central Europe, northwards to Sweden and southwards to Sicily and Macedonia. Similar plants have been described from Russia, Ukraine and the Baltic Republics as *P. neglectum* Besser and *P. scythicum* Klokov.

P. rurivagum was treated as a species by Moss (1914), but not fully understood in Britain until Styles (1962) revised the *P. aviculare* aggregate. It is superficially very similar to *P. aviculare*, of which it is probably a segetal ecotype.

J. R. Akeroyd

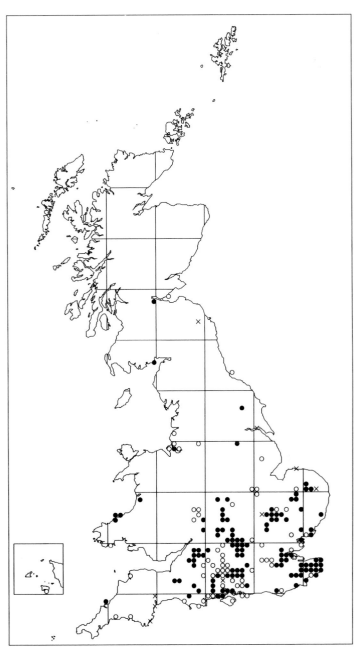

Current map	No	Atlas (S)	No
1970 →	116		
Pre-1970	64		
Introductions	9	All records	43

Polypodium cambricum L.
Status: not scarce

Southern polypody

In its British localities *P. cambricum* is mainly found on the steep slopes or vertical cliffs of base-rich rocky outcrops in whose cracks and crevices it finds secure anchorage and a moist root-run with a gritty, humus-rich, sharply drained soil. Such situations also provide some protection from the wind, especially when partially shaded by trees. Although generally considered to be a calcicole and often found on Carboniferous and other limestones, it occurs on a wide range of rock types such as basalt, calciferous sandstone, conglomerate, dolerite, shale and volcanic tuffs. In a few coastal sites it has been found on base-deficient rocks whose crevices have become filled with shelly sand, and as an epiphyte on trees. It is also widely found in man-made habitats, but apparently not in Scotland: on ancient walls with crumbling lime-mortar and also on the sides and rubble of disused limestone quarries and occasionally on base-rich hedgebanks. Soil samples from a number of Welsh localities gave pH values of 6.0-6.85 (Hughes 1969). In its more northerly localities it appears to favour sites with a more southerly aspect but even there it is not entirely restricted to them. It reaches its northern limit in Europe on Lismore (Rutherford & Stirling 1973). It is mainly restricted to the lowlands, but reaches 460 metres in Merioneth and near Malham Tarn.

Established plants can spread vegetatively by rhizomes to a limited extent. Spores are produced abundantly under optimum conditions. Frond size and shape, pinna serration and fertility are considerably modified by environmental conditions: under extreme shading and humidity, fronds achieve maximum size and modification of frond form, but fail to produce sporangia.

Invasion of habitats by scrub following change of management has reduced some populations almost to extinction and large populations on old walls, for example at Conway Castle, Dryslwyn Castle and Tintern Abbey, have been completely destroyed during cleaning of the masonry.

P. cambricum also occurs in western and southern Europe (Jalas & Suominen 1972), reaching its northern limit in Britain. It is also found in North Africa and in south-west Asia.

The British *Polypodium* species are somewhat critical, and microscopic examination of the sporangia is often needed for a certain identification. *P. cambricum* is therefore likely to be under-recorded in some areas.

R. H. Roberts

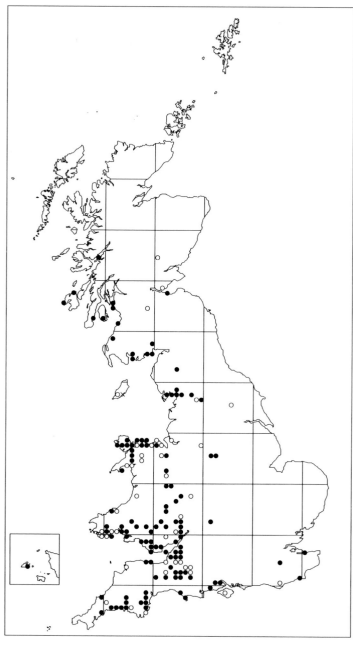

Current map	No	Atlas (S)	No
1970 →	116		
Pre-1970	42		
Introductions	1	All records	46

Polypogon monspeliensis (L.) Desf.

Status: scarce

Annual beard-grass

P. monspeliensis occurs with several other grasses, such as *Hordeum marinum*, *Puccinellia distans*, *P. fasciculata* and *P. rupestris*, on open, frequently saline, coastal soils. Typical habitats include the edges of pools, creeks or recently cleared ditches, where it often appears with *Spergularia marina*; bare patches along the berms and counter dykes behind sea walls; and open parts of cattle-poached marshland where, depending on the salinity levels, it may be found with *Agrostis stolonifera* (with which it occasionally hybridises), *Aster tripolium*, *Bolboschoenus maritimus*, *Juncus gerardii*, *Salicornia* species and *Ranunculus sceleratus*. It is sometimes found inland on waste ground and refuse tips, where it is often introduced in bird-seed mixtures. It is confined to the lowlands.

P. monspeliensis is an inbreeding annual, reproducing entirely by seed which may be spread by cattle. The seed may survive for many years in the soil as evidenced by the sudden reappearance of populations at, or near to, former known sites, often when new sea walls or ditches are constructed. It requires bare ground for germination and successful seedling establishment.

The species is probably declining as a result of widespread changes including the conversion of coastal pasture to arable, alterations in the management of remaining pasture and the draining and filling-in of brackish ditches and pools. It appears not to survive competition with perennial grasses, and so it may quickly disappear from drained and reseeded pastures.

P. monspeliensis is widespread in Europe, northern and southern Africa and Asia, and introduced into North America (where it has spread rapidly in some areas). In Europe it reaches its northern limit in Britain.

A. J. Gray

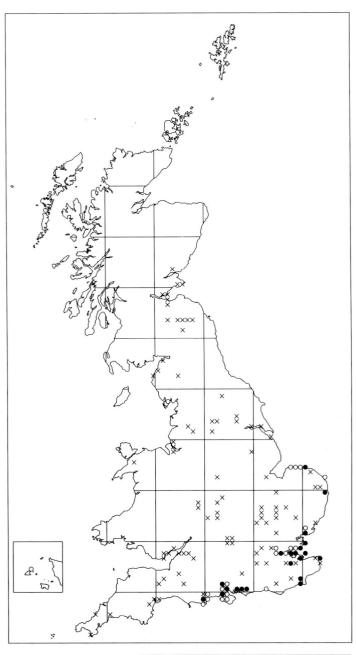

Current map	No	Atlas	No
1970 →	21	1930 →	14
Pre-1970	20	Pre-1930	14
Introductions	93	Introductions	53

Potamogeton coloratus Hornem.
Status: scarce

Fen pondweed

This aquatic species is usually found in shallow, base-rich but nutrient-poor water. It grows in pools and ditches in calcareous fenland, in slow-flowing streams, in flooded clay and marl pits and in lakes on limestone or at the landward edge of calcareous sand dunes. In fens it can also be found growing sub-terrestrially on damp moss carpets. It is found over a range of substrates including peat, clay and fine or stony sediments derived from limestone. Charophytes, including *Chara hispida*, *C. pedunculata* and *C. vulgaris*, are often found growing with it. It is a lowland species, notably absent from the more elevated Carboniferous limestone areas of northern England where there are many apparently suitable habitats.

P. coloratus is a rhizomatous perennial. The rhizome system allows it to persist through brief periods when its habitat dries out. It flowers freely in shallow water and produces numerous seeds. Little is known of the conditions under which it reproduces by seed. At some fenland sites it has reappeared following disturbance of peat (e.g. in pools created when invasive shrubs were extracted), which suggests that the seeds can retain viability for some years in moist peat.

A number of *P. coloratus* sites have been lost through drainage or eutrophication. Many of its remaining localities are species-rich calcareous wetlands which are nature reserves or SSSIs. These are presumably safeguarded from habitat destruction but are probably not immune from the more insidious effects of a falling water table or nutrient enrichment. In addition, *P. coloratus* has colonised some newly available habitats and it is, for example, locally frequent in flooded brick-pits in the Peterborough area.

It is found in western, central and southern Europe, extending north to Scotland and southern Sweden. Outside Europe it is known only from north-western Africa and south-western Asia. It is listed as a most vulnerable species in The Netherlands.

The species of *Potamogeton* have often been misidentified, and many older records are erroneous. Records made before 1940 have been accepted for these maps only if supported by expertly determined herbarium specimens. The maps must consequently under-estimate the former distribution of some species.

C. D. Preston

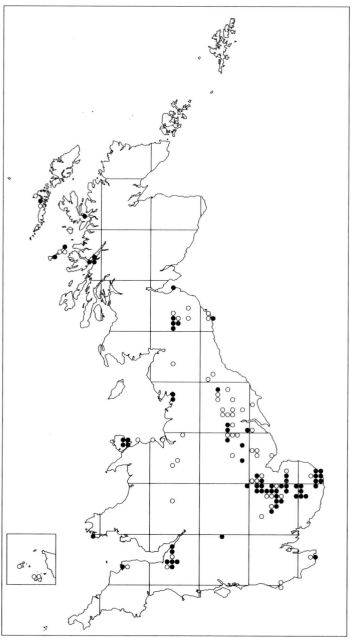

Current map	No	Atlas	No
1970 →	70		
Pre-1970	58		
Introductions	0	All records	99

Potamogeton compressus L.

Status: scarce

Grass-wrack pondweed

The natural habitat of this aquatic species is apparently slowly-flowing lowland rivers and nearby ox-bows, and calcareous lowland lakes. It has, however, also colonised canals and drainage ditches. Most of the records from the English Midlands and the Welsh Borders are from canals. In the Norfolk Broads it grows in mesotrophic grazing marsh ditches in a diverse community which includes other scarce aquatics such as *Hydrocharis morsus-ranae* and *Stratiotes aloides*.

P. compressus sometimes sets seed, but vegetative reproduction is probably more frequent than regeneration by seed. This is accomplished by specialised turions, which also act as agents of dispersal.

As the map shows, *P. compressus* has decreased markedly in Britain. It is extinct in the Cambridgeshire fenland, where it was last collected in 1912, and in the Thames valley, where it was last recorded from Oxfordshire in 1947. The reasons for these disappearances are not fully understood; in Cambridgeshire it became extinct before other scarce aquatics declined. Eutrophication was certainly responsible for its extinction at other sites such as Balgavies Loch and Rescobie Loch, and in the Broads. Its decline in canals can be attributed to some falling into disuse and drying out, whereas the flora of others has deteriorated as they have become increasingly used for pleasure boating. It may, however, still survive in some canals for which we have no recent record. The mesotrophic drainage ditches in Broadland in which it survives are very vulnerable to eutrophication; many have become floristically impoverished in the last seventeen years in non-intensive grazing marshes, even in areas where management had been aimed at maintaining their botanical interest (Doarks 1990).

P. compressus is widespread in temperate Eurasia. In North America it is replaced by *P. zosteriformis* Fernald, which is regarded by some authorities as a subspecies of *P. compressus*.

A similar species, *P. acutifolius*, is a plant of grazing marsh ditches which has also declined in Britain and now qualifies for inclusion in the *Red Data Book*.

C. D. Preston

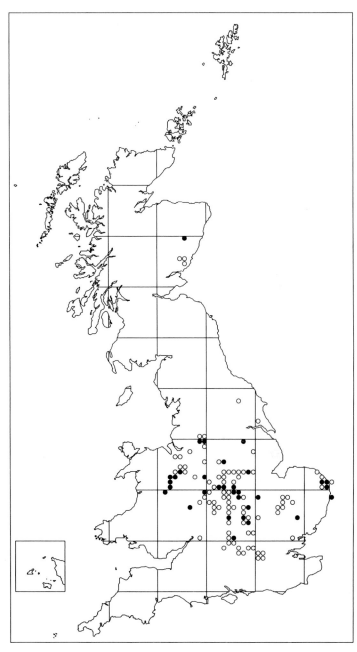

Current map	No	Atlas	No
1970 →	32		
Pre-1970	84		
Introductions	0	All records	89

Potamogeton filiformis Pers.
Status: scarce

Slender-leaved pondweed

P. filiformis, a plant of shallow water, is usually found over soft sediments such as sand, silt or marl on the gently sloping sides of lakes. It is most often found in water 5-50 cm deep, but in such habitats the water level tends to be very variable. The lakes in which it grows are usually over limestone (as on Lismore) or are enriched by bases derived from nearby basalt, limestone, glacial deposits or dune sand, or receive sea-spray. In lakes over limestone the water can be highly calcareous but nutrient-poor, but most *P. filiformis* sites are mesotrophic or eutrophic. *P. filiformis* often grows with charophytes, including *Chara aspera*, *C. hispida*, *C. vulgaris* and *Tolypella nidifica* var. *glomerata*. In addition to lakes, this species also grows in outflow streams and nearby ditches, as well as in other slow-flowing streams and rivers, in flooded quarries and, rarely, in cliff-top rock pools. It is primarily a lowland species, reaching 350 metres at Drumore Loch.

P. filiformis is a perennial with a strong rhizome. Plants spread vegetatively by rhizomatous growth, and plants can flower and fruit freely in water as shallow as 1 cm. Plants overwinter as tubers which develop on the rhizome, and when washed out of the substrate these doubtless also act as a means of dispersal.

P. filiformis is extinct in Anglesey, where it was first collected in 1798 (the first British record) and last seen in 1826; later records are erroneous (Preston 1990). The reason for its disappearance is unknown. In Scotland there is no evidence that it has suffered any decline. It is probably under-recorded, particularly on the west coast.

A widespread circumboreal species, found in Europe, Asia and North America. In Europe it is primarily a northern species, which is also found at high altitudes in the Alps and has scattered localities in Spain, Italy and Yugoslavia.

P. filiformis, like *Callitriche hermaphroditica*, is unusual in being a northern aquatic which prefers mesotrophic or eutrophic, lowland waters, and consequently has a predominantly eastern distribution. Fossil evidence demonstrates that it was widespread in Britain in the last glacial period (Godwin 1975), but has since retreated to its current range.

C. D. Preston

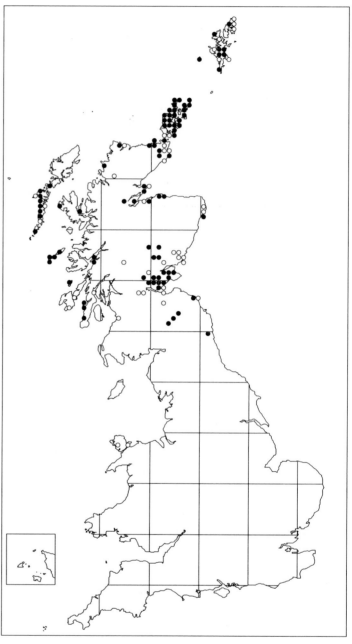

Current map	No	Atlas	No
1970 →	88		
Pre-1970	42		
Introductions	0	All records	72

Potamogeton friesii Rupr.

Status: not scarce

Flat-stalked pondweed

This species grows in still or slowly-flowing water. In England and Wales its main habitats are lowland rivers, canals, fenland lodes and species-rich ditches in grazing marshes. Here it grows with species such as *Ceratophyllum demersum, Potamogeton crispus, P. pectinatus, P. perfoliatus, P. pusillus* and *Ranunculus circinatus*. In Scotland it is also found in canals in the industrial lowlands, but most records are from lakes where the water is enriched by bases derived from limestone, calcareous sand dunes or calcareous glacial drift. It is a characteristic species of the 'machair lochs' on the west coast of the Outer Hebrides. It is usually found in relatively eutrophic water, but it is unable to withstand very high levels of dissolved nutrients. It is confined to the lowlands.

P. friesii is a non-rhizomatous species which flowers and fruits rather sparingly. Its normal mode of reproduction and dispersal is by turions, which develop in the leaf axils and at the end of short axillary branches in July and August.

This species was recorded in the 19th century in a number of canals in southern England which have now disappeared from the landscape. In some other canals which are still extant, and in some rivers in this area, it has not been recorded since before 1950. Since 1950 there have been few further losses in southern England, where its tolerance of eutrophic water and its ability to persist in canals and fenland lodes which carry light boat traffic is advantageous. It appeared in the Thurne Valley broads in the 1930s, when the charophyte communities in the calcium-rich but hitherto nutrient-poor lakes were replaced by vegetation dominated by vascular plants as nutrient levels increased. However, it was unable to persist when nutrient levels increased even further (George 1992). It sometimes colonises newly available habitats, such as flooded gravel pits. It is extinct in Balgavies Loch and Rescobie Loch, where the aquatic flora has also been greatly impoverished by eutrophication (Ingram & Noltie 1981).

It is a widespread species, which has a predominantly northern distribution in Europe and is also found in Asia and North America.

C. D. Preston

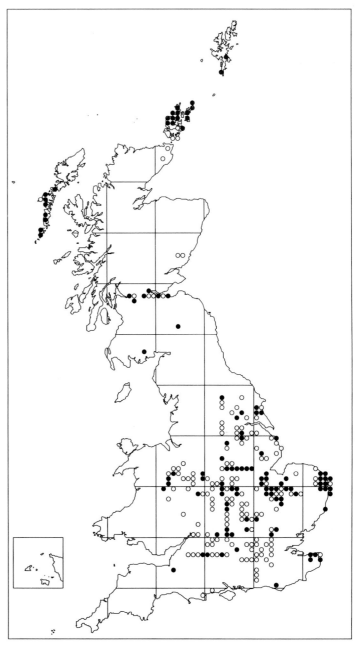

Current map	No	Atlas	No
1970 →	112		
Pre-1970	143		
Introductions	0	All records	169

Potamogeton praelongus Wulfen
Status: not scarce

Long-stalked pondweed

This species usually grows in water at least 1 metre deep, and can occur as a dominant below 1.5-3 metres. It is most frequently found in mesotrophic lakes, both in limestone areas and in lakes which are in predominantly acidic catchments but receive drainage from outcrops of base-rich rocks such as basalt or limestone. In Scotland and northern England it also occurs in slowly-flowing rivers and flooded quarries. Species which characteristically grow in the same water bodies include *Potamogeton gramineus*, *P. perfoliatus* and *P. × zizii*. In southern England and Wales *P. praelongus* is recorded from rivers, canals, the Broads and larger fenland drains. It grows in water bodies from sea-level up to 790 metres at Lochan an Tairbh-uisge.

It is a rhizomatous perennial which overwinters as leafy shoots. In some habitats the water is too deep for plants to flower but if plants do flower they fruit freely. Little information is available about its germination requirements.

P. praelongus has decreased markedly in the lowlands. Much of this decline has taken place since 1950: this species was frequent in the Cambridgeshire fenland in the 1950s (Perring, Sell & Walters 1964) but is now known from only two localities. It seems likely that eutrophication, perhaps coupled with unsympathetic management, is responsible for this dramatic decline, but there is only circumstantial evidence for this. As a deep-water species it does not grow in habitats such as grazing marsh ditches, in which other pollution-sensitive species have persisted after they disappeared from larger water bodies. It is still frequent in parts of Scotland, where it is probably somewhat under-recorded.

P. praelongus is widespread in northern and central Europe, extending north to Iceland and northern Scandinavia and south to France and Bulgaria. It has declined in some other areas of lowland Europe, including the Netherlands (Ploeg 1990). It is a circumboreal species, found in Asia and North America with an isolated occurrence in Mexico.

C. D. Preston

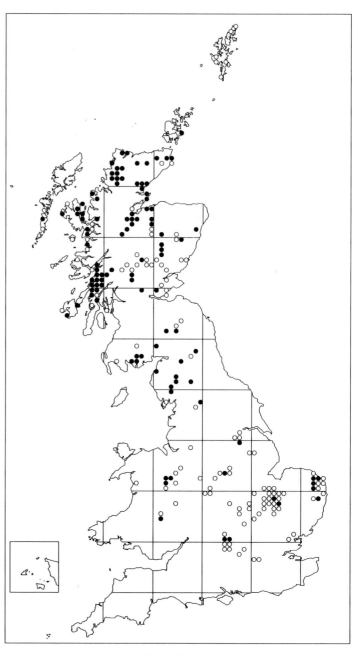

Current map	No	Atlas	No
1970 →	107		
Pre-1970	115		
Introductions	0	All records	141

330

Potamogeton trichoides Cham. & Schldl.
Status: scarce

Hairlike pondweed

P. trichoides is found in shallow, still or slowly-flowing water in a wide range of habitats, including lakes, reservoirs, ponds, lowland rivers, canals, drainage ditches and flooded clay, sand and gravel pits. It is usually found in meso-eutrophic or eutrophic water, often with *Elodea canadensis* or *E. nuttallii* and frequently with *Myriophyllum spicatum*, *Potamogeton crispus* and other linear-leaved pondweeds, especially *P. pectinatus* and *P. pusillus*. In some sites it has been noted as an early colonist of freshly cleared canals and ditches. It is confined to the lowlands.

P. trichoides is an annual which flowers and fruits sparingly. New colonies are probably established by seed, but reproduction in established populations is primarily by turions, which develop throughout the summer on the ends of stems and branches.

This species is one of the less conspicuous linear-leaved *Potamogeton* species, a group which is troublesome to identify and often avoided by botanists. Although it was first recognised in Britain in 1850, many early records were erroneous (Dandy & Taylor 1938). It is almost certainly under-recorded in some areas, but plants of *P. pusillus* are sometimes misidentified and reported as this species. A few years ago it was thought to be declining, but there have subsequently been many new records and there is little doubt that it was simply being overlooked. In some areas it may actually be increasing: these include the Somerset Levels, where it was first recorded in 1972 and is now locally abundant.

P. trichoides is widespread in Europe, north to Scotland and southern Sweden. Its world distribution is more southerly than that of *P. friesii* or *P. praelongus*: it is found in western and central Asia and eastern and southern Africa.

C. D. Preston

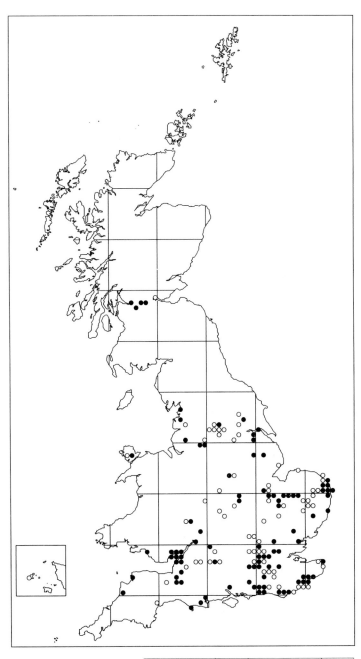

Current map	No	Atlas	No
1970 →	94		
Pre-1970	68		
Introductions	0	All records	70

Potentilla argentea L.

Status: not scarce

Hoary cinquefoil

This is a plant of dry, warm, sandy, free-draining soils, found on open short grass swards and on slopes and banks. Its associates are mainly low grasses and herbs and include *Claytonia perfoliata*, *Festuca brevipila*, *F. ovina*, *F. rubra* and *Genista tinctoria*. In years when rabbit populations are reduced, it may be crowded out by *Arrhenatherum elatius* and *Dactylis glomerata*. Provided that open spaces are available, this plant is also found near low bushes of *Ulex europaeus* and may benefit from nitrogen released from the root nodules of *Ulex*.

It is a perennial herb which reproduces by seed. The number of plants in an area is very variable and may be affected by the spread of more competitive species. Whatever the precise regulation of successful reproduction, this plant is a survivor. It is recorded by Relhan (1785) "among furze at Hildersham" and in the same place by Babington (1860). Trist (1988) reported that it is "annually variable in quantity" there. It does not readily colonise new sites.

Its distribution in eastern England, particularly on the red crag and coarse sands of Breckland, indicates a preference for light soils of heathland and uncultivated areas not subject to disturbance. It is probably in decline through loss of suitable habitats.

P. argentea occurs throughout most of Europe, to western and central Asia. It is also found in the northern United States, westwards to Kansas.

P. J. O. Trist

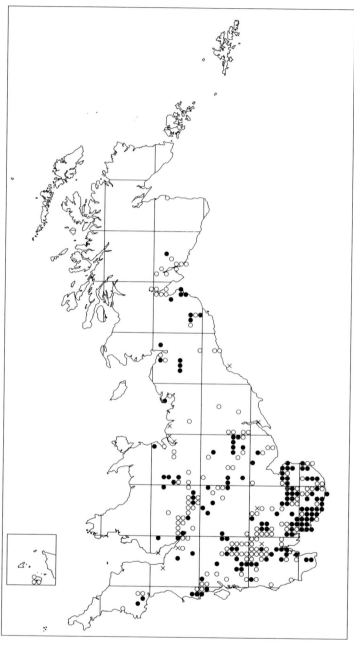

Current map	No	Atlas	No
1970 →	138	1930 →	147
Pre-1970	148	Pre-1930	56
Introductions	10	Introductions	5

Potentilla crantzii (Crantz) G. Beck ex Fritsch

Alpine cinquefoil

Status: scarce

P. crantzii is a calcicolous mountain plant of steep, dry rock faces and ledges, growing on a wide range of basic rocks, on both shady and sun-exposed aspects. Its associated plants on cliffs include *Alchemilla alpina, Dryas octopetala, Galium boreale, Linum catharticum, Persicaria vivipara, Saxifraga aizoides, S. oppositifolia* and *Silene acaulis*. It also grows in close-grazed calcareous grassland, often on slopes below the crags, but also on level ground. Here it may be subjected to rabbit grazing, especially at the lower altitude sites (Raven & Walters 1956). *P. crantzii* reaches 1000 metres in Snowdonia and 1035 metres on Ben Alder, but descends to 300 metres in northern England and 250 metres in Assynt.

P. crantzii is a perennial. Colonies consist of discrete individuals which apparently arise from seed. Vegetative spread is very limited. The plant is a pseudogamous apomict: the flowers are pollinated mainly by hover-flies, but the pollen only stimulates the formation of seed.

There is little evidence that the distribution of this species has changed in recent years, and colonies appear to show little variation in size from year to year. Heavy grazing is a threat to populations in accessible situations

P. crantzii has a typical arctic-alpine distribution. It is almost circumpolar but it is missing from the lands on either side of the Bering Straits.

Unlike those of *P. neumanniana*, British populations of *P. crantzii* are relatively homogeneous, although both hexaploids and heptaploids occur (Smith 1963b; Smith 1971).

A. Slack

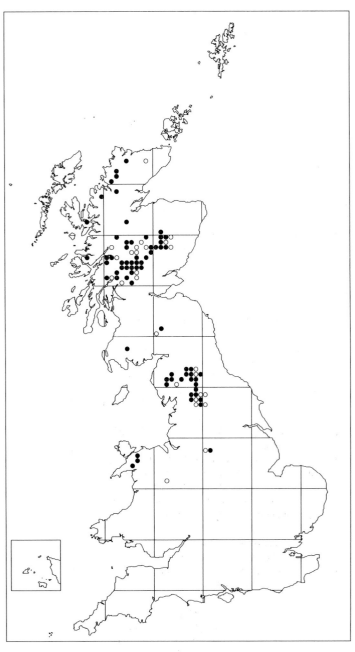

Current map	No	Atlas	No
1970 →	69	1930 →	48
Pre-1970	26	Pre-1930	12
Introductions	0	Introductions	0

Potentilla neumanniana Reichb.
Status: scarce

Spring cinquefoil

This is a plant of open ground and seasonally parched, skeletal soils in various base-rich habitats. These include coastal limestone exposures, inland limestone crags and screes, other base-rich crags and dry chalk grasslands. Associates on limestone formations include *Galium sterneri*, *Geranium sanguineum*, *Helianthemum canum*, *Hornungia petraea*, *Sesleria caerulea* and *Veronica spicata*. In the principal populations on eastern chalk, *P. neumanniana* occurs on periglacial patterned ground in association with *Astragalus danicus*, *Thalictrum minus* and *Veronica spicata*.

This is a perennial, woody, prostrate dwarf shrub. Reproduction is by both seed and vegetative means. The woody stolons will root at the nodes. The plant is a pseudogamous apomict (Smith 1963a). It flowers freely and sets seed which germinates in bare ground. The reappearance of the species following clearance of scrub and rank vegetation suggests that the seed has a relatively long viability.

In the lowlands *P. neumanniana* has suffered a marked decline. In many classic localities (such as the Suffolk brecks and the Lincolnshire warrens) this species has become extinct with the cessation of extensive pastoral grazing and commercial warrens in which parched bare ground was locally abundant. Where well-established, *P. neumanniana* will persist under light scrub. Prolonged exposure to shade appears to result in plants dying out. A number of sites have been lost through dominance by rank grasses, scrub invasion and the deliberate planting of trees. Limestone and upland sites appear more stable with skeletal soils and open screes being more resistant to fluctuations in rank vegetation and scrub associated with changes in grazing pressure.

This species is confined to Europe. It is predominantly a plant of central Europe, extending north to southern Scandinavia and south to the mountains of Spain, Italy and the Balkans.

British *P. neumanniana* is both cytologically and morphologically variable: hexaploids, heptaploids and higher polyploids occur. Some populations of *Potentilla*, notably at Craig an Dail Bheag and Grassington, are intermediate between *P. crantzii* and *P. neumanniana* (Smith 1971).

C. Chatters

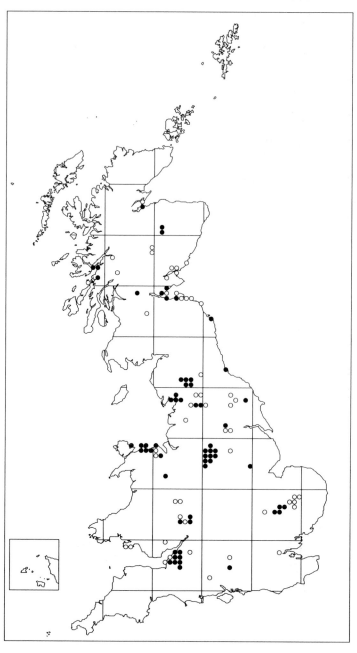

Current map	No	Atlas	No
1970 →	62	1930 →	45
Pre-1970	51	Pre-1930	23
Introductions	0	Introductions	0

continued →

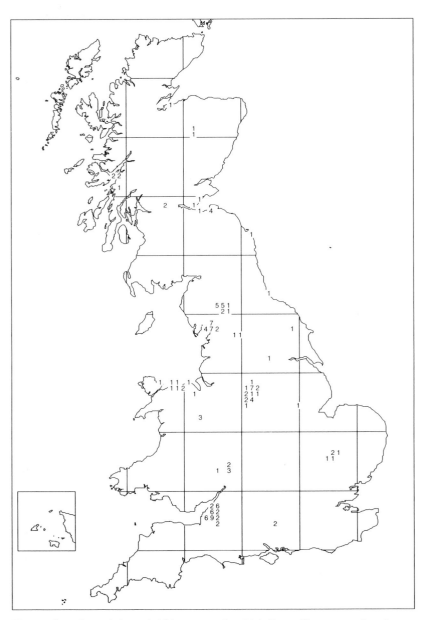

The number of tetrads in each 10 km square in which *Potentilla neumanniana* has been recorded as a native species from 1970 onwards. Squares in which the species is recorded in 9 or more tetrads are plotted as 9: *P. neumanniana* is actually recorded from 11 tetrads in ST45. The species has been found in a total of 142 tetrads from 1970 onwards.

Primula elatior (L.) Hill

Status: scarce

Oxlip

P. elatior is a shade-tolerant species. It is most frequent in woods dominated by ash, field maple and pedunculate oak (with an understorey of hazel) on soils derived from calcareous boulder clay and it persists when these trees are replaced by invasive elm clones. Within these woods it is locally abundant in areas where the vigour of *Mercurialis perennis*, usually a dominant herb, is reduced by seasonal flooding. The woods are traditionally managed as coppices with scattered oak standards. *P. elatior* flowers profusely in the second year after coppicing but much less freely as the coppice stools grow and shade increases. Other, much rarer, habitats include wet alder woods, damp meadows and ancient hedgerows; at its only Norfolk locality it formerly grew in a *Phragmites*-dominated fen community over peat (Woodell 1965). It is confined to the lowlands.

P. elatior is a highly sedentary perennial. Many of the woods in which it grows are probably primary. It also grows in some ancient secondary woods but spreads very slowly into recent woods, even if these are adjacent to existing populations, and rarely colonises hedgerows. Plants are almost completely self-incompatible. Viable seed is produced but little is known about the longevity of plants or the circumstances under which they reproduce by seed. The response to coppicing reflects an increase in the vigour of existing plants.

P. elatior meadows have been almost or entirely eliminated by agricultural improvement, and the species has become increasingly restricted to woodland. In woods it is tenacious; numbers are reduced when coppicing ceases or woods are coniferised but plants continue to grow in open areas such as rides. Numbers have apparently declined in some well-studied woods since 1945, for reasons which are unclear (Rackham 1992). In recent years spectacular displays of *P. elatior* in flower have become rarer, as deer have increased in numbers and often eat the young inflorescences.

P. elatior is a widespread and variable species, extending from Britain east to the Altai mountains of central Asia. It is a montane species in the southern and eastern parts of its range.

The compact range of *P. elatior* in Britain was first documented by Christy (1897). Within this area it tends to replace *P. vulgaris*; the two species hybridise where they meet. For further accounts of this well-studied species, see Preston (1993), Rackham (1980), and Richards (1989).

C. D. Preston

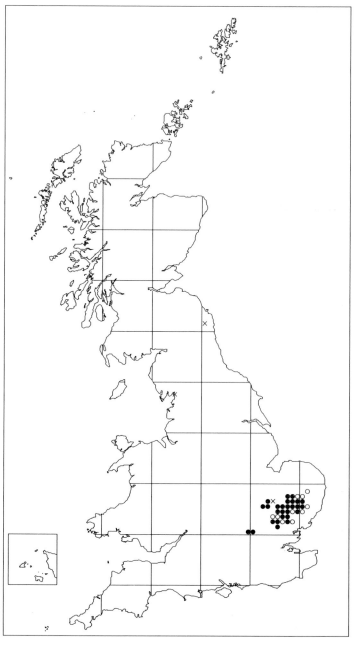

Current map	No	Atlas	No
1970 →	27	1930 →	25
Pre-1970	10	Pre-1930	7
Introductions	3	Introductions	0

Primula farinosa L.
Status: scarce

Bird's-eye primrose

P. farinosa is a characteristic species of the calcareous mires of the northern Pennines. Its favourite sites are amongst grasses and sedges on the low hummocks of calcareous gravelly clay which are a residual feature of erosion around springs and stream-banks on gently undulating ground. Here it grows with *Parnassia palustris*, *Pinguicula vulgaris*, *Selaginella selaginoides*, *Valeriana dioica* and many other plants. It grows also on the more steeply sloping banks of streams and rivers on glacial till, where slippage opens up the plant cover. In some places it survives - too often precariously - in remnants of closely-grazed moist pasture. Locally it remains very abundant, often in damp and sloping pastures below the cliffs in steep-sided valleys. It is especially a plant of the lower hills, but it is found from near sea-level to 570 metres in Wensleydale.

P. farinosa is a short-lived perennial, which reproduces by seed. Plants are almost completely self-incompatible and are pollinated by syrphids, bee-flies and day-flying moths.

This plant has disappeared from a great many sites, especially those in the valley bottoms, and on the magnesian limestone in Durham, as these have been drained, manured, fertilised or resown. Although an amount of 'poaching' by stock may help to open the ground for colonisation, and on flatter sites grazing helps to restrict competition, present levels of over-stocking, with winter feed-stations concentrating animals in small areas, are causing damage both locally and over large areas. The remoter upland mires may be more resistant to such damage, but uprooted plants can often be found in such places, apparently plucked by sheep and then discarded.

P. farinosa has a very wide distribution across northern Eurasia as far as the Pacific. Although it shows a clearly montane distribution in much of Europe, occurring up to 2900 metres in the Alps (where it is less restricted to base-rich soils), it does not penetrate into the Scandinavian or Scottish mountains, occurring around the Baltic, for instance, only on lower limestone exposures.

F. J. Roberts

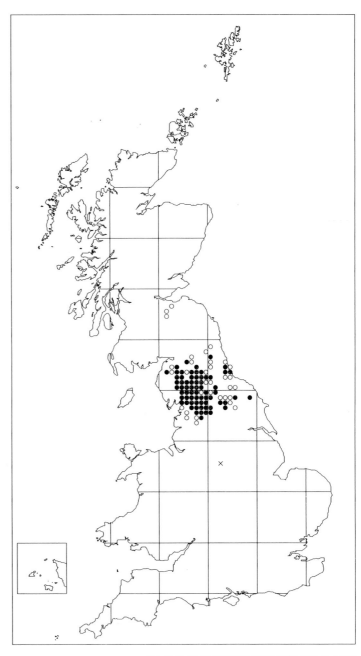

Current map	No	Atlas	No
1970 →	67	1930 →	57
Pre-1970	33	Pre-1930	25
Introductions	1	Introductions	0

continued →

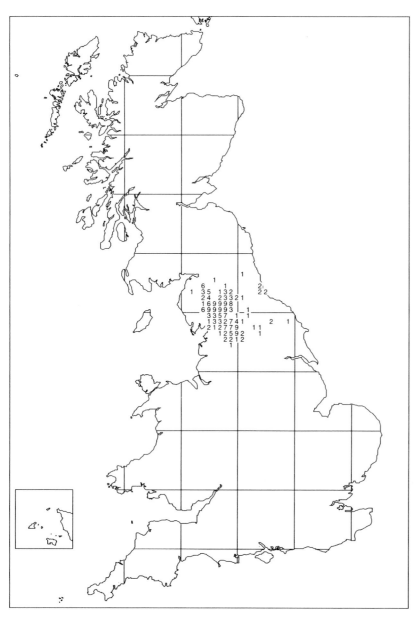

The number of tetrads in each 10 km square in which *Primula farinosa* has been recorded as a native species from 1970 onwards. Squares in which the species is recorded in 9 or more tetrads are plotted as 9: *P. farinosa* is actually recorded in 9 tetrads in NY40 and NY71, 10 in NY60, 11 in NY51, 12 in NY50 and NY70, 14 in NY61, 15 in SD97 and 16 in SD96. The species has been found in a total of 264 tetrads from 1970 onwards.

Primula scotica Hook.

Status: scarce

P. scotica occurs in a characteristic and species-rich short sward. This may occur in the transitional zone between the *Armeria/Plantago* sward and maritime heath, as a mosaic with maritime heath, as a mosaic with coarse machair, or with rock outcrops. It is accompanied by *Agrostis capillaris, Carex flacca, Danthonia decumbens, Euphrasia* spp., *Festuca ovina, F. rubra, Plantago lanceolata, P. maritima* and *Thymus polytrichus*, and is rarely found more than 5 km from the sea or above 100 metres.

Although often behaving as a biennial in cultivation, it is perennial in the wild. It reproduces entirely from seed and is heavily dependent on good seed-bed conditions, both edaphic and climatic. Although it is fully self-fertile in the absence of insects, it is visited by syrphids and cross-pollination may result in more vigorous plants with greater longevity. Mature plants persist long after a site has become unsuitable for germination. There is high mortality among young plants after severe winters.

Many of its major habitats are amenable to cultivation and almost all are grazed. Both over-grazing and under-grazing can be harmful, according to the exposure of the site, and most site losses, which continue, are due to one of these causes.

P. scotica is endemic. Its closest relative, *P. scandinavica*, is found in Norway and north-western Sweden.

For a more detailed discussion of the ecology and conservation of this species, see Bullard (1987).

E. R. Bullard

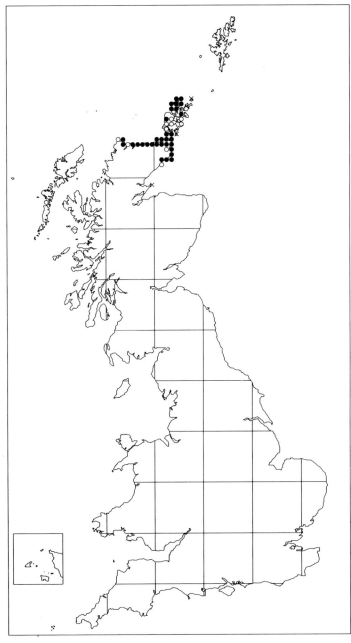

Current map	No	Atlas	No
1970 →	31		
Pre-1970	11		
Introductions	3	All records	33

Puccinellia fasciculata (Torrey) E. Bickn.

Status: scarce

Borrer's saltmarsh-grass

One of a group of scarce grasses found in bare, frequently disturbed, normally saline ground close to the sea, *P. fasciculata* is rather '*Poa annua*-like' and may be overlooked as such. Its associates are rather more distinctive and include *Hordeum marinum*, *Polypogon monspeliensis*, *Puccinellia rupestris* and *Spergularia marina*. Favoured habitats are the bare mud dredged from ditches and counter dykes in coastal reclaimed land, vehicle tracks and cattle-poached mud - indeed any open saline areas around sea walls and embankments, though more commonly on the landward side of the sea wall. It has also been recorded from roadsides in Kent (Kitchener 1983).

P. fasciculata is a short-lived perennial which is self-pollinating and spreads entirely by seed. Plants have often flowered and the above-ground parts dried up by early summer. The seeds are probably distributed with soil during bank or ditch construction and plants have appeared now and then in inland sites on salt-affected roadside verges. This species spread extensively in the Netherlands following the 1953 floods and subsequent construction work. As with many similar grasses, it appears to produce seed from even the most depauperate plants.

The distribution of this species reflects the fact that it is an early successional opportunist plant of bare ground. Local populations may therefore disappear for several years and new populations become established when the ground is disturbed - indeed a regular programme of dredging of ditches or controlled disturbance, as well as cattle poaching, may have been the major factors conserving the species in its stronghold areas, the sea-walls and coastal grazing marshes of Essex and Kent.

It occurs along the coasts of western Europe as far north as Britain and the Netherlands. It is also native to North America and South Africa.

A. J. Gray

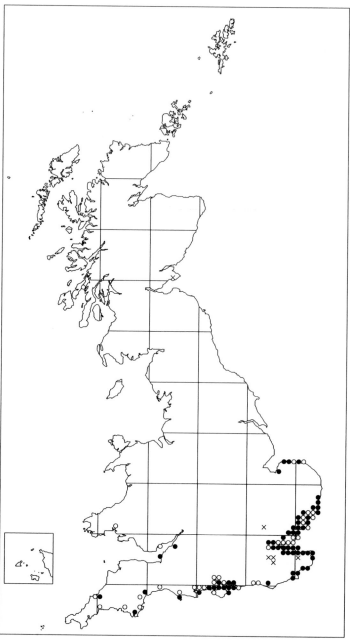

Current map	No	Atlas	No
1970 →	60	1930 →	51
Pre-1970	36	Pre-1930	10
Introductions	6	Introductions	0

Puccinellia rupestris (With.) Fern. & Weath.   **Stiff saltmarsh-grass**
Status: scarce

This attractive grass has a very similar ecology to its close relative *P. fasciculata* and is often found with it and other coastal grasses such as *Hordeum marinum* and *P. distans* on bare, often cattle-poached ground, along trackways and the edges of brackish pools and ditches and in open ephemeral vegetation behind sea-walls; despite its English name, only very rarely on the disturbed upper parts of saltmarshes. Other associates include *Parapholis strigosa*, *Polypogon monspeliensis*, *Spergularia marina* and, in less saline areas, *Agrostis stolonifera* and *Sagina procumbens*. It is also found on muddy shingle and in rock crevices, such as the facing stones of sea walls (where it often resembles *Catapodium rigidum* in general appearance). It appears to withstand trampling on tracks. It has been recorded in Kent on salt-affected roadside verges. Like its short-lived associates it avoids closed coastal grasslands, particularly where these are dominated by *Elytrigia atherica*.

P. rupestris plants are either annual or biennial, flowering only once and being distributed by seed. It is self-fertilising, single individuals sometimes founding colonies on newly disturbed mud before other plants shade them out. It can reappear after many years' absence when soils are disturbed. The populations on muddy shingle are more persistent but vary greatly in size from year to year.

This species appears to be retreating southwards but northern populations may yet be refound. The reason for its retreat is not known. The plant is favoured by a regime of periodic disturbance such as the cleaning out of coastal drainage ditches.

P. rupestris occurs on the coasts of northern and western Europe, from Britain and the Netherlands to Spain; it is also recorded from Syria.

A. J. Gray

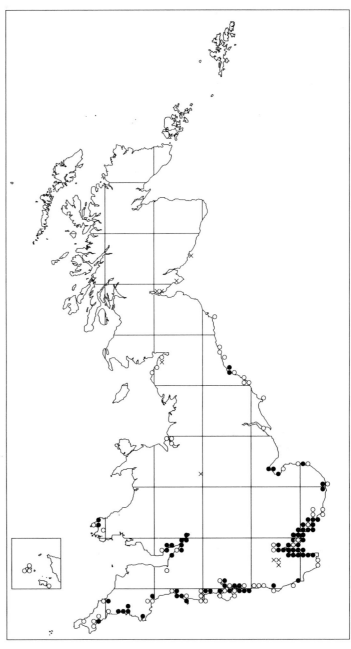

Current map	No	Atlas	No
1970 →	73	1930 →	51
Pre-1970	62	Pre-1930	43
Introductions	9	Introductions	0

341

Pulmonaria longifolia (Bast.) Boreau

Status: scarce

Narrow-leaved lungwort

This perennial is found in lightly shaded places, predominantly overlying relatively base-rich clays supporting gleys and brown earth soils. The plant is strongly associated with areas of ancient countryside (Rackham 1976) in the lowlands, most notably working and relic woodpasture, ancient enclosed woodlands, particularly coppices, species-rich *Pteridium aquilinum* heathland, hedgebanks, scrubby marl pits and woodland edge grasslands. *P. longifolia* tolerates dense shade, the presence of grazing animals, and some physical disturbance, but cannot survive combinations of these three elements. Thus under high grazing pressure, it requires relatively well illuminated undisturbed conditions and protection from the excesses of grazing through a seasonal *P. aquilinum* canopy or the presence of *Prunus spinosa*, *Rosa* and *Rubus* scrub. The plant may persist in suboptimal conditions at low population levels, but can become locally abundant where shading vegetation is cleared. Associated species are very varied but regularly include *Anemone nemorosa*, *Hyacinthoides non-scripta*, *Primula vulgaris*, *Serratula tinctoria*, *Stachys officinalis* and *Succisa pratensis*.

P. longifolia flowers freely and sets viable seeds which germinate on bare ground. The plant also reproduces vegetatively by natural division of rootstock. Rooted stems and fragments of root have readily re-established themselves as viable plants following disturbances such as the construction of woodbanks and railway cuttings.

Despite the vigorous nature of many colonies, they seldom spread to apparently suitable contiguous habitats. As areas of ancient countryside have been modified by intensive farming and plantation forestry, or have become derelict through the cessation of traditional management, the number and vigour of populations have declined. It is likely that additional colonies await discovery, particularly within ancient enclosed landscapes and *P. aquilinum* heaths. As this species is becoming increasingly fashionable in cultivation it is possible that naturalised colonies may emerge outside the range of the native populations.

It is restricted to a small area of western Europe, from northern Spain and Portugal through France to Britain. Its distribution is confused with that of its close ally *P. angustifolia*, which occurs from eastern France eastwards.

The historic and current distribution of *P. longifolia* is confined to the catchment of the Pleistocene Solent River (West 1980).

C. Chatters

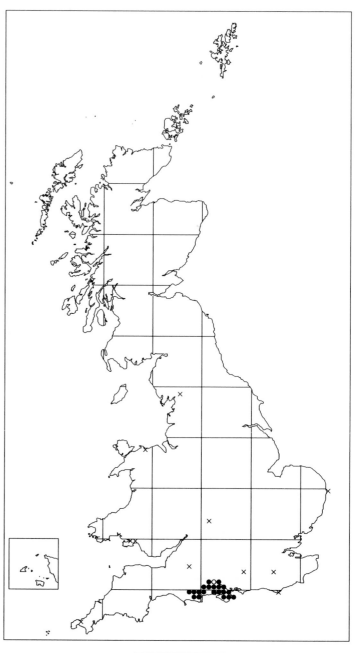

Current map	No	Atlas	No
1970 →	20	1930 →	17
Pre-1970	1	Pre-1930	2
Introductions	11	Introductions	7

continued →

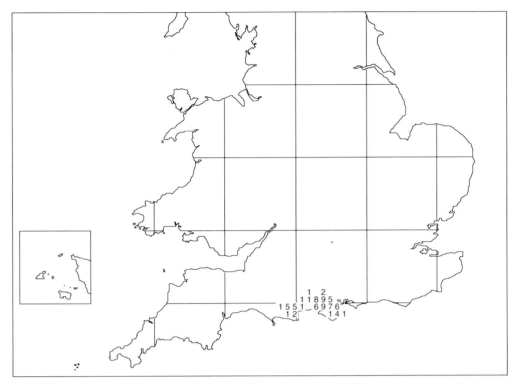

The number of tetrads in each 10 km square in which *Pulmonaria longifolia* has been recorded as a native species from 1970 onwards. Squares in which the species is recorded in 9 or more tetrads are plotted as 9: *P. longifolia* is actually recorded in 11 tetrads in SZ39 and 14 in SU30. The species has been found in a total of 83 tetrads from 1970 onwards.

Pulsatilla vulgaris Miller

Status: scarce

Pasqueflower

This is a perennial herb of grazed and ungrazed grasslands, confined in England to relatively shallow (5-15 cm), calcareous soils. Most colonies occur on steep south to south-west facing slopes on the escarpment of the chalk or Jurassic limestone, or in similar grassland in old quarries and on ancient earthworks. At sites where *P. vulgaris* is common, the grassland is characteristically rich in species, with a high proportion of dicotyledons including, most commonly, *Asperula cynanchica, Campanula rotundifolia, Centaurea nigra, Filipendula vulgaris, Hippocrepis comosa, Lotus corniculatus, Pilosella officinarum, Pimpinella saxifraga, Plantago lanceolata, P. media, Thymus polytrichus* and *T. pulegioides. Briza media, Bromopsis erecta, Carex caryophyllea, C. flacca, Festuca ovina* and *Koeleria macrantha* are also common associates.

P. vulgaris is a long-lived perennial with an extensive rootstock. It reproduces mostly vegetatively, by the growth of adventitious buds on the rhizome which form small daughter rosettes near to the mother plant. Plants can be found in flower from the middle of March to late June, but the main period of flowering is from about 6 April to 20 May. Flower production varies considerably from year to year, even at sites where the turf remains short. Flower production decreases as competition from tall grasses increases, a sharp fall in flowering occurring when the average height of the vegetation reaches 10-15 cm. Although some colonies regularly produce considerable amounts of viable seed, establishment from seed is a rare event. Colonisation of new sites is unknown, partly because of lack of a dispersal mechanism but, more importantly, because of the combination of special requirements for germination and establishment. Reports of 'new' sites far-removed from known sites should always be treated with suspicion.

P. vulgaris has been lost from many of its former localities, mainly because of habitat destruction (Wells 1968). Lack of management and scrub encroachment pose a serious threat to about half of the localities from which it is still known. Small populations are particularly at risk.

P. vulgaris subsp. *vulgaris* is widely distributed across north-west Europe on calcareous and sandy soils, but diminishing as habitat destruction continues (Jalas & Suominen 1989). It is replaced by subsp. *grandis* (Wenderoth) Zamels in eastern Europe.

For further information on this species, see Wells & Barling (1971).

T. C. E. Wells

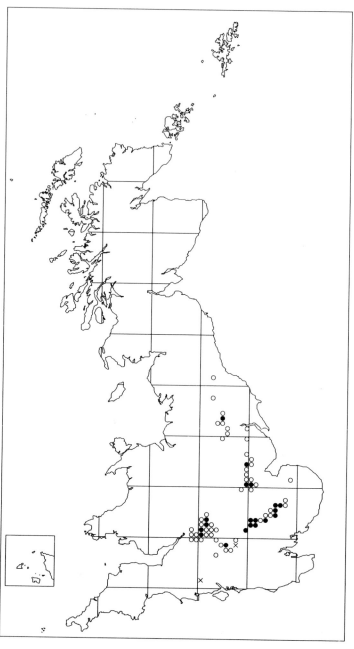

Current map	No	Atlas	No
1970 →	19	1930 →	27
Pre-1970	48	Pre-1930	35
Introductions	2	Introductions	0

continued →

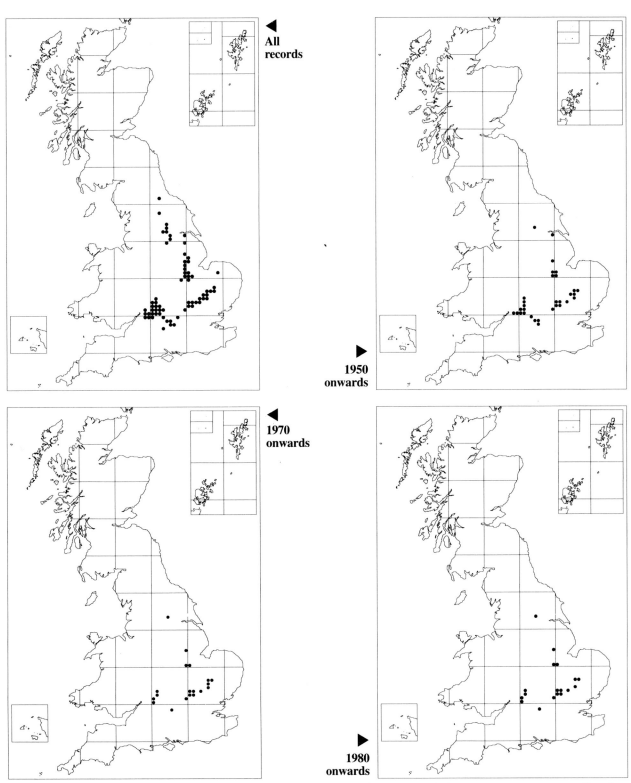

The distribution of *Pulsatilla vulgaris*, illustrated by a series of maps for different time periods.

continued →

continued

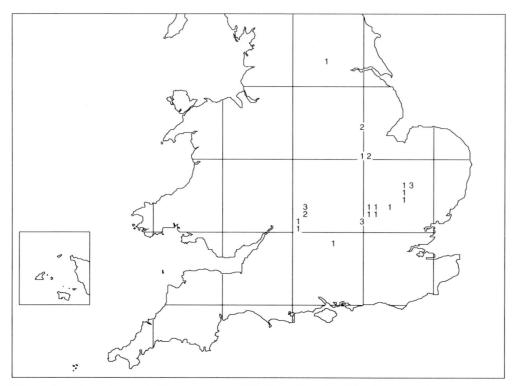

The number of tetrads in each 10 km square in which *Pulsatilla vulgaris* has been recorded as a native species from 1970 onwards. The species has been found in a total of 28 tetrads from 1970 onwards.

Pyrola media Sw.
Status: scarce

P. media usually grows on mildly acidic to slightly basic, well-drained soils in woods (especially pinewoods) and heaths. In pinewoods, it grows in the mossy dwarf-shrub field layer amongst *Vaccinium myrtillus* and *V. vitis-idaea*, and in association with *Goodyera repens*, *Gymnocarpium dryopteris*, *Listera cordata*, *Melampyrum pratense* and *Pyrola minor*. It is also a member of a distinctive sub-montane dwarf shrub heath - usually derived from former woodland - with co-dominance of *Arctostaphylos uva-ursi* and *Calluna vulgaris*, but on slightly basic brown earths with an abundance of *Genista anglica* and herbs such as *Anemone nemorosa*, *Lathyrus linifolius*, *Lotus corniculatus* and *Viola riviniana*. Its altitudinal range is from near sea-level in Banff to 550 metres on Coire Garbhlach above Glen Feshie.

Little seems to be known about the reproduction of this evergreen perennial herb, but it has evident powers of recovery after moorland fires, despite the appearance of widespread decline.

This is a mysterious plant. In the *Atlas of the British flora* (Perring & Walters 1962), a high proportion of mapped records were pre-1930, and although some new records have been made since 1970, they are mainly in the north-east of Scotland where most of the extant populations occur. Either there has been a substantial decline, even within the Highlands, or there was previous confusion of identity with *P. minor*. Unfavourable woodland management might have been a factor in its decline, and some colonies have been lost through afforestation, unless they can survive the thicket stage of growth. Many heathland sites are subject to burning, but the plant appears able to regenerate with the rest of the community. Heavy grazing which destroyed the dwarf shrub heath would also remove this species, and could have contributed to its decline.

Matthews (1955) classifies this species as continental-northern, and it occurs from arctic Scandinavia to the mountains of central Europe, the Caucasus and Asia Minor.

D. A. Ratcliffe

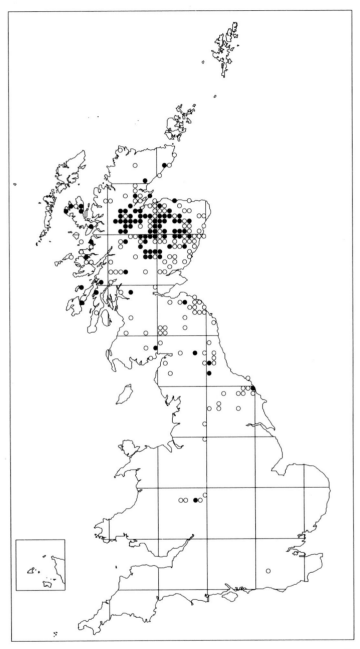

Current map	No	Atlas	No
1970 →	85	1930 →	59
Pre-1970	138	Pre-1930	89
Introductions	0	Introductions	0

Pyrola rotundifolia L. subsp. *maritima* (Kenyon) E. Warb.

Status: scarce

Round-leaved wintergreen

An attractive perennial herb of damp dune-slacks. Within the dune system its ecological requirements are wide-ranging, from habitats which are quite wet to fairly dry ones, but most of them are on calcareous sand and apparently with a high water table. It is most frequently found on the drier margins of wet slacks where *Salix repens* is abundant, on the slopes of low *S. repens* hummocks, and even on the sides of low fixed dunes. Where the dunes have been planted with conifers and the canopy is fairly open, e.g. under Corsican pine, the shade is often sufficient to suppress *S. repens* and other species, while *P. rotundifolia* subsp. *maritima* thrives. Few exceptions to the coastal habitat are known; one in a calcareous upland marsh at 120 m altitude and another among scrub over wet limestone-quarry waste. Like other members of the Pyrolaceae, it is strongly mycorrhizal, drawing inorganic and also some organic nutrients from its symbiotic mycorrhizal fungus, with complete dependence on the fungus during the germination and establishment phase.

It is a patch-forming clonal perennial, spreading by slender creeping rhizomes. Single patches frequently appear in isolation, and may spread rapidly (c. 20-30 cm or more in a year) but often do not persist for long, disappearing completely and unexpectedly with no apparent cause. Established populations with many plants persist but fluctuate in numbers. Flowering tends to be rather sporadic and irregular, with a well-marked peak in July but with much variation from clone to clone. The seeds are numerous and extremely small. Local dispersal of seeds is probably mainly by wind, with occasional wider dispersal between dune-systems on the feet of waterfowl, and on footwear or the tyres of vehicles; there may also have been occasional dispersal with planted conifers, but this does not appear to be the primary reason for its recent spread.

P. rotundifolia subsp. *maritima* was originally described from Lancashire by Bennett (1893), and subsequently discovered in Norfolk. Since 1926 it has colonised a series of new sites in Wales and south-western England (Kay, Roberts & Vaughan 1974). Cessation of grazing may have favoured its spread but its survival and persistence at individual dune-slack sites seem to be finely balanced.

The *P. rotundifolia* complex has a circumboreal distribution. *P. rotundifolia* subsp. *maritima* is confined to north-west Europe, from Britain, Ireland and France to southern Scandinavia.

Q. O. N. Kay & R. H. Roberts

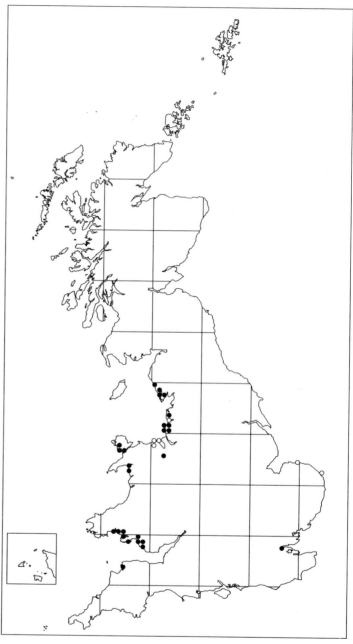

Current map	No	Atlas (S)	No
1970 →	26		
Pre-1970	6		
Introductions	0	All records	15

Pyrola rotundifolia L. subsp. *rotundifolia*

Round-leaved wintergreen

Status: scarce

This species occupies diverse habitats, which are, however, usually calcareous and damp. In England it is primarily a plant of scrubby fens, e.g. former turf ponds in the Norfolk Broads, seasonally damp areas in disused chalk pits, and in coastal dune slacks. In these sites it grows in luxuriant mossy communities, often dominated by *Calliergon cuspidatum* and *Drepanocladus* spp. Usually it is found under willows, with which it may share a mycorrhizal partner. In Scotland it is recorded from open pine woodland, the banks of burns and in gullies on open moorland, and damp montane cliff ledges. It ascends to 680 metres on Guala Mhor, and there are unlocalised records from *c.* 760 metres in the Breadalbanes.

It is an evergreen rhizomatous perennial, flowering from July to September. It is homogamous, pollinated by various insects or self-pollinating. Its seeds are very small, capable of long range wind-borne dispersal, and reliant on a mycobiont for seedling growth and establishment.

It is declining to near extinction in the Norfolk Broads through cessation of turf cutting and reed mowing. It has been lost from at least one disused chalk pit through rubbish tipping. Its ability to colonise such habitats argues for efficient wind-borne seed dispersal, and records from atypical habitats may thus represent chance colonisation where the plant rarely persists. It has been lost from some Scottish moorland sites because of intensive afforestation. It has perhaps been under-recorded as it is vegetatively similar to the other *Pyrola* species.

The *P. rotundifolia* complex has a circumboreal distribution. *P. rotundifolia* subsp. *rotundifolia* occurs in Europe from Scandinavia to the mountains of northern Spain, northern Italy, Bulgaria and the Crimea. It is widespread in Asia east to 120 °E.

An interesting parallel can be drawn with *Liparis loeselii*, a past associate in many Norfolk sites. Both have declining eastern nominate races and slowly increasing west coast dune-slack variants.

F. J. Rumsey

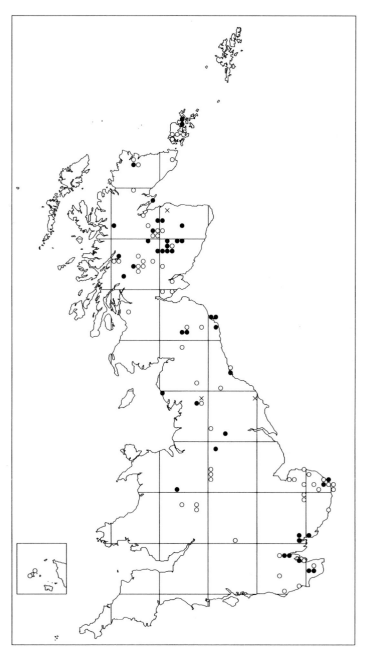

Current map	No	Atlas	No
1970 →	42	1930 →	30
Pre-1970	62	Pre-1930	28
Introductions	3	Introductions	2

Ranunculus arvensis L.
Status: not scarce

Corn buttercup

An annual of cultivated and waste land, this former scourge of cereal crops is normally seen on heavy, and sometimes calcareous, soils. Very few large populations still occur. *R. arvensis*, where it occurs in any quantity, is often found with other rare weeds, including *Euphorbia platyphyllos*, *Petroselinum segetum*, *Scandix pecten-veneris*, *Torilis arvensis* and *Valerianella rimosa*. It has been found to increase in years with no spring cultivations and in years with wet summers and is almost entirely restricted to winter-sown crops.

An annual, its germination is greatest in autumn, with a few further seedlings cropping up in spring. Curved spiny projections on the fruit, which presumably aid dispersal by animals, give this the folk name of Devil's Curry-comb. Buried fruits can remain viable for many years although in one experiment Wilson (1990) found that over 60% of seed germinated within 5 months of sowing.

Once a pernicious weed of arable land, earning it such names as Worrywheat and Starveacre, it was formerly widespread throughout lowland England and Wales and, to a lesser extent, Scotland. It was controlled to some extent by seed-screening but good control was obtained with the herbicides MCPA and 2,4-D developed in the 1940s and 1950s. The distribution of this species has therefore retracted at an astonishing rate, onto isolated arable sites, and it is now found at all frequently only in the midland counties of Warwickshire and Worcestershire. Nevertheless, it has been recorded in over 100 10 km squares since 1980, and it does not yet qualify as a scarce species.

A southern species, it occurs throughout much of lowland Europe, but is declining rapidly in the countries of north-west Europe (Jalas & Suominen 1989). It is also found in north-west Africa and south-west Asia. It is widely introduced elsewhere.

A. Smith

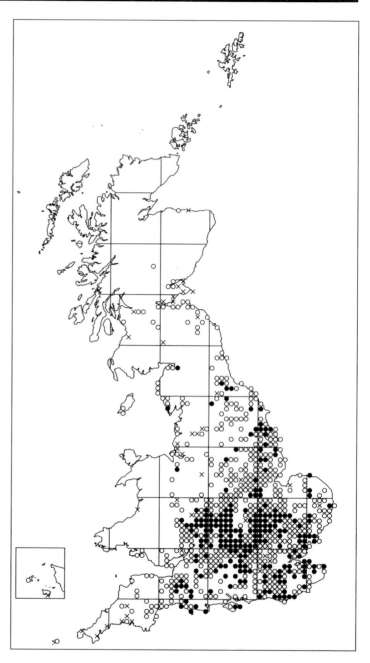

Current map	No	Atlas	No
1970 →	221	1930 →	431
Pre-1970	472	Pre-1930	51
Introductions	39	Introductions	0

continued →

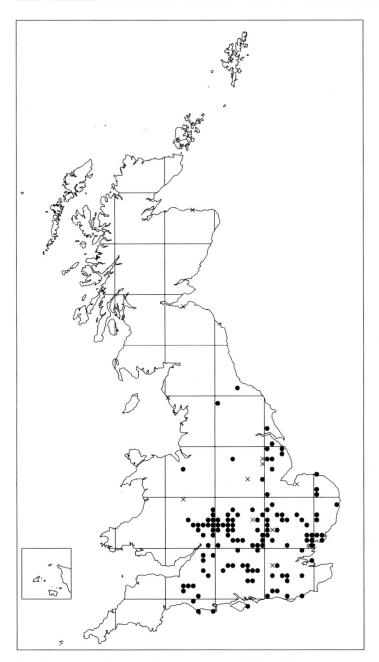

The distribution of *Ranunculus arvensis* from 1980 to 1992.

Ranunculus baudotii Godron

Status: not scarce

Brackish water-crowfoot

R. baudotii is the characteristic water-crowfoot of brackish water that is still or slow-moving. It is now most frequent in ditches in grazing marshes on former saltmarsh, but it also occurs occasionally in pools (including transient pools in dune slacks) and on mud-flats which are only very briefly inundated by the sea. There are a few inland sites with past tidal influence or where the water is brackish due to salt-bearing rocks. It is usually found in shallow water, rarely rooting in over 30 cm of water, and can survive exposure, growing prostrate on wet mud. *R. baudotii* grows in species-poor vegetation, often with *Callitriche* spp., *Potamogeton pectinatus* (particularly if there is some water movement) and *Zannichellia palustris*, where tall emergents are uncommon or suppressed by management. In grazing marshes, it is strongly associated with unfenced ditches in pasture, where stock graze the water's edge and trample the mud. Such conditions occur also in arable land where the drainage channel is regularly managed using a weed bucket. It may be accompanied by *Ceratophyllum submersum* in still water, and by *Ruppia maritima* or very occasionally *R. cirrhosa* on mud flats. In grazing marsh ditches, *R. baudotii* is dominant at intermediate salinity, forming a transition between the richer macrophyte vegetation of fresh water and *Ruppia* beds at high salinities. It is strictly lowland, almost confined to land below 10 metres.

R. baudotii may be either annual or perennial. Although it produces good seed, in disturbed sites or where the ditch vegetation is liable to cutting or dredging, *R. baudotii* spreads by fragments rooting on bare mud (either exposed or submerged). It is thereby able to colonise new sites, but it cannot compete with dense emergents such as *Bolboschoenus maritimus*.

R. baudotii has declined in the last 150 years, particularly on the west coast of Britain and at its few inland sites. Conversion of much coastal pasture to arable, together with the more effective control of tidal water, appear to be responsible for the decline of *R. baudotii* and its associated vegetation.

R. baudotii is distributed along the coasts of Europe south of the Arctic Circle, but is absent from Norway and Iceland; it also occurs in North Africa. It is apparently rare in the eastern Mediterranean. A map of its European distribution is given by Jalas & Suominen (1989).

J. O. Mountford

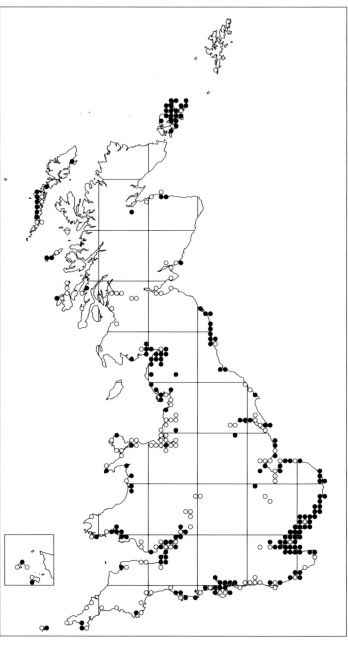

Current map	No	Atlas	No
1970 →	186	1930 →	85
Pre-1970	135	Pre-1930	69
Introductions	0	Introductions	0

Ranunculus parviflorus L.

Status: not scarce

One of the few annual buttercups found in Britain, *R. parviflorus* is a plant of dry open ground, growing in a variety of temporary habitats such as rabbit scrapes, track sides, flower beds, gravel paths, broken turf on cliff edges and building sites. Low competition and some disturbance seem necessary. Associated species are usually commoner annual weeds such as *Cardamine hirsuta*, *Cerastium glomeratum*, *Fumaria* spp., *Veronica arvensis* and *V. polita*.

Strongly opportunist, this species adapts easily to available water and nutrients. Plants can vary from tiny rosettes with a single flower which fruit quickly and dry up, to many-branched individuals up to 30 cm across which may continue flowering from April to Christmas in a damp mild year. Seed is set freely, and winter germination produces cohorts of juveniles which compete for adult space. It appears to have a seedbank as the species may appear irregularly but persistently in an area for decades.

Like many of the more continental annual weeds, *R. parviflorus* has declined from intensive farming, the use of herbicides, and the general 'tidying' of the countryside and settlements.

R. parviflorus is a Mediterranean and western European species, which extends northwards to Britain and Ireland (Jalas & Suominen 1989).

R. FitzGerald

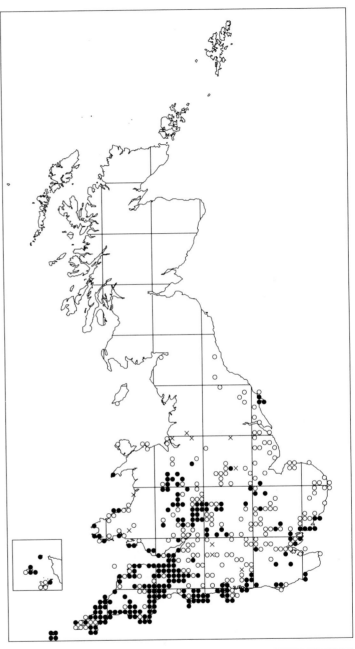

Current map	No	Atlas	No
1970 →	218	1930 →	131
Pre-1970	216	Pre-1930	127
Introductions	10	Introductions	0

Ranunculus tripartitus DC.

Status: scarce

Three-lobed crowfoot

R. tripartitus occurs in shallow but seasonal bodies of water among heaths or related communities, especially shallow ditches and ponds, cart-tracks and gate-ways, wet in winter and spring but dry by summer. The soil base-status and pH are moderately high. Associates include *Apium inundatum*, *Cicendia filiformis*, *Eleogiton fluitans*, *Juncus pygmaeus* (Lizard Peninsula only), *Lythrum portula*, *Pilularia globulifera*, *Potamogeton polygonifolius* and a variety of charophytes. Like other pond and trackway species of heaths and commons, *R. tripartitus* is intolerant of competition from other plant species, needing open sites maintained by fluctuating water levels, grazing and poaching by livestock, and disturbance by traffic.

Typically a winter annual, germinating in autumn and flowering in April and May, earlier than related species. Its sites often dry out completely by June.

R. tripartitus may be under-recorded, partly because of its early flowering, partly from problems of identification. Typical *R. tripartitus* is very local and diminishing through the destruction of heaths, draining or infilling of its habitats, and the cessation of grazing and disturbance which allow development of *Salix aurita* and *S. cinerea* carr. The long viability of its seed allows it to recover if overgrown sites are cleared, provided drainage has not been too severe. The Lizard Peninsula is the only area in Britain where *R. tripartitus* is at all frequent. Plants recorded as *R. lutarius* auct. in the New Forest are actually a pentaploid hybrid between *R. omiophyllus* and *R. tripartitus* (*R.* × *novae-forestae*); the presence of pure *R. tripartitus* in the New Forest has not been confirmed although some of these hybrids are very similar to it (Cook 1966; Webster 1990).

R. tripartitus is very local globally, occurring in north-western Europe from south-west Spain to northern Germany, and is also reported from Greece and Morocco (Jalas & Suominen 1989). It is declining throughout the northern part of its range.

A. J. Byfield

Current map	No	Atlas	No
1970 →	19	1930 →	28
Pre-1970	57	Pre-1930	33
Introductions	0	Introductions	0

continued →

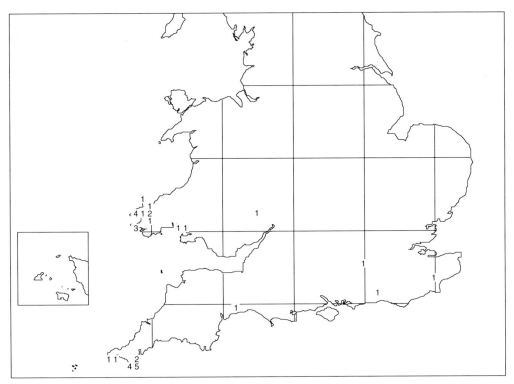

The number of tetrads in each 10 km square in which *Ranunculus tripartitus* has been recorded as a native species from 1970 onwards. The species has been found in a total of 33 tetrads from 1970 onwards.

Rhynchospora fusca (L.) Aiton f.

Status: scarce

Brown beak-sedge

This is a perennial found on wet heaths and the margins of acid bogs, often on bare peat. It usually avoids the very wettest areas. It can be found with *Eleocharis multicaulis*, *Eriophorum angustifolium*, *Juncus bulbosus*, *Narthecium ossifragum*, *Rhynchospora alba* and *Sphagnum* species, and occasionally with *Lycopodiella inundata*, but on bare peat it is often the only species present. It will gradually give way to other plants, particularly *Molinia caerulea*, as the habitat dries out. It is confined to the lowlands.

R. fusca actively spreads by rhizomes. It will readily colonise bare peat, and has re-established itself in sites where the invading vegetation and top 2 cm of peat has been removed. This suggests reproduction by seed, but further work is necessary to establish this. Colonies are usually small, but can occasionally be very large indeed. Dead flowering stems persist through the winter and can be identified as late as March.

The species is certainly declining in southern Britain. It has not been seen in Somerset since 1970, when the site was destroyed by peat cutting. In areas where it has survived habitat destruction, cessation of grazing is a much greater threat now than drainage or improvement. In Dorset, 17 of the 27 sites in which it was recorded in a survey made in 1932-38 are now lost, almost entirely to invading carr. It is holding its own in Wales and it has been discovered at several Scottish localities in recent years: it is currently known in five Scottish vice-counties, compared to two in 1962.

It is widespread in western Ireland, but its current status in central Ireland is unknown. It also occurs in north-western and central Europe, being commoner in the north and west, and in north-eastern America.

D. A. Pearman

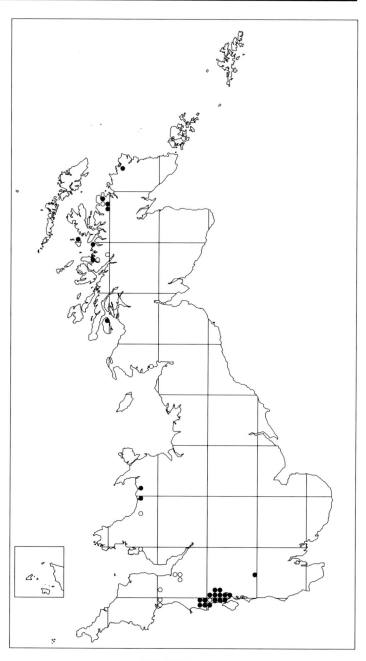

Current map	No	Atlas	No
1970 →	26	1930 →	18
Pre-1970	13	Pre-1930	9
Introductions	0	Introductions	0

continued →

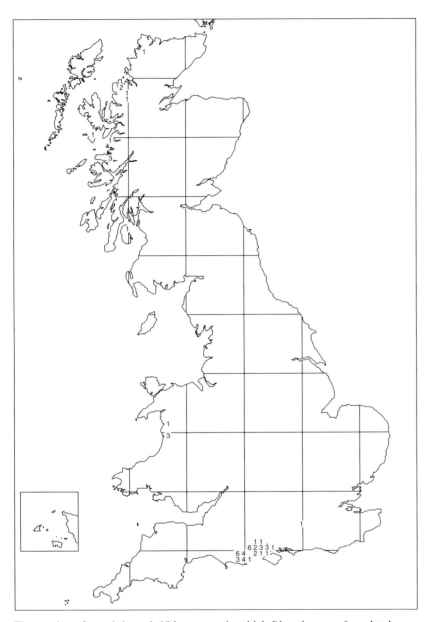

The number of tetrads in each 10 km square in which *Rhynchospora fusca* has been recorded as a native species from 1970 onwards. The species has been found in a total of 55 tetrads from 1970 onwards.

Ribes alpinum L.
Status: scarce

Mountain currant

This is an undershrub of steeply sloping ash woodland on Carboniferous or, more rarely, magnesian limestone. Other woody species such as *Corylus avellana*, *Rhamnus cathartica* and *Taxus baccata* may be present at some sites. It can usually be identified from habit alone, forming trailing mats or 'curtains' over the edges of vertical rocks and small cliffs and in ravines. At woodland margins and in places more accessible to grazing animals, it loses its trailing habit, forming instead small bushes which may be overlooked. Patches can be very large, and very occasionally it is the dominant species. Aspect seems to be unimportant, most colonies being in the sheltered, damper dale bottoms. Formerly it was extensively planted for ornament and hedging, thus explaining its widespread occurrence as an introduction. Even within its native area, the origins of some populations are unclear as some native sites are near to villages. In Britain, it is not, as its name suggests, a mountain species, but a hill plant. It reaches a maximum altitude of 365 metres at Wormhill.

It is dioecious, both sexes being present in most populations. Fruit production is variable, some native populations providing sufficient currants for jelly to be made. It spreads both by fruit dispersal and vegetatively. There is evidence that native populations are able to colonise new sites through seeds dispersed by birds.

Although sites are well-known to local botanists, they are rarely reported; therefore it is unlikely that the plant has diminished as the map suggests. Where colonisation takes place, seedlings thrive only if both grazing and competition from other shrubs are removed.

R. alpinum occurs in the mountains of Europe from Scandinavia south to northern Spain and east to Bulgaria. It is also found in the Caucasus and the Atlas Mountains of Morocco.

R. Smith

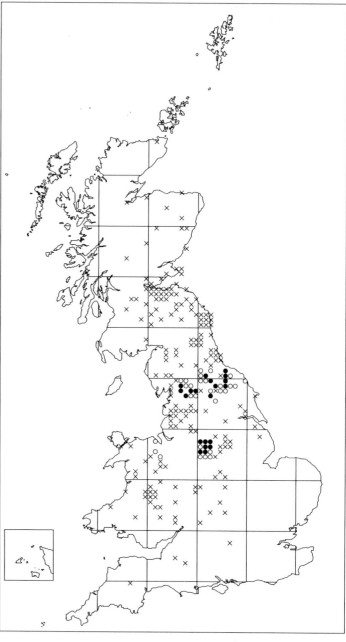

Current map	No	Atlas	No
1970 →	20	1930 →	31
Pre-1970	28	Pre-1930	7
Introductions	179	Introductions	92

Ribes spicatum Robson

Status: scarce

Downy currant

This is a plant of rocky woods on basic soils. In its headquarters in the northern Pennines the plant is very largely restricted to the Carboniferous limestone, and it is locally frequent here in scrubby woodland, and especially in the deeper grikes (or fissures) in limestone pavements. It also grows in strong colonies along some of the streams and rivers draining from the uplands, both in wooded ravines and in broader valleys where a thin strip of trees has been left along rocky river banks. Where it occurs in hedges and along roadsides it is generally impossible to determine whether it has colonised from native sites, been cast-out from cultivation, or been planted. It is a lowland species, but reaching 465 metres above Malham.

R. spicatum is a straggling bush. It is pollinated by insects, but fruit-set seems less frequent than in *R. rubrum*.

R, spicatum is often said to be declining, but many of its habitats are fairly secure, and Graham (1988) suggests that it is more frequently recorded in Durham now than in the past. Identification can only be certain when flowers are present: these pass quickly early in the season, and for this reason the plant is readily overlooked and probably under-recorded.

It is found in northern, and especially eastern, Europe, south to Poland and Romania. Further east it is replaced by related species.

The plant varies a great deal, especially in leaf pubescence, posture of the raceme at flowering, and the prominence of the floral characters. When well-marked, *R. spicatum* is readily distinguishable; less distinct populations, such as some along the Cumbrian R. Eden, may be derived from cultivated plants, or show past or present hybridisation with *R. rubrum*, which is a frequent associate. Indeed, some cultivated currants are said to be a hybrid between the two.

F. J. Roberts

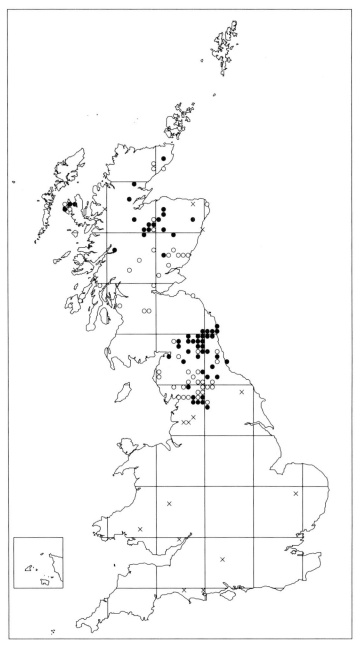

Current map	No	Atlas	No
1970 →	57	1930 →	20
Pre-1970	52	Pre-1930	33
Introductions	16	Introductions	2

Rumex maritimus L.

Status: not scarce

Golden dock

Like its relatives *R. palustris*, *Persicaria laxiflora* and *P. minor*, this species is part of the distinctive vegetation that develops on wet nutrient-rich mud as the water-level in ditches, pools and reservoirs falls through the summer. Other typical associates include *Bidens* spp. and *Chenopodium* spp. *R. maritimus* prefers wet, well-illuminated sites that are often calcareous and rich in both nitrogen and phosphorus. Despite the scientific name, *R. maritimus* is not confined to the coastal zone, though it is tolerant of mildly saline conditions. Although most common on silt and wet gravel in the flood plains of major rivers, suitable situations occur also on old peat cuttings or in wet hollows within grassland. Its chief requirement is for sites with a strongly varying water level where water lies through winter and late into the spring, creating conditions that are inimical for both exacting aquatic and terrestrial species. Such conditions occur on the shores of Breckland meres, for example. *R. maritimus* is a rare casual on spent ballast and other dry open habitats. Its native distribution is strictly lowland.

R. maritimus is an annual, producing ample seed, and is a pioneer species that is able to colonise new habitats efficiently. Plants can sometimes overwinter and flower again in their second year. In Europe it is an indicator of warm areas, needing a long summer and autumn that evaporates pools and allows seed to mature.

R. maritimus has declined sharply in Britain in the last 150 years, due to the elimination of farm ponds and surplus ditches, the drainage of wet grassland and the increased regulation of water levels (Mountford & Sheail 1989). However, its late flowering and fruiting, together with its use of transient habitats, may lead to it having been overlooked in some areas recently. For example, it is certainly more widespread than was thought in the Cambridgeshire Fenland. It may be encouraged by a more *laissez faire* attitude to water management and the continued use of ponds by stock and waterfowl.

R. maritimus is somewhat continental in its distribution, being found throughout most of Europe but absent toward the Arctic and the Mediterranean, and rare on the Atlantic seaboard (Jalas & Suominen 1979). It occurs through temperate Asia as far as northern India, China and Japan. In the Americas, it is represented by subsp. *fueginus* which is found from Quebec and Alaska to Tierra del Fuego, but is mainly montane in the tropics.

J. O. Mountford

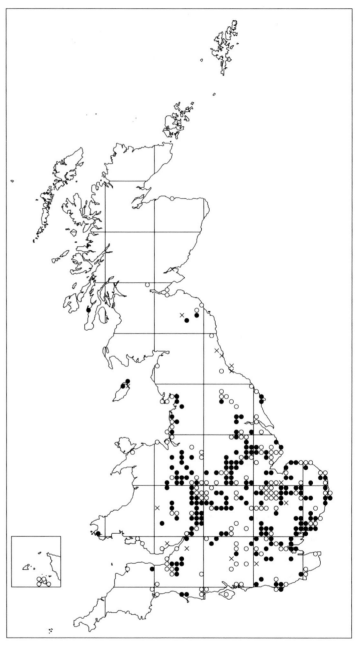

Current map	No	Atlas	No
1970 →	191	1930 →	83
Pre-1970	148	Pre-1930	61
Introductions	14	Introductions	3

Rumex palustris Smith

Status: not scarce

Marsh dock

R. palustris grows in very similar habitats to *R. maritimus*; indeed the two species have often been observed together. Typical of wet nutrient-rich mud exposed in late summer and autumn, *R. palustris* is somewhat more terrestrial and ruderal than its relative. Although most common by ponds and ditches, *R. palustris* also occurs in wet depressions in grassland, on newly cut peat, by gravel pits and, within its core range, as a frequent weed of spoil dredged from rivers and drainage channels. Like *R. maritimus*, it is a rare weed in dry open sites, particularly as a ballast casual. It occurs naturally only in the lowlands.

R. palustris is normally a biennial or short-lived perennial, although occasionally behaving as an annual. It reproduces entirely by seed, which is produced in great numbers. Like *R. maritimus*, it is a pioneer, being able to colonise new sites where competition is low. Its dependence on wet mud and varying water levels means that its population size in any one year may be greatly affected by the weather.

Although *R. palustris* is declining in Britain, the trend is not so pronounced as in *R. maritimus*, and, though less widespread overall, it remains significantly commoner than its relative in some areas e.g. the Fenland and the Somerset Levels and Moors. *R. palustris* has also suffered from the landscape being more intensively managed and would benefit from the creation of more ponds, particularly if their level was allowed to vary naturally and their shores were to be grazed and trampled by stock or waterfowl.

R. palustris is much less widespread than *R. maritimus*. It occurs through most of central Europe, but is absent from Ireland, Fennoscandia and the Iberian peninsula, and rare in Italy and the Balkans (Jalas & Suominen 1979). It extends into European Russia and temperate western Asia, but reaches neither Siberia nor the Americas.

J. O. Mountford

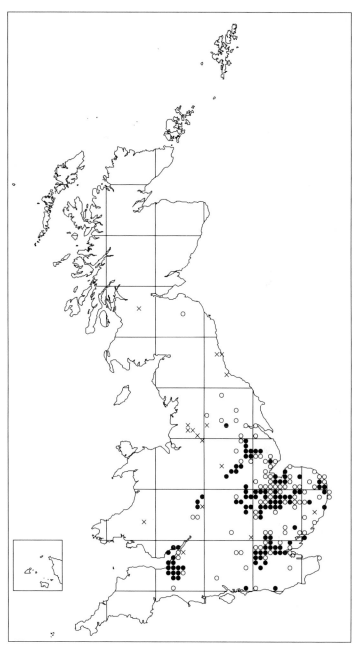

Current map	No	Atlas	No
1970 →	101	1930 →	69
Pre-1970	92	Pre-1930	33
Introductions	16	Introductions	6

Ruppia cirrhosa (Petagna) Grande
Status: scarce

Spiral tasselweed

This is an aquatic species which grows in soft sediments in brackish water in ditches, ponds, coastal lagoons, tidal inlets and lakes near the sea. Unlike the commoner *R. maritima*, *R. cirrhosa* is rarely found in very shallow water. It can be dominant in brackish sites in which few other vascular macrophytes grow. In The Fleet, a coastal lagoon separated from the sea by Chesil Beach, it grows in abundance with *Zostera angustifolia* and *Z. noltii*.

R. cirrhosa is a perennial species which flowers rather sparingly. Flowering plants regularly set seed, but little is known of the circumstances required for germination.

R. cirrhosa is similar to *R. maritima*, and vegetative plants cannot always be identified with certainty. This taxonomic difficulty, coupled with the fact that aquatics are less well recorded than terrestrial species, means that it is probably under-recorded. Despite the relatively high proportion of pre-1970 records, there is no conclusive evidence that this species has declined.

It is widespread on the coasts of Europe from the Mediterranean area to Iceland and northern Scandinavia. The world distribution of *R. cirrhosa* is in doubt because of confusion with related species, but it is reported from Asia, Africa, North and South America and Australasia.

C. D. Preston

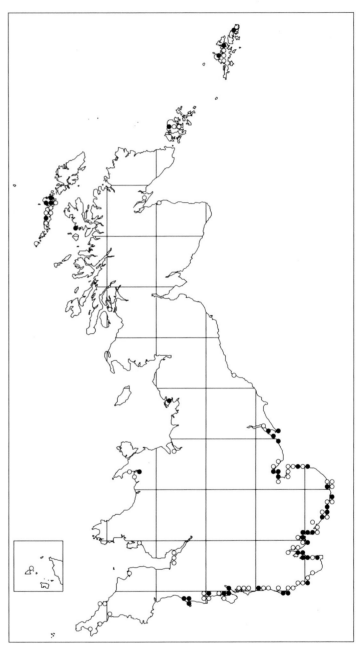

Current map	No	Atlas	No
1970 →	46	1930 →	13
Pre-1970	70	Pre-1930	43
Introductions	0	Introductions	0

Sagina saginoides (L.) Karsten

Status: scarce

Alpine pearlwort

S. saginoides is a relict, high montane plant which descends to low levels in the far north of Scotland. It is a small herb needing freedom from competition, which it finds on unstable, frost-heaved soils or steep ground, and in places blasted by wind or covered with snow until well into the spring. Its substrates are usually fairly base-rich and well-drained, though sometimes slightly moist through water seepage. Its associates include a wide variety of mosses, liverworts and lichens, and low herbs such as *Alchemilla alpina, Carex bigelowii, Festuca ovina* agg., *Gnaphalium supinum, Juncus trifidus, J. triglumis, Minuartia sedoides, Persicaria vivipara, Saxifraga aizoides, Sibbaldia procumbens, Silene acaulis* and *Thalictrum alpinum*. Most of its sites are in the range of 700-900 metres reaching 1200 metres on Ben Lawers and falling to 460 metres on the Old Man of Storr.

This is a perennial herb, but little is known about its modes of reproduction.

S. saginoides has rather few post-1970 records, but this is probably because of lack of recent recording rather than any decline. It is also readily overlooked, and its small size gives protection against the direct effects of grazing. Global warming would be the most obvious threat to its status, which otherwise seems fairly secure.

S. saginoides is a widespread arctic-alpine plant of northern latitudes and high mountain ranges of temperate regions in both the Old and New Worlds. Its European distribution is mapped by Jalas & Suominen (1983).

D. A. Ratcliffe

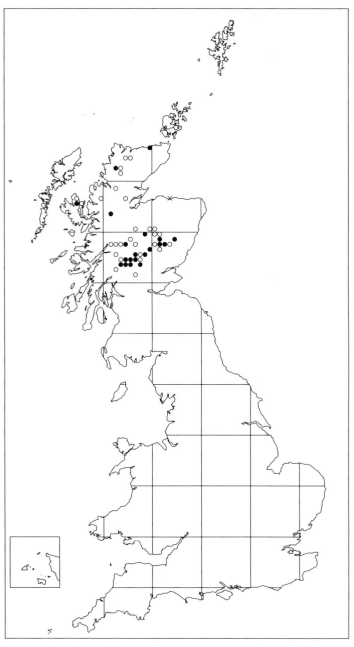

Current map	No	Atlas	No
1970 →	20	1930 →	29
Pre-1970	28	Pre-1930	10
Introductions	1	Introductions	0

Salicornia pusilla J. Woods
Status: scarce

One-flowered glasswort

S. pusilla is confined to the uppermost levels of coastal saltmarshes, especially at about the level of normal tides. Dense stands, perhaps mixed with other diploid *Salicornia* species, grow in saltmarsh pans and amongst upper marsh *Puccinellia maritima*. It may be commoner on saltmarshes with low sediment accretion rates. An additional habitat is saline fields behind sea walls, where there is saltwater seepage and where cattle maintain patches of disturbed ground.

This species is always annual, and reproduces exclusively by seed. Dispersal is by mature branches (containing the seeds) becoming detached from the plant and either falling directly to the ground, or being moved by water currents for varying distances.

There is little to suggest that this species has declined nationally. However, the spread of *Spartina anglica* has been blamed for its disappearance from Poole Harbour.

Outside the British Isles, *S. pusilla* appears to be restricted to the north coast of Brittany and the Pas de Calais (Jalas & Suominen 1980).

This species is morphologically plastic, ranging from unbranched forms (possibly caused by nutrient- or water- stress), to very strongly branched plants on upturned turfs and earth dug from borrow pits and drains. An occasional variant is grey-green with the fertile segments scarcely compressed and the branches consequently nearly cylindrical, but these apparently distinctive features vanish in cultivation. The strikingly prostrate variant is genetically controlled. This species is sometimes confused with other diploids, especially before the normal three-flowered cymules have developed fully and only the larger central flower is visible. The one-flowered cymules characteristic of this species are very rare in other members of the genus, and are confined to genetic mutations.

D. H. Dalby

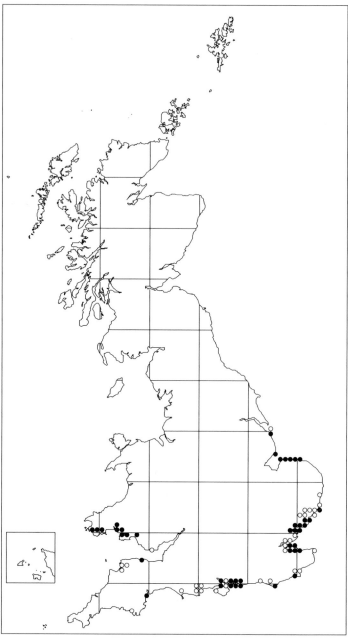

Current map	No	Atlas	No
1970 →	42	1930 →	32
Pre-1970	32	Pre-1930	11
Introductions	0	Introductions	0

Salix arbuscula L.
Status: scarce

Mountain willow

This low shrub grows on base-rich mountains. It is found in moist or wet conditions such as flushes, in gravelly soil inundated by mountain burns, or on damp ledges on calcareous rock. Its main associates are *Alchemilla glabra*, *Saxifraga aizoides* and *S. oppositifolia*. Other patterns of association depend on grazing pressure, and on ungrazed ledges it often grows with a wide range of calcicolous tall herbs. It occurs at altitudes ranging from 460 metres on Ben Lui to 870 metres on Carn Gorm in Glen Lyon.

Seed is produced in quantity in dense colonies, and must be the main means of reproduction. The discrete form of most bushes indicates that vegetative spread is not a significant factor in reproduction. As seedlings require predominantly bare soil and freedom from competition in order to establish (Stace 1975), few will develop under stable conditions. It is likely that the landslips and rockfalls occurring in montane habitats are necessary in order to create the conditions for significant seedling establishment.

In the Southern Uplands *S. arbuscula* has not been recorded since 1934. There are insufficient data to show any changes in its distribution in the Scottish Highlands. Grazing, and the habitat changes resulting from it, have undoubtedly affected its distribution by destroying plants or parts of plants, thereby reducing seed production and preventing regeneration. However, some dense stands of procumbent plants, surviving heavy sheep-grazing, suggest that mature *S. arbuscula* may be more tolerant of grazing than most other montane willows. Scattered or isolated individuals may represent occasional colonists but are more probably survivors of once more numerous populations.

It is an arctic-alpine, Eurasiatic species, found in Scotland, Scandinavia, arctic Russia and the Urals, to Siberia and central Asia. Its European distribution is mapped by Jalas & Suominen (1976). Records from mountain ranges further south in Europe are based on misidentifications of other members of the *S. arbuscula* group (Meikle 1984).

Its distribution in Britain, especially at the edges of its range, is somewhat unclear because of confusion with small-leaved plants of *S. myrsinifolia*, *S. myrsinites*, *S. phylicifolia* and with large plants of *S. herbacea*.

D. K. Mardon

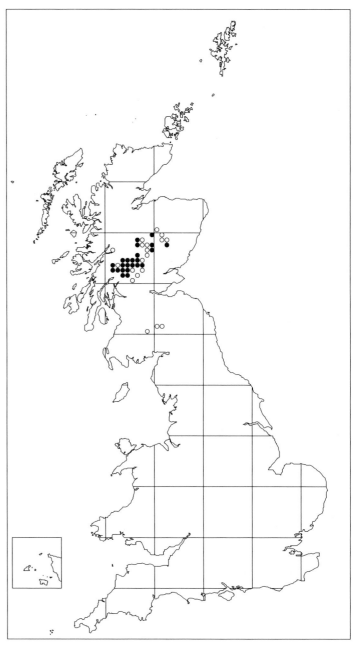

Current map	No	Atlas	No
1970 →	23	1930 →	15
Pre-1970	19	Pre-1930	9
Introductions	0	Introductions	0

Salix lapponum L.
Status: scarce

Downy willow

This is a shrub of moist to wet, enriched sites on mountains. It tolerates a wider range of soil conditions than most other montane willows, but its natural range and habitat preferences are masked by the pressure of grazing, which confines *S. lapponum* largely to cliffs or rocky sites. Associated species are many but often include *Deschampsia cespitosa*, *Luzula sylvatica*, *S. myrsinifolia* or *S. phylicifolia* and *Vaccinium myrtillus*. On base-rich sites it can occur with rarer montane willows such as *S. lanata* and, on ungrazed ledges, with tall herbs such as *Geranium sylvaticum* and *Solidago virgaurea*. It grows at altitudes from 200 metres in the Ochils to 900 metres at Coire Garbhlach.

Seed is produced in quantity in colonies with numerous male and female plants, and significant reproduction by seed can occur on sites with regular landslips and rockfalls. However, at many sites plants are too isolated for effective pollination to occur (Mardon 1990) and few if any seeds are produced. But, as seedlings require predominantly bare soil and freedom from competition in order to establish (Meikle 1975), few will develop under stable conditions. Where such stable conditions develop, the ground stratum may provide a good medium for vegetative spread.

At many of the montane sites on which *S. lapponum* can survive, with protection from grazing, the natural instability results in progressive loss of plants. Small colonies or isolated plants produce little or no seed and are unable to reproduce. Such colonies observed regularly appear to be in steady decline (Mardon 1990). However, data are not available to demonstrate that a clear decline in range has taken place.

S. lapponum is a Eurasian species which is widely distributed in Scandinavia, northern Russia, and Siberia, but rare in central France, the Pyrenees, central Europe, the Balkans and southern Russia. In the Alps it is replaced by the closely related *S. helvetica* Vill. For a map of the European distribution of *S. lapponum*, see Jalas & Suominen (1976).

D. K. Mardon

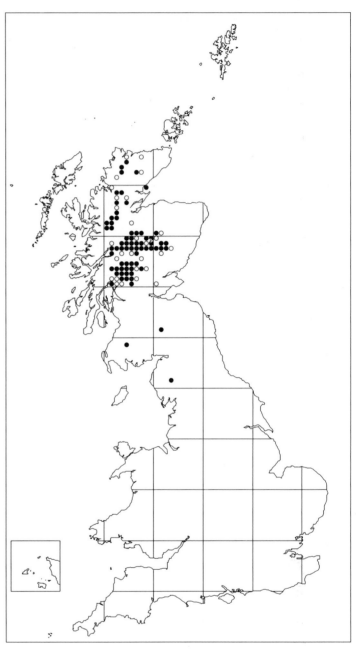

Current map	No	Atlas	No
1970 →	68	1930 →	50
Pre-1970	28	Pre-1930	11
Introductions	0	Introductions	0

Salix myrsinifolia Salisb.

Status: not scarce

Dark-leaved willow

This species is a shrub, or less often a small tree up to 4 metres high, locally abundant on rocky or gravelly river-banks and lake-shores, less frequent in thickets on marshy ground or by the margins of wet woodland. It is commonly associated with *S. aurita*, *S. caprea* and *S. cinerea*, with which it hybridises. Like most willows, it is intolerant of shade, and will not survive for long under taller trees. It is usually a lowland species, but in Scotland it sometimes grows as a dwarf, spreading shrub on wet rock-faces at altitudes up to 940 metres on Stob Binnein.

The distribution of *S. myrsinifolia* appears to be stable. In East Anglia it was reported from Norfolk in 1820, but subsequently overlooked by British botanists until it was discovered in quantity in Cambridgeshire in 1980 (Donald 1981).

S. myrsinifolia spreads by seed, and is an efficient colonist of moist, open sites. Old specimens will occasionally fall and layer themselves, forming small single-clone thickets.

It is widely distributed in northern and central Europe eastwards to Siberia, and south to Italy (Jalas & Suominen 1976). In Ireland, *S. myrsinifolia* is restricted as a native to a few of the northern counties where it is rare (Harron 1992) and apparently declining. It occurs elsewhere in Ireland as an introduction, sometimes becoming a locally successful colonist.

Normally *S. myrsinifolia* is readily distinguishable from similar species by the fact that damaged or bruised leaves rapidly turn black and most bushes exhibit some blackened foliage. In central Scotland it tends to hybridise with *S. phylicifolia* forming populations of *S. × tetrapla* Walker. Such populations mask the distinctions between the two parent species and are evidently of ancient origin, since they are to be found in areas where pure *S. phylicifolia* is no longer present (Meikle 1992).

R. D. Meikle

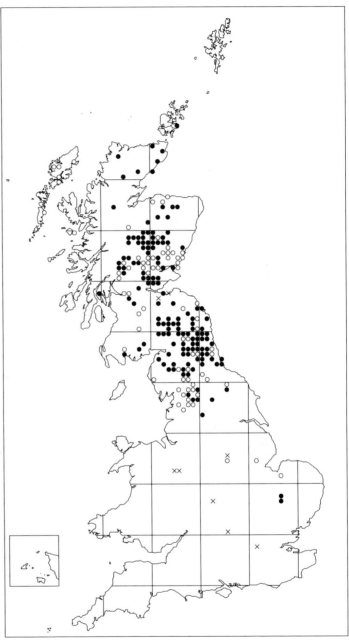

Current map	No	Atlas	No
1970 →	141	1930 →	75
Pre-1970	73	Pre-1930	32
Introductions	8	Introductions	7

Salix myrsinites L.
Status: scarce

Whortle-leaved willow

This low shrub grows in enriched moist or wet sites, mainly on mountains, where it is largely restricted to ungrazed or lightly grazed areas. The variety of associated species appears to reflect the wide range of soil conditions tolerated by *S. myrsinites*, e.g. *Calluna vulgaris*, *Dryas octopetala*, *Salix reticulata* and a wide range of tall herbs on base-rich mountain cliff ledges. Constant associations have not been recorded. Its sites range in altitude from 220 metres at Inchnadamph to 915 metres on Ben Alder.

Observations of *S. myrsinites* plants at Inchnadamph National Nature Reserve, where some are within exclosures built in 1959, suggest that vegetative spread is insignificant and that seedling establishment is constrained by the surrounding vegetation cover. Apparently fertile but immature fruits were observed in quantity. As seedlings require predominantly bare soil and freedom from competition in order to establish (Meikle 1975), few will develop under stable conditions. Presumably the areas of bare soil and freedom from competition resulting from landslips and rockfalls on montane sites provide the conditions for reproduction by seed.

Data are insufficient to show current trends in the species' abundance and range. There is some evidence that, like *S. lapponum*, isolated colonies may be in decline. However, like *S. arbuscula*, the procumbent habit predominant among British *S. myrsinites* plants may render them more tolerant of grazing than *S. lapponum*.

S. myrsinites is an arctic-alpine, Eurasiatic species recorded from Scotland, Scandinavia, northern Russia, the Urals, Siberia and north-eastern Asia. Records from the Pyrenees and central Europe are misidentifications (Meikle 1984). For a map of its European distribution, see Jalas & Suominen (1976).

D. K. Mardon

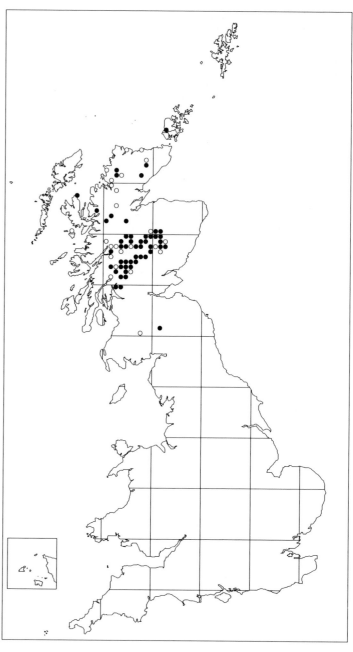

Current map	No	Atlas	No
1970 →	50	1930 →	30
Pre-1970	24	Pre-1930	9
Introductions	0	Introductions	0

Salix reticulata L.

Status: scarce

Net-leaved willow

S. reticulata is a plant of montane rock-ledges. It has stringent soil requirements, growing with few exceptions on limestone or calcareous schist. On large outcrops it is better able to survive rock-falls, droughts and grazing, as vegetative spread from surrounding plants can re-populate a denuded area. Small outcrops rarely harbour the plant. Associates include *Dryas octopetala*, *Galium boreale*, *Persicaria vivipara*, *Polystichum lonchitis*, *Saxifraga nivalis* and *Silene acaulis*. Only found in the higher hills of Scotland, its altitude range is 680 metres in Glen Doll to 1125 metres on Ben Lawers; it is rarely found at the lower end of its altitudinal range.

S. reticulata is a creeping perennial dwarf shrub spreading by means of rhizomes and rooting stems. It usually flowers well but on Creag an Lochain Meikle (1977) found that nearly all the plants were male. Nevertheless regeneration appeared active. Regeneration is usually obvious elsewhere.

It is not clear whether this species is currently spreading or is in decline. Donald Patton studied Beinn Laoigh in 1920-1923 (Patton 1924), and was unable to find *S. reticulata*, even though Peter Ewing had found it years before. Since about 1960 it has become quite easy to find there (Roger 1975) suggesting that the plant may be subject to periods of advance and withdrawal (or that more people have been searching!).

The distribution of *S. reticulata* is typically arctic-alpine, being almost circumpolar but absent from Iceland and Greenland. Its European distribution is mapped by Jalas & Suominen (1976).

A. Slack

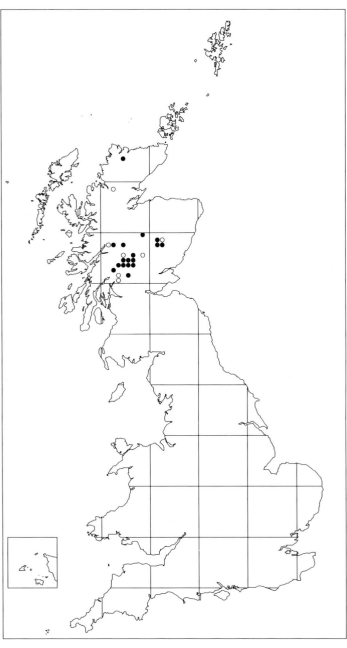

Current map	No	Atlas	No
1970 →	17	1930 →	12
Pre-1970	7	Pre-1930	5
Introductions	0	Introductions	0

Sarcocornia perennis (Miller) A.J. Scott

Status: scarce

Perennial glasswort

This is a plant of saltmarshes and drift-lines, especially on bare or sparsely vegetated areas and gravelly substrates. It occurs at many levels on the shore, on eroding lower parts of saltmarshes, and at higher levels along drift-lines and on shell and shingle banks. Occasionally it can also be found on bare ground above the drift-line, for example on trackways behind sea-walls. Unlike *Suaeda vera*, with which it often occurs, it rarely forms extensive stands. Other associated species depend on the situation, but in saltmarshes they frequently include *Atriplex portulacoides*, *Limonium vulgare*, *Puccinellia maritima* and *Salicornia europaea sensu lato*.

S. perennis is a woody perennial, flowering from August to September and fruiting from October to November. Germination is in the spring. Seedlings can be easily overlooked amongst annual *Salicornia* spp., but adult plants form conspicuous 'bushes' up to 1 metre across.

S. perennis has probably always been scarce in Britain, and its distributional limits have changed very little during the present century. At many of its currently known localities it occurs in small and fragmentary stands or as just a few widely scattered 'bushes'; this suggests that it could be present but undetected in many of the squares from which it has not been reported since 1970.

This species grows on the coasts of southern and western Europe, and is at its northern limit in Britain (Jalas & Suominen 1980). It also occurs in Algeria.

S. J. Leach

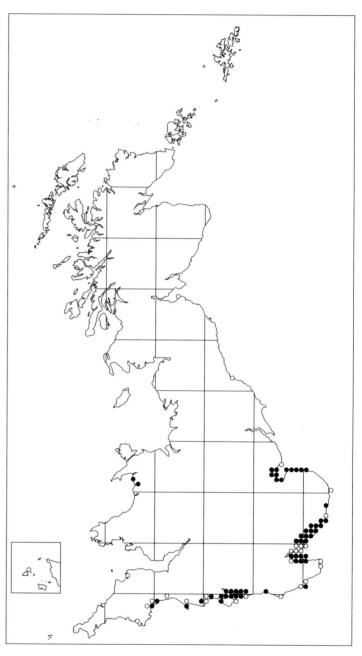

Current map	No	Atlas	No
1970 →	53	1930 →	37
Pre-1970	27	Pre-1930	13
Introductions	0	Introductions	0

Saxifraga nivalis L.

Status: scarce

Alpine saxifrage

This is a plant of periodically irrigated rocks or open vegetation on the ledges of mountain crags, usually in shaded sites where the rock is strongly base-rich. It seems rather intolerant of competition and is absent from the tall herb-rich vegetation on the larger ledges of montane crags. It is most frequent in pockets and crevices of damp, calcareous, mica-schist crags where associates may include *Cystopteris fragilis*, *Saxifraga oppositifolia*, *Sedum rosea* and, more rarely, *Veronica fruticans* and *Woodsia alpina*. Frequent bryophyte associates include *Grimmia funalis* and *G. torquata*. It reaches 1125 metres on Ben Lawers, but descends to lower altitudes in the west, down to 365 metres on Quiraing.

S. nivalis is a perennial species, readily setting seed in its Scottish localities but not in Cumbria.

There is no real evidence of any decline in Scotland. It is probably still present in many of the 10 km squares for which only pre-1970 records are available. Cumbrian populations are extremely small and vulnerable.

It has a circumboreal distribution, extending south in Europe to northern Germany, and occurring in Asia, eastern North America and Greenland.

G. P. Rothero

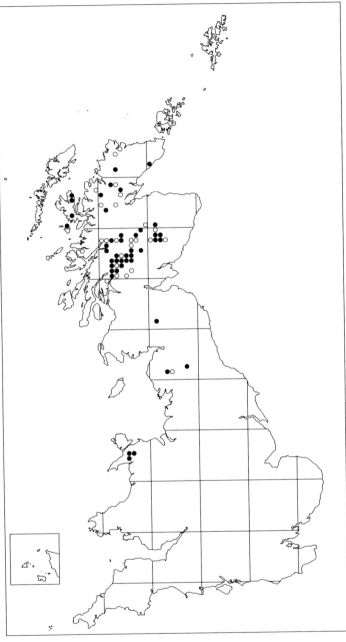

Current map	No	Atlas	No
1970 →	43	1930 →	42
Pre-1970	25	Pre-1930	14
Introductions	0	Introductions	0

Scandix pecten-veneris L.

Status: scarce

Shepherd's-needle

This is characteristically an arable weed on soils which are dry in summer, often heavy, calcareous clays. It is associated with other uncommon weed species, such as *Euphorbia platyphyllos*, *Fumaria densiflora*, *Lithospermum arvense*, *Kickxia elatine*, *Papaver argemone*, *P. hybridum*, *Petroselinum segetum*, *Ranunculus arvensis* and *Valerianella dentata*. However, it often occurs in species-poor weed communities where it is the only uncommon species. It is also known to occur in a number of semi-natural sites on coastal screes, perhaps indicating its mode of existence prior to the development of agriculture, and maybe serving as refugia.

An annual, *S. pecten-veneris* has its main period of germination from October to early November, followed by a smaller crop of seedlings in spring. Its autumn-germinating seedlings are prone to being eradicated by pre-sowing cultivations associated with winter cereal crops but it is nevertheless almost entirely restricted to winter-sown crops. Wilson (1990) has shown that in one experiment 53-99.5% of seeds germinated within 3 months of sowing, indicating a low level of seed dormancy, and reducing the species' ability to survive those periods of farming which are detrimental to its growth.

This is a lowland species which was once widespread as a weed of arable land and so abundant at times that it impeded mechanical harvesters. After 1955, the introduction of chemical herbicides such as MCPA and 2,4-D initiated a rapid decline, as demonstrated on the Broadbalk plots at the Rothamsted Experimental Station. It appears to have fared best in a small area of West Suffolk where it still regularly achieves pest proportions and where it seems resistant to the herbicides used and competes well with the intensively farmed winter cereal crops. Although there are records from 131 10 km squares from 1970 onwards, this declining species is classified as scarce as it has been recorded in only 85 10 km squares since 1980.

Its distribution in Europe is centred on the Mediterranean, extending westwards to Britain and northwards to Denmark; the species occurs only as a casual in Scandinavia. It has declined considerably in north-west Europe as well as in eastern Europe. Its range includes North Africa and an area extending from south-west Asia to the borders of India. It occurs as an introduction in North and South America, southern Africa, Australia and New Zealand.

A. Smith

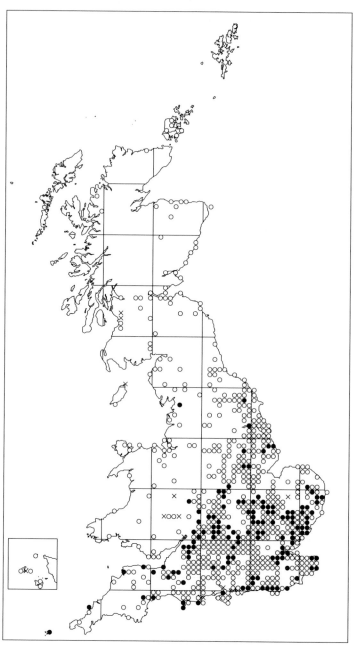

Current map	No	Atlas	No
1970 →	131	1930 →	451
Pre-1970	534	Pre-1930	54
Introductions	11	Introductions	0

continued →

Scandix pecten-veneris
continued

Shepherd's-needle

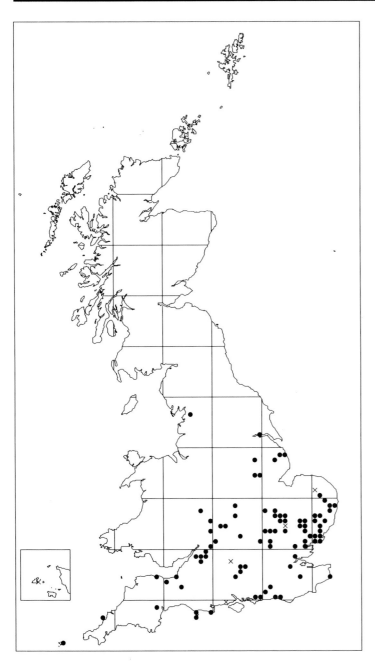

The distribution of *Scandix pecten-veneris* from 1980 to 1992.

Scilla autumnalis L.

Status: scarce

Autumn squill

S. autumnalis grows on terrace gravels by the Thames, dune sands on the Isle of Wight, and Carboniferous and Devonian limestones, schists, serpentine and greenstone in south-west England. It survives near the Thames in acidic grass-heath on golf courses where the dominants include *Agrostis capillaris*, *A. vinealis*, *Calluna vulgaris* and *Festuca ovina*. The Devonian limestones support *Bupleurum baldense* and *Helianthemum apenninum* as well as abundant *S. autumnalis*. At the Lizard Peninsula its open habitats support numerous associates including *Herniaria ciliolata* and *Minuartia verna*. In the Channel Islands it is abundant on gneiss with other geophytes such as *Ophioglossum lusitanicum* and *Romulea columnae* and therophytes including *Poa infirma*. It is confined to the lowlands.

The bulbs of *S. autumnalis* tolerate long dry periods but promptly resume growth when moistened. Flowering in late summer precedes the appearance of the overwintering leaves. Bulbs are long-lived; seed is freely produced and may be scattered from the capsules of the persistent infructescences up to 40 cm. Germination usually takes place in autumn.

Some of its Thames valley sites (e.g. Chelsea) have been built over, and it has greatly decreased in the Avon Gorge at Bristol since the 18th century, but it remains locally very abundant on, or near, the coasts of Devon, Cornwall and the Channel Islands, especially where periodic droughts on the shallow skeletal soils reduce competition from more aggressive but more mesophytic species such as *Prunus spinosa* and *Ulex europaeus*, or introduced species such as *Quercus ilex*. Only on deeper soils (often with *Scilla verna*) are grazing, mowing or burning necessary to prevent succession to heath or scrub.

A species of southern and western Europe, extending along the Atlantic coast to Britain. It is also found in north-west Africa and Asia east to Iran.

Two cytological races occur in Britain: a tetraploid from E. Cornwall eastwards, and also in Jersey, and a hexaploid in the south of Cornwall and in Guernsey (Ainsworth, Parker & Horton 1983, J.S. Parker and L.C. Frost *in litt.*).

C. Chatters & D. E. Coombe

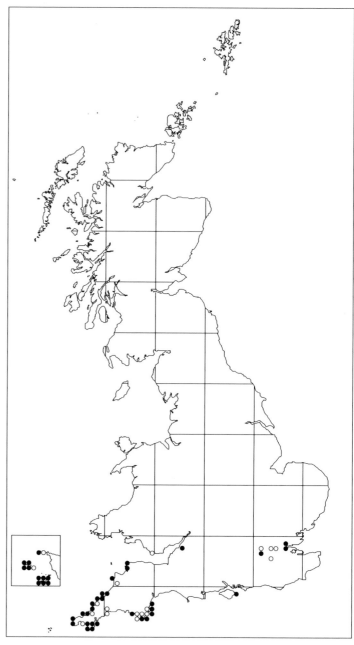

Current map	No	Atlas	No
1970 →	29	1930 →	23
Pre-1970	16	Pre-1930	9
Introductions	0	Introductions	0

Scrophularia umbrosa Dumort.

Status: not scarce

Green figwort

This species usually grows at the sides of rivers and streams, but is also found in damp woodland. It grows in fertile soils, often in vegetation dominated by *Phalaris arundinacea* and with associates such as *Butomus umbellatus*, *Caltha palustris*, *Iris pseudacorus*, *Oenanthe crocata*, *Schoenoplectus lacustris* and *Scirpus sylvaticus*. There is some negative association with *S. auriculata*, which may replace it, at least in more open situations in the south where *S. auriculata* is common. *S. umbrosa* occurs in both open and shaded situations. At one locality it grows in cracks in sun-baked retaining walls near a river, though there is some water seepage through the soil. It is confined to the lowlands.

S. umbrosa is a perennial which spreads by a compact rhizome. It reproduces by seed, which probably germinates mainly in the spring and does not form a persistent seed bank. Individuals may be scattered amongst other species or form small stands.

S. umbrosa has increased markedly in abundance this century in several of the regions in which it is now frequent. It was, for example, first recorded as a rarity in Norfolk in 1904, in Berwickshire in 1852 and in Angus in 1910, in all of which it is now locally frequent. Despite its similarity with *S. auriculata*, former confusion between the two species does not seem to explain the apparent increase. *S. umbrosa* may even be a relatively recent coloniser of Britain, perhaps distributed by wildfowl, which could explain its scattered distribution outwith its main centres.

It is a continental species, occurring in central and eastern Europe, north to southern Scandinavia, and Asia as far east as Tibet.

M. E. Braithwaite

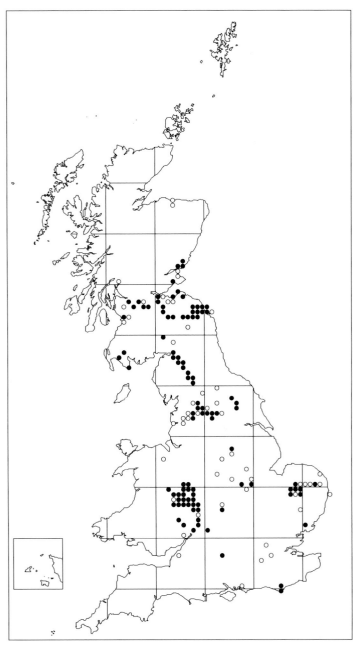

Current map	No	Atlas	No
1970 →	101	1930 →	36
Pre-1970	52	Pre-1930	32
Introductions	0	Introductions	0

Sedum forsterianum Smith

Rock stonecrop

Status: scarce

This is a very local species occurring on rocks and screes. It can grow in open, dry situations, or in wet woodland. In Britain the more usual habitat is open rock faces and broken cliffs, often near the sea. It is found in open grassland communities and occurs with other rare or scarce species, including *Helianthemum apenninum*, *Inula conyza*, *Scilla autumnalis* and *Trinia glauca*. Its commoner associates include *Dactylis glomerata*, *Festuca ovina*, *Koeleria macrantha*, *Pilosella officinarum*, *Plantago lanceolata*, *Sedum acre*, *S. album* and *Thymus polytrichus*. It is grown as a rockery plant in gardens and over graves in churchyards, and it has occasionally become established in the wild from discarded stock. The altitudinal range of *S. forsterianum* is from sea level on the west coast to 600 metres at Llyn-y-fan Fach in the Black Mountains.

It is a perennial plant with creeping stems forming mats. Short ascending stems are sterile, whilst flowering stems are much longer. It is known to spread vegetatively.

S. forsterianum seems to have become more common throughout its western range. It may have benefited from increased grazing as it can easily spread into open ground by broken-off stems, and it is not palatable.

In Europe it has an essentially western distribution, occurring from southern Spain north to Britain, and it is often found in damper situations than in Britain. It is also reported from Morocco

Populations are variable and it was previously thought that two subspecies could be recognised. They have not been maintained by Stace (1991).

L. Farrell

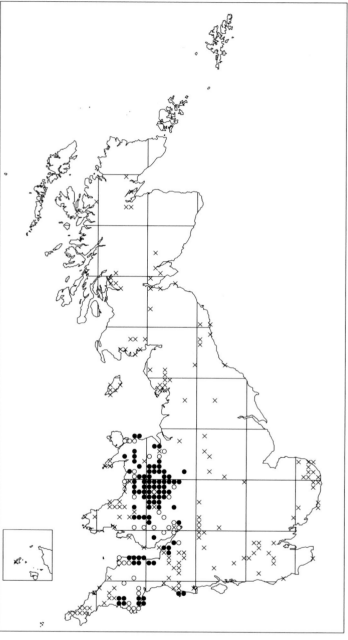

Current map	No	Atlas	No
1970 →	87	1930 →	53
Pre-1970	36	Pre-1930	20
Introductions	152	Introductions	54

Sedum villosum L.

Status: scarce

Hairy stonecrop

This species is found in stony bryophyte-dominated flushes that are only slightly base-rich, often on rather level ground beside streams amongst species-poor hill grassland or heather moorland. Most sites are in areas which receive 75-150 cm of rainfall per annum. The bryophytes *Calliergon cuspidatum* and *Philonotis fontana* are typical associates, often with *Plagiomnium ellipticum*, but *Cratoneuron commutatum* is infrequent. Higher plants in association are often dwarfed and sparse and are a variable mix of such species as *Bellis perennis*, *Caltha palustris*, *Cardamine pratensis*, *Carex echinata*, *C. nigra*, *Juncus articulatus*, *Prunella vulgaris*, *Ranunculus acris* and *Trifolium repens*. In some areas *Galium uliginosum* is a typical associate. In Cumbria and the Craven Pennines it occurs in stony flushes which are not dominated by bryophytes. In its montane sites in the western Highlands it is limited to gravel flushes on the Tertiary basalt of Mull and Morvern where associates include *Juncus triglumis* and *Koenigia islandica*. *S. villosum* is most frequent between 250 metres and 500 metres but occurs at over 1000 metres on Ben Lawers.

It is a perennial, or sometimes biennial, plant. The stem is branched at the base and spreads by producing offsets. Nevertheless, reproduction is probably mainly by seed.

S. villosum colonises a habitat that is, by its nature, scattered and scarce but despite this it remains very locally frequent, at least in the Southern Uplands. However, many of its more lowland sites have been lost to drainage and others to forestry. It may colonise shallow ditches or little-used stony tracks, occasionally in profusion. It is still likely to persist in many of the upland 10 km squares in which it has not been recorded recently.

It is a species with a mainly northern distribution, occurring in Greenland, Iceland and Scandinavia, but extending south to the mountains of Spain, Portugal and Morocco.

M. E. Braithwaite

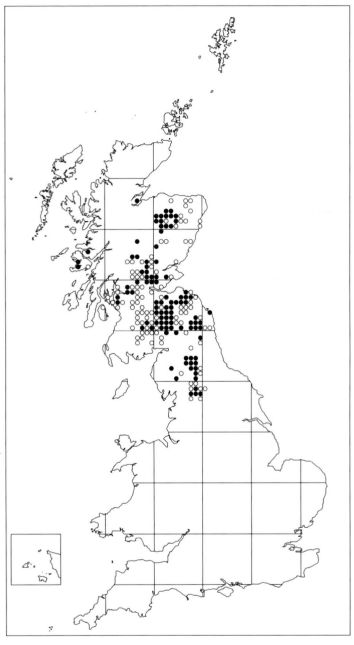

Current map	No	Atlas	No
1970 →	99	1930 →	75
Pre-1970	102	Pre-1930	54
Introductions	0	Introductions	0

Sesleria caerulea (L.) Ard.

Status: scarce

Blue moor-grass

This is a characteristic and often dominant grass of the sheep-grazed Carboniferous limestone of northern England. In the Pennines it grows on shallow well-drained rendzina soils. Although such sites may be subject to summer drought, this has little effect on the competitive ability and vigour of *S. caerulea*. It characteristically occurs in open communities in scree, in crevices and on ledges of scars, extending back from the edge of the scars on to the usually non-calcareous, overlying drift. Although it can tolerate a pH as low as 5, with increasing depth of drift it becomes patchy and eventually disappears. It is also able to grow under the light shade of limestone ash woodland. The open communities are species-rich with, at the upland sites, such characteristically montane species as *Draba incana*, *Galium boreale*, *G. sterneri*, *Minuartia verna* and *Persicaria vivipara*, while lowland sites have more southern, thermophilous species such as *Asperula cynanchica*, *Centaurea scabiosa* and *Hippocrepis comosa*. Occurring throughout the altitudinal range are *Helianthemum nummularium*, *Scabiosa columbaria* and *Thymus polytrichus*. There is a small, recently discovered, relict population in the Peak District. It also occurs in a limited area of east Durham on the drier Permian limestone and locally in the Breadalbanes on strongly calcareous mica schist rocks, where it occurs up to 980 metres and is associated with *Dryas octopetala*, *Saxifraga oppositifolia*, *Silene acaulis* and dwarf willows.

The flowers appear early, often in March, and the culms elongate considerably after flowering, becoming very conspicuous. They may be grazed by both rabbits and sheep. Fruit production, viability and germination are good.

This species is widespread over large areas in northern England and is not under threat.

S. caerulea is a European endemic, occurring chiefly in the mountains of central Europe from the Pyrenees to the Carpathians. There are isolated records from southern Iceland, southern Spain and Albania. It also occurs in western Ireland, where it grows on limestone and coastal sands, and from northern France to central Germany.

For a detailed account of the ecology of this species, see Dixon (1982).

G. Halliday

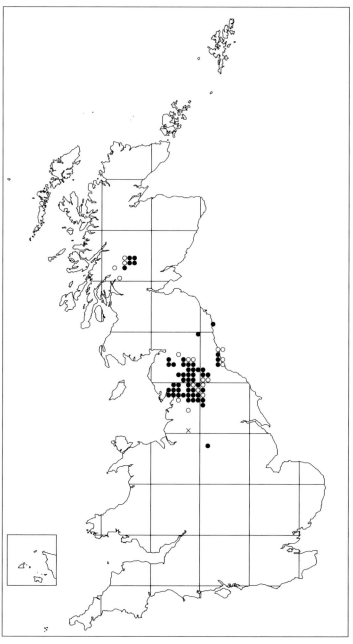

Current map	No	Atlas	No
1970 →	53	1930 →	58
Pre-1970	19	Pre-1930	2
Introductions	1	Introductions	0

Sibbaldia procumbens L.

Status: scarce

S. procumbens is a montane plant of the Scottish Highlands, with two main habitats, both characterised by sparse and open vegetation. The first, where it is more abundant, is in situations where snow lies late into the spring, in high corries and hollows, and especially along the line of snow cornices under a ridge or plateau rim. The other main habitat is on the bare, stony ablation surfaces of high plateaux with fell-field terrain, where wind exposure is severe and the winter snow cover usually slight and ephemeral. It also grows in dwarf herb communities on intermittently flushed soils on high slopes, sometimes beneath cliffs. *S. procumbens* tends to be calcicolous in the southern part of its range, but becomes indifferent to pH further north and grows on a wide range of parent rocks (McVean & Ratcliffe 1962). In areas of non-calcareous rock, associated species include *Alchemilla alpina, Carex bigelowii, Deschampsia cespitosa, Festuca ovina, Galium saxatile, Gnaphalium supinum, Luzula spicata* and *Persicaria vivipara*. Over calcareous substrates, *Minuartia sedoides, Silene acaulis* and *Thymus polytrichus* can also be found with it. *S. procumbens* ascends from 580 metres on Ben More Assynt to 1300 metres in the Cairngorms (Hadley 1985; Wilson 1956).

S. procumbens has a branched, woody, perennial stock with short stems bearing inconspicuous flowers. These, with their few stamens, appear to have little chance of insect pollination, but nectar is attractive to flies and it seems that insect pollination is the rule (Clapham, Tutin & Warburg 1962). Vegetative propagation also takes place from the branches.

There are few threats to this montane species. It is under-recorded in some areas and is almost certainly still present in most of the 10 km squares in which it has not been seen since 1970.

S. procumbens is an arctic-alpine plant. The typical form is mainly European, growing in the Alps, north to Scandinavia and the Kola peninsula, south to Spanish Sierra Nevada, and west to Scotland, Iceland and Greenland. In Siberia and North America, subspecies or closely related species complete the circumpolar distribution (Clapham, Tutin & Warburg 1962).

For a detailed account of this species, see Coker (1966).

A. Slack

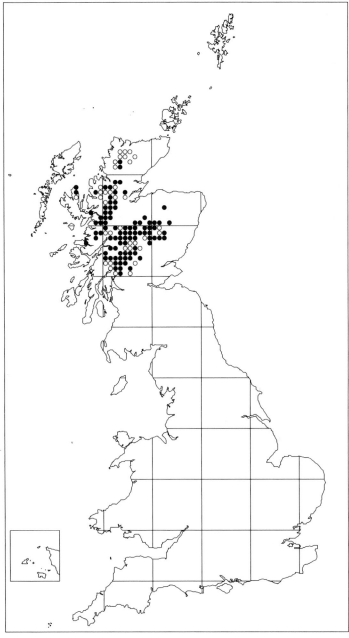

Current map	No	Atlas	No
1970 →	89	1930 →	74
Pre-1970	36	Pre-1930	6
Introductions	0	Introductions	0

Sibthorpia europaea L.
Status: scarce

Cornish moneywort

S. europaea grows in humid microclimates in sheltered lowland sites. It is most frequently found above small streams and ditches, growing over a thin layer of soil on granite walls or other masonry or on the earthy banks of rivulets and ditches. Most sites are shaded by walls, banks or trees. *S. europaea* usually creeps over a carpet of mosses with vascular plants present only as scattered individuals. It is occasionally found on moist, flat, sometimes cattle-poached soils by streams; it also occurs in abundance in a moist lawn and on the wet rock of a disused railway cutting. It is restricted to acidic soils (pH 4.1-6.5). In Cornwall and Devon it is most frequent between 100 and 200 metres at the edge of granite massifs where there are numerous small streams. It reaches 300 metres on Carnedd Llwyd.

S. europaea is an evergreen perennial which reproduces by vegetative spread and from seed. Plants are usually self-pollinating and seed is set very freely in cultivation (Hedberg 1975), though not always in the wild. Colonies are reduced in size in prolonged summer droughts, but subsequently grow back from surviving fragments (Rilstone 1948). Frost damage also occurs in the wild during harsh winters, and plants cultivated outdoors in Cambridge are completely defoliated by winter cold.

This inconspicuous plant has not decreased markedly in range or abundance, although it may have declined locally where roadside streams have been piped. It has only recently been found in Monmouthshire (1990) and Dorset (1992) and may be overlooked at other sites on the fringe of its range.

It occurs in western Europe from the Azores, Spain and Portugal to south-western Ireland and Wales. It also occurs in Greece (Mt Pelion), Crete and in the mountains of tropical Africa.

Several British bryophytes and ferns with a mainly western distribution have, like *S. europaea*, outliers in the Weald. Its disjunct world distribution suggests that *S. europaea* was formerly more widespread, perhaps in Tertiary times. Western European populations are quite uniform whereas those in Africa are variable (Hedberg 1955).

C. D. Preston

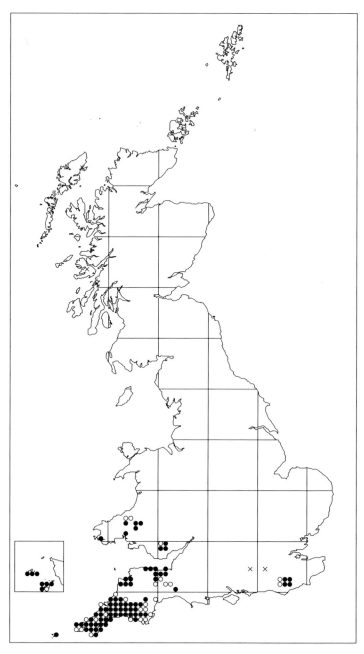

Current map	No	Atlas	No
1970 →	74	1930 →	56
Pre-1970	26	Pre-1930	27
Introductions	4	Introductions	0

continued →

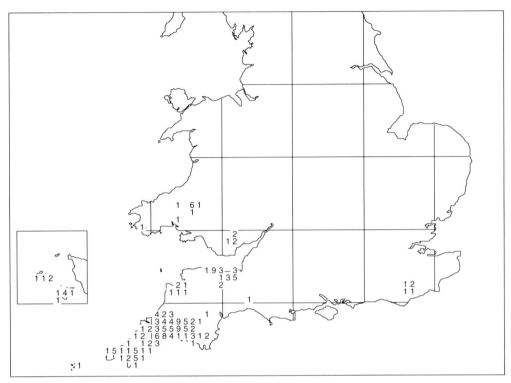

The number of tetrads in each 10 km square in which *Sibthorpia europaea* has been recorded as a native species from 1970 onwards. Squares in which the species is recorded in 9 or more tetrads are plotted as 9: *S. europaea* is actually recorded from 9 tetrads in SX36 and SX37 and 10 in SS84. The species is recorded from a total of 200 tetrads from 1970 onwards.

Silene conica L.
Status: scarce

Sand catchfly

S. conica is a plant of sandy soils, now mainly found on fixed dunes, and pastures or waste ground near the sea. In East Anglia *S. conica* is found, usually on disturbed ground, at the margins of fields, by tracks across heaths, and in abandoned arable fields. The non-native records are of casual plants on sandy waste ground and sandy edges to lakes. Characteristic associates are *Arenaria serpyllifolia, Cerastium semidecandrum, Plantago lanceolata* and *Sedum acre*. A large West Sussex colony on maritime dunes grows with *Aira praecox, Carex arenaria, Cerastium semidecandrum, Phleum arenarium, Poa bulbosa* and *Vulpia fasciculata*. The inland locality in Worcestershire on a sandy common, has been known since at least the end of the last century, and still survives.

It is an annual, which flowers freely, particularly in warm summers, but is dependant on hot summers for good seed production. Populations in Britain vary considerably in size from year to year.

The plant has not decreased in Breckland although it appears to have declined elsewhere in East Anglia. In Kent, the species is just holding its own with two localities, but the West Sussex colony at Clymping has, since 1950, spread along the dunes and at the back of the shingle beach. Here the number of plants increased considerably after the hot summers of 1989 and 1990, followed by the wet springs of 1990 and 1991.

This is a species of south-western and central Europe, occurring through most of the Mediterranean region, but absent from some of the islands (Jalas & Suominen 1986); it is also found in North Africa and south-west Asia. In Europe three subspecies are recognised: subsp. *conica*, which is the British plant, extends throughout the range of the species except for south-eastern Europe and the Ukraine.

M. Briggs

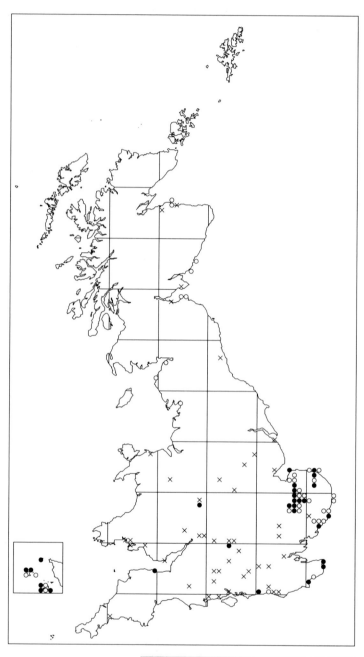

Current map	No	Atlas	No
1970 →	22	1930 →	21
Pre-1970	31	Pre-1930	21
Introductions	46	Introductions	37

Silene gallica L.
Status: scarce

Small-flowered catchfly

This plant is characteristically found as a weed of cultivated or disturbed ground, most frequently on sandy soils. It occasionally grows on sandy sea-shores, and it is frequent on dunes in the Channel Islands.

This is a winter annual, germinating predominantly in the autumn. However, as the seedlings cannot tolerate temperatures of -10 °C, many are killed off in extreme conditions.

S. gallica is restricted to lowland zones by its intolerance of low temperatures. Salisbury (1961) described it as "locally frequent" but it has declined considerably and now occurs only very locally in southern Britain, often in coastal regions. The BSBI Arable Weed Survey of 1986-1987 (Smith 1989) elicited very few records for this species in Britain. It has probably been unable to survive the intensification of agriculture with the routine use of herbicides and heavy applications of fertiliser. It is occasionally introduced with imported clover seed.

This species is widespread in central and southern Europe and the Mediterranean region, extending into the northern parts of France and to Britain, and eastwards to Bulgaria and Romania (Jalas & Suominen 1986). Elsewhere it has an almost cosmopolitan distribution as a weed. It has, however, virtually disappeared from northern Europe.

The flowers of this species are very variable, and differently coloured variants have been given varietal names.

A. Smith

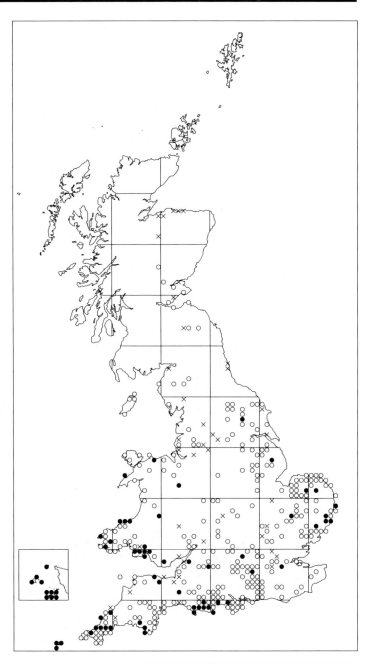

Current map	No	Atlas	No
1970 →	57	1930 →	137
Pre-1970	283	Pre-1930	90
Introductions	42	Introductions	21

continued →

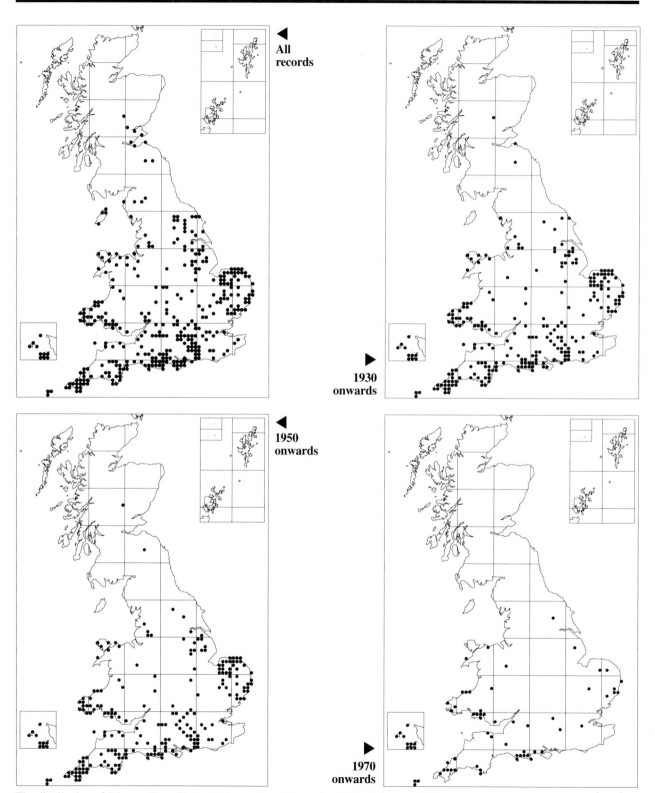

The distribution of *Silene gallica*, illustrated by a series of maps for different time periods.

continued →

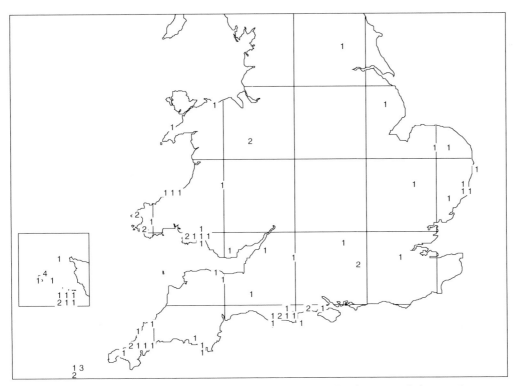

The number of tetrads in each 10 km square in which *Silene gallica* has been recorded as a native species from 1970 onwards. The species has been found in a total of 82 tetrads from 1970 onwards.

Silene noctiflora L.
Status: not scarce

Night-flowering catchfly

This is a plant of cultivated ground and rarely of open waste land, on dry, often sandy and calcareous soils. It also occurs on the heavier, oolitic limestone soils of the Cotswolds and Lincolnshire Wolds. It is most frequent where crop-rotations include spring-sown crops. It is often associated with other uncommon species such as *Fumaria densiflora*, *Papaver argemone* and *P. hybridum*.

An annual, it germinates predominantly in the spring, with a few seedlings developing in the autumn. Wilson (1990) found that plants developed best in crops sown towards the end of March. As it generally flowers rather late, in July, it is more successful at setting seed in crops such as sugar beet which are harvested in the autumn or winter. It also does well when stubble is left after harvest. It demonstrates poor reproductive capacity in wet years but its seed may be quite long-lived in the soil seed bank.

This species has declined considerably since the 1950s. It is now rare throughout most of its range, but perhaps more frequent in East Anglia than elsewhere. It is susceptible to herbicides and to high rates of nitrogen application, but it has benefited from the establishment of 'conservation headlands'.

S. noctiflora is widespread in Europe and Asia. In Europe it has a somewhat continental distribution, and it is rare in both northern Europe and the Mediterranean region (Jalas & Suominen 1986). It is an established introduction in North America.

A. Smith

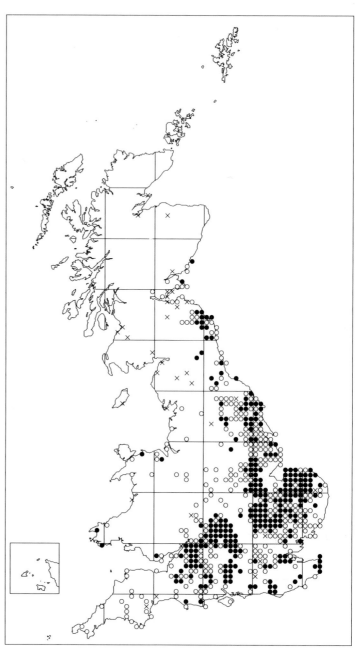

Current map	No	Atlas	No
1970 →	260	1930 →	304
Pre-1970	301	Pre-1930	30
Introductions	33	Introductions	17

Silene nutans L.

Status: scarce

Nottingham catchfly

This is a plant of chalk and limestone grassland and open communities, usually on shallow, well-drained soils. It is normally found on calcareous rock outcrops but it grows in acidic soil over shingle. In Britain it is characteristic of coastal cliffs, sandbanks and, especially, shingle beaches. It is locally very abundant, as on parts of the coast of Hampshire and Kent.

S. nutans is a long-lived perennial with floral adaptation for outcrossing. The drooping flowers are inconspicuous by day, with the perianth-lobes rolled inwards. In the evening they unroll and the flowers are conspicuous and fragrant, attracting moths. The flowers, which are markedly protandrous (Proctor & Yeo 1973), are produced from May to July. Although it usually spreads by seed, fallen stems root readily at the nodes (Hepper 1956).

S. nutans is apparently one of the species which spread in post-glacial times but now survives only in open habitats. It is still widespread in its stronghold on the coasts of southern and south-eastern England from East Devon to East Kent. However, it has declined in its scattered inland stations and is now extinct at Nottingham Castle where it was first recorded by John Ray before 1670.

The species occurs over most of Europe, southwards to central Spain, Calabria and Macedonia; in northern Europe to Finland and Sweden (Jalas & Suominen 1986); and outside Europe it occurs through Siberia as far east as Lake Baikal (Meusel, Jäger & Weinert 1965). It is extremely variable, with several regional variants having been recognised at different ranks. The robust British plants have been called subsp. *smithiana* (Jeanmond & Bocquet 1983), but do not seem to be separable from subsp. *nutans*.

J. R. Akeroyd

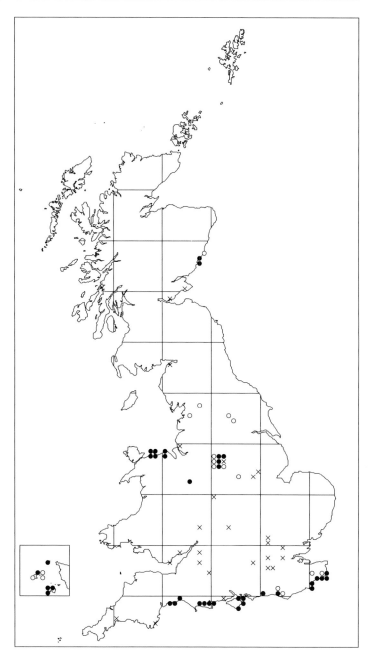

Current map	No	Atlas	No
1970 →	32	1930 →	29
Pre-1970	14	Pre-1930	15
Introductions	26	Introductions	14

continued →

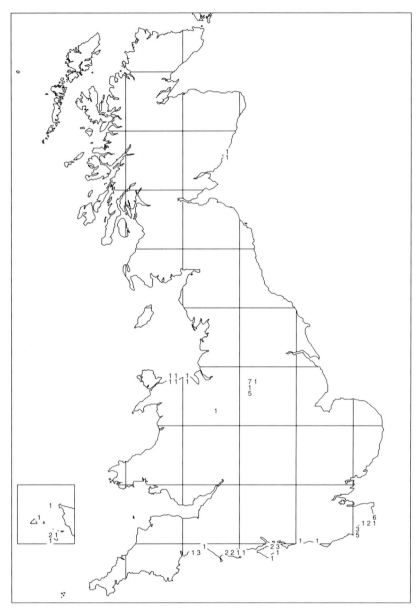

The number of tetrads in each 10 km square in which *Silene nutans* has been recorded as a native species from 1970 onwards. The species has been found in a total of 65 tetrads from 1970 onwards.

Sium latifolium L.
Status: scarce

Greater water-parsnip

The natural habitat of *S. latifolium* is the very wet, species-rich, tall-herb fen that develops as a semi-floating raft at the margins of lakes and large rivers. This vegetation is often dominated by *Phragmites australis* or *Typha angustifolia*, and *S. latifolium* is sometimes accompanied by the other scarce umbellifers *Cicuta virosa* and *Peucedanum palustre*. However, following the drainage and reclamation of most fens in Britain, *S. latifolium* is now most often met in drainage ditches, growing in a more species-poor reed-swamp or, more rarely, with a floating mat of *Hydrocharis morsus-ranae*, Lemnaceae and, in Broadland, *Stratiotes aloides*. It is frequent in old cuttings in fen peat. *S. latifolium* prefers shallow, still or slow-moving water that is alkaline, rich in nitrogen and on a peat or alluvial soil. It is able to tolerate the light shade produced by reeds, but is excluded from carr. Although often growing in stands of *Bolboschoenus maritimus*, *S. latifolium* is rarely, if ever, found in brackish water. It is confined to the lowlands of Britain, being most common in the coastal levels and flood plains of major rivers.

S. latifolium can live submerged for some years without flowering. It is a perennial which produces abundant seed, but opportunities for seedling establishment are few in tall fen. In ditches, particular individuals survive in tall reed for over 10 years, but recruits are usually only seen following the cutting of the vegetation or the use of a weed bucket.

S. latifolium has undergone a catastrophic decline in Britain in the last 200 years, probably as a result of fen drainage and the elimination or over-engineering of watercourses. Even in many protected sites, decline has been observed and new individuals are rare. Since it is intolerant of grazing and frequent cutting, *S. latifolium* is often most common in ditches adjacent to unreclaimed fen or arable land, provided the water is kept open by *occasional* use of a weed bucket or scythe.

S. latifolium is widespread in Europe, but is very rare near the Mediterranean and absent from Portugal. It is rare and mainly southern in Fennoscandia, having also markedly declined in Finland. *S. latifolium* extends into temperate Siberia, and is recorded in south-eastern Australia, but is unknown in Japan and the Americas.

J. O. Mountford

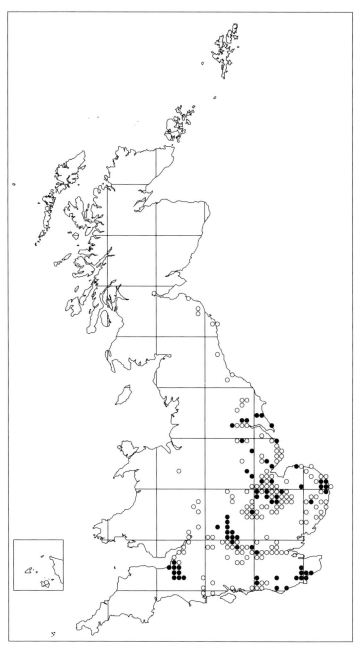

Current map	No	Atlas	No
1970 →	66	1930 →	98
Pre-1970	149	Pre-1930	66
Introductions	0	Introductions	0

Sonchus palustris L.

Status: scarce

Marsh sow-thistle

In England, *S. palustris* is most often recorded in tall vegetation by major lowland rivers. In Broadland and by the Thames, it characteristically occurs among *Phragmites australis* in strips of marshy land fringing the river's lower reaches ('ronds'), but elsewhere in England (as in continental Europe) it is typical of tall-herb vegetation along watercourses, with *Filipendula ulmaria*, *Lythrum salicaria* and *Stachys palustris*. It occasionally grows with *Lathyrus palustris*, *Peucedanum palustre*, *Sium latifolium* and other scarce species in tall-herb fen. It will tolerate partial shade within stands of *Phragmites australis* and *Cladium mariscus*, but does not persist in carr. *S. palustris* grows in wet peaty or alluvial soils which are neutral to alkaline and rich in nitrogen. It is also moderately tolerant of salinity, occurring by the tidal parts of some rivers.

S. palustris is a tall perennial with an erect rootstock. It reproduces entirely by seed. The achenes have a pappus of long hairs and are wind dispersed.

S. palustris demonstrates different trends in distribution in different parts of its British range. Along the Thames and in Kent, it has declined where industry and housing have destroyed its populations. In contrast, in Broadland and in eastern Suffolk, it is at least as common as in the nineteenth century and there is some evidence that it is increasing. In the Cambridgeshire Fens, it became extinct as a result of the drainage of most of its sites, but in the last 30 years has spread from stock introduced into Woodwalton Fen. The Hampshire population was not discovered until 1959, but appears to be native. The species is probably favoured by regular (but infrequent) winter cutting of reeds.

S. palustris extends from eastern England and Spain through Denmark, southern Sweden and Serbia to central Russia, Transcaucasia and north-eastern Anatolia. The sub-continental nature of its range is shown by its absence from the oceanic, Mediterranean and Arctic extremes of Europe.

J. O. Mountford

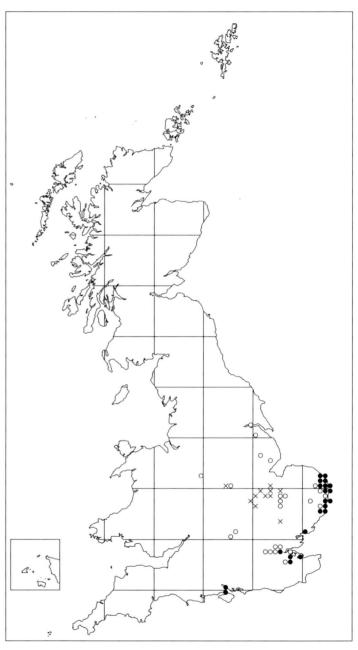

Current map	No	Atlas	No
1970 →	21	1930 →	15
Pre-1970	24	Pre-1930	18
Introductions	11	Introductions	4

Sorbus devoniensis E. Warb.

Status: scarce

This species is locally frequent in hedgerows, where it may grow into a substantial tree but is more often seen as a hedgerow shrub, growing with species such as *Corylus avellana*, *Ilex aquifolium* and *Quercus* spp., and trimmed along with the other woody species of the hedge. Most of its core range in Devon is on non-calcareous Devonian and Carboniferous shale, slates and grits. It is very local on the North Devon coast in steep rocky oak scrub (less often in open rocky moorland) above Old Red Sandstone sea-cliffs between Combe Martin and Countisbury, with an inland population (slightly differentiated in morphological and isoenzyme characters) in rocky oakwoods in the valley of the East Lyn River. It sometimes extends into scrubby heath or moorland margins inland, as on Roborough Down north of Plymouth and the Cretaceous gravel summit of Little Haldon south of Exeter. It is a lowland plant.

It is apomictic, though slight variation in morphology and peroxidase phenotype suggests the possibility of occasional outcrossing (Proctor, Proctor & Groenhof 1989, and unpublished data). Fruit production varies greatly from year to year, with seasons of heavy fruiting often, but not necessarily, followed by seasons of sparse fruit-set. Fruits are eaten, and the seeds probably generally dispersed, by birds. This species establishes readily from seed and young trees are frequent in suitable habitats.

S. devoniensis was not described as a species until 1957, having previously been confused with other members of the *S. latifolia* aggregate. Its distribution in Devon appears to be stable, and plants were rediscovered in Cornwall in 1986, over 100 years since the last record from that county.

S. devoniensis is endemic to Britain and Ireland. There are related (probably apomictic) species in France and central Europe (Sell 1989a).

The distribution pattern of *S. devoniensis*, with a compact main area in North Devon, subsidiary areas in south-eastern Ireland and South Devon, and an outlying occurrence in Co. Down, suggests local dispersal, probably largely by birds, combined with occasional long-distance dispersal either by birds or deliberate planting. The population in the East Lyn valley, with glossier, more deeply toothed and somewhat narrower leaves ('*S. admonita*'), may possibly have originated through outcrossing with *S. subcuneata*. In addition to the localities shown on the map, *S. devoniensis* probably occurs in the Isle of Man but this requires confirmation (Sell 1989a).

M. C. F. Proctor

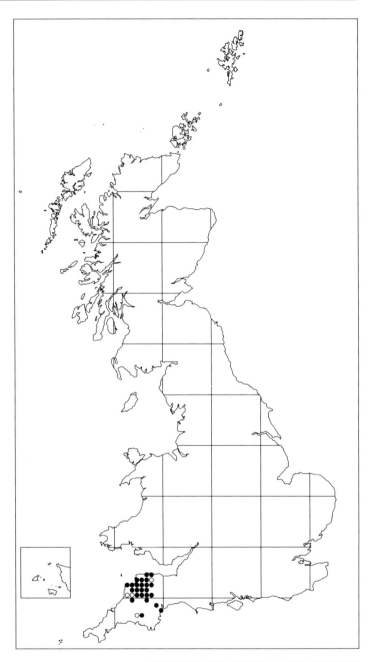

Current map	No	Atlas (S)	No
1970 →	24		
Pre-1970	4		
Introductions	0	All records	20

continued →

Sorbus devoniensis
continued

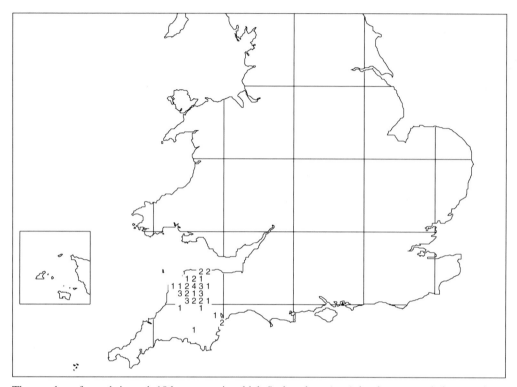

The number of tetrads in each 10 km square in which *Sorbus devoniensis* has been recorded as a native species from 1970 onwards. The species has been found in a total of 43 tetrads from 1970 onwards.

Sorbus porrigentiformis E. Warb.

Status: scarce

This tree is usually rooted into the crevices of cliffs and outcrops of Carboniferous limestone, other similar hard limestones (Lower Devonian in South Devon, Ordovician in Radnor) or very rarely Old Red Sandstone (North Devon). *S. porrigentiformis* most characteristically occurs in open well-lit situations; the plants sometimes found in deep shade under a close tree canopy are probably always relics from formerly more open conditions. It seldom occurs on cliffs or outcrops completely devoid of other woody species. It is commonly associated with *Crataegus monogyna*, *Fraxinus excelsior*, *Prunus spinosa*, *Taxus baccata* and other calcicolous shrubs. It grows from near sea-level to *c*. 530 metres on Craig Cerrig-gleisiad.

S. porrigentiformis is apomictic and reproduces by seed. Fruit is set freely, but the amount varies greatly from year to year. The fruits are eaten, and probably dispersed, by birds. Young plants are frequent in populations providing suitably open conditions for establishment. Vegetative regrowth from the base may be important to the survival of damaged plants, but is not a significant means of spread.

The distribution of *S. porrigentiformis* appears to be stable, but the population at Asham Wood may have been destroyed by quarrying.

It is endemic to Britain, but there appear to be similar apomictic microspecies in comparable habitats in southern-central and south-eastern Europe in the zone of contact between *S. aria* and *S. graeca* (Tutin *et al*. 1968).

S. porrigentiformis is a uniform and well-circumscribed microspecies. It has been much confused with other taxa, some closely related, others not. Records from North Wales are based on plants closer to *S. eminens* and *S. hibernica*; some from the Black Mountains and adjacent areas, and from the west Somerset coast relate to undescribed apomictic species differing from *S. porrigentiformis* in leaf and fruit morphology, growth-habit, ecology and peroxidase phenotype (Proctor & Groenhof 1992).

M. C. F. Proctor

Current map	No	Atlas (S)	No
1970 →	21		
Pre-1970	2		
Introductions	0	All records	16

continued →

Sorbus porrigentiformis
continued

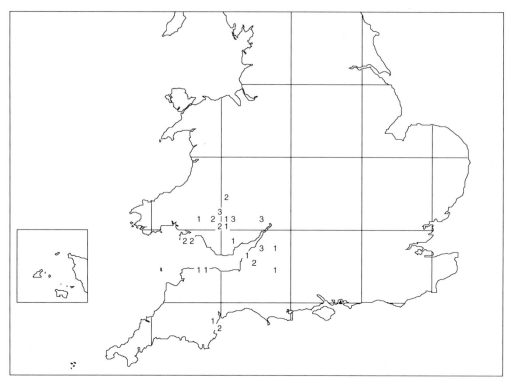

The number of tetrads in each 10 km square in which *Sorbus porrigentiformis* has been recorded as a native species from 1970 onwards. The species has been found in a total of 36 tetrads from 1970 onwards.

Sorbus rupicola (Syme) Hedlund
Status: scarce

This tree is found on steep rocky slopes or cliffs of basic rock at low to moderate altitude. In England and Wales it is practically confined to areas of Carboniferous limestone, but in Scotland it is found on a wide variety of rock types including Old Red Sandstone, Tertiary basalt, Dalradian limestone and Moine schist. It often grows in inaccessible situations. It reaches 500 metres at Creag Bhuilg in Glen Avon.

Mature individuals readily produce flowers and fruit. The latter are probably distributed by birds, leading to regeneration in new sites.

Populations of *S. rupicola* are often small and it is quite common for them to consist of only a single tree. They appear to be stable.

It is endemic to north-western Europe, where it is recorded from Britain, Ireland, Estonia, Norway and Sweden. In Scandinavia it has a predominantly southern distribution, but it extends north in western Norway to the Arctic Circle (Hultén & Fries 1986).

A. McG. Stirling

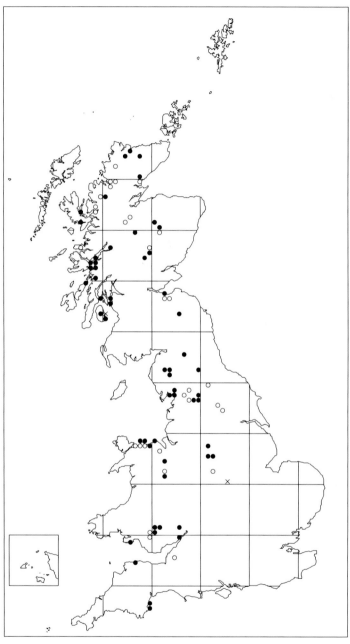

Current map	No	Atlas (S)	No
1970 →	56		
Pre-1970	31		
Introductions	2	All records	60

Spartina maritima (Curtis) Fern.

Status: scarce

Small cord-grass

S. maritima typically occurs in the higher levels of saltmarshes, with species of the so-called general saltmarsh community such as *Limonium vulgare*, *Plantago maritima*, *Puccinellia maritima*, *Salicornia europaea*, *Suaeda maritima* and *Triglochin maritima*. The first of these is the most common companion whilst the presence of *Aster tripolium* or *Atriplex portulacoides* at more than a fairly low density usually signals that *S. maritima* will not be found. It is very occasionally found as a pioneer on bare mud, but not the deep, rapidly accreting muds occupied by its allopolyploid derivative *S. anglica*. In the very mixed communities of the higher saltmarsh it is often scattered and patchy, seeming to prefer lower 'turf', the wetter, possibly more saline depressions and open areas within the sward and the edges of salt pans.

S. maritima is perennial, appears rarely to set seed in Britain, and persists almost entirely by vegetative spread (by tough and quite persistent narrow rhizomes). The lack of seed may be related to the fact that the plant is at its northern limit on the east coast of England (in Spain and the southern part of its range it is a tall, sward-forming plant), and it is generally late flowering. Its method of photosynthesis is more typical of tropical species and renders its growth very temperature-dependent. Recent discoveries of new sites in Suffolk may represent formerly overlooked populations rather than the establishment of new ones.

S. maritima is clearly declining in range and for a variety of reasons (Raybould *et al.* 1991). These include land claim of saltmarshes, erosion, successional changes (notably the invasion of tall *Atriplex portulacoides* and *Puccinellia maritima* on better-drained soils), and possibly even changes in salinity. Interestingly *S. anglica*, frequently blamed for ousting its progenitor, is unlikely to be a major factor in its decline. There are still a few large populations at its centre of distribution in southern Suffolk and Essex.

Native to the coasts of southern and western Europe and at its northern limit in eastern England. It is also widespread in Africa.

For more details of the ecology of this species, see Marchant & Goodman (1969).

A. J. Gray

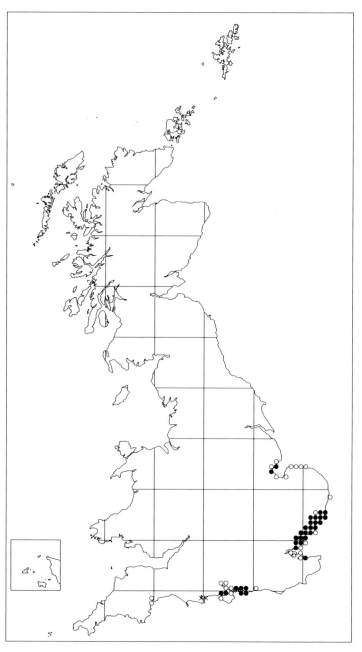

Current map	No	Atlas	No
1970 →	31	1930 →	26
Pre-1970	25	Pre-1930	21
Introductions	2	Introductions	0

continued →

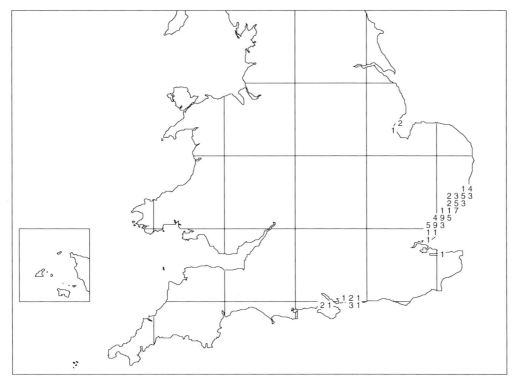

The number of tetrads in each 10 km square in which *Spartina maritima* has been recorded as a native species from 1970 onwards. Squares in which the species is recorded in 9 or more tetrads are plotted as 9: *S. maritima* is actually recorded from 9 tetrads in TM01 and 11 in TL90. The species has been found in a total of 92 tetrads from 1970 onwards.

Spiranthes romanzoffiana Cham.
Status: scarce

Irish lady's-tresses

This is a plant with a distinctive habitat, this being the *Molinia caerulea* carpet on old lazy beds grazed by cattle. Some sites are subject to inundation in winter. However, three of the five largest known populations in Britain are not inundated, but have trickles flowing through them from occasional flushes. Ideally, sites should be grazed by cattle when the plant is dormant. In 1972, John Raven noted that the species was unusually abundant in an area where cattle had been fed throughout the preceding winter. It is confined to the lowlands.

There is no direct evidence of cross-pollination in Britain, and our populations are believed to reproduce entirely vegetatively. A lateral bud (very rarely two) develops at the base of the stem during the growing season. This bud overwinters, and produces the following year's aerial parts. Disturbance seems to stimulate dormant plants. One of our largest populations has produced approximately one hundred flowering spikes consistently for at least the last five years (J.H. Robarts pers. comm.).

Though formerly included in the *Red Data Book* (Perring & Farrell 1983) more sites have been found recently because the species has been deliberately searched for in likely places. It may have been under-recorded in the past as it is very difficult to see when not in flower because of its grass-like leaves.

S. romanzoffiana is a member of the small North American element in our flora. It is confined to Britain and Ireland in Europe, but it is widespread in North America, including the Aleutian Islands.

F. Horsman

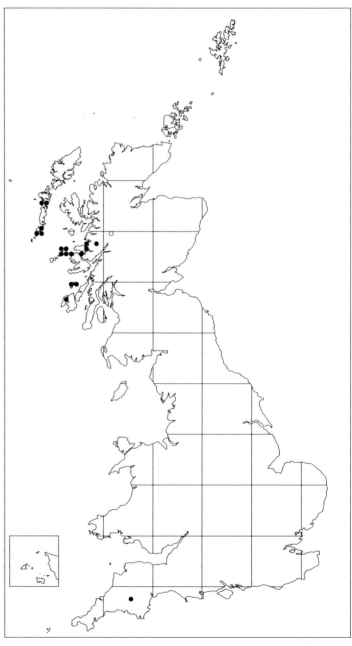

Current map	No	Atlas	No
1970 →	18	1930 →	7
Pre-1970	2	Pre-1930	0
Introductions	0	Introductions	0

Stratiotes aloides L.

Status: scarce

Water-soldier

S. aloides is a characteristic dominant in the submerged layer of a macrophyte community with *Ceratophyllum demersum* and *Utricularia vulgaris* where *Callitriche platycarpa*, *Hydrocharis morsus-ranae* and Lemnaceae form a floating mat on the surface. Other scarce species which may be present in this community include *Potamogeton compressus* and *Sium latifolium*. *S. aloides* grows in the still water of grazing marsh ditches, appearing to prefer water that is moderately rich in nutrients and calcareous. It is most often found where there are enhanced levels of calcium, magnesium and inorganic nitrogen, notably towards the upper margin of the fen basin (Wheeler & Giller 1982). *S. aloides* grows where regular cleaning of the ditches or ponds (often with grazing of the margins) suppresses the growth of reed and other tall emergents. It requires well-lit conditions, and is absent from turbid water or where bank vegetation and dense emergent growth shade the water surface. Outside its relict native range, *S. aloides* has been widely introduced into ponds and lakes. It is confined to sites below 50 metres in the warm lowlands.

S. aloides is free-floating and stoloniferous. In Britain it reproduces only by offsets and fruit are never set, since the species is dioecious and only the female plant is found here. When introduced as whole plants into a new site, *S. aloides* increases rapidly. However, without seed it is unable to spread naturally from one drainage system to another.

The native range of *S. aloides* has contracted sharply in the last 150 years. However, in the Netherlands *S. aloides* has increased, apparently favoured by nitrogenous fertiliser run-off from farmland (Westhoff & Held 1969). The decline in Britain may follow the rise in phosphate content of the water from sewage, farm slurry or detergents. *S. aloides* is now only frequent in Broadland, and has largely disappeared from its previous strongholds in the Cambridgeshire Fens, Lincolnshire and Yorkshire. However, due to its attractive appearance *S. aloides* is often grown in ponds and can be encountered as a casual introduction throughout lowland Britain. It can spread rapidly in water with a low phosphate level and in some sites, such as the Pevensey Levels, it is thoroughly naturalised.

S. aloides is widespread in the temperate and warmer parts of Europe and western Asia, though rare in the far south and west. For example, it is absent from both Greece and Portugal.

J. O. Mountford

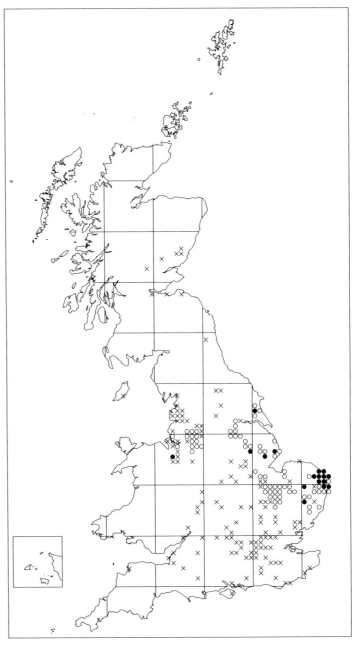

Current map	No	Atlas	No
1970 →	17	1930 →	14
Pre-1970	68	Pre-1930	37
Introductions	128	Introductions	41

continued →

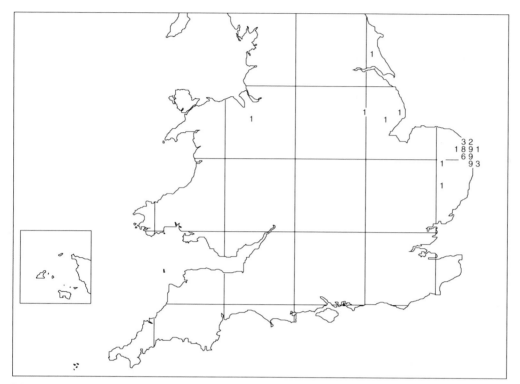

The number of tetrads in each 10 km square in which *Stratiotes aloides* has been recorded as a native species from 1970 onwards. Squares in which the species is recorded in 9 or more tetrads are plotted as 9: *S. aloides* is actually recorded in 9 tetrads in TG40, 10 in TG41 and 11 in TM49. The species has been found in a total of 61 tetrads from 1970 onwards.

Suaeda vera Forsskål ex J. Gmelin

Status: scarce

Shrubby sea-blite

This is a conspicuous shrub of shingle drift-lines and the dry upper parts of saltmarshes, especially where these adjoin shingle banks or sand dunes. It also occurs along sea-wall drift-lines and, more rarely, adjoining brackish 'creeks' and ditches in coastal grazing marshes. On shingle it can form dense monospecific stands, but in saltmarshes it is usually co-dominant with *Atriplex portulacoides* and/or *Elytrigia atherica*. In Norfolk it is also a prominent member of a distinctive community of saltmarsh - sand dune transitions, with such species as *Armeria maritima*, *Atriplex portulacoides*, *Frankenia laevis*, *Limonium bellidifolium*, *L. binervosum* and *Puccinellia maritima*.

S. vera is a small evergreen shrub, flowering from July to September and fruiting from September to November. Water-borne seeds are washed up and accumulate amongst drift-line litter, germinating in the spring. Vegetative fragments detached during winter storms may also be involved in the colonisation of new sites. Lateral vegetative spread is by means of freely rooting subterranean stems.

S. vera has probably always been scarce in Britain, and its distribution has clearly changed very little in recent times. There are relatively few cases of the species having been lost from sites, although at its northern limit in Lincolnshire it has apparently "come and gone and returned several times" (Gibbons 1975). Some stands of *S. vera* may be at risk from sea defence and other coastal engineering schemes, although most of the larger populations are within SSSIs. Nevertheless, accelerated sea-level rise as a result of climate-change could represent a significant long-term threat.

It is found on the coasts of southern and western Europe and inland in Spain (Jalas & Suominen 1980); also in Madeira, the Canary Islands, St Helena, Angola, Somalia, south-western Asia and inland in southern Russia, Afghanistan and India. It reaches its northern limit in Britain, which correlates with the 16 °C isotherm for August (Chapman 1976).

For an account of the ecology of this species, see Chapman (1947).

S. J. Leach

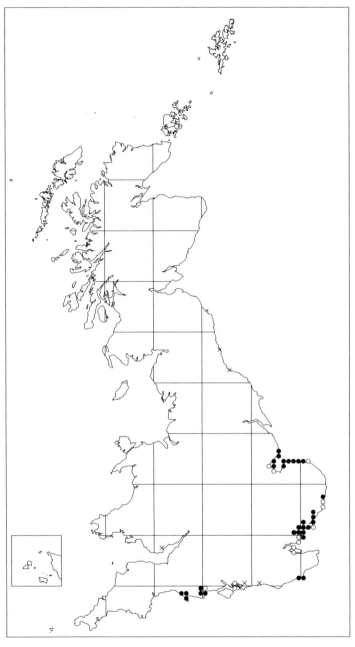

Current map	No	Atlas	No
1970 →	30	1930 →	30
Pre-1970	13	Pre-1930	5
Introductions	6	Introductions	2

Subularia aquatica L.

Awlwort

Status: not scarce

This rooted aquatic plant is typically found in oligotrophic and base-poor lakes. However, on Skye it is found in a few sites of a higher base status which are located on basalt but which also receive some acid influence. It usually occurs in shallow water (less than 1 metre), although in clear water it may grow at greater depths. Plants are often isolated or in small groups of two to three and are commonly found growing amongst *Littorella uniflora*. It is usually found on rocky substrates and may grow between stones and boulders, although it also occurs less commonly on silt and on sandy substrates. It is found in lochs with a peaty influence, although it is generally absent from peaty pools. In Scotland, it has been found as low as 5 metres altitude (Loch Hope and Loch Evelix) and up to 795 metres (Sandy Loch and the Cairngorms).

This is an annual plant, which is usually self-pollinated.

Owing to its small size and superficial similarity to *Littorella uniflora*, *S. aquatica* has been poorly recorded in the past and is commoner than was once supposed. During survey work in the north of Scotland conducted by the Nature Conservancy Council freshwater loch survey team, *S. aquatica* was found in many new sites, and it no longer qualifies as nationally scarce. In areas which have not yet been covered by this project it is probably still under-recorded.

Abroad it is known from the mountains of western Europe and in northern Europe from Ireland and Scandinavia to northern Russia; also from Siberia, Greenland, and North America.

For a more detailed description of the ecology of this species, see Woodhead (1951).

S. L. Bell

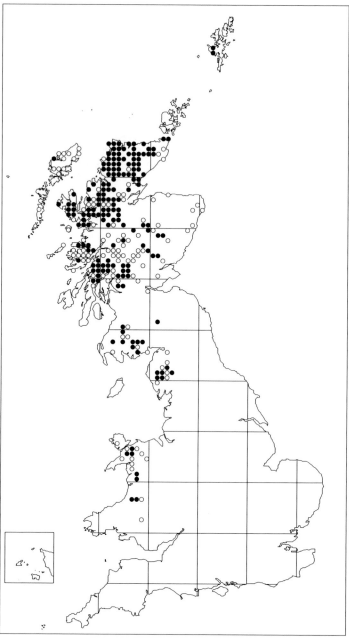

Current map	No	Atlas	No
1970 →	168	1930 →	84
Pre-1970	111	Pre-1930	29
Introductions	0	Introductions	0

Teesdalia nudicaulis (L.) R. Br.

Status: not scarce

Shepherd's cress

This species occurs on sand and gravel, always in open patches, and often on ground disturbed either by rabbits, other animals, natural erosion or trampling. It is often associated with *Aira caryophyllea*, *A. praecox*, *Hypochaeris glabra*, *Ornithopus perpusillus*, *Rumex acetosella* and *Trifolium arvense* on slightly acid soils. It is found in a range of habitats including heathy grassland, sand dunes, scree and boulders, river shingle, track sides and disused railways. It ranges from sea-level to 450 metres on Ben More, Mull.

It is an annual and populations can fluctuate from year to year. About 90% of the seeds germinate in the autumn and performance in the following spring is dependent on weather conditions. For detailed accounts of the reproductive biology of this species, see Newman (1963, 1964, 1965).

This small plant is often overlooked when in flower in spring, and is more conspicuous when in fruit. An increase in records from Scotland, the Welsh Borders and south-western England may be the result of more intensive fieldwork in these areas. This species has decreased in south-eastern England as a result of urban development, the reversion of commons to scrub following cessation of grazing, the ploughing of heathland and (in East Anglia) commercial afforestation.

T. nudicaulis is a characteristic member of grass heath communities on sandy soils in western and central Europe (Matthews 1955), and its range extends to Sweden, Russia and Yugoslavia (Tutin *et al*. 1993). It has been introduced to North America (Rich 1991).

L. Farrell

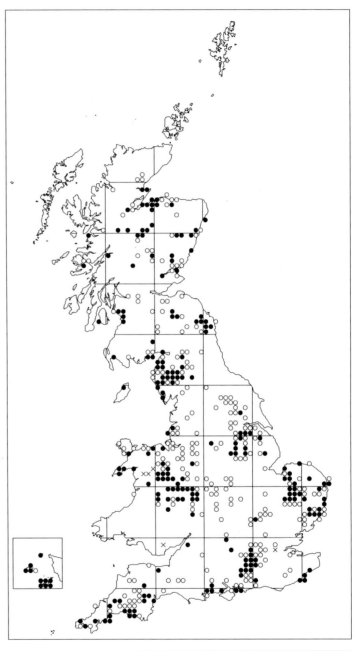

Current map	No	Atlas	No
1970 →	202	1930 →	165
Pre-1970	246	Pre-1930	110
Introductions	5	Introductions	2

Tephroseris integrifolia (L.) Holub subsp. *integrifolia*   **Field fleawort**
Status: scarce

This is a short-lived rosette-forming perennial of short calcareous *Festuca* grassland, mainly on the chalk but also on the Cotswold oolite. Typical associates in the ancient grasslands where it occurs include *Asperula cynanchica, Helianthemum nummularium, Helictotrichon pratense, Hippocrepis comosa, Koeleria macrantha, Thesium humifusum* and, more locally, *Phyteuma orbiculare, Polygala calcarea, Pulsatilla vulgaris* and various orchids. It is virtually confined to the lowlands, but it was recorded at 550 metres in its isolated stations near Brough.

It reproduces mainly by seed, which germinates freely in cultivation, but it can also produce offsets which form new plants. It seems to require warm, dry sites, especially on south-facing slopes, but it is much less restricted to these aspects than is *Polygala calcarea*. It has a relict distribution, often associated with ancient earthworks or trackbanks (U.K. Smith pers. comm.) and seems to have little or no capacity to colonise new sites today. This species has an endotrophic mycorrhiza (Smith 1979) like many terrestrial orchids and, like them, is very variable in numbers from one year to another.

This species has decreased considerably over the last century. This seems to be due to the destruction, 'improvement' or scrub invasion of old sheepwalks, and the abandonment of sheep grazing. It seems now to be extinct in all the sites on the oolite, except for one in the northern Cotswolds, but it is still locally much more frequent and locally plentiful on the Sussex and Wiltshire downs than is evident from the map, though it is now nearly extinct in Kent due to lack of grazing. It is apparently extinct in Westmorland, where the population was perhaps intermediate between this subspecies and subsp. *maritima*.

It is one of the few British chalk grassland species that are (strangely) absent from France, though its place is taken there locally by the closely related *T. helenitis*. Further afield, it has a very scattered distribution in calcareous grasslands in northern Denmark, southern Sweden, Estonia, Karelia, the Swiss Jura, Austria and in dry areas of eastern Europe. Other members of the *T. integrifolia* complex occur in Asia and in western North America.

T. integrifolia subsp. *maritima*, a British endemic, is confined to coastal sites on Holy Island, Anglesey. It is not covered by the above account.

F. Rose

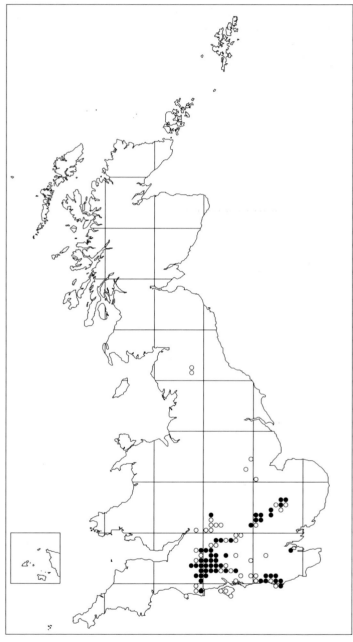

Current map	No	Atlas	No
1970 →	51	1930 →	52
Pre-1970	44	Pre-1930	22
Introductions	0	Introductions	0

404

Thelypteris palustris Schott

Status: scarce

Marsh fern

This fern is a dominant plant in lowland primary reedswamp characteristic of the mesotrophic mires of Broadland. It also colonises new peat cuttings in those deeper valley mires on neutral or slightly alkaline peats where there is a high winter water table. Associated species include *Carex acutiformis*, *C. riparia*, *Cladium mariscus*, *Juncus subnodulosus*, *Lysimachia vulgaris* and *Menyanthes trifoliata*. It persists in closed fen carr under the shade of *Frangula alnus*, *Rhamnus cathartica* or *Salix cinerea*. It is a lowland species, but it was recorded at 335 metres at Castleton, Aberdeen.

T. palustris is a rhizomatous perennial. It produces copious spores, and establishment is a common occurrence, providing that the peat surface is not too acid.

The main reason for the decline of this species throughout lowland Britain is the drainage of mires. Acidification and the natural trend of fens to develop into *Sphagnum* communities may also be contributory factors.

In Europe this species occurs rather rarely along the Atlantic and Mediterranean seaboard, but is widespread throughout central and eastern Europe as far north as 65 °N (Jalas & Suominen 1972). Elsewhere, it occurs throughout Asia to Japan and in North America south to Florida and Texas.

A. C. Jermy

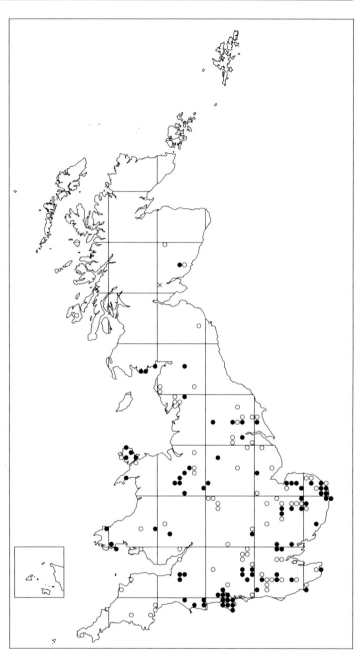

Current map	No	Atlas	No
1970 →	85	1930 →	59
Pre-1970	79	Pre-1930	40
Introductions	1	Introductions	1

continued →

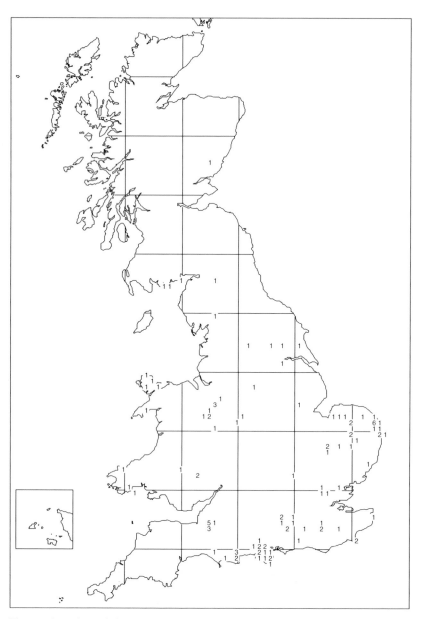

The number of tetrads in each 10 km square in which *Thelypteris palustris* has been recorded as a native species from 1970 onwards. The species has been found in a total of 115 tetrads from 1970 onwards.

Thesium humifusum DC.

Status: scarce

Bastard-toadflax

This plant is found in short, species-rich calcicolous grassland, chiefly on chalk, less frequently on oolitic limestone and rarely on calcareous sandy soils near the coast. In Wiltshire, it is usually associated with *Carex humilis* and is mostly confined to warm, south-west facing slopes. On the oolitic limestone, at sites such as Barnsley Warren, it grows in association with *Pulsatilla vulgaris* and *Polygala calcarea*. On the Isle of Portland it grows on rather bare, shallow clayey soils overlying limestone.

T. humifusum is a perennial hemiparasitic herb having haustoria on its roots by means of which it attaches itself to the roots of other plants. The mature plant has a woody rootstock from which in May it produces slender, yellowish-green shoots with a prostrate habit of growth. The plant is probably long-lived. It flowers freely from June onwards and produces a small ovoid fruit, but little is known concerning the fate of the seeds and conditions required for germination.

Locally, it may be relatively abundant with cover values of up to 30%, but it is easily overlooked and probably under-recorded. It has been lost from some of its former localities as a result of ploughing of downland and is also threatened by application of inorganic fertilisers and by scrub encroachment.

It is confined to western Europe (Belgium, France, Great Britain, Netherlands and Spain) and has a distinctly southern oceanic distribution (Jalas & Suominen 1976).

T. C. E. Wells

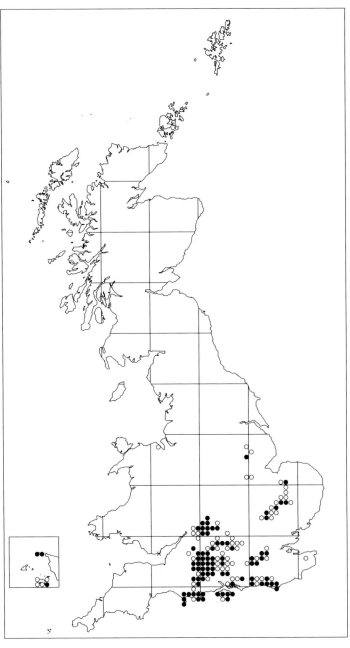

Current map	No	Atlas	No
1970 →	81	1930 →	72
Pre-1970	62	Pre-1930	48
Introductions	1	Introductions	1

Thlaspi caerulescens J.S. Presl & C. Presl

Status: scarce

Alpine penny-cress

The distribution of *T. caerulescens* in England and Wales reflects a distinct association with derelict lead- and zinc-mine workings, particularly in limestone areas but also on shales. It is often a pioneer colonist of metalliferous mine wastes and river gravels contaminated with lead, zinc and cadmium, where it is frequently associated with *Minuartia verna*. It is occasionally found on non-metalliferous substrata (limestone outcrops and scree, whinstone). In Scotland, isolated montane populations occur on a variety of substrata including limestone, serpentine, basalt, shales and porphyritic gravels. Although typically a plant of very open conditions, it can persist in a more closed turf over mine wastes or at its montane sites. It is mainly an upland plant, reaching 940 metres on Caenlochan, but also growing down to near sea-level in western Wales.

In the British Isles *T. caerulescens* is a perennial, or rarely a biennial. Plants are almost entirely self-pollinated and populations are inbreeding (Riley 1956). Reproduction is largely by seed but daughter rosettes are produced on old plants and these rosettes can become independent plants. Seed dispersal is not long-range, seedlings frequently establishing on bare soil close to parent plants. Germination occurs in the early autumn. There is no persistent seed bank.

Whilst many of its populations are isolated and often very small, *T. caerulescens* can be locally abundant at its mine sites. Reworking of lead mine spoil and land reclamation may have already exterminated some populations. The unstable nature of metal-contaminated river gravels confers a precarious status to important populations beside the Afon Ystwyth, Rivers South Tyne and West Allen. It appears now to be extinct at its only serpentine locality at Grey Hill.

This species is widely, although locally, distributed in the mountains of southern, western and central Europe and on metalliferous (calamine, serpentine) soils at lower altitude, extending eastwards to Poland and Yugoslavia. It has been introduced into Scandinavia. The British populations represent the north-western limit of its range. Closely related taxa occur in Asia and in western North America.

This is a very variable plant morphologically, which has led to considerable taxonomic confusion (Ingrouille & Smirnoff 1986). *Flora Europaea* (Tutin *et al.* 1993) now recognises only two subspecies: subsp. *caerulescens* and subsp. *virens*. The former name should be applied to all British material.

A. J. M. Baker

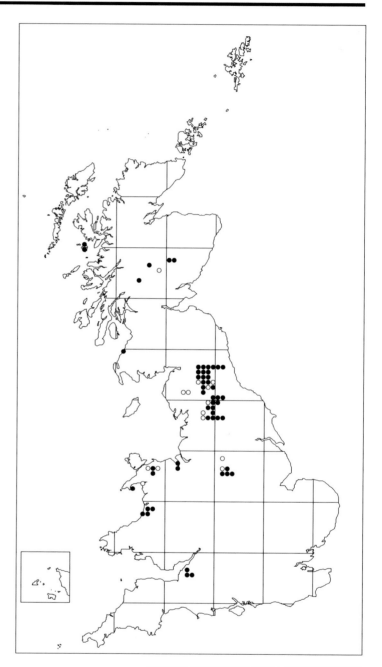

Current map	No	Atlas	No
1970 →	52	1930 →	38
Pre-1970	14	Pre-1930	13
Introductions	0	Introductions	0

continued →

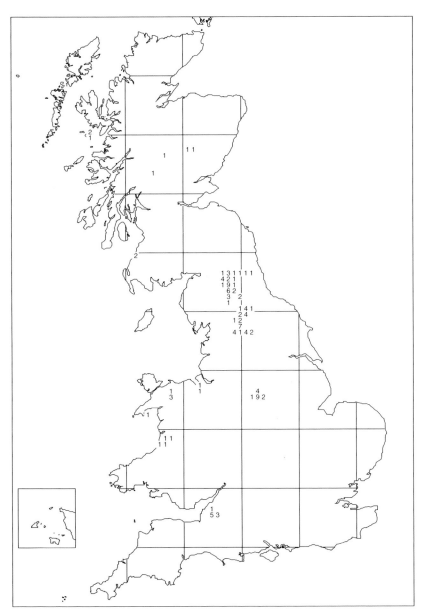

The number of tetrads in each 10 km square in which *Thlaspi caerulescens* has been
recorded as a native species from 1970 onwards. Squares in which the species is
recorded in 9 or more tetrads are plotted as 9: *T. caerulescens* is actually recorded in
9 tetrads in SK25 and 15 in NY74. The species has been found in a total of 124 tetrads
from 1970 onwards. The tetrad data are inadequate in Northumberland, as recording
in this county has been in 5 × 5 km grid squares (Swan 1993).

Tilia platyphyllos Scop.
Status: scarce

Large-leaved lime

Typically this species occurs as a large tree or coppice stool in old woodland, where it is usually associated with a mixed canopy of *Acer campestre*, *A. pseudoplatanus*, *Fagus sylvatica*, *Fraxinus excelsior*, *Quercus robur*, *Taxus baccata* and *Ulmus glabra*, with the field layer dominated by *Mercurialis perennis* (Rodwell 1991a). It also grows on ledges of cliffs, where it is associated with some of these species and often with apomictic *Sorbus* species. It is usually found on calcareous soils of very variable depth, or, more rarely, on acid soils derived from volcanic rocks. It occurs on the lower slopes of hills up to about 400 metres at Craig y Cilau.

It is a very long-lived tree (probably reaching 500-700 years) and reproduces vegetatively by new shoots springing from the junction of stem and root and from fallen stems. Suckers from the roots are not normally produced. Fruits are usually fertile (in contrast to *T. cordata* at the north of its range) and seedlings are frequent but saplings rare. Saplings survive in deep shade but strong growth of young trees occurs mainly in gaps.

T. platyphyllos behaves in its natural habitats as a relict species of both old woodlands and such situations as ravines and cliffs. It has been widely planted since at least the sixteenth century and has sometimes spread by seeding from planted sources. It is tolerant of silvicultural neglect and is lost only when woodland is grubbed out.

It is native throughout central and western Europe, reaching its northern limit in a single Swedish locality at latitude 59 °N and its eastern limit at longitude 25 °E in Ukraine. Southwards it extends to the hills bordering the Mediterranean in Europe and into Turkey.

It has often been regarded as doubtfully native in Britain but its fossil fruits and pollen occur in post-glacial (Flandrian) deposits and it appears to have spread into Britain about 7000 years ago. In several localities it grows with natural hybrids (*T. × vulgaris* L.) but more rarely with *T. cordata*.

C. D. Pigott

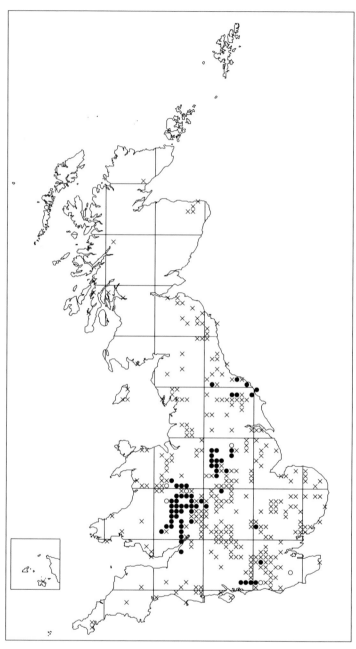

Current map	No	Atlas *	No
1970 →	63	1930 →	14
Pre-1970	6	Pre-1930	3
Introductions	294	Introductions	0

* Only records of native plants were mapped in the *Atlas*.

Tofieldia pusilla (Michaux) Pers.

Status: not scarce

Scottish asphodel

T. pusilla is distinctly calcicole, requiring a reliably damp but not flooded situation; it cannot withstand much exposure. It grows in calcareous flushes from near sea-level at Durness to 915 metres at Coire Coulavie, Glen Affric. These flushes are usually narrow strips of grass and sedge around springs and beside burns, sufficiently far down the mountain to ensure constant water. The flushes are limited by taller vegetation on the drier zones along each side. At low altitude associates include *Carex hostiana, Drosera longifolia, Eriophorum latifolium, Pinguicula lusitanica, Schoenus nigricans* and *Scorpidium scorpioides* but in higher flushes it may be accompanied by *Carex panicea, Juncus triglumis, Pinguicula vulgaris, Saxifraga aizoides, Thalictrum alpinum* and even *Carex saxatilis* (McVean & Ratcliffe 1962).

T. pusilla is a perennial, growing from a rooting stock which gives rise to a cluster of sword-like leaves. Between June and September a taller inflorescence stalk is produced headed by a short raceme of a few small green-white flowers. These rarely open wide, have no nectary and are not long-lasting. Though tiny insects may pollinate them, self-pollination is more likely as the anthers dehisce inwards. Fruits and seeds are produced and vegetative reproduction also occurs by the formation of basal leaf clusters.

John Ray first found *T. pusilla* in 1671, two miles from Berwick. It was new to science. The precise spot is unclear but it could have been a flush beside the River Tweed. There having been railways, roads and many other developments since that time, there is no chance of its survival there, but in its now more well-known mountain haunts it is not threatened. The isolated record in Leicestershire is based on a nineteenth century specimen. There is no information about the habitat it came from.

T. pusilla is a circumpolar arctic-alpine plant. In Europe its only sites south of Britain are in the Alps and the Tatra mountains.

A. Slack

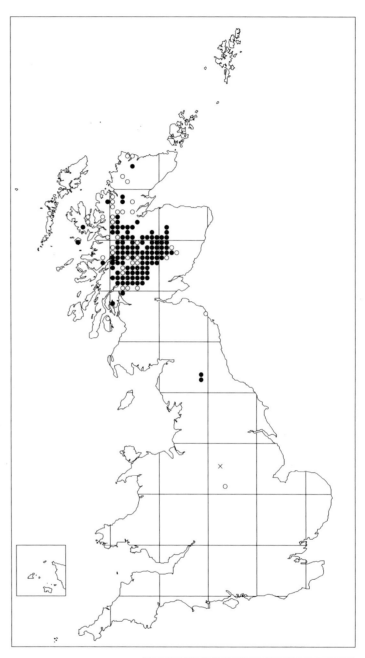

Current map	No	Atlas	No
1970 →	106	1930 →	81
Pre-1970	37	Pre-1930	9
Introductions	1	Introductions	0

Torilis arvensis (Hudson) Link

Status: scarce

Spreading hedge-parsley

A rare weed, most frequent on heavy calcareous clay soils, almost exclusively found in winter-sown cereal crops. It also occurs occasionally in other crops and on waste land in open, well-drained situations. It has poor powers of dispersal and tends not to colonise far from the location of parent plants. It is usually associated with other uncommon weeds such as *Euphorbia platyphyllos*, *Lathyrus aphaca*, *Lithospermum arvense*, *Petroselinum segetum*, *Ranunculus arvensis* and *Valerianella dentata*.

T. arvensis is an annual or rarely a biennial: most seeds germinate in autumn, some in spring. Germination is intermittent, and seed is thought to remain dormant in the soil for several years. Cool, damp summers are known to inhibit seed-set, whilst harsh winters eliminate autumn-germinated seedlings.

Once widespread on the chalk and limestone soils of southern Britain, its range and frequency have diminished considerably since the 1950s as it has proved to be vulnerable to herbicide treatments. It also competes poorly with heavily fertilised modern crop varieties

It ranges throughout western, southern and central Europe and south-western Asia but is declining and is threatened in most countries of north-western Europe. The centre of distribution is probably southern and central Europe, and it is probably at the edge of its range in Britain.

The fruits of *T. arvensis* are covered with bristly hairs which have incurved tips. The hooked tips of bristles on the fruit would cause them to cling to the fur of passing animals, as well as to clothing. In the absence of livestock, dispersal tends to be restricted.

A. Smith

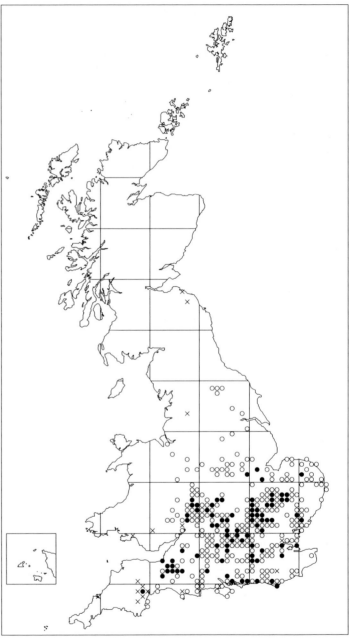

Current map	No	Atlas	No
1970 →	82	1930 →	137
Pre-1970	252	Pre-1930	104
Introductions	16	Introductions	0

Trifolium glomeratum L.
Status: scarce

Clustered clover

A plant typically occurring in short, open communities on sandy drought-prone soils near the sea. It is found in a wide variety of situations, including the tops of stone walls, beside sandy tracks and rides, newly sown lawns, sandy arable fields, golf course fairways and railway sidings; in the Isles of Scilly it is frequent as a bulb field and garden weed. In open, rather base-poor grasslands its associates include *Aira caryophyllea, A. praecox, Crepis capillaris, Erodium cicutarium, Medicago arabica, Ornithopus perpusillus, Trifolium dubium, T. striatum* and *Vulpia bromoides*. It can occur with several other nationally scarce species, for example in south-west England with *Erodium moschatum, Lotus subbiflorus* and *Medicago polymorpha* and the nationally rare *Lotus angustissimus*, and on the Suffolk coast with *Crassula tillaea, Poa bulbosa* and *Trifolium suffocatum*. It is occasionally found as a casual inland.

T. glomeratum is an annual, germinating in the autumn (as early as August in a wet summer) and flowering the following spring. Populations may suffer as a result of spring drought.

It is very erratic in time, space and vigour. Populations range from fewer than five plants to being 'dominant' and 30 cm tall to the exclusion of 'all else' in Jersey in 1979. Plants in a Guernsey granite quarry were about a metre across. It has 'good years' (e.g. 1991, in Dorset, when it was recorded in nine localities). In some areas it is difficult to locate or deemed extinct. On Kew Green, it has appeared irregularly since 1805.

T. glomeratum is more or less restricted to southern and western Europe, from the Mediterranean region and the Canary Islands northwards to western France, southern Britain and south-east Ireland. It is also found in North Africa and in south-west Asia.

D. E. Coombe & S. J. Leach

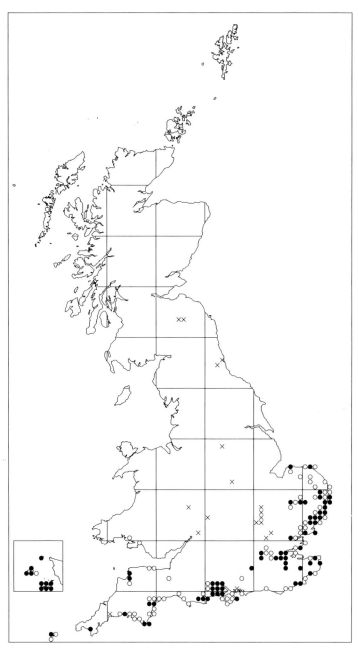

Current map	No	Atlas	No
1970 →	61	1930 →	32
Pre-1970	71	Pre-1930	56
Introductions	18	Introductions	10

Trifolium occidentale Coombe
Status: scarce

Western clover

This is a strictly maritime plant, found in dry species-rich short grasslands, rarely more than 100 metres from very exposed coasts. The soils are either shallow over hard basic or acidic rocks, or of stabilised sand. Its Welsh locality is on limestone (with *Helianthemum canum*); only two sites are known on shales. It extends from the spray-zone, with *Crithmum maritimum*, *Cynodon dactylon*, *Spergularia rupicola* and *Trifolium incarnatum* subsp. *molinerii*, to slightly less exposed grassland characterised by *Jasione montana* and *Scilla autumnalis*: in this, sparse *Calluna vulgaris* and *Erica cinerea* indicate lesser salt spray effects. Seventy-eight vascular plants were recorded by Coombe (1961) in eight 1 m² quadrats from Cornwall and Guernsey including *Armeria maritima*, *Isoetes histrix* (once), *Minuartia verna*, *Scilla verna* (infrequent) and *Sedum anglicum*. *T. occidentale* occurs on calcareous sand in Cornwall, but dune sites in north-western Guernsey are much richer: one square metre there had 39 species, including *Bupleurum baldense*, *Mibora minima* and *Polycarpon tetraphyllum*. Nearby, it grows with *Lagurus ovatus* and *Matthiola sinuata*. Soils range from acid (pH 5.1) on schists to alkaline (pH 7.6) on calcareous sand. It is not found above 70 metres altitude.

It is a stoloniferous, early-flowering (late March to June) perennial, fruiting particularly where stolons extend over sunny rocks. Severe droughts kill it, as in 1959 and 1976, but on these occasions copious seedlings re-established it in 1960 and 1977. In 1990, January hurricanes destroyed many plants on western cliffs.

T. occidentale was first detected in Britain in 1957 and described, new to science, by Coombe (1961). Over three decades it has on average changed very little in distribution and abundance. It recovered slowly from local toxic detergent spillage on cliffs after the Torrey Canyon disaster of 1968. One 'permanent' quadrat established in Guernsey in 1959 was destroyed by a runaway oil rig in 1978.

It is frequent on the coasts of north-western France (Cotentin and Brittany) and south-eastern Ireland; and rare in northern Spain and in Portugal. For a map of its world distribution, see Preston (1980).

It is a diploid species. Spontaneous hybrids with the tetraploid *Trifolium repens* have not been found.

D. E. Coombe

Current map	No	Atlas (S)	No
1970 →	17	1930 →	11
Pre-1970	2	Pre-1930	0
Introductions	0	Introductions	0

Trifolium ochroleucon Hudson

Sulphur clover

Status: scarce

This clover is usually found on the chalky boulder clay, less commonly on chalk, in the lowlands. Most records are from roadside verges or old trackways, less commonly from old pastures and railway embankments and cuttings. As it rarely exceeds 50 centimetres in height it cannot withstand competition from tall grasses such as *Calamagrostis epigejos* and *Festuca arundinacea*. It is thus usually associated with shorter mesophytic grasses including *Anthoxanthum odoratum*, *Briza media*, *Festuca rubra*, *Helictotrichon pubescens*, *Lolium perenne*, *Trisetum flavescens* and the sedge *Carex flacca*. These occur with *T. ochroleucon* on verges mown in high summer, less commonly in lightly grazed pasture. Associated species such as *Cirsium acaule*, *Filipendula vulgaris*, *Pimpinella saxifraga*, *Plantago media*, *Primula veris* and *Sanguisorba minor* indicate calcareous soil, while *Betonica officinalis*, *Lysimachia nummularium*, *Pulicaria dysenterica*, *Silaum silaus* and *Valeriana officinalis* suggest seasonally wet soil. *Melampyrum cristatum* and *Pimpinella major* are characteristic associates on wood-borders in East Anglia.

T. ochroleucon is a long-lived caespitose perennial. Little is known about its reproductive biology, but it has obviously colonised habitats such as railway cuttings from seed.

Many of its old roadside localities have been destroyed in the re-alignment and widening of roads, the use of verges for public utilities such as telephone cables, and the fashion of manicuring verges near farms and villages in the interests of tidiness. *T. ochroleucon* in England occurs in a predominantly arable landscape, and the relatively few old pastures not ploughed up have usually received dressings of phosphate (as basic slag) and nitrogenous spring dressings which favour the palatable grasses *Lolium perenne* and *Dactylis glomerata* at the expense of plants of low competitive ability. Verges left uncut soon develop into tall (1.8 metres) stands of *Festuca arundinacea* and other coarse grasses: their mattress of dead leaves allows few associates to survive.

T. ochroleucon is fairly widespread in western, southern and central Europe, predominantly on clay soils. It extends eastwards to Iran and is also recorded from North Africa.

D. E. Coombe

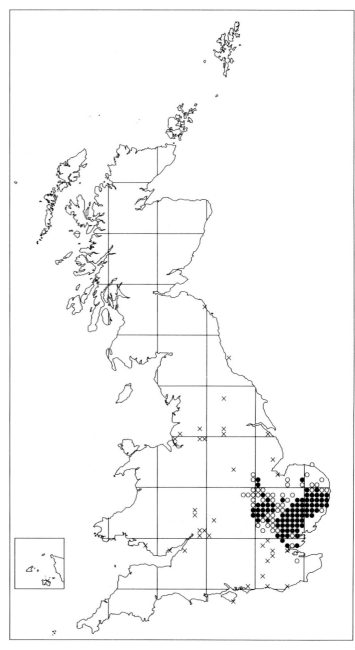

Current map	No	Atlas	No
1970 →	79	1930 →	67
Pre-1970	47	Pre-1930	45
Introductions	36	Introductions	27

Trifolium ornithopodioides L.
Status: not scarce

Bird's-foot clover

This is a plant of barish places, usually near the sea. *T. ornithopodioides* is a calcifuge, occurring on acid sands and gravels, coastal shingle, and on sea-walls and disturbed ground along the upper fringes of saltmarshes. It does particularly well on heavily trampled sites such as car-parks, trackways, viewing points and picnic sites, and has occasionally been recorded on lawns. Its preference is for sites which are parched in summer and moist, even water-logged, in winter. It is tolerant of winter flooding, with its long internodes and petioles enabling the leaves to float on the water surface; in car-parks, for example, it frequently occurs in and around puddles and flooded wheelruts. As befitting a plant of bare ground, it occurs with a wide range of other species: for example, with *Herniaria ciliolata* and *Poa infirma* on low rocky knolls on ground used for car-parking at Lizard Town; elsewhere in Cornwall on dune-sand and cliffs with *Scilla autumnalis*, *Trifolium scabrum* and *T. suffocatum*; on sea-walls and trackways adjoining salt marsh at Bridgwater Bay with *Bupleurum tenuissimum*, *Hordeum marinum* and *Plantago coronopus*; and on lawns in Essex with *Trifolium micranthum*, *T. subterraneum* and the alien *Pratia angulata*. It is confined to the lowlands.

It is usually an annual, germinating in autumn and overwintering in moist sites. It flowers from May to July, or sometimes until September. It is readily overlooked.

It was, perhaps, under-recorded previously (Perring & Walters 1962) and has probably spread into recently disturbed coastal sites. It is scarce inland on commons: 'at risk' in Surrey, sporadic around London, casual in West Suffolk and long gone from Lincolnshire. Perhaps 'improvement' of grassland is responsible for its decline in these counties.

In addition to its British localities, it occurs in south-eastern Ireland, southern and western Europe north to Denmark, and north-western Africa.

D. E. Coombe

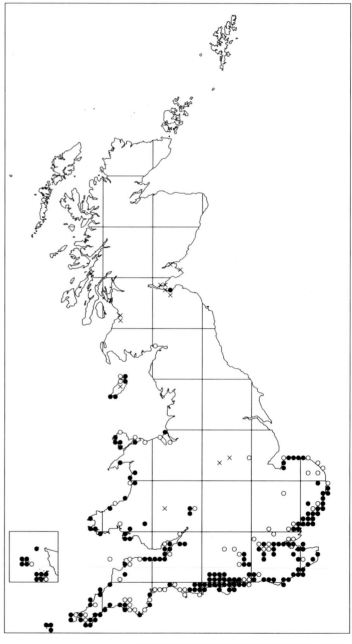

Current map	No	Atlas	No
1970 →	161	1930 →	80
Pre-1970	70	Pre-1930	26
Introductions	13	Introductions	6

Trifolium squamosum L.

Sea clover

Status: scarce

This plant is usually maritime, being found on the edges of saltmarshes and eroded saltings, on sea-walls, in brackish meadows, on drained estuarine marshes and on tidal rivers or creeks; rarely on sand or on low limestone cliffs; and as a casual in waste places and by railways. The soil is usually salty clay, but at two Somerset sites it persists in green lanes on salt-free gleys at 19 km and 27 km from the sea at sites where it was first recorded by Murray (1882). It grows about 10 km inland on the tidal Sussex Ouse. On the Isle of Portland it grows on low limestone cliff edges with *Festuca rubra*, *Inula crithmoides*, *Limonium recurvum* and *Trifolium fragiferum*. On the landward side of a grassy Essex sea-wall it grows with *Lathyrus nissolia*, *Puccinellia distans*, *P. fasciculata*, *P. rupestris* and *Spergularia marina*, and elsewhere with *Bupleurum tenuissimum* and *Hordeum marinum*. Its highest recorded altitude is 50 metres at Yarley Hill.

It is an erect annual, reaching to 40 cm, tolerant of some competition but not trampling or grazing. All recent Somerset records are dated mid-April to early July. It is best sought in May or June.

It has declined greatly over much of its range this century, in part through re-building of coastal defences. Felixstowe Docks were built (1980) on its last known Suffolk site. The Portway from Bristol to Avonmouth destroyed the colonies discovered in 1773 by J. Banks and J. Lightfoot. It is easily confused with similar native or alien species, e.g. *T. alexandrinum*. It occurs rarely as a wool alien. It is perhaps under-recorded since 1970, as it flowers early and disintegrates rapidly. It has been reported from new sites in Somerset, Dorset and Sussex since 1987.

Abroad, it occurs in western and southern Europe, western Asia and North Africa. It is at its northern limit in Britain.

D. E. Coombe

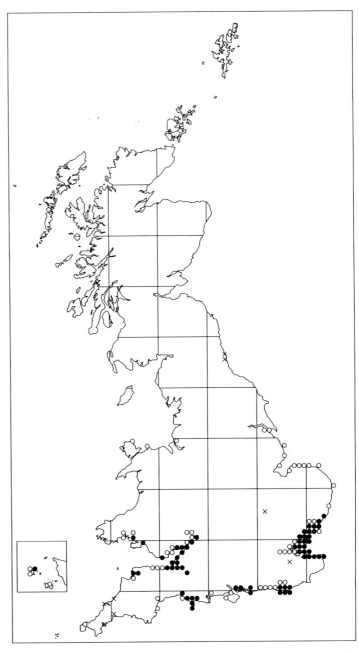

Current map	No	Atlas	No
1970 →	60	1930 →	40
Pre-1970	52	Pre-1930	32
Introductions	8	Introductions	6

Trifolium suffocatum L.
Status: scarce

Suffocated clover

This submaritime plant is rather sparse in species-rich habitats, especially in Cornwall, the Isles of Scilly and the Channel Islands, but gregarious in heavily trampled but less species-rich sites, both on the coast and inland in W. Suffolk. It occurs almost always on sunny, very thin, dry soils on rocky coasts, or on acidic compacted sand and shingle in south-eastern England. In Suffolk and the Channel Islands, thousands of plants can be found in car parks, at picnic sites and on trampled lawns. In eastern England, associates include *Aphanes inexspectata, Crassula tillaea, Ornithopus perpusillus, Poa annua, P. bulbosa, Plantago coronopus, Scleranthus annuus* and other calcifuges, many being annual submaritime *Trifolium* species, e.g. *T. glomeratum*. When found with *T. ornithopodioides*, it is probably on slightly moister soils. In Cornwall and the Channel Islands on sand and on rocky (granitic) coasts the floristic richness is astonishing: commonly 35 to 40 vascular plant species occur in 1 m², plus rare hepatics (e.g. *Riccia nigrella*). It is frequently found with *Scilla autumnalis*, and can occur with many other uncommon species such as *Anisantha madritensis, Crassula tillaea, Euphorbia portlandica, Filago minima, Mibora minima, Moenchia erecta, Ophioglossum lusitanicum, Poa infirma, Polycarpon tetraphyllum, Romulea columnae, Teesdalia nudicaulis, Trifolium incarnatum* subsp. *molinerii, T. strictum, T. subterraneum, Tuberaria guttata* and *Viola kitaibeliana*. It sometimes grows with *Isoetes histrix* and *Juncus capitatus* (Guernsey) and *Ranunculus paludosus* (Jersey) and these associates indicate soils which are moist in winter but dry in summer.

It is a short-lived, autumn-germinating small annual of low competitive ability. It flowers from March to May and then disintegrates. Seeds can germinate in wet summers and a second generation of plants flowers in August.

This species is much overlooked: the increase in records this century may reflect the growth of coastal holiday traffic, but, except in Suffolk, it has mostly gone from inland sites. It is occasionally recorded inland as an alien from both wool and spent tan (*Quercus macrolepis*).

Its broader distribution is western Europe from England southwards and the Mediterranean region, extending eastwards to Iran.

D. E. Coombe

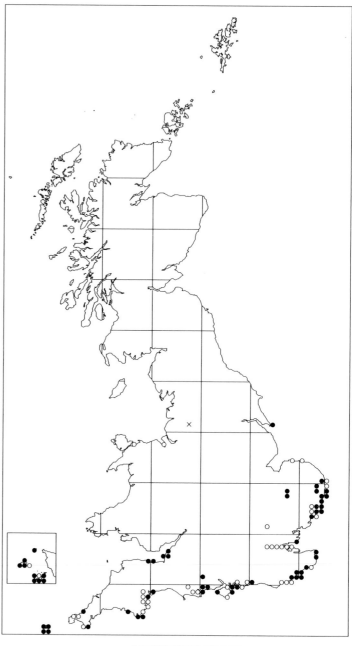

Current map	No	Atlas	No
1970 →	49	1930 →	35
Pre-1970	37	Pre-1930	31
Introductions	1	Introductions	3

Ulex minor Roth

Dwarf gorse

Status: not scarce

This shrub is locally frequent in dry or somewhat moist *Calluna vulgaris-Erica cinerea* heath, occurring locally with *Agrostis curtisii* and/or *Molinia caerulea*, on acid, nutrient-poor soils on podzolised sands and gravels. These soils are mainly of Cretaceous (Wealden, Lower Greensand) or Tertiary (Eocene, Oligocene) age, but *U. minor* is also a component of 'chalk heaths' on thin superficial deposits overlying chalk, and occurs in heaths on sandy glacial drift in the East Midlands. It occurs locally along heathy roadsides and rides in acid woodland, perhaps always a relic of pre-existing heath. It is a palatable species which is suppressed by heavy grazing. *U. minor* has a similar (but narrower) ecological niche to *U. gallii*, which replaces *U. minor* in western and northern Britain. The boundary between the distributions of the two species is remarkably sharp, with little geographical overlap. *U. europaeus* differs from both in being primarily a plant of heath margins, acid grassland and scrub, generally on acid brown-earth soils rather than heath podzols. *U. minor* grows from near sea-level to *c.* 240 metres altitude at Hindhead.

It is a low spiny shrub, reproducing entirely by seed, and generally flowering and fruiting freely every year. The seeds are hard-coated and germination tends to be slow and erratic, but seedling establishment takes place readily, especially after fire.

The map show that there has been little decline in the overall distribution of this species; the pre-1970 records in Sussex are due to the lack of recent recording of a locally common species. It has, however, been lost from many sites over the last half-century owing to the destruction of heathland by agriculture, forestry, building and industrial development, and the spread of scrub and woodland when tree growth is no longer prevented by grazing or burning.

U. minor occurs in central and western France, northern, north-western and south-western Spain, and Portugal.

U. minor is often confused with *U. gallii*. Both are very plastic, especially in the size of vegetative parts, and show parallel ranges of variation. Populations of *U. minor* generally have a mean calyx length less than 9 mm and, in low-growing heathland plants, often 8 mm or less. *U. gallii* populations usually have a mean calyx length of more than 10 mm and even starved populations on thin soils rarely have a mean calyx length as short as 9 mm (Proctor 1965).

M. C. F. Proctor

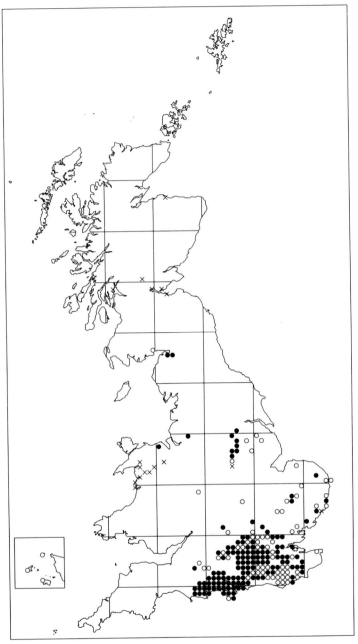

Current map	No	Atlas	No
1970 →	131	1930 →	133
Pre-1970	67	Pre-1930	13
Introductions	17	Introductions	0

Ulmus plotii Druce

Status: scarce

Plot's elm

This elm is typically a constituent of lowland hedgerows and shelter belts. It is believed by some authorities to be endemic in the flood plains of the river systems in the North Midlands of England, and to have been spread elsewhere by artificial means. When closely trimmed, it is indistinguishable from several other typical hedgerow elms, but it becomes identifiable when allowed to grow untrimmed for several years.

Regeneration from seed in the wild has not yet been proved, but it has been raised from seed in botanic gardens and arboreta. Well grown trees flower freely in most years and produce crops of fruit. Suckers are produced in the wild, but not as freely as in other elms, and it is only conjectural that this is an effective means of propagation, or of regeneration after trees have been felled.

Many authorities believe it capable of hybridisation with other British taxa, but doubt whether this occurs freely in the wild, or that its products survive in significant numbers. However, it is one possible explanation of the comparative scarcity of *U. plotii* even before the outbreak of Dutch Elm Disease in the 1970s. Fewer than 50 populations are known to have survived that outbreak, and of those only four or five contain mature trees. Vegetative propagation probably accounts for the remainder, and the grubbing out of hedges after the felling of diseased trees for a significant proportion of those that have not survived.

It is not known to occur in the wild outside Great Britain.

The oldest authenticated records date from 1910, but it was misunderstood until Melville's (1940) account of it. For an account of this species, see Richens (1983).

K. G. Messenger

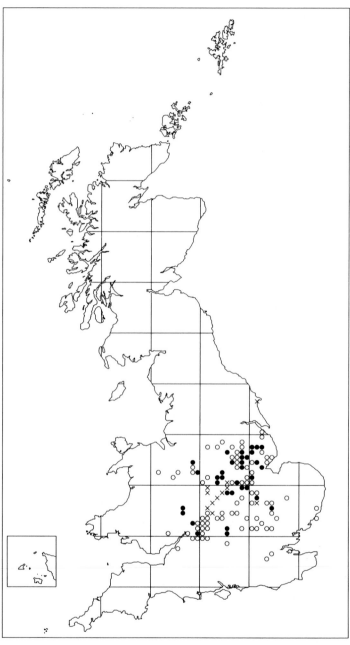

Current map	No
1970	33
Pre-1970	77
Introductions	11

Vaccinium microcarpum (Turcz. ex Rupr.) Schmalh.　Small cranberry

Status: scarce

This is exclusively a species of *Sphagnum* mires, often occurring with its close relative *V. oxycoccos* and sometimes growing intermixed with it, but generally forming small discrete colonies in somewhat drier microhabitats. It typically grows on small hummocks of glacial origin within blanket mires, but also occurs at the top of *Sphagnum* hummocks in raised and valley mires. Compared to *V. oxycoccos*, it tends to predominate further north and at higher altitudes, up to 800 metres on Bogha-cloiche above Dalwhinnie.

It is an evergreen perennial plant which spreads vegetatively by creeping stems to make small clonal colonies which tend to grow more erect and not to be so extensive as those of *V. oxycoccos*. It is pollinated by bees, but is probably self-fertile, although not automatically self-pollinating. Berries are produced freely and seeds are dispersed after ingestion by birds such as grouse.

Due to taxonomic problems, the distribution is poorly understood. It was previously thought to be limited in Britain to the Scottish Highlands, but it has been recently recorded from several sites in Northumberland. The number of 10 km squares for which this species has been recorded has nearly trebled since the *Atlas* (Perring & Walters 1962), but this has almost certainly arisen through a more thorough understanding of the characters and habitat preferences of this species. It is most common and widespread in the Cairngorms and in the 'flow country' of Caithness.

Abroad it is found in Iceland and Scandinavia (almost completely replacing *V. oxycoccos* in Lapland), and the whole of Siberia south to north-western Ukraine; the Alps and Carpathians, tending to occur at higher altitudes than *V. oxycoccus*; and mountains of North America, but absent from Greenland.

It is a diploid which tends to have smaller, darker-coloured flowers on glabrous pedicels, filaments hairy outside, more triangular leaves, and pear-shaped fruits in comparison with the tetraploid *V. oxycoccos*. However, in many British populations, many confusing intermediates occur, and even diploids rarely have 'pure' *V. microcarpum* characters. Triploid hybrids also occur. It is probably best treated as a subspecies of *V. oxycoccos*.

A. J. Richards

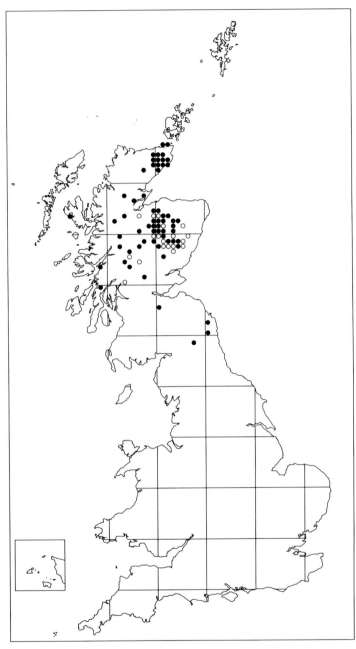

Current map	No	Atlas	No
1970 →	61	1930 →	19
Pre-1970	19	Pre-1930	4
Introductions	0	Introductions	0

Valerianella dentata (L.) Pollich

Status: not scarce

Narrow-fruited cornsalad

This is characteristically a cornfield plant found on lighter, more calcareous arable land, particularly overlying chalk. It often forms part of an association which includes *Anagallis arvensis*, *Aphanes arvensis*, *Chaenorhinum minus*, *Euphorbia exigua*, *Fumaria officinalis* and other fumitories (*F. densiflora* in the south-east), *Legousia hybrida*, *Lithospermum arvense*, *Kickxia elatine*, *K. spuria*, *Myosotis arvensis*, *Papaver* spp., *Sherardia arvensis*, *Veronica arvensis*, *V. persica* and *Viola arvensis*, as well as occasional uncommon weeds such as *Geranium columbinum*, *Petroselinum segetum*, *Ranunculus arvensis*, *Scandix pecten-veneris*, *Torilis arvensis* and *Valerianella rimosa*.

V. dentata is an annual, germinating both in spring and autumn but surviving best in less competitive spring-sown crops.

The British distribution of this species has diminished considerably from that of the 1930-1960 period as mapped by Perring & Walters (1962). This decline has been as a result of the regular use of herbicide and the application of nitrogenous fertilisers to highly competitive modern crop varieties. In counties such as Dorset it is hardly ever seen, although *V. carinata* and *V. locusta* remain common.

V. dentata occurs throughout most of southern and central lowland Europe, and through Turkey to the western shores of the Caspian Sea. It is also found in North Africa.

A. Smith

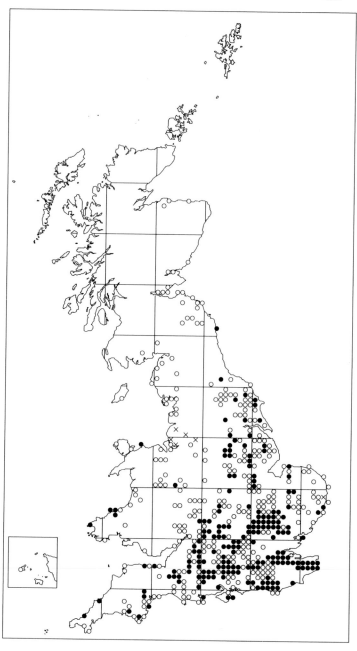

Current map	No	Atlas	No
1970 →	189	1930 →	222
Pre-1970	296	Pre-1930	83
Introductions	6	Introductions	0

Verbascum lychnitis L.

Status: scarce

White mullein

Primarily a plant of waste places and disturbed ground, usually on calcareous soils, *V. lychnitis* often occurs in large numbers in recently-felled woodland, on railway embankments and on the verges of new roads or tracks. It often grows in association with arable weeds, and with other species of *Verbascum* with which it freely hybridises.

V. lychnitis is usually regarded as a biennial, but observations on marked plants show that many produce a flower-spike in two successive years. It reproduces by means of its copious seed production. The seeds are able to remain viable for many years when buried in the soil. Felling of woodland and the dragging-out of timber can unearth seeds and cause large colonies to arise on disturbed ground. Such colonies decline again as other, more permanent, vegetation recolonises the area.

V. lychnitis requires periodic soil disturbance for its survival and occasional felling of woodland within its main areas of distribution appears to provide this. The native population increased markedly following the Great Storm of October 1987 and the subsequent clearance of uprooted trees.

Elsewhere in the world, *V. lychnitis* can be found in France, Holland, Germany, Belgium, Italy, Denmark and Morocco, and is naturalised in parts of Scandinavia and North America.

The British plants are normally white-flowered, but small numbers of yellow-flowered plants occur sporadically around Minehead on the north coast of Somerset, and as casuals or garden escapes in other parts of England, Scotland and Wales.

V. A. Johnstone

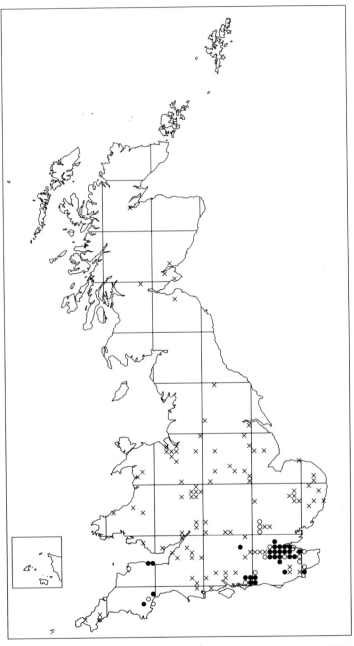

Current map	No	Atlas	No
1970 →	29	1930 →	24
Pre-1970	15	Pre-1930	28
Introductions	96	Introductions	53

Verbascum pulverulentum Villars

Status: scarce

Hoary mullein

The only natural habitat for this species in East Anglia is the coastal shingle bank on the eastern shores of the Wash. However, it is also found in carstone and gravel pits, on roadside verges and railway banks and on waste ground. It may have been spread to some of these localities with gravel. Outside its main area of regular distribution, plants occur as casuals, but rarely persist long unless they find a really suitable habitat. One place where they have done this is by a railway line in Norwich where a fine colony persists.

V. pulverulentum is usually described as a biennial, but it really acts as a monocarpic perennial, taking from two to four years to build up a sufficient rosette for successful flowering. Seeds germinate freely within weeks of falling from the plant and quickly make flat rosettes which remain evergreen during the winter. Plants which have their main stem damaged, and this is a not infrequent occurrence, throw up many new shoots from the leaf axils and will flower and fruit.

In north-west Norfolk *V. pulverulentum* has become reduced in number. It was formerly found on many roadsides where the plants were often cared for by local roadmen, but they do not survive well with modern mechanical cutting. Field headlands also supported many plants but again these no longer survive. Their seed, however, seems long-lived as the site of a roadside pipeline was covered in rosettes the following spring in a site where they had not been seen for some years. At present they are safe in the Snettisham Country Park and are to be found in the area wherever there is suitable bare ground. They are distinctive enough for several non-botanical people to take an interest in them: one fine colony lies behind a garage, whose owner is very proud of them, so they are in no danger.

V. pulverulentum is a native of south-western Europe, not occurring further north than the Netherlands, nor further east than the Rhineland. It is just possible that it is not completely hardy in severe winters and this may help to explain the fluctuations in its appearance away from the coastal fringe.

For a detailed account of the distribution of this species, with lists of associated species, see Parker (1985).

G. Beckett

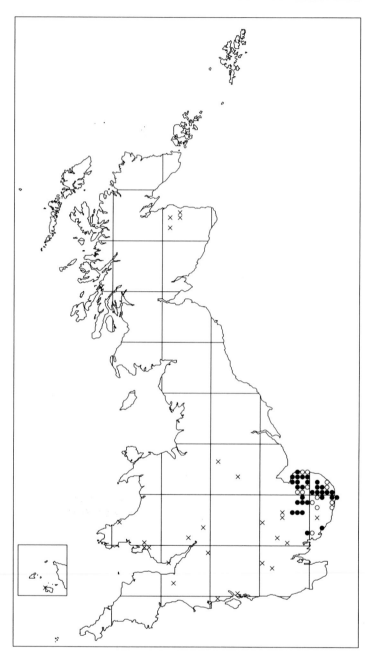

Current map	No	Atlas	No
1970 →	30	1930 →	9
Pre-1970	13	Pre-1930	14
Introductions	25	Introductions	13

continued →

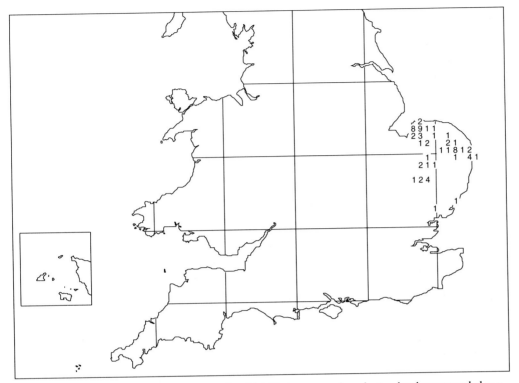

The number of tetrads in each 10 km square in which *Verbascum pulverulentum* has been recorded as a native species from 1970 onwards. Squares in which the species is recorded in 9 or more tetrads are plotted as 9: *V. pulverulentum* is actually recorded in 11 tetrads in TF73. The species has been found in a total of 69 tetrads from 1970 onwards.

Verbascum virgatum Stokes
Status: scarce

Twiggy mullein

This plant is probably native in some parts of south-west England. In Cornwall and Devon it is recorded from dry banks, old walls and pastures; it has also been reported from sheltered sea-cliffs. On the Lizard Peninsula, it grows on a steep, rocky, roughly grazed field with many small annuals including the nationally rare *Polycarpon tetraphyllum*. It is now seldom seen in gardens, but when cultivated its abundant production of seeds allows it to escape with ease. It occurs as a casual on waste ground, rubbish tips, re-seeded roadside verges, disused railways, forest tracks, disused sandpits inland and disturbed dunes by the sea. It will grow in most soil types.

V. virgatum is a biennial, reproducing entirely by seed, which is very small and easily wind-dispersed. This plant cannot survive much competition and often disappears from a site when lack of management allows coarse grassland or scrub to colonise.

V. virgatum is endemic to western Europe, from the Azores, Spain and Portugal to Britain. It is doubtfully native in Italy. The species reaches its northern limit in Britain.

The hybrid between *V. virgatum* and *V. thapsus* has been recorded as a casual in Warwickshire (Stace 1991).

V. A. Johnstone

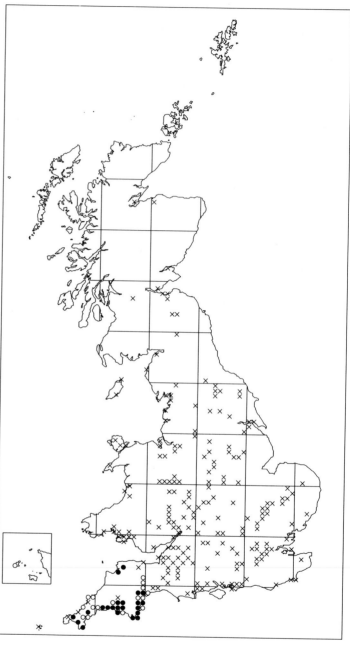

Current map	No	Atlas	No
1970 →	22	1930 →	13
Pre-1970	16	Pre-1930	13
Introductions	204	Introductions	93

Veronica alpina L.
Status: scarce

Alpine speedwell

This is a strictly montane species, growing mainly where snow lies late, in open, often rocky, places with little competition from taller plants. The high corries of the central Scottish Highlands, from the Ben Nevis range to the Cairngorms and the Lochnagar massif, are its chief stronghold. Many localities are on acidic rocks such as granite, but most habitats receive some base enrichment by flushing, and there are occurrences on calcareous substrates. The ground is well-drained but often slightly moist. *V. alpina* often grows in the bryophyte carpets of late snow areas, with vascular plant associates such as *Alchemilla alpina, Carex lachenalii, Deschampsia cespitosa, Epilobium anagallidifolium, Ranunculus acris, Saxifraga stellaris, Sibbaldia procumbens, Thalictrum alpinum, Veronica serpyllifolia* subsp. *humifusa* and *Viola palustris*. On more basic soils, *V. alpina* grows in alpine dwarf herb swards, with *Carex capillaris, Cerastium alpinum, Festuca rubra, Persicaria vivipara, Saxifraga aizoides, S. oppositifolia, Selaginella selaginoides, Silene acaulis* and *Thymus polytrichus*. The altitudinal range is from 760 metres above Loch Callater to 1035 metres in Glen Coe; it has also been recorded from 1160 metres on Ben Lawers.

It is a perennial which flowers quite freely in many of its localities, but there is no information about its propagation in the wild.

Many habitats are accessible to red deer and sheep, so *V. alpina* must tolerate light grazing, but it may be restricted indirectly where grazing has promoted increase of coarser grasses such as *Deschampsia cespitosa*. Most colonies from which there are only pre-1970 records are probably still extant.

This is an arctic-alpine species of both the Old and New Worlds, widespread in northern regions and the high mountains of central Europe and the Rockies.

D. A. Ratcliffe

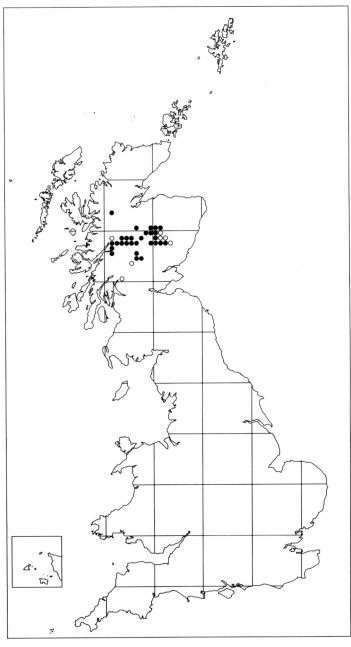

Current map	No	Atlas	No
1970 →	28	1930 →	20
Pre-1970	7	Pre-1930	5
Introductions	0	Introductions	0

Veronica spicata L. subsp. *hybrida* (L.) Gaudin

Status: scarce

Spiked speedwell

V. spicata subsp. *hybrida* is a strikingly attractive plant found on Carboniferous limestone and other hard basic rocks. It grows mainly on inaccessible cliff ledges and in rock crevices, but also occurs on shallow, often humic soils on cliff-tops near rock outcrops. Associates include *Scabiosa columbaria*, which has very similar rosette leaves, and many extremely local or rare species, for example *Aster linosyris*, *Helianthemum canum* and *Hypochaeris maculata*, which may have grown in these western limestone refuges since the late-glacial period. It is found at altitudes from nearly sea-level to 400 metres on Moughton Fell.

It is a long-lived, sometimes shy-flowering perennial, spreading slowly (about 2-4 cm a year) by prostrate rooting stems. Isolated plants set seed, but seed-set per capsule is low and variable (2-10 seeds), perhaps because of incomplete self-compatibility. The small, oily-surfaced, rugose seeds are *c.* 0.8-1 mm long and are dispersed locally by wind and rain-splash. In cultivation, germination and seedling establishment is erratic and sparse, with seedlings occasionally establishing from seeds apparently transported up to 1.5 metres away by ants.

Quarrying was the main threat to its limestone refuges in the past. Many are now protected as nature reserves and are comparatively safe. The main threats are native scrub encroachment and overgrowth by invading *Cotoneaster* spp.

V. spicata is widespread and variable in continental Europe, with five subspecies (Tutin *et al.* 1972). Plants in western British populations vary in size (Avon Gorge plants have flowering spikes up to 45 cm high, most other populations only up to 25 cm at most) and leaf shape, with many differences being maintained in cultivation. They are thought to have survived in their present scattered refuge sites since the late-glacial period about 10,000 years ago, when *V. spicata* was probably widespread in 'steppe-tundra' vegetation (Pigott & Walters 1954). Their genetic differences are likely to result from fragmentation of late-glacial clines, supplemented by selection and genetic drift in small, long-isolated populations. Contact between populations and colonisation of new sites has probably been very rare, if it has occurred at all, although accidental transport of *V. spicata* seeds by far-ranging site-specific birds (e.g. nesting peregrine falcons) is a possible means for this.

V. spicata subsp. *spicata* is found in a few localities in East Anglia. It is included in the *Red Data Book* (Perring & Farrell 1983).

Q. O. N. Kay

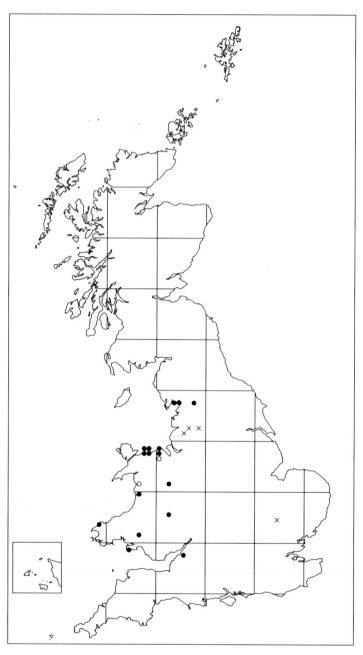

Current map	No	Atlas	No
1970 →	16	1930 →	15
Pre-1970	2	Pre-1930	3
Introductions	4	Introductions	0

continued →

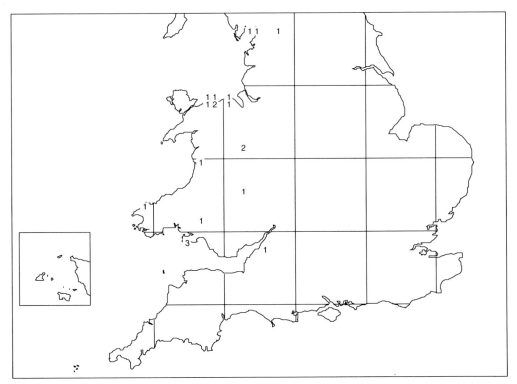

The number of tetrads in each 10 km square in which *Veronica spicata* subsp. *hybrida* has been recorded as a native species from 1970 onwards. The species has been found in a total of 20 tetrads from 1970 onwards.

Vicia bithynica (L.) L.
Status: scarce

Bithynian vetch

This is a mainly coastal species usually growing on clays and found on undercliffs, the backs of beaches and bare ground. It is often associated with other uncommon legumes, notably *Lathyrus aphaca*, *L. nissolia*, *L. sylvestris* and *Vicia lutea*. It is rare inland, where it tends to be a climber in hedges and bushes. Occasionally it occurs on the bare ground of old railway lines.

It is an annual, although sometimes erroneously described as a perennial, usually germinating in early spring and flowering in autumn (White 1912). The seed germinates well: in garden tests 11 seedlings germinated, albeit erratically, from 14 seeds sown. Some seedlings appeared two or even three years afterwards.

This species is apparently becoming rarer. It has certainly disappeared from many coastal sites in the north and east of its range for reasons that are not obvious. In its undercliff habitats in Dorset, it appears to be thriving and abundant.

Abroad it occurs from western Europe to north-western Africa, and east through the Mediterranean to Cyprus, Syria, Turkey and the Crimea.

It is difficult to distinguish localities where this species is native from those where it is a long-established alien. It is probably not native in Cornwall, for example, though it has persisted in one site on the Lizard Peninsula for over 90 years.

D. A. Pearman

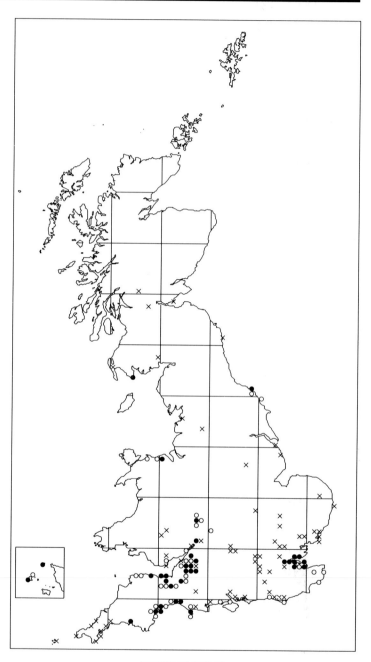

Current map	No	Atlas	No
1970 →	33	1930 →	24
Pre-1970	35	Pre-1930	36
Introductions	64	Introductions	37

continued →

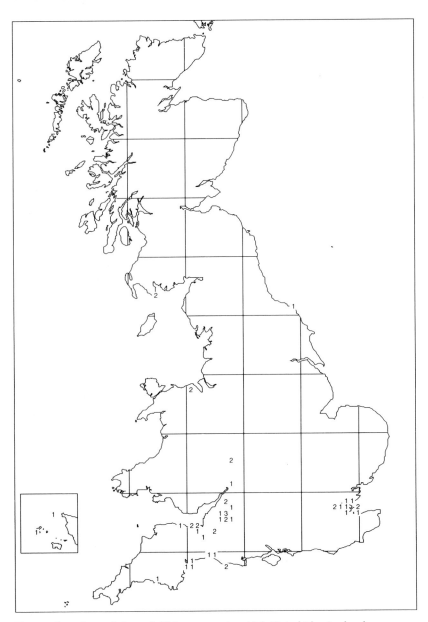

The number of tetrads in each 10 km square in which *Vicia bithynica* has been recorded as a native species from 1970 onwards. The species has been found in a total of 48 tetrads from 1970 onwards.

Vicia lutea L.

Status: scarce

Yellow-vetch

V. lutea grows as a native in several coastal habitats, including sparsely vegetated but stable shingle, *Festuca rubra* grassland and on cliffs in the transition zone between grassland and *Prunus spinosa* scrub. It also occurs in less natural habitats including roadside banks and verges and the sides of disused limestone and serpentine quarries. At the northernmost extant localities, in south-west Scotland, it is confined to south-facing cliff slopes in sheltered bays. Characteristic associates include *Armeria maritima, Dactylis glomerata, Plantago lanceolata, Poa humilis* and *Silene maritima*. In Sussex *V. lutea* is also found in chalk grassland, but there is some doubt whether these plants are native or established aliens. The species is also found as a casual inland, and some inland populations can persist for some years in habitats such as railway embankments and disused gravel pits.

V. lutea is an annual which germinates in autumn, flowers in the following June and fruits freely. Plants on shingle can produce a few flowers underground, which also set seed. Populations vary greatly in size from year to year, and can be particularly abundant in the year following a hot summer when perennial species have been killed by drought. Plants can also appear in abundance after gorse scrub has been burnt.

This species has not been seen at many of its sites in northern England and Scotland since 1930. There is always the possibility that the species could be rediscovered at some of these sites in a particularly favourable year, and at other sites where it is thought to be native it may have been only a casual. In southern England one population was destroyed many years ago by coastal development and another may have been lost because of natural erosion, but the distribution currently seems to be stable.

V. lutea is a southern and western European species which is at the northern edge of its range in Britain. It also occurs in N. Africa and Asia eastwards to Iran. The species is described as polymorphic in Turkey (Davis 1970), but native British populations are rather uniform except for slight variation in flower colour.

C. D. Preston

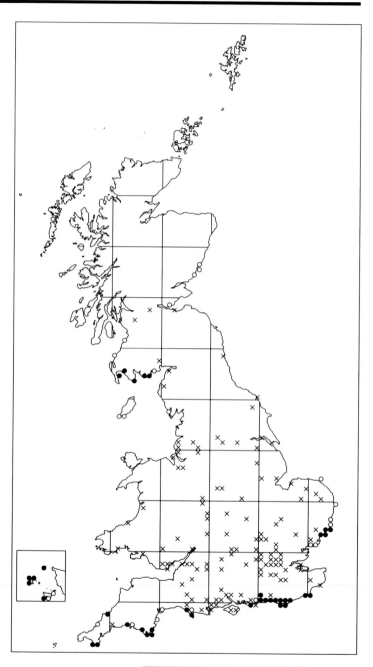

Current map	No	Atlas	No
1970 →	32	1930 →	12
Pre-1970	22	Pre-1930	24
Introductions	123	Introductions	85

continued →

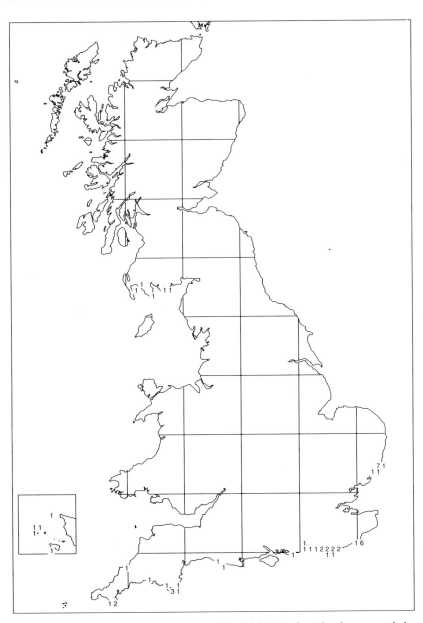

The number of tetrads in each 10 km square in which *Vicia lutea* has been recorded as a native species from 1970 onwards. The species has been found in a total of 55 tetrads from 1970 onwards.

Vicia orobus DC.

Status: not scarce

Wood bitter-vetch

A characteristic species of well-drained old species-rich grassland in fertile, somewhat base enriched soil. It is intolerant of grazing and of competition from scrub. It occurs especially on banks and among boulders and thorny bushes, which give some protection from grazing stock, and on grassy sides of roads and tracks where there is no grazing but an occasional cut prevents the development of scrub. A favourite habitat is the stony edges of small enclosed fields of unimproved grassland from which sheep are excluded in summer to allow a hay crop to grow. It has a wide range of associates including *Alchemilla glabra, Carex pallescens, Coeloglossum viride, Euphrasia arctica* subsp. *borealis, Genista anglica, Pseudorchis albida, Rhinanthus minor, Serratula tinctoria, Stachys officinalis, Succisa pratensis* and *Viola lutea*. It is primarily an upland species, usually found between 200 metres and 300 metres, reaching 430 metres in Afton Glen, but descending to sea-level north of Lochinver.

A long-lived perennial which germinates readily from seed.

Although more widespread in its core areas than previously thought, it is intolerant of both grazing and competition from scrub, and thus affected both by too much and too little management. It has suffered from grassland improvement in some areas.

It is confined to western Europe, from North Spain to Denmark and south-west Norway, but on the European mainland it is a plant of shrub and forest edges. It is closely allied to *V. cassubica* L., which replaces it from central France eastwards.

D. A. Pearman & P. M. Benoit

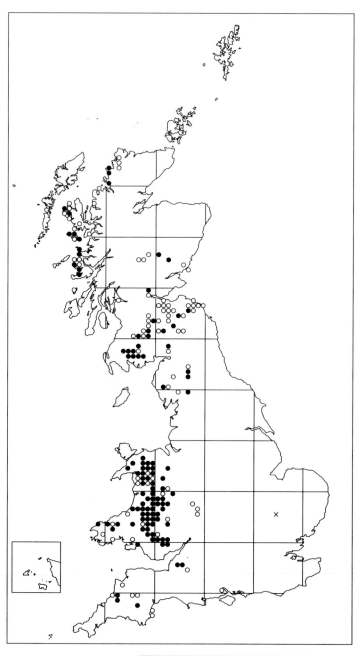

Current map	No	Atlas	No
1970 →	107	1930 →	62
Pre-1970	82	Pre-1930	49
Introductions	1	Introductions	0

Vicia parviflora Cav.

Status: scarce

Slender tare

This species grows in cornfields, hedgebanks and grassy areas on calcareous clay soils. It is an early coloniser of open areas and may require occasional disturbance. In Dorset it grows on crumbling lias soils on sea cliffs, with other legumes including *Lathyrus aphaca*, *L. nissolia*, *L. sylvestris* and occasionally with *Vicia bithynica*. In this area it has recently been found in cliff-top set-aside fields (Preston & Pearman 1992).

It is an annual species which reproduces by seed.

Its noticeable decline in recent years is a cause for concern (Smith 1986), although the plant may have been overlooked or optimistically recorded in error because of confusion with *V. tetrasperma*. The reasons for its decline are not clear, although it may be modern farming practices that are responsible, as is the case in the Netherlands and Germany.

It is widely distributed in southern and western Europe.

L. Farrell

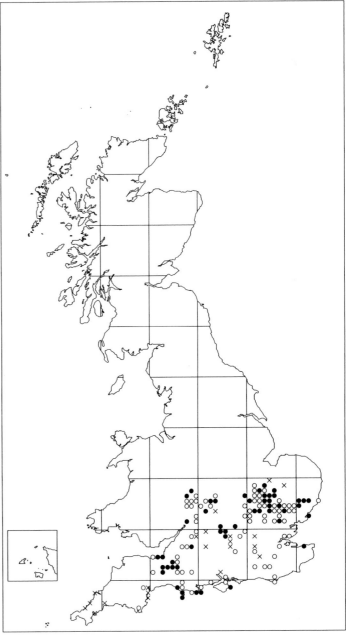

Current map	No	Atlas	No
1970 →	49	1930 →	39
Pre-1970	74	Pre-1930	34
Introductions	21	Introductions	12

Viola lactea Smith

Status: scarce

Pale dog-violet

This lowland species grows on open heaths and moors. It is tolerant of soil disturbance although the longevity of the seed in its abundant soil seed bank is unknown. Because of its inability to compete with taller vegetation it occurs mainly on patchy or open heathland. It occurs on level to gently sloping sites with soils varying from those which are shallow and dry to those which are partially waterlogged in winter. Most sites have *Calluna vulgaris, Potentilla erecta* and *Ulex gallii* whilst the drier locations have frequent *Erica cinerea* and sometimes scattered fronds of *Pteridium aquilinum. Carex flacca, Lotus corniculatus* and *Thymus polytrichus* are typical associates on more calcareous heaths. Typical associates on the wetter hyperoceanic Welsh sites include *Molinia caerulea* and occasionally *Erica tetralix, Juncus acutiflorus* and *Succisa pratensis.* On sea-cliffs in Cornwall and Pembrokeshire *V. lactea* is found with *Plantago maritima* and *Scilla verna* but it seems to avoid the most salt-drenched maritime heathland. The soil pH of its sites varies from 4.7 to 6.5 (F. Evans 1989; Moore 1958).

Reproduction is wholly by seed and can be prolific. After soil disturbance or winter heathland fires, abundant seedlings can become established (F. Evans 1989).

V. lactea is decreasing in Britain owing to the reduction in the extent of open lowland heathland, combined with the decline of the active management once associated with traditional heathland pastoral regimes. As it prefers the better-drained soils, *V. lactea* can suffer more than many other heathland species from improvement or lack of management. Grazing, general soil disturbance along tracks and paths, regular mowing and, in particular, short winter burning rotations favour its survival.

It has a scattered distribution along the Atlantic coast of Europe from Connemara, Republic of Ireland, in the north to Portugal in the south.

V. lactea frequently hybridises with *V. riviniana* to form large floriferous clumps which are highly sterile but reproduce vegetatively. It is less commonly found with *V. canina* so the hybrid with that species is rare. This hybrid is also vigorous and floriferous but is thought to have a generally low fertility (Moore 1957; Moore 1958; Stace 1975).

S. B. Evans

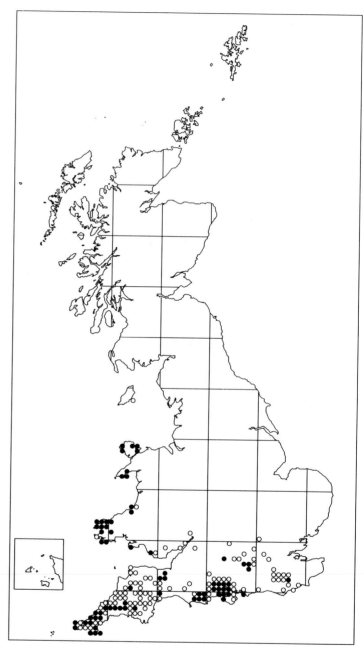

Current map	No	Atlas	No
1970 →	71	1930 →	65
Pre-1970	98	Pre-1930	70
Introductions	0	Introductions	0

continued →

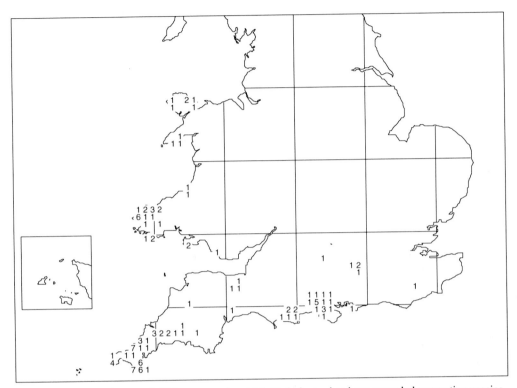

The number of tetrads in each 10 km square in which *Viola lactea* has been recorded as a native species from 1970 onwards. The species has been found in a total of 123 tetrads from 1970 onwards. The tetrad data are inadequate for the New Forest, where the species is still regarded as so common that it has not been recorded at tetrad level.

Vulpia ciliata Dumort. subsp. *ambigua* (Le Gall) Stace & Auq.   **Bearded fescue**

Status: scarce

Populations of this species are found on disturbed sandy soil of neutral or high pH which has a low percentage cover of perennial grasses. Most observed populations are found alongside roads and tracks. Common associates include *Aira praecox, Bromus hordeaceus, Carex arenaria, Festuca rubra, Holcus mollis, Plantago coronopus, Rumex acetosa, R. acetosella, Sedum acre, Trifolium arvense* and *T. dubium*. At Holme-next-the-Sea it has occurred with *Vulpia bromoides, V. fasciculata* and *V. myuros* in an area of 4 m². An exceptional population at Honey Pot Wood exists on the broken concrete of a disused airfield. This is a strictly lowland species.

V. ciliata is a winter annual grass which has no seed bank and a mean dispersal distance of 60 mm (Carey 1991; Carey & Watkinson 1993). Seed production is strongly influenced by competition from perennial grasses (Carey 1991). Populations and individuals vary dramatically in size from year to year. For example, at Santon Warren the number of seeds produced per plant was approximately 10 in 1987 and over 100 in 1990. The life-history characteristics of this species lead to a high turnover of populations. New populations can establish from one seed in a few years given hot dry summers and open ground. As there is no seed bank one disastrous year will lead to a population disappearing. Normally germination starts in September although in the wet July of 1987 seeds started germinating whilst still attached to their infructescence. If plants survive their first few weeks there is a high probability of them surviving to flower in May or June. High seed production appears to be favoured by a wet and warm spring followed by hot and dry conditions in June and July.

This species is restricted to the south of England by both climatic and habitat factors (Carey, Watkinson & Gerard in press) and its distribution is likely to remain relatively stable although populations are likely to appear and disappear at regular intervals. Current research suggests it may increase if the climate becomes hotter and drier. As it is a species of disturbed ground the only management needed to preserve populations is regular removal of perennial vegetation.

From an international perspective, *V. ciliata* subsp. *ambigua* is one of Britain's more important taxa. Only a few populations exist outside Britain, in northern France and Belgium. *V. ciliata* subsp. *ciliata* is a plant of southern Europe and the Mediterranean area which is found in Britain only as an alien.

P. D. Carey

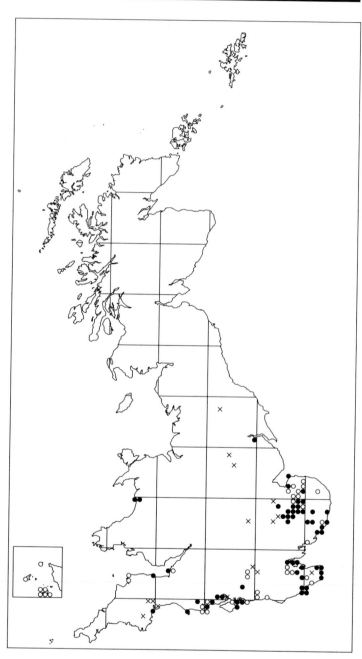

Current map	No	Atlas	No
1970 →	54	1930 →	38
Pre-1970	31	Pre-1930	8
Introductions	15	Introductions	0

Vulpia fasciculata (Forsskål) Fritsch

Status: scarce

Dune fescue

This is a small annual grass of coastal areas, forming small colonies or locally very abundant. It occurs both on dunes and on sandy shingle, on soils which are infertile, free draining and usually very dry during the summer months. The soil pH typically lies between 6.6 and 9.0. Plants occur in open communities through the mobile and later yellow dune phases dominated by *Ammophila arenaria*, to the fixed dunes where there is only remnant *A. arenaria* and the vegetation is dominated by a range of annual and prostrate perennial dicots, mosses, lichens and scattered shoots of *Carex arenaria* and *Festuca rubra*. *V. fasciculata* is frequently associated with other winter annuals such as *Aira praecox*, *Cerastium diffusum* and *Phleum arenarium*. Populations may persist in a given locality for many years where the vegetation is open and there is some movement of sand.

V. fasciculata is a winter annual. Germination occurs in the autumn (September-December) when soil moisture reaches favourable levels. Germination occurs whether the seeds are buried or on the surface of the sand but establishment depends critically upon the seeds being slightly buried (Watkinson 1990). Plants overwinter and flower following vernalisation in late May and June. The florets are hermaphrodite and generally self-fertilising. Dispersal occurs when the fruits are ripe towards the end of June or early July and they then remain dormant over the summer months. There is no permanent seed bank.

The distribution of the species is generally well recorded in Great Britain, whereas on the continent there is some confusion with *V. membranacea*. The abundance of plants within sites is thought to have increased since 1954 when myxomatosis reduced rabbit populations.

The world distribution is broadly circum-Mediterranean, extending to western Europe. The species is at its northern limit in the British Isles. On the continent *V. fasciculata* is known as far north as the Somme Département in France. Native inland localities occur only in Egypt, Israel and Jordan. It has been introduced into Australia where it has become a weed in some localities.

For a detailed account of this species, see Watkinson (1978).

A. R. Watkinson

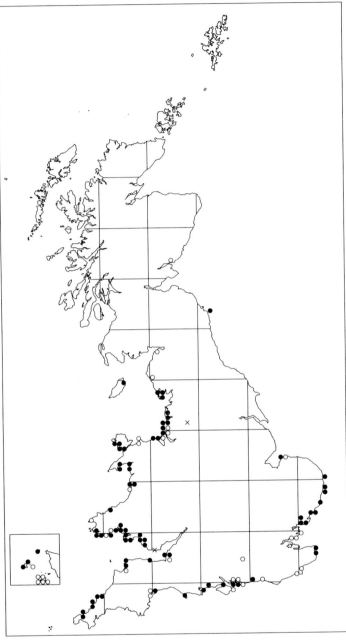

Current map	No	Atlas	No
1970 →	70	1930 →	41
Pre-1970	28	Pre-1930	14
Introductions	2	Introductions	2

Vulpia unilateralis (L.) Stace

Status: scarce

Mat-grass fescue

This grass grows in dry, open and very bare, often rubbly, places on lowland chalk or limestone. In addition to these possibly native habitats it has also occurred in a variety of relatively ephemeral sites, including railway tracks, walls and rubbish tips, arriving at some of these sites with contaminated seed. It is extremely intolerant of competition, growing on its own, or with slightly more robust annuals such as *Catapodium rigidum*, *Cerastium pumilum*, *Minuartia hybrida* and *Vulpia bromoides*. Presumably for this reason it is sometimes found on anthills.

It is an annual. It germinates in spring, flowers early and quickly disarticulates, usually by the end of May or early June. Nothing is known of seed viability.

Although not recorded in Britain before 1903, and only rarely before 1949, *V. unilateralis* is thought on balance to be a native plant. Stace (1961) argues that its range is very similar to another species, *Orchis simia*, of the continental southern element in the British flora. It is very difficult to say whether this species is increasing or decreasing because of the probability that not only was it overlooked or confused in the past, but also that this is still the case. Certainly cessation of quarrying and disturbance have accounted for the loss of some sites, though on the other hand roadworks and building sites may provide additional opportunities.

This species is found throughout southern Europe, north to the Pas de Calais and Belgium and east at least to the Crimea and Syria.

D. A. Pearman

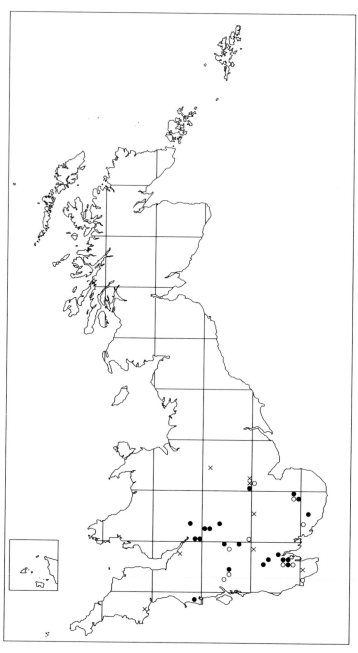

Current map	No	Atlas	No
1970 →	20	1930 →	10
Pre-1970	10	Pre-1930	1
Introductions	8	Introductions	5

continued →

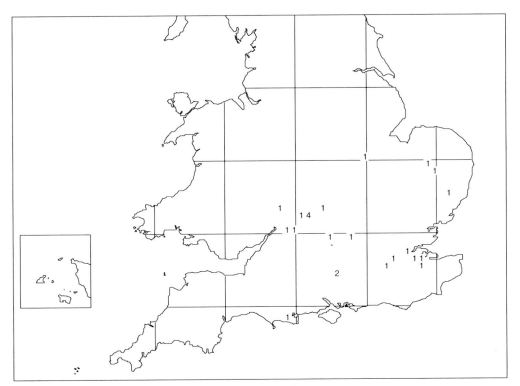

The number of tetrads in each 10 km square in which *Vulpia unilateralis* has been recorded as a native species from 1970 onwards. The species has been found in a total of 24 tetrads from 1970 onwards.

Wolffia arrhiza (L.) Horkel ex Wimmer
Status: scarce

Rootless duckweed

W. arrhiza normally occurs in still water as scattered thalli in a floating carpet of other Lemnaceae and *Hydrocharis morsus-ranae*, growing over submerged *Ceratophyllum demersum*. *W. arrhiza* is particularly common where *Lemna gibba* and *Spirodela polyrhiza* are abundant, but where *L. trisulca* is rare or absent. Most British sites are in species-rich grazing marsh ditches, particularly the wider rhynes and drains that are regularly (often annually) cleaned of emergent and submerged vegetation. The water is normally neutral and rich in nitrogen. Data from Somerset and Kent support the Dutch observation that *W. arrhiza* (and *Lemna gibba*) can become dominant in sites near sewer and factory outfalls where the water is eutrophic (Mountford & Sheail 1984; Westhoff & Held 1969). *W. arrhiza* will also occur in slightly saline water, and is most common in ditches on estuarine alluvium, although it also occurs inland on peat.

Although *W. arrhiza* is the smallest 'flowering plant' in Britain, its flowers have never been observed anywhere in Europe. Reproduction is vegetative, by budding of the thalli to form daughters. The plants sink in late autumn and over-winter as submerged thalli. The minute size of the plant means that short-distance dispersal between sites is possible attached to waterfowl, stock, machinery or botanists. Long distance dispersal by these means is unlikely, since *W. arrhiza* soon dies when removed from the water.

W. arrhiza displays conflicting trends in distribution in different areas of Britain, although it is highly likely that this species was missed in some sites before the present century. Sites near London may have been eliminated by urban sprawl, whilst in Romney Marsh it has remained unchanged or declined where ditches have become shaded by reeds or bank vegetation following conversion of the surrounding grassland to arable. In the Somerset Levels and Moors, however, *W. arrhiza* appears more widespread than in the nineteenth century, possibly due to eutrophication and transport between sites on ditch-cleaning equipment. Effective conservation of *W. arrhiza* requires the control of emergent communities (using a weed bucket rather than herbicides) and the mowing or grazing of bank vegetation.

W. arrhiza is found throughout the warm and temperate regions of the Old World, and in Australia. In Europe, it is absent from Fennoscandia, but otherwise widespread (if local or overlooked) from Britain and Lithuania south to Portugal, Sicily and Bulgaria. *W. arrhiza* has recently been recorded in Saskatchewan, Canada (Looman 1983).

J. O. Mountford

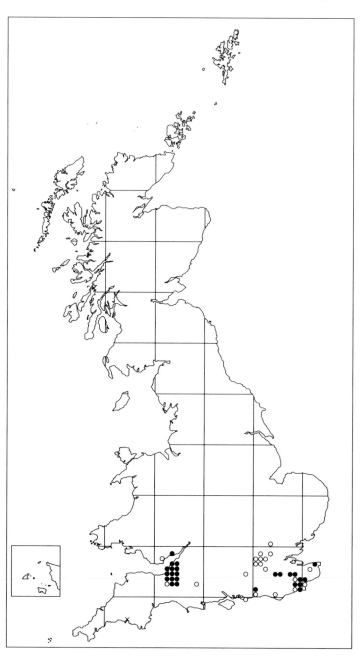

Current map	No	Atlas	No
1970 →	25	1930 →	17
Pre-1970	20	Pre-1930	12
Introductions	1	Introductions	1

continued →

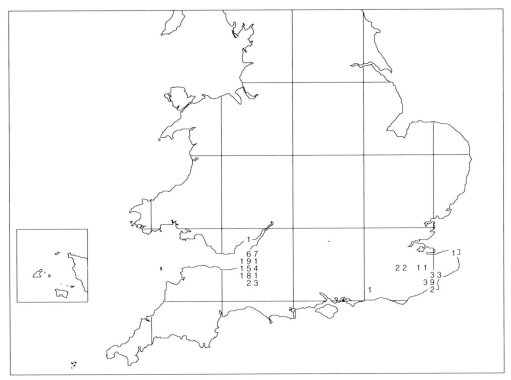

The number of tetrads in each 10 km square in which *Wolffia arrhiza* has been recorded as a native species from 1970 onwards. Square in which the species is recorded in 9 or more tetrads are plotted as 9: *W. arrhiza* is actually recorded from 10 tetrads in ST35 and 12 in TQ92. The species has been found in a total of 82 tetrads from 1970 onwards.

Zostera angustifolia (Hornem.) Reichb.
Status: scarce

Narrow-leaved eelgrass

This is a marine species of mudflats and estuaries which are always well sheltered from violent waves. It is recorded from half-tide to low-tide mark, and more rarely down to 4 metres, generally in shallower but more turbid water than *Z. marina* (Tutin 1942), especially on muds and muddy sands (Gubbay 1988). It grows in waters of variable salinity, often about 25 g dm^{-3} (i.e. fairly brackish (Tutin 1942)), although it has been recorded in salinities up to 42 g dm^{-3} (highly saline (Clapham, Tutin & Moore 1987)). It is usually found in pure stands (although rarely as extensive as *Z. marina*), or sometimes with the green seaweed *Chaetomorpha* spp. It also grows in some coastal lagoons, including The Fleet where it is accompanied by *Ruppia cirrhosa*, *R. maritima* and *Zostera noltii* and the charophyte *Lamprothamnium papulosum*.

The rhizome is perennial and long-lived, although the flowering shoots are annual. Short lengths of rhizome readily break off and are dispersed by the tide, providing the main means for establishing new colonies. It flowers in sea temperatures above 15 °C (usually around July), shedding its seeds in August and September. Germination occurs in autumn and early winter, but seedlings are always scarce, and absent in some years.

No major declines have been noted in this species, which did not suffer the wasting disease reported for *Z. marina*. Changes in salinity and substrate distribution as a result of estuarine 'reclamation' is the most serious threat at some sites.

Z. angustifolia is recorded in Europe from Denmark, Ireland and Sweden, but its distribution is imperfectly known because of confusion with *Z. noltii* and narrow-leaved variants of *Z. marina*.

Some of the mapped records for this species may well be a confusion with narrow-leaved forms of *Z. marina*, which can, in exposed habitats or turbulent waters, have leaves as narrow as 2 mm (Evans 1985). Stace (1991) suggests that this plant may only be a variety (var. *angustifolia* Hornem.) of *Z. marina*.

M. Scott

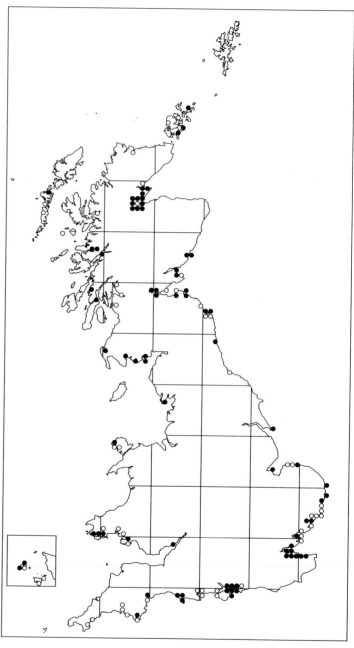

Current map	No	Atlas	No
1970 →	74	1930 →	27
Pre-1970	49	Pre-1930	19
Introductions	0	Introductions	0

Zostera marina L.

Status: scarce

Eelgrass

The most truly marine of the *Zostera* species, this is essentially a subtidal plant, extending from slightly above low water of spring tides to a depth of about 4 metres on British coasts but 10 metres in the Mediterranean, depending on the clarity of the water (Tutin 1942). It is generally found on coarser substrates than *Z. angustifolia*, such as sand and sandy mud (Gubbay 1988) or fine gravel (Clapham, Tutin & Moore 1987), but avoiding brackish water or very exposed coasts. In places it forms dense subtidal meadows. It can support significant communities of marine organisms and is an important food for some wildfowl.

The reproduction of this perennial species is similar to that of the closely related *Z. angustifolia*.

This species showed a marked decline throughout its range from 1931 to 1934, after a major outbreak of a wasting disease. This is generally attributed to the micro-organism *Labyrinthula macrocystis*, but other environmental factors may have put populations under stress, allowing the parasite to flourish. Populations made some recovery after the 1930s outbreak, but rarely to their former abundance and *Labyrinthula* may have remained endemic. Tutin (1942) suggests that the plant might still be found in small quantities at most of its old localities, but it may be overlooked at some of these sites due to lower densities. Trawling, cockle-fishing, bait-digging and other human activities can have localised effects, leading to erosion and eventual displacement of *Zostera*. Short, Ibelings & Hartog (1988) and Turk (1989) recorded a re-appearance of the wasting disease in the late 1980s, which, together with the long-term consequences of increased human pressure on coastal sites, could lead to further declines in future.

Z. marina is recorded from the Mediterranean to the coasts of Norwegian Lapland, and on the Atlantic and Pacific coasts of North America.

While a considerable part of the decline apparent on the map can be attributed to disease and environmental factors, some reflects stricter recording standards. Many early records undoubtedly refer to leaves or uprooted plants on the strandline (Turk 1986). On the other hand, many established colonies are inaccessible even at spring tides, and may be overlooked by land-locked botanists.

M. & S. Scott

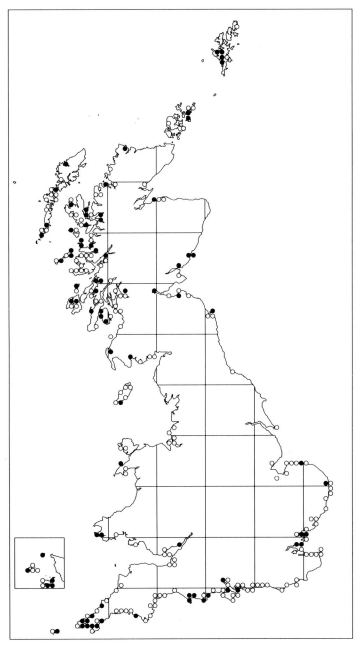

Current map	No	Atlas	No
1970 →	77	1930 →	70
Pre-1970	162	Pre-1930	81
Introductions	0	Introductions	0

Zostera noltii Hornem.
Status: scarce

Dwarf eelgrass

This is usually the most accessible of the three British *Zostera* species. It is found highest on the shore in sheltered estuaries and harbours, often adjacent to lower saltmarsh communities, and never below the low-water mark. It is found typically on mixtures of sand and mud, varying in consistency from firm to soft (Gubbay 1988), often in pools or runnels, although it is able to withstand more prolonged exposure than the other *Zostera* species. It can form extensive populations, as at Maplin Sands, where it covers 325 ha., and sometimes grows amongst stands of *Spartina anglica* (Gubbay 1988).

Z. noltii is a perennial, flowering in mid-late summer, with seed germination in the autumn. Vegetative dispersal of rhizome fragments is probably the usual means of colonising new sites.

Some of the apparent decline may be attributable to past misidentification, the recording of strandline specimens, or to purely temporal effects of natural variation of estuarine substrates. Whilst the apparent decline from the Moray Firth, Firth of Forth or Solent area might be attributed to pollution, it is difficult to reconcile this with the survival of populations around the Thames estuary. Invasive stands of *Spartina anglica* could pose a threat at some sites.

The plant is recorded around European coasts from the Mediterranean to south-western Norway and Sweden.

M. Scott

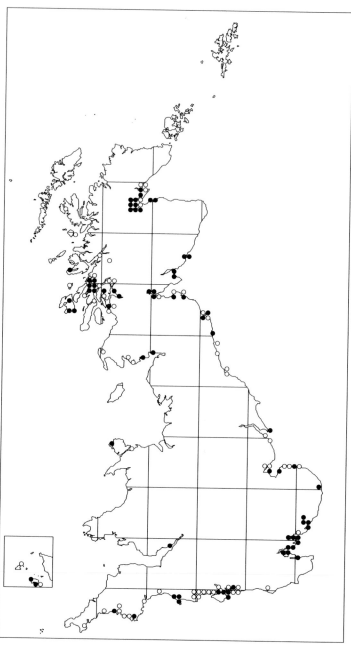

Current map	No	Atlas	No
1970 →	69	1930 →	40
Pre-1970	61	Pre-1930	15
Introductions	0	Introductions	0

Habitats of scarce species in Britain

Two different approaches to the conservation of the flora and fauna of Britain can be recognised. One is concerned with the conservation of particular habitats. Habitats are classified, their importance assessed and efforts made to protect representative or special examples of each. This approach is exemplified by *A Nature Conservation Review* (Ratcliffe 1977) which discusses the major semi-natural habitats of Britain and details the individual sites which are of particular importance for each habitat. The second line of approach is based on a consideration of individual species. The Red Data Books for vascular plants and other taxonomic groups are the products of this tradition. There is sometimes tension between these different approaches, especially when their advocates are competing for limited and inadequate resources. However, both are essential if effective conservation measures are to be developed and applied. It is a truism that a species cannot be protected without the conservation of its habitat. It is less obvious, but equally true, that a species-based approach is also necessary. The conservation of many species will require more than the protection of good examples of particular habitat types. The specific areas in which they occur need to be identified and protected. Within these areas particular species may have individual, and often rather subtle, habitat requirements and sites may have to be managed in particular ways to provide these. Species which are characteristic of particular habitats can be used to identify historic trends in those habitats, by drawing on the detailed historical records available for the more popular plant and animal groups. The distribution of these characteristic species provides an independent index of the effectiveness with which their habitats are being conserved. Other species may not grow in habitats which are recognised and valued by conservationists. A study of these will highlight neglected habitats or draw attention to taxa which are found in areas which do not easily fit into our classification of semi-natural vegetation. Finally, some species attract the attention of the wider public and can be used to draw attention to the need for the conservation of their habitats.

The survey of scarce plants in Britain summarised in this book is clearly a species-based approach to conservation, but it has many implications for habitat conservation. The species included in the revised list of scarce species (Table 1) and the rarer species (Table 2) can be allocated to ten major habitat types. The allocation of some species to these broad habitat types is admittedly rather arbitrary, as some species could be placed in more than one category. Species which occur in a diversity of habitats or in habitats which cannot be assigned to one of the major categories have not been classified. The number of species in each major habitat is shown in Table 4. A comparison with the equivalent total for species in the *Red Data Book* reveals a remarkable similarity.

Table 4 The proportion of scarce and rare species in ten major habitat types. The classification of habitats differs from that given in the *Red Data Book* (Perring & Farrell 1983, p. 93) and the rare species have therefore been assigned to habitat types on the basis of the information given in the species accounts.

	Scarce	%	Rare	%
Montane habitats	38	14	43	14
Heaths, moors and bogs	13	5	17	6
Neutral and acid grassland	10	4	16	5
Calcicolous grassland and basic rock outcrops	44	17	61	19
Fens and calcareous flushes	17	6	20	6
Water margins and damp mud	8	3	17	5
Freshwater habitats	13	5	8	3
Woods, scrub and hedges	28	11	20	6
Arable weeds	13	5	17	6
Coastal habitats	61	23	58	18
Unclassified	18	7	38	12

Montane habitats

The 38 scarce species of montane habitats are listed in Table 5; their distribution is mapped in Figures 10, 11 and 12. The reduction in species recorded in north-west Scotland and in the Aberdeenshire Cairngorms almost certainly reflects a lack of recent recording in these areas.

There is little doubt that most, if not all, of the montane species listed in Table 5 have a relict distribution. Fossil evidence for at least 10 of the 38 species indicates that they were present in the last glacial period at sites in England and Wales which are now well south of their current range. *Dryas octopetala*, *Potentilla crantzii* and *Salix reticulata* have a particularly well documented fossil record; all three were found, for example, in deposits at Barnwell Station in the Cam valley near Cambridge which date from the last glacial some 19,500 years B.P. (Godwin 1975, Bell & Dickson 1971). The subsequent climatic amelioration, accompanied by the spread of woodland, eliminated these species from lowland areas, and in the north and west their range contracted as the mineral soils exposed after the retreat of the ice gradually became leached and large areas were covered by blanket bog. The plants therefore became restricted to the few remaining habitats where mineral soils were available but competition from more vigorous species was restricted by climatic factors. In historical times it is likely that heavy grazing in the uplands has eliminated many of the more palatable montane species from areas which are accessible to sheep; some species such as the montane willows may also have suffered from the effects of burning.

The montane species now grow in habitats such as wind-exposed summits, sheltered and shaded sites where snow accumulates in the winter and lies late into the spring and early summer, rock-ledges on cliffs and the sides of gullies, block screes, and in springs and flushes. Species which can withstand grazing are also found in montane grassland communities. The species in this group differ in their soil preferences: some are markedly calcicole whereas others are distinctly calcifuge. They also differ in the extent to which they are confined to high altitudes. Species such as *Carex saxatilis* and *Juncus castaneus* are strictly montane but others such as *Carex rupestris* and *Dryas octopetala* occur at sea level in the north of Scotland.

Two species which are not included in this habitat group nevertheless have strong affinities with it. *Equisetum variegatum* occurs in both coastal dune slacks and calcareous flushes in the uplands; its unusual habitat preferences and British distribution resemble those of the bryophytes *Amblyodon dealbatus*, *Catoscopium nigritum* and *Meesia uliginosa*. *Circaea alpina* is a plant of submontane woodland and a range of treeless habitats, but cannot be considered a truly montane species.

The habitats of the montane species are often remote and many are too inhospitable and unproductive to have suffered from human exploitation. Few species show any evidence of having declined in the period for which we have botanical records. There is no evidence that any species in this group has undergone a decline in recent years, although an assessment of recent trends is handicapped by the under-recording of some montane areas since 1970. The montane species do not rely on human intervention to maintain specific habitat conditions, although some would probably benefit from action to restrict grazing pressure in upland areas. Specific localities are threatened by proposals for the development of skiing and other tourist facilities. At lower altitudes species have suffered from the effects of afforestation and some sites are threatened by quarrying. Drainage is also a minor threat, as is the damage to tracksides and stony flushes caused by off-the-road vehicles and scrambler motorbikes. None of these is likely to cause a significant contraction in the range of the montane species. The depredations of botanists were probably a significant threat to some of the rarer species in the heyday of the private herbarium collection, but can scarcely have any impact today.

Table 5 Scarce species of montane habitats. Species covered by the project but recorded in 15 or fewer 10 km squares are listed in brackets. Species found in over 100 10 km squares are not listed.

Alchemilla glomerulans	Carex vaginata	Juncus castaneus	Salix arbuscula
Alchemilla wichurae	Cerastium alpinum	(Luzula arcuata)	Salix lapponum
Alopecurus borealis	Cerastium arcticum	Lycopodium annotinum	Salix myrsinites
Arabis petraea	Cerastium cerastoides	Minuartia sedoides	Salix reticulata
Arctostaphylos alpinus	(Cystopteris montana)	Myosotis stolonifera	Saxifraga nivalis
Athyrium distentifolium	Draba norvegica	Phleum alpinum	Sedum villosum
Carex atrata	Dryas octopetala	Poa alpina	Sibbaldia procumbens
Carex capillaris	Euphrasia frigida	Poa glauca	Veronica alpina
Carex rupestris	Juncus alpinoarticulatus	Potentilla crantzii	
Carex saxatilis	Juncus biglumis	Sagina saginoides	

One potential threat to the montane species could, however, have a marked impact in future years. Significant global warming has been predicted for future decades as a result of the emission of 'greenhouse gases'. The 'best guess' of Wigley & Raper (1992) is for a warming of 2.5°C between 1990 and 2100, but there is considerable uncertainty attached to these predictions. In Britain summer temperature rises of 2.5-3°C and winter temperature rises of *c*. 3°C are forecast for the same period, accompanied by an increase of 5-15% in annual rainfall (Rotmans, Hulme & Downing 1994). The distribution of many montane species, including *Dryas octopetala*, *Juncus castaneus* and *Salix reticulata*, is closely correlated with summer isotherms (Conolly & Dahl 1970). The reasons for the absence of these plants from warmer areas probably involve both physiological and ecological constraints, and doubtless differ from species to species. Substantial climate warming is likely to have an adverse impact on the montane scarce species, some of which may be more severely affected than others.

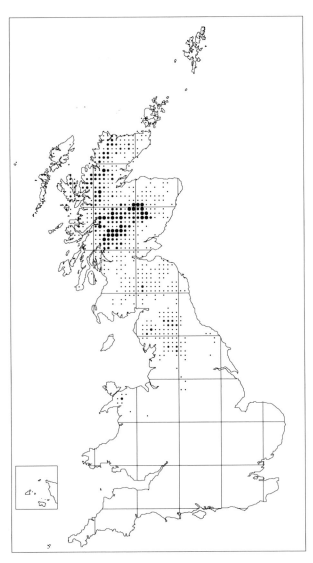

Figure 10 Number of scarce species of montane habitats recorded in each 10 km square. The species mapped are listed in Table 5. Dots of increasing size indicate 1-4 species, 5-10 species, 10-19 species and 20 or more species per square.

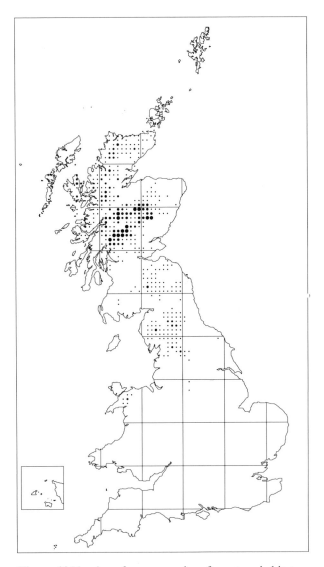

Figure 11 Number of scarce species of montane habitats recorded from 1970 onwards in each 10 km square. The species mapped are listed in Table 5. Dots of increasing size indicate 1-4 species, 5-10 species, 10-19 species and 20 or more species per square.

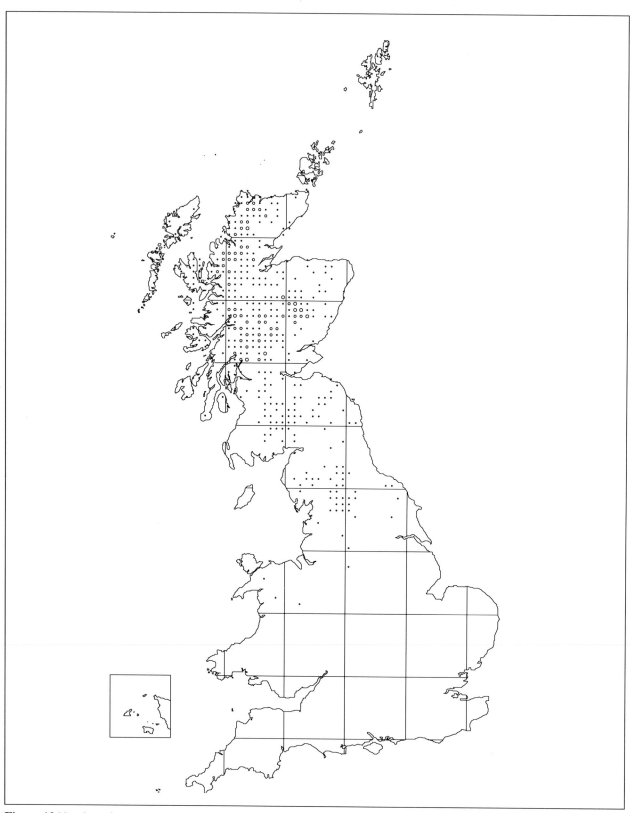

Figure 12 Number of scarce species of montane habitats in each 10 km square which were recorded before 1970 but have not subsequently been refound. The species mapped are listed in Table 5. Circles of increasing size indicate 1-4 species, 5-9 species and 10-19 species per square.

Heaths, moors and bogs

The 13 scarce species of heaths, moors and bogs are listed in Table 6 and mapped in Figures 13, 14 and 15. Half of the species of this habitat have predominantly southern distributions, a fact that reflects the restricted areas now available to heathland and bog species which are limited by climatic or other factors to the southern counties.

The bogs of Britain developed at a relatively late stage in this interglacial. Fossil evidence indicates a considerable expansion of blanket bog and raised mire in northern and western Britain in the period between 7000 and 5000 B.P. There was also a more limited development of raised mires in the lowlands. Natural heathland communities almost certainly occurred in exposed areas of thin, rocky or sandy soil on the coast or in the mountains, but the large areas of inland lowland heath are almost certainly the result of tree clearance by man in the Neolithic and the Bronze Age, followed by grazing, burning or a period of cultivation. The treeless tracts dominated by a few shrubby species of Ericaceae are the western European equivalent of the degraded garigue of the Mediterranean lands.

The only scarce species in this group with an adequate fossil record is *Betula nana*. Remains of this species are frequent in glacial and late glacial deposits throughout Britain and indeed in Ireland, where it is no longer present (Godwin 1975). Thereafter it retracted to its present range. It is, however, a species with many affinities to the plants of montane habitats listed in Table 5, and its history is not necessarily typical of the other species of more lowland habitats. The history of most scarce bog species is probably similar to that of commoner plants such as *Rhynchospora alba*, which is recorded from the late glacial but is far more frequent in later deposits.

There are still extensive tracts of moorland and bog in the thinly populated north and west of Britain, although these have been reduced in extent in recent decades by afforestation or degraded by draining, excessive burning or overgrazing. In the south and east heathlands and bogs have gradually been whittled away by habitat destruction. The results can be seen in the distribution maps of species such as *Gentiana pneumonanthe*, *Hammarbya paludosa* and *Lycopodiella inundata*. Many populations of these species were eliminated by the agricultural improvers in the 18th and 19th centuries. *H. paludosa*, for example, was last recorded in Bedfordshire in 1798, Lincolnshire in 1820, Cambridgeshire in 1855 and had gone from Suffolk by the end of that century. The heathland and bogs of the southern counties survived longer than those in the east, but have nevertheless been considerably reduced in area. Moore's (1962) paper on the destruction and fragmentation of the heaths of Dorset has become a classic of historical ecology. He showed that some heathland was lost to urban development in the period between 1811 and 1896, and to urbanisation and forestry plantations from 1896 to 1934. Thereafter the rate of loss increased as heath was reclaimed for agriculture and mineral workings and lost to building development and forestry. Chapman, Clarke & Webb (1989) estimated that the 40,000 hectares of heath present in Dorset in 1750 had shrunk to 7900 hectares by 1978; by 1987 a further 425 hectares had been lost, mainly to agriculture, buildings and roads (Webb 1990). And Dorset is still one of the most rural of the southern counties.

Even though destruction of heathland and bogs continues, it does not now constitute the main threat to the scarce species of these habitats. Inland lowland heaths rapidly revert to woodland unless the growth of trees is prevented by grazing, burning or similar disturbances. As the traditional agricultural management of heaths has decreased they have become increasingly invaded by trees and shrubs, and many areas which were once heath are now secondary woodland. Webb (1990) found that the area of the Dorset heaths covered by gorse, birch and pine had increased by 15% between 1978 and 1987. Even if a heath survives, this does not ensure the persistence of some scarce species. Plants such as *Cicendia filiformis*, *Gentiana pneumonanthe* and *Lycopodiella inundata* require some degree of disturbance if they are to persist in damp heathland vegetation. This may be caused by grazing animals, periodic burning, by the occasional vehicle passing along unsurfaced tracks, or, in the case of *Lycopodiella inundata*, by peat cutting. The absence of disturbance will inevitably lead to the decline of these species. Tiny annuals such as *Cicendia filiformis* are all too easily eliminated by the well-intentioned 'improvement' of heathland paths and tracks which is just as likely to happen within nature reserves as it is outside them.

Table 6   List of the scarce species of heaths, moors and bogs. Species found in over 100 10 km squares are not listed.

Ajuga pyramidalis	Hammarbya paludosa
Betula nana	Illecebrum verticillatum
Carex magellanica	Lycopodiella inundata
Cicendia filiformis	Rhynchospora fusca
Crassula tillaea	Vaccinium microcarpum
Deschampsia setacea	Viola lactea
Gentiana pneumonanthe	

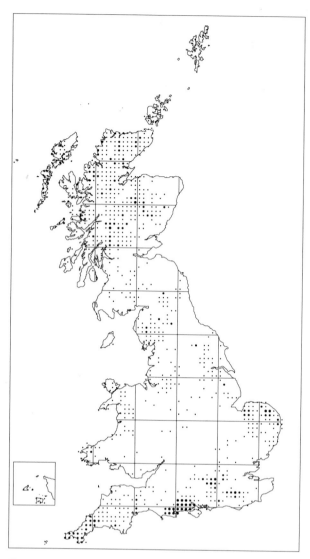

Figure 13 Number of scarce species of heaths, moors and bogs recorded in each 10 km square. The species mapped are listed in Table 6. Dots of increasing size indicate 1-2 species, 3-4 species and 5-9 species per square.

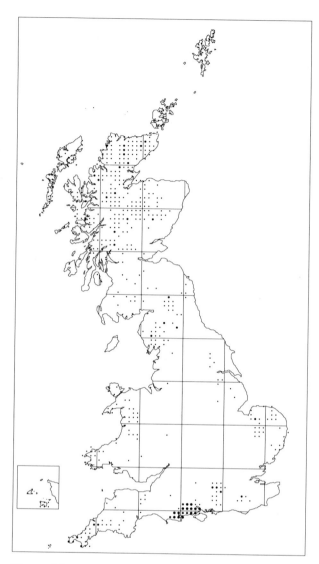

Figure 14 Number of scarce species of heaths, moors and bogs recorded from 1970 onwards in each 10 km square. The species mapped are listed in Table 6. Dots of increasing size indicate 1-2 species, 3-4 species and 5-9 species per square.

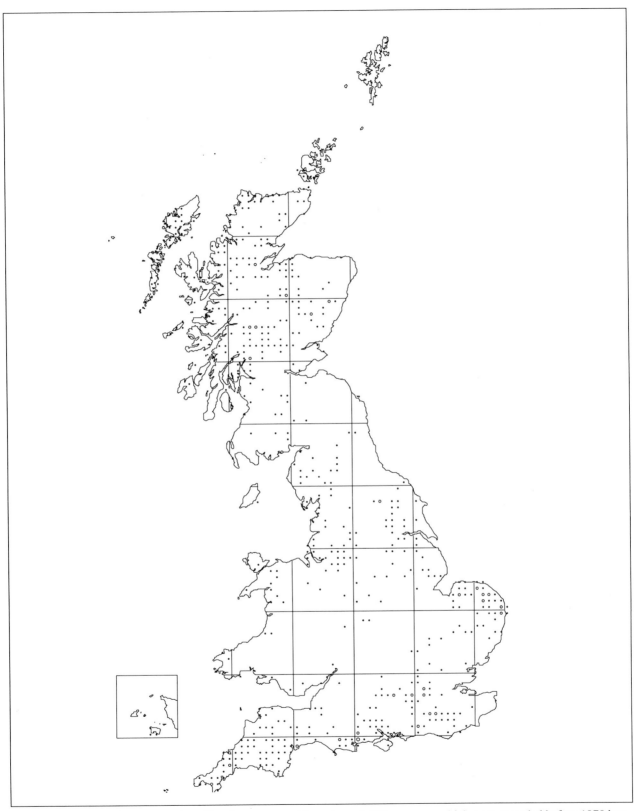

Figure 15 Number of scarce species of heaths, moors and bogs in each 10 km square which were recorded before 1970 but have not subsequently been refound. The species mapped are listed in Table 6. Circles of increasing size indicate 1-2 species, 3-4 species and 5-9 species per square.

Neutral and acid grassland

The ten species of neutral and acid grassland are listed in Table 7 and mapped in Figures 16, 17 and 18. They include species of two distinct ecological groups. Five are plants of hay meadows and the remaining five of less productive acid and sometimes heathy grassland.

Hay meadows are found on relatively fertile sites in both the uplands and the lowlands; in the lowlands they often occur on the floodplains of rivers. Unimproved hay meadows often have a species-rich sward which, unlike calcicolous grassland, is not usually marked by scarce or rare species. The few scarce species which are characteristically found in this habitat are *Euphrasia rostkoviana* subsp. *montana*, *E. rostkoviana* subsp. *rostkoviana*, *Fritillaria meleagris*, *Meum athamanticum* and *Oenanthe silaifolia*. *Alchemilla glomerulans* is a montane species but it also has significant populations in hay meadows in Teesdale. Species-rich lowland hay meadows are now a rare habitat. Those in situations where arable crops can be grown have often been ploughed up. Many are still managed as grassland but by intensive methods. Ploughing and resowing replaces species-rich swards by grassland which is composed almost exclusively of a few selected species. Many remaining flood plain grasslands are threatened by destruction during sand and gravel excavation. However, the loss of species-rich meadows has also been caused simply by the use of artificial fertilisers, which encourages grasses at the expense of less competitive herbs and soon results in a floristically impoverished plant community. As a result of these changes species-rich hay meadows in the uplands can be found only on the occasional steep bank, which has not been 'improved', or in specially protected sites.

The loss of species-rich hay meadows is a symptom of the virtual elimination of unimproved neutral grassland from the countryside. Within living memory herb-rich lowland pastures were taken for granted. Grigson (1950) described the 'old, somewhat neglected meadows, or the rough grazings; of which together...there are still millions of acres in England and Wales'. Unfortunately his conclusion that 'by and large there are few if any meadow plants we were able to pick as children that we shall not be able to pick as old men' was too optimistic. Since Grigson wrote most of the meadows he was describing have been destroyed by ploughing or by intensive grassland management. The most notable species of this habitat is *Orchis morio*, which although covered by the project is still too frequent to qualify as a scarce species.

The remaining five species in Table 7 are plants of less productive, acid grassland, although each occurs in a distinct range of habitats: *Carex montana*, *Chamaemelum nobile*, *Dianthus armeria*, *Hypericum undulatum* and *Spiranthes romanzoffiana*. The four southern species have also suffered from the conversion of pasture to arable, agricultural improvements including the drainage of damp fields and the fertilisation or ploughing and reseeding of pastures, and the loss of agriculturally marginal land to building. Populations have also disappeared as a result of the reduction of grazing levels on heathy grassland, with the consequent spread of coarse herbs or scrub.

Table 7 Scarce species of neutral and acid grassland. Species of hay meadows are annotated '(H)'. Species found in over 100 10 km squares are not listed.

Carex montana	Fritillaria meleagris (H)
Chamaemelum nobile	Hypericum undulatum
Dianthus armeria	Meum athamanticum (H)
Euphrasia rostkoviana	Oenanthe silaifolia (H)
subsp. montana (H)	Spiranthes romanzoffiana
Euphrasia rostkoviana	
subsp. rostkoviana (H)	

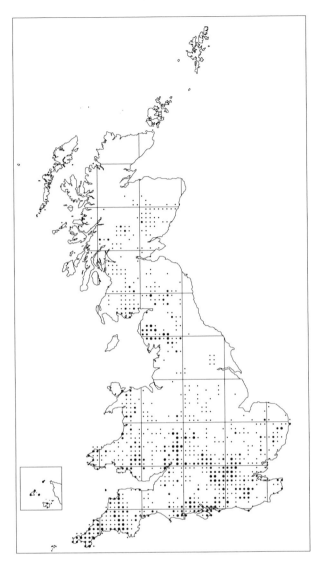

Figure 16 Number of scarce species of neutral and acid grassland recorded in each 10 km square. The species mapped are listed in Table 7. Dots of increasing size indicate 1 species, 2 species and 3-4 species per square.

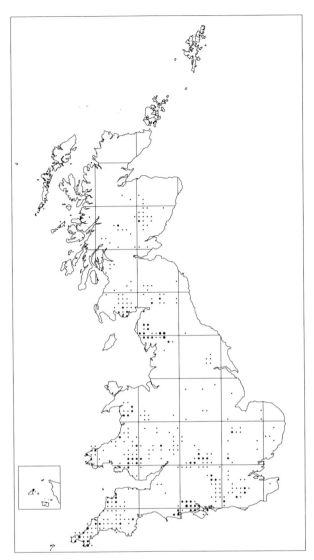

Figure 17 Number of scarce species of neutral and acid grassland recorded from 1970 onwards in each 10 km square. The species mapped are listed in Table 7. Dots of increasing size indicate 1 species, 2 species and 3-4 species per square.

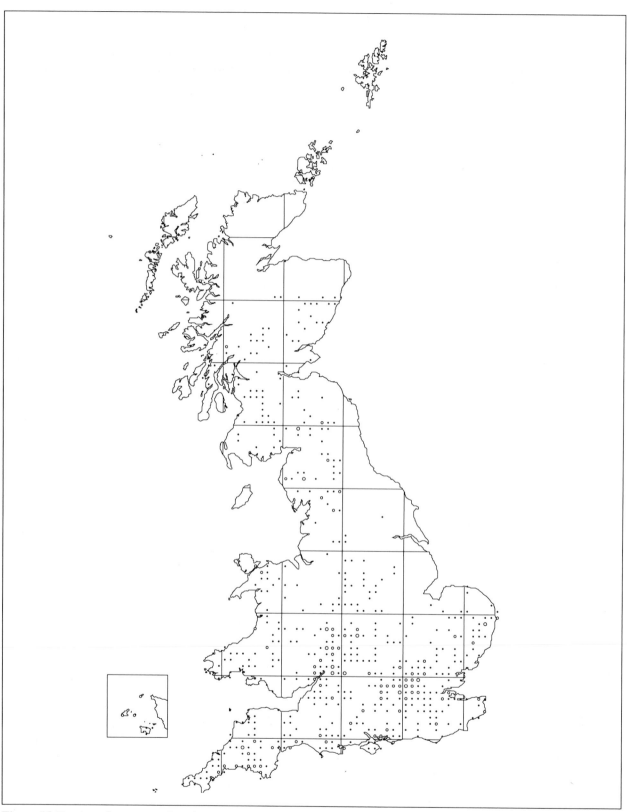

Figure 18 Number of scarce species of neutral and acid grassland in each 10 km square which were recorded before 1970 but have not subsequently been refound. The species mapped are listed in Table 7. Circles of increasing size indicate 1 species, 2 species and 3-4 species per square.

Calcicolous grassland and basic rock outcrops

The 44 scarce species in this group are those of calcicolous grassland and basic rock outcrops (including limestone pavement). They are listed in Table 8 and mapped in Figures 19, 20 and 21. Most of the British calcicolous grasslands occur over chalk or limestone rocks, but some are found over other base-rich substrates such as dune sand. The main basic rock outcrops are limestone, with Carboniferous limestone being particularly significant. Some of the grassland and rock outcrop species extend onto base-rich substrates such as basalt or serpentine. Two species (*Minuartia verna*, *Thlaspi caerulescens*) have a particular affinity for rocks and soil containing high levels of heavy metals.

The grassland species vary in their habitat preferences. Some are plants of short, heavily grazed turf (e.g. *Carex ericetorum*, *Galium pumilum*), whereas others are favoured by longer grass swards or even the edge of scrub (e.g. *Aceras anthropophorum*, *Linum perenne*). A few species have a relatively plastic growth habit which enables them to adapt to swards of different height (e.g. *Phyteuma orbiculare*). Several of the scarce species of calcicolous grassland are dependent on gaps in the sward for their survival; these gaps may be created by drought, rabbit activity or human disturbance. The species of rocks and limestone pavements are distinguished in Table 8. Some of these can be found in open conditions whereas others tolerate or require shade or shelter.

The direct fossil evidence for the history of these plants in Britain is meagre. Three of the species, *Helianthemum canum*, *Linum perenne* and *Minuartia verna*, are recorded from deposits dating from the middle and end of the last glacial period (Godwin 1975). It would be unwise to assume that the history of these three species is typical of those listed in Table 8, some of which have more southerly or more oceanic distributions. Most of the calcicolous grassland species must have been very local in Britain before the clearance of woodland by man. Species of open grassland are thought to have persisted through this period in refugia such as sea cliffs and sand dunes, inland rock outcrops, cliffs and eroding banks alongside rivers and perhaps on steep chalk and limestone slopes where soils were shallow and woodland cover light. A classic statement of this hypothesis was made by Pigott & Walters (1954) with particular reference to several scarce species including *Carex ericetorum*, *C. humilis*, *Sesleria caerulea*, *Tephroseris integrifolia* and *Veronica spicata*. With woodland clearance from the Neolithic onwards, anthropogenic grasslands became available and were colonised by species spreading from naturally open habitats. The colonisation of open habitats appears to have continued into historic times, as several sites with a rich chalk or limestone flora are prehistoric, Roman or post-Roman earthworks or even disused medieval quarries. Species which are currently confined to limestone rock outcrops were clearly unable to expand into grassland habitats, perhaps in some cases because of an inability to withstand grazing.

In more recent times the chalk grassland of southern England has become reduced in extent and the existing sites have been fragmented. The great sheepwalks of eastern England were ploughed by the agricultural improvers of the 18th and 19th centuries. C.C. Babington's lament for the Cambridgeshire chalk grassland is often cited. 'Until recently (within 60 years) most of the chalk district was open and covered with a beautiful coating of turf, profusely decorated with *Anemone Pulsatilla*, *Astragalus Hypoglottis*, and other interesting plants. It is now converted to arable land, and its peculiar plants mostly confined to small waste spots by road-sides, pits, and the very few banks which are too steep for the plough. Even the tumuli, entrenchments, and other interesting works of the ancient inhabitants have seldom escaped the rapacity of the modern agriculturist, who too frequently looks upon the native plants of the country as weeds, and its antiquities as deformities' (Babington 1860). One of the sites Babington had in mind

Table 8 Scarce species of calcicolous grassland and basic rock outcrops. Species found in over 100 10 km squares are not listed. Plants of rock outcrops (including limestone pavement) are annotated '(R)'.

Aceras anthropophorum	Iberis amara
Actaea spicata (R)	Lathyrus aphaca
Adiantum capillus-veneris (R)	Linum perenne
Ajuga chamaepitys	Minuartia verna (R)
Allium schoenoprasum (R)	Orchis ustulata
Carex digitata (R)	Orobanche alba
Carex ericetorum	Phyteuma orbiculare
Carex humilis	Polygonatum odoratum (R)
Cerastium pumilum	Potentilla neumanniana
Clinopodium calamintha	Pulsatilla vulgáris
Crepis mollis	Ribes alpinum (R)
Draba muralis (R)	Ribes spicatum (R)
Dryopteris submontana (R)	Sedum forsterianum (R)
Epipactis atrorubens (R)	Sesleria caerulea
Euphrasia pseudokerneri	Silene nutans (R)
Galium pumilum	Sorbus porrigentiformis (R)
Gentianella anglica	Sorbus rupicola (R)
Gentianella germanica	Tephroseris integrifolia subsp. integrifolia
Gymnocarpium robertianum (R)	Thesium humifusum
Helianthemum canum (R)	Thlaspi caerulescens (R)
Herminium monorchis	Trifolium ochroleucon
Hornungia petraea (R)	Veronica spicata subsp. hybrida (R)

was probably Triplow Heath south of Cambridge, where at least five species which are now scarce or rare (*Ajuga chamaepitys*, *Hypochaeris maculata*, *Minuartia hybrida*, *Pulsatilla vulgaris* and *Thesium humifusum*) were extirpated when the site was enclosed and ploughed in the 1840s; by 1847 Babington described it as 'quite spoiled for botany' (Crompton 1959). The chalk and limestone downland of the southern counties was not ploughed up to the same extent as that in the east in this period, but large areas were ploughed during the Second World War and in the subsequent period of intensive arable farming. Some of the largest areas of chalk grassland are in sites which were owned by the Ministry of Defence, and were not managed as agricultural land.

Many of the smaller chalk grassland sites which escaped the plough were grazed by rabbits until the 1950s. The spread of myxomatosis led to a crash in the rabbit population and to the rapid spread of scrub in these areas. Areas of grassland which were still maintained as pasture were often fertilised, and many of their calcicolous herbs disappeared because of their inability to compete in a lush grassy sward. Other pressures which have destroyed chalk grassland sites or led to the loss of many species from extant sites include the use of chalk-pits and quarries for 'land-fill', the deliberate spraying or unsympathetic management of roadside verges and public pressure on the more popular 'beauty spots'.

The surviving areas of ancient chalk and limestone downland in southern England are prized by conservationists; the best sites are notified as SSSIs and many are managed as nature reserves. Nevertheless, the conservation of chalk grassland is not straightforward. The threat of scrub invasion is always present on sites which are too small, or too exposed to the dog-walking public, to be grazed. Scrub must be controlled in these areas by mowing or by labour-intensive manual clearance. Once an area has been colonised by scrub it is difficult to re-establish a chalk grassland community, as the nutrient levels in the soil increase under a scrub cover and cleared areas tend to be invaded by rank weeds unless a grassy sward can be established rapidly (Stanier 1993). Many chalk grasslands which have escaped scrub invasion have nevertheless become dominated by coarse grass species such as *Brachypodium pinnatum* and *Bromopsis erecta*, probably because of the reduction in grazing in recent years. This has eliminated the low sward which is required by some species, or the disturbed areas needed by others. Small sites may be subject to spray- or fertiliser-drift from nearby arable land. All sites receive rainfall which may contain significant levels of nitrogen. It is not clear whether this is responsible for some of the recent changes in British chalk grassland, but in the Netherlands, where there is much intensive animal husbandry, it has been suggested that enhanced nitrogen levels in rainfall have been responsible for the increased dominance of *Brachypodium pinnatum* in chalk grassland (Bobbink & Willems 1987). Finally, it may be difficult to manage a small site for a range of chalk grassland plants and animals with subtly different ecological requirements.

The grassland over magnesian limestone in northern England has also been reduced to fragmentary stands by ploughing and, locally, by quarrying. However, there are still large areas of grassland over Carboniferous limestone in upland areas which are still dominated by pastoral farming. The threats to these are largely those associated with agricultural intensification. Limestone rock outcrops are of little agricultural importance but can be threatened by quarrying, which has even taken place within National Parks. The limestone pavements of northern England are of great geomorphological and botanical interest, but they have been threatened by legal and illegal removal for sale as ornamental stones or rock gardens.

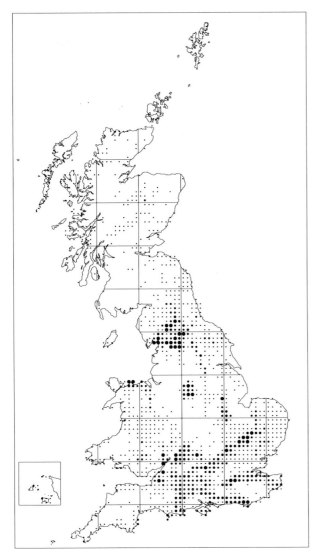

Figure 19 Number of scarce species of calcicolous grassland and basic rock outcrops recorded in each 10 km square. The species mapped are listed in Table 8. Dots of increasing size indicate 1-3 species, 4-6 species, 7-9 species and 10 or more species per square.

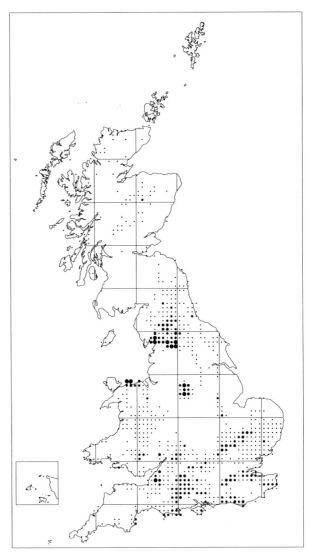

Figure 20 Number of scarce species of calcicolous grassland and basic rock outcrops recorded from 1970 onwards in each 10 km square. The species mapped are listed in Table 8. Dots of increasing size indicate 1-3 species, 4-6 species, 7-9 species and 10 or more species per square.

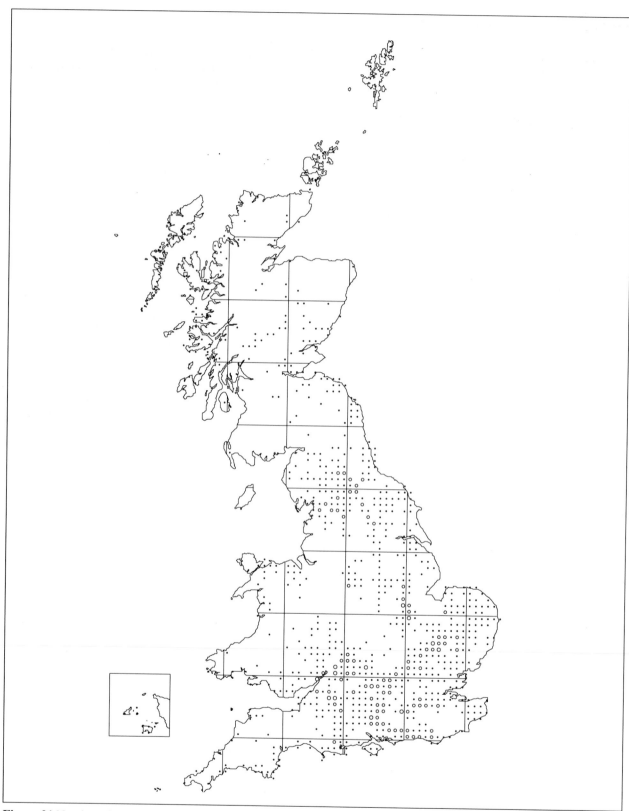

Figure 21 Number of scarce species of calcicolous grassland and basic rock outcrops in each 10 km square which were recorded before 1970 but have not subsequently been refound. The species mapped are listed in Table 8. Circles of increasing size indicate 1-3 species, 4-6 species and 7-9 species per square.

Fens and calcareous flushes

The 17 scarce species characteristic of these habitats are listed in Table 9 and mapped in Figures 22, 23 and 24. This group includes species which are characteristic of a variety of plant communities. One significant group consists of tall herbs which are characteristic of true fens. These include *Carex appropinquata*, *Cicuta virosa*, *Lathyrus palustris*, *Peucedanum palustre*, *Sium latifolium* and *Sonchus palustris*. All these have suffered to a greater or lesser extent by the gradual drainage of the lowland fens from the 17th century onwards, and the canalisation of the larger lowland rivers. This has led to the elimination of these fenland species from some areas and the fragmentation of their distribution in others. These same causes have resulted in the extinction of *Tephroseris palustris* and the virtual extinction of *Senecio paludosus*, two species of similar ecology, in Britain. Most of the tall fenland herbs listed in Table 9 are apparently unable to spread from their existing localities and are rarely if ever found as colonists of new sites. *Sonchus palustris*, which has spread into new areas in recent years, is an exception.

Many of the remaining remnants of fenland are of considerable conservation interest, and are protected as nature reserves. Some have suffered in recent years from falling water tables which have led to the drying out of fenland plant communities and their subsequent invasion by scrub. However, modern techniques can now be used to seal isolated reserves such as Wicken Fen from the surrounding arable land and thus allow the maintenance of a high water table. This has proved to be a much more effective in enhancing the growth of fenland species than programmes of scrub clearance.

Some of the taller plants of fens and ditchsides, such as *Althaea officinalis* and *Sium latifolium*, are intolerant of grazing. A few of the scarce species of fens and calcareous flushes are plants of smaller stature such as *Dactylorhiza traunsteineri* and *Primula farinosa*, and these are sometimes dependent on grazing for the maintenance of a low sward in which they can survive. Other shorter species such as *Carex appropinquata*, *C. elongata* and *Thelypteris palustris* are able to persist or even thrive in damp carr and woodland.

Table 9 Scarce species of fens and calcareous flushes. Species covered by the project but recorded in 15 or fewer 10 km squares are listed in brackets. Species found in over 100 10 km squares are not listed.

Althaea officinalis	Dactylorhiza traunsteineri
(Calamagrostis stricta)	Lathyrus palustris
Carex appropinquata	Lysimachia thyrsiflora
Carex elongata	Peucedanum palustre
(Carex vulpina)	Primula farinosa
Cicuta virosa	Sium latifolium
Cuscuta europaea	Sonchus palustris
Cyperus longus	Thelypteris palustris
Cystopteris montana	

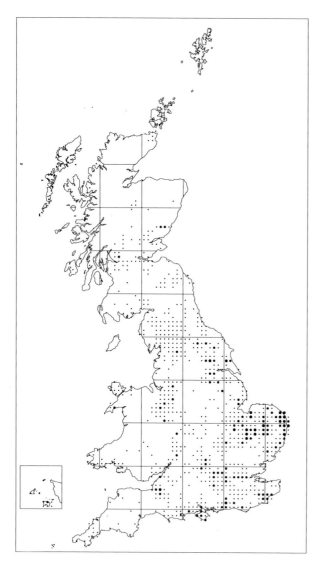

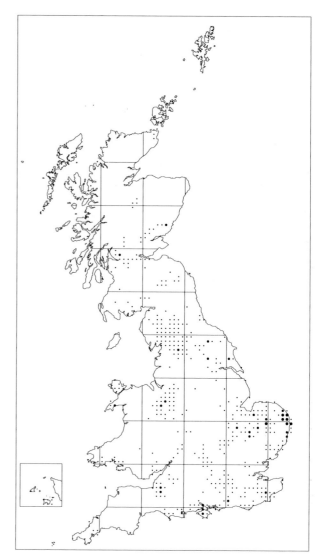

Figure 22 Number of scarce species of fens and calcareous flushes recorded in each 10 km square. The species mapped are listed in Table 9. Dots of increasing size indicate 1-2 species, 3-4 species and 5 or more species per square.

Figure 23 Number of scarce species of fens and calcareous flushes recorded from 1970 onwards in each 10 km square. The species mapped are listed in Table 9. Dots of increasing size indicate 1-2 species, 3-4 species and 5 or more species per square.

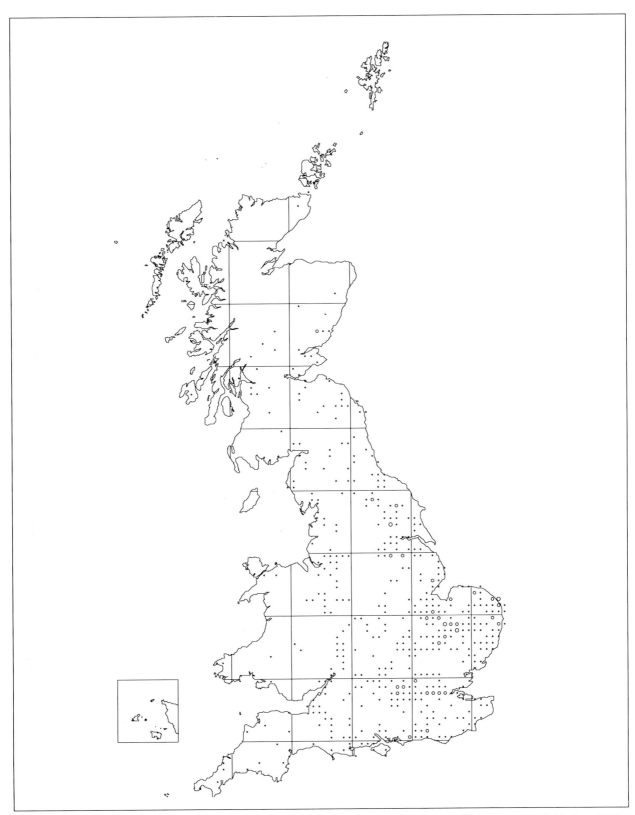

Figure 24 Number of scarce species of fens and calcareous flushes in each 10 km square which were recorded before 1970 but have not subsequently been refound. The species mapped are listed in Table 9. Circles of increasing size indicate 1-2 species, 3-4 species and 5 or more species per square.

Water margins and damp mud

Eight species are listed in Table 10 and mapped in Figures 25, 26 and 27. All are small plants of low competitive ability which grow in shallow water, on exposed mud or in short grazed swards by water. Most are annuals or short-lived perennials which can fluctuate markedly in abundance from season to season. Many of their sites are small water bodies such as seasonally flooded ruts and hollows, ponds and ditches. These are artificial but often ancient habitats which were more frequent in the days when the countryside was scruffier than it is now, and when commons and village greens were grazed by cattle, horses, pigs and geese. In addition to these smaller habitats, some of the species in this group are found in shallow water around the edge of larger ponds, lakes and reservoirs, or on damp mud exposed by a falling water table. We have no detailed knowledge of the history of the species in this group. They probably spread into their current habitats from natural communities by the edge of large rivers, or on floodplains, which have long been destroyed.

Salisbury (1970) drew attention to the decline of species found in these habitats, and this is amply confirmed by the results of the current project. With the exception of *Juncus filiformis*, all the species we have covered show a significant decline in at least part of, and in some cases throughout, their British range. This has been caused by the gradual disappearance of rutted tracks and roads, the drainage or infilling of ponds or the loss of small water bodies under bricks and mortar as towns and villages have expanded. Even where ponds survive, the cessation of grazing on commons and village greens has often led to the replacement of short swards around their edge by rank vegetation or by willow scrub. The reduction in the area of grazing marshes has also contributed to the decrease of species which are found on cattle-trampled ditch-sides.

The most threatened species in the group are *Mentha pulegium* and *Ranunculus tripartitus*. *M. pulegium* must be amongst the most threatened plants in Britain, and *R. tripartitus* may be one of Europe's most vulnerable species. Other species which have undoubtedly declined in some areas have increased in others as they have spread to reservoirs or have colonised newly available habitats such as sand and gravel diggings. *Juncus filiformis* is probably as common as it ever was, as it has also colonised artificial reservoirs from its natural habitats by the edge of lakes.

Table 10 Scarce species of water margins and damp mud. Species covered by the project but recorded in 15 or fewer 10 km squares are listed in brackets. Species found in over 100 10 km squares are not listed.

Elatine hexandra	(Mentha pulegium)
Elatine hydropiper	Persicaria laxiflora
Juncus filiformis	Pilularia globulifera
Limosella aquatica	Ranunculus tripartitus

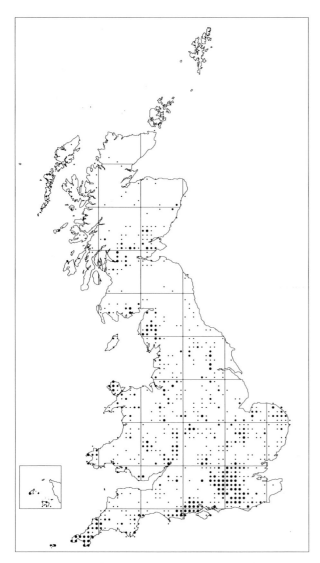

Figure 25 Number of scarce species of water margins and damp mud recorded in each 10 km square. The species mapped are listed in Table 10. Dots of increasing size indicate 1 species, 2 species and 3 or more species per square.

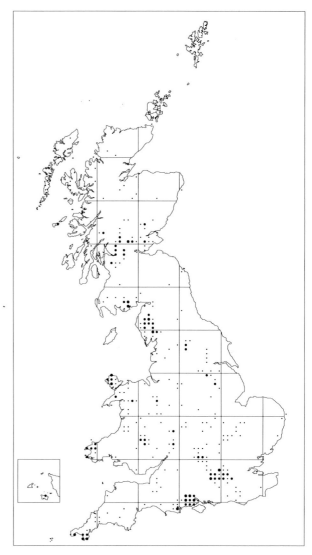

Figure 26 Number of scarce species of water margins and damp mud recorded from 1970 onwards in each 10 km square. The species mapped are listed in Table 10. Dots of increasing size indicate 1 species, 2 species and 3 or more species per square.

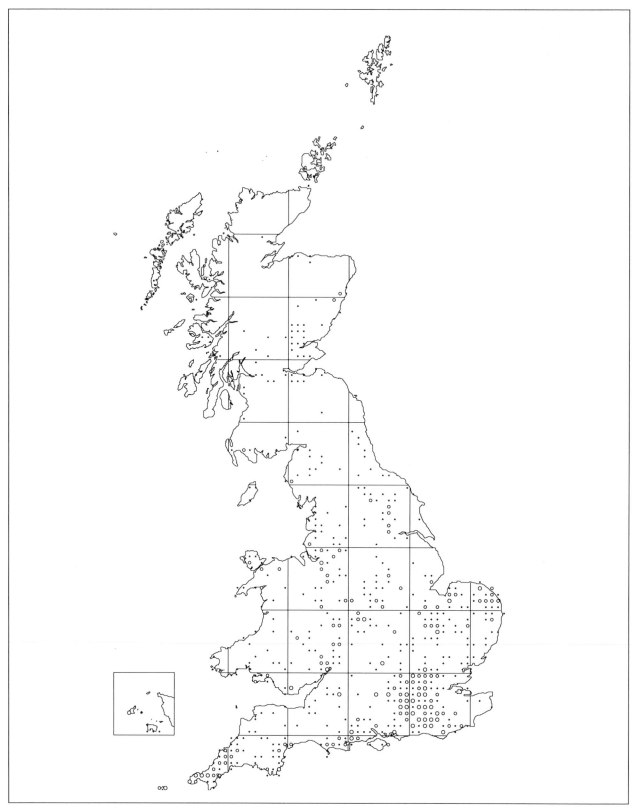

Figure 27 Number of scarce species of water margins and damp mud in each 10 km square which were recorded before 1970 but have not subsequently been refound. The species mapped are listed in Table 10. Circles of increasing size indicate 1 species, 2 species and 3 or more species per square.

Freshwater habitats

The larger natural freshwaters of Britain have not suffered to the same extent as other wetland habitats from habitat destruction. Nevertheless they have been profoundly altered by man. Streams and rivers have been canalised, and their complex channels with stretches of fast and slower water and varied backwaters have been reduced in many cases to uniformity. The nutrient status of rivers, ponds and lakes has been increased as they have received inputs from sewage or, more recently, drainage from fertilised agricultural land. These changes, many of which have had an adverse effect on the natural flora, have been compensated for by the creation of new water-bodies such as the Norfolk Broads (flooded peat diggings), ditches dug when wetlands are drained, canals initially constructed for transport in the late 18th and early 19th centuries and gravel pits abandoned to flooding after the extraction of minerals had been completed. Aquatic plants are often good colonisers and recently created water bodies can have as rich a flora as natural sites.

The 13 scarce species of permanent freshwaters are listed in Table 11 and mapped in Figures 28, 29 and 30. It is not surprising that few of them are plants of acid and nutrient-poor waters, as such habitats are very frequent in the north and west. The only scarce plant which is usually found in such habitats is *Isoetes echinospora*, and this is an under-recorded species which may be discovered in over 100 10 km squares eventually. *Luronium natans* also occurs naturally in oligotrophic lakes but has spread into mesotrophic canals.

The remaining species grow in mesotrophic or eutrophic waters. The most threatened plants are those of mesotrophic habitats, particularly if they have a predominantly southern distribution. The gradual eutrophication of freshwaters which has taken place in lowland Britain is very difficult to combat in specific nature reserves or other protected sites, as few of these are hydrologically isolated. Some canals have had a rich assemblage of the aquatics of mesotrophic water but the increase in leisure boat traffic in recent years has reduced their floristic interest. The flora of ditches in grazing marshes has also suffered a major decline as pastoral land has been converted to arable and the ditches filled or allowed to become overgrown. The effects of all these factors can be seen in the distribution map of a species such as *Potamogeton compressus*. Lakes in the uplands of the north and west are rarely threatened by endemic eutrophication, but are often polluted from individual sources such as agricultural buildings, houses and tourist chalets or fish farms.

Species of nutrient-rich water have sometimes benefited from eutrophication. Most of these are too frequent to qualify as scarce, but the apparent increase of *Potamogeton trichoides* and *Wolffia arrhiza* in the Somerset Levels is perhaps attributable to this cause. It is not easy to account for the restricted distribution of two scarce species, *Callitriche truncata* and *P. trichoides*, which judging from their habitat requirements might be expected to be more widespread.

Table 11 Scarce species of freshwater habitats. Species covered by the project but recorded in 15 or fewer 10 km squares are listed in brackets. Species found in over 100 10 km squares are not listed.

Callitriche truncata	Nymphoides peltata
Isoetes echinospora	Potamogeton coloratus
Luronium natans	Potamogeton compressus
Myriophyllum	Potamogeton filiformis
verticillatum	Potamogeton trichoides
(Najas flexilis)	Stratiotes aloides
Nuphar pumila	Wolffia arrhiza

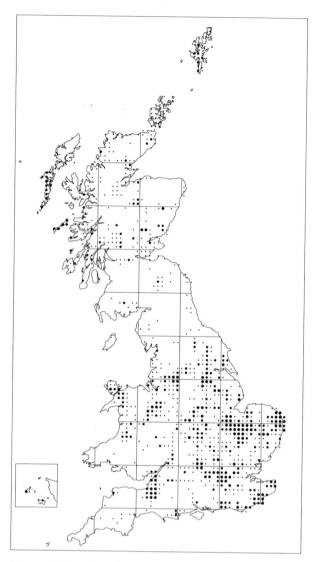

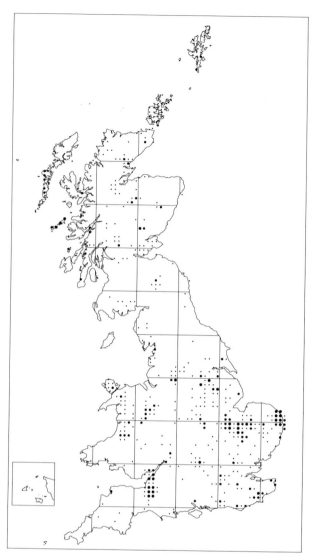

Figure 28 Number of scarce species of freshwater habitats recorded in each 10 km square. The species mapped are listed in Table 11. Dots of increasing size indicate 1 species, 2 species and 3 or more species per square.

Figure 29 Number of scarce species of freshwater habitats recorded from 1970 onwards in each 10 km square. The species mapped are listed in Table 11. Dots of increasing size indicate 1 species, 2 species and 3 or more species per square.

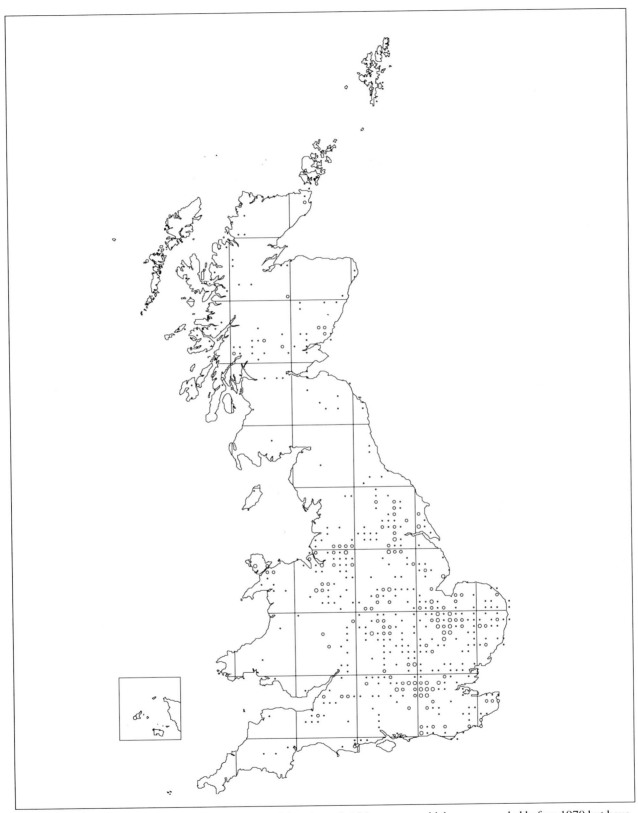

Figure 30 Number of scarce species of freshwater habitats in each 10 km square which were recorded before 1970 but have not subsequently been refound. The species mapped are listed in Table 11. Circles of increasing size indicate 1 species, 2 species and 3 or more species per square.

Woods, scrub and hedges

The wildwood which developed in Britain after the last glacial period covered most of the lowlands and much of the uplands. Significant woodland clearances began in the Neolithic and the tempo increased in the Bronze Age, the Iron Age and in the Roman period (Rackham 1980). By Anglo-Saxon times most of the wildwood had been cleared, and was only represented by small fragments, or by narrow strips retained as hedges. Many of the remaining areas of woodland were intensively managed, and this has often resulted in modifications to the composition of the tree canopy and perhaps to the herb layer as well. In subsequent times the area of woodland increased when farmland was abandoned in periods of agricultural depression or when the population was reduced by disease, or decreased when fragments of wildwood were cleared in times of agricultural prosperity.

The history of trees and woodland has been reconstructed in some detail by pollen analysis, but we have little knowledge of the postglacial history of many woodland herbs. From the late 17th century onwards we have detailed botanical records which can be used to assess their more recent history. Few woodland species have shown the dramatic decline demonstrated by many species of lowland heath or exposed mud in south-east England. In part this must reflect the survival of woods, which were initially maintained in many areas because wood was essential for building and as fuel, and later safeguarded for sporting purposes or simply because of their amenity value. Within woods herbs also appear to be resilient to changes in management, which may alter the size of populations but rarely exterminate species entirely. A study of five woods in eastern England with a long history of botanical recording shows that many species that were formerly recorded are no longer present, but these tend to be light-demanding plants of grassland and woodland edges. Few species of permanently shaded habitats or coppiced woodland have been lost, except in the one wood which was partially grubbed out for arable in the late 17th century and only later reverted to woodland (Rackham 1980). The persistence of species within woods is elegantly demonstrated by *Primula elatior*. This species survives in most of the woods in which it has been recorded, including those which foresters have attempted to coniferise in recent years; the complete destruction of a wood appears to be the only reliable way of exterminating it. However, *P. elatior* also grew in damp streamside meadows, a habitat from which they have totally disappeared (Preston 1993). Most of the sites from which *Cardamine bulbifera* has been lost have also disappeared because of woodland clearance, but coniferisation is now the most significant threat to this species (Showler & Rich 1993).

The 28 scarce species of woods and hedges are listed in Table 12 and mapped in Figures 31, 32 and 33. Some of the species are found in characteristic lowland woodland communities, but have an abnormally restricted native distribution. These species include *Aconitum anglicum*, *Arum italicum*, *Cardamine bulbifera*, *Impatiens noli-tangere*, *Orchis purpurea*, *Ornithogalum pyrenaicum*, *Primula elatior* and *Pulmonaria longifolia*. Several species are more widespread plants of woods over shallow, calcareous soils, including *Bromus benekenii*, *Cephalanthera longifolia*, *Daphne mezereum*, and *Hordelymus europaeus*. Woodland species which do not fit easily into either of these categories include *Epipactis phyllanthes* and *Tilia platyphyllos*. Most of these species have a stable distribution. The only major exceptions are *Cephalanthera longifolia*, which demonstrates a rather mysterious decline, and *Epipactis phyllanthes*, which tends to colonise new sites but disappear from areas in which it is established.

Table 12 also includes a number of species which are typical of northern pine or birch woodland. Native pine woods have declined as they are open to grazing animals such as sheep and deer and have therefore failed to regenerate. Other woods have been deliberately cleared and replanted by exotic conifers. The native *Pinus sylvestris* is itself a scarce species, and other scarce plants of northern woodland are *Corallorhiza trifida*, *Goodyera repens* and *Linnaea borealis*. These plants are able to invade old plantations, and *G. repens* is now found well south of its former native range in the coniferous tracts of Breckland, but their existence in such habitats is precarious as populations are constantly threatened by felling and replanting. *Melampyrum sylvaticum* is also a plant of northern woods, and has a preference for birch.

Table 12 Scarce species of woods, scrub and hedges. Species found in over 100 10 km squares are not listed.

Aconitum napellus	Linnaea borealis
Arum italicum	Melampyrum cristatum
Bromopsis benekenii	Melampyrum sylvaticum
Campanula patula	Melittis melissophyllum
Cardamine bulbifera	Orchis purpurea
Cephalanthera longifolia	Ornithogalum pyrenaicum
Corallorhiza trifida	Orobanche rapum-genistae
Daphne mezereum	Pinus sylvestris
Epipactis phyllanthes	Primula elatior
Fallopia dumetorum	Pulmonaria longifolia
Goodyera repens	Pyrola media
Helleborus foetidus	Sorbus devoniensis
Hordelymus europaeus	Tilia platyphyllos
Impatiens noli-tangere	Ulmus plotii

Scarce species of hedges, woodland margins and open woodland are *Campanula patula*, *Fallopia dumetorum*, *Helleborus foetidus*, *Melampyrum cristatum*, *Melittis melissophyllum*, *Sorbus devoniensis* and *Ulmus plotii*. *Orobanche rapum-genistae* is a plant of open scrub. The distribution of these herbs is less stable than that of the truly woodland species, and factors which have affected individual plants include hedgerow destruction, the drift of agricultural fertilisers and herbicide sprays from arable fields onto adjacent hedges and tracksides, and the decline of coppice management which has reduced the areas of light shade in woodland. *Ulmus plotii* has suffered from disease, which has reduced the number of mature trees, and from hedgerow removal. Many other elms are probably equally worthy of recognition as species but the results of recent critical studies have not yet been published. The individual elm taxa tend to have rather local distributions and many are threatened for the same reasons. The remarkable decline of *Orobanche rapum-genistae* is discussed under that species. The reasons are not understood but the distribution of the species now appears to have attained stability.

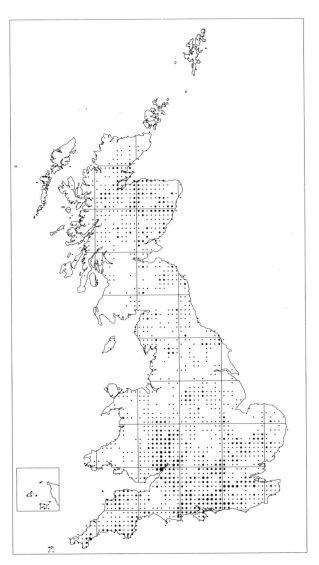

Figure 31 Number of scarce species of woods, scrub and hedges recorded in each 10 km square. The species mapped are listed in Table 12. Dots of increasing size indicate 1-2 species, 3-5 species, 6-8 species and 9 or more species per square.

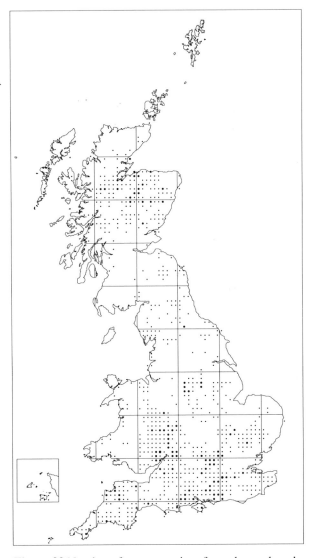

Figure 32 Number of scarce species of woods, scrub and hedges recorded from 1970 onwards in each 10 km square. The species mapped are listed in Table 12. Dots of increasing size indicate 1-2 species, 3-5 species and 6-8 species per square.

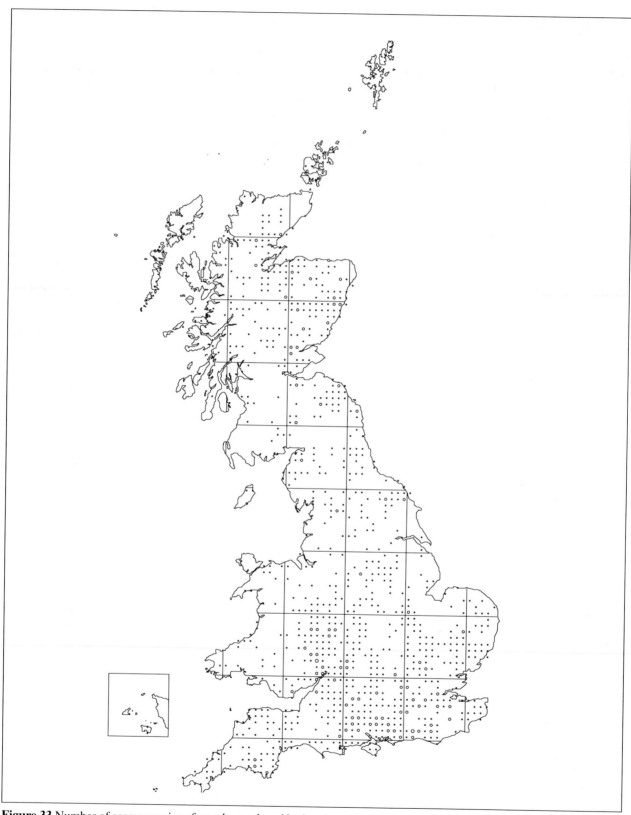

Figure 33 Number of scarce species of woods, scrub and hedges in each 10 km square which were recorded before 1970 but have not subsequently been refound. The species mapped are listed in Table 12. Circles of increasing size indicate 1-2 species, 3-5 species and 6-8 species per square.

Arable weeds

All 19 arable weeds covered by the scarce species project are listed in Table 13 and mapped in Figures 34, 35 and 36. Only eight of these species have been recorded in 100 or fewer 10 km squares since 1970; a further five are included in the revised list of scarce species as they have been recorded in 100 or fewer squares since 1980. However, it is particularly difficult to establish the current status of arable weeds. Many have declined very rapidly in Britain in the last 40 years, and are likely to have disappeared from some of the squares in which they have been recorded since 1970. The extant populations may be small, and those species which have a reservoir of dormant seed in the soil may appear only sporadically when conditions are suitable. These small populations are easily overlooked in large and otherwise unrewarding tracts of arable land. Finally, the picture has been complicated in recent years by the fact that some of the more attractive weeds have been included in 'wild flower' seed mixes and these transient stands are not always easy to separate from established populations.

Some British arable weeds are thought to be native plants which spread from naturally open habitats to invade cultivated land. Other species are believed to have spread with arable farming and therefore to be ancient introductions. There is no conclusive evidence that any of the species listed in Table 13 are native. *Centaurea cyanus* is known to have been present in natural plant communities in the late glacial vegetation of western Europe, and a single pollen grain has been found in British deposits dating from this period (Godwin 1975). It is, however, uncertain whether it persisted in Britain until the beginning of arable farming or whether it became extinct and was subsequently introduced by man. Arable weeds such as those listed in Table 13 are conventionally described as natives of Britain, but their true native distribution is impossible to delimit with any certainty.

Some of the weeds covered by the current project were until recently familiar plants, and even agriculturally significant pest species. They have declined dramatically this century as a result of improved farming techniques. More rigorous seed cleaning was the first of these procedures to make an impact on the weed flora, and as a result one species which was dependent on repeated re-introduction (*Agrostemma githago*) was virtually eliminated; it is now listed in the *Red Data Book*. More species were affected by the development of chemical herbicides in the 1940s and 1950s. Species differ in their sensitivity to herbicides. Some of the species which have declined most dramatically are those such as *Ranunculus arvensis* and *Scandix pecten-veneris* which combine a sensitivity to herbicide applications with the absence of a large bank of dormant seed in the soil. In addition to the direct impact of seed-cleaning and herbicides, weeds have suffered indirectly from the development of improved crop varieties which are much more competitive when grown in heavily fertilised fields. Whereas many stubble fields were left unploughed for several weeks after harvest and not sown until the following spring, the current tendency is to sow cereals soon after the harvest in autumn. This has led to a reduction in species which germinate in spring and flower and fruit in the autumn stubble.

As a result of all these changes, there has been a dramatic change in the weed flora of arable fields. Many species have disappeared from some areas entirely. Some species appear to have retracted onto arable fields on chalky soils, for reasons which are not well understood. Where the scarcer weeds survive they tend to be present at the borders of fields, where the stand of cereals thins out, in corners which have escaped herbicide sprays or in the very occasional field which for one reason or another is not farmed by intensive methods. In most fields the traditional weeds have been replaced by a group of species, including *Alopecurus myosuroides* and *Galium aparine*, which are resistant to herbicides or can take advantage of the high levels of nutrients in fertilised fields.

Ornithologists have recently recognised a long-term decline in the birds of arable land. Species such as grey partridge and corn bunting have suffered from agricultural intensification in a similar way to the arable weeds. The main causes of the decline in farmland birds are thought to be the switch to autumn-sown crops and consequent loss of winter stubble fields, the increasing use of inorganic fertilisers, herbicides and insecticides and the destruction or degradation of habitats such as hedgerows and wet meadows (Gibbons, Reid & Chapman 1993).

Table 13 Arable weeds covered by the project. The list includes species which occur in 16-100 and those which occur in over 100 10 km squares.

Apera interrupta	Fumaria densiflora	Papaver hybridum	Silene noctiflora
Apera spica-venti	Fumaria parviflora	Polygonum rurivagum	Torilis arvensis
Centaurea cyanus	Fumaria vaillantii	Ranunculus arvensis	Valerianella dentata
Euphorbia platyphyllos	Galeopsis angustifolia	Scandix pecten-veneris	Vicia parviflora
Fumaria bastardii	Papaver argemone	Silene gallica	

The conservation of arable weeds is a difficult problem. A few devoted enthusiasts have championed their cause in the face of considerable indifference from other conservationists, who have considered that semi-natural habitats should have priority or have been unwilling to face the ridicule that they feared might be provoked by plans to conserve species hitherto regarded as pests. The most imaginative proposals have been those for 'conservation headlands', unsprayed strips of land six metres wide left around the edge of arable fields. These were originally developed by the Game Conservancy as a means of increasing the number of game birds on a farm, but they have also proved to be of value to arable weeds. Another possibility is to manage fields with particularly rich arable weed communities as reserves specifically for the weeds. Part of the Weeting Heath National Nature Reserve is already managed as arable land to protect rare Breckland weeds.

A more detailed account of the ecology and conservation of the British weed flora is given by Wilson (1992).

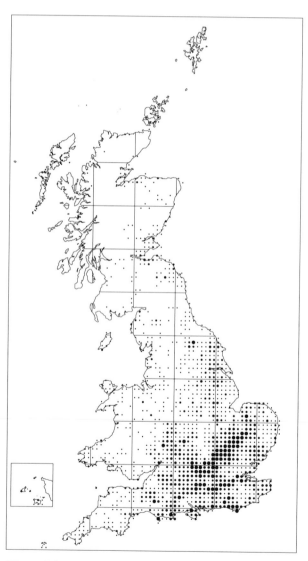

Figure 34 Number of arable weed species covered by the project recorded in each 10 km square. The species mapped are listed in Table 13. Dots of increasing size indicate 1-2 species, 3-4 species, 5-6 species and 7 or more species per square.

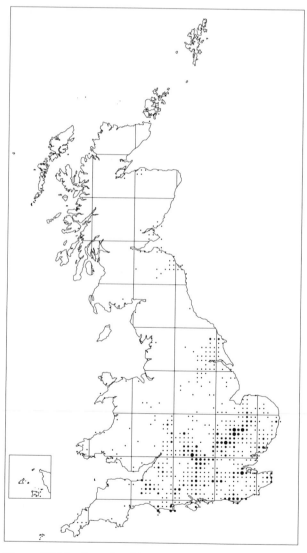

Figure 35 Number of arable weed species covered by the project recorded from 1970 onwards in each 10 km square. The species mapped are listed in Table 13. Dots of increasing size indicate 1-2 species, 3-4 species, 5-6 species and 7 or more species per square.

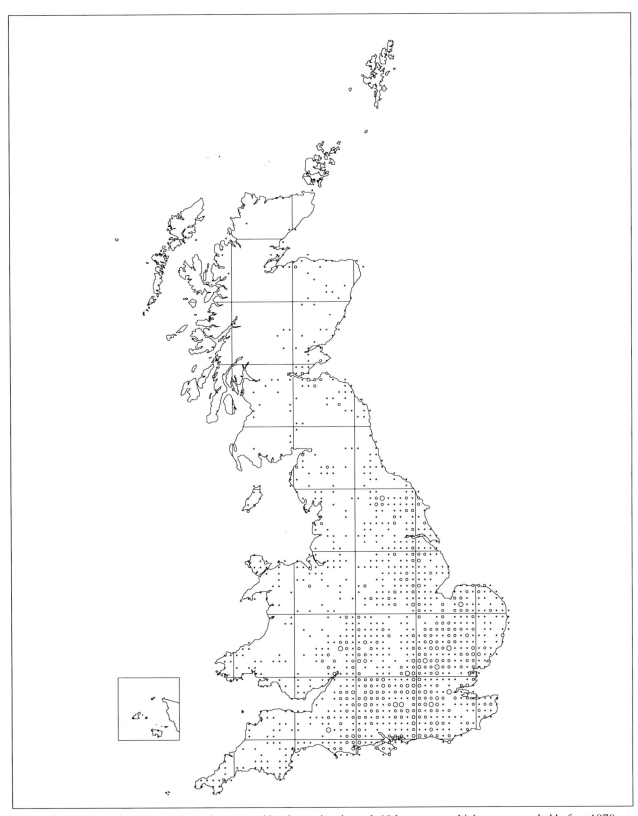

Figure 36 Number of arable weed species covered by the project in each 10 km square which were recorded before 1970 but have not subsequently been refound. The species mapped are listed in Table 13. Circles of increasing size indicate 1-2 species, 3-4 species, 5-6 species and 7 or more species per square.

Coastal habitats

The large suite of scarce species which is found in coastal habitats is listed in Table 14 and mapped in Figures 37, 38 and 39. Separate maps are provided for subsets of the coastal species which are found in sand dunes, shingle beaches and strandlines (Figures 40, 41 and 42), in salt marshes and brackish pastures (Figures 43, 44 and 45) and in brackish or sea water (Figures 46, 47 and 48).

Table 14 Scarce species of coastal habitats. Species covered by the project but recorded in 15 or fewer 10 km squares are listed in brackets. Species found in over 100 10 km squares are not listed. Plants of sand dunes, shingle beaches and strandlines are annotated '(SD)', those of salt marshes and brackish pastures '(SM)' and those of brackish or sea water '(BW)'.

Alopecurus bulbosus (SM)	Medicago minima (SD)
Asplenium obovatum	Medicago polymorpha
Atriplex longipes (SM)	Mertensia maritima (SD)
Atriplex praecox (SM)	Ophioglossum azoricum
Brassica oleracea	Orobanche hederae
Bupleurum tenuissimum	Parapholis incurva
Carex divisa (SM)	Poa bulbosa (SD)
Carex maritima (SD)	Polypogon monspeliensis
Carex punctata	(SM)
Centaurium littorale	Primula scotica
(Chenopodium	Puccinellia fasciculata
chenopodioides) (SM)	(SM)
Coincya monensis subsp.	Puccinellia rupestris (SM)
monensis	Pyrola rotundifolia subsp.
(Corynephorus canescens)	maritima (SD)
(SD)	Ruppia cirrhosa (BW)
Equisetum variegatum	Salicornia pusilla (SM)
(SD)	Sarcocornia perennis (SM)
Erodium moschatum	Scilla autumnalis
Euphorbia portlandica	Silene conica (SD)
Euphrasia foulaensis	Spartina maritima (SM)
(Euphrasia marshallii)	Suaeda vera (SM)
Festuca arenaria (SD)	Trifolium glomeratum
Frankenia laevis (SM)	(SD)
Hippophae rhamnoides	Trifolium occidentale
(SD)	Trifolium squamosum
Hordeum marinum	Trifolium suffocatum (SD)
Hypochaeris glabra (SD)	Vicia bithynica
Inula crithmoides (SM)	Vicia lutea
Juncus acutus (SD)	Vulpia ciliata subsp.
Juncus balticus (SD)	ambigua (SD)
Lathyrus japonicus (SD)	Vulpia fasciculata (SD)
Lepidium latifolium	Zostera angustifolia (BW)
Limonium humile (SM)	Zostera marina (BW)
Lotus subbiflorus	Zostera noltii (BW)
Marrubium vulgare	

With the possible exception of the steepest and most maritime cliffs, few coastal habitats have been unmodified by man and most have been subjected to centuries of grazing or other disturbance. Nevertheless, the coastal zone includes some of the most natural habitats in Britain. Many sand dunes, salt marshes, strandlines and coastal rocks are probably still not dissimilar to a hypothetical 'natural' condition.

Many species of coastal habitats have apparently had stable distributions over the period for which we have historical records, and do not appear to be under any particularly serious threat today. This is true of many plants of cliffs, exposed coastal slopes and rocks, sand dunes and the lower parts of salt marshes. Some of the more vulnerable habitats are discussed in the following paragraphs, but this concentration on the threatened areas should not be allowed to obscure the relatively healthy state of much coastal vegetation. This relatively secure nature of coastal sites is shown by the marked decline at inland localities of *Bupleurum tenuissimum*, *Crassula tillaea*, *Scilla autumnalis* and *Trifolium suffocatum*, all of which remain locally frequent by the sea.

Coastal grazing marshes and the upper edge of salt marshes provide a complex of habitats which can be rich in scarce species. These habitats include heavily grazed brackish turf with bare patches where cattle congregate, winter-flooded hollows and permanent pools, ditches between the fields and rutted and trampled muddy tracks which lead to them. Many traditional grazing marshes in south-east England have been drained, ploughed and converted into arable land in recent years, and others have been taken for industrial development or house building. In an Essex study area of 16000 ha the area of coastal grassland decreased from 11749 to 2083 ha between 1938 and 1981. Over 90% of the losses were attributable to conversion to arable, most of which took place in the 1939-45 war or after the U.K. joined the European Community (Williams & Hall 1987). Even if land remains managed as grazing land, ponds may be filled, tracks surfaced, water levels in ditches stabilised and ditches fenced: all developments which can remove the special micro-habitat which are required by some species. Species which are vulnerable to the destruction of coastal grazing marshes or their more intensive management include *Alopecurus bulbosus*, *Carex divisa*, *Chenopodium chenopodioides*, *Polypogon monspeliensis*, *Puccinellia fasciculata* and *P. rupestris*.

Species of coastal habitats can be vulnerable to a wide range of development and disturbance including building for tourism, large-scale improvement in sea defences, excavation of sand and shingle and public trampling of sand dunes and shingle beaches. The remote shingle spit of Orford Ness, for example, has been subject to military activity (as a bombing range and for atomic weapons research), damaged by coastal defence works and used for gravel extraction. Many of these operations have been unco-ordinated and unnecessarily damaging (Fuller & Randall 1988). Species which have decreased because of coastal disturbance include *Carex maritima* and *Mertensia maritima*; these have tended to retreat to less disturbed northern beaches.

In common with other areas of agriculturally marginal land, many coastal slopes and cliffs are now less heavily grazed than they once were. The southern cliffs of Guernsey provide one of many examples: cliffs which appear in old paintings as rocky grassland with a few stunted gorse bushes are now covered in many areas by a dense thicket of scrub. These cliffs bear a rich assemblage of scarce and rare species which are now restricted to pathsides and the shallowest, most droughted or exposed soils where scrub cannot become established. Although under-grazing has reduced the size of populations of a number of coastal species, relaxation of grazing has probably enabled some more palatable species such as *Pyrola rotundifolia* subsp. *maritima* and *Vulpia fasciculata* to increase in abundance or spread.

Some coastal plants are winter annuals which flower and fruit in spring and then pass through the summer as dormant seed. This life cycle has enabled scarce species such as *Poa bulbosa* and *Trifolium suffocatum*, as well as more frequent plants such as *Erodium maritimum* and *Trifolium ornithopodioides*, to spread into sites such as cliff-tops, car parks and pathsides which are heavily trampled by tourists in midsummer. These species might be expected to benefit from global warming, which could increase the habitats where perennials are reduced in vigour or eliminated by summer drought. A consequence of the predicted global warming is a rise in sea level which might amount to 40 cm by 2100 (Wigley & Raper 1992). This could adversely affect salt marshes and other low coastal habitats if they become squeezed between the rising sea and coastal defence works. Another long term but potentially serious threat to these communities lies in proposals for estuarine barrages.

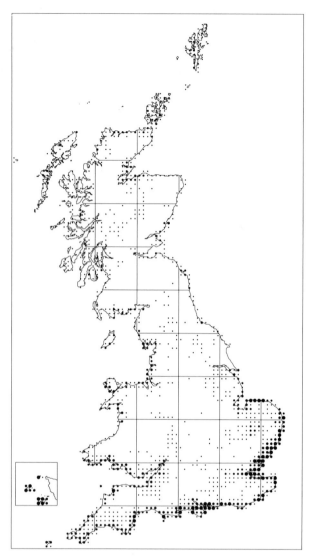

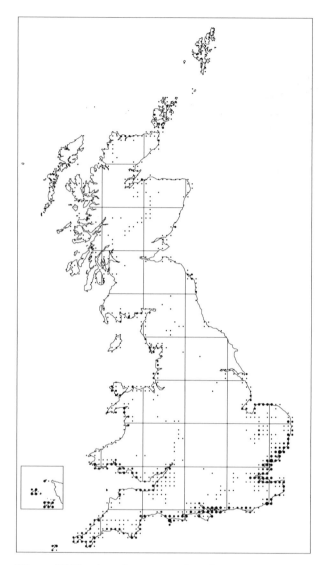

Figure 37 Number of scarce species of coastal habitats recorded in each 10 km square. The species mapped are listed in Table 14. Dots of increasing size indicate 1-4 species, 5-9 species, 10-19 species and 20 or more species per square.

Figure 38 Number of scarce species of coastal habitats recorded from 1970 onwards in each 10 km square. The species mapped are listed in Table 14. Dots of increasing size indicate 1-4 species, 5-9 species and 10-19 species per square.

478

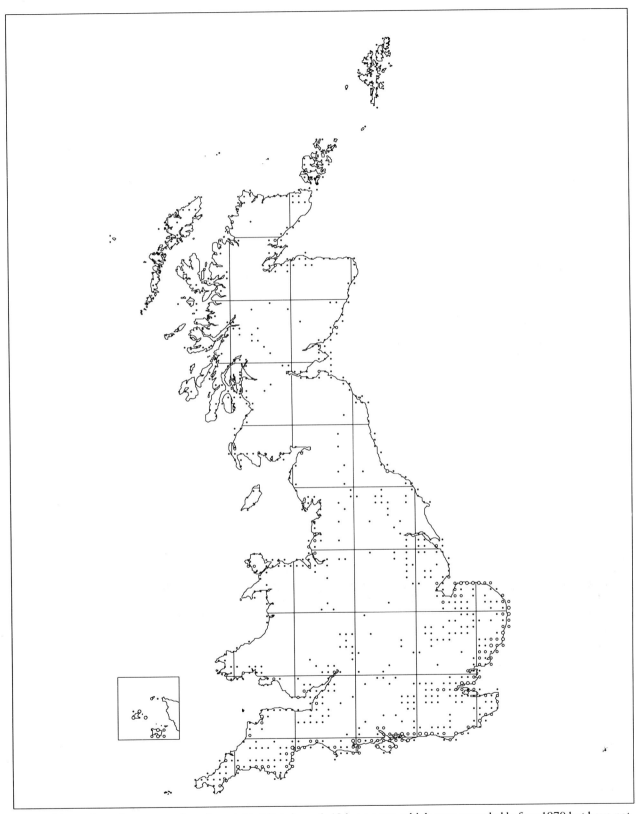

Figure 39 Number of scarce species of coastal habitats in each 10 km square which were recorded before 1970 but have not subsequently been refound. The species mapped are listed in Table 14. Circles of increasing size indicate 1-4 species, 5-9 species and 10-19 species per square.

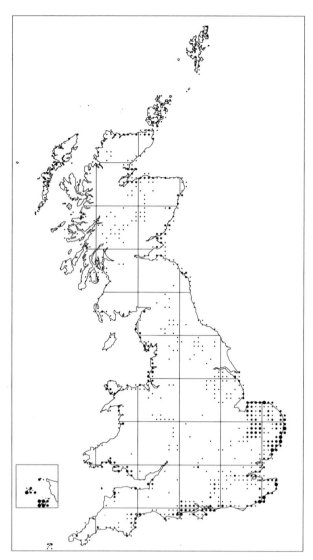

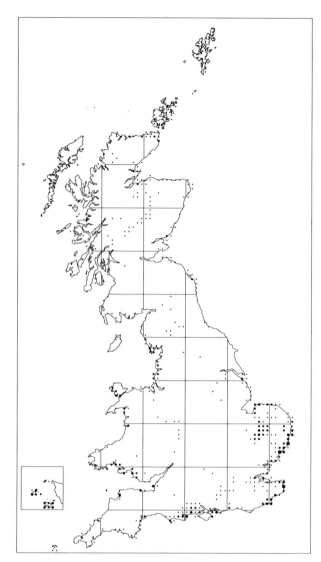

Figure 40 Number of scarce species of sand dunes, shingle beaches and strandlines recorded in each 10 km square. The species mapped are listed in Table 14. Dots of increasing size indicate 1-2 species, 3-5 species, 6-9 species and 10 or more species per square.

Figure 41 Number of scarce species of sand dunes, shingle beaches and strandlines recorded from 1970 onwards in each 10 km square. The species mapped are listed in Table 14. Dots of increasing size indicate 1-2 species, 3-5 species, 6-9 species and 10 or more species per square.

480

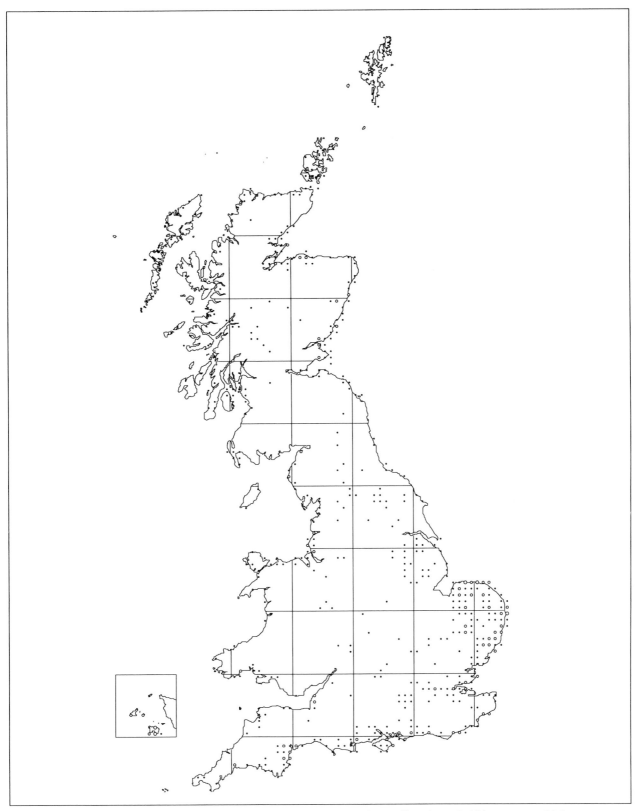

Figure 42 Number of scarce species of sand dunes, shingle beaches and strandlines in each 10 km square which were recorded before 1970 but have not subsequently been refound. The species mapped are listed in Table 14. Circles of increasing size indicate 1-2 species, 3-5 species and 6-9 species per square.

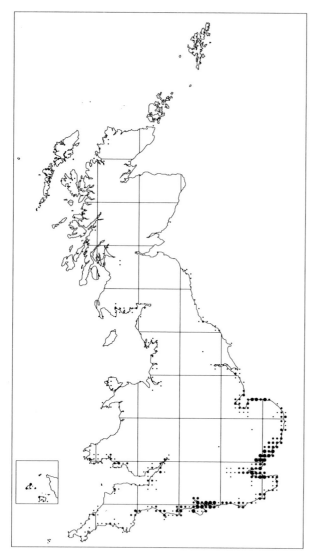

Figure 43 Number of scarce species of salt marshes and brackish pastures recorded in each 10 km square. The species mapped are listed in Table 14. Dots of increasing size indicate 1-2 species, 3-4 species, 5-9 species and 10 or more species per square.

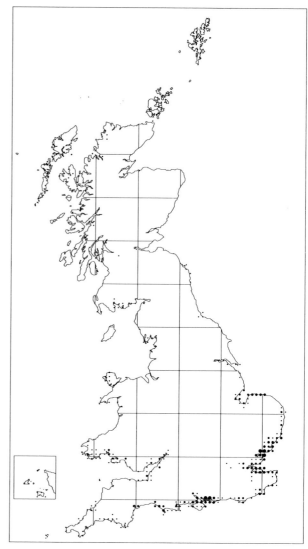

Figure 44 Number of scarce species of salt marshes and brackish pastures recorded from 1970 onwards in each 10 km square. The species mapped are listed in Table 14. Dots of increasing size indicate 1-2 species, 3-4 species, 5-9 species and 10 or more species per square.

482

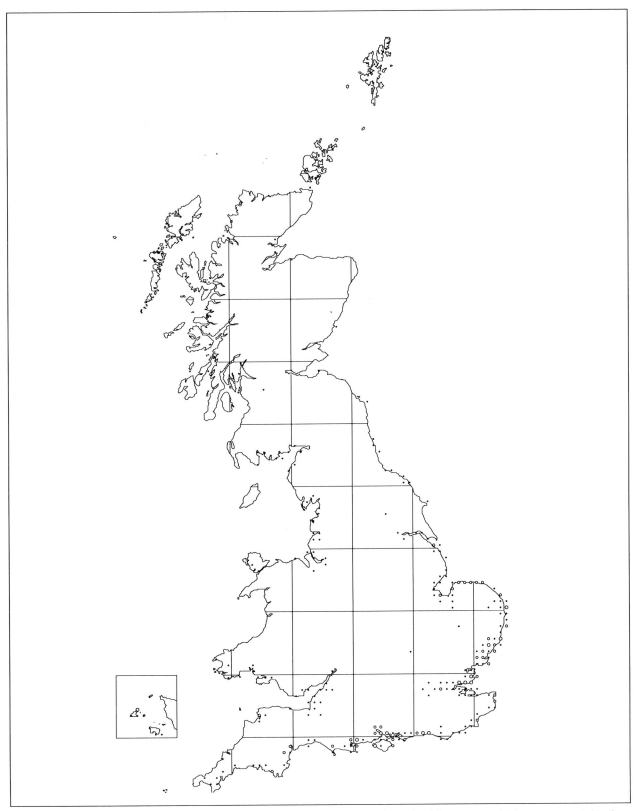

Figure 45 Number of scarce species of salt marshes and brackish pastures in each 10 km square which were recorded before 1970 but have not subsequently been refound. The species mapped are listed in Table 14. Circles of increasing size indicate 1-2 species, 3-4 species and 5-9 species per square.

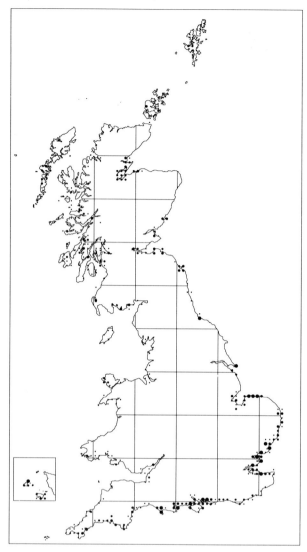

Figure 46 Number of scarce species of brackish water or sea water recorded in each 10 km square. The species mapped are listed in Table 14. Dots of increasing size indicate 1 species, 2 species, 3 species and 4 species per square.

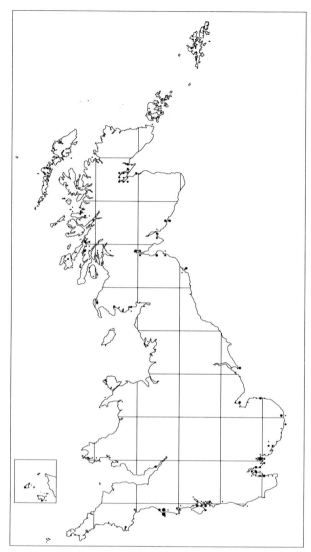

Figure 47 Number of scarce species of brackish water or sea water recorded from 1970 onwards in each 10 km square. The species mapped are listed in Table 14. Dots of increasing size indicate 1 species, 2 species, 3 species and 4 species per square.

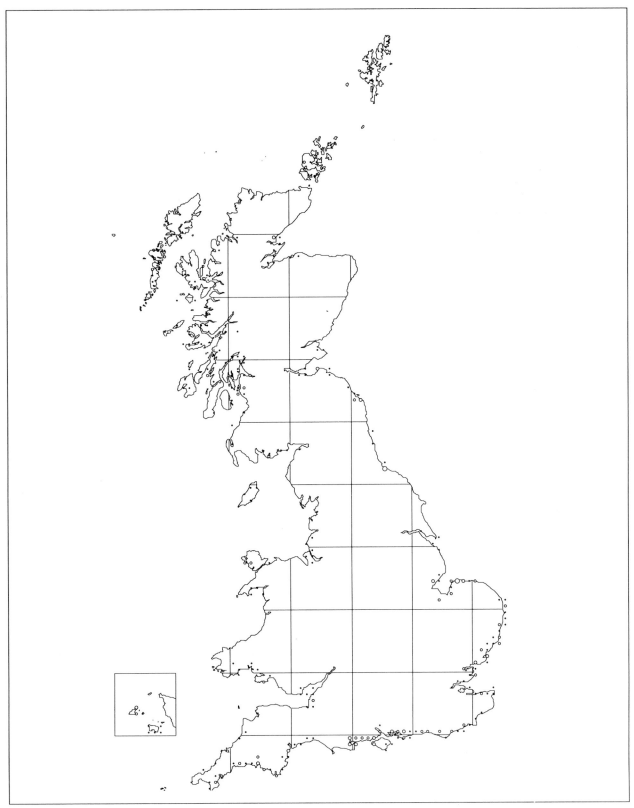

Figure 48 Number of scarce species of brackish water or sea water in each 10 km square which were recorded before 1970 but have not subsequently been refound. The species mapped are listed in Table 14. Circles of increasing size indicate 1 species, 2 species, 3 species and 4 species per square.

Changes in our knowledge of the distribution of species, 1962-1992

One of the main reasons for setting up a project to gather data on scarce species was the realisation that the maps in the *Atlas of the British Flora* (Perring & Walters 1962) were very outdated. Nevertheless, they were the only source of information on the national distribution of vascular plant species available to the compilers of the official list of scarce species (Nature Conservancy Council 1989). The completion of the project allows us to compare the current records of these species to those published in the *Atlas* some 30 years ago.

Most of the recording for the *Atlas of the British Flora* took place over five field seasons (1955-1959), but the project was also able to draw on records collected for a number of vice-counties in the 1930s. The aim of the fieldwork was to visit all 10 km squares, but some areas were less well recorded than others. The editors of the *Atlas* attempted to obtain records from all the 10 km squares in which the rarest of species ('A species') had been recorded. However, for the less rare species ('B species' and 'C species') they could only attempt to ensure that they had at least one record from all the vice-counties in which the species was known to occur. The *Atlas* maps might therefore under-estimate the known distribution of the 'B' and 'C' species. The distribution of coastal species is likely to be under-estimated for an additional reason. Records from coastal 10 km squares which contained a small area of land were plotted in an adjacent square, so that the dots did not appear to be in the sea.

The publication of the *Atlas* established the 10 km square as the fundamental unit of botanical recording. It also stimulated the development of the B.S.B.I. vice-county recorder system, and most recorders attempted to maintain lists of species for each square in their county. In many vice-counties detailed flora projects were launched to map the distribution of plants in tetrads or 5 × 5 km squares. There have also been a number of surveys of particular habitats organised by the conservation agencies. Many areas have now been recorded much more systematically and thoroughly than they were at the time of the *Atlas*. In the current scarce species project we have been able to draw upon the results of many of these recording schemes. This has had two benefits: we have had access to a substantial body of existing data, and recorders who were carrying out fieldwork to establish the distribution of scarce species in 1991-92 often had previous records to guide them in their search. There are, however, a few vice-counties in which there has been little systematic

recording since the 1950s.

It is clear from the history of recording outlined above that the maps in the *Atlas of the British Flora* show records for a 30-year period from 1930 to 1959 or 1960, but most records were made in five years of concentrated recording by botanists who were often exploring terrain with which they were unfamiliar. Those in the present book were acquired over a period of approximately 20 years, in which recording has been much more intensive in many areas. In view of this, it is not surprising that many species are now known from more 10 km squares than they were in 1962. The number of post-1970 10 km squares in which plants are mapped in this book exceeds the number of post-1930 squares recorded in the 1962 *Atlas* for 231 of the 286 plants for which recent records were distinguished in the 1962 *Atlas*. Species which are now known from twice as many recent squares as they were then are listed in Table 15. Many of these are species with a northern but not montane distribution (e.g. *Ajuga pyramidalis*, *Andromeda polifolia*, *Carex aquatilis*, *Festuca altissima*), suggesting that areas of northern England and Scotland which were not exciting enough to attract visiting botanists were not well recorded in the *Atlas*. The increase of records in the north has transformed our view of the distribution of some species, which are now known to have important populations in areas from which they were scarcely known in 1962. Striking examples include *Elatine hexandra*, *Limosella aquatica* and *Persicaria minor*. In addition to the northern species, there is a group of species in Table 15 which have southern distributions but which are rather inconspicuous, and often only apparent for a limited period of the year (e.g. *Alopecurus bulbosus*, *Oenanthe silaifolia*, *Trifolium ornithopodioides*). A substantial proportion of the plants in Table 15 are ones which were probably known only to more expert botanists in the 1950s, as their taxonomy had only recently been elucidated (*Dactylorhiza traunsteineri*, *Polygonum rurivagum*, *Polypodium cambricum*). A few were not mapped in the *Atlas* at all as they were only recognised in Britain after its publication (*Atriplex longipes*, *Atriplex praecox*). Some of these species are now known to most British botanists; others are still the preserve of the expert but we now have records collected over a much longer period than was the case in the 1950s.

The greatly increased number of records available for the species in Table 15 can be attributed almost entirely to increased recording. For the majority of species there is no evidence that the range of the plants themselves has expanded. Indeed, it seems likely that the increase in records of a few of the species in the table actually masks a decline in the number of sites in which the plant occurs. This is almost certainly the case for *Euphorbia platyphyllos* and *Oenanthe silaifolia* and perhaps also for *Linnaea borealis*. Evidence for the decline of these species comes from vice-counties which have been well-recorded over a long period. In Surrey, for example, *Oenanthe silaifolia* has become 'much reduced in some localities, due to ploughing or use of sprays' (Leslie 1987). There are a few species in Table 15 which may have genuinely increased in frequency. These include *Elatine hydropiper* in Scotland, *Poa bulbosa* and *Scrophularia umbrosa*.

In view of the general tendency for the number of recent 10 km squares from which species have been recorded to be greater now than in 1962, the fact that a particular species is recorded from substantially fewer recent squares now is likely to be significant. Those species which have been recorded since 1970 in less than 80% of the total number of post-1930 squares in which they were mapped in the 1962 *Atlas* are listed in Table 16. The reduction in the number of recent squares for *Cochlearia scotica* is due to the taxonomic uncertainty that now surrounds that species, and that for *Minuartia sedoides* to under-recording in the mountains of north-west Scotland. Most of the other species have almost certainly declined, and

Table 15 List of the species covered by the project for which there are at least twice as many recent 10 km squares now as there were in the *Atlas of the British Flora* (Perring & Walters 1962). The number of recent squares in each publication is tabulated together with the increase, expressed as the new total divided by the old. Recent records in the *Atlas* are records made in or after 1930; recent records now are those made in or after 1970. Square totals exclude the Channel Islands.

Species	Atlas	Current	Increase
Atriplex longipes		27	
Atriplex praecox		43	
Elatine hydropiper	4	19	4.8
Tilia platyphyllos	14	63	4.5
Festuca arenaria	12	52	4.3
Oenanthe silaifolia	13	49	3.8
Dactylorhiza traunsteineri	12	44	3.7
Ruppia cirrhosa	13	45	3.5
Corallorhiza trifida	19	65	3.4
Verbascum pulverulentum	9	30	3.3
Vaccinium microcarpum	19	61	3.2
Carex aquatilis	44	136	3.1
Crepis mollis	9	28	3.1
Ceratophyllum submersum	37	111	3.0
Carex maritima	14	41	2.9
Persicaria minor	45	130	2.9
Ribes spicatum	20	57	2.9
Equisetum pratense	32	89	2.8
Juncus acutus	10	28	2.8
Scrophularia umbrosa	36	101	2.8
Orobanche rapum-genistae	36	97	2.7
Polygonum rurivagum	43	116	2.7
Zostera angustifolia	27	73	2.7
Vicia lutea	12	32	2.7
Elatine hexandra	38	97	2.6
Euphorbia platyphyllos	42	109	2.6

Species	Atlas	Current	Increase
Festuca altissima	56	148	2.6
Spiranthes romanzoffiana	7	18	2.6
Callitriche truncata	11	28	2.5
Limosella aquatica	22	55	2.5
Polypodium cambricum	46	116	2.5
Asplenium obovatum	34	77	2.3
Myosotis stolonifera	32	75	2.3
Poa bulbosa	23	52	2.3
Rumex maritimus	83	191	2.3
Cicuta virosa	29	63	2.2
Nuphar pumila	16	35	2.2
Ranunculus baudotii	85	186	2.2
Ajuga pyramidalis	25	53	2.1
Alopecurus bulbosus	26	54	2.1
Apera interrupta	17	35	2.1
Callitriche hermaphroditica	83	178	2.1
Carex rupestris	14	29	2.1
Andromeda polifolia	69	140	2.0
Daphne mezereum	12	24	2.0
Draba norvegica	12	24	2.0
Hypericum undulatum	24	49	2.0
Juncus filiformis	10	20	2.0
Linnaea borealis	16	32	2.0
Trifolium ornithopodioides	80	161	2.0
Vulpia unilateralis	10	20	2.0

this decrease is attested for many species by a wealth of independent evidence. The arable weeds, for example, are prominent amongst the plants in Table 16. It is interesting to see that the presence of *Gnaphalium sylvaticum* in this list appears to confirm the conclusion of the BSBI Monitoring Scheme that this species is declining, a decline which had not hitherto been suspected.

The species listed in Tables 15 and 16 are extreme examples of species which have been under-recorded in the past or have declined in recent years. Most of the species covered by the project fall between these two extremes. The nature and degree of the difference between the number of recent 10 km squares in which the species was recorded in the 1962 *Atlas* and by the current project depend on the effectiveness with which the species was originally recorded, the extent to which the areas in which it occurs have been surveyed subsequently and any changes in the distribution of the plant itself, coupled (where relevant) by any changes in the taxonomy of the species and the ease with which it can be identified. These factors can be assessed individually in a rather subjective manner, but the changes in the number of recent records can certainly not be used as a simple index of changes in the distribution of the plant.

Table 16   List of the species for which the number of recent 10 km square records is less than 80% of the recent 10 km square records mapped in the *Atlas of the British Flora* (Perring & Walters 1962). The number of recent squares in each publication is tabulated and the current recent records expressed as a percentage of the *Atlas* records. Recent records in the *Atlas* are records made in or after 1930; recent records now are those made in or after 1970. Square totals exclude the Channel Islands. The table excludes species of *Euphrasia*, *Fumaria* and *Potamogeton* as recent records were not distinguished in the *Atlas*.

Species	Atlas	Current	%
Scandix pecten-veneris	451	131	29
Polygonum boreale	49	19	38
Cochlearia scotica	76	30	39
Silene gallica	137	55	40
Mentha pulegium	43	20	46
Centaurea cyanus	267	127	47
Galeopsis angustifolia	233	116	50
Gnaphalium sylvaticum	525	290	55
Minuartia sedoides	47	27	57
Torilis arvensis	137	82	60
Hypochaeris glabra	134	81	60
Carex vulpina	19	12	63
Deschampsia cespitosa subsp. alpina s.l.	52	33	63
Ribes alpinum	31	20	64
Chamaemelum nobile	148	96	65
Sium latifolium	98	66	67
Ranunculus tripartitus	28	19	68
Sagina saginoides	29	20	69
Pulsatilla vulgaris	27	19	70
Minuartia hybrida	100	72	72
Impatiens noli-tangere	22	16	73
Chenopodium chenopodioides	16	12	75
Hydrocharis morsus-ranae	173	134	77
Papaver argemone	394	308	78
Galium parisiense	24	19	79

List of localities cited in the text

Localities mentioned in the text are given below with their vice-counties and grid references. Where possible, the 10-km square or squares are given, but for larger areas (e.g. Breckland, Snowdonia) the 100-km squares are given and the vice-counties omitted. The accompanying map gives the numerical equivalents of the 100-km square alphabetical codes used below.

A

Afon Ystwyth, Cards., SN57,67,77,87
Afton Glen, Ayrs., NS60
Airedale, SD, SE
Am Binnein, Mid Perth, NN42
Aonach air Crith, W. Ross, NH00
Aonach Beag, Westerness, NN17
Armboth Fells, Cumberland, NY21
Arran, NR, NS
Asham Wood, N. Somerset, ST64
Askham Bog, Mid-W. Yorks., SE54
Assynt, NC
Avielochan, Moray, NH91
Avon Gorge, N. Somerset, W. Gloucs., ST57

B

Balgavies Loch, Angus, NO55
Barnack Hills and Holes, Northants., TF00
Barnsley Warren, E. Gloucs., SP00
Barnwell Station, Cambs., TL45
Bath, N. Somerset, ST76
Beinn Dearg, E. Ross, NH28
Beinn Heasgarnich, Mid Perth, NN43
Beinn na Socaich, Westerness, NN27
Ben Alder, Easterness, Westerness, NN47
Ben Avon, Banffs., S. Aberdeen, NJ10
Ben Chonzie, Mid Perth, NN73
Ben Lawers, Mid Perth, NN64
Ben Lui (=Beinn Laoigh), Mid Perth, W. Perth, NN22
Ben Macdui, Banffs., S. Aberdeen, NN99
Ben More Assynt, E. Sutherland, NC32
Ben More, Mid Ebudes, NM53
Ben Nevis, Westerness, NN17
Ben Wyvis, E. Ross, NH46
Berwick, Cheviot, NT95
Bidean nam Bian, Main Argyll, NN15
Black Mountains, SO
Blake Rigg, Westmorland, NY20
Blandford Camp, Dorset, ST90
Blyth, S. Northumb., NZ38
Bodmin Moor, SX
Bogha-cloiche, Easterness, NN78

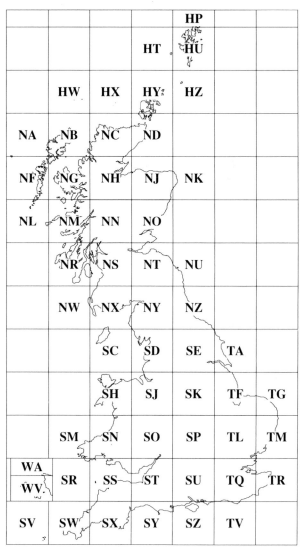

Figure 49 The 100 km squares of the Ordnance Survey national grid.

489

Bottom Head Fell, W. Lancs., SD65
Braemar, S. Aberdeen, NO19
Braeriach, Easterness, S. Aberdeen, NN99, NH90
Braunton Burrows, N. Devon, SS43
Breadalbane, NN
Brean Down, N. Somerset, ST25
Breckland, TF,TL
Bridgwater Bay, N. Somerset, S. Somerset, ST24,25
Broadland, TG
Brough, Westmorland, NY71
Burton Bradstock, Dorset, SY48
Buxton, Derbys., SK07

C

Caenlochan, Angus, NO17
Cairn Toul, S. Aberdeen, NN99
Cairngorms, NH, NJ, NN, NO
Cambridge, Cambs., TL45
Cambridgeshire Fens, TF, TL
Carn Gorm, Glen Lyon, Mid Perth, NN65
Carnedd Llwyd, Glam., ST19
Carreg yr Ogof, Carms., SN72
Castleton, S. Aberdeen, NO19
Cheddar Gorge, N. Somerset, ST45
Chelsea, Middlesex, TQ27
Chesil Beach, Dorset, SY58,67,68
Chichester, W. Sussex, SU80
Chilterns, SP,SU
Choire Ghamhnain, Main Argyll, NN23
Clova, Angus, NO27
Clymping, W. Sussex, TV00
Coire Coulavie, Easterness, NH12
Coire Garbhlach, Easterness, NN89
Colley Hill, Surrey, TQ25
Combe Martin, N. Devon, SS54
Cononish, Mid Perth, NN32
Conway Castle, Caerns., SH77
Cotswolds, SO,SP,ST
Countisbury, N. Devon, SS74
Cow Green, Co. Durham, Westmorland, NY73,83
Craig an Dail Bheag, S. Aberdeen, NO19
Craig Cerrig-gleisiad, Brecs., SN92
Craig y Cilau, Brecs., SO11
Craven Pennines, SD
Creag an Lochain, Mid Perth, NN54
Creag Bhuilg, Glen Avon, Banffs., NJ10
Creag Mhor, Mid Perth, NN33
Cronkley Fell, N.W. Yorks., NY82
Crosby Ravensworth Fell, Westmorland, NY61
Cross Fell, Cumberland, Westmorland, NY63
Cul Mor, W. Ross, NC11
Culbin Sands, Moray, NH96, NJ06
Cwmorthin, Merioneth, SH64

D

Dalmellington, Ayrs., NS40
Dartmoor, SX
Dolgellau, Merioneth, SH71
Dovedale, Derbys., Staffs., SK15
Dover, E. Kent, TR34
Drumore Loch, Angus, NO16
Dryslwyn Castle, Carms., SN52
Durness, W. Sutherland, NC46

E

East Lyn River, N. Devon, SS74
Eigg, N. Ebudes, NM48,49
Esthwaite Water, Westmorland, SD39

F

Fealar, E. Perth, NO07
Felixstowe Docks, E. Suffolk, TM23
Fetlar, Shetland, HU58,59,68,69
Fin Glen, Glen Lyon, Mid Perth, NN64
Firth of Forth, NT
Fleet, The, Dorset, SY58,67,68
Foula, Shetland, HT93,94
Fraochaidh, Main Argyll, NN05

G

Glas Maol, Angus, S. Aberdeen, W. Perth, NO17
Glen Beg, E. Perth, NO17
Glen Cannich, Easterness, E. Ross, NH13,23
Glen Clunie, S. Aberdeen, NO18
Glen Doll, Angus, NO27
Glen Coe, Main Argyll, NN15
Gog Magog Hills, Cambs., TL45
Goss Moor, E. Cornwall, SW96
Grampians, NJ, NN
Grassington, Mid-W. Yorks., SE06
Great Close Scar, Mid-W. Yorks., SD96
Great Glen, NH, NN
Great Orme, Caerns., SH78
Grey Corries, Westerness, NN27
Grey Hill, Ayrs., NX19
Guala Mhor, Main Argyll, NN44
Guernsey, WV

H

Hawes, N.W. Yorks., SD88
Hawkswick Clowder, Mid-W. Yorks., SD96
Helvellyn, Cumberland, Westmorland, NY31
Heysham Docks, W. Lancs., SD46
Highfolds Scar, Mid-W. Yorks., SD86
Hildersham, Cambs., TL54
Hindhead, Surrey, SU83
Holme-next-the-Sea, W. Norfolk, TF74

Q

Quarnford, Staffs., SK06
Quiraing, N. Ebudes, NG46

R

Rescobie Loch, Angus, NO55
Ribblehead, Mid-W. Yorks., SD77
Ribblesdale, SD
River Avon, ST
River Clyde estuary, NS
River Dove, SK
River Eden, NY
River Ouse, E. Sussex, TQ40
River Severn, SJ,SO
River South Tyne, NY
River Tees, NY,NZ
River Thames, SP, SU, TQ
River Trent, SE, SJ, SK
River Tweed, NT
River Ure, SD, SE
River West Allen, NY
River Wye, SN, SO, ST
Roborough Down, S. Devon, SX56
Romney Marsh, TQ, TR
Rothamsted Experimental Station, Herts., TL11
Roudsea Wood, Westmorland, SD38
Rum, N. Ebudes, NG30,40, NM39,49

S

Sandy Loch, S. Aberdeen, NO28
Santon Warren, W. Norfolk, TL88
Seana Braigh, E. Ross, NH28
Sedbergh, N.W. Yorks., SD69
Sgorr Dhearg, Glencoe, Main Argyll, NN05
Sgurr na Lapaich, Easterness, E. Ross, NH13
Shap, Westmorland, NY51
Sidmouth, S. Devon, SY18
Silverdale, W. Lancs., SD47
Skeggles Water, Westmorland, NY40
Slioch, W. Ross, NH06
Slochd Mor, Easterness, NH82
Snettisham, W. Norfolk, TF63
Snowdon, Caerns., SH65
Snowdonia, SH
Solent, The, SU, SZ
Somerset Levels and Moors, ST
Southern Uplands, NS, NT, NX, NY
Speyside, NH, NJ, NN
St Andrews, Fife, NO51
Stob Binnein, W. Perth, NN42
Stonehenge, S. Wilts, SU14
Strath Carron, E. Ross, NH49,59
Symond's Yat, W. Gloucs., SO51

T

Teesdale, NY
Thurne Valley, E. Norfolk, TG41
Tintern Abbey, Mons., SO50
Tom a'Choinich, Easterness, E. Ross, NH12
Tottenham, Middlesex, TQ39
Totternhoe, Beds., SP92
Triplow Heath, Cambs., TL44
Trotternish, N. Ebudes, NG
Troutbeck, Westmorland, NY40
Tynemouth, S. Northumb., NZ36
Tywyn Burrows, Carms., SN30

U

Unst, Shetland, HP60
Upper Teesdale, NY

V

Vale of York, SE

W

Walton on the Naze, N. Essex, TM22
Ward's Stone, W. Lancs., SD55
Wash, The, TF
Weald, The, TQ
Weeting Heath, W. Norfolk, TL78
Wensleydale, N.W. Yorks., SD98, SE08
West Penwith, SW
Westbury-sub-Mendip, N. Somerset, ST54
Whin Sill, NY, NZ
White Coombe, Dumfries., NT11
Wicken Fen, Cambs., TL56,57
Widdybank Fell, Co. Durham, NY83
Widecombe, S. Devon, SX77
Woodwalton Fen, Hunts., TL28
Wormhill, Derbys., SK17

Y

Yarley Hill, N. Somerset, ST44

Acknowledgements

Our greatest debt is to the BSBI vice-county recorders who devoted so much of their time to checking the printouts and maps, and who supplied so many additional records of scarce species. The recorders who took part in the project were Mrs P.P. Abbott, Dr K.J. Adams, G.H. Ballantyne, Mrs M. Barron, N. Batchelor, Mrs G. Beckett, P.M. Benoit, C.R. Boon, Dr H.J.M. Bowen, M.E. Braithwaite, Lady Anne Brewis, Mrs M. Briggs, N.H. Brown, A.L. Bull, Miss E.R. Bullard, Mrs L.B. Burt, J.K. Butler, A.O. Chater, A.R. Church, Mrs P. Copson, Dr R.W.M. Corner, Dr F.E. Crackles, Mrs G. Crompton, A. Currie, J.J. Day, J.R. Edelsten, Mrs P.A. Evans, S.B. Evans, T.G. Evans, B.R.W. Fowler, Dr L.S. Garrad, Mrs G.M. Gent, Miss V. Gordon, Rev. G.G. Graham, D.E. Green, I.P. Green, Mrs J.A. Green, P.R. Green, E.F. Greenwood, Dr R.L. Gulliver, Dr G. Halliday, P.A. Harmes, Prof. D.M. Henderson, Dr J. Hodgson, Dr M.G.B. Hughes, Dr D.R. Humphreys, Miss A.M. Hutchison, Mrs E.M. Hyde, Miss E.H. Jackson, T. J. James, M.B. Jeeves, P.A. Jones, Dr S.L. Jury, G.M. Kay, Dr Q.O.N. Kay, D.H. Kent, H.J. Killick, M.A.R. & Mrs C. Kitchen, Mrs F. Le Sueur, P.S. Lusby, Dr P. Macpherson, Mrs M.E.R. Martin, R. Maycock, D.J. McCosh, D.R. McKean, T.F. Medd, K.G. Messenger, Miss R.J. Murphy, Mrs C.W. Murray, Miss J. Muscott, Mrs R.E. Parslow, E.G. Philp, M. Porter, R.D. Pryce, C. Riley, A.B. Ritchie, R.H. Roberts, Capt. R.G.B. Roe, Dr J. Rogers, Miss A. Rutherford, Dr H. Salzen, W. Scott, B. Shepard, Dr A.J. Silverside, A.A.P. Slack, Mrs J.E. Smith, Dr R.A.H. Smith, R. Smith, N.F. Stewart, Mrs O.M. Stewart, A.McG. Stirling, Prof. G.A. Swan, Dr R.E. Thomas, B.H. Thompson, Mrs S.E. Thomson, W.H. Tucker, Mrs M. Wainwright, Dr A. Walker, Dr D. Welch, T.C.E. Wells, Mrs I. Weston, Prof. A.J. Willis, D.C. Wood and Dr G. Wynne.

We are also grateful to the following members of the BSBI, the Wild Flower Society, the conservation agencies or other organisations who adopted species or supplied records to the project: D.J. Armstrong, Dr A.J.M. Baker, Mrs J. Banks (La Société Jersiaise), Rev. A. Beddow, Dr P. Berry, E.L. Birse, B.J. Bonnard, R.P. Bowman, Dr S.J. Bungard, A.J. Byfield, Dr P.D. Carey, Dr S.B. Chapman, C. Chatters, Miss A.P. Conolly, Mrs V. Cornell, Cornwall Biological Records Centre, M.J. Cragg-Barker, Dr R.D. Cundall, M. Currie, J.P. Curtis, R.W. David, B. Dellow, T.E. Dixon, Ms J. Duncan, R.M. Edgar, R.G. Ellis, Miss L. Farrell, Ms C. Ferguson, Lady Rosemary FitzGerald, M.J.Y. Foley, T.H. Fowler, A.N. Gagg, Ms D. Gilbert, Dr A.J. Gray, Mr & Mrs S. Hartley, S. Hedley, Mrs B.G. Hogarth, M.N. Jenkinson, P. Jepson, A.C. Jermy, V.A. Johnstone, A. Jones, P. Hope Jones, Ms J. Lambert, D.C. Lang, S.J. Leach, Mrs M.L. Long (La Société Jersiaise), Ms E.J. MacKintosh, Dr A.J.C. Malloch, L.J. Margetts, Mrs M.H. Marsden (La Société Serquiaise), Ms G. McKnight, J. McPhail, J. Mitchell, Miss B. Mortimer, A.L. Newton, Mrs E. Norman, M.J. O'Leary, J. Ounsted, Mrs P. Parker (Shropshire Wildlife Trust), J.M. Patmore, A.G. Payne, Dr C.D. Pigott, J. Poingdestre, M.S. Porter, Dr M.C.F. Proctor, Miss R.D. Rabey, Dr D.A. Ratcliffe, Mrs G.H. Read, Dr T.C.G. Rich, F.J. Roberts, F. Rose, R.J. Rose, G.P. Rothero, M.W. Rowe, M.N. Sanford (Suffolk Biological Records Centre), Ms S. Scott-White (Wiltshire Biological Records Centre), P.J. Selby, Dr A.J. Showler, Mrs A. Smith, M.J. Southam, R.E.N. Smith, Prof. C.A. Stace, Miss H.E. Stace, Dr L.A. Storer, Mrs T.M.J. Tarpey (Colchester Natural History Society), T. Taylor, R.M. Walls, D.A. Wells, Mrs G.W. Wheeldon, N. Willby, L.R. Williams, R. Wilson, Miss H.R. Winship (Hampshire Wildlife Trust), P.C.H. Wortham. We also thank the many other botanists who contributed to the scheme by making records on field meetings or sending their records to the vice-county recorders.

The authors of the species texts are acknowledged under their contributions; the value of their contribution is self-evident. Many people made valuable comments on individual draft texts, and we are particularly grateful to C. Chatters, Dr D.E. Coombe, Dr G. Halliday, S.J. Leach, R.D. Pryce, Dr D.A. Ratcliffe, Mrs J.E. Smith, Dr R.A.H. Smith, and Dr P.J. Wilson for their expert comments on a large number of accounts.

At the Biological Records Centre Miss C. Ward and Miss S.E. Yates undertook the mammoth task of entering the records into the database. Many of the records of scarce aquatic plants were compiled and processed by Mrs J.M. Croft in a project which received financial support from the National Rivers Authority. We are grateful to P.T. Harding, the head of BRC, for his support throughout the project and to H.R. Arnold, Mrs J.M. Croft, Mrs W. Forrest, Miss C.L. Wilson and the BRC data manager J.C.M. Dring for assistance in many different ways. We also thank Dr A.J. Morton of Imperial College, London, for advice on the use of his DMAP program, which has been used to plot the distribution maps.

The BSBI provided financial support from the Welch Fund towards the end of the project; without this it would have been difficult to complete the work within a reasonable timescale. We appreciate the sympathetic response of the BSBI treasurer, M. Walpole, to our applications for money. We are grateful to the members of the BSBI Records Committee for their interest and encouragement.

Finally we would like to thank the Nature Conservancy Council for finding the money to initiate the project. We are particularly grateful to Miss L. Farrell for her enthusiastic support, which enabled us to obtain NCC funding, and for managing the project until it became the responsibility of JNCC. Mrs M.A. Palmer was responsible for the project when it was inherited by JNCC. We received valuable comments on the manuscript from Dr F.H. Perring and Prof. A.J. Willis. We thank Ms L. Wright of the JNCC Publications Branch for her work on this book and her colleague J.H. Bratton for his critical scrutiny of every page.

References

Ainsworth, C.C., Parker, J.S., & Horton, D.M. 1983. Chromosome variation and evolution in *Scilla autumnalis*. *In*: *Kew Chromosome Conference II*, ed. by P.E. Brandham and M.D. Bennett, 261-268. London, George Allen & Unwin.

Al-Bermani, A.-K.K.A. 1991. *Taxonomic, cytogenetic and breeding relationships of* Festuca rubra sensu lato. Ph.D. Thesis, University of Leicester.

Allen, D.E. 1984. *Flora of the Isle of Man*. Douglas, Manx Museum and National Trust.

Anderson, K., & Murphy, K.J. 1987. *The aquatic vegetation of the Union Canal (Lothian and Central Regions, Scotland)*. Unpublished report to Nature Conservancy Council, Edinburgh.

Aston, H.I. 1973. *Aquatic plants of Australia*. Carlton, Melbourne University Press.

Babington, C.C. 1860. *Flora of Cambridgeshire*. London, John Van Voorst.

Baker, J.G. 1866. On *Aira uliginosa* as a British plant. *Journal of Botany*, *4*: 176-178.

Ballantyne, G.H. 1992. *Orobanche alba* Steph. ex Willd. in Fife (v.c. 85). *Watsonia*, *19*: 39-40.

Barrett, S.C.H., & Helenurm, K. 1987. The reproductive biology of boreal forest herbs. I. Breeding systems and pollination. *Canadian Journal of Botany*, *65*: 2036-2046.

Barry, R., & Wade, P.M. 1986. *Callitriche truncata* Guss. Biological Flora of the British Isles, No. 162. *Journal of Ecology*, *74*: 289-294.

Bateman, R.M., & Denholm, I. 1983. A reappraisal of British and Irish dactylorchids, 1. The tetraploid marsh-orchids. *Watsonia*, *14*: 347-376.

Bateman, R.M., & Denholm, I. 1989. A reappraisal of the British and Irish dactylorchids, 3. The spotted-orchids. *Watsonia*, *17*: 319-349.

Beattie, E.P. 1965. July 6th to 13th, 1963. Fort William. *Proceedings of the Botanical Society of the British Isles*, *6*: 192-195.

Bell, F.G., & Dickson, C.A. 1971. The Barnwell Station arctic flora: a reappraisal of some plant identifications. *New Phytologist*, *70*: 627-638.

Bennett, A. 1893. *Pyrola rotundifolia* and its European forms. *Journal of Botany*, *31*: 332-334.

Birse, E.L. 1980. *Andromeda polifolia* L. on Mount Keen. *Transactions of the Botanical Society of Edinburgh*, *43*: 245-246.

Blackstock, T.H. 1981. The distribution of *Juncus filiformis* L. in Britain. *Watsonia*, *13*: 209-214.

Bobbink, R., & Willems, J.H. 1987. Increasing dominance of *Brachypodium pinnatum* (L.) Beauv. in chalk grasslands: a threat to a species-rich ecosystem. *Biological Conservation*, *40*: 301-314.

Boorman, L.A. 1967. *Limonium vulgare* Mill. and *L. humile* Mill. Biological Flora of the British Isles, No. 106. *Journal of Ecology*, *55*: 221-232.

Bougourd, S.M. 1977. *The genetics and cytology of natural populations of* Allium schoenoprasum L. Ph.D. Thesis, University of London.

Bougourd, S.M., & Parker, J.S. 1975. The B-chromosome system of *Allium schoenoprasum* I. B-distribution. *Chromosoma*, *53*: 273-282.

Bougourd, S.M., & Parker, J.S. 1979. The B-chromosome system of *Allium schoenoprasum* III. An abrupt change in B-frequency. *Chromosoma*, *75*: 385-392.

Bratton, J. 1990. Seasonal pools - an overlooked invertebrate habitat. *British Wildlife*, *2*: 22-29.

Brewis, A. 1990. Yellow ivy broomrape. *Watsonia*, *18*: 81-82.

Briggs, M. 1990. *Sussex plant atlas selected supplement*. Brighton, Booth Museum of Natural History.

Brightmore, D. 1979. *Frankenia laevis* L. Biological Flora of the British Isles, No. 146. *Journal of Ecology*, *67*: 1097-1107.

Brightmore, D., & White, P.H.F. 1963. *Lathyrus japonicus* Wild. Biological Flora of the British Isles, No. 94. *Journal of Ecology*, *51*: 795-801.

Brummitt, R.K., Kent, D.H., Lusby, P.S., & Palmer, R.C. 1987. The history and nomenclature of Thomas Edmondston's endemic Shetland *Cerastium*. *Watsonia, 16*: 291-297.

Bullard, E.R. 1987. *Primula scotica* Hook. A new passenger pigeon? *BSE News*, No. 48: 2-6.

Byfield, A. 1991. Classic British wildlife sites - the Lizard Peninsula. *British Wildlife, 3*: 92-105.

Carey, P.D. 1991. *The population ecology of* Vulpia ciliata *ssp.* ambigua *(Le Gall) Stace & Auquier*. Ph.D. Thesis, University of East Anglia.

Carey, P.D., & Watkinson, A.R. 1993. The dispersal and fates of seeds of the winter annual grass *Vulpia ciliata*. *Journal of Ecology, 81*: 759-767.

Carey, P.D., Watkinson, A.R., & Gerard, F. In press. The determinants of the distribution and abundance of the winter annual grass *Vulpia ciliata. Journal of Ecology*.

Carlisle, A., & Brown, A.H.F. 1968. *Pinus sylvestris* L. Biological Flora of the British Isles, No. 109. *Journal of Ecology, 56*: 269-307.

Chapman, S.B., Clarke, R.T., & Webb, N.R. 1989. The survey and assessment of heathland in Dorset, England, for conservation. *Biological Conservation, 47*: 137-152.

Chapman, S.B., Rose, R.J., & Clarke, R.T. 1989. The behaviour of populations of the marsh gentian (*Gentiana pneumonanthe*): a modelling approach. *Journal of Applied Ecology, 26*: 1059-1072.

Chapman, V.J. 1947. *Suaeda fruticosa* Forsk. Biological Flora of the British Isles, No. 22. *Journal of Ecology, 35*: 303-310.

Chapman, V.J. 1976. *Coastal vegetation*. 2nd ed. Oxford, Pergamon Press.

Christy, M. 1897. *Primula elatior* in Britain: its distribution, peculiarities, hybrids and allies. *Journal of the Linnean Society (Botany), 33*: 172-201.

Clapham, A.R., *ed.* 1978. *Upper Teesdale, the area and its natural history*. London, Collins.

Clapham, A.R., Tutin, T.G., & Moore, D.M. 1987. *Flora of the British Isles*. 3rd ed. Cambridge, Cambridge University Press.

Clapham, A.R., Tutin, T.G., & Warburg, E.F. 1962. *Flora of the British Isles*. 2nd ed. Cambridge, Cambridge University Press.

Coker, P.D. 1966. *Sibbaldia procumbens* L. Biological Flora of the British Isles, No. 104. *Journal of Ecology, 54*: 823-831.

Conolly, A.P., & Dahl, E. 1970. Maximum summer temperature in relation to the modern and Quaternary distributions of certain arctic-montane species in the British Isles. *In: Studies in the vegetational history of the British Isles*, ed. by D. Walker and R.G. West, 159-223. Cambridge, Cambridge University Press.

Cook, C.D.K. 1966. A monographic study of *Ranunculus* subgenus *Batrachium* (DC.) A. Gray. *Mitteilungen der Botanischen Staatssammlung München, 6*: 47-237.

Cook, C.D.K. 1990. Seed dispersal of *Nymphoides peltata* (S.G. Gmelin) O. Kuntze (Menyanthaceae). *Aquatic Botany, 37*: 325-340.

Coombe, D.E. 1956. Notes on some British plants seen in Austria. *Veröffentlichungen des Geobotanischen Instituts, Eidgenössische technische Hochschule Rübel in Zürich, 35*: 128-137.

Coombe, D.E. 1961. *Trifolium occidentale*, a new species related to *T. repens* L. *Watsonia, 5*: 68-87.

Cooper, M.R., & Johnson, A.W. 1984. *Poisonous plants in Britain and their effects on animals and man*. London, Her Majesty's Stationery Office.

Corner, R.W.M. 1970. The status of *Juncus alpinoarticulatus* Chaix in southern Scotland. *Transactions of the Botanical Society of Edinburgh, 40*: 622-623.

Corner, R.W.M. 1990. *Cardamine amara* L.: its occurrence in montane habitats in Britain. *Watsonia, 18*: 200-201.

Crompton, G. 1959. The Peat Holes of Triplow. *Nature in Cambridgeshire*, No. 2: 24-34.

Curtis, T.G.F., & McGough, H.N. 1988. *The Irish Red Data Book. 1. Vascular plants*. Dublin, Stationery Office.

Curtis, W. 1777-1798. *Flora Londinensis*. London.

Dandy, J.E., & Taylor, G. 1938. Studies of British potamogetons. - II. Some British records of *Potamogeton trichoides*. *Journal of Botany, 76*: 166-171.

David, R.W. 1977. The distribution of *Carex montana* L. in Britain. *Watsonia, 11*: 377-378.

David, R.W. 1978a. The distribution of *Carex digitata* L. in Britain. *Watsonia, 12*: 47-49.

David, R.W. 1978b. The distribution of *Carex elongata* L. in the British Isles. *Watsonia*, *12*: 158-160.

David, R.W. 1979a. The distribution of *Carex humilis* Leyss. in Britain. *Watsonia*, *12*: 257-258.

David, R.W. 1979b. The distribution of *Carex rupestris* All. in Britain. *Watsonia*, *12*: 335-337.

David, R.W. 1981a. The distribution of *Carex ericetorum* Poll. in Britain. *Watsonia*, *13*: 225-226.

David, R.W. 1981b. The distribution of *Carex punctata* Gaud. in Britain, Ireland and Isle of Man. *Watsonia*, *13*: 318-321.

David, R.W. 1982a. The British distribution of uncommon *Carices*: addenda and corrigenda. *Watsonia*, *14*: 68-70.

David, R.W. 1982b. The distribution of *Carex maritima* Gunn. in Britain. *Watsonia*, *14*: 178-180.

Davis, P.H., *ed.* 1970. *Flora of Turkey and the East Aegean Islands. Vol. 3*. Edinburgh, Edinburgh University Press.

Dawson, H.J. 1990. Chromosome numbers in two *Limonium* species. *Watsonia*, *18*: 82-84.

Devon Wildlife Trust. 1992. *Survey of culm grasslands in Devon, 1991*. Exeter, Devon Wildlife Trust.

Dixon, J.M. 1982. *Sesleria albicans* Kit. ex Schultes. Biological Flora of the British Isles, No. 151. *Journal of Ecology*, *70*: 667-684.

Doarks, C. 1990. *Changes in the flora of grazing marsh dykes in Broadland, between 1972-74 and 1988-89*. Unpublished, Nature Conservancy Council. (England Field Unit Report.)

Donald, D. 1981. Dark-leaved willow *Salix nigricans* in Cambridgeshire. *Nature in Cambridgeshire*, No. 24: 50-52.

Driscoll, R.J. 1985. Floating water-plantain, *Luronium natans*, in Norfolk. *Transactions of the Norfolk and Norwich Naturalists' Society*, *27*: 43-44.

Druce, G.C. 1900. *G. sylvestre*, Poll., var. *nitidulum* (Thuill.). *Report of the Botanical Exchange Club of the British Isles*, *1*: 577.

Druce, G.C. 1926. *The Flora of Buckinghamshire*. Arbroath, T. Buncle & Co.

Duncan, U.K. 1970. *Lathyrus maritimus* Bigel. subsp. *acutifolius* (Bab.) Pedersen in eastern Scotland. *Watsonia*, *8*: 87.

Easy, G. 1992. 'Breckland bent' in Cambridgeshire. *Nature in Cambridgeshire*, No. 34: 43-45.

Elkington, T.T. 1968. Introgressive hybridization between *Betula nana* L. and *B. pubescens* Ehrh. in north-west Iceland. *New Phytologist*, *67*: 109-118.

Elkington, T.T. 1971. *Dryas octopetala* L. Biological Flora of the British Isles, No. 124. *Journal of Ecology*, *59*: 887-905.

Ericson, L. 1977. The influence of voles and lemmings on the vegetation in a coniferous forest, during a 4-year period, in northern Sweden. *Wahlenbergia*, *4*: 1-114.

Evans, F. 1989. *A review of management of lowland wet heath in Dyfed, West Wales*. Peterborough, Nature Conservancy Council. (Contract surveys, No. 42.)

Evans, S. 1989. *Carex appropinquata* in Pembs., v.c. 45 - a misidentification for *C. diandra*. *BSBI News*, No. 53: 17-18.

Evans, T.G. 1985. *Zostera* of the Severn Estuary (v.c. 35). *Watsonia*, *15*: 425.

Fitt, G. 1844. Remarks on some species of *Chenopodium*. *Phytologist*, *1*: 1136-1138.

Fitter, A.H., & Smith, C.J., *eds.* 1979. *A wood in Ascam*. York, William Sessions.

FitzGerald, R. 1989. "Lost and found" - *Alopecurus bulbosus* Gouan in S.E. England. *Watsonia*, *17*: 425-428.

Foley, M.J.Y. 1990. An assessment of populations of *Dactylorhiza traunsteineri* (Sauter) Soó in the British Isles and a comparison with others from Continental Europe. *Watsonia*, *18*: 153-172.

Foley, M.J.Y. 1992. The current distribution and abundance of *Orchis ustulata* L. (Orchidaceae) in the British Isles - an updated summary. *Watsonia*, *19*: 121-126.

Fone, A.L. 1989. Competition in mixtures of the annual *Hypochoeris glabra* and perennial *H. radicata*. *Journal of Ecology*, *77*: 484-494.

Forestry Commission. 1989. *Native pinewood grants and guidelines*. London, HMSO.

Forest Enterprise. 1992. *A future for Forest Enterprise native pinewoods*. Inverness, Forest Enterprise.

Fuller, R.M., & Randall, R.E. 1988. The Orford Shingles, UK - classic conflicts in coastline management. *Biological Conservation*, *46*: 95-114.

Garnett, P.M., & Sledge, W.A. 1967. The distribution of *Actaea spicata* L. *Naturalist*, 1967: 73-76.

George, M. 1992. *The land use, ecology and conservation of Broadland*. Chichester, Packard Publishing.

Gerarde, J. 1597. *The herball or generall historie of plantes*. London.

Gibbons, D.W., Reid, J.B., & Chapman, R.A. 1993. *The new atlas of breeding birds in Britain and Ireland: 1988-1991*. London, T. & A.D. Poyser.

Gibbons, E.J. 1975. *The Flora of Lincolnshire*. Lincoln, Lincolnshire Naturalists' Union.

Giertych, M., & Mátyás, C., *eds*. 1991. *Genetics of Scots pine*. Amsterdam, Elsevier. (Developments in plant genetics and breeding, No. 3.)

Gilbert, O.L. 1966. *Dryopteris villarii* in Britain. *British Fern Gazette*, 9: 263-268.

Gilbert, O.L. 1970. *Dryopteris villarii* (Bellardi) Woynar. Biological Flora of the British Isles, No. 118. *Journal of Ecology*, 58: 301-313.

Godwin, H. 1975. *The history of the British flora*. 2nd ed. Cambridge, Cambridge University Press.

Good, R. 1948. *A geographical handbook of the Dorset flora*. Dorchester, Dorset Natural History and Archaeological Society.

Goodway, K.M. 1955. The forms of *Galium pumilum* in Britain. *Proceedings of the Botanical Society of the British Isles, 1*: 383.

Graham, G.G. 1988. *The flora and vegetation of County Durham*. Durham, Durham Flora Committee and Durham County Conservation Trust.

Grieve, M. 1931. *A modern herbal*. 2 vols. London, Jonathan Cape.

Griffiths, M.E., & Proctor, M.C.F. 1956. *Helianthemum canum* (L.) Baumg. Biological Flora of the British Isles, No. 59. *Journal of Ecology, 44*: 677-692.

Grigson, G. 1950. *Flowers of the meadow*. Harmondsworth, Penguin Books.

Grime, J.P., Hodgson, J.G., & Hunt, R. 1988. *Comparative plant ecology*. London, Unwin Hyman.

Grubb, P.J. 1976. A theoretical background to the conservation of ecologically distinct groups of annuals and biennials in the chalk grassland ecosystem. *Biological Conservation, 10*: 53-76.

Gubbay, S. 1988. *A coastal directory for marine nature conservation*. Ross-on-Wye, Marine Conservation Society.

Hadley, G., *ed.* 1985. *A Map Flora of mainland Inverness-shire*. Edinburgh, Botanical Society of Edinburgh and Botanical Society of the British Isles.

Haeupler, H., & Schönfelder, P. 1989. *Atlas der Farn- und Blütenpflanzen der Bundesrepublik Deutschland*. Stuttgart, Eugen Ulmer.

Hagerup, O. 1921. *The structure and biology of arctic flowering plants. Vol. 2, part 10. Caprifoliaceae*. Kjøbenhavn, C.A. Reitzel Boghandel.

Halliday, G. 1960. *Taxonomic and ecological studies in the* Arenaria ciliata *and* Minuartia verna *complexes*. Ph.D. Thesis, University of Cambridge.

Hanbury, F.J., & Marshall, E.S. 1899. *Flora of Kent*. London, Frederick J. Hanbury.

Hare, T. 1990. Lesser fleabane - a plant of seasonal hollows. *British Wildlife, 2*: 77-79.

Harron, J. 1992. The present distribution of the dark-leaved willow *Salix myrsinifolia* Salisb., in north-east Ireland. *Irish Naturalists' Journal, 24*: 8-11.

Harvey, H.J., & Meredith, T.C. 1981. Ecological studies of *Peucedanum palustre* and their implications for conservation management at Wicken Fen, Cambridgeshire. *In: The biological aspects of rare plant conservation*, ed. by H. Synge, 365-378. Chichester, John Wiley & Sons.

Hatcher, P.E., & Alexander, K.N.A. 1994. The status and conservation of the netted carpet *Eustroma reticulatum* (Denis & Schiffermüller, 1775) (Lepidoptera: Geometridae), a threatened moth species in Britain. *Biological Conservation, 67*: 41-47.

Hedberg, O. 1955. A taxonomic revision of the genus *Sibthorpia* L. *Botaniska Notiser, 108*: 161-183.

Hedberg, O. 1975. A cytogenetic study of the genus *Sibthorpia* L. (Scrophulariaceae). *Caryologia, 28*: 251-260.

Hennedy, R. 1891. *The Clydesdale Flora*. 5th ed. Glasgow, Hugh Hopkins.

Hepper, F.N. 1956. *Silene nutans* L. Biological Flora of the British Isles, No. 60. *Journal of Ecology, 44*: 693-700.

Heslop-Harrison, Y. 1953. *Nuphar intermedia* Ledeb., a presumed relict hybrid, in Britain. *Watsonia, 3*: 7-25.

Heslop-Harrison, Y. 1955. *Nuphar pumila* (Timm) DC. Biological Flora of the British Isles, No. 49. *Journal of Ecology, 43*: 355-360.

Holland, S.C., *ed.* 1986. *Supplement to the Flora of Gloucestershire*. Bristol, Grenfell Publications.

Hooker, J.D. 1870. *The student's Flora of the British Islands*. London, Macmillan & Co.

Hooker, J.D. 1884. *The student's Flora of the British Islands*. 3rd ed. London, Macmillan & Co.

Hooker, W.J. 1821. *Flora Scotica*. Edinburgh, Archibald Constable & Co.

Horrill, A.D. 1972. *Melampyrum cristatum* L. Biological Flora of the British Isles, No. 125. *Journal of Ecology, 60*: 235-244.

Hubbard, C.E. 1954. *Grasses*. Harmondsworth, Penguin Books.

Hughes, M.G.B. 1983. Conservation of the nationally rare *Deschampsia setacea* (bog hair-grass) on the Lizard Downs. *In*: *University of Bristol Lizard Project Restricted Report no. 6*, 12-21. Unpublished, University of Bristol.

Hughes, M.G.B. 1984. *Deschampsia setacea* (Hudson) Hackel new to south-western England. *Watsonia, 15*: 34-36.

Hughes, W.E. 1969. The distribution of *Polypodium vulgare* L. subspecies *serratulum* Arcangeli in North Wales. *Nature in Wales, 11*: 194-198.

Hultén, E. 1956. The *Cerastium alpinum* complex. *Svensk Botanisk Tidskrift, 50*: 411-495.

Hultén, E. 1958. The amphi-Atlantic plants and their phytogeographical connections. *Kungliga Svenska Vetenskapsakademiens Handlingar, Fjarde Serien, 7*: 1-340.

Hultén, E. 1970. The circumpolar plants. II. Dicotyledons. *Kungliga Svenska Vetenskapsakademiens Handlingar, Fjarde Serien, 13*: 1-463.

Hultén, E., & Fries, M. 1986. *Atlas of North European vascular plants north of the Tropic of Cancer*. 3 vols. Königstein, Koeltz Scientific Books.

Huxley, A., *ed.* 1992. *The new Royal Horticultural Society dictionary of gardening*. 4 vols. London, Macmillan Press.

Ingram, R., & Noltie, H.J. 1981. *The Flora of Angus (Forfar, v.c. 90)*. Dundee, Dundee Museums and Art Galleries.

Ingrouille, M.J., & Smirnoff, N. 1986. *Thlaspi caerulescens* J. and C. Presl (*T. alpestre* L.) in Britain. *New Phytologist, 102*: 219-233.

Ingrouille, M.J., & Stace, C.A. 1986. The *Limonium binervosum* aggregate (Plumbaginaceae) in the British Isles. *Botanical Journal of the Linnean Society, 92*: 177-217.

Ivimey-Cook, R.B. 1984. *Atlas of the Devon Flora*. Exeter, Devonshire Association for the Advancement of Science, Literature and Art.

Jalas, J., & Suominen, J., *eds.* 1972. *Atlas Florae Europaeae. Vol. 1. Pteridophyta (Psilotaceae to Azollaceae)*. Helsinki, Committee for Mapping the Flora of Europe and Societas Biologica Fennica Vanamo.

Jalas, J., & Suominen, J., *eds.* 1973. *Atlas Florae Europaeae. Vol. 2. Gymnospermae Pinaceae to Ephedraceae)*. Helsinki, Committee for Mapping the Flora of Europe and Societas Biologica Fennica Vanamo.

Jalas, J., & Suominen, J., *eds.* 1976. *Atlas Florae Europaeae. Vol. 3. Salicaceae to Balanophoraceae*. Helsinki, Committee for Mapping the Flora of Europe and Societas Biologica Fennica Vanamo.

Jalas, J., & Suominen, J., *eds.* 1979. *Atlas Florae Europaeae. Vol. 4. Polygonaceae*. Helsinki, Committee for Mapping the Flora of Europe and Societas Biologica Fennica Vanamo.

Jalas, J., & Suominen, J., *eds.* 1980. *Atlas Florae Europaeae. Vol. 5. Chenopodiaceae to Basellaceae*. Helsinki, Committee for Mapping the Flora of Europe and Societas Biologica Fennica Vanamo.

Jalas, J., & Suominen, J., *eds.* 1983. *Atlas Florae Europaeae. Vol. 6. Caryophyllaceae (Alsinoideae and Paronychioideae)*. Helsinki, Committee for Mapping the Flora of Europe and Societas Biologica Fennica Vanamo.

Jalas, J., & Suominen, J., *eds.* 1986. *Atlas Florae Europaeae. Vol. 7. Caryophyllaceae (Silenoideae)*. Helsinki, Committee for Mapping the Flora of Europe and Societas Biologica Fennica Vanamo.

Jalas, J., & Suominen, J., *eds.* 1989. *Atlas Florae Europaeae. Vol. 8. Nymphaeaceae to Ranunculaceae*. Helsinki, Committee for Mapping the Flora of Europe and Societas Biologica Fennica Vanamo.

Jalas, J., & Suominen, J., *eds.* 1991. *Atlas Florae Europaeae. Vol. 9. Paeoniaceae to Capparaceae*. Helsinki, Committee for Mapping the Flora of Europe and Societas Biologica Fennica Vanamo.

Jeanmonod, D., & Bocquet, G. 1983. Propositions pour un traitement biosystématique du *Silene nutans* L. (Caryophyllaceae). *Candollea, 38*: 267-295.

Jermy, A.C., Arnold, H.R., Farrell, L., & Perring, F.H. 1978. *Atlas of ferns of the British Isles*. London, Botanical Society of the British Isles & British Pteridological Society.

Jermy, A.C., Chater, A.O., & David, R.W. 1982. *Sedges of the British Isles*. London, Botanical Society of the British Isles. (BSBI Handbook No. 1, 2nd ed.)

Jermyn, S.T. 1974. *Flora of Essex*. Colchester, Essex Naturalists' Trust.

Jones, M. 1987. *Orobanche hederae* Duby in the British Isles. *In*: *Parasitic flowering plants*, ed. by H.C. Weber and W. Fortstreuter, 457-471. Marburg. (Proceedings of the 4th International Symposium on Parasitic Flowering Plants.)

Jones, V., & Richards, P.W. 1954. *Juncus acutus* L. Biological Flora of the British Isles, No. 47. *Journal of Ecology, 42*: 639-650.

Kay, Q.O.N., Roberts, R.H., & Vaughan, I.M. 1974. The spread of *Pyrola rotundifolia* L. subsp. *maritima* (Kenyon) E.F. Warb. in Wales. *Watsonia, 10*: 61-67.

Kemp, R.J. 1987. Reappearance of *Orchis purpurea* Hudson in Oxfordshire. *Watsonia, 16*: 435-436.

Kent, D.H. 1992. *List of vascular plants of the British Isles*. London, Botanical Society of the British Isles.

King, N., & Wells, D. 1993. *Fritillaria meleagris* L. Fritillary. *In*: *The Wiltshire Flora*, ed. by B. Gillam, 95-97. Newbury, Pisces Publications.

Kinloch, B.B., Westfall, R.D., & Forrest, G.I. 1986. Caledonian Scots pine: origins and genetic structure. *New Phytologist, 104*: 703-729.

Kitchener, G. 1983. Maritime plants on inland roads of West Kent. *Transactions of the Kent Field Club, 9*: 87-94.

Knuth, P., trans. J.R. Ainsworth Davis. 1906-1909. *Handbook of flower pollination*. 3 vols. Oxford, Clarendon Press.

Kümpel, H., & Mrkvicka, A.C. 1990. Untersuchungen zur Abtrennung der *Orchis ustulata* L. subsp. *aestivalis* (Kümpel) Kümpel & Mrkvicka. *Mitteilungsblatt, Arbeitskreis Heimische Orchideen Baden-Württembug, 22*: 306-324.

Lamb, H.H. 1977. *Climate: present, past and future. Vol. 2. Climatic history and the future*. London, Methuen & Co.

Leach, S.J. 1986. The rediscovery of *Carex maritima* Gunn. on the fairways at St Andrews Links, Fife. *Watsonia, 16*: 80-81.

Leach, S.J., Stewart, N.F., & Ballantyne, G.H. 1984. *Limosella aquatica* L. in Fife: a declining species making a come-back. *Watsonia, 15*: 118-119.

Lees, E. 1851. *The botanical looker-out*. 2nd ed. London, Hamilton, Adams, & Co.

Lees, E. 1867. *The botany of Worcestershire*. Worcester, Worcestershire Naturalists' Club.

Lees, F.A. 1888. *The Flora of West Yorkshire*. London, Lovell Reeve & Co.

Leslie, A.C. 1987. *Flora of Surrey supplement and checklist*. Guildford, A.C. & P. Leslie.

Lidén, M. 1986. Synopsis of Fumarioideae (Papaveraceae) with a monograph of the tribe Fumarieae. *Opera Botanica, 88*: 1-133.

Lightfoot, J. 1777. *Flora Scotica*. 2 vols. London.

Looman, J. 1983. Water meal, *Wolffia arrhiza* (Lemnaceae) in Saskatchewan. *Canadian Field-Naturalist, 97*: 220-222.

Lousley, J.E. 1976. *Flora of Surrey*. Newton Abbot, David & Charles.

Lovatt, C.M. 1982. *The history, ecology and status of the rare plants and the vegetation of the Avon Gorge, Bristol*. Ph.D. Thesis, University of Bristol.

McAllister, H.A., & Rutherford, A. 1990. *Hedera helix* L. and *H. hibernica* (Kirchner) Bean (Araliaceae) in the British Isles. *Watsonia, 18*: 7-15.

McCallum Webster, M. 1978. *Flora of Moray, Nairn and East Inverness*. Aberdeen, Aberdeen University Press.

McNaughton, I.H., & Harper, J.L. 1964a. *Papaver argemone* L. Biological Flora of the British Isles, No. 99. *Journal of Ecology, 52*: 786-789.

McNaughton, I.H., & Harper, J.L. 1964b. *Papaver hybridum* L. Biological Flora of the British Isles, No. 99. *Journal of Ecology, 52*: 789-793.

McVean, D.N., & Ratcliffe, D.A. 1962. *Plant communities of the Scottish Highlands*. London, Her Majesty's Stationery Office. (Monographs of the Nature Conservancy no. 1.)

Marchant, C.J., & Goodman, P.J. 1969. *Spartina maritima* (Curtis) Fernald. Biological Flora of the British Isles, No. 116. *Journal of Ecology, 57*: 287-291.

Mardon, D.K. 1990. Conservation of montane willow scrub in Scotland. *Transactions of the Botanical Society of Edinburgh, 45*: 427-436.

Margetts, L.J. 1987. 79th report on botany. *Report and Transactions of the Devonshire Association for the Advancement of Science, Literature and Art, 119*: 253-259.

Margetts, L.J. 1988. *The difficult and critical plants of the Lizard district of Cornwall*. Bristol, Grenfell Publications.

Marshall, J.K. 1967. *Corynephorus canescens* (L.) Beauv. Biological Flora of the British Isles, No. 105. *Journal of Ecology, 55*: 207-220.

Matthews, J.R. 1955. *Origin and distribution of the British flora*. London, Hutchinson & Co.

Meikle, R.D. 1977. Willow meeting, Kindrogan, Perthshire. 24th-29th June 1976. *BSE News*, No. 23: 8-13.

Meikle, R.D. 1984. *Willows and poplars of Great Britain and Ireland*. London, Botanical Society of the British Isles. (BSBI Handbook No. 4)

Meikle, R.D. 1992. British willows; some hybrids and some problems. *Proceedings of the Royal Society of Edinburgh, 98B*: 13-20.

Melville, R. 1940. Contributions to the study of British elms.- III. The plot elm, *Ulmus plotii* Druce. *Journal of Botany, 78*: 181-192.

Meredith, T.C., & Grubb, P.J. 1993. *Peucedanum palustre* (L.) Moench. Biological Flora of the British Isles, No. 179. *Journal of Ecology, 81*: 813-826.

Meusel, H., & Jäger, E.J. 1992. *Vergleichende Chorologie der zentraleuropäischen Flora. Vol. 3*. Jena, Gustav Fischer.

Meusel, H., Jäger, E., Rauschert, S., & Weinert, E. 1978. *Vergleichende Chorologie der zentraleuropäischen Flora. Vol. 2*. Jena, Gustav Fischer.

Meusel, H., Jäger, E., & Weinert, E. 1965. *Vergleichende Chorologie der zentraleuropäischen Flora. Vol. 1*. Jena, Gustav Fischer.

Mitchell, N.D. 1976. The status of *Brassica oleracea* L. subsp. *oleracea* (wild cabbage) in the British Isles. *Watsonia, 11*: 97-103.

Mitchell, N.D., & Richards, A.J. 1979. *Brassica oleracea* L. ssp. *oleracea*. Biological Flora of the British Isles, No.145. *Journal of Ecology, 67*: 1087-1096.

Moore, D.M. 1957. The status of *Viola lactea. In: Progress in the study of the British flora*, ed. by J.E. Lousley, 97-102. London, Botanical Society of the British Isles.

Moore, D.M. 1958. *Viola lactea* Sm. Biological Flora of the British Isles, No. 67. *Journal of Ecology, 46*: 527-535.

Moore, N.W. 1962. The heaths of Dorset and their conservation. *Journal of Ecology, 50*: 369-391.

Moss, C.E. 1914. *The Cambridge British Flora. Vol. 2*. Cambridge, Cambridge University Press.

Mountford, J.O., & Sheail, J. 1984. Plant life and the watercourses of the Somerset Levels and Moors. *Nature Conservancy Council, CSD Report*, No. 560.

Mountford, J.O., & Sheail, J. 1989. *The effects of agricultural land use change on the flora of three grazing marsh areas*. Peterborough, Nature Conservancy Council. (Focus on Nature Conservation, No. 20.)

Murray, C.W. 1991. *Arctostaphylos alpinus* in the Isle of Skye - reinstated after more than 200 years. *Botanical Journal of Scotland, 46*: 152.

Murray, R.P. 1882. Somerset notes. *Journal of Botany, 20*: 328.

Musselman, L.J. 1982. The Orobanchaceae of Virginia. *Castanea, 47*: 266-275.

Nature Conservancy Council. 1989. *Guidelines for selection of biological SSSIs*. Peterborough, Nature Conservancy Council.

Newman, E.I. 1963. Factors controlling the germination date of winter annuals. *Journal of Ecology, 51*: 625-638.

Newman, E.I. 1964. Factors affecting the seed production of *Teesdalia nudicaulis*. I. Germination date. *Journal of Ecology, 52*: 391-404.

Newman, E.I. 1965. Factors affecting the seed production of *Teesdalia nudicaulis*. II. Soil moisture in spring. *Journal of Ecology, 53*: 211-232.

Nordal, I., & Stabbetorp, O.E. 1990. Morphology and taxonomy of the genus *Cochlearia* (Brassicaceae) in northern Scandinavia. *Nordic Journal of Botany, 10*: 249-263.

Ockendon, D.J. 1968. *Linum perenne* ssp. *anglicum* (Miller) Ockendon. Biological Flora of the British Isles, No. 114. *Journal of Ecology, 56*: 871-882.

Oswald, P. 1993. Native and naturalised garlics in the Cambridge University Botanic Garden. *Nature in Cambridgeshire*, No. 35: 67-75.

Page, C.N. 1982. *The ferns of Britain and Ireland*. Cambridge, Cambridge University Press.

Page, C.N. 1988. *Ferns: their habitats in the British and Irish landscape*. London, Collins. (New Naturalist, No. 74.)

Parker, P.F. 1985. The distribution and ecology of *Verbascum pulverulentum* Vill. in eastern England. *Boletim da Sociedade Broteriana (ser. 2), 58*: 249-257.

Parkinson, J. 1640. *Theatrum Botanicum*. London.

Patton, D. 1924. The vegetation of Beinn Laoigh. *Report of the Botanical Society and Exchange Club of the British Isles, 7*: 268-319.

Paul, A.M. 1987. The status of *Ophioglossum azoricum* (Ophioglossaceae: Pteridophyta) in the British Isles. *Fern Gazette, 13*: 173-187.

Pearman, D. 1990. *Alopecurus bulbosus* Gouan in Dorset. *Watsonia, 18*: 206-207.

Pearson, M.C., & Rogers, J.A. 1962. *Hippophaë rhamnoides* L. Biological Flora of the British Isles, No. 85. *Journal of Ecology, 50*: 501-513.

Perring, F.H., & Farrell, L. 1977. *British Red Data Books: 1. Vascular plants*. Lincoln, Society for the Promotion of Nature Conservation.

Perring, F.H., & Farrell, L. 1983. *British Red Data Books: 1. Vascular plants*. 2nd ed. Lincoln, Royal Society for Nature Conservation.

Perring, F.H., & Sell, P.D., *eds*. 1968. *Critical supplement to the atlas of the British flora*. London, Thomas Nelson & Sons.

Perring, F.H., Sell, P.D., & Walters, S.M. 1964. *A Flora of Cambridgeshire*. Cambridge, Cambridge University Press.

Perring, F.H., & Walters, S.M. 1962. *Atlas of the British Flora*. London, Thomas Nelson & Sons.

Petch, C.P., & Swann, E.L. 1968. *Flora of Norfolk*. Norwich, Jarrold & Sons.

Pigott, C.D., & Walters, S.M. 1954. On the interpretation of the discontinuous distributions shown by certain British species of open habitats. *Journal of Ecology, 42*: 95-116.

Ploeg, D.T.E. van der. 1990. *De Nedelandse breedbladige fonteinkruiden*. Utrecht, Stichting Uitgeverij Koninklijke Nederlandse Natuurhistorische Vereniging.

Potterton, D., *ed*. 1983. *Culpeper's colour herbal*. London, W. Foulsham & Co.

Preston, C.D. 1980. *Trifolium occidentale* D.E. Coombe, new to Ireland. *Irish Naturalists' Journal, 20*: 37-40.

Preston, C.D. 1990. *Potamogeton filiformis* Pers. in Anglesey. *Watsonia, 18*: 90-91.

Preston, C.D. 1993. The distribution of the oxlip *Primula elatior* (L.) Hill in Cambridgeshire. *Nature in Cambridgeshire*, No. 35: 29-60.

Preston, C.D., & Croft, J.M. 1992. Database and atlas of aquatic vascular plants in the British Isles. Phase II: interim report. *JNCC Report*, No. 34.

Preston, C.D., & Pearman, D.A. 1992. A second extant Dorset locality for *Gastridium ventricosum*. *Proceedings of the Dorset Natural History and Archaeological Society, 113*: 207-210.

Price Evans, E. 1932. Cader Idris: a study of certain plant communities in south-west Merionethshire. *Journal of Ecology, 20*: 1-52.

Price Evans, E. 1944. Cader Idris and Craig-y-Benglog. The study of the distribution of floristically rich localities in relation to bed-rock. *Journal of Ecology, 32*: 167-179.

Prime, C.T. 1954. *Arum neglectum* (Towns.) Ridley. Biological Flora of the British Isles, No. 42. *Journal of Ecology, 42*: 241-248.

Prime, C.T. 1960. *Lords and ladies*. London, Collins. (New Naturalist Monograph, No. 17.)

Pritchard, N.M. 1961. *Gentianella* in Britain. III. *Gentianella germanica* (Willd.) Börner. *Watsonia, 4*: 290-303.

Proctor, M.C.F. 1965. The distinguishing characters and geographical distributions of *Ulex minor* and *Ulex gallii*. *Watsonia, 6*: 177-187.

Proctor, M.C.F., & Groenhof, A.C. 1992. Peroxidase isoenzyme and morphological variation in *Sorbus* L. in South Wales and adjacent areas, with particular reference to *S. porrigentiformis* E.F. Warb. *Watsonia, 19*: 21-37.

Proctor, M.C.F., Proctor, M.E., & Groenhof, A.C. 1989. Evidence from peroxidase polymorphism on the taxonomy and reproduction of some *Sorbus* populations in south-west England. *New Phytologist, 112*: 569-575.

Proctor, M.[C.F.] & Yeo, P. 1973. *The pollination of flowers*. London, Collins. (New Naturalist, No. 54.)

Pugsley, H.W. 1940. Notes on *Orobanche* L. *Journal of Botany*, *78*: 105-116.

Rackham, O. 1976. *Trees and woodland in the British landscape*. London, J.M. Dent & Sons.

Rackham, O. 1980. *Ancient woodland: its history, vegetation and uses in England*. London, Edward Arnold.

Rackham, O. 1992. Gamlingay Wood. *Nature in Cambridgeshire*, No. 34: 3-15.

Randall, R.E. 1977. The past and present status and distribution of sea pea, *Lathyrus japonicus* Willd., in the British Isles. *Watsonia*, *11*: 247-251.

Ranwell, D.S., *ed.* 1972. *The management of sea buckthorn* Hippophaë rhamnoides *L. on selected sites in Great Britain*. Norwich, Nature Conservancy. (Report of *Hippophaë* Study Group.)

Ratcliffe, D. 1959. *Hornungia petraea* (L.) Rchb. Biological Flora of the British Isles, No. 70. *Journal of Ecology*, *47*: 241-247.

Ratcliffe, D. 1960. *Draba muralis* L. Biological Flora of the British Isles, No. 75. *Journal of Ecology*, *48*: 737-744.

Ratcliffe, D.A. 1959. The mountain plants of the Moffat Hills. *Transactions of the Botanical Society of Edinburgh*, *37*: 257-271.

Ratcliffe, D.A., *ed.* 1977. *A nature conservation review*. 2 vols. Cambridge, Cambridge University Press.

Ratcliffe, D.A., & Eddy, A. 1960. *Alopecurus alpinus* Sm. in Britain. *Proceedings of the Botanical Society of the British Isles*, *3*: 389-391.

Raven, J., & Walters, M. 1956. *Mountain flowers*. London, Collins. (New Naturalist, No. 33.)

Raven, P.H. 1963. *Circaea* in the British Isles. *Watsonia*, *5*: 262-272.

Ray, J. 1724. *Synopsis methodica stirpium Britannicarum*. 3rd ed. London.

Raybould, A.F., Gray, A.J., Lawrence, M.J., & Marshall, D.F. 1991. The evolution of *Spartina anglica* C.E. Hubbard (Gramineae): genetic variation and status of the parental species in Britain. *Biological Journal of the Linnean Society*, *44*: 369-380.

Rea, C., *ed.* 1897. *The Transactions of the Worcestershire Naturalists' Club 1847-1896*. Worcester, Worcestershire Naturalists' Club.

Relhan, R. 1785. *Flora Cantabrigiensis*. Cambridge.

Rich, T.C.G. 1991. *Crucifers of Great Britain and Ireland*. London, Botanical Society of the British Isles. (BSBI Handbook No. 6.)

Rich, T.C.G., & Rich, M.D.B., *comps.* 1988. *Plant crib*. London, Botanical Society of the British Isles.

Rich, T.C.G., & Woodruff, E.R. 1990. BSBI Monitoring Scheme 1987-1988. 2 vols. *Nature Conservancy Council, CSD Report*, No. 1265.

Richards, A.J. 1986. Cross-pollination by wasps in *Epipactis leptochila* (Godf.) Godf. *s.l. Watsonia*, *16*: 180-182.

Richards, [A.]J. 1989. *Primulas of the British Isles*. Princes Risborough, Shire Publications.

Richards, A.J., & Swan, G.A. 1976. *Epipactis leptochila* (Godfery) Godfery and *E. phyllanthes* G.E. Sm. occurring in South Northumberland on lead and zinc soils. *Watsonia*, *11*: 1-5.

Richards, P.W. 1943. *Juncus filiformis* L. Biological Flora of the British Isles, No. 10. *Journal of Ecology*, *31*: 60-65.

Richens, R.H. 1983. *Elm*. Cambridge, Cambridge University Press.

Ridley, H.N. 1930. *The dispersal of plants throughout the world*. Ashford, L. Reeve & Co.

Riley, R. 1956. The influence of the breeding system on the genecology of *Thlaspi alpestre* L. *New Phytologist*, *55*: 319-330.

Rilstone, F. 1948. Fluctuations of *Sibthorpia europaea* L. *The North Western Naturalist*, *23*: 130-131.

Roberts, H.A., & Boddrell, J.E. 1983. Seed survival and periodicity of seedling emergence in ten species of annual weeds. *Annals of Applied Biology*, *102*: 523-532.

Roberts, H.A., & Feast, P.M. 1973. Emergence and longevity of seeds of annual weeds in cultivated and undisturbed soil. *Journal of Applied Ecology*, *10*: 133-143.

Roberts, R.H. 1975. *Frankenia laevis* L. in Anglesey. *Watsonia*, *10*: 291-292.

Roberts, R.H. 1988. The occurrence of *Dactylorhiza traunsteineri* (Sauter) Soó in Britain and Ireland. *Watsonia, 17*: 43-47.

Rodwell, J.S., *ed.* 1991a. *British plant communities. Vol. 1. Woodlands and scrub.* Cambridge, Cambridge University Press.

Rodwell, J.S., *ed.* 1991b. *British plant communities. Vol. 2. Mires and heaths.* Cambridge, Cambridge University Press.

Roe, R.G.B. 1981. *The Flora of Somerset.* Taunton, Somerset Archaeological and Natural History Society.

Roger, J.G. 1975. Alpine section excursion to Beinn Laoigh (Ben Lui), Argyll and Perthshire (grid ref. NN 265263), 29.6.74. *BSE News*, No. 14: 5-6.

Rose, F. 1948. *Orchis purpurea* Huds. Biological Flora of the British Isles, No. 26. *Journal of Ecology, 36*: 366-377.

Rose, F., & Géhu, J.M. 1960. Comparaison floristique entre les comtés anglais du Kent et du Sussex et le département français du Pas-de-Calais. *Bulletin de la Société de botanique du nord de la France, 13*: 125-139.

Rotmans, J., Hulme, M., & Downing, T.E. 1994. Climate change implications for Europe: an application of the ESCAPE model. *Global Environmental Change, 4*: 97-124.

Rutherford, A., & Stirling, A.McG. 1973. *Polypodium australe* Fée and the tetraploid hybrid in Scotland. *British Fern Gazette, 10*: 233-235.

Salisbury, E. 1952. *Downs and dunes.* London, G. Bell & Sons.

Salisbury, E. 1961. *Weeds & aliens.* London, Collins. (New Naturalist, No. 43.)

Salisbury, E.J. 1967. The reproduction and germination of *Limosella aquatica. Annals of Botany, new series, 31*: 147-162.

Salisbury, E.[J.] 1970. The pioneer vegetation of exposed muds and its biological features. *Philosophical Transactions of the Royal Society, 259B*: 207-255.

Sandwith, C. 1927. The hornworts and their occurrence in Britain. *Proceedings of the Bristol Naturalists' Society, 6*: 303-311.

Sanford, M. 1991. *The orchids of Suffolk.* Ipswich, Suffolk Naturalists' Society.

Scott, G.A.M. 1963. *Mertensia maritima* (L.) S.F. Gray. Biological Flora of the British Isles, No. 89.

Journal of Ecology, 51: 733-742.

Scott, G.A.M., & Randall, R.E. 1976. *Crambe maritima* L. Biological Flora of the British Isles, No. 139. *Journal of Ecology, 64*: 1077-1091.

Scott, W., & Palmer, R.C. 1987. *The flowering plants and ferns of the Shetland Islands.* Lerwick, Shetland Times.

Seddon, B. 1965. Occurrence of *Isoetes echinospora* in eutrophic lakes in Wales. *Ecology, 46*: 747-748.

Sell, P.D. 1985. A field of fumitories. *BSBI News*, No. 41: 16-17.

Sell, P.D. 1989a. The *Sorbus latifolia* (Lam.) Pers. aggregate in the British Isles. *Watsonia, 17*: 385-399.

Sell, P.D. 1989b. The *Fumaria bastardii* Boreau/ *F. muralis* Sonder ex Koch complex in the British Isles. *BSBI News*, No. 51: 24-26.

Short, F.T., Ibelings, B.W., & Hartog, C. den. 1988. Comparison of a current eelgrass disease to the wasting disease in the 1930s. *Aquatic Botany, 30*: 295-304.

Showler, A.J., & Rich, T.C.G. 1993. *Cardamine bulbifera* (L.) Crantz (Cruciferae) in the British Isles. *Watsonia, 19*: 231-245.

Silverside, A.J. 1990. Dandelions and their allies. *In: A guide to some difficult plants. Illustrated articles from the Wild Flower Society magazine 1973-1988*, 41-67. Wild Flower Society.

Silverside, A.J. 1991. The identity of *Euphrasia officinalis* L. and its nomenclatural implications. *Watsonia, 18*: 343-350.

Simmonds, N.W. 1946. *Gentiana pneumonanthe* L. Biological Flora of the British Isles, No. 16. *Journal of Ecology, 33*: 295-307.

Sinker, C.A., Packham, J.R., Trueman, I.C., Oswald, P.H., Perring, F.H., & Prestwood, W.V. 1985. *Ecological Flora of the Shropshire region.* Shrewsbury, Shropshire Trust for Nature Conservation.

Small, E., & Jomphe, M. 1989. A synopsis of the genus *Medicago* (Leguminosae). *Canadian Journal of Botany, 67*: 3260-3294.

Smith, A. 1986. Endangered species of disturbed habitats. *Nature Conservancy Council, CSD Report*, No. 644.

Smith, A. 1989. *Summary of BSBI Arable Weed Survey 1986-87.* Peterborough, Nature Conservancy Council. (Contract Surveys, No. 48.)

Smith, G.L. 1963a. Studies in *Potentilla* L. I. Embryological investigations into the mechanism of agamospermy in British *P. tabernaemontani* Aschers. *New Phytologist*, *62*: 264-282.

Smith, G.L. 1963b. Studies in *Potentilla* L. II. Cytological aspects of apomixis in *P. crantzii* (Cr.) Beck ex Fritsch. *New Phytologist*, *62*: 283-300.

Smith, G.L. 1971. Studies in *Potentilla* L. III. Variation in British *P. tabernaemontani* Aschers. and *P. crantzii* (Cr.) Beck ex Fritsch. *New Phytologist*, *70*: 607-618.

Smith, P.H. 1984. The distribution, status and conservation of *Juncus balticus* Willd. in England. *Watsonia*, *15*: 15-26.

Smith, U.K. 1979. *Senecio integrifolius* (L.) Clairv. Biological Flora of the British Isles, No. 147. *Journal of Ecology*, *67*: 1109-1124.

Stace, C.A. 1961. *Nardurus maritimus* (L.) Murb. in Britain. *Proceedings of the Botanical Society of the British Isles*, *4*: 248-261.

Stace, C.A. 1975. *Hybridization and the flora of the British Isles*. London, Academic Press.

Stace, C.A. 1991. *New Flora of the British Isles*. Cambridge, Cambridge University Press.

Stanier, M. 1993. The restoration of grassland on the Devil's Ditch, Cambridgeshire. *Nature in Cambridgeshire*, No. 35: 13-17.

Steven, H.M., & Carlisle, A. 1959. *The native pinewoods of Scotland*. Edinburgh, Oliver and Boyd.

Stevens, J.P. 1985. *The meiotic and breeding systems of* Allium schoenoprasum *in natural populations*. D. Phil. Thesis, University of York.

Stevens, J.P., & Bougourd, S.M. 1988a. Genetic analysis of flower colour variation in *Allium schoenoprasum* L. (wild chives). *Heredity*, *60*: 253-256.

Stevens, J.P., & Bougourd, S.M. 1988b. Inbreeding depression and the outcrossing rate in natural populations of *Allium schoenoprasum* L. (wild chives). *Heredity*, *60*: 257-261.

Stevens, J.P., & Bougourd, S.M. 1991. The frequency and meiotic behaviour of structural chromosome variants in natural populations of *Allium schoenoprasum* L. (wild chives) in Europe. *Heredity*, *66*: 391-401.

Styles, B.T. 1962. The taxonomy of *Polygonum aviculare* and its allies in Britain. *Watsonia*, *5*: 177-214.

Summerhayes, V.S. 1951. *Wild orchids of Britain*. London, Collins. (New Naturalist, No. 19.)

Svensson, R., & Wigren, M. 1985. Blåklintens historia och biologi i Sverige. *Svensk Botanisk Tidskrift*, *79*: 273-297

Swan, G.A. 1993. *Flora of Northumberland*. Newcastle upon Tyne, Natural History Society of Northumbria.

Syme, J.T. Boswell, *ed.* 1870. *English Botany. Vol. 3. Juncaceae to Cyperaceae*. 3rd ed. London, Robert Hardwicke.

Tarpey, T., & Heath, J. 1990. *Wild flowers of North East Essex*. Colchester, Colchester Natural History Society.

Taschereau, P.M. 1977. *Atriplex praecox* Hülphers: a species new to the British Isles. *Watsonia*, *11*: 195-198.

Taschereau, P.M. 1985. Taxonomy of *Atriplex* species indigenous to the British Isles. *Watsonia*, *15*: 183-209.

Townsend, F. 1883. *Flora of Hampshire*. London, L. Reeve & Co.

Trist, P.J.O., *ed.* 1979. *An Ecological Flora of Breckland*. East Ardsley, EP Publishing.

Trist, P.J.O. 1981. The survival of *Alopecurus bulbosus* Gouan in former sea-flooded marshes in East Suffolk. *Watsonia*, *13*: 313-316.

Trist, P.J.O. 1986. The distribution, ecology, history and status of *Gastridium ventricosum* (Gouan) Schinz & Thell. in the British Isles. *Watsonia*, *16*: 43-54.

Trist, P.J.O. 1988. Hildersham Furze Hills. *Nature in Cambridgeshire*, No. 30: 4-12.

Trist, P.J.O. 1993. *Corynephorus canescens* (L.) Beauv. (Poaceae) on the west coast of Scotland. *Watsonia*, *19*: 192-193.

Tubbs, C.R. 1986. *The New Forest*. London, Collins. (New Naturalist, No. 73.)

Turk, S.M. 1986. The three species of eelgrass (*Zostera*) on the Cornish coast. *Cornish Studies*, *14*: 15-22.

Turk, S.M. 1989. Eelgrass decline hits Cornwall. *Marine Conservation*, *2*: 37.

Turner, D., & Dillwyn, L.W. 1805. *The botanist's guide through England and Wales*. 2 vols. London, Phillips & Fardon.

Tutin, T.G. 1942. *Zostera* L. Biological Flora of the British Isles, No. 7. *Journal of Ecology*, *30*: 217-226.

Tutin, T.G., Burges, N.A., Chater, A.O., Edmondson, J.R., Heywood, V.H., Moore, D.M., Valentine, D.H., Walters, S.M., & Webb, D.A., *eds*. 1993. *Flora Europaea. Vol. 1. Psilotaceae to Platanaceae*. 2nd ed. Cambridge, Cambridge University Press.

Tutin, T.G., Heywood, V.H., Burges, N.A., Moore, D.M., Valentine, D.H., Walters, S.M., & Webb, D.A., *eds*. 1968. *Flora Europaea. Vol. 2. Rosaceae to Umbelliferae*. Cambridge, Cambridge University Press.

Tutin, T.G., Heywood, V.H., Burges, N.A., Moore, D.M., Valentine, D.H., Walters, S.M., & Webb, D.A., *eds*. 1972. *Flora Europaea. Vol. 3. Diapensiaceae to Myoporaceae*. Cambridge, Cambridge University Press.

Tutin, T.G., Heywood, V.H., Burges, N.A., Moore, D.M., Valentine, D.H., Walters, S.M., & Webb, D.A., *eds*. 1980. *Flora Europaea. Vol. 5. Alismataceae to Orchidaceae (Monocotyledones)*. Cambridge, Cambridge University Press.

Tutin, T.G., Heywood, V.H., Burges, N.A., Valentine, D.H., Walters, S.M., & Webb, D.A., *eds*. 1964. *Flora Europaea. Vol. 1. Lycopodiaceae to Platanaceae*. Cambridge, Cambridge University Press.

Vaughan, I.M. 1978. *Lathyrus palustris* L. var. *pilosus* (Cham.) Ledeb in v.c. 44. *BSBI News*, No. 20: 14.

Velde, G. van der & Heijden, L.A. van der. 1981. The floral biology and seed production of *Nymphoides peltata* (Gmel.) O. Kuntze (Menyanthaceae). *Aquatic Botany*, *10*: 261-293.

Verdcourt, B. 1948. *Cuscuta europaea* L. Biological Flora of the British Isles, No. 25. *Journal of Ecology*, *36*: 358-365.

Waldren, S. 1982. *Frankenia laevis* L. in mid Glamorgan. *Watsonia*, *14*: 185-186.

Ward, S.D., & Evans, D.F. 1976. Conservation assessment of British limestone pavements based on floristic criteria. *Biological Conservation*, *9*: 217-233.

Watkinson, A.R. 1978. *Vulpia fasciculata* (Forskål) Samp. Biological Flora of the British Isles, No. 143. *Journal of Ecology*, *66*: 1033-1049.

Watkinson, A.R. 1990. The population dynamics of *Vulpia fasciculata*: a nine-year study. *Journal of Ecology*, *78*: 196-209.

Webb, D.A. 1985. What are the criteria for presuming native status? *Watsonia*, *15*: 231-236.

Webb, D.A., & Akeroyd, J.R. 1991. Inconstancy of sea-shore plants. *Irish Naturalists' Journal*, *23*: 384-385.

Webb, N.R. 1990. Changes on the heathlands of Dorset, England, between 1978 and 1987. *Biological Conservation*, *51*: 273-286.

Webster, S.D. 1990. Three natural hybrids in *Ranunculus* L. subgenus *Batrachium* (DC.) A. Gray. *Watsonia*, *18*: 139-146.

Wells, T.C.E. 1967. *Dianthus armeria* L. at Woodwalton Fen, Hunts. *Proceedings of the Botanical Society of the British Isles*, *6*: 337-342.

Wells, T.C.E. 1968. Land-use changes affecting *Pulsatilla vulgaris* in England. *Biological Conservation*, *1*: 37-43.

Wells, T.C.E., & Barling, D.M. 1971. *Pulsatilla vulgaris* Mill. Biological Flora of the British Isles, No. 120. *Journal of Ecology*, *59*: 275-292.

West, I.M. 1980. Geology of the Solent estuarine system. *In*: *The Solent estuarine system: an assessment of present knowledge*, 6-18. Swindon, Natural Environment Research Council. (The Natural Environment Research Council Publications Series C, No. 22.)

Westerhoff, D., & Clark, M.J. 1992. *The New Forest heathlands, grasslands and mires. A management review and strategy*. Lyndhurst, English Nature.

Westhoff, V., & Held, A.J. den. 1969. *Plantengemeenschappen in Nederland*. Zutphen, Thieme & Cie.

Wheeler, B.D., & Giller, K.E. 1982. Status of aquatic macrophytes in an undrained area of fen in the Norfolk Broads, England. *Aquatic Botany*, *12*: 277-296.

White, F.B.W. 1898. *The Flora of Perthshire*. Edinburgh, Perthshire Society of Natural Science.

White, J.W. 1912. *The Flora of Bristol*. Bristol, John Wright & Sons.

Wigley, T.M.L., & Raper, S.C.B. 1992. Implications for climate and sea level of revised IPCC emissions scenarios. *Nature*, *357*: 293-300.

Wilkins, D.A. 1963. Plasticity and establishment in *Euphrasia*. *Annals of Botany*, *27*: 533-552.

Willby, N.J., & Eaton, J.W. 1993. The distribution, ecology and conservation of *Luronium natans* (L.) Raf. in Britain. *Journal of Aquatic Plant Management*, *31*: 70-76.

Williams, G., & Hall, M. 1987. The loss of coastal grazing marshes in south and east England, with special reference to East Essex, England. *Biological Conservation*, *39*: 243-253.

Willis, A.J. 1985. Plant diversity and change in a species-rich dune system. *Transactions of the Botanical Society of Edinburgh*, *44*: 291-308.

Willis, A.J. 1989. Effects of the addition of mineral nutrients on the vegetation of the Avon Gorge, Bristol. *Proceedings of the Bristol Naturalists' Society*, *49*: 55-68.

Willis, A.J., Martin, M.H., & Taylor, K.B. 1991. *Orchis purpurea* Hudson in the Avon Gorge, Bristol. *Watsonia*, *18*: 387-390.

Wilmot-Dear, M. 1985. *Ceratophyllum* revised - a study in fruit and leaf variation. *Kew Bulletin*, *40*: 243-271.

Wilson, A. 1956. *The altitudinal range of British plants*. 2nd ed. Arbroath, T. Buncle & Co.

Wilson, P.J. 1990. *The ecology and conservation of rare arable weed species and communities*. Ph.D. Thesis, University of Southampton.

Wilson, P.J. 1992. Britain's arable weeds. *British Wildlife*, *3*: 149-161.

Wisheu, I.C., & Keddy, P.A. 1991. Seed banks of a rare wetland plant community: distribution patterns and effects of human-induced disturbance. *Journal of Vegetation Science*, *2*: 181-188.

Witte, R.H. 1992. Nieuwe standplaatsen van *Minuartia hybrida* (Vill.) Schischkin (Tengere veldmuur) in Nederland. *Gorteria*, *18*: 125-126.

Woodell, S.R.J. 1965. *Primula elatior* in Norfolk; immigrant or relic? *Proceedings of the Botanical Society of the British Isles*, *6*: 37-39.

Woodhead, N. 1951. *Subularia aquatica* L. Biological Flora of the British Isles, No. 35. *Journal of Ecology*, *39*: 465-469.

Yeo, P.F. 1961. Germination, seedlings, and the formation of haustoria in *Euphrasia*. *Watsonia*, *5*: 11-22.

Yeo, P.F. 1971. Revisional notes on *Euphrasia*. *Botanical Journal of the Linnean Society*, *64*: 353-361.

Zhang, L. 1983. Vegetation ecology and population biology of *Fritillaria meleagris* L. at the Kungsängen Nature Reserve, eastern Sweden. *Acta Phytogeographica Suecica*, *73*: 1-95.

Index

This index is intended as a list of rare and scarce vascular plants in Britain as well as an index to the species covered in detail in this book.

Species which are thought as a result of the current project to be scarce are indexed in bold type with the relevant page reference in this book:

Aceras anthropophorum 26

Those species which were treated in detail by the scarce species project but are now known from fewer than 16 10 km squares and would therefore qualify for inclusion in the Red Data Book under existing criteria are indexed similarly but with an 'R' after the species name:

Carex vulpina (R) 98

All species which are treated in detail in this book but are not regarded as scarce because they are known in more than 100 10 km squares, or for other reasons, are indexed in roman type:

Subularia aquatica 402

Species which are included in the *Red Data Book* (Perring and Farrell 1983) are listed in roman type with a reference to the relevant page number of the Red Data Book prefixed by 'RDB':

Physospermum cornubiense ....(RDB 28)

Species which are not included in the *Red Data Book* but which were recognised as qualifying for inclusion before the start of the scarce species project are listed in roman type, followed by 'RDB' but no page number:

Adonis annua...(RDB)

The nomenclature follows Stace (1991). Synonyms are indexed in italics (and are followed by the accepted name in brackets) but are otherwise treated in the same way as the species to which they refer.

513